The Atlantic Book
of
British and American
Poetry

The Atlantic Book

of
British and American
Poetry

Edited by

DAME EDITH SITWELL

An Atlantic Monthly Press Book
Boston · Little, Brown and Company · *Toronto*

Copyright Notices and Acknowledgments

The editor wishes to thank the following for permission to reprint the material included in this anthology:

GEORGE ALLEN & UNWIN LTD. — for selections from *Chinese Poems* translated by
Dr. Arthur Waley.

BRANDT & BRANDT — for selection from *Collected Poems*. Oxford University Press.
Copyright © 1925, 1953 by Conrad Aiken; — for selections from *Selected Works
of Stephen Vincent Benét*. Rinehart & Company, Inc. Copyright 1925, 1927,
1928 by Stephen Vincent Benét. Copyright renewed 1953, 1955, 1956 by
Rosemary Carr Benét; — for selections from *Poems 1923–1954*. Harcourt, Brace

To
Father Philip Caraman, S.J.

Introduction

My gratitude to Edward Weeks, who suggested the compilation of this anthology (the fulfillment of a life devoted to the cause of poetry), and to my publishers, Atlantic–Little, Brown, is unending. I have lived in delight, and hope this will be shared by my readers.

This is not a collection comprising all names. I have omitted those great prose writers who are in no sense poets, but who have written verse — Swift and Thoreau, for instance, and that prose writer of genius who is the author of *Wuthering Heights* but whose verse is, to my feeling, unworthy of her. It is doing them no service to admit them.

There are many gaps in the verse of the eighteenth century, but that which has been omitted is juiceless and sapless. The lesser Augustans do not find a place in this book. Nor does much of the poetry written between 1880 and 1915. The content of many of the earliest verses of that period, though usually of no importance, was frequently too heavy for the frail structure. When intended to be light, the poems did not "run upon pleasant feet." When intended to be serious, "instead of a covey of poetic partridges, with whirring wings of music," to quote Coleridge's most unfair accusation against one of his own poems, "up came a metaphysical bustard, winging its slow, laborious, earth-skimming flight over dreary and level wastes."

The metaphysical bustard was at her most prolific between 1800 and 1880. But she has been nesting again recently, and whereas she had for a mate in the earlier period a religious bustard, her mate is now the even worse political-piety bustard. With what results may be imagined. At this time, anybody who has read Marx (irrespective of whether he has the slightest understanding of poetry) believes this has conferred poetic genius on him. Genius of this order has found no place in this book.

But to return to the 1880's. It was at about this time that a frightened rush began among the minor versifiers to conform to the mind of the Man in the Street, to provide simple vehicles for his simple thoughts and scratchy cotton gloves to protect his hands from the touch of reality.

There is now a general clamoring for the use of the Vulgar Tongue, "to which," said Dante (who would, I fear, be disdained were he of our day), "infants, when they first begin to distinguish sounds, are accustomed by those about them. Or still more shortly, we call that the Vulgar Tongue which, without any rules at all, we get by imitating our nurses." (*De Vulgari Eloquio*). But in most cases poetry should, to quote a phrase of Ben Jonson, "speak above a mortal mouth."

I have written a number of individual Prefaces, although it was obviously impossible to discuss all the poets represented. In many cases these are only a series of technical notes. Some, again, were written for the purpose of including from longer poems of varying quality exquisite fragments which have given me great delight.

The order in which the poets are placed in the book is in general chronological but not always so; I have placed them in a juxtaposition where I believe they can be seen to the best advantage.

In the matter of style — spelling, punctuation, and capitalization — I have followed what are in my judgment the best editions for the text. In the early poems I have in general altered *u* for *v* and *i* for *j* to the modern usage, but otherwise I have preserved the ancient spelling. Glossaries have been provided where help seemed necessary. For Shakespeare I have followed the guidance of the Nonesuch Edition of the First Folio with Herbert Farjeon's discerning notes.

In an exquisite phrase, Mr. Robert Frost summed up the perfume, the flower of poetry. He said that it "begins in delight, and ends in wisdom." Such has been the purpose of this book.

EDITH SITWELL

London, June, 1958

Contents

Contents

Contents

Contents

Contents   xxxvii

The Atlantic Book
of
British and American
Poetry

Anonymous Early Religious Poems

Some of these poems, or refrains from poems, such as *Eva's Lament, Sunset on Calvary, Luveli ter of loveli eyghe, O my harte is wo,* and *An Evening Prayer* have not, before, appeared in general anthologies, only in those devoted to a certain century, and then but rarely. They are almost unknown.

In the Early Religious and Early Secular sections, there is more difference in the chronological arrangements than in any of the other sections of the book.

> Modyr whyt as lyly flowr,
> Your lullyng lessyth my langowr —

included for the ineffable falling music of this refrain, which is as wonderful as Desdemona's "Sing all a greene Willough must be my Garland" — is of the fifteenth century. So is:

> Of a rose, a lovely rose,
> Of a rose is al myn song . . .

but "Ah my dere, ah my dere Son" belongs to a century later.

Both in this section and in the Anonymous Early Secular section I have included a poem to which authorship has been ascribed. This is for convenience' sake; for instance, the poem, presumed to be by King Canute, which begins the Secular section has, surely, its place there.

Much of the earliest English poetry, with its crude and unskilled thumping, or creaking, alliteration, echoes the sound of those earthy occupations which accompany the work of food growing and gathering.

The creaking and thumping of the wagons, the sharp sound of the flail threshing the corn, these are echoed even in certain devotional poems. But these are not to be found in the body of this book.

Yet in one such poem (*The Orison of Our Lady,* the date of which is not much later than 1200), suddenly, from the rough earth, from the creaking sound, these lines are born — they refer to the Blessed in Heaven:

> Heo beoth so read so rose so hwit so the lilie
> And ever more heo beoth glad and singeth thuruhut murie,
> Mid brihte gimstones hore krune is al biset
> And al heo doth thet hem liketh, so that no thing ham let,

heo beoth] they be.   hwit] white.   brihte gimstones] bright gemstones.   hore krune] their crown.   ham let] prevents them.

> Thi leowe sune is hore king, and thu ert hore kwene,
> Ne beoth heo never i-dreaved mid winde ne mid reine.

leowe sune] loved son.   ne beoth heo] nor be they.   i-dreaved] troubled.

This suddenly delightful sound was to become, at a later time, the foundation of one form of ballad rhythm.

Another form, of a different order, is foreshadowed in these wonderful lines from *Love Ron* (*Love Song*), whose author was Thomas of Hales, a Minorite, who wrote it at the instance of a young nun — the date being before 1240.

> Under molde hi leggeth colde
> And faleweth so doth medewe gras.

leggeth] lieth.   faleweth] falleth.   medewe gras] meadow grass.

Saintsbury says, "The very bones of an Englishman under the cold mould itself ought to start and tremble at the hearing of them."

Then there is the miraculous music, brought about in part by the long echoing vowels, in part by those two lines that each consist of two syllables only, of these stanzas from *Our Lady's Song* (*The Crucifixion: Towneley Plays*). What poet, having read these, could resist quoting them!

> Alas! may ever be my sang, whiles I may lyf in leid,
> Me thynk now that I lyf to lang to se my barne thus blede.
> Iewes wyrke with hym al wrang, wherefore do they this dede?
> Lo, so hy they have him hang — they let for no drede.
>   Why so
> His foman is he amang? No freynde he has but fo.

> Alas Dede! thou dwellys to lang! whi art thou hid fro me,
> Who kend the to my childe to gang? all blak thou makys
>   his ble.
> Now witterly thou wyrkis wrang, the more I will wyte thee,
> But if thou will my harte stang, that I might with hym dee,
>   And byde:
> Sore syghyng is my sang, for thyrlyd is his hyde.

leid] grief.   Iewes] Jews.   dede] death.   let for no drede] prevented by no dread.
kend] taught.   ble] countenance.   wyte] implore.   but if] that.
thyrlyd] beaten.

It is true that "dark ages clasp the daisy root." And from those dark ages grew that miracle *I sing of a maiden,* with its absolute stillness (with the exception of the faint flutter caused by the double-syllabled "Aprille," the rhyme to "stille"). The stillness arises, in part, from the long pauses ending the lines. One can only say that "To create a little flower is the labour of ages," that this mysterious growth is the flower itself, not only the name of the flower, and that it is one of the masterpieces of our language.

From EVA'S LAMENT

Alas! that evyr that speche was spokyn,
That the fals aungel seyd onto me,
Alas! oure makers byddyng is brokyn,
For I have towchyd his owyn dere tre.

ADAM LAY I–BOWNDYN

Adam lay i-bowndyn,
  Bowndyn in a bond —
Fowre thousand wynter
  Thoght he not too long;
And al was for an appil,
  An appil that he tok,
As clerkes fynden,
  Writen in here book. —

Ne hadde the appil takë ben,
  The appil taken ben,
Ne haddë never our lady
  A ben hevenë quene.
Blyssid be the tyme
  That appil takë was,
Ther fore we mown syngyn
  Deo Gracias.

here] their.   ne hadde] had not.   a ben] have been.   mown] must.

I SING OF A MAIDEN

I sing of a maiden
  That is makeles;
King of alle kinges
  To here sone che ches.

He cam also stille
  Ther his moder was,
As dew in Aprille
  That fallith on the gras.

He cam also stille
  To his moderes bowr,
As dew in Aprille
  That fallith on the flowr.

He cam also stille
  Ther his moder lay,
As dew in Aprille
  That fallith on the spray.

Moder and maiden
  Was never non but che;
Wel may swich a lady
  Godes moder be.

makeles] matchless.   che ches] she chose.   also] as.

OF A ROSE, A LOVELY ROSE

Of a rose, a lovely rose,
Of a rose is al myn song.

Lestynt, lordynges, both elde and ynge,
How this rosë began to sprynge;
Swych a rosë to myn lykynge
    In all this world ne knowe I non.

The aungil cam fro hevenë tour,
To grete Marye with gret honour,
And seidë sche schuld bere the flour,
    That schuldë breke the fendës bond.

The flour sprong in heye Bedlem,
That is bothë bryght and schene,
The rose is Mary, hevenë quene,
    Out of her bosum the blosmë sprong.

The ferstë braunche is full of might,
That sprong on Crystemesse nyght:
The sterre schon over Bedlem bryght,
    That is bothë brod and long.

The second braunchë sprong to helle,
The fendës power down to felle;
Therein myght non sowlë dwelle
    Blessed be the tyme the rosë sprong.

The threddë braunche is good and swote,
It sprong to hevenë crop and rote,
Therein to dwelle and ben our bote;
    Every day it schewit in prestes hand.

Prey we to here with gret honour,
Sche that bare the blessid flour,
Sche be our helpe and our socour,
    And schild us fro the fendës hand.

---

lestynt] listen.   fendës] fiend's, Devil's.   schene] beautiful, shining.   swote] sweet.
crop] new shoot.   rote] root.   bote] salvation.   schild] shield.

THE VIRGIN'S SONG

Iesu, swete sone dere!
On porful bed list thou here,
  And that me greveth sore;
For thi cradel is ase a bere,
Oxe and asse beth thi fere:
  Weepe ich mai tharfore.
Iesu, swete, beo noth wroth,
Thot ich nabbe clout ne cloth
  The on for to folde,
The on to folde ne to wrappe,
For ich nabbe clout ne lappe;
Bote ley thou thi fet to my pappe,
  And wite the from the colde.

porful] poverty-full.   list] lyest.   fere] companions.   ich nabbe] I have not.
lappe] fold of a garment.   wite] keep.

From MODYR WHYT AS LYLY FLOWR

Modyr whyt as lyly flowr,
Your lullyng lessyth my langowr.

As I ros up in a mornyng,
My thowth was on a mayd yyng,
That song aslep with hyr lullyng
  Her swet son, owr Savowr.

As sche hym held in hyr lape,
He toke hyr lovely by the pape,
And therof swetly he toke an appe,
  And sok hys fyll of the lycowr.

To hys modyr gen he seye,
For this mylke me must deye,
It ys my kynd therwith to playe,
  My swet modyr par amowr.

yyng] young.   appe] draught, drink.   gen] gently (*also*, began).   For this mylke
me must deye] Presumably this means that by drinking this milk He recognized that He
had taken on human flesh, and therefore must die as all flesh dies.   my kynd] my
nature (as a human being).

The maydyn frely gen to syng,
And in hyr song she mad mournyng,
How he that is owr hevyn kyng
     Shuld shed hys blod with gret dolowr.

Modyr, thi wepyng grevyth me sor,
But I wold dey, thu haddys be lor;
So awey, modyr, and wep no more;
     Thy lullyng lessyth my langowr.

thu haddys be lor] thou hadst by the law.

THERE IS A FLOURE SPRUNG OF A TREE

There is a floure sprung of a tree,
The rote thereof is called Jesse;
*   A floure of price,*
There is none seche in Paradise!

This flour is faire and fresche of heue;
Hit fadès never, bot ever is new;
The blissful branche this flour on grew
Was Mary mild that bare Jesu.
          A flour of grace,
Ayains all sorow hit is solas!

The sede hereof was Godès sond,
That God him selve sew with his hond
In Bedlem in that holy londe;
Amedis here herbere there he hir fond.
          This blissful floure
Sprang never bot in Marys boure.

When Gabrael this maid met,
With *"Ave Maria"* he here gret;
Betwene hem two this flour was set,
And kept was, no mon schul wit;
          But on a day
In Bedlem hit con spred and spray.

When that floure began to spred,
And his blosum to brede,
Riche and pore of every lede

Godès sond] God's sending.   amedis] amidst.   herbere] garden.   **non mon schul
wit**] no man may know.   con] began.   lede] speech.

Thay marvelt hou this flour might sprede;
  And kingès three
That blessful floure come to see.

Angeles there cam out of here toure
To loke apon this freschele floure,
Houe faire he was in his coloure,
And hou sote in his savoure,
  And to behold
How soche a flour might spring in golde.

Of lilly, of rose of rise,
Of primrol, and of flour-de-lyse,
Of all the flours at my devise,
That floure of Jesse yet bers the pris,
  As most of hele
To slake oure sorows every dele.

I pray youe flours of this cuntrè,
Where evere ye go, where ever ye be,
Hold hup the flour of good Jesse
Fore your frescheness and youre beutè,
  As fairest of all,
And ever was, and ever schall.

sote] sweet.   golde] mould.   rise] twig, branch.   hele] health.

VENI, CORONABERIS

Surge mea sponsa, swete in sight,
  And se thi sone thou gafe souke so scheene;
Thou schalt abide with thi babe so bright,
  And in my glorie be callide a queene.
  Thi mammillis, moder, ful weel y meene,
    Y had to my meete that y myght not mys;
  Above all creaturis, my moder clene,
    Veni, coronaberis.

Come, clenner than cristal, to my cage;
  Columba mea, y thee calle,
And se thi sone that in servage
  For mannis soule was made a thralle.
  In thi paliys so principal
    I pleyde privyli withoute mys;

scheene] bright, beautiful.   myght not mys, withoute mys, etc.] in each case all was
ordained.   clene] pure.   servage] servitude.

Myn high cage, moder, have thou schal;
    Veni, coronaberis.

For macula, moder, was nevere in thee;
    Filia syon, thou art the flour;
Ful sweteli schalt thou sitte bi me,
    And bere a crowne with me in tour,
    And alle my seintis to thin honour
        Schal honoure thee, moder, in my blis,
    That blessid bodi that bare me in bowur,
    Veni, coronaberis.

Tota pulcra thou art to my plesynge,
    My moder, princes of paradiys,
Of thee a watir ful well gan sprynge
    That schal agen alle my rightis rise;
    The welle of mercy in thee, moder, liys
        To bringe thi blessid bodi to blis;
    And my seintis schulen do thee service,
    Veni, coronaberis.

Veni, electa mea, meekeli chosen,
    Holi moder and maiden queene,
On sege to sitte semeli bi him an high,
    Thi sone and eek thi childe.
    Here, moder, with me to dwelle,
        With thi swete babe that sittith in blis,
    There in joie and blis that schal nevere mys,
    Veni, coronaberis.

Veni, electa mea, my moder swete,
    Whanne thou bad me, babe, be ful stille,
Ful goodli oure lippis than gan mete,
    With bright braunchis as blosmes on hille.
    Favus distillans it wente with wille,
        Oute of oure lippis whanne we dide kis,
    Therfore, moder, now ful stille,
    Veni, coronaberis.

Veni de libano, thou lylye in launche,
    That lappid me loveli with loulynge song,
Thou schalt abide with thi blessid braunche,
    That so semeli of thi bodi sprong.

---

watir ful well] a well full of water.   schulen] shall.   sege] throne.
favus] honeycomb.   launche] branch, stalk.

Ego, flos campi, thi flour, was solde,
  That on calveri to thee cried y-wys:
Moder, thou woost this is as y wolde;
  Veni, coronaberis.

Pulcra ut luna, thou berist the lamme,
  As the sunne that schineth clere,
Veni in ortum meum, thou deintiest damme,
  To smelle my spicis that here ben in fere.
  My paliys is pight for thi pleasure,
    Ful of bright braunchis and blosmes of blis;
Come now, moder, to thi derling dere!
    Veni, coronaberis.

Quid est ista so vertuose
  That is evere lastyng for hir mekenes?
Aurora consurgens graciouse,
  So benigne a ladi, of such brightnes,
  This is the colour of kinde clennes,
    Regina celi that nevere dide mys;
  Thus endith the song of greet sweettnes,
    Veni, coronaberis.

woost] knowest.   lamme] light.   fere] company, quantity.   pight] pitched.

AL THE MERYERE

Al the meryere is that place
The sunne of grace hym schynit in.

The sunne of grace hym schynit in
  In on day quan it was morwe
Quan our Lord God born was
  Withoute wem or sorwe.

The sunne of grace hym schynit in
  On a day quan it was non
Quan our Lord God born was
  And on the rode don.

The sunne of grace hym schynit in
  On a day quan it was pryme
Quan our Lord God born was
  So wel he knew his tyme.

The sunne of grace hym schynit in
  On a day quan it was undyrn
Quan our Lord God born was
  And to the herte stongyn.

schynit] shone.   quan] when.   wem] stain.   non] noon.   rode] rood, cross.
don] down.   undyrn] mid-afternoon.   stongyn] stung.

HAYLL, COMLY AND CLENE

PRIMUS PASTOR

Hayll, comly and clene!
  Hayll, yong child!
Hayll, maker, as I meyne,
  Of a madyn so mylde!
Thou hast waryd, I weyne,
  The warlo so wylde;
The fals gyler of teyn
  Now goys he begylde.
    Lo, he merys;
Lo, he laphys, my swetyng,
A welfare metyng,
I have holden my hetyng;
    Have a bob of cherys.

SECUNDUS PASTOR

Hayll, sufferan savyoure!
  For thou has us soght:
Hayll, frely foyde and floure
  That all thyng has wroght!
Hayll, full of favoure,
  That made all of noght!

Hayll! I kneyll and I cowre.
  A byrd have I broght
    To my barne.
Hayll, lytell tynë mop,
Of oure crede thou art crop:
I wold drynk on thy cop,
    Lytyll day starne.

TERTIUS PASTOR

Hayll, derlyng dere,
  Full of godhede!
I pray the be nere
  When that I have nede.
Hayll! swete is thy chere!
  My hart wold blede
To se the sytt here
  In so poore wede,
    With no pennys.
Hayll! put furth thy dall!
I bryng the bot a ball:
Have and play the with all,
    And go to the tenys.

waryd] cursed.	warlo] wizard.	gyler] beguiler.	teyn] evil. goys] goes.
merys] merry is.	hetyng] promise.	bob] bunch.	frely foyde] noble child.
barne] bairn.	mop] moppet.	crop] twig.	cop] cup. chere] face,
countenance.	dall] hand. tenys] tennis.		

TERLY TERLOW

Terly terlow, terly terlow,
So merily the shepardes began to blow!

About the feld they piped full right,
Even about the middës of the night;
Adown from heven they saw cum a light.
    Terly terlow.

Of angels there came a company
With mery songes and melody;
The shepardes anon gan them aspy.
    Terly terlow.

"*Gloria in excelsis*" the angels song
And said that peace was present among
To every man that to the faith wold long.
    Terly terlow.

The shepardes hied them to Bethleme,
To see that blessèd sonnès beme;
And there they found that glorious streme.
    Terly terlow.

Now pray we to that mekè child,
And to his moder that is so mild
The which was never defiled.
    Terly terlow.

streme] ray of light.   mekè] gentle.

QUIA AMORE LANGUEO

I

In the vaile of restless mind
  I sought in mountein and in mede,
Trusting a treulove for to find:
    Upon an hill than toke I hede;
    A voise I herd (and nere I yede)
    In gret dolour complaining tho,
    "See, dere soule, my sides blede
    Quia amore langueo."

Upon this mount I fand a tree;
  Undir this tree a man sitting;
From hede to fote woundid was he,
    His herte blode I saw bleding;
    A semely man to be a king,
    A graciose face to loke unto.
    I askid him how he had paining,
    He said, "*Quia amore langueo.*

"I am treulove that fals was never;
  My sistur, mannis soule, I loved hir thus;
By-cause I wold on no wise dissevere,
  I left my kingdome gloriouse;

treulove] truelove grass, a four-leaf clover.   yede] went.   tho] then.   fand] found.

I purveyd hir a place full preciouse;
 She flitt, I folowid, I luffed her soo
That I suffred these paines piteouse
 Quia amore langueo.

"My faire love and my spouse bright,
 I saved hir fro beting, and she hath me bett;
I clothed hir in grace and hevenly light,
 This blody surcote she hath on me sett;
 For langing love I will not lett;
  Swete strokis be thes, loo;
 I haf loved ever als I hett,
  Quia amore langueo.

"I crownid hir with blisse and she me with thorne,
 I led hir to chambre and she me to die;
I brought hir to worship and she me to scorne,
 I did hir reverence and she me velanye.
 To love that loveth is no maistrye,
  Hir hate made never my love hir foo;
 Ask than no moo questions whye,
  But *Quia amore langueo.*

II

"Loke unto min handis, man!
 Thes gloves were geven me whan I hir sought;
They be nat white, but rede and wan,
 Embrodred with blode my spouse them brought;
 They will not of, I lefe them nought,
  I wowe hir with them where ever she goo;
 Thes handes full frendly for hir fought,
  Quia amore langueo.

"Marvell not, man, thof I sitt still,
 My love hath shod me wondir straite;
She boklid my fete as was hir will
 With sharp nailes, loo thou mayst waite!
 In my love was never dissaite,
  For all my membres I haf opind hir to;
 My body I made hir hertis baite,
  Quia amore langueo.

purveyd] prepared. flitt] fled. beting] beating. bett] beaten.
langing] longing. lett] cease. als] as. hett] promised. velanye] discourtesy.
maistrye] mastery, domination. wan] discolored of] off. lefe] leave.
wowe] woo. thof] though. waite] look. dissaite] deceit.

"In my side I haf made hir nest,
  Loke, in me how wide a wound is here!
This is hir chambre, here shall she rest,
  That she and I may slepe in fere.
Here may she wasshe, if any filth were;
  Here is socour for all hir woo;
Cum if she will, she shall haf chere,
  Quia amore langueo.

"I will abide till she be redy,
  I will to hir send if she sey nay;
If she be rechelesse I will be gredy,
  If she be daungerouse I will hir pray.
If she do wepe, than bid I nay;
  Min armes ben spred to clipp hir to;
Crye onis, 'I cum!' now, soule, assaye!
  Quia amore langueo.

"I sitt on an hille for to se farre,
  I loke to the vaile, my spouse I see;
Now rinneth she awayward, now cummith she narre,
  Yet fro min eyesight she may nat be;
Sum waite ther pray, to make hir flee,
  I rinne tofore to chastise hir foo;
Recover, my soule, againe to me,
  Quia amore langueo.

III

"My swete spouse, will we goo play?
  Apples ben ripe in my gardine;
I shall clothe thee in new array,
  Thy mete shall be milk, honye, and wine;
Now, dere soule, latt us go dine,
  Thy sustenance is in my scripp, loo!
Tary not now, faire spouse mine,
  Quia amore langueo.

"If thou be foule, I shall make thee clene,
  If thou be seke, I shall thee hele;
If thou ought morne, I shall be-mene;
  Spouse, why will thou nought with me dele?
Thou foundist never love so lele;

in fere] together.   rechelesse] heedless.   gredy] importunate, insistent.
daungerouse] disdainful.   clipp] embrace.   narre] nearer.   recover] return.
scripp] wallet.   seke] sick.   morne] mourn.   be-mene] lament.
dele] treat.   lele] loyal, true.

What wilt thou, soule, that I shall do?
  I may of unkindnes thee appele,
    Quia amore langueo.

"What shall I do now with my spouse?
  Abide I will hire jantilnesse;
Wold she loke onis out of hir house
  Of flesshely affeccions and unclennesse;
Hir bed is made, hir bolstar is blisse,
  Hir chambre is chosen, suche ar no moo;
Loke out at the windows of kindnesse,
    Quia amore langueo.

"Long and love thou never so high,
  Yit is my love more than thin may be;
Thou gladdist, thou wepist, I sitt thee bygh.
  Yit might thou, spouse, loke onis at me!
Spouse, shuld I alway fede thee
  With childis mete? nay, love, nat so!
I preve thee, love, with adversite,
    Quia amore langueo.

"My spouse is in chambre, hald youre pease!
  Make no noise, but lat hir slepe;
My babe shall sofre noo disease,
  I may not here my dere childe wepe,
For with my pappe I shall hir kepe;
  No wondir though I tend hir to,
This hoole in my side had never been so depe,
  But *Quia amore langueo.*

"Wax not wery, min owne dere wife!
  What mede is aye to liffe in comfort?
For in tribulacion, I rin more rife
  Ofter times than in disport;
In welth, in woo, ever I support;
  Than, dere soule, go never me fro!
Thy mede is markid, whan thou art mort,
  In blisse; *Quia amore langueo.*"

appele] accuse.   jantilnesse] gentleness.   suche ar no moo] there are no others
like it.   thin] thine.   preve] test, try.   disease] distress.   mede] reward.
liffe] live.   rin more rife] run more often.   markid] destined.   mort] dead.

AH MY DERE

"Ah my dere, ah my dere Son,"
  Said Mary, "ah my dere,
Kiss thy mother, Jesu,
  With a laughing chere."

This enders night
I saw a sight
  All in my slepe;
Mary, that may,
She sang "Lullay"
  And sore did weep.

To kepe she soght
Full fast about
  Her son fro colde.
Joseph said "Wyfe,
My joye, my lyfe,
  Say what ye wolde."

"No thing, my spouse,
Is in this house,
  Unto my pay;
My son, a kyng,

That made all thyng,
  Lyeth in hay."

"My mother dere
Amend your chere
  And now be still;
Thus for to lye
It is soothly
  My Father's will.

Derisyon,
Great passyon.
  Infinitely,
As it is found,
Many a wound
  Suffer shall I.

On Calvary
That is so hye,
  There shall I be,
Man to restore,
Naylit full sore
  Upon a tree."

chere] face.   enders] recent, past.   may] maid.

SUNSET ON CALVARY

Nou goth sonne under wod, —
Me reweth, Marie, thy faire Rode.
Nou goth sonne under tre, —
Me reweth, Marie, thy sonne and the.

under wod] into the wood; that is, the shade.   me reweth] I sorrow for.
rode] rood, cross.

LUVELI TER OF LOVELI EYGHE *

Luveli ter of loveli eyghe,
Qui dostu me so wo?
Sorful ter of sorful eyghe,
Thu brekst myn herte a-to.

ter] tear.   eyghe] eye.   a-to] in two.

O MY HARTE IS WO

"O my harte is wo!"
Mary she said so,
"For to see my dere son die,
And sones have I no mo."

When that my swetė sone
Was thirty winter old,
Than the traitor Judas
Wexėd very bold;
For thirty plates of money
His master he had sold.
But whan I it wist,
Lord, my hart was cold!

Upon Shere Thursday
Than truly it was,
On my sonnès deth
That Judas did compass.
Many were the fals Jewes
That folowed him by trace,
And there beffore them all
He kissed my sonnès face.

My son beffore Pilat
Brought was he,
And Peter said three times
He knew him not, parde.
Pilat said unto the Jewes
"What say ye?"
They criėd with one voice,
"Crucifige, crucifige."

wist] knew.   parde] certainly (from *par Dieu*).

* This refrain was written about 1372 and has been attributed to Johan de Grimestone.

On Good Friday
    At the mount of Calvary
My son was don on the crosse,
    Nailéd with nailés three.
Of all the frendés that he had
    Never one could he see,
But jentill John the evangelist
    That still stode him by.

Though I were sorowfull,
    No man have at it wonder;
For houge was the erth quake,
    Horible was the thonder.
I loked on my swete son
    On the crosse that I stode under;
Then cam Lungeus with a spere
    And clift his hart in sonder.

From A PRAYER OF THE FIVE WOUNDS

Jhesu cryst, myn leman swete,
    That for me deye-des on rode tre,
With al myn herte i the bi-seke
    For thi wndes to and thre,
That al so faste in myn herte
    Thi love roted mute be,
As was the spere in-to thi side,
    Whan thow suffredis ded for me.

       leman] lover.   rode] rood, cross.

AN EVENING PRAYER

Upon my Ryght syde y me leye,
Blesid lady, to the y pray,
Ffor the teres that ye lete
Upone yowr swete sonnys feete,
Sende me grace for to slepe
And good dremys for to mete,
Slepyng, wakyng, til morowe daye bee.
Owre lorde is the frwte, oure lady is the tree;
Blessid be the blossome that sprange, lady, of the!

        lete] drop, shed.

Richard Rolle
1300?-1349

MY TREWEST TRESOWRE *

My trewest tresowre sa trayturly was taken,
   Sa bytterly bondyn wyth bytand bandes,
How sone of thi servandes was thou forsaken,
   And lathly for my lufe hurld with thair handes.

My well of my wele sa wrangwysly wryed,
   Sa pulled owt of preson to pilate at prime;
Thaire dulles and thaire dyntes ful drerely thou dreed
   Whan thai schot in thi syght bath slaver and slyme.

My hope of my hele sa hyed to be hanged,
   Sa charged with thi crosce and corond with thorne,
Ful sare to thi hert thi steppes tha stanged —
   Me thynk thi bak burd breke; it bendes for-borne.

My salve of my sare sa saryful in syght,
   Sa naked and nayled thi ryg on the rode,
Ful hydusly hyngand, thai heved the on hyght,
   Thai lete the stab in the stane all stekked that thar stode.

My dere-worthly derlyng, sa dolefully dyght,
   Sa straytly upryght streyned on the rode;
For thi mykel mekenes, thi mercy, thi myght,
   Thow bete al my bales with bote of thi blode.

My fender of my fose, sa fonden in the felde,
   Sa lufly lyghtand at the evensang tyde;
Thi moder and hir menghe unlaced thi scheld —
   All weped that thar were, thi woundes was sa wyde.

bytand] biting.   sone] soon.   lathly] vilely.   lufe] love.
wrangwysly] wrongfully.   wryed] accused.   prime] the first hour.
dulles] wounds.   dyntes] blows.   dreed] suffered.   hele] salvation.
stanged] stung.   burd] must.   ryg] back.   rode] rood, cross.   mykel] much,
great.   bales] sorrows.   bote] help, bounty.   fender] defender.   fonden] tested.
menghe] companions.

* Sometimes held to be by one of Rolle's followers.

My pereles prynce als pure I the pray,
The mynde of this myrour thou lat me noght mysse;
Bot wynd up my wylle to won wyth the ay,
That thou be beryd in my brest and bryng me to blysse.
AMEN.

won] dwell.

Anonymous Early Secular Poems

The earliest poem in this section, *Merie sungen the muneches,* is ascribed to King Canute (994[?]–1035). It is taken from the twelfth-century *Liber Eliensis.* But it is possible that it may have been written by the King's court poet, Toraren the Icelander, also called Thorar Luvtunge.

I owe to that great poet Mr. David Jones the information about this minstrel. He sent me these strange lines by him:

> Canute rules the land
> As Christ, the shepherd of Greece, doth the heavens.

These Mr. Jones found in Christopher Dawson's *Religion and the Rise of Western Culture,* which contains also another poem by the minstrel, *The Song of the Sea Calm,* quoted from a translation from the Norse of the Heimskringla by E. Monsen and A. H. Smith.

The poems in this section, however, are far from sea sorrows, and sea voices, or sea calms.

Layaman, in his *Brut,* the date of which is about 1189, says that after an Arthurian battle "There weren in thissen lande blissful songes" — songs of a youth that will never grow old.

We can hear the anonymous poets saying, as a poet of many centuries later said:

> . . . pour moi voici
> Toujours que ton sourire éblouissant prolonge
> La même rose avec son bel été qui plonge
> Dans autrefois et puis dans le futur aussi.*

How simple seems the enchanter's art: "I say a flower, and out of the oblivion to which my voice consigns every contour, as far as anything save the known calyx, musically arises, ideal and exquisite, the one flower absent from all bouquets."

Such was the young girl Alisoun. The poet said "a flower" and she arose in music.

* Stéphane Mallarmé.

The slow movement of *Now sprinkes the spray* is managed with great beauty.

Part of the impression, in *Spring Song,* that small sharp leaf-buds are breaking into being is given by the particular places in which the alliteration is used — sometimes far separated in a line, sometimes put close together.

And part of the feeling of an eternal budding spring, in *Alisoun,* is conveyed by the *r*'s in the first two lines, which give a little trembling sound, like that of small budding leaves being blown by the wind.

MERIE SUNGEN THE MUNECHES *

Merie sungen the muneches binnen Ely
Tha Cnut ching rew therby.
Roweth cnihtes neer the land
And here we thes muneches sang.

muneches] monks.   binnen] near.   ching] king.   rew] rowed.
cnihtes] knights.   here] hear.

From BLOU NORTHERNE WYND

Ichot a burde in boure bryht,
That fully semly is on syht,
Menksful maiden of myht;
    Feir ant fre to fonde;
In al this wurhliche won
A burde of blod ant of bon,
Never yete y nuste non
    Lussomore in londe.
Blou northerne wynd!
Send thou me my suetyng!
Blou northerne wynd!
Blou! blou! blou!

ichot] I know.   burde] maiden.   menksful] worshipful.   feir] fair.
fonde] take, prove.   wurhliche] noble.   won] multitude.   y nuste] I knew not.
lussomore in londe] lovelier on earth.   suetyng] sweetheart.

* Attributed to King Canute (994[?]–1035), and also to his court poet, Toraren the Icelander.

With lokkes lefliche ant longe,
With frount ant face feir to fonde
With murthes monie mote heo monge,
   That brid so breme in boure.
With lossom eye grete ant gode,
With browen blysfol under hode,
He that rest him on the rode,
   That leflych lyf honoure.

Hire lure lumes liht
Ase a launterne a nyht,
Hire bleo blykyeth so bryht,
   So feyr heo is ant fyn.
A suetly swyre heo hath to holde,
With armes shuldre ase mon wolde,
Ant fingres feyre forte folde,
   God wolde hue were myn! . . .

Heo is coral of godnesse,
Heo is rubie of ryhtfulnesse,
Heo is cristal of clannesse,
   Ant baner of bealte.
Heo is lilie of largesse,
Heo is parvenke of prouesse,
Heo is solsecle of suetnesse,
   Ant lady of lealte. . . .

For hire love y carke ant care,
For hire love y droupne ant dare,
For hire love my blisse is bare
   Ant al ich waxe won,
For hire in slep y slake,
For hire love al nyht ich wake,
For hire love mournynge y make
   More then eny mon.
     Blou northerne wynd!
     Send thou me my suetyng!
     Blou northerne wynd!
     Blou! blou! blou!

lefliche] lovely.   fonde] take between the hands.   murthes] mirths, joys.   mote heo monge] may she mingle.   brid] bird.   breme] full of life.   lossom] lovely. rode] rood, cross.   lure] face.   lumes] beams.   bleo] color.   heo] she. suetly swyre] darling neck.   forte] for to.   hue] she.   clannesse] cleanness, purity.   parvenke] periwinkle.   solsecle] sunflower.   droupne] droop. won] wan.

NOW SPRINKES THE SPRAY

Now sprinkes the spray,
Al for love ich am so seek
That slepen I ne may.

Als I me rode this endre day
  O my playinge,
Seigh I whar a litel may
    Bigan to singe,
    "The clot him clinge!
Way es him i love-longinge
Sal libben ay!"

Son ich herde that mirye note,
  Thider I drogh.

I fonde hire in an herber swot
  Under a bogh,
  With joye ynogh.
  Son I asked, "Thou mirye may,
  Why sinkestou ay?"

Then answerde that maiden swote
  Mid wordes fewe,
  "My lemman me haves bihot
  Of love trewe:
  He chaunges anewe.
  Yif I may, it shal him rewe,
  By this day."

sprinkes] springs.   seek] sick.   this endre] the other.   o] on.   seigh] saw.
may] maid.   way] woe.   i] in.   sal libben] shall live.   herber swot] arbor
sweet.   sinkestou] do you sing.   lemman] lover.   bihot] promised.

SPRING

Lenten ys come with love to toune,
With blosmen and with briddes
    roune,
  That al this blisse bryngeth;
Dayes-eyes in this dales,
Notes suete of nyhtegales,
  Uch foul song singeth;
The threstelcoc him threteth oo,
Away is huere wynter wo,
  When woderove springeth;
Thise foules singeth ferly fele
Ant wlyteth on huere winne wele,
  That al the wode ryngeth.

The rose rayleth hire rode,
The leves on the lyhte wode
  Waxen al with wille;
The mone mandeth hire bleo,
The lilie is lossom to seo,
  The fenyl and the fille;
Wowes thise wilde drakes,
Males murgeth huere makes
  On strem that striketh
    stille.
Mody meneth; so doth mo
(Ichot ych am on of tho)
  For love that likes ille.

roune] voice.   dayes-eyes] daisies.   threteth] treadeth.   huere] their.
woderove] woodruff.   ferly fele] marvelous many.   wlyteth on huere winne
wele] whistle, in their wealth of joy.   rayleth hire rode] clothes herself in red.
mandeth hire bleo] sends forth her light.   lossom to seo] lovely to see.   fille] thyme.
wowes] woo.   murgeth] make merry.   makes] mates.   striketh] flows.   mody
meneth] the passionate man makes moan.   so doth mo] so do others.   ichot] I know.
likes ille] are troubled.

The mone mandeth hire lyht,
So douth the semly sonne bryht,
  When briddes singeth breme;
Deawes donketh the dounes,
Deores whisperes derne rounes
  Domes for to deme;
Wormes woweth under cloude,
Wymmen waxeth wounder proude.
  So wel hit wol hem seme,
Yef me shal wonte wille of on,
This wunne weole wole forgon
  Ant wyht in wode be fleme.

breme] lustily.　　deawes] dews.　　donketh] make dank.　　deores] animals.
derne rounes] secret cries.　　domes for to deme] whereby they converse.
cloude] clod.　　wunne weole] wealth of joy.　　fleme] fugitive.

AL NIST BY THE ROSE

Al nist by the rose, rose —
  Al nist by the rose i lay;
Darf ich noust the rose stele,
  Ant yet ich bar the flour away.

nist] night.　　darf] dared.　　noust] not.

ALISOUN

Bytuene Mershe and Averil
  When spray biginneth to springe,
The lutel foul hath hire wyl
  On hyre lud to synge:
Ich libbe in love-longinge
For semlokest of alle thynge,
  He may me blisse bringe,
  Ich am in hire baundoun.
An hendy hap ichabbe y-hent,
Ichot from hevene it is me sent,
From alle wymmen my love is lent
  And lyht on Alisoun.

On heu hire her is fayr ynoh,
  Hire browe broune, hire eye blake;
With lossum chere he on me loh;
  With middel smal and wel y-make;
Bote he me wolle to hire take

on hyre lud] in her language.　　ich libbe] I live.　　semlokest] seemliest.　　he] she.
baundoun] thralldom.　　hendy] gracious.　　y-hent] received.　　ichot] I know.
hire her] her hair.　　lossum chere] lovely face.　　loh] smiled.　　bote he] unless she.

For to buen hire owen make,
Long to lyven ichulle foresake
    And feye fallen adoun.

Nightes when I wende and wake,
    For-thi myn wonges waxeth won,
Levedi, al for thine sake
    Longinge is y-lent me on
    In world his non so wyter mon
    That al hire bounte telle con;
    Hire swyre is whittore than the swon,
        And feyrest may in toune.

Ich am for wowyng al for-wake,
    Wery so water in wore;
Lest eny reve me my make
    Ichabbe y-yerned yore.
    Betere is tholien whyle sore
    Then mournen evermore.
    Geynest under gore,
        Herkne to my roun.
An hendy hap ichabbe y-hent,
Ichot from hevene it is me sent,
From alle wymmen my love is lent
    And lyht on Alisoun.

buen] be.   make] mate.   feye] like to die.   wende] turn.   for-thi] on that account.   wonges] cheeks.   won] wan.   levedi] lady.   y-lent me on] come upon
me.   so wyter mon] so wise a man.   swyre] neck.   may] maid.
wowyng] wooing.   for-wake] worn out with vigils.   so water in wore] as water in a
weir.   reve] rob.   y-yerned yore] long desired.   tholien] to endure.   geynest
under gore] comeliest under robe.   roun] voice.

ICH AM OF IRLONDE

Ich am of Irlonde
    Ant of the holy londe
        Of Irlonde.
    Gode sire, pray ich the,
        For of saynte charitè,
    Come ant dance wyth me
        In Irlonde.

MAIDEN IN THE MOR

Maiden in the mor lay,
  In the mor lay,
Sevenist fulle, sevenist fulle,
Maiden in the mor lay,
  In the mor lay,
Sevenistes fulle ant a day.

Welle was hire dring
  Wat was hire dring?
The chelde water of the —
The chelde water of the —
Welle was hire dring.
  Wat was hire dring?
The chelde water of the welle-spring.

Welle was hire mete,
  Wat was hire mete?
The primerole ant the —
The primerole ant the —
Welle was hire mete,
  Wat was hire mete?
The primerole ant the violet.

Welle was hire bowr.
  Wat was hire bowr?
The rede rose an te —
The rede rose an te —
Welle was hire bowr.
  Wat was hire bowr?
The rede rose an te lilye flowr.

mor] moor.   sevenist] seven-night.   welle] good.   hire mete] her meat.
primerole] primrose.   dring] drink.   chelde] cold.   an te] and the.

A FAREWELL TO HIS MISTRESS

Farewell now my lady gaye,
  Farewell floure most freshest of hew,
Farewell sapher yn all assey,
  Farewell harte of whyte and blewe,
  Farewell kynde, curteys and trewe,
    Farewell woman withowten any evyll,
  Farewell the cumlyst that ever I knewe —
    I take my leve agaynst my wyll.

Farewell now my derlyng dere,
  Farewell most wysyst and womanly,
Farewell my love from yere to yere,
  Farewell byrall bryghtest of blee,
  Farewell kynde, curteys and free
    Farewell that may me save and spyll;
  How-ever I fare, well fare ye —
    I take my leve agaynst my wyll.

sapher yn all assey] all-tested sapphire.   byrall] beryl.   blee] gleam.   spyll] kill.

Farewell goodly grond of grace,
  Farewell the well of worthynes,
Farewell my comforth yn every case,
  Farewell my helpe ferthe of dystresse,
  Farewell my werrour from al sykenes,
    Farewell my lady of voyce soo shryll,
    Farewell nurter and all gentylnesse —
    I take my leve ageynst my wyll.

Farewell my wershype and my welthe,
  Farewell my myrthes with-owten mysse,
Farewell my hartye hope and helthe,
  Farewell freshe and lustye to kysse,
  Farewell all welthes that men can wyshe,
    Farewell as bryght as sonne over hyll,
    Farewell, god bryng yow to his blysse,
    I take my leve a-gaynst my wyll.

grond] ground.   ferthe of] out of.   werrour] defender.   nurter] nurture.
myrthes] joys.   mysse] wrong.

From SIR ORFEO

His harp, whereon was al his gle,
He hidde in an holwe tre;
And, when the weder was clere and bright,
He toke his harp, to him wel right,
And harped at his owhen wille.
Into alle the wode the soun gan schille,
That alle the wilde bestes that ther beth
For joie abouten him thai teth;
And alle the foules that ther were
Come and sete, on ech a brere,
To here his harping afine,
So miche melody was therin;
And when he his harping lete wold,
No best bi him abide nold.
He might se him bisides
Oft in hot undertides
The king o fairy with his rout
Com to hunt him al about,
With dim cri and bloweing;

schille] shrill.   teth] draw.   lete wold] would lay by.   undertides] mid-mornings.

And houndes also with him berking;
Ac no best thai no nome,
No never he nist whider thai bicome.
And other while he might him se
As a gret ost bi him te
Wele atourned ten hundred knightes,
Ech y-armed to his rightes,
Of contenaunce stout and fers,
With mani desplaid baners,
And ech his swerd ydrawe hold,
Ac never he nist whider thai wold.
And other while he seghe other thing:
Knightes and levedis com daunceing
In queynt atire, gisely,
With queynt pas and softly;
Tabours and trunpes gede hem bi,
And al maner menstraci.

ac] but.   no nome] no name.   ost] host.   bi him te] by him draw.
atourned] accoutred.   his swerd ydrawe hold] held his drawn sword.   seghe] saw.
levedis] ladies.   gisely] skillfully.   gede] went.   menstraci] minstrels.

King James I of Scotland

1394-1437

From THE KINGIS QUAIR

Blissit mot be the heye goddis all,
So fair that glateren in the firmament!
And blissit be thare myght celestiall,
That have convoyit hale, with one assent,
My lufe, and to so glade a consequent!
And thankit be fortunys exiltree
And quhile, that thus so wele has quhirlit me.

Thankit mot be, and fair and lufe befall
The nychtingale, that, with so gud entent,
Sang thare of lufe the notis suete and small,
Quhair my fair hertis lady was present,
Hir with to glad, or that sche forthir went!

lufe] love.   exiltree] axletree.   quhile] wheel.   quhirlit] whirled.
fair] fortune.   quhair] where.   or] before.

And thou gerafloure mot ithankit be
All othir flouris for the lufe of the!

And thankit be the fair castell wall,
   Quhare as I quhilom lukit furth and lent.
Thankit mot be the sanctis marciall,
   That me first causit hath this accident.
   Thankit mot be the grene bewis bent,
Throu quhom, and under, first fortunyt me
My hertis hele and my confort to be.

For to the presence suete and delitable,
   Rycht of this floure that full is of plesance,
By process and by menys favorable,
   First of the blisfull goddis purveyance,
   And syne throu long and trew contynuance
Of veray faith in lufe and trew service,
I cum am, and yit forthir in this wis.

gerafloure] gillyflower.   lukit] looked.   sanctis] saints.   bewis] boughs.

Geoffrey Chaucer
1340?-1400

In his *Descriptive Catalogue,* William Blake said of Chaucer: "As
Newton numbered the stars, and as Linnaeus numbered the plants, so
Chaucer numbered the classes of men."

Those fresh and shining poems, *The Canterbury Tales,* have a curiously strong and resilient line, an urgent life. Their strength is of nature;
and the will which is in them, and which forms their purpose and guides
their direction, is instinctive. Close to the earth as are these poems, often
the strength and movement of the lines, for all the warmth and humanity in them, are like the strength and movement of a slow plant life.

Sometimes the line is divided by a pause that is both long and deep,
but the two halves divided by the pause have a movement and impetus
of a peculiar strength, and this is not the rushing, tumultuous, swelling
movement of the march of waves (for it is often slow, and it has more
direction than that of waves); it has, rather, the inevitability and urgency
of sap rising in a plant. At moments the growth is horizontal, its urgency
keeps close to the earth, as with a melon (because the vowels are equal
in length, in height, or in depth); but more often, owing to a rising

system of sharp vowels, it springs into the air, like sap rising in a tree.

In the "ardent harmony, the heat of spiritual life guiding the movement" of *O Blisful Light,* the supreme magnificence is indeed a song of the morning.

Chaucer, when he wrote of love, had that "sublimity in tenderness" that Swinburne, with truth, said was the reason for Wordsworth's genius at its highest. Chaucer had also the sublimity in sweetness which Wordsworth had not, and which is one of the rarest of qualities; yet, although Chaucer had all the lightness and brightness of a fiery spirit, he had not, like Wordsworth, seen the Burning Bush. Indeed, Chaucer's was a different sublimity and a different tenderness from that of Wordsworth. The sublimity and tenderness of Wordsworth were those of a man who had learned godship, who had worked that he might attain it — teaching and healing with wise and soothing words that little child, the dust. The sublimity and tenderness of Chaucer, whose love poems are among the most noble, most gentle, most moving, and most honey-sweet of our language, neither teach nor heal. They are not those of a god who has once been a man, they are those of a gentle giant who has retained all his humanity and whose preferred companions are men. If he writes of the poor, he has the sweet compassion of the warm human giant for the little, the cold, the hungry.

He is a poet of light. It is interesting to compare the peculiar shining quality of Chaucer with the lucency of Marlowe. The former glitters, like dew upon a forest under the sun. The latter has a still, bright lucency like that upon still water, or a "faint eternal eventide of gems."

Chaucer knew nothing of the black powers that rule the world, or the dark places of the heart. It was to the sweet things of the earth, and the "blisful light," to an earthy God of growing things, that this gentle giant knelt, "with dredful hart and glad devocioun."

MERCILES BEAUTE: FIRST ROUNDEL

Your yën two wol slee me sodenly;
I may the beautee of hem not sustene,
So woundeth hit thourghout my herte kene.

And but your word wol helen hastily
My hertes wounde, while that hit is grene,
    Your yën two wol slee me sodenly;
    I may the beautee of hem not sustene.

Upon my trouthe I sey you feithfully
That ye ben of my lyf and deeth the quene;

yën] eyes.

For with my deeth the trouthe shal be sene.
Your yën two wol slee me sodenly;
I may the beautee of hem not sustene,
So woundeth it thourghout my herte kene.

From TROILUS AND CRISEIDE

CANTICUS TROILI (from Book I)

If no love is, O God, what fele I so?
And if love is, what thing and which is he?
If love be good, from whennes comth my woo?
If it be wikke, a wonder thynketh me,
When every torment and adversite
That cometh of hym, may to me savory thinke,
For ay thurst I, the more that ich it drynke.

And if that at myn owen lust I brenne,
From whennes cometh my waillynge and my
pleynte?
If harm agree me, wherto pleyne I thenne?
I noot, ne whi unwery that I feynte.
O quike deth, O swete harm so queynte,
How may of the in me swich quantite,
But if that I consente that it be?

And if that I consente, I wrongfully
Compleyne, iwis. Thus possed to and fro,
Al sterelees withinne a boot am I
Amydde the see, bitwixen wyndes two,
That in contrarie stonden evere mo.
Allas! what is this wondre maladie?
For hete of cold, for cold of hete, I dye.

wikke] wicked.	savory] pleasant.	brenne] burn.	noot] know not.
possed] tossed.	sterelees] without a rudder.	boot] boat.	

O BLISFUL LIGHT (from Book III)

O blisful light, of which the bemes clere
Adorneth al the thridde heven faire!
O sonnes lief, O Joves doughter deere,
Plesance of love, O goodly debonaire,
In gentil hertes ay redy to repaire!

light] the planet Venus.   thridde] third.   sonnes lief] beloved of the sun.

O veray cause of heele and of gladnesse,
Yheried be thy might and thy goodnesse!

In hevene and helle, in erthe and salte see
   Is felt thy might, if that I wel descerne;
As man, brid, best, fissh, herbe, and grene tree
    Thee fele in times with vapour eterne.
    God loveth, and to love wol nought werne;
And in this world no lives creature
Withouten love is worth, or may endure.

Ye Joves first to thilk effectes glade,
   Thorugh which that thinges liven alle and be,
Comeveden, and amorous him made
    On mortal thing, and as you list, ay ye
    Yeve him in love ese or adversitee;
And in a thousand formes down him sente
For love is erthe, and whom you liste, he hente.

Ye fierse Mars apaisen of his ire,
   And as you list, ye maken hertes digne;
Algates hem that ye wol sette a-fire,
    They dreden shame, and vices they resigne;
    Ye do hem corteis be, fresshe and benigne;
And heighe or lowe, after a wight entendeth,
The joyes that he hath, youre might him sendeth.

Ye holden regne and hous in unitee;
   Ye sothfast cause of frendshipe ben also;
Ye knowe al thilke covered qualitee
    Of thinges, which that folk on wondren so,
    Whan they can nought construe how it may jo,
She loveth him, or why he loveth here,
As why this fissh, and naught that, comth to were.

Ye folk a lawe han set in universe,
   And this knowe I by hem that lovers be,
That whoso striveth with you hath the werse.
    Now, lady bright, for thy benignite,
    At reverence of hem that serven thee,
Whos clerk I am, so techeth me devise
Som joye of that is felt in thy servise.

heele] welfare.   yheried] praised.   werne] refuse.   lives] living.   Joves] Jove (*object of* comeveden).   thilk] the same.   comeveden] excited.   list] please. yeve] give.   hente] seized.   apaisen] appease.   digne] worthy.   algates] at all times.   hem] them.   do] make.   after] according as.   wight] creature. thilke covered] that secret.   jo] come about.   were] weir.   devise] describe.

Ye in my naked herte sentement
　　Inhielde, and do me shewe of thy swetnesse—
Caliope, thy vois be now present,
　　For now is nede; sestou not my destresse,
　　How I mot telle anonright the gladnesse
Of Troilus, to Venus heryinge?
To which gladnesse, who nede hath, God him bringe!

inhielde] infuse.　　sestou] do you see.　　mot] must.　　to Venus heryinge] for Venus'
glory.

BUT WHAN THE COK (from Book III)

But whan the cok, comune astrologer,
　　Gan on his brest to bete and after crowe,
And Lucifer, the dayes messager,
　　Gan for to rise, and out hire bemes throwe,
　　And estward roos, to him that coude it knowe,
Fortuna Major, than anoon Criseide,
With herte soor, to Troilus thus seide:

"Min hertes lif, my trist, and my plesaunce,
　　That I was born, allas, what me is wo,
That day of us moot make disseveraunce!
　　For time it is to rise and hennes go,
　　Or ellis I am lost for evere mo!
O night, allas! why niltou over us hove,
As longe as when Almena lay by Jove?

"O blake night, as folk in bokes rede,
　　That shapen art by God this world to hide
At certein times with thy derke wede,
　　That under that men mighte in reste abide,
　　Wel oughten bestes pleine, and folk thee chide,
That there as day with labour wolde us breste,
That thou thus fleest, and deinest us nought reste.

"Thou doost, allas, to shortly thin office,
　　Thou rakle night, ther God, maker of kinde,
Thee, for thin haste and thin unkinde vice,
　　So faste ay to oure hemisperye binde,
　　That nevere more under the ground thou winde!

trist] trust.　　moot] must.　　hennes] hence.　　niltou hove] will you not hover.
bestes] beasts.　　pleine] complain.　　breste] afflict.　　rakle] hasty.　　ther] may.
kinde] nature.　　hemisperye] hemisphere.　　winde] return.

For now, for thou so hiest out of Troye,
Have I forgon thus hastily my joye!"

This Troilus, that with tho wordes felte,
  As thoughte him tho, for piëtous distresse,
The blody teris from his herte melte,
  As he that nevere yet swich hevinesse
  Assayed hadde, out of so gret gladnesse,
Gan therwithal Criseide, his lady deere,
In armes streine, and seide in this manere:

"O cruel day, accusour of the joye
  That night and love han stole and faste ywrien,
Accorsed be thy coming into Troye,
  For every bore hath oon of thy brighte yën!
  Envious day, what list thee so to spyen?
What hastou lost, why sekestou this place?
Ther God thy light so quenche, for his grace.

"Allas! what have thise loveris thee agilt,
  Dispitous day? Thin be the peine of helle!
For many a lovere hastou slain, and wilt;
  Thy pouringe in wol nowher lat hem dwelle.
  What profrestou thy light here for to selle?
Go selle it hem that smale selis grave;
We wol thee nought, us nedeth no day have."

And ek the sonne Titan gan he chide,
  And seide, "O fool, wel may men thee dispise,
That hast the dawing al night by thy side,
  And suffrest hire so soone up fro thee rise,
  For to disese loveris in this wise.
What! holde youre bed ther, thou, and ek thy Morwe!
I bidde God, so yeve you bothe sorwe!"

Therwith ful soore he sighte, and thus he seide:
  "My lady right, and of my wele or wo
The welle and roote, O goodly min, Criseide,
  And shal I rise, allas, and shal I so?
  Now fele I that min herte moot a-two.
For how sholde I my lif an houre save,
Sin that with you is al the lif ich have?

---

tho] then.   accusour] betrayer.   ywrien] hidden.   bore] chink.   agilt] wronged.
selis] seals.   grave] engrave.   wol] want.   dawing] dawn.   disese] discomfit.
bidde] pray to.   sighte] sighed.

"What shal I don? For, certes, I not how,
Ne whan, allas! I shal the time see
That in this plit I may ben eft with you.
And of my lif, God woot how that shall be,
Sin that desir right now so biteth me,
That I am ded anon, but I retourne.
How sholde I longe, allas, fro you sojourne?

"But natheles, min owen lady bright,
Yit were it so that I wiste outrely
That I, youre humble servant and youre knight,
Were in youre herte yset as fermely
As ye in min, the which thing, trewely,
Me levere were than thise worldes tweine,
Yet sholde I bet enduren al my peine."

To that Criseide answerde right anon,
And with a sik she seide, "O herte deere,
The game, ywis, so forforth now is gon,
That first shal Phebus fallen fro his spere,
And everich egle ben the douves feere,
And every roche out of his place sterte,
Er Troilus out of Criseides herte."

not] know not.   eft] again.   but] unless.   outrely] absolutely.   bet] better.
sik] sigh.   forforth] far.   spere] sphere.   feere] mate.   roche] rock.

From THE CANTERBURY TALES

PROLOGE OF THE PRIORESSES TALE

"O Lord, oure Lord, thy name how merveillous
Is in this large world ysprad," quod she;
"For noght oonly thy laude precious
Parfourned is by men of dignitee,
But by the mouth of children thy bountee
Parfourned is, for on the brest soukynge
Somtyme shewen they thyn heriynge.

"Wherfore in laude, as I best kan or may,
Of thee and of the white lylye flour
Which that the bar, and is a mayde alway,
To telle a storie I wol do my labour;
Nat that I may encreessen hir honour,

ysprad] spread.   parfourned] fulfilled.   heriynge] praise.   bar] bare.

For she hirself is honour and the roote
Of bountee, next hir Sone, and soules boote.

"O mooder Mayde! o mayde Mooder free!
  O bussh unbrent, brennynge in Moyses sighte,
That ravyshedest doun fro the Deitee,
    Thurgh thyn humblesse, the Goost that in th' alighte,
    Of whos vertu, whan he thyn herte lighte,
Conceyved was the Fadres sapience,
Helpe me to telle it in thy reverence!

"Lady, thy bountee, thy magnificence,
  Thy vertu, and thy grete humylitee,
Ther may no tonge expresse in no science;
    For somtyme, Lady, er men praye to thee,
    Thou goost biforn of thy benyngnytee,
And getest us the lyght, thurg thy preyere,
To gyden us unto thy Sone so deere.

"My konnyng is so wayk, o blisful Queene,
  For to declare thy grete worthynesse
That I ne may the weighte nat susteene;
    But as a child of twelf month oold, or lesse,
    That kan unnethes any word expresse,
Right so fare I, and therfore I yow preye,
Gydeth my song that I shal of yow seye."

boote] bounty.   konnyng] skill, cunning.   wayk] weak.   unnethes] hardly.

THE NUN'S PRIEST'S TALE

A povre widwe, somdeel stape in age
Was whilom dwelling in a narwe cotage,
Biside a grove, stondinge in a dale.
This widwe, of which I telle you my tale,
Sin thilke day that she was last a wif,
In pacience ladde a ful simple lif,
For litel was hir catel and hir rente.
By housbondrye of swich as God hire sente
She foond hirself and eek hir doghtren two.
Thre large sowes hadde she, and namo,
Three keen, and eek a sheep that highte Malle.
Ful sooty was hire bowr and eek hir halle,

somdeel] somewhat.   stape] advanced.   namo] no more.   keen] cows.

In which she eet ful many a sklendre meel.
O poinaunt sauce hir neded never a deel.
No deintee morsel passed thurgh hir throte;
Hir diete was accordant to hir cote.
Repleccioun ne made hire nevere sik;
Attempree diete was al hir physik,
And exercise, and hertes suffisaunce.
The goute lette hire nothing for to daunce,
N'apoplexye shente nat hir heed.
No win ne drank she, neither whit ne reed;
Hir bord was served moost with whit and blak,
Milk and brown breed, in which she foond no lak,
Seind bacoun, and somtime an ey or tweye;
For she was, as it were, a maner deye.
    A yeerd she hadde, enclosed al aboute
With stickes, and a drye dich withoute,
In which she hadde a cok, hight Chauntecleer.
In al the land of crowing nas his peer.
His vois was murier than the murye orgon
On messe-dayes that in the chirche gon.
Wel sikerer was his crowing in his logge
Than is a clocke or an abbey orlogge.
By nature he knew ech ascencioun
Of the equinoxial in thilke town;
For whan degrees fiftene weren ascended,
Thanne crew he, that it mighte nat been amended.
His coomb was redder than the fin coral,
And batailled as it were a castel wal;
His bile was blak, and as the jeet it shoon;
Lik asure were his legges and his toon;
His nailes whitter than the lilye flowr,
And lik the burned gold was his colour.
This gentil cok hadde in his governaunce
Sevene hennes for to doon al his plesaunce,
Whiche were his sustres and his paramours,
And wonder lik to him, as of colours;
Of whiche the faireste hewed on hir throte
Was cleped faire damoisele Pertelote.
Curteis she was, discreet, and debonaire,
And compaignable, and bar hirself so faire,
Sin thilke day that she was seven night oold,
That trewely she hath the herte in hoold

poinaunt] piquant.   deel] bit.   lette . . . daunce] in no way hindered her from
dancing.   shente] hurt.   seind] broiled.   ey] egg.   deye] dairywoman.
sikerer] more reliable.   logge] resting place.   orlogge] clock.
batailled] embattled, *here* crenellated.   toon] toes.

Of Chauntecleer, loken in every lith;
He loved hire so that wel was him therwith.
But swich a joye was it to here hem singe,
Whan that the brighte sonne gan to springe,
In sweete accord, "My lief is faren in londe!"
For thilke time, as I have understonde,
Beestes and briddes coude speke and singe.

  And so bifel that in a daweninge,
As Chauntecleer among his wives alle
Sat on his perche, that was in the halle,
And next him sat this faire Pertelote,
This Chauntecleer gan gronen in his throte,
As man that in his dreem is drecched soore.
And whan that Pertelote thus herde him roore,
She was agast, and seide, "Herte deere,
What eileth you, to grone in this manere?
Ye been a verray sleper; fy, for shame!"

  And he answerde, and seide thus: "Madame,
I pray you that ye take it nat agrief.
By God, me mette I was in swich meschief
Right now, that yet min herte is soore afright.
Now God," quod he, "my swevene recche aright,
And kepe my body out of foul prisoun!
Me mette how that I romed up and down
Withinne our yeerd, wheer as I saugh a beest
Was lik an hound, and wolde han maad areest
Upon my body, and wolde han had me deed.
His colour was bitwixe yelow and reed,
And tipped was his tail and bothe his eeris
With blak, unlik the remenant of his heeris;
His snoute smal, with glowinge eyen tweye.
Yet of his look for feere almoost I deye;
This caused me my groning, doutelees."

  "Avoy!" quod she, "fy on you, hertelees!
Allas!" quod she, "for, by that God above,
Now han ye lost min herte and al my love.
I can nat love a coward, by my feith!
For certes, what so any womman seith,
We alle desiren, if it mighte bee,
To han housbondes hardy, wise, and free,
And secree, and no nigard, ne no fool,
Ne him that is agast of every tool,

---

loken in every lith] locked in every limb.   lief] dear one.   faren] gone.
drecched] troubled.   swevene] dream.   recche aright] read aright.
remenant] rest.   heeris] hairs, coat.   secree] discreet.

Ne noon avauntour, by that God above!
How dorste ye seyn, for shame, unto youre love
That any thing mighte make you aferd?
Have ye no mannes herte, and han a berd?
Allas! and conne ye been agast of swevenis?
Nothing, God woot, but vanitee in sweven is.
Swevenes engendren of replecciouns,
And ofte of fume and of complecciouns,
Whan humours been to habundant in a wight.
Certes this dreem, which ye han met tonight,
Cometh of the greete superfluitee
Of youre rede colera, pardee,
Which causeth folk to dreden in hir dremes
Or arwes, and of fir with rede lemes,
Of rede beestes, that they wol hem bite,
Of contek, and of whelpes, grete and lite;
Right as the humour of malencolye
Causeth ful many a man in sleep to crye
For feere of blake beres, or boles blake,
Or elles blake develes wole hem take.
Of othere humours coude I telle also
That werken many a man in sleep ful wo;
But I wol passe as lightly as I can.
  Lo Catoun, which that was so wis a man,
Seide he nat thus, 'Ne do no fors of dremes'?
  Now sire," quod she, "whan we flee fro the bemes,
For Goddes love, as taak som laxatif.
Up peril of my soule and of my lif,
I conseille you the beste, I wol nat lie,
That bothe of colere and of malencolye
Ye purge you; and for ye shal not tarye,
Though in this town is noon apothecarye,
I shal myself to herbes techen you
That shul been for youre hele and for youre prow;
And in oure yeerd tho herbes shal I finde
The whiche han of hire propretee by kinde
To purge you binethe and eek above.
Foryet nat this, for Goddes owene love!
Ye been ful colerik of compleccioun;
Ware the sonne in his ascencioun
Ne finde you nat repleet of humours hoote.
And if it do, I dar wel leye a grote,
That ye shul have a fevere terciane,

---

avauntour] braggart, boaster.   **engendren**] begin in.   **replecciouns**] overindul-
gence.   **fume**] vapor.   **colera**] choler.   **arwes**] arrows.   **lemes**] flames.
contek] strife.   **boles**] bulls.   **do no fors of**] pay no heed to.   **prow**] benefit.

Or an agu, that may be youre bane.
A day or two ye shul have digestives
Of wormes, er ye take youre laxatives
Of lauriol, centaure, and fumetere,
Or elles of ellebor, that groweth there,
Of catapuce, or of gaitris beryis,
Of herbe ive, growing in oure yeerd, ther mery is;
Pekke hem up right as they growe and ete hem in.
Be mirye, housbonde, for youre fader kin!
Dredeth no dreem, I can sey you namoore."
    "Madame," quod he, "graunt mercy of youre
        loore.
But nathelees, as touching daun Catoun,
That hath of wisdom swich a greet renown,
Though that he bad no dremes for to drede,
By God, men may in olde bookes rede
Of many a man moore of auctorite
Than evere Caton was, so moot I thee,
That al the revers seyn of this sentence,
And han wel founden by experience
That dremes been significaciouns
As wel of joye as of tribulaciouns
That folk enduren in this lif present.
Ther nedeth make of this noon argument;
The verray preeve sheweth it in dede.
    Oon of the gretteste auctour that men rede
Seith thus; that whilom two felawes wente
On pilgrimage, in a ful good entente;
And happed so, they coomen in a town
Wher as ther was swich congregacioun
Of peple, and eek so streit of herbergage,
That they ne founde as muche as o cotage
In which they bothe mighte ylogged bee.
Wherfore they mosten of necessitee,
As for that night, departen compaignye;
And ech of hem gooth to his hostelrye,
And took his logging as it wolde falle.
That oon of hem was logged in a stalle,
Fer in a yeerd, with oxen of the plough;
That oother man was logged wel ynough,
As was his aventure or his fortune,
That us governeth alle as in commune.
    And so bifel that, longe er it were day,
This man mette in his bed, ther as he lay,

---

daun] don (lord).   moot I thee] may I thrive.   verray preeve] actual proof.
herbergage] lodging.   mette] dreamed.

How that his felawe gan upon him calle,
And seide, 'Allas! for in an oxes stalle
This night I shal be mordred ther I lie.
Now help me, deere brother, or I die.
In alle haste com to me!' he saide.
This man out of his sleep for feere abraide;
But whan that he was wakened of his sleep,
He turned him, and took of this no keep.
Him thoughte his dreem nas but a vanitee.
Thus twies in his sleping dremed hee;
And atte thridde time yet his felawe
Cam, as him thoughte, and seide, 'I am now slawe.
Bihoold my bloody woundes depe and wide!
Aris up erly in the morwe tide,
And at the west gate of the town,' quod he,
'A carte ful of dong ther shaltou se,
In which my body is hid ful prively;
Do thilke carte arresten boldely.
My gold caused my mordre, sooth to sayn.'
And tolde him every point how he was slain,
With a ful pitous face, pale of hewe.
And truste wel, his dreem he foond ful trewe,
For on the morwe, as soone as it was day,
To his felawes in he took the way;
And whan that he cam to this oxes stalle,
After his felawe he bigan to calle.
　　The hostiler answerede him anon,
And seide, 'Sire, your felawe is agon.
As soone as day he wente out of the town.'
　　This man gan fallen in suspecioun,
Remembringe on his dremes that he mette,
And forth he gooth — nolenger wolde he lette —
Unto the west gate of the town, and fond
A dong-carte, as it were to donge lond,
That was arrayed in that same wise
As ye han herd the dede man devise.
And with an hardy herte he gan to crye
Vengeance and justice of this felonye.
'My felawe mordred is this same night,
And in this carte he lith gaping upright.
I crye out on the ministres,' quod he,
'That sholden kepe and reulen this citee.
Harrow! allas! heere lith my felawe slain!'
What sholde I moore unto this tale sayn?
The peple out sterte and caste the cart to grounde,

abraide] awoke.　　lette] wait.　　upright] flat.　　harrow] help.

And in the middel of the dong they founde
The dede man, that mordred was al newe.

O blisful God, that art so just and trewe,
Lo, how that thou biwreyest mordre alway!

Mordre wol out, that se we day by day.
Mordre is so wlatsom and abhominable
To God, that is so just and resonable,
That he ne wol nat suffre it heled be,
Though it abide a yeer, or two, or thre.
Mordre wol out, this my conclusioun.
An right anon, ministres of that town
Han hent the carter and so soore him pined,
And eek the hostiler so soore engined,
That they biknewe hire wickednesse anon,
And were anhanged by the necke-bon.

Heere may men seen that dremes been to drede.
And certes in the same book I rede,
Right in the nexte chapitre after this —
I gabbe nat, so have I joye or blis —
Two men that wolde han passed over see,
For certein cause, into a fer contree,
If that the wind ne hadde been contrarye,
That made hem in a citee for to tarye
That stood ful mirye upon an haven-side;
But on a day, again the even-tide,
The wind gan chaunge, and blew right as hem leste.
Jolif and glad they wente unto hir reste,
And casten hem ful erly for to saille.
But to that o man fil a greet mervaille:
That oon of hem, in sleping as he lay,
Him mette a wonder dreem again the day.
Him thoughte a man stood by his beddes side,
And him comanded that he sholde abide,
And seide him thus, 'If thou tomorwe wende,
Thou shalt be dreint; my tale is at an ende.'
He wook, and tolde his felawe what he mette,
And preyde him his viage for to lette;
As for that day, he preyde him to abide.
His felawe, that lay by his beddes side,
Gan for to laughe, and scorned him ful faste.
'No dreem,' quod he, 'may so min herte agaste
That I wol lette for to do my thinges.
I sette nat a straw by thy dreminges,

biwreyest] disclose.   wlatsom] loathesome.   heled] concealed.   hent] caught.
pined] tortured.   engined] racked.   biknewe] confessed.   gabbe] lie.   o] one.
fil] befell.   dreint] drowned.

For swevenes been but vanitees and japes.
Men dreme alday of owles and of apes,
And eek of many a maze therwithal;
Men dreme of thing that nevere was ne shal.
But sith I see that thou wolt heere abide,
And thus forsleuthen wilfully thy tide,
God woot, it reweth me; and have good day!'
And thus he took his leve, and wente his way.
But er that he hadde half his cours yseiled,
Noot I nat why, ne what mischaunce it eiled,
But casuelly the shippes botme rente,
And ship and man under the water wente
In sighte of othere shippes it biside,
That with hem seiled at the same tide.
And therfore, faire Pertelote so deere,
By swiche ensamples of olde maystou leere
That no man sholde been to recchelees
Of dremes; for I seye thee, doutelees,
That many a dreem ful soore is for to drede.
   Lo, in the lif of Seint Kenelm I rede,
That was Kenulphus sone, the noble king
Of Mercenrike, how Kenelm mette a thing.
A lite er he was mordred, on a day,
His mordre in his avisioun he say.
His norice him expouned every deel
His sweven, and bad him for to kepe him weel
For traisoun; but he nas but seven yeer oold,
And therfore litel tale hath he toold
Of any dreem, so hooly was his herte.
By God! I hadde levere than my sherte
That ye hadde rad his legende, as have I.
   Dame Pertelote, I sey you trewely,
Marcrobeus, that writ the avisioun
In Affrike of the worthy Sipioun,
Affermeth dremes, and seith that they been
Warninge of thinges that men after seen.
And forthermoore, I pray you, looketh wel
In the Olde Testament, of Daniel,
If he heeld dremes any vanitee.
Reed eek of Joseph, and ther shul ye see
Wher dremes be somtime — I sey nat alle —
Warninge of thinges that shul after falle.

alday] constantly.   maze] delusion.   forsleuthen] waste in sloth.   noot] know not.
mischaunce it eiled] was the matter.   casuelly] by accident.   leere] learn.
reccheless] careless.   Mercenrike] Mercia.   lite] little.   avisioun] vision,
dream.   norice] nurse.   litel tale hath he toold] set no store by.

Looke of Egypte the king, daun Pharao,
His bakere and his butiller also,
Wher they ne felte noon effect in dremes.
Whoso wol seken actes of sondry remes
May rede of dremes many a wonder thing.
Lo Cresus, which that was of Lyde king,
Mette he nat that he sat upon a tree,
Which signified he sholde anhanged bee?
Lo heere Andromacha, Ectores wif,
That day that Ector sholde lese his lif,
She dremed on the same night biforn
How that the lif of Ector sholde be lorn,
If thilke day he wente into bataille.
She warned him, but it mighte nat availle;
He wente for to fighte natheles,
But he was slain anon of Achilles.
But thilke tale is al to longe to telle,
And eek it is ny day, I may nat dwelle.
Shortly I seye, as for conclusioun,
That I shal han of this avisioun
Adversitee; and I seye forthermoor,
That I ne telle of laxatives no stoor,
For they been venimous, I woot it weel;
I hem diffye, I love hem never a deel!
　　Now let us speke of mirthe, and stinte al **this.**
Madame Pertelote, so have I blis,
Of o thing God hath sent me large grace;
For whan I se the beautee of youre face,
Ye been so scarlet reed aboute youre yën,
It maketh al my drede for to dien;
For al so siker as *In principio,*
Mulier est hominis confusio, —
Madame, the sentence of this Latin is,
'Womman is mannes joye and al his blis.'
For whan I feele a-night your softe side,
Al be it that I may nat on you ride,
For that oure perce is maad so narwe, allas!
I am so ful of joye and of solas,
That I diffye bothe sweven and dreem."
And with that word he fley down fro the beem,
For it was day, and eke his hennes alle,
And with a chuk he gan hem for to calle,
For he hadde founde a corn, lay in the yerd.
Real he was, he was namoore aferd.

wher] whether.　　remes] realms.　　lorn] lost.　　telle . . . no stoor] set **no store by.**
yën] eyes.　　siker] sure.　　sentence] meaning, theme.　　real] **regal.**

He fethered Pertelote twenty time,
And trad hire eke as ofte, er it was prime.
He looketh as it were a grim leoun,
And on his toos he rometh up and down;
Him deigned nat to sette his foot to grounde.
He chucketh, whan he hath a corn yfounde,
And to him rennen thanne his wives alle.
Thus royal, as a prince is in his halle,
Leve I this Chauntecleer in his pasture,
And after wol I telle his aventure.
    Whan that the month in which the world bigan,
That highte March, whan God first maked man,
Was compleet, and passed were also,
Sin March bigan, thritty dayes and two,
Bifel that Chauntecleer in al his pride,
His sevene wves walkinge by his side,
Caste up his eyen to the brighte sonne,
That in the signe of Taurus hadde yronne
Twenty degrees and oon, and somewhat moore,
And knew by kinde, and by noon oother loore,
That it was prime, and crew with blisful stevene.
"The sonne," he seide, "is clomben up on hevene
Fourty degrees and oon, and moore ywis.
Madame Pertelote, my worldes blis,
Herkneth thise blisful briddes how they singe,
And se the fresshe flowres how they springe,
Ful is min herte or revel and solas!"
But sodeinly him fil a sorweful cas,
For evere the latter ende of joye is wo.
God woot that worldly joye is soone ago;
And if a rethor coude faire endite,
He in a cronicle saufly mighte it write
As for a soverein notabilitee.
Now every wis man, lat him herkne me;
This storye is also trewe, I undertake,
As is the book of Launcelot de Lake,
That wommen holde in ful greet reverence.
Now wol I torne again to my sentence.
    A col-fox, ful of sly iniquitee,
That in the grove hadde woned yeres three,
By heigh imaginacioun forncast,
The same night thurghout the hegges brast

by kinde] by the instinct of his species.   stevene] voice.   ywis] indeed.
cas] accident.   rethor] rhetorician.   col-fox] coal-fox, fox with black markings.
woned] lived.   by heigh imaginacioun forncast] by divine will predestined.
hegges] hedges.   brast] broke.

Into the yerd ther Chauntecleer the faire
Was wont, and eek his wives, to repaire;
And in a bed of wortes stille he lay,
Til it was passed undren of the day,
Waitinge his time on Chauntecleer to falle,
As gladly doon thise homicides alle
That in await liggen to mordre men.
O false mordrour, lurkinge in thy den!
O newe Scariot, newe Genilon,
False dissimulour, o Greek Sinon,
That broghtest Troye al outrely to sorwe!
O Chauntecleer, acursed be that morwe
That thou into that yerd flaugh fro the bemes!
Thou were ful wel ywarned by thy dremes
That thilke day was perilous to thee;
But what that God forwoot moot nedes bee,
After the opinioun of certein clerkis.
Witnesse on him that any parfit clerk is,
That in scole is greet altercacioun
In this mateere, and greet disputisoun,
And hath been of an hundred thousand men.
But I ne can nat bulte it to the bren,
As can the hooly doctour Augustin,
Or Boece, or the Bisshop Bradwardin,
Wheither that Goddes worthy forwiting
Streineth me nedely for to doon a thing, —
"Nedely" clepe I simple necessitee;
Or elles, if free chois be graunted me
To do that same thing, or do it noght,
Though God forwoot it er that it was wroght;
Or if his witing streineth never a deel
But by necessitee condicioneel.
I wol nat han to do of swich mateere;
My tale is of a cok, as ye may heere,
That tok his conseil of his wif, with sorwe,
To walken in the yerd upon that morwe
That he hadde met that dreem that I you tolde.
Wommennes conseils been ful ofte colde;
Wommannes conseil broghte us first to wo,
And made Adam fro Paradis to go,
Ther as he was ful mirye and wel at ese.
But for I noot to whom it might displese,
If I conseil of wommen wolde blame,
Passe over, for I seide it in my game.

wortes] weeds.　　　undren] mid-morning.　　　forwoot] foresees.　　　bulte to the
bren] sift to the husk.　　　clepe] call, name.

Rede auctours, where they trete of swich mateere,
And what they seyn of wommen ye may heere.
Thise been the cockes wordes, and nat mine;
I can noon harm of no womman divine.

 Faire in the soond, to bathe hire mirily,
Lith Pertelote, and alle hire sustres by,
Again the sonne, and Chauntecleer so free
Soong murier than the mermaide in the see;
But Physiologus seith sikerly
How that they singen wel and mirily.
And so bifel that, as he caste his yë
Among the wortes on a boterflye,
He was war of this fox, that lay ful lowe.
Nothinge ne liste him thanne for to crowe,
But cride anon, "Cok! Cok!" and up he sterte
As man that was affrayed in his herte.
For natureelly a beest desireth flee
Fro his contrarye, if he may it see,
Though he never erst hadde sein it with his yë.

 This Chauntecleer, whan he gan him espye,
He wolde han fled, but that the fox anon
Seide, "Gentil sire, allas! wher wol ye gon?
Be ye affrayed of me that am youre freend?
Now, certes, I were worse than a feend,
If I to you wolde harm or vileinye!
I am nat come youre conseil for t'espye,
But trewely, for cause of my cominge
Was oonly for to herkne how that ye singe.
For trewely, ye have as mirye a stevene
As any aungel hath that is in hevene.
Therwith ye han in musik moore feelinge
Than hadde Boece, or any that can singe.
My lord youre fader — God his soule blesse! —
And eek youre mooder, of hire gentillesse,
Han in min hous ybeen to my greet ese;
And certes, sire, ful fain wolde I you plese.
But for men speke of singing, I wol seye,
So moote I brouke wel mine eyen tweye,
Save you, I herde nevere man so singe
As dide your fader in the morweninge.
Certes, it was of herte, al that he song.
And for to make his vois the moore strong,
He wolde so peine him that with bothe his yën
He moste winke, so loude he wolde cryen,
And stonden on his tiptoon therwithal,

soond] sand.   liste] pleased.   brouke] use, enjoy.   peine] take pains,

And strecche forth his necke long and smal.
And eek he was of swich discrecioun
That ther nas no man in no regioun
That him in song or wisedom mighte passe.
I have wel rad in 'Daun Burnel the Asse,'
Among his vers, how that ther was cok,
For that a preestes sone yaf him a knok
Upon his leg whil he was yong and nice,
He made him for to lese his benefice.
But certein, ther nis no comparisoun
Bitwixe the wisedom and discrecioun
Of youre fader and of his subtiltee.
Now singeth, sire, for seinte charitee;
Lta se, conne ye youre fader countrefete?"
    This Chauntecleer his winges gan to bete,
As man that coude his traisoun nat espye,
So was he ravisshed with his flaterye.
    Allas! ye lordes, many a fals flatour
Is in youre courtes, and many a losengeour,
That plesen you wel moore, by my feith,
Than he that soothfastnesse unto you seith.
Redeth Ecclesiaste of flaterye;
Beth war, ye lordes, of hir trecherye.
    This Chauntecleer stood hye upon his toos,
Strecchinge his necke, and heeld his eyen cloos,
And gan to crowe loude for the nones.
And daun Russell the fox stirte up atones,
And by the gargat hente Chauntecleer,
And on his bak toward the wode him beer,
For yet ne was ther no man that him sewed.
    O destinee, that mayst nat been eschewed!
Allas, that Chauntecleer fleigh fro the bemes!
Allas, his wif ne roghte nat of dremes!
And on a Friday fil al this meschaunce.
    O Venus, that art goddesse of plesaunce,
Sin that thy servant was this Chauntecleer,
And in thy service dide al his poweer,
Moore for delit than world to multiplye,
Why woldestou suffre him on thy day to die?
    O Gaufred, deere maister soverain,
That whan thy worthy king Richard was slain
With shot, compleinedest his deeth so soore,
Why ne hadde I now thy sentence and thy loore
The Friday for to chide, as diden ye?

yaf] gave.   losengeour] deceiver.   nones] nonce, occasion.   atones] at once.
gargat] throat.   sewed] pursued.   roghte nat of] set no store by.   shot] a missile.

For on a Friday, soothly, slain was he,
Thanne wolde I shewe you how that I coude pleine
For Chauntecleres drede and for his peine.
　Certes, swich cry ne lamentacion,
Was nevere of ladies maad whan Ilion
Was wonne, and Pyrrus with his streite swerd,
Whan he hadde hent king Priam by the berd,
And slain him, as seith us *Eneidos,*
As maden alle the hennes in the clos,
Whan they had sein of Chauntecleer the sighte.
But sovereinly dame Pertelote shrighte,
Ful louder than dide Hasdrubales wif,
Whan that hir housbonde hadde lost his lif,
And that the Romains hadde brend Cartage.
She was so ful of torment and of rage
That wilfully into the fir she sterte,
And brende hirselven with a stedefast herte.
　O woful hennes, right so criden ye,
As, whan that Nero brende the citee
Of Rome, criden senatoures wives
For that hir husbondes losten alle hir lives;
Withouten gilt this Nero hath hem slain.
Now wole I turne to my tale again.
　This sely widwe and eek hir doghtres two
Herden thise hennes crye and maken wo,
And out at dores stirten they anon,
And sien the fox toward the grove gon,
And bar upon his bak the cok away,
And criden, "Out! harrow! and weilaway!
Ha! Ha! the fox!" and after him they ran,
And eek with staves many another man.
Ran Colle oure dogge, and Talbot, and Gerland,
And Malkin, with a distaf in hir hand;
Ran cow and calf, and eek the verray hogges,
So fered for the berking of the dogges
And shouting of the men and wommen eeke,
They ronne so hem thoughte hir herte breeke.
They yolleden as feendes doon in helle;
The dokes criden as men wolde hem quelle;
The gees for feere flowen over the trees;
Out of the hive cam the swarm of bees.
So hidous was the noise, a, *benedicitee!*
Certes, he Jacke Straw and his meinee
Ne made nevere shoutes half so shrille,

---

sein] seen.　　　shrighte] shrieked.　　　sterte] rushed.　　　sely] simple, poor.
yolleden] yelled.　　dokes] ducks.　　quelle] kill.　　　meinee] followers.

Whan that they wolden any Fleming kille,
As thilke day was maad upon the fox.
Of bras they broghten bemes, and of box,
Of horn, of boon, in whiche they blewe and pouped,
And therwithal they skriked and they houped.
It semed as that hevene sholde falle.

Now, goode men, I prey you herkneth alle:
Lo, how Fortune turneth sodeinly
The hope and pride eek of hir enemy!
This cok, that lay upon the foxes bak,
In al his drede unto the fox he spak,
And seide, "Sire, if that I were as ye,
Yet sholde I seyn, as wis God helpe me,
'Turneth again, ye proude cherles alle!
A verray pestilence upon you falle!
Now am I come unto the wodes side;
Maugree youre heed, the cok shal heere abide.
I wol him ete, in feith, and that anon!'"

The fox answerde, "In feith, it shal be don."
And as he spak that word, al sodeinly
This cok brak from his mouth deliverly,
And heighe upon a tree he fleigh anon.
And whan the fox saugh that the cok was gon,
"Alas!" quod he, "O Chauntecleer, allas!
I have to you," quod he, "ydoon trespas,
In as muche as I maked you aferd
Whan I you hente and broghte out of the yerd.
But, sire, I dide it in no wicke entente.
Com down, and I shal telle you what I mente;
I shal seye sooth to you, God help me so!"

"Nay thanne," quod he, "I shrewe us bothe two.
And first I shrewe myself, bothe blood and bones,
If thou bigile me ofter than ones.
Thou shalt namoore, thurgh thy flaterye,
Do me to singe and winke with min yë;
For he that winketh, whan he sholde se,
Al wilfully, God lat him nevere thee!"

"Nay," quod the fox, "but God yeve him meschaunce,
That is so undiscreet of governaunce
That jangleth whan he sholde holde his pees."

Lo, swich it is for to be recchelees
And necligent, and truste on flaterye.
But ye that holden this tale a folye,

bemes] trumpets.   pouped] tooted.   houped] whooped.   maugree your
heed] despite all you can do.   delivery] nimbly.   shrewe] curse.   thee] prosper.
jangleth] chatters.

As of a fox, or of a cok and hen
Taketh the moralite, goode men.
For seint Paul seith that al that writen is,
To oure doctrine it is ywrite, ywis;
Taketh the fruit, and lat the chaf be stille.
Now, goode God, if that it be thy wille,
As seith my lord, so make us alle goode men,
And bringe us to his heighe blisse! Amen.

From THE LEGEND OF GOOD WOMEN: PROLOGUE

WHAN THAT THE MONTH OF MAY

Whan that the month of May
Is comen, and that I here the foules synge,
And that the floures gynnen for to sprynge,
Farewel my bok, and my devocioun!
Now have I thanne eek this condicioun
That, of al the floures in the mede,
Thanne love I most thise floures white and rede,
Swiche as men callen daysyes in our toun.
To hem have I so gret affeccioun,
As I seyde erst, whanne comen is the May,
That in my bed ther daweth me no day
That I nam up and walkyng in the mede
To seen this flour ayein the sonne sprede,
Whan it upryseth erly by the morwe.
That blisful sighte softneth al my sorwe,
So glad am I, whan that I have presence
Of it, to doon it alle reverence,
As she that is of alle floures flour,
Fulfilled of al vertu and honour,
And evere ilyke faire, and fressh of hewe;
And I love it, and ever ylike newe,
And evere shal, til that myn herte dye.
Al swere I nat, of this I wol nat lye,
Ther loved no wight hotter in his lyve.
And whan that hit ys eve, I renne blyve,
As sone as evere the sonne gynneth weste,
To seen this flour, how it wol go to reste,
For fere of nyght, so hateth she derknesse.
Hire chere is pleynly sprad in the brightnesse

rede] red, golden.   erst] first.   nam] am not.   ayein] against.   ilyke] alike.
al] although.   blyve] swiftly.   chere] face, countenance.

Of the sonne, for ther yt wol unclose.
Allas, that I ne had Englyssh, ryme or prose,
Suffisant this flour to preyse aryght! . . .

She is the clernesse and the verray lyght
That in this derke world me wynt and ledeth.
The hert in-with my sorwfull brest yow dredeth
And loveth so sore that ye ben verrayly
The maistresse of my wit, and nothing I.
My word, my werk ys knyt so in youre bond
That, as an harpe obeieth to the hond
And maketh it soune after his fyngerynge,
Ryght so mowe ye oute of myn herte bringe
Swich vois, ryght as yow lyst, to laughe or pleyne.
Be ye my gide and lady sovereyne!
As to myn erthly god to yow I calle,
Bothe in this werk and in my sorwes alle. . . .

And doun on knes anoon-ryght I me sette,
And, as I koude, this fresshe flour I grette,
Knelyng alwey, til it unclosed was,
Upon the smale, softe, swote gras,
That was with floures swote enbrouded al,
Of swich swetnesse and swich odour overal,
That, for to speke of gomme, or herbe, or tree,
Comparisoun may noon ymaked bee;
For yt surmounteth pleynly alle odoures,
And of riche beaute alle floures.
Forgeten hadde the erthe his pore estat
Of wynter, that hym naked made and mat,
And with his swerd of cold so sore greved;
Now hath th' atempre sonne all that releved,
That naked was, and clad him new agayn.
The smale foules, of the sesoun fayn,
That from the panter and the net ben scaped,
Upon the foweler, that hem made awhaped
In wynter, and distroyed hadde hire brood,
In his dispit hem thoghte yt did hem good
To synge of hym, and in hir song despise
The foule cherl that, for his coveytise,
Had hem betrayed with his sophistrye.
This was hire song, "The foweler we deffye,

---

wynt] turns, directs. pleyne] complain. anoon-ryght] immediately.
swote] sweet. noon] none. mat] dead. atempre] mild. fayn] glad.
panter] bag-net. awhaped] scared.

And al his craft." And somme songen clere
Layes of love, that joye it was to here,
In worship and in preysinge of hir make;
And for the newe blisful somers sake,
Upon the braunches ful of blosmes softe,
In hire delyt they turned hem ful ofte,
And songen, "Blessed be Seynt Valentyn,
For on this day I chees yow to be myn,
Withouten repentyng, myn herte swete!"

make] mate.

BALADE

Hyd, Absolon, thy gilte tresses clere;
   Ester, ley thou thy meknesse al adown;
Hyd, Jonathas, al thy frendly manere;
   Penalopee and Marcia Catoun,
   Make of youre wifhod no comparysoun;
Hyde ye youre beautes, Ysoude and Eleyne:
My lady cometh, that al this may disteyne.
Thy faire body, lat yt nat appere,
   Lavyne; and thou, Lucresse of Rome toun,
And Polixene, that boghten love so dere,
   And Cleopatre, with al thy passyoun,
   Hyde ye your trouthe of love and your renoun;
And thou, Tisbe, that hast for love swich peyne:
My lady cometh, that al this may disteyne.
Herro, Dido, Laudomia, alle yfere,
   And Phillis, hangyng for thy Demophoun,
And Canace, espied by thy chere,
   Ysiphile, betrayed with Jasoun,
   Maketh of your trouthe neythir boost ne soun;
Nor Ypermystre or Adriane, ye tweyen:
My lady cometh, that al this may dysteyne.

disteyne] dim.   trouthe] fidelity.   yfere] together, in company.   chere] face.
soun] vaunt.

John Gower
d. 1408

From CONFESSIO AMANTIS: CEIX AND ALCEONE

THE HOUSE OF SLEEP

This Yris, fro the high stage
Which undertake hath the message,
Her reyny cope dede upon,
The which was wonderli begon
With colours of diverse hewe,
An hundred mo than men it knewe;
The hevene light unto a bowe
She bende, and so she cam down lowe,
The god of Slep wher that she fond;
And that was in a strange lond,
Which marcheth upon Chymerie:
For there, as saith the Poesie,
The God of Slep hath made his hous,
Which of entaille is merveilous.
    Under an hell ther is a cave,
Which of the sonne mai noght have,
So that noman mai knowe ariht
The point betwen the dai and nyht:
Ther is no fyr, ther is no sparke,
Ther is no dore, which mai charke,
Wherof an yhe should unschette,
So that inward there is no lette.
And for to speke of that withoute,
Ther stands no gret tree nyh aboute
Wher on ther myhte crowe or pie
Alihte, for to clepe or crie;
Ther is no cok to crowe day,
Ne beste non which noise may;
The hell bot al aboute round
Ther is growende upon the ground
Popi, which berth the sed of slep,
With othre herbes suche an hep.
A stille water for the nones

---

reyny] rainy.   dede upon] put on.   begon] adorned.   marcheth] borders.
entaille] fashion.   hell] hall.   charke] creak.   yhe should unschette] eye should
unclose.   lette] obstacle.   clepe] call.   beste] beast.   the hell bot al aboute
round] all round about the hall.   sed] seed.   nones] nonce.

Rennende upon the smale stones,
Which hihte of Lethes the rivere,
Under that hell in such manere
Ther is, which gifth gret appetit
To slepe. And thus full of delit
Slep hath his hous; and of his couche
Withinne his chambre if I schal touche,
Of hebenus that slepi tree
The bordes al aboute be,
And for he scholde slepe softe,
Upon a fethrebed alofte
He lith with many a pilwe of doun.
The chambre is strowed up and doun
With swevenes many thousendfold.
 Thus cam Yris into this hold,
And to the bedd, which is al blak,
Sche goth, and ther with Slep sche spak.

rennende] running.   hihte] is called.   hebenus] ebony.   bordes] borders.
lith] lieth.   swevenes] dreams.

From CONFESSIO AMANTIS: JASON AND MEDEA

The Flees he tok and goth to Bote,
The Sonne schyneth bryhte and hote,
The Flees of gold schon forth withal,
The water glistreth overal.
 Medea wepte and sigheth ofte,
And stod upon a Tour alofte:
And prively withinne hirselve,
Ther herde it nouther ten ne tuelve,
Sche preide, and seide, "O, God him spede,
The kniht which hath mi maidenhiede!"
And ay sche loketh toward thyle.
Bot whan sche sih withinne a while
The Flees glistrende ayein the Sonne,
Sche saide, "Ha lord, now al is wonne,
Mi kniht the field hath overcome:
Nou wolde god he were come;
Ha lord, that he ne were alonde!"
Bot I dar take this on honde,
If that sche hadde wynges tuo,
Sche wolde have flowe unto him tho
Strawht ther he was into the Bot.

ther herde it nouther ten ne tuelve] in other words, she did not heed the passing of
time.   thyle] the isle.   alonde] on land.   dar take this on honde] dare swear.

John Lydgate

1370?-1450?

LAT NOMAN BOOSTE OF KONNYNG NOR VERTU

I

Lat noman booste of konnyng nor vertu,
  Of tresour, richesse nor of sapience,
Of worldly support, for al comyth of Jesu:
  Connsayl, confort, discrecion and prudence,
  Provision, forsight and providence,
    Like as the lord of grace list dispose.
  Somman hath wisdam, somman hath elloquence,
    Al stant on chaung lyke a mydsomyr rose.

Holsom in smellyng be the soote fflourys,
  Ful delitable outward to the sight.
The thorn is sharp curyd with fresh colouris,
  Al is nat gold that outward shewith bright,
  A stokfyssh boon in dirknesse yevith a light,
    Twen fair and foul as God list dispose,
  A difference atwix day and nyght.
    Al stant on chaung lyke a mydsomyr rose.

Floures open upon every grene
  Whan the larke messager of day
Salueth the uprist of the sonne shene
  Moost amerously in *Apryl* and in *May,*
  And *Aurora* ageyn the morwe gray
    Causith the dayeseye hir crowne to unclose.
  Worldly cladnesse is medlyd with affray.
    Al stant on chaung lyke a mydsomyr rose.

Atwen the Cokkow and the Nightyngale
  Ther is a maner straunge difference.
On fressh braunchys syngith the woode wale,
  Jayes in musyk have smal experyence,
  Chateryng *pyes* whan they come in presence
    Moost malapert ther verdite to purpose.

chaung] change.   soote] sweet.   boon] bone.   dayeseye] daisy.
cladnesse] gladness.   affray] fear.   woode wale] green woodpecker.

Al thyng hath favour breffly in sentence,
Of soffte or sharp, lyke a mydsomyr rose.

II

Wher is now *David* the moost worthy kyng
　Of Juda and Israel moost famous and notable?
And wher is *Salomon* moost sovereyn of konnyng
　Richest of bildyng of tresour incomparable?
　Face of *Absolon* moost fair moost amyable?
　　Rekne up echon of trouthe, make no glose
　Rekne up *Jonathas* of frenship immutable:
　　Al stant on chaung lyke a mydsomyr rose.

Wher is *Julius* proudest in his empyre
　With his tryumphes moost imperyal?
Wher is *Pirrus* that was lord and sire
　Of Ynde in his estat roial?
　And wher is *Alisaundir* that conqueryd al,
　　Failed leiser his testament to dispose?
　Nabugodonosor or *Sardonapal?*
　　Al stant on chaung like a mydsomyr rose.

Wher is *Tullius* with his sugryd tonge?
　Or *Crisistomus* with his goldene mouth,
The aureat ditees that he red and songe
　Of *Omerus* in Grece both north and south,
　The tragedyes divers and unkouth
　　Of moral Senek the mysteryes to unclose?
　By many example this mateer is ful kouth:
　　Al stant on chaung like a mydsomyr rose.

Wher been of Fraunce al the dozepeers
　Which in Gawle hadde the governaunce?
Vowes of the pecok with al ther proude cheers?
　The worthy nyne with al ther hih bobbaunce?
　Troian knyhtis grettest of alliaunce?
　　The flees of gold conqueryd in Colchos?
　Rome and Cartage moost sovereyn of puissaunce?
　　Al stant on chaung like a mydsomyr rose.

---

echon] each one.　make glose] gloss over.　leiser] leisure, time.　unkouth] curious, strange.　kouth] known.　dozepeers] douzepers, the Twelve Peers of France,
among whom was Roland.　bobbaunce] pomp.

William Dunbar
1465-1520?

"Poets," Swinburne said in his *Miscellanies,* "may be divided into two exhaustive but not exclusive classes,—the gods of harmony and creation, the giants of energy and invention."

If this be so, Dunbar and Dryden are ungodlike giants of our poetry.

The sounds arising from these Titans vary from the hot earthy sound, the rumbling noise of volcanoes about to burst into flames, of Dryden, to the sound of the huge thundering footsteps of that Blind Harry, William Dunbar.

Sometimes Dunbar is a blinded, blundering, earthy giant; sometimes he has the vastness and strength of a genial, blustering, boisterous north wind — a geniality that can blacken and turn dangerous. Yet even when he is most windlike, his spirit has at the same time a queerly animal quality — almost a smell; his genius has a terrible animal force, stinking and rank like that of Swift, but it is for the most part a genial and friendly rankness, unlike that of Swift. This rank darkness and animal stink is present, or can be present, in nearly all genius, but in most, "the angel that stands near the naked man" has interfused it with sweetness and light.

Writing, elsewhere, of texture, of the relationship of consonants and vowels, I said that the vowels are, perhaps, the spirit, the consonants and labials the physical identity, with all the variations of harshness, hairiness, coldness, roughness and smoothness, "the garment of the spirit; thus distinguished, marked off, and announced . . . to the outer world" as "the animal by the skin, the tree by its bark."

"In the deepest tones of harmony," so Wagner quotes Schopenhauer* as saying, "in the fundamental bass-notes, I recognised the lowest degree of the objectivation of the Will, inorganic nature, the mass of the planet. All the higher tones . . . are to be regarded . . . as the accessory vibrations of the deep fundamental tone, at the sound of which they are always to be heard softly vibrating. . . . This is analogous to the view which requires that all bodies and organisations of nature shall be taken as arising in course of gradual evolution from the mass of the planet: this development is their support as well as their source. . . . Thus the ground bass is to us in harmony, as inorganic nature is to the rest of the world, the rude mass upon which everything rests, and from which everything rises and is developed."

If we apply, as we may do, the above to poetry, we may substitute consonants for the bass notes, vowels for the higher tones.

* Wagner: *Opera and Drama,* Part II, Prose Works. Translated by W. A. Ellis.

It would be impossible to say that the higher tones, the vowels, of the terrific Blind Harry can "be heard softly vibrating." But certainly the huge consonantal system is "the rude mass upon which everything rests," only endowed with a gigantic Will.

Dunbar's poems are roared out by a genial, blustering, boisterous north wind, caring nothing for smoothness — invigorating, not appeasing. Sometimes the roughness dies down, and the sound is like that of a stilled cold wind blowing in the branches of a tree heavy with leaves, creaking discordantly in the tree's veins.

LAMENT FOR THE MAKARIS

"Quhen He Wes Seik"

I that in heill wes and gladnes,
Am trublit now with gret seiknes,
And feblit with infermite;
   Timor mortis conturbat me.

Our plesance heir is all vane glory,
This fals warld is bot transitory,
The flesche is brukle, the Fend is sle;
   Timor mortis conturbat me.

The stait of man dois change and vary,
Now sound, now seik, now blith, now sary,
Now dansand mery, now like to dee;
   Timor mortis conturbat me.

No stait in erd heir standis sickir;
As with the wynd wavis the wickir,
Wavis this warldis vanite;
   Timor mortis conturbat me.

On to the ded gois all Estatis,
Princis, Prelotis, and Potestatis,
Baith riche and pur of al degre;
   Timor mortis conturbat me.

He takis the knychtis in to feild,
Anarmit under helme and scheild;
Victour he is at all mellie;
   Timor mortis conturbat me.

makaris] poets, makers.   heill] health.   brukle] brittle.   sle] sly.   erd] earth.
wickir] the osier.   pur] poor.   anarmit] armed.

That strang unmercifull tyrand
Takis, on the moderis breist sowkand,
The bab full of benignite;
 Timor mortis conturbat me.

He takis the campion in the stour,
The capitane closit in the towr,
The lady in bowr full of bewte;
 Timor mortis conturbat me.

He sparis no lord for his piscence,
Na clerk for his intelligence;
His awfull strak may no man fle;
 Timor mortis conturbat me.

Art, magicianis, and astrologgis,
Rethoris, logicianis, and theologgis,
Thame helpis no conclusionis sle;
 Timor mortis conturbat me.

In medicyne the most practicianis,
Lechis, surrigianis, and phisicianis,
Thame self fra ded may not supple;
 Timor mortis conturbat me.

I se that makaris amang the laif
Playis heir ther pageant, syne gois to graif;
Sparit is nocht ther faculte;
 Timor mortis conturbat me.

He hes done petuously devour,
The noble Chaucer, of makaris flour,
The Monk of Bery, and Gower, all thre;
 Timor mortis conturbat me.

The gude Syr Hew of Eglintoun,
And eik Heryot, and Wyntoun,
He hes tane out of this cuntre;
 Timor mortis conturbat me.

stour] battle. piscence] power. strak] stroke. conclusionis] reasoning.
supple] rescue. laif] the rest. syne] then. faculte] profession. **hes done
devour**] has devoured. the Monk of Bery] John Lydgate.

That scorpion fell hes done infek
Maister Johne Clerk, and James Afflek,
Fra balat making and tragidie;
    Timor mortis conturbat me.

Holland and Barbour he hes berevit;
Allace! that he nocht with us levit
Schir Mungo Lokert of the Le;
    Timor mortis conturbat me.

Clerk of Tranent eik he hes tane,
That maid the Anteris of Gawane;
Schir Gilbert Hay endit hes he;
    Timor mortis conturbat me.

He hes Blind Hary and Sandy Traill
Slaine with his schour of mortall haill,
Quhilk Patrik Johnestoun mycht nocht fle;
    Timor mortis conturbat me.

He hes reft Merseir his endite,
That did in luf so lifly write,
So schort, so quyk, of sentence hie;
    Timor mortis conturbat me.

He hes tane Roull of Aberdene,
And gentill Roull of Corstorphin;
Two bettir fallowis did no man se;
    Timor mortis conturbat me.

In Dumfermelyne he hes done roune
With Maister Robert Henrisoun;
Schir Johne the Ros enbrast hes he;
    Timor mortis conturbat me.

And he hes now tane, last of aw,
Gud gentill Stobo and Quintyne Schaw,
Of quham all wichtis hes pete:
    Timor mortis conturbat me.

Gud Maister Walter Kennedy
In poynt of ded lyis veraly,
Gret reuth it wer that so suld be;
    Timor mortis conturbat me.

hes done infek] has infected.   nocht] not.   quhilk] which.   endite] writing.
luf] love.   roune] run.   quham] whom.   wichtis] beings, wights.   pete] pity.
reuth] pity.

Sen he hes all my brether tane,
He will nocht lat me lif alane,
On forse I man his nyxt pray be;
   Timor mortis conturbat me.

Sen for the deid remeid is none,
Best is that we for dede dispone,
Eftir our deid that lif may we;
   Timor mortis conturbat me.

From THE FLYTING OF DUMBAR AND KENNEDIE

QUOD DUMBAR TO KENNEDY

Iersch brybour baird, vyle beggar with thy brattis,
  Cuntbittin crawdoun Kennedy, coward of kynd,
Evill farit and dryit, as Denseman on the rattis,
    Lyke as the gleddis had on thy gule snowt dynd;
    Mismaid monstour, ilk mone owt of thy mynd,
     Renunce, rebald, thy rymyng, thow bot royis,
    Thy trechour tung hes tane ane heland strynd;
    Ane lawland ers wald mak a bettir noyis.

Revin, raggit ruke, and full of rebaldrie,
  Scarth fra scorpione, scaldit in scurrilitie,
I see the haltane in thy harlotrie,
    And in to uthir science no thing slie,
    Off every vertew voyd, as men may sie;
     Quytclame clergie, and cleik to the ane club,
    Ane baird blasphemar in brybrie ay to be;
    For wit and wisdome ane wisp fra the may rub.

Thow speiris, dastard, gif I dar with the fecht?
  Ye dagone, dowbart, thairof haif thow no dowt!
Quhair evir we meit, thairto my hand I hecht
    To red thy rebald ryming with a rowt:

on forse] of necessity.   man] must.

Iersch brybour baird] Irish beggar bard.   brattis] ? rags.   cuntbittin] infected.
crawdoun] coward.   of kynd] by nature.   Denseman on the rattis] Dane on the
wheels (on which criminals were executed and exposed).   gleddis] red kites.   gule
snowt] red nose.   mone] must.   royis] ravest.   heland strynd] highland strain.
revin] raven.   ruke] rook.   scarth] a hairy dwarfish creature.   haltane] haughty.
slie] skilled.   quytclame] renounce.   clergie] learning.   cleik] seize.
brybrie] beggary, thieving.   speiris] asks.   fecht] fight.   dagone] Dagon, chief of
the devils.   dowbart] dull, stupid fellow.   hecht] promise.   red] set to rights.
rowt] heavy blow.

Throw all Bretane it salbe blawin owt
　　How that thow, poysonit pelor, gat thy paikis;
With ane doig leich I schepe to gar the schowt,
　　And nowther to the tak knyfe, swerd, nor aix.

Thow crop and rute of traitouris tressonable,
　　The fathir and moder of morthour and mischeif,
Dissaitfull tyrand, with serpentis tung, unstable;
　　Cukcald cradoun, cowart, and commoun theif;
　　Thow purpest for to undo our Lordis cheif
　　　In Paislay, with ane poysone that wes fell,
　　For quhilk, brybour, yit sall thow thoill a breif;
　　　Pelour, on the I sall it preif my sell.

Thocht I wald lie, thy frawart phisnomy,
　　Dois manifest thy malice to all men;
Fy! tratour theif; Fy! glengoir loun, fy! fy!
　　Fy! feyndly front, far fowlar than ane fen.
　　My freyindis thow reprovit with thy pen!
　　　Thow leis, tratour! quhilk I sall on the preif,
　　Suppois thy heid war armit tymis ten,
　　　Thow sall recryat, or thy croun sall cleif.

QUOD KENNEDY TO DUMBAR
Conspiratour, cursit cocatrice, hell caa,
　　Turk, trumpour, traitour, tyran intemperate;
Thow irefull attircop, Pilate apostata,
　　Judas, jow, juglour, Lollard laureate;
　　Sarazene, symonyte provit, Pagane pronunciate,
　　　Machomete, manesuorne, bugrist abhominabile,
　　　Devill, dampnit dog, sodomyte insatiable,
　　With Gog and Magog grete glorificate.

Nero thy nevow, Golyas thy grantsire,
　　Pharao thy fader, Egipya thy dame,
Deulbere, thir are the causis that I conspire,
　　Termygantis temptise the, and Vaspasius thine eme;
　　Belzebub thy full brothir will clame
　　　To be thyne air, and Cayphas thy sectour;
　　　Pluto thy hede of kyn and protectour,
　　To hell to lede the on lycht day and leme.

pelor] thief.　　　paikis] blows.　　schepe] undertake.　　　thoill] suffer, endure.
breif] summons.　　preif] prove.　　glengoir] venereal disease.　　loun] worthless
fellow.　　leis] liest.　　cleif] cleave.　　attircop] a repulsive person (literally, spider).
jow] Jew.　　Lollard] follower of Wycliffe, hence a heretic.　　deulbere] devilborn.
eme] uncle.　　sectour] executor.　　leme] bright.

Herode thyne othir eme, and grete Egeas,
　Marciane, Machomete, and Maxencius,
Thy trew kynnismen, Antenor and Eneas,
　Throp thy nere nece, and austerne Olibrius,
　Puttidew, Baal, and Eyobulus;
　　Thir fendis ar the flour of thy four branchis,
　　Sterand the potis of hell, and nevir stanchis,
　Dout not, Deulbere, *Tu es Dyabolus.*

Duelbere, thy spere of were, but feir, thou yelde,
　Hangit, mangit, eddir-strangit, strynde stultorum,
To me, maist hie Kenydie, and flee the felde,
　Pickit, wickit, convickit Lamp Lollardorum.
Defamyt, blamyt, schamyt, Primas Paganorum.
　Out! out! I schout, apon that snout that snevillis,
　　Tale tellare, rebellare, induellar wyth the devillis,
　Spynk, sink with stynk *ad Tertera Termagorum.*

were] war.　　but feir] without equal.　　mangit] bruised.　　eddir-stangit] adder-
stung.　　spynk] vagabond.

THE MANERE OF THE CRYING OF ANE PLAYE

　　　Harry, Harry, hobbillschowe!
　　　Se quha is cummyn nowe,
　　　Bot I wait nevir howe,
　　　　With the quhorle wynd?
　　　A soldane owt of Seriand land,
　　　A gyand strang for to stand,
　　　That with the strength of my hand
　　　　Beres may bynd.
　　　Yit I trowe that I vary,
　　　I am the nakit Blynd Hary,
　　　That lang has bene in the fary
　　　　Farleis to fynd:
　　　And yit gif this be nocht I,
　　　I wait I am the spreit of Gy,
　　　Or ellis go by the sky,
　　　　Licht as the lynd.

　　　The God of most magnificence
　　　Conserf this fair presens,
　　　And saif this amyable audiens
　　　　Grete of renoune.

hobbillschowe] uproar.　　quha] who.　　quhorle wynd] whirlwind.　　soldane] sultan.
Seriand] Syrian.　　fary] fairyland.　　farleis] wonders.　　wait] think.

Provest, baillies, officeris,
And honorable induellaris,
Marchandis and familiaris
    Of all this fair towne.
Quha is cummyn heir bot I,
    A bauld, bustuos bellamy,
At your cors to mak a cry
    With a hie sowne?
Quhilk generit am of gyandis kynd,
Fra strang Hercules be strynd;
Off all the Occident of Ynd,
    My eldaris bair the croune.

My foregrantschir hecht Fyn McKowle,
That dang the Devill and gart him yowle,
The skyis ranyd quhen he wald scowle
    And trublit all the aire:
He gat my grantschir Gog Magog;
Ay quhen he dansit, the warld wald schog;
Five thousand ellis yeid in his frog
    Of Hieland pladdis of haire.
Yit he was bot of tender youth;
Bot eftir he grew mekle at fouth,
Ellevyne ell wyde met was his mouth,
    His teith was tene myle sqwaire.
He wald apone his tais stand,
And tak the sternis doune with his hand,
And set tham in a gold garland
    Abone his wyfis haire.

He had a wyf was lang of clift,
Hir heid wan heiar than the lift;
The hevyne rerdit quhen scho walk rift;
    The las was no think sklender.
Scho spittit Lochlomond with hir lippis;
Thunner and fyreflaucht flewe fra hir hippis;
Quhen scho was crabit the son tholit clips;
    The Fende durst nocht offend hir.
For cald scho tuke the fever cartane,
For all the claith of Fraunce and Bertane
Wald nocht be till hir leg a gartane,

induellaris] inhabitants.   bauld] bold.   bellamy] good friend.   cors] cross.
hecht] was called.   dang] struck.   gart] made.   schog] shake.   yeid] went.
frog] coat.   mekle] great.   fouth] size.   sternis] stars.   lang of clift] long-legged.
lift] sky.   rerdit] roared.   rift] belch.   tholit] suffered.   cartane] quartan.
claith] cloth.

Thocht scho was ying and tender;
Apon a nycht heire in the north,
Scho tuke the gravell and stalit Cragorth,
Scho pischit the mekle watter of Forth,
    Sic tyde ran eftirhend hir.

A thing writtin of hir I fynd:
In Irland quhen scho blewe behynd,
At Noroway costis scho rasit the wynd,
    And gret schippis drownit thare.
Scho fischit all the Spanye seis,
With hir sark lape before hir theis;
Sevyne dayis saling betuix hir kneis
    Was estymit and maire.
The hyngand brayis on athir syde
Scho poltit with hir lymmis wyde;
Lassis micht leir at hir to stryd,
    Wald ga to lufis laire.
Scho merkit syne to land with myrth;
And pischit fyf quhalis in the Firth,
That cropyn war in hir count for girth,
    Welterand amang the waire.

My fader, mekle Gow MakMorne,
Out of that wyfis wame was schorne;
For litilnes scho was forlorne
    Sic a kempe to beire:
Or he of eld was yeris thre,
He wald stepe oure the occeane se;
The mone sprang never abone his kne,
    The heyvn had of him feire.
Ane thousand yere is past fra mynd,
Sen I was generit of his kynd,
Full far amang the desertis of Ynde,
    Amang lyoun and beire:
Baith the King Arthour and Gawane,
And mony bald berne in Brettane,
Ar deid and in the weiris slane,
    Sen I couth weild a speire.

I have bene forthwart ever in feild,
And now so lang I haf borne scheld,

---

sark] shirt.   theis] thighs.   poltit] knocked against.   leir] learn.
merkit] approached.   quhalis] whales.   cropyn] crept.   girth] refuge.
waire] seaweed.   kempe] champion.   berne] bairn, lad.   weiris] wars.

That I am all crynd in for eild
  This litill, as ye may se.
I have bene bannist under the lynd
Full lang that no man couth me fynd,
And now with this last southin wynd,
  I am cummyn heir parde.
My name is Welth, thairfor be blyth,
I come heire comfort yow to kyth,
Suppos that wretchis wryng and wryth,
  All darth I sall gar de;
For sekerly, the treuth to tell,
I come amang yow hiere to duell,
Fra sound of Sanct Gelis bell
  Nevir think I to fle.

Sophea and the Soldane strang,
With weiris that has lestit lang,
Furth of thar boundis maid me to gang,
  And turn to Turky tyte.
The King of Frauncis gret army
Has brocht in darth in Lombardy,
And in ane cuntre he and I
  May nocht baith stand perfyte.
In Denmark, Swetherik, and Noroway,
Na in the Steidis I dar nocht ga,
Amang thaim is bot tak and sla,
  Cut thropillis and mak quyte.
Irland for evir I have refusit,
All wichtis suld hald me excusit,
For never in land quhar Erische was usit,
  To duell had I delyte.

Quharfor in Scotland come I heire
With yow to byde and perseveire,
In Edinburgh quhar is meriast cheire,
  Plesans, disport, and play,
Quhilk is the lampe and *A per se*
Of this regioun in all degre,
Of welefaire and of honeste
  Renoune and riche aray.
Sen I am Welth cummyn to this wane,
Ye noble merchandis everilkane
Addres yow furth with bow and flane
  In lusty grene lufraye,

crynd] shriveled.   eild] age.   kyth] show.   tyte] quickly.   thropillis] throats.
wane] dwelling.   everilkane] everyone.   flane] arrow.   lufraye] livery.

And follow furth on Robyn Hude,
With hartis coragious and gud,
And thocht that wretchis wald ga wod,
    Of worschipe hald the way.

For and I and my thre feres aye,
Weilfaire, Wantones, and Play,
Sall byde with yow in all affray,
    And cair put clene to flicht,
And we sall dredles us addres
To bannis derth and all distres
And with all sportis and merynes
    Your hartis hald ever on hicht.
I am of mekle quantite
Of gyand kynd, as ye may se,
Quhar sall be gottin a wyf to me
    Siclyke of breid and hicht?
I dreid that thair be nocht a maide
In all this towne may me abyd,
Quha wait gif ony heir besyd,
    Micht suffir me all nycht.

With yow sen I mon leid my lyf,
Gar sers baith Louthiane and Fyf
And wale to me a mekle wyf,
    A gret ungracious gan,
Sen scho is gane, the Gret Forlore. . . .

Adow, fair weill! for now I go,
Bot I will nocht lang byd yow fro;
Chryst yow conserve fra every wo,
    Both madin, wyf, and man;
God bliss thame, and the Haly Rude,
Givis me a drink so it be gude;
And quha trowis best that I do lude,
    Skynk first to me the can.

feres] companions.   dredles] fearlessly.   sers] search.   wale] choose.
skynk] fill up.

Gavin Douglas
1474?-1522

From KING HART

HART'S CASTLE

King Hart, into his cumlye castell strang
   Closit about with craft and meikill ure,
So semlye wes he set his folk amang,
   That he no dout had of misaventure:
So proudlye wes he polist, plane and pure,
    With youthheid and his lustye levis grene;
So fair, so fresche, so liklye to endure,
    And als so blith as bird in simmer schene.

For wes he never yit with schowris schot,
   Nor yit ourrun with rouk, or ony raine;
In all his lusty lecam nocht ane spot,
   Na never had experience into paine,
Bot alway into liking, nocht to laine;
    Onlye to love, and verrye gentilnes,
He was inclinit cleinlye to ramane,
    And wonn under the wing of wantounes. . . .

So strang this King him thocht his castell stude,
   With mony towre and turat crownit hye:
About the wall their ran ane water wude,
   Blak, stinkand, sour, and salt as is the sey,
That on the wallis wiskit, gre by gre,
    Boldning to ryis the castell to confound;
Bot thay within maid sa grit melody,
    That for thair reird they micht nocht heir the sound.

strang] strong.   meikill ure] great labor.   dout] fear, suspicion.   plane] smooth.
als so] as.   schene] fair.   schot] assailed.   rouk] mist.   lecam] body.
liking] pleasure.   nocht to laine] to hide nothing.   cleinlye] permanently.
wonn] dwell.   stude] stood.   wude] raging.   wiskit] lapped.   gre] step.
boldning] swelling.   ryis] rise.   sa grit] so great.   reird] noise.

From THE PROLOUG OF THE TWELFT BUIK
OF THE ÆNEAD

Quhill schortly, with the blesand torch of day,
Abilyeit in his lemand fresch array,
Furth of hys palyce ryall ischyt Phebus,
Wyth goldin crown and vissage gloryus,
Crysp haris, brycht as chrysolite or topace,
For quhais hew mycht nane behald his face,
The fyry sparkis brastyng fra his ene,
To purge the ayr; and gylt the tendyr grene,
Defundand from hys sege etheriall
Glaid influent aspectis celicall.
Before his regale hie magnificens
Mysty vapour uppringand, sweit as sens,
In smoky soppis of donk dewis wak,
Moich hailsum stovis ourheildand the slak;
The aureat fanes of hys trone soverane
With glytrand glans ourspred the occiane,
The large fludis lemand all of lycht
Bot with a blenk of his supernale sycht.
For to behald, it was a gloir to see
The stabillit wyndis and the cawmyt see,
The soft sessoun, the firmament serene,
The lowne illumynat air, and fyrth amene;
The sylver scalyt fyschis on the greit
Ourthwort cleir stremis sprynkland for the heyt,
Wyth fynnis schynand brown as synopar,
And chyssell talis, stowrand heyr and thar;
The new cullour alychtnyng all the landis,
Forgane thir stannyris schane the beryall strandis.

quhill] while.   abilyeit] attired.   lemand] shining, blazing.   quhais] whose.
defundand] pouring out   sege] throne.   celicall] celestial.   soppis] mixture.
wak] watery.   moich] much.   stovis] vapors.   slak] gap between two hills.
occiane] ocean.   lowne] serene.   amene] pleasant.   greit] sand.
sprynkland] sparkling.   synopar] cinnamon.   chyssell] chisel-shaped.

Anonymous

QUHEN ALYSANDYR OUR KING WAS DEDE

Quhen Alysandyr our king was dede
  That Scotland led in luve and le,
Away was sons of ale and brede,
  Of wine and wax, of gamyn and gle;
Our gold was changit into lede.
  Christ, born into virginite,
Succour Scotland and remede,
  That stad is in perplexite.

quhen] when.   le] law.   sons] plenty.   gamyn] gaming.   stad] bestead.

LULLY LULLEY

Lully lulley lully lulley,
The fawcon hath born my mak away.

He bare hym up, he bare hym down,
He bare him into an orchard brown.
  Lully lulley lully lulley,
  The fawcon hath born my mak away.

In that orchard ther was an hall
That was hangid with purpil and pall.

And in that hall ther was a bede,
Hitt was hangid with gold so rede.

And yn that bed ther lythe a knyght,
His wowndis bledyng day and nyght.

By that bede side ther kneleth a may,
And she wepeth both nyght and day.

And by that bede side ther stondith a ston,
Corpus Christi wretyn ther-on.
  Lully lulley lully lulley,
  The fawcon hath born my mak away.

mak] mate.   may] maid.

EPITAPH ON QUEEN ELIZABETH, WIFE OF HENRY VII

Here lith the fresshe flowr of Plantagenet,
Here lith the white rose in the rede sete.
Here lith the nobull quen Elyzabeth,
Here lith the princes departid by deth.
Here lith blode of owr contray royall,
Here lith fame of Ynglond immortall.
Here lith of Edward the IIIIth a picture,
Here lith his dowghter and perle pure.
Here lith the wyff of Harry owr trew kyng,
Here lith the hart the joy and the gold rynge.
Here lith the lady so lyberall and gracius,
Here lith the pleasure of thy hows.
Here lith very love of man and child,
Here lith insampull owre myndez to bild.
Here lith all bewte of lyvyng a myrrour,
Here lith all vertu good maner and honour.
God grant her now hevyn to encrese,
And owr kyn Harry long lyff and pease.

From DALYAUNCE

MUNDUS. Welcome, fayre chylde, what is thy name?
INFANS. I wote not, syr, withouten blame.
But ofte tyme my moder in her game
Called me dalyaunce.
MUNDUS. Dalyaunce, my swetë chylde,
It is a name that is ryght wylde,
For whan thou waxest olde.
It is a name of no substaunce
But, my fayre chylde, what woldest thou have?
INFANS. Syr of some comforte I you crave —
Mete and clothe my lyfe to save:
And I your true servaunt shall be.
MUNDUS. Fayre chylde, I graunte thee thyne askynge.
I wyll thee fynde whyle thou art yinge
So thou wylte be obedyent to my byddynge.
These garments gaye I gyve to thee.
And also I gyve to thee a name,
And clepe thee Wanton, in every game;

fynde] keep.   yinge] young.

Tyll XIII yere be come and gone,
And than come agayne to me.

Infans is now called Wanton.

WANTON. Gramercy, Worlde, for myne araye,
For now I purpose me to playe.
MUNDUS. Fare well, fayre chylde, and have good daye.
All rychelesnesse is kynde for thee.

Mundus goes out leaving Wanton alone.

WANTON. Aha, Wanton is my name!
I can many a quayntë game.
Lo, my toppe I dryve in same,
    Se, it torneth rounde!
I can with my scorgë-stycke
My felowe upon the heed hytte,
And wyghtly from hym make a skyppe
    And blere on hym my tonge.
If brother or syster do me chyde
I wyll scratche and also byte.
I can crye, and also kyke,
    And mocke them all berewe.
If fader or mother wyll me smyte,
I wyll wryngë with my lyppe;
And lyghtly from hym make a skyppe;
    And call my damë shrewe.
Aha, a newe game have I founde:
Se this gynne it renneth rounde;
And here another have I founde,
    And yet mo can I fynde.
I can mowë on a man;
And make a lesynge well I can,
And mayntayne it ryght well than.
    This connynge came me of kynde.
Ye, syrs, I can well gelde a snayle;
And catche a cowe by the tayle;
    This is a fayre connynge!
I can daunce, and also skyppe;
I can playe at the chery pytte;
And I can wystell you a fytte,
    Syres, in a whylowe ryne.

---

rychelesnesse] heedlessness.   kynde] natural.   wyghtly] nimbly.   blere] stick
out.   wryngë] squiggle.   gynne] toy or trap.   mowë] make grimaces.
lesynge] falsehood.   connynge] learning.   fytte] air, tune, stave.   whylowe
ryne] willow rind.

Ye, syrs, and every daye
Whan I to scole shall take the waye
Some good mannes gardyn I wyll assaye,
  Perys and plommes to plucke.
I can spye a sparowes nest.
I wyll not go to scole but whan me lest,
For there begynneth a sory fest
  Whan the mayster sholde lyfte my docke.
But, syrs, whan I was seven yere of age,
I was sent to the Worlde to takë wage.
And this seven yere I have ben his page
  And kept his commaundëment. . . .

perys] pears.   me lest] it pleases me.   fest] feast or fast.   docke] gown or coattail.

Sir David Lindsay
1490?-1555

From THE COMPLAYNT OF SCHIR DAVID LINDESAY

THE CHILDHOOD OF JAMES V

I tak the Queenis Grace, thy mother,
My lord Chanclare, and mony other,
Thy nowreis, and thy auld maistress,
I tak them all, to bear witness.
Auld Willie Dile, were he on live,
My life well he could descrive:
How as ane chapman bearis his pack,
I bore thy grace upon my back,
And sometimes stridlingis on my neck,
Dancing with mony bend and beck.
The first sillabis that thou did mute
Was *Pa, Da Lyn:* upon the lute
Then playit I twenty springis, perqueir,
Which was great piete for to hear.
Fra play thou let me never rest,
Bot *Gynkartoun* thou luvit, ay, best.
And, ay, when thou come from the scule,
Then I behuffit to play the fule:
As I at length, into my *Dreme,*

nowreis] nurse.   mute] utter.   piete] pity.   I behuffit] it behooved me.

My sundry service did expreme.
Though it bene better, as sayis the wise,
Hap to the Court, nor gude service,
I wot thou luvit me better than,
Nor, now, some wife dois her gude man.
Then men till other did record,
Said Lindesay would be made ane lord.
Thou hast made lordis, sir, be Sanct Geill,
Of some that has nocht servit so weill.
    To you, my lordis, that standis by,
I shall you show the causis why.
If ye list tarry, I sall tell,
How my infortune first befell.
I prayit daily, on my knee,
My young maister that I mycht see
Of eild, in his estate royal,
Having power imperial,
Then traistit I, without demand,
To be promovit to some land.
Bot my asking I gat owre soon,
Because ane clipse fell in the moon,
The which all Scotland made astir.
Then did my purpose rin arreir,
The which were longsome to declare,
And all my heart is wonder sair,
When I have in remembrance
The sudden change, to my mischance.
The King was bot twelf yearis of age,
When new ruleris come, in their rage,
For common weill making no care,
Bot for their profit singulair.
    Imprudently, like witless fulis,
They took the young Prince from the sculis,
Where he, under obedience,
Was learning virtue and science,
And hastily put in his hand
The governance of all Scotland;
As who would in a stormy blast,
When marineris bene all aghast
Through danger of the seis rage,
Would tak a child of tender age,
Which never had bene on the sea,
And to his bidding all obey,
Giving him whole the governall

---

expreme] express.   of eild] of age.   clipse] eclipse.

Of ship, marchand, and marinall,
For dreid of rockis and foreland,
To put the rudder in his hand.
Without Goddis grace is no refuge:
If there be danger, ye may judge.
I give them to the Devil of Hell,
Which first devisit that counsell.
I will not say that it was treason,
Bot I dar swear, it was no reason.
I pray God let me never see ryng
Into this realm so young ane King.

ryng] reign.

John Skelton
1460?-1529

It is interesting to compare (or contrast) the strong growth and sense of direction of Chaucer with the sharpness and shrillness, the brightness, both of color and light, of Skelton's poems. Sometimes the shape and movement are like those of flames, at moments flickering and crackling, at other times leaping upwards; and those flames have the brightness and the shrillness of a parrot's feathers.

Other poems, again — those celebrating the beauty of young girls — have the notes we hear in the woods in spring, wild bird songs, a murmuration of starlings, a watch of nightingales, and a charm of goldfinches. Sometimes they have the sharpness and coldness of an early spring flower's petals.

In the lovely *To Mistress Isabell Pennell,* after the first three lines, each line is the shape of a honeycomb.

"In the construction," say Tickner Edwardes in his book on the honey-bee, "of the six-sided cell, with its base composed of three rhombs or diamonds, the bee has adapted a form which our great arithmeticians admit to be the best possible for her requirements."

Here, then, is the six-sided cell, with its base composed of six rhombs or diamonds:

My maiden Isabell,
Reflaring rosabell,
The flagrant camamell;
The ruddy rosary,
The soveraine rosemary,
The praty strawbery.

and the "endeles welth" of which we hear at the end of the poem is that which the dusky workers in fields and gardens bring home to their hives when they:

> having laboured hard from light to light
> With golden thighes come singing home at night.*

To Mistress Isabell Pennell, as Walter de la Mare has said in *Come Hither,* is "the loveliest and gayest song of praise and sweetness to 'a young thing' I have ever seen."

In the twist of this poem we have the spring bird's song, and the closely juxtaposed assonances "May" and "Maidenly demure" in the last line of the sixth verse and the first line of the seventh are round like buds.

"Ieloffer," says de la Mare in a note upon this poem in *Come Hither,* "gelofer, gelofre, gillofre, gelevor, gillyvor, gillofer, jerefloure, gerraflour — all these are ways of spelling 'gillyflower,' 'gelofre' coming nearest to its original French: *giroflée* meaning spiced like a clove.† There were of old, I find, three kinds of gillyflowers: the clove, the stock, and the wall. It was the first of these kinds that was meant in the earlier writers by the small clove carnation (or Coronation, because it was made into chaplets or garlands). Its Greek name was dianthus (the flower divine); and its twin sister is the Pink, so called because its edges are pinked, that is, jagged, notched, scalloped. Country names for it are Sweet John, Pagiants, Blunket, and Sops-in-Wine, for it spices what it floats in, and used to be candied for a sweetmeat. Blossoming in July, the gillyflower suggests July-flower, and if Julia is one's sweetheart, it may also be a Julie-flower. So one name may carry many echoes."

Lullay, lullay is one of the most drowsy-sounding poems in the language.

The sleepy movement owes much to the drone-sound of the alliteration. I know no poem to equal it for drowsiness excepting the lines about the House of Sleep in John Gower's *Ceix and Alceone,* the even earlier (fourteenth century) anonymous poem *Maiden in the mor* discovered by Kenneth Sisam, and the lovely refrain of the ballad *The Broomfield Hill* (page 492).

---

* John Day, *The Parliament of Bees.*

† Gelevor: a sweet red fire coming after the frost? — E.S.

From PHILIP SPARROW

PLACEBO

Pla-ce-bo,
Who is there, who?
Di-le-xi,
Dame Margery;
Fa, re, mi, mi,
Wherefore and why, why?
For the soule of Philip Sparowe,
That was late slain at Carowe,
Among the Nones Blake,
For that swete soules sake,
And for all sparowes soules,
Set in our bederolles,
Pater noster qui,
With an *Ave Mari* . . .

It was so prety a fole,
It wold sit on a stole,
And lerned after my scole
For to kepe his cut,
With, Phillip, kepe your cut!
It had a velvet cap,
And wold sit upon my lap,
And seke after small wormes,
And somtime white bred crommes;
And many times and ofte
Betwene my brestes softe
It wolde lie and rest;
It was propre and prest.
Somtime he wolde gaspe
Whan he sawe a waspe;
A fly or a gnat,
He wolde flye at that;
And pritely he wold pant
Whan he saw an ant;
Lord, how he wolde pry
After the butterfly!
Lorde, how he wolde hop
After the gressop!
And whan I said, Phip, Phip,
Than he wold lepe and skip,

And take me by the lip.
Alas, it will me slo,
That Phillip is gone me fro! . . .

Alas, I wold ride and go
A thousand mile of grounde!
If any such might be found,
It were worth an hundreth pound
Of kinge Cresus golde,
Or of Attalus the olde,
The riche prince of Pargame,
Who so list the story to se.
Cadmus, that his sister sought,
And he shold be bought
For golde and fee,
He shuld over the see,
To wete if he coulde bringe
Any of the ofspringe,
Or any of the blode.
But whoso understode
Of Medeas arte,
I wolde I had a parte
Of her crafty magike!
My sparowe than shuld be quicke
With a charme or twaine,
And playe with me againe.
But all this is in vaine
Thus for to complaine. . . .

All maner of birdes in your kind;
Se none be left behinde.
To mourninge loke that ye fall
With dolorous songes funerall,
Some to singe, and some to say,
Some to wepe, and some to pray,
Every birde in his laye.
The goldfinche, the wagtaile;
The janglinge jay to raile,
The fleckid pye to chatter
Of this dolorous mater;

bederolles] prayer lists.   propre and prest] neat and keen.   wete] know.

And robin redbrest,
He shall be the preest
The requiem masse to singe,
Softly warbelinge,
With helpe of the red sparow,
And the chattringe swallow,
This herse for to halow;
The larke with his longe to;
The spinke, and the martinet
    also;
The shovelar with his brode bek;
The doterell, that folishe pek,
And also the mad coote,
With a balde face to toote;
The feldefare, and the snite;
The crowe, and the kite;
The ravin, called Rolfe,
His plaine songe to solfe;
The partriche, the quaile;
The plover with us to waile;
The woodhacke, that singeth
    "chur"
Horsly, as he had the mur;
The lusty chaunting nightingale;
The popingay to tell her tale,
That toteth oft in a glasse,
Shal rede the Gospell at masse;
The mavis with her whistell
Shal rede there the pistell.
But with a large and a longe
To kepe just plaine songe,
Our chaunters shalbe the
    cuckoue,
The culver, the stockedowue,
With "puwit" the lapwing,
The versicles shall sing.
    The bitter with his "bumpe,"
The crane with his trumpe,
The swan of Menander,
The gose and the gander,
The duck and the drake,
Shall watche at this wake;

The pecocke so proude,
Because his voice is loude,
And hath a glorious taile,
He shall sing the graile;
The owle, that is so foule,
Must helpe us to howle;
The heron so gaunte,
And the cormoraunte,
With the fesaunte,
And the gaglinge gaunte,
And the churlisshe chough;
The route and the rough;
The barnacle, the bussarde,
With the wilde mallarde;
The divendop to slepe;
The water hen to wepe;
The puffin and the tele
Money they shall dele
To poore folke at large,
That shall be their charge;
The semewe and the titmose;
The wodcocke with the longe
    nose;
The threstil with her warbling;
The starling with her brabling;
The roke, with the ospraye
That putteth fisshes to a fraye;
And the denty curlewe,
With the turtill most trew.
    At this *Placebo*
We may not well forgo
The countringe of the coe:
The storke also,
That maketh his nest
In chimneyes to rest;
Within those walles
No broken galles
May there abide
Of cokoldry side,
Or els philosophy
Maketh a great lie.
    The estrige, that will eate

longe to] long toe.   spinke] finch.   pek] dolt.   toote] peer **at.**   solfe] sing.
mur] catarrh.   toteth] peers.   gaglinge gaunte] gobbling gannet.   route] a kind
of goose.   rough] sandpiper.   divendop] dabchick.

An horshowe so great,
In the stede of meate,
Such fervent heat
His stomacke doth freat;
He can not well fly,
Nor singe tunably,
Yet at a braide
He hath well assaide
To solfe above ela,
Fa, lorell, fa, fa;
Ne quando
Male cantando,
The best that we can,
To make him our belman,
And let him ring the bellis;
He can do nothing ellis.
   Chaunteclere, our coke,
Must tell what is of the clocke
By the astrology
That he hath naturally
Conceived and cought,
And was never tought
By Albumazer
The astronomer,
Nor by Ptholomy
Prince of astronomy,
Nor yet by Haly;
And yet he croweth daily
And nightly the tides
That no man abides,
With Partlot his hen,
Whom now and then
Hee plucketh by the hede
Whan he doth her trede.
   The birde of Araby,
That potencially
May never die,
And yet there is none
But one alone;
A phenex it is
This herse that must blis
With armaticke gummes

That cost great summes,
The way of thurification
To make a fumigation,
Swete of reflare,
And redolent of eire,
This corse for to sence
With greate reverence,
As patriarke or pope
In a blacke cope;
Whiles he senseth the herse,
He shall singe the verse,
Libera me,
In de, la, soll, re,
Softly bemole
For my sparowes soule.
Plinny sheweth all
In his story naturall
What he doth finde
Of the phenix kinde;
Of whose incineracion
There riseth a new creacion
Of the same facion
Without alteracion.
Saving that olde age
Is turned into corage
Of fresshe youth againe;
This matter trew and plaine,
Plaine matter indede,
Who so list to rede.
   But for the egle doth flye
Hyest in the skye,
He shall be the sedeane,
The quere to demeane,
As provost principall,
To teach them their ordinall;
Also the noble faucon,
With the gerfaucon,
The tarsell gentill,
They shall morne soft and still
In their amisse of gray;
The sacre with them shall say
Dirige for Phillippes soule;

reflare] odor.   sedeane] subdean.   sacre] a kind of falcon.

The goshauke shall have a role
The queresters to controll;
The lanners and the marlions
Shall stand in their morning
    gownes;
The hobby and the muskette
The sensers and the crosse shall
    fet;
The kestrell in all this warke
Shall be holy water clarke. . . .

  Credo videre bona Domini,
I pray God Phillip to heven may fly!
Domine, exaudi orationem meam!
To heven he shall, from heven he
    cam!
    Do-mi-nus vo-bis-cum!
Of al good prayers God send him
    sum!

Oremus
Deus, cui proprium est misereri et
    parcere,
On Phillips soule have pite!
For he was a prety cocke,
And came of a gentill stocke,
And wrapt in a maidenes smocke,
And cherisshed full daintely,
Till cruell fate made him to dy:
Alas, for dolefull desteny!
But whereto shuld I
Lenger morne or crye?
To Jupiter I call,
Of heven emperiall,
That Phillip may fly
Above the starry sky,
To treade the prety wren,
That is our Ladyes hen:
Amen, amen, amen!

    lanner, marlion, hobby] types of falcon.   muskette] sparrowhawk.

From THE GARLAND OF LAUREL

TO MISTRESS ISABELL PENNELL

By Saint Mary, my lady,
Your mammy and your dady
Brought forth a godely baby!
  My maiden Isabell,
Reflaring rosabell,
The flagrant camamell;
  The ruddy rosary,
The soveraine rosemary,
The praty strawbery;
  The columbine, the nepte,
The jeloffer well set,
The propre violet;
  Enuwid your coloure
Is like the dasy flowre
After the Aprill showre;
  Sterre of the morow gray,

The blossom on the spray,
The fresshest flowre of
  May;
  Maidenly demure,
Of womanhode the lure;
Wherfore I make you sure,
  It were an hevenly helth,
It were an endeles welth,
A life for God himselfe,
  To here this nightingale,
Amonge the birdes smale,
Warbelinge in the vale,
    Dug, dug,
    Jug, jug,
Good yere and good luk,
With chuk, chuk, chuk, chuk!

    reflaring] redolent.   nepte] catnip.

TO MISTRESS MARGARET HUSSEY

Mirry Margaret,
As midsomer flowre,
Jentill as faucoun
Or hawke of the towre;
    With solace and gladnes,
Moche mirthe and no madnes,
All good and no badnes,
So joyously,
So maidenly,
So womanly
Her demening
In every thinge,
Far, far passinge
That I can endight,
Or suffice to wright
Of mirry Margarete,
As midsomer flowre,

Jentill as facoun
Or hawke of the towre;
    As pacient and as still,
And as full of good will,
As faire Ysaphill;
Coliaunder,
Swete pomaunder,
Good Cassaunder;
Stedfast of thought,
Wele made, wele wrought;
Far may be sought
Erst that ye can finde
So corteise, so kinde
As mirry Margarete,
This midsomer flowre,
Jentill as faucoun
Or hawke of the towre.

LULLAY, LULLAY

With, Lullay, lullay, like a childe,
Thou slepist to long, thou art begilde.

"My darling dere, my daisy flowre,
    Let me," quod he, "ly in your lap."
"Ly still," quod she, "my paramoure,
    Ly still hardely, and take a nap."
    His hed was hevy, such was his hap,
All drowsy dreming, drownd in slepe,
That of his love he toke no kepe.

With ba, ba, ba, and bas, bas, bas,
    She cherished him both cheke and chin,
That he wist never where he was;
    He had forgoten all dedely sin.
    He wantid wit her love to win:
He trusted her payment, and lost all his pay:
She left him sleping, and stale away.

kepe] heed.

The rivers routh, the waters wan;
　She sparid not to wete her fete;
She wadid over, she found a man
　　That halsid her hartely and kist her swete:
　　Thus after her cold she cought a hete.
"My lefe," she said, "routith in his bed;
Ywis he hath an hevy hed."

What dremist thou, drunchard, drousy pate!
　Thy lust and liking is from thee gone;
Thou blinkerd blowboll, thou wakist to late,
　　Behold, thou lieste, luggard, alone!
　　Well may thou sigh, well may thou grone,
To dele with her so cowardly:
Ywis, poule-hachet, she blerid thine eye.

　　With, Hey, lullay, like a childe,
　　Thou slepist to long, thou art begilde.

halsid] hugged.　　routith] snores.

Anonymous

AND CAN THE PHYSICIAN MAKE SICK MEN WELL

And can the physician make sick men well?
And can the magician a fortune divine?
Without lily, germander, and sops-in-wine,
　　With sweet-briar
　　And bon-fire
　　And strawberry wire
　　And columbine.

Within and out, in and out, round as a ball,
With hither and thither, as straight as a line,
With lily, germander, and sops-in-wine,
　　With sweet-briar
　　And bon-fire
　　And strawberry wire
　　And columbine.

When Saturn did live, there lived no poor,
The king and the beggar with roots did dine,

With lily, germander, and sops-in-wine,
 With sweet-briar
 And bon-fire
 And strawberry wire
 And columbine.

THE MAIDENS CAME

The maidens came
When I was in my mothers bower.
I hade all that I wolde.
The baily berith the bell away,
The lilly, the rose, the rose I lay,
The silver is whit, red is the golde,
The robes that lay in fold;
The baily berith the bell away,
The lilly, the rose, the rose I lay;
And through the glasse window
Shines the sone.
How shuld I love and I so young?
The baily berith the bell away,
The lilly, the rose, the rose I lay.

WHO SHALL HAVE MY FAIRE LADY

Who shall have my faire lady?
Who shall have my faire lady?
Who but I, who but I, who but I?
Under the levis grene!

The fairest man
That best love can,
Dandirly, dandirly,
Dandirly, dan,
Under the levis grene.

WESTRON WINDE, WHEN WILL THOU BLOW

Westron winde, when will thou blow,
The smalle raine downe can raine?
Crist, if my love wer in my armis,
And I in my bed againe.

Sir Thomas Wyatt
1503?-1542

WHO SO LIST TO HOUNT

Who so list to hount, I knowe where is an hynde,
But as for me, helas, I may no more:
The vayne travaill hath weried me so sore.
I ame of theim that farthest commeth behinde;
Yet may I by no meanes my weried mynde
Drawe from the Diere: but as she fleeth afore,
Faynting I folowe. I leve off therefore,
Sins in a nett I seke to hold the wynde.
Who list her hount, I put him owte of dowbte,
As well as I may spend his tyme in vain:
And, graven with Diamonds, in letters plain
There is written her faier neck rounde abowte:
    Noli me tangere, for Cesars I ame;
    And wylde for to hold, though I seme tame.

THE LOVER COMPLAYNETH THE UNKINDNESS
OF HIS LOVE

My lute awake! perfourme the last
Labor that thou and I shall wast,
    And end that I have now begon;
For when this song is sung and past,
    My lute be still, for I have done.

As to be herd where ere is none,
As lede to grave in marbill stone,
    My song may perse her hert as sone;
Should we then sigh, or syng, or mone?
    No, no, my lute, for I have done.

The Rokkes do not so cruelly
Repulse the waves continuelly,
    As she my suyte and affection,
So that I ame past remedy:
    Whereby my lute and I have done.

Prowd of the spoyll that thou hast gott
Of simple hertes thorough loves shot,
    By whome, unkynd, thou hast theim wone,

Thinck not he haith his bow forgot,
    All tho my lute and I have done.

Vengeaunce shall fall on thy disdain,
That makest but game on ernest pain;
    Thinck not alone under the sonne
Unquyt to cause thy lover's plain,
    All tho my lute and I have done.

Perchaunce the lye wethered and old,
The wynter nyghtes that are so cold,
    Playnyng in vain unto the mone;
Thy wisshes then dare not be told;
    Care then who lyst, for I have done.

And then may chaunce the to repent
The tyme that thou hast lost and spent
    To cause thy lovers sigh and swoune;
Then shalt thou knowe beaultie but lent,
    And wisshe and want as I have done.

Now cesse, my lute, this is the last
Labour that thou and I shall wast,
    And ended is that we begon;
Now is this song boeth sung and past:
    My lute be still, for I have done.

FORGET NOT YET THE TRYDE ENTENT

Forget not yet the tryde entent
Of suche a truthe as I have ment,
My gret travayle so gladly spent
    Forget not yet.

Forget not yet when fyrst began
The weary lyffe ye know syns whan,
The sute, the servys none tell can,
    Forget not yett.

Forget not yet the gret assays,
The cruell wrong, the skornfull ways,
The paynfull pacyence in denays,
    Forgett not yet.

Forget not yet, forget not thys,
How long ago hathe ben and ys
The mynd that never ment amys,
    Forget not yet.

Forget not then thyn owne aprovyd,
The whyche so long hathe thee so lovyd,
Whose stedfast faythe yet never movyd,
    Forget not thys.

in denays] in spite of denials.

WHAT SHULDE I SAYE

What shulde I saye
  Sins faithe is dede,
And truthe awaye
  From you ys fled?
  Shulde I be led
With doblenesse?
Naye, naye, mistresse!

I promiside you
  And you promisid me
To be as true
  As I wolde bee;
  But sins I se
Your doble herte,
Farewell my perte!

Though for to take
  Yt ys not my minde
But to forsake —
  I am not blind —
  And as I finde
So will I truste.
Farewell, unjuste!

Can ye saye naye?
  But you saide
That I allwaye
  Shulde be obeide;
  And thus betraide
Or that I wiste —
Fare well, unkiste!

or] ere.

AND WYLT THOW LEVE ME THUS

And wylt thow leve me thus?
Say nay, say nay, ffor shame,
To save the from the Blame
Of all my greffe and grame;
And wylt thow leve me thus?
  Say nay, Say nay!

And wylt thow leve me thus,
That hathe lovyd the so long,
In welthe and woe among?
And ys thy hart so strong
As for to leve me thus?
  Say nay, Say nay!

And wylt thow leve me thus,
That hathe gevyn the my hart,
Never for to Depart,
Nother for payn nor smart;
And wylt thow leve me thus?
  Say nay, Say nay!

And wylt thow leve me thus
And have nomore Pyttye
Of hym that lovythe the?
Helas thy cruellte!
And wylt thow leve me thus?
  Say nay, Say nay!

greffe] grief.   grame] sorrow.   nother] neither.

A! MY HERTE, A! WHAT AILETH THE

A! my herte, a! what aileth the
To sett so light my libretye,
Making me bonde when I was fre?
  A! my herte, a! what aileth thee?

When thou ware rid from all distresse,
Voyde of all paine and pensifnesse,
To chose againe a new mistresse,
   A! my herte, a! what aileth thee?

When thou ware well, thou could not hold;
To tourne agayne that ware too bold:
Thus to renue my sorrowes olde,
   A! my herte, a! what aileth thee?

Thou knoist full well that but of late
I was tournid out of loves gate,
And now to guide me to this mate,
   A! my herte, a! what aileth thee?

I hopte full well all had ben done,
But nowe my hope is tane and won,
To my tourment to yelde so sone,
   A! my herte, a! what aileth thee?

THE LOVER SHEWETH HOW HE IS FORSAKEN OF SUCH AS HE SOMETIME ENJOYED

They fle from me that sometyme did me seke
   With naked fote stalking in my chambre.
I have sene theim gentill tame and meke
   That nowe are wyld and do not remembre
   That sometyme they put theimself in daunger
To take bred at my hand; and nowe they raunge
Busily seking with a continuell chaunge.

Thancked be fortune, it hath ben othrewise
   Twenty tymes better; but ons in speciall,
In thyn arraye after a pleasaunt gyse,
   When her lose gowne from her shoulders did fall,
   And she me caught in her armes long and small;
Therewithall swetely did me kysse,
And softely saide, *dere hert, howe like you this?*

It was no dreme: I lay brode waking.
   But all is torned thorough my gentilnes
Into a straunge fasshion of forsaking;
   And I have leve to goo of her goodenes,
   And she also to use new fangilnes.
But syns that I so kyndely ame served,
I would fain knowe what she hath deserved.

Henry Howard, Earl of Surrey
1516-1547

DESCRIPTION OF THE SPRING
Wherein each thing renewes, save onelie the lover

The soote season, that bud and blome furth bringes,
With grene hath clad the hill and eke the vale;
The nightingale with fethers new she singes;
The turtle to her make hath tolde her tale.
Somer is come, for every spray nowe springes;
The hart hath hong his olde hed on the pale;
The buck in brake his winter cote he flinges;
The fishes flote with newe repaired scale;
The adder all her sloughe awaye she slinges;
The swift swalow pursueth the flyes smale;
The busy bee her honye now she minges.
Winter is worne, that was the flowers bale.
   And thus I see among these pleasant thinges
   Eche care decayes, and yet my sorow springes.

      soote] sweet, gentle.   make] mate.

Ballads

The gigantic *Tom o' Bedlam's Song* is rarely seen excepting in a caponized version, emasculated, relaxed and prettified. In its original version, stark, rank-smelling, so hot with fever (for all the cold of the heartless world in which it is a prisoner) that it might set the world on fire, it stands even above *Edward* as the greatest ballad Britain has produced. Not all "the starres att bloudie warres" have let fall more fiery tears.

This poem has come down to us as written by one unknown. But for many years I have believed I recognized the hand that took down this cry from the depths, this cry from the living specter — suffering flesh and blood for all that it is a ghost, a phantom that has gathered upon itself flesh and blood in order to confront one who could voice its pain.

I believe the hand to be that of William Shakespeare. And Robert Graves shares this belief.

Of *Lully lulley,* W. P. Ker wrote in *Form and Style in Poetry:* "The whole mystery of Christendom, the story of the Passion, has been turned into a song with a ballad-burden. It is the frailest of all poetic creatures, and no words can fully express its beauty. The meaning can scarcely be apprehended till just at the close."

There is, as he remarked, "nothing that can outrival the ballad phrase" — in such lines, for instance, as these from *Babylon, or the Bonnie Banks o' Fordie,* not included in this book:

> He's killed the may, and he's laid her by
> For to bear the red rose company.

The ballads and the nursery rhymes are haunted by the dream of Babylon: "How many miles to Babylon?"

In the nursery rhymes Babylon becomes, at times, Barley Bridge. In *The Bonnie Banks o' Fordie,* Babylon is no longer a city but an outlaw, haunting a dewy wood.

Many of the refrains of the lesser ballads are to be found echoed in each other. For instance, *Babylon,* from which I have quoted the above lines, has for a variant the following opening stanza:

> There wond three ladies in a bower,
>   Annet and Margret and Marjorie,
> And they have gone out to pu' a flower
>   And the dew it lyes on the wood gay ladie.

— the singularly lovely last line of which is a variation of the refrain of another ballad, *The Cruel Brother.*

Another version of the first verse of *Babylon* runs thus:

> There were three sisters on a road,
>   Gilly flower, gentle and rosemary,
> And there they met a banished lord,
>   And the dove it hings over the mulberry tree.

— which has almost the same refrain as that of *The Riddling Knight* (page 493).

The refrains are almost always of great beauty, even in cases when the ballad is inferior — as in *The Water o' Wearies' Well,* where the refrain runs thus:

> There came a bird out o' a bush
>   On water for to dine,
> And sighing sair sang the king's daughter,
>   O wae's this heart o' mine.

But infinitely more beautiful is the ineffably sweet and drowsy refrain from *The Broomfield Hill* (page 492). It is very old. Child says: "A Song

of 'Brume, brume on hill' is named in *The Complaynt of Scotland*,
1549."

I think it must have been sung to the Maiden in the Mor by some passing honeybee.

TOM O' BEDLAM'S SONG

From the hagg and hungrie goblin
That into raggs would rend ye,
And the spirit that stands by the naked man
In the Book of Moones defend yee!
That of your five sounde sences
You never be forsaken,
Nor wander from your selves with Tom
Abroad to begg your bacon.
   While I doe sing "any foode, any feeding,
   Feedinge, drinke or clothing,"
   Come dame or maid, be not afraid,
   Poor Tom will injure nothing.

Of thirty bare years have I
Twice twenty bin enraged,
And of forty bin three tymes fifteene
In durance soundlie caged.
On the lordlie loftes of Bedlam,
With stubble softe and dainty,
Brave braceletts strong, sweet whips ding-dong,
With wholsome hunger plenty.
   And nowe I sing, etc.

With a thought I tooke for Maudlin,
And a cruse of cockle pottage,
With a thing thus tall, skie blesse you all,
I befell into this dotage.
I slept not since the Conquest,
Till then I never waked,
Till the rogysh boy of love where I lay
Mee found and strip't mee naked.
   And nowe I sing, etc.

When I short have shorne my sowre face
And swigg'd my horny barrel,
In an oaken inne I pound my skin
As a suit of gilt apparell.

The moon's my constant Mistrisse,
And the lowlie owle my morrowe,
The flaming Drake and the Nightcrowe make
Mee musicke to my sorrowe.
   While I doe sing, etc.

The palsie plagues my pulses
When I prigg your pigs or pullen,
Your culvers take, or matchles make
Your Chanticleare, or sullen.
When I want provant, with Humfrie
I sup, and when benighted,
I repose in Powles with waking soules
Yet nevere am affrighted.
   But I doe sing, etc.

I knowe more then Apollo,
For oft, when hee ly's sleeping,
I see the starres att bloudie warres
In the wounded welkin weeping;
The moone embrace her shepheard,
And the quene of Love her warryor,
While the first doth borne the star of morne,
And the next the heavenly Farrier.
   While I doe sing, etc.

The Gipsie Snap and Pedro
Are none of Tom's comradoes.
The punk I skorne and the cut-purse sworn
And the roaring boyes bravadoe.
The meeke, the white, the gentle,
Me handle touch and spare not
But those that crosse Tom Rynosseros
Doe what the panther dare not.
   Although I sing, etc.

With an host of furious fancies,
Whereof I am commander,
With a burning speare, and a horse of aire,
To the wildernesse I wander.
By a knight of ghostes and shadowes
I summon'd am to tourney

---

prigg] steal.   pullen] poultry.   culvers] pigeons.   provant] food, provisions.
Humfrie] To "dine with Duke Humphrey" was to go dinnerless.   Powles] St. Paul's
churchyard.

Ten leagues beyond the wide world's end.
Me thinke it is noe journey.
Yet will I sing "any foode, any feeding,
Feedinge, drinke or clothing,"
Come dame or maid, be not afraid,
Poor Tom will injure nothing.

HIERUSALEM, MY HAPPIE HOME

Hierusalem, my happie home,
   When shall I come to thee?
When shall my sorrowes have an end,
   Thy joyes when shall I see?

O happie harbour of the saintes,
   O sweete and pleasant soyle:
In thee noe sorrow may be founde,
   Noe greefe, noe care, noe toyle.

In thee noe sickenesse may be seene,
   Noe hurt, noe ache, noe sore;
There is no Death, nor uglie Devill,
   There is life for evermore.

Noe Dampishe mist is seene in thee,
   Nor cold nor Darksome night;
There everie soule shines as the sunne,
   There god himselfe gives light.

There lust and lukar cannot dwell,
   There envie beares noe sway;
There is noe hunger, heate nor colde,
   But pleasure everie way.

Hierusalem, Hierusalem,
   God grant I once may see
Thy endlesse joyes, and of the same
   Partaker aye to bee.

Thy walls are made of precious stones,
   Thy bulwarkes Diamondes square;
Thy gates are of right Orient pearle,
   Exceedinge riche and rare.

Thy terettes, and thy Pinacles
  With Carbuncles Doe shine;
Thy verie streetes are paved with gould,
  Surpassinge cleare, and fine.

Thy houses are of Ivorie,
  Thy windoes Cristale cleare;
Thy tyles are made of beaten gold:
  O god that I were there!

Within thy gates nothinge doth come
  That is not passinge cleane;
Noe spiders web, noe Durt, noe Dust,
  Noe filthe may there be seene.

Ay my sweete home, Hierusaleme,
  Would god I were in thee!
Would god my woes were at an end,
  Thy joyes that I might see!

Thy saintes are crownd with glorie great;
  They see god face to face;
They triumph still; they still rejoyce:
  Most happie is their case.

Wee that are heere in banishment
  Continuallie doe mourne;
We sighe and sobbe, we weepe and weale,
  Perpetually we groane.

Our sweete is mixt with bitter gaule;
  Our pleasure is but paine,
Our joyes scarce last the lookeing on:
  Our sorrowes still remaine.

But there they live in such delight,
  Such pleasure and such play,
As that to them a thousand yeares
  Doth seeme as yesterday.

Thy Viniardes and thy Orchardes are
  Most beutifull and faire,
Full furnished with trees and fruites
  Most wonderful and rare.

Thy gardens and thy gallant walkes
    Continually are greene;
There groes such sweete and pleasant flowers
    As noe where eles are seene.

There is nector and Ambrosia made;
    There is muske and Civette sweete;
There manie a faire and daintie Drugge
    Are troden under feete.

There Cinomon, there sugar groes;
    There narde and balme abound:
What tounge can tell or hart conceive
    Thy joyes that there are found.

Thy happy Saints (Hierusalem)
    Doe bathe in endlesse blisse;
None but those blessed soules can tell
    How great thy glory is.

Quyt through the streetes with silver sound
    The flood of life doe flowe,
Upon whose bankes on everie syde
    The wood of life doth growe.

There trees for evermore beare fruite
    And evermore doe springe:
There evermore the Angels sit
    And evermore doe singe.

There David standes with harpe in hand
    As maister of the Quier:
Tenne thousand times that man were blest
    That might this musique heare.

Our Ladie singes magnificat
    With tune surpassinge sweete,
And all the virginns beare their partes,
    Sitinge above her feete.

Te Deum doth Sant Ambrose singe,
    Saint Augustine dothe the like,
Ould Simeon and Zacharie
    Have not their songes to seeke.

There Magdalene hath left her mone,
    And cheerefullie doth singe
With blessed saintes, whose harmonie
    In everie streete doth ringe.

Hierusalem, my happie home,
    Would god I were in thee!
Would god my woes were at an end,
    Thy joyes that I might see!

LADIE GREENSLEEVES

Alas, my love, ye do me wrong,
    To cast me off discurteously:
And I have loved you so long,
    Delighting in your companie.
        Greensleeves was all my joy,
        Greensleeves was my delight:
    Greensleeves was my hart of gold,
        And who but Ladie Greensleeves?

I have been readie at your hand,
    To grant what ever you would crave.
I have both waged life and land,
    Your love and good will for to have.

I bought thee kerchers to thy head,
    That were wrought fine and gallantly:
I kept thee both at boord and bed,
    Which cost my purse wel favouredly.

I bought thee peticotes of the best,
    The cloth so fine as fine might be:
I gave thee jewels for thy chest,
    And all this cost I spent on thee.

Thy smock of silk, both faire and white,
    With gold embrodered gorgeously:
Thy peticote of Sendall right:
    And this I bought thee gladly.

Thy girdle of gold so red,
    With pearles bedecked sumptuously:
The like no other lasses had,
    And yet thou wouldst not love me.

Thy purse and eke thy gay gilt knives,
　Thy pincase gallant to the eie:
No better wore the Burgesse wives,
　And yet thou wouldst not love me.

Thy crimson stockings all of silk,
　With golde all wrought above the knee,
Thy pumps as white as was the milk,
　And yet thou wouldst not love me.

Thy gown was of the grossie green,
　Thy sleeves of Satten hanging by:
Which made thee be our harvest Queen,
　And yet thou wouldst not love me.

Thy garters fringed with the golde,
　And silver aglets hanging by,
Which made thee blithe for to beholde,
　And yet thou wouldst not love me.

My gayest gelding I thee gave,
　To ride where ever liked thee,
No Ladie ever was so brave,
　And yet thou wouldst not love me.

My men were clothed all in green,
　And they did ever wait on thee:
Al this was gallant to be seen,
　And yet thou wouldst not love me.

They set thee up, they took thee downe,
　They servd thee with humilitie,
Thy foote might not once touch the ground,
　And yet thou wouldst not love me.

For everie morning when thou rose,
　I sent thee dainties orderly:
To cheare thy stomack from all woes,
　And yet thou wouldst not love me.

Thou couldst desire no earthly thing.
　But stil thou hadst it readily:
Thy musicke still to play and sing,
　And yet thou wouldst not love me.

And who did pay for all this geare,
    That thou didst spend when pleased thee?
Even I that am rejected here,
    And thou disdainst to love me.

Wel, I wil pray to God on hie,
    That thou my constancie maist see:
And that yet once before I die,
    Thou wilt vouchsafe to love me.

Greensleeves now farewel adue,
    God I pray to prosper thee:
For I am stil thy lover true,
    Come once againe and love me.
        Greensleeves was all my joy,
        Greensleeves was my delight:
        Greensleeves was my hart of gold,
        And who but Ladie Greensleeves?

From MY HEART IS HIGH ABOVE

My heart is high above,
    My body is full of bliss,
For I am set in love,
    As well as I would wish;
I love my lady pure,
    And she loves me again;
I am her serviture,
    She is my soverane.

She is my very heart,
    I am her hope and heal;
She is my joy inwart,
    I am her lover leal;
I am her bound and thrall,
    She is at my command;
I am perpetual
    Her man, both foot and hand.

The thing that may her please
    My body sall fulfil;
Whatever her disease,
    It does my body ill.

My bird, my bonny one,
    My tender babe venust,
My love, my life alone
    My liking and my lust.

We interchange our hearts
    In other's armis soft;
Spreitless we twa departs
    Usand our loves oft;
We mourn when light day dawns,
    We plain the night is short,
We curse the cock that crows,
    That hinders our disport. . . .

Lovers in pain, I pray
    God send you such remead
As I have night and day,
    You to defend from death.
Therefore be ever true
    Unto your ladies free,
And they will on you rue,
    As mine has done on me.

venust] of Venus.

A LYKE–WAKE DIRGE

This ae nighte, this ae nighte,
    Every night and alle,
Fire, and sleete, and candle lighte,
    And Christe receive thye saule.

When thou from hence away are past,
    Every night and alle,
To Whinny-muir thou comest at last,
    And Christe receive thye saule.

If ever thou gavest hosen and shoon,
    Every night and alle,
Sit thee down and put them on,
    And Christe receive thye saule.

If hosen and shoon thou ne'er gavest nane,
    Every night and alle,
The whinnes shall pricke thee to the bare bane,
    And Christe receive thye saule.

From Whinny-muir when thou mayst passe,
    Every night and alle,
To Brigg o' Dread thou comest at laste,
    *And Christe receive thye saule.**

From Brigg o' Dread when thou mayst passe,
    Every night and alle,
To purgatory fire thou comest at laste,
    And Christe receive thye saule.

If ever thou gavest meat or drink
    Every night and alle,
The fire shall never make thee shrinke,
    And Christe receive thye saule.

If meate or drinke thou never gavest nane,
    Every night and alle,
The fire will burn thee to the bare bane,
    And Christe receive thye saule.

* According to Sir Walter Scott, *Minstrelsy of the Scottish Border,* there is a stanza missing here.

This ae nighte, this ae nighte,
  Every night and alle,
Fire, and sleete, and candle lighte,
  And Christe receive thye saule.

EDWARD

"Why dois your brand sae drap wi bluid,
    Edward, Edward,
Why dois your brand sae drap wi bluid,
  And why sae sad gang yee O?"
"O I hae killed my hauke sae guid,
    Mither, mither,
O I hae killed my hauke sae guid,
  And I had nae mair bot hee O."

"Your haukis bluid was nevir sae reid,
    Edward, Edward,
Your haukis bluid was nevir sae reid,
  My deir son I tell thee O."
"O I hae killed my reid-roan steid,
    Mither, mither,
O I hae killed my reid-roan steid,
  That erst was sae fair and frie O."

"Your steid was auld, and ye hae gat mair,
    Edward, Edward,
Your steid was auld, and ye hae gat mair,
  Sum other dule ye drie O."
"O I hae killed my fadir deir,
    Mither, mither,
O I hae killed my fadir deir,
  Alas, and wae is mee O!"

"And whatten penance wul ye drie for that,
    Edward, Edward?
And whatten penance will ye drie for that?
  My deir son, now tell me O."
"Ile set my feit in yonder boat,
    Mither, mither,
Ile set my feit in yonder boat,
  And Ile fare ovir the sea O."

"And what wul ye doe wi your towirs and your ha,
    Edward, Edward?

And what wul ye doe wi your towirs and your ha,
  That were sae fair to see O?"
"Ile let thame stand tul they doun fa,
    Mither, mither,
Ile let thame stand tul they doun fa,
  For here nevir mair maun I bee O."

"And what wul ye leive to your bairns and your wife,
    Edward, Edward?
And what wul ye leive to your bairns and your wife,
  When ye gang ovir the sea O?"
"The warldis room, late them beg thrae life,
    Mither, mither,
The warldis room, late them beg thrae life,
  For thame nevir mair wul I see O."

"And what wul ye leive to your ain mither deir,
    Edward, Edward?
And what wul ye leive to your ain mither deir?
  My deir son, now tell me O."
"The curse of hell frae me sall ye beir,
    Mither, mither,
The curse of hell frae me sall ye beir,
  Sic counseils ye gave to me O."

THE THREE RAVENS

There were three ravens sat on a tree
  Downe a downe, hay downe, hay downe.
There were three ravens sat on a tree,
  With a downe, hay downe, hay downe.
There were three ravens sat on a tree,
They were as blacke as they might be.
  With a downe derrie, derrie, derrie, downe, downe.

The one of them said to his mate,
"Where shall we our breakefast take?"

"Downe in yonder greene field,
There lies a knight slain under his shield.

"His hounds they lie downe at his feete,
So well they can their master keepe.

"His haukes they flie so eagerly,
There's no fowle dare him come nie."

Downe there comes a fallow doe,
As great with yong as she might goe.

She lift up his bloudy hed,
And kist his wounds that were so red.

She got him up upon her backe,
And carried him to earthen lake.

She buried him before the prime,
She was dead herselfe ere even-song time.

God send every gentleman,
  Downe a downe, hay downe, hay downe.
God send every gentleman,
  With a downe, hay downe, hay downe.
God send every gentleman,
Such haukes, such hounds, and such a leman.
  With a downe derrie, derrie, derrie, downe, downe.

LORD RANDAL

"O where have you been, Lord Randal, my son?
O where have you been, my handsome young man?" —
"I have been to the greenwood; O make my bed soon,
For I'm weary with hunting, and fain would lie down."

"And what met ye there, Lord Randal, my son?
And what met ye there, my handsome young man?" —
"I met with my true love; O make my bed soon,
For I'm weary with hunting, and fain would lie down."

"And what did she give you, Lord Randal, my son?
And what did she give you, my handsome young man?" —
"Eels fried in a pan; O make my bed soon,
For I'm weary with hunting, and fain would lie down."

"What colour were they, Lord Randal, my son?
What colour were they, my handsome young man?" —
"They were speckled and blotched; O make my bed soon,
For I'm weary with hunting, and fain would lie down."

"O where did she get them, Lord Randal, my son?
O where did she get them, my handsome young man?" —
"From hedges and ditches; O make my bed soon,
For I'm weary with hunting, and fain would lie down."

"O where are your bloodhounds, Lord Randal, my son?
O where are your bloodhounds, my handsome young man?" —
"They swelled and they died; Mother, make my bed soon,
For I'm sick at the heart, and I fain would lie down."

"O that was strong poison, Lord Randal, my son!
O that was strong poison, my handsome young man!" —
"O yes, I am poisoned; So make my bed soon,
For I'm sick at the heart, and I fain would lie down."

THE WIFE OF USHER'S WELL

There lived a wife at Usher's Well,
    And a wealthy wife was she;
She had three stout and stalwart sons,
    And sent them oer the sea.

They hadna been a week from her,
    A week but barely ane,
Whan word came to the carlin wife
    That her three sons were gane.

They hadna been a week from her,
    A week but barely three,
Whan word came to the carlin wife
    That her sons she'd never see.

"I wish the wind may never cease,
    Nor fashes in the flood,
Till my three sons come hame to me,
    In earthly flesh and blood."

It fell about the Martinmass,
    When nights are lang and mirk,
The carlin wife's three sons came hame,
    And their hats were o the birk.

It neither grew in syke nor ditch,
    Nor yet in ony sheugh;
But at the gates o Paradise,
    That birk grew fair eneugh.

"Blow up the fire, my maidens,
    Bring water from the well;

carlin] country.   fashes] troubles.   syke] marsh.   sheugh] trench.

For a' my house shall feast this night,
  Since my three sons are well."

And she has made to them a bed,
  She's made it large and wide,
And she's taen her mantle her about,
  Sat down at the bed-side.

Up then crew the red, red cock,
  And up and crew the gray;
The eldest to the youngest said,
  " 'Tis time we were away."

The cock he hadna crawd but once,
  And clappd his wings at a',
When the youngest to the eldest said,
  "Brother, we must awa.

"The cock doth craw, the day doth daw;
  The channerin worm doth chide;
Gin we be mist out o our place,
  A sair pain we maun bide.

"Fare ye weel, my mother dear!
  Fareweel to barn and byre!
And fare ye weel, the bonny lass
  That kindles my mother's fire!"

channerin] fretting.

THE UNQUIET GRAVE

"The wind doth blow today, my love,
  And a few small drops of rain;
I never had but one true-love,
  In cold grave she was lain.

"I'll do as much for my true-love
  As any young man may;
I'll sit and mourn all at her grave
  For a twelvemonth and a day."

The twelvemonth and a day being up,
  The dead began to speak:
"Oh who sits weeping on my grave,
  And will not let me sleep?"

" 'Tis I, my love, sits on your grave,
　And will not let you sleep;
For I crave one kiss of your clay-cold lips,
　And that is all I seek."

"You crave one kiss of my clay-cold lips;
　But my breath smells earthy strong;
If you have one kiss of my clay-cold lips,
　Your time will not be long.

" 'Tis down in yonder garden green,
　Love, where we used to walk,
The finest flower that e'er was seen
　Is withered to a stalk.

"The stalk is withered dry, my love,
　So will our hearts decay;
So make yourself content, my love,
　Till God calls you away."

SIR PATRICK SPENS

The king sits in Dumferling toune,
　Drinking the blude-reid wine:
"O whar will I get a guid sailor,
　To sail this schip of mine?"

Up and spak an eldern knicht,
　Sat at the kings richt kne:
"Sir Patrick Spens is the best sailor
　That sails upon the se."

The king has written a braid letter,
　And signd it wi his hand,
And sent it to Sir Patrick Spens,
　Was walking on the sand.

The first line that Sir Patrick red,
　A loud lauch lauched he;
The next line that Sir Patrick red,
　The teir blinded his ee.

"O wha is this has don this deid,
　This ill deid don to me,
To send me out this time o' the yeir,
　To sail upon the se!

"Mak hast, mak haste, my mirry men all,
    Our guid schip sails the morne."
"O say na sae, my master deir,
    For I feir a deadlie storme.

"Late late yestreen I saw the new moone,
    Wi the auld moone in hir arme,
And I feir, I feir, my deir master,
    That we will cum to harme."

O our Scots nobles wer richt laith
    To weet their cork-heild schoone:
Bot lang owre a' the play wer playd,
    Thair hats they swam aboone.

O lang, lang may their ladies sit,
    With thair fans into their hand,
Or eir they se Sir Patrick Spens
    Cum sailing to the land.

O lang, lang may the ladies stand,
    Wi thair gold kems in thair hair,
Waiting for thair ain deir lords,
    For they'll se thame na mair.

Haf owre, haf owre to Aberdour,
    It's fiftie fadom deip,
And thair lies guid Sir Patrick Spens,
    Wi the Scots lords at his feit.

richt laith] right loth.   weet] wet.   lang owre] long ere.   aboone] **above.**

THE GOULDEN VANITIE

There was a gallant ship, and a gallant ship was she,
    Eck iddle du, and the Lowlands low;
And she was called The Goulden Vanitie,
    As she sailed to the Lowlands low.

She had not sailed a league, a league but only three,
When she came up with a French gallee,
    As she sailed to the Lowlands low.

Out spoke the little cabin-boy, out spoke he;
"What will you give me if I sink that French gallee
    As ye sail to the Lowlands low?"

"I'll give thee gold, and I'll give thee fee,
And my eldest daughter thy wife shall be
   If you sink her off the Lowlands low."

"Then sew me up ticht in a black bull's skin,
And throw me oer deck-buird, sink I or swim
   As ye sail to the Lowlands low."

So they've sewed him up ticht in a black bull's skin,
And have thrown him oer deck-buird, sink he or swim
   As they sail to the Lowlands low.

About, and about, and about went he,
Until he cam up with the French gallee
   As they sailed to the Lowlands low.

O some were playing cards, and some were playing dice,
The boy he had an auger bored holes two at twice;
He let the water in, and it dazzled in their eyes,
   As they sailed to the Lowlands low.

Then some they ran with cloaks, and some they ran with caps,
To try if they could stap the saut-water draps
   As they sailed to the Lowlands low.

About, and about, and about went he,
Until he cam back to The Goulden Vanitie
   As they sailed to the Lowlands low.

"Now throw me oer a rope and pu me up on buird,
And prove unto me as guid as your word
   As ye sail to the Lowlands low."

"We'll no throw ye oer a rope, nor pu you up on buird,
Nor prove unto you as guid as our word
   As we sail to the Lowlands low."

"You promised me gold, and you promised me fee,
Your eldest daughter my wife she should be
   As ye sail to the Lowlands low."

"You shall have gold, and you shall have fee,
But my eldest daughter your wife shall never be
   As we sail to the Lowlands low."

Out spoke the little cabin-boy, out spoke he;
"Then hang me, I'll sink ye as I sunk the French gallee
As ye sail to the Lowlands low."

The boy he swam round all by the starboard side,
When they pu'd him up on buird it's there he soon died;
They threw him oer deck-buird to go down with the tide,
And sink off the Lowlands low.

THE WANDERING SPECTRE
(THE CAULD LAD O' HILTON)

Wae's me, wae's me,
The acorn's not yet
Fallen from the tree
That's to grow the wood,
That's to make the cradle,
That's to rock the bairn,
That's to grow a man,
That's to lay me.

Alexander Montgomerie
1556?-1610?

From THE NICHT IS NEIR GONE

Hey! now the day dawis;
The jolly cock crawis;
Now shroudis the shawis
    Thro' Nature anon.
The thissel-cock cryis
On lovers wha lyis:
Now skaillis the skyis;
    The nicht is neir gone.

The fieldis overflowis
With gowans that growis,
Quhair lilies like low is
    As red as the rone.

shroudis] array themselves.   shawis] woods.   skaillis] clears.   gowans] daisies.
low] flame, fire.   rone] rowan.

> The turtle that true is,
> With notes that renewis,
> Her pairty pursuis:
>   The nicht is neir gone.
>
> Now hairtis with hindis
> Conform to their kindis,
> Hie tursis their tyndis
>   On ground quhair they grone.
> Now hurchonis, with hairis,
> Aye passis in pairis;
> Quhilk duly declaris
>   The nicht is neir gone.

pairty] mate.   tursis] carry.   tyndis] antlers.   grone] groan, or bell.
hurchonis] hedgehogs.

Sir Edward Dyer
c. 1540-1607

THE LOWEST TREES HAVE TOPPS

The lowest trees have topps, the ante her gall,
  The flie her spleene, the little sparke his heat:
The slender hairs cast shadows, though but small,
  And bees have stinges, although they be not great;
Seas have their sourse, and soe have shallow springes:
And Love is Love, in beggers and in Kinges.

Wher waters smothest ronne, ther deepest are the foords,
  The diall stirs, yet none perceives it moove;
The firmest fayth is fownd in fewest woordes,
  The turtles doe not singe, and yet they love;
True heartes have ears and eyes, no tongues to speake:
They heare and see, and sigh, and then they breake.

MY MYNDE TO ME A KYNGDOME IS

My mynde to me a kyngdome is,
  Such perfect joy therin I fynde,
That it excells all other blisse
  That worlde afords or growes by kynde:
Though muche I wante which moste would have,
Yet still my mynde forbides to crave.

No princely pompe, no wealthy store,
   Nor force to win the victorye,
No wily witt to salve a sore,
   No shape to feade a lovinge eye;
To none of these I yealde as thrall:
For why? my minde dothe serve for all.

I see how plenty suffers ofte,
   And hastye clymers sone do fall:
I see that those whiche are alofte
   Myshapp dothe threaten moste of all:
They get with toylle, they keepe with feare;
Such cares my mynde coulde never beare.

Contente I live, this is my staye:
   I seeke no more than may suffyse,
I presse to beare no haughtie swaye;
   Look, what I lack my mynde suppliese:
Lo, thus I tryumphe lyke a kynge,
Content with that my mynde doth bringe.

Some have too muche, yet still do crave,
   I little have, and seeke no more:
They are but poore, though muche they have,
   And I am ryche with lytle store:
They poore, I ryche; they begg, I geve:
They lacke, I leave; they pyne, I lyve.

I laugh not at an others loss,
   I grudge not at an others gaine:
No worldly waves my mynde can toss,
   My state at one dothe still remayne:
I feare no foe, I fawne no freende,
I lothe not lyfe, nor dread no ende.

Some weighe theyre pleasure by theyre luste,
   Their wisdom by theyre rage of will:
Theire treasure is theire only truste,
   A cloked crafte theyre store of skyll:
But all the pleasure that I fynde
Is to mayntayne a quiet mynde.

My wealthe is healthe and perfecte ease,
   My conscience cleere my chiefe defense:
I neither seeke by brybes to please,
   Nor by deserte to breede offence:
Thus do I lyve, thus will I dye;
Would all did so, as well as I.

Sir Walter Raleigh
1552?-1618

THE LIE

Goe soule the bodies guest
　Upon a thankelesse arrant,
Fear not to touch the best
　The truth shall be thy warrant:
Goe since I needs must die,
And give the world the lie.

Say to the Court it glowes,
　And shines like rotten wood,
Say to the Church it showes
　Whats good, and doth no good.
If Church and Court reply,
Then give them both the lie.

Tell Potentates they live
　Acting by others action,
Not lovd unlesse they give,
　Not strong but by affection.
If Potentates reply,
Give Potentates the lie.

Tell men of high condition,
　That mannage the estate,
Their purpose is ambition,
　Their practise onely hate:
And if they once reply,
Then give them all the lie.

Tell them that brave it most,
　They beg for more by spending,
Who in their greatest cost
　Like nothing but commending.
And if they make replie,
Then give them all the lie.

Tell zeale it wants devotion
　Tell love it is but lust,
Tell time it meets but motion,
　Tell flesh it is but dust.
And wish them not replie
For thou must give the lie.

Tell age it daily wasteth,
　Tell honour how it alters.
Tell beauty how she blasteth
　Tell favour how it falters
And as they shall reply,
Give every one the lie.

Tell wit how much it wrangles
　In tickle points of nycenesse,
Tell wisedome she entangles
　Her selfe in over wisenesse.
And when they doe reply
Straight give them both the lie.

Tell Phisicke of her boldnes,
　Tell skill it is prevention:
Tell charity of coldnes,
　Tell law it is contention,
And as they doe reply
So give them still the lie.

Tell fortune of her blindnesse,
　Tell nature of decay,
Tell friendship of unkindnesse,
　Tell justice of delay.
And if they will reply,
Then give them all the lie.

Tell Arts they have no soundnesse,
  But vary by esteeming,
Tell schooles they want pro-
    foundnes
  And stand so much on seeming.
If Arts and schooles reply,
Give arts and schooles the lie.

Tell faith its fled the Citie,
  Tell how the country erreth,
Tell manhood shakes off pittie,

Tell vertue least preferred.
And if they doe reply,
Spare not to give the lie.

So when thou hast, as I
  Commanded thee, done blab-
    bing,
Because to give the lie
  Deserves no lesse than stabbing,
Stab at thee he that will,
No stab thy soule can kill.

THE PASSIONATE MANS PILGRIMAGE
Supposed to be written by one at the point of death

Give me my Scallop shell of quiet,
  My staffe of Faith to walke upon,
My Scrip of Joy, Immortall diet,
  My bottle of salvation:
My Gowne of Glory, hopes true gage,
And thus Ile take my pilgrimage.

Blood must be my bodies balmer,
  No other balme will there be given
Whilst my soule like a white Palmer
  Travels to the land of heaven,
Over the silver mountaines,
Where spring the Nectar fountaines:
And there Ile kisse
The Bowle of blisse,
And drinke my eternall fill
On every milken hill.
My soule will be a drie before,
But after it, will nere thirst more.

And by the happie blisfull way
  More peacefull Pilgrims I shall see,
That have shooke off their gownes of clay,
  And goe appareld fresh like mee.
Ile bring them first
To slake their thirst,
  And then to taste those Nectar suckets
At the cleare wells
Where sweetnes dwells,
  Drawne up by Saints in Christall buckets.

And when our bottle and all we,
Are fild with immortalitie:
Then the holy paths weele travell
Strewde with Rubies thicke as gravell,
Ceilings of Diamonds, Saphire floores,
High walles of Corall and Pearl Bowres.

From thence to heavens Bribeles hall
Where no corrupted voyces brall,
No Conscience molten into gold,
Nor forgd accusers bought and sold,
No cause deferd, nor vaine spent Jorney,
For there Christ is the Kings Atturney:
Who pleades for all without degrees,
And he hath Angells, but no fees.

When the grand twelve million Jury,
Of our sinnes with sinfull fury,
Gainst our soules blacke verdicts give,
Christ pleades his death, and then we live,
Be thou my speaker taintles pleader,
Unblotted Lawyer, true proceeder,
Thou movest salvation even for almes:
Not with a bribed Lawyers palmes.

And this is my eternall plea,
To him that made Heaven, Earth and Sea,
Seeing my flesh must die so soone,
And want a head to dine next noone,
Just at the stroke when my vaines start and spred
Set on my soul an everlasting head.
Then am I readie like a palmer fit,
To tread those blest paths which before I writ.

AS YOU CAME FROM THE HOLY LAND *

As you came from the holy land
    Of Walsinghame,
Mett you not with my tru love
    By the way as you came?

How shall I know your trew love,
    That have mett many one
As I went to the holy lande,
    That have come, that have gone?

* Sometimes attributed to Raleigh.

She is neyther whyte nor browne,
    Butt as the heavens fayre:
There is none hathe a forme so divine
    In the earth or the ayre:

Such an one did I meet, good Sir,
    Suche an Angelyke face,
Who lyke a queene, lyke a nymph, did appere,
    By her gaite, by her grace:

She hath lefte me here all alone,
    All allone as unkowne,
Who somtymes did me lead with her selfe
    And me lovde as her owne:

Whats the cause that she leaves you alone
    And a new waye doth take:
Who loved you once as her owne,
    And her joye did you make?

I have lovde her all my youth,
    Butt now ould as you see,
Love lykes not the fallyng frute
    From the wythered tree:

Know that love is a careless chylld
    And forgets promyse paste:
He is blynd, he is deaff, when he lyste
    And in faythe never faste:

His desyre is a dureless contente
    And a trustless joye;
He is wonn with a world of despayre
    And is lost with a toye:

Of women kynde suche indeed is the love
    Or the word Love abused,
Under which many chyldysh desyres
    And conceytes are excusde:

Butt Love is a durable fyre,
    In the mynde ever burnynge:
Never sycke, never ould, never dead,
    From itt selfe never turnynge.

        dureless] not lasting.

Robert Southwell
1561?-1595

THE BURNING BABE

As I in hoarie Winters night
  Stood shivering in the snow,
Surpriz'd I was with sudden heat,
  Which made my heart to glow;
And lifting up a fearefull eye
  To view what fire was neere,
A prettie Babe all burning bright
  Did in the aire appeare;
Who, scorched with excessive heat,
  Such flouds of teares did shed,
As though his flouds should quench
    his flames,
  Which with his teares were bred:
Alas, (quoth he) but newly borne,
  In fierie heats I frie,
Yet none approach to warme their
    hearts,

Or feele my fire but I;
My faultlesse brest the furnace is,
  The fuell wounding thornes:
Love is the fire, and sighs the smoke,
  The ashes shames and scornes;
The fuell justice layeth on,
  And mercy blowes the coales,
The metall in this Furnace wrought,
  Are mens defiled soules:
For which, as now on fire I am,
  To worke them to their good,
So will I melt into a bath,
  To wash them in my blood.
With this he vanisht out of sight,
  And swiftly shrunke away,
And straight I called unto minde,
  That it was Christmasse day.

Phineas Fletcher
1580-1650

A LITANY

Drop, drop, slow tears,
  And bathe those beauteous feet
Which brought from Heaven
  The news and Prince of peace:
Cease not, wet eyes,
  His mercy to intreat;
To crie for vengeance
  Sinne doth never cease:
In your deep floods
  Drown all my faults and fears,
Nor let his eye
  See sinne, but through my tears.

Sir Philip Sidney
1554-1586

The metrical wonders of this singing flame, one of the greatest lyrical poets in our language, are endless.

As Saintsbury * said, "There was nobody in English, not even Chaucer, from whom Sidney could have learnt the art of playing on a word for its sound and echo as he does . . . on the word 'you' " — in the song:

> Doubt you to whom my Muse these notes entendeth,
> Which now my breast, orecharg'd, to musick lendeth?
> To you, to you, all song of praise is due,
> Only in you my song begins and endeth.

— "and old as double rhymes are, they have never been made to yield quite such sweetness."

The *Double Sestine* has a strange hive-humming music, like that of shepherds' oaten pipes; and this changes, sometimes, to a hard dark drumming sound, like that of great drops of water falling over the rocks of a forest cavern. This effect was brought about by the female endings.

We find almost the same effect in the first two verses of *When to my deadlie pleasure;* here the drumming music is caused by the first accent of the line falling on the first syllable of the first word, and by the fact that all the lines either end with a double-syllabled word, or seem, almost, to do so (the accent falling on the word before, in that case), so that one hears "harts fort" nearly, if not quite, as if it were "hartsfort," with little, if any, separation between the words.

In *Get hence foule Griefe,* the beauty is largely due to the deep pauses dividing the line. In *Who hath his fancie pleased* it is due to the deep pauses ending each line.

THE NIGHTINGALE
To the tune of
"Non credo già che più infelice amante"

The Nightingale as soone as Aprill bringeth
Unto her rested sense a perfect waking,
While late bare earth, proud of new clothing springeth,
Sings out her woes, a thorne her song-booke making:
And mournfully bewailing,

* *The History of English Prosody.*

Her throate in tunes expresseth
What griefe her breaste oppresseth,
For *Thereus* force on her chaste will prevailing.
O *Philomela* faire, O take some gladnesse,
That here is juster cause of plaintfull sadnesse:
Thine earth now springs, mine fadeth,
Thy thorne without, my thorne my heart invadeth.

Alas she hath no other cause of anguish
But *Thereus* love, on her by strong hand wrokne,
Wherein she suffring all her spirits languish,
Full womanlike complaines her will was brokne.
But I who dayly craving,
Cannot have to content me,
Have more cause to lament me,
Since wanting is more woe then too much having.
O *Philomela* faire, O take some gladnesse,
That here is juster cause of plaintfull sadnesse:
Thine earth now springs, mine fadeth:
Thy thorne without, my thorne my heart invadeth.

O FAIRE! O SWEETE!
*To the tune of the Spanish song, "Se tu señnora no
dueles de mi"*

O faire! O sweete! when I do looke on thee,
In whome all joyes so well agree,
Heart and soul do sing in me.
This you heare is not my tongue,
Which once said what I conceaved,
For it was of use bereaved,
With a cruell answer stong.
No; though tongue to roofe be cleaved,
Fearing lest he chastisde be,
Heart and soule do singe in me.

O faire! O sweete! when I do looke on thee,
In whome all joyes so well agree,
Heart and soul do sing in me.
Just accord all musicke makes;
In thee just accord excelleth,
Where each part in such peace dwelleth,
One of other, beautie takes.
Since, then, truth to all mindes telleth
That in thee lives harmonie,
Heart and soule do sing in me.

O faire! O sweete! when I do looke on thee,
In whome all joyes so well agree,
Heart and soul do sing in me.
   They that heaven have knowne do say,
That whoso that grace obtaineth,
To see what faire sight there raigneth,
   Forced are to sing alway:
So, then, since that heaven remaineth
   In thy face I plainly see,
   Heart and soule do singe in me.

O faire! O sweete! when I do looke on thee,
In whome all joyes so well agree,
Heart and soul do sing in me.
   Sweete, thinke not I am at ease,
For because my cheefe part singeth;
This song from deathe's sorrow springeth,
   As to swanne in last disease:
For no dumbnesse nor death bringeth
   Stay to true love's melody:
   Heart and soul do sing in me.

WHEN TO MY DEADLIE PLEASURE

When to my deadlie pleasure,
When to my livelie torment,
Ladie mine eyes remained,
Joyned alas to your beames.

With violence of heav'nly
Beautie tied, to vertue,
Reason abasht retyred,
Gladly my senses yeelded.

Gladly my senses yeelding,
Thus to betray my hart's fort,
Left me devoid of all life.

They to the beamie Sunnes went,
Where by the death of all deaths,
Finde to what harme they hastned.

Like to the silly *Sylvan*,
Burn'd by the light he best liked,
When with a fire he first met.

Yet, yet a life to their death,
Lady you have reserved,
Lady the life of all love.

For though my sense be from me,
And I be dead who want sense,
Yet do we both live in you.

Turned anew by your meanes,
Unto the flowre that ay turnes,
As you, alas, my Sunne bends.

Thus do I fall to rise thus,
Thus do I dye to live thus,
Changed to a change, I change not.

Thus may I not be from you:
Thus be my senses on you:
Thus what I thinke is of you:
Thus what I seeke is in you:
   All what I am, it is you.

WHO HATH HIS FANCIE PLEASED
To the tune of "Wilhelmus van Nassau"

Who hath his fancie pleased
  With fruits of happie sight,
Let here his eyes be raised
  On Nature's sweetest light;
A light which doth dissever,
  And yet unite the eyes;
A light which — dying never —
  Is cause the looker dyes.

She never dies, but lasteth
  In life of lover's hart,
He ever dies that wasteth
  In love his chiefest part.
Thus is her life still guarded
  In never-dying faith;
Thus is his death rewarded,
  Since she lives in his death.

Looke then, and dye; the pleasure
  Doth answere well the paine;
Small losse of mortall treasure,
  Who may immortall gaine.
Immortall be her graces,
  Immortall is her minde;
They, fit for heavenly places,
  This heaven in it doth bind.

But eyes these beauties see not,
  Nor sence that grace descryes;
Yet eyes deprived be not
  From sight of her faire eyes,
Which, as of inward glorie
  They are the outward seale;
So may they live still sorie,
  Which die not in that weale.

But who hath fancies pleased
  With fruits of happie sight,
Let here his eyes be raysed
  On Nature's sweetest light.

From ASTROPHEL AND STELLA

FIRST SONG

Doubt you to whom my Muse these notes entendeth,
Which now my breast, orecharg'd, to musick lendeth?
   To you, to you, all song of praise is due,
Only in you my song begins and endeth.

Who hath the eyes which marrie state with pleasure?
Who keeps the key of Nature's chiefest treasure?
   To you, to you, all song of praise is due,
Only for you the heav'n forgate all measure.

Who hath the lips, where wit in fairenesse raigneth?
Who womankind at once both deckes and stayneth?
   To you, to you, all song of praise is due,
Onely by you Cupid his crowne maintaineth.

Who hath the feet, whose step all sweetnesse planteth?
Who else, for whom Fame worthy trumpets wanteth?
   To you, to you, all song of praise is due,
Onely to you her scepter Venus granteth.

Who hath the breast, whose milk doth patience nourish?
Whose grace is such, that when it chides doth cherish?
   To you, to you, all song of praise is due,
Onelie through you the tree of life doth flourish.

Who hath the hand which, without stroke, subdueth?
Who long-dead beauties with increase reneueth?
   To you, to you, all song of praise is due,
Onely at you all envie hopelesse rueth.

Who hath the haire, which, loosest, fastest tieth?
Who makes a man live, then glad when he dieth?
   To you, to you, all song of praise is due,
Only of you the flatterer never lieth.

Who hath the voyce, which soule from sences sunders?
Whose force, but yours, the bolts of beautie thunders?
   To you, to you, all song of praise is due,
Only with you not miracles are wonders.

Doubt you, to whome my Muse these notes intendeth,
Which now my breast, orecharg'd, to musicke lendeth?
 To you, to you, all song of praise is due:
Only in you my song begins and endeth.

FOURTH SONG

Onely Joy, now here you are,
Fit to heare and ease my care,
Let my whispering voyce obtaine
Sweete reward for sharpest paine;
Take me to thee, and thee to mee:
"No, no, no, no, my Deare, let bee."

Night hath closde all in her cloke,
Twinkling starres love-thoughts provoke,
Danger hence, good care doth keepe,
Jealouzie himselfe doth sleepe;
Take me to thee, and thee to mee:
"No, no, no, no, my Deare, let bee."

Better place no wit can finde,
Cupid's knot to loose or binde;
These sweet flowers our fine bed too,
Us in their best language woo:
Take me to thee, and thee to mee:
"No, no, no, no, my Deare, let bee."

This small light the moone bestowes
Serves thy beames but to disclose;
So to raise my hap more hie,
Feare not else, none can us spie;
Take me to thee, and thee to mee:
"No, no, no, no, my Deare, let bee."

That you heard was but a mouse,
Dumbe Sleepe holdeth all the house:
Yet asleepe, me thinkes they say,
Yong fooles take time while you may;
Take me to thee, and thee to mee:
"No, no, no, no, my Deare, let bee."

Niggard time threates, if we misse
This large offer of our blisse,
Long stay, ere he graunt the same:
Sweet, then, while ech thing doth frame,
Take me to thee, and thee to mee:
"No, no, no, no, my Deare, let bee."

Your faire mother is a-bed,
Candles out and curtaines spread;
She thinkes you do letters write;
Write, but first let me endite;
Take me to thee, and thee to mee:
"No, no, no, no, my Deare, let bee."

Sweete, alas, why strive you thus?
Concord better fitteth us;
Leave to Mars the force of hands,
Your power in your beautie stands;
Take thee to me, and me to thee:
"No, no, no, no, my Deare, let bee."

Wo to mee, and do you sweare
Me to hate? but I forbeare;
Cursed be my destines all,
That brought me so high to fall;
Soone with my death I will please thee:
"No, no, no, no, my Deare, let bee."

ELEVENTH SONG

"Who is it that this darke night,
  Underneath my window playneth?"
It is one who from thy sight,
  Being (ah) exild, disdayneth
Every other vulgar light.

"Why alas, and are you he?
  Be not yet those fancies changed?"
Deere when you find change in me,
  Though from me you be estranged,
Let my chaunge to ruine be.

"Well, in absence this will dy,
   Leave to see, and leave to wonder."
Absence sure will helpe, if I
   Can learne, how my selfe to sunder
From what in my hart doth ly.

"But time will these thoughts remove:
   Time doth worke what no man knoweth."
Time doth as the subject prove,
   With time still the affection groweth
In the faithfull Turtle dove.

"What if you new beauties see,
   Will not they stir new affection?"
I will thinke they pictures be,
   (Imagelike of Saints perfection)
Poorely counterfeting thee.

"But your reasons purest light,
   Bids you leave such minds to nourish?"
Deere, do reason no such spite,
   Never doth thy beauty florish
More, then in my reasons sight.

"But the wrongs love beares, will make
   Love at length leave undertaking."
No the more fooles it do shake,
   In a ground of so firme making,
Deeper still they drive the stake.

"Peace, I thinke that some give eare:
   Come no more, lest I get anger."
Blisse, I will my blisse forbeare,
   Fearing (sweete) you to endanger,
But my soule shall harbour there.

"Well, be gone, be gone I say,
   Lest that *Argus* eyes perceive you."
O unjust fortunes sway,
   Which can make me thus to leave you,
And from lowts to run away.

SONNET XXXI

With how sad steps, O Moone, thou climb'st the skies,
How silently, and with how wanne a face,
What may it be, that even in heav'nly place
That busie archer his sharpe arrowes tries?
Sure if that long with *Love* acquainted eyes
Can judge of *Love,* thou feel'st a Lovers case;
I reade it in thy lookes, thy languisht grace
To me that feele the like, thy state descries.
Then ev'n of fellowship, O Moone, tell me,
Is constant *Love* deem'd there but want of wit?
Are Beauties there as proud as here they be?
Do they above love to be lov'd, and yet
    Those Lovers scorne whom that *Love* doth possesse?
    Do they call *Vertue* there ungratefulnesse?

SONNET XLVII

What have I thus betrayed my libertie?
Can those blacke beames such burning markes engrave
In my free side? or am I borne a slave,
Whose necke becomes such yoke of tyranny?
Or want I sense to feele my miserie?
Or sprite, disdaine of such disdaine to have?
Who for long faith, tho dayly helpe I crave,
May get no almes but scorne of beggerie.
Vertue awake, Beautie but beautie is,
I may, I must, I can, I will, I do
Leave following that, which it is gaine to misse.
Let her go: soft, but here she comes, go to,
    Unkind, I love you not: O me, that eye
    Doth make my heart give to my tongue the lie.

From THE COUNTESS OF PEMBROKE'S ARCADIA

O SWEET WOODS

O sweet woods the delight of solitarines!
O how much I do like your solitarines!
Where mans mind hath a freed consideration
Of goodnes to receive lovely direction.
Where senses do behold th' order of heav'nly hoste,
And wise thoughts do behold what the creator is:

Contemplation here holdeth his only seate:
Bownded with no limitts, borne with a wing of hope,
Clymes even unto the starres, Nature is under it.
Nought disturbs thy quiet, all to thy service yeelds,
Each sight draws on a thought, thought mother of science,
Sweet birds kindly do graunt harmony unto thee,
Faire trees shade is enough fortification,
Nor danger to thy selfe if be not in thy selfe.

O sweete woods the delight of solitarines!
O how much I do like your solitarines!
Here nor treason is hidd, vailed in innocence,
Nor envies snaky ey, finds any harbor here,
Nor flatterers venomous insinuations,
Nor cunning humorists puddled opinions,
Nor courteous ruin of proffered usury,
Nor time pratled away, cradle of ignorance,
Nor causeless duty, nor comber of arrogance,
Nor trifling title of vanity dazleth us,
Nor golden manacles, stand for a paradise,
Here wrongs name is unheard: slander a monster is,
Keepe thy sprite from abuse, here no abuse doth haunte.
What man grafts in a tree dissimulation?

O sweete woods the delight of solitarines!
O how well I do like your solitarines!
Yet deare soile, if a soule closed in a mansion
As sweete as violetts, faire as lilly is,
Streight as Cedar, a voice staines the Cannary birds,
Whose shade safely doth hold, danger avoideth her:
Such wisedome, that in her lives speculation:
Such goodnes that in her simplicitie triumphs:
Where envies snaky ey, winketh or els dyeth,
Slander wants a pretext, flattery gone beyond:
Oh! if such a one have bent, to a lonely life,
Her stepps gladd we receave, gladd we receave her eys.
    And thinke not she doth hurt our solitarines,
    For such company decks such solitarines.

DOUBLE SESTINE

STREPHON. You Gote-heard Gods, that love the grassie mountaines,
           You Nimphes that haunt the springs in pleasant vallies,
           You Satyrs joyde with free and quiet forrests,

Vouchsafe your silent eares to playning musique,
Which to my woes gives still an early morning:
And drawes the dolor on till wery evening.

KLAIUS.   O *Mercurie*, foregoer to the evening,
O heavenlie huntresse of the savage mountaines,
O lovelie starre, entitled of the morning,
While that my voice doth fill these wofull vallies,
Vouchsafe your silent eares to plaining musique,
Which oft hath *Echo* tir'd in secrete forrests.

STREPHON.   I that was once free-burges of the forrests,
Where shade from Sunne, and sports I sought at evening,
I that was once esteem'd for pleasant musique,
Am banisht now among the monstrous mountaines
Of huge despaire, and foule afflictions vallies,
Am growne a shrich-owle to my selfe each morning.

KLAIUS.   I that was once delighted every morning,
Hunting the wilde inhabiters of forrests,
I that was once the musique of these vallies,
So darkened am, that all my day is evening,
Heart-broken so, that molehilles seeme high mountaines,
And fill the vales with cries in steed of musique.

STREPHON.   Long since alas, my deadly Swannish musique
Hath made it selfe a crier of the morning,
And hath with wailing strength climb'd highest mountaines:
Long since my thoughts more desert be then forrests:
Long since I see my joyes come to their evening,
And state throwen downe to over-troden vallies.

KLAIUS.   Long since the happie dwellers of these vallies,
Have praide me leave my strange exclaiming musique,
Which troubles their dayes works, and joyes of evening:
Long since I hate the night, more hate the morning:
Long since my thoughts chase me like beasts in forrests,
And make me wishe my selfe layd under mountaines.

STREPHON.   Me seemes I see the high and stately mountaines,
Transforme themselves to lowe dejected vallies:
Me seemes I heare in these ill-changed forrests,
The Nightingales doo learne of Owles their musique:
Me seemes I feele the comfort of the morning
Turnde to the mortall serene of an evening.

KLAIUS.   Me seemes I see a filthie clowdie evening,
                As soon as Sunne begins to clime the mountaines:
                Me seemes I feele a noysome scent, the morning
                When I doo smell the flowers of these vallies:
                Me seemes I heare, when I doo heare sweete musique,
                The dreadfull cries of murdred men in forrests.

STREPHON.   I wish to fire the trees of all these forrests;
                I give the Sunne a last farewell each evening;
                I curse the fidling finders out of Musicke:
                With envie I doo hate the loftie mountaines;
                And with despite despise the humble vallies:
                I doo detest night, evening, day, and morning.

KLAIUS.   Curse to my selfe my prayer is, the morning:
                My fire is more, then can be made with forrests;
                My state more base, then are the basest vallies:
                I wish no evenings more to see, each evening;
                Shamed I have my selfe in sight of mountaines,
                And stoppe mine eares, lest I growe mad with Musicke.

STREPHON.   For she, whose parts maintainde a perfect musique,
                Whose beautie shin'de more then the blushing morning,
                Who much did passe in state the stately mountaines,
                In straightnes past the Cedars of the forrests,
                Hath cast me wretch into eternall evening,
                By taking her two Sunnes from these darke vallies.

KLAIUS.   For she, to whom compar'd, the Alpes are vallies,
                She, whose least word brings from the spheares their
                          musique,
                At whose approach the Sunne rose in the evening,
                Who, where she went, bare in her forhead morning,
                Is gone, is gone from these our spyled forrests,
                Turning to desarts our best pastur'de mountaines.

STREPHON AND KLAIUS.   These mountaines witnesse shall, so shall these
                        vallies,
                These forrests eke, made wretched by our musique,
                Our morning hymne is this, and song at evening.

MY TRUE LOVE HATH MY HART

My true love hath my hart, and I have his,
By just exchange, one for the other giv'ne.
I holde his deare, and myne he cannot misse:
There never was a better bargaine driv'ne.
His hart in me, keepes me and him in one,
My hart in him, his thoughts and senses guides:
He loves my hart, for once it was his owne:
I cherish his, because in me it bides.
His hart his wound receaved from my sight:
My hart was wounded, with his wounded hart,
For as from me, on him his hurt did light,
So still me thought in me his hurt did smart:
    Both equall hurt, in this change sought our blisse:
    My true love hath my hart and I have his.

GET HENCE FOULE GRIEFE

Get hence foule Griefe, the canker of the minde:
    Farewell Complaint, the misers only pleasure:
Away vayne Cares, by which fewe men do finde
        Their sought-for treasure.

Ye helplesse Sighes, blowe out your breath to nought,
    Teares, drowne your selves, for woe (your cause) is
        wasted,
Thought, thinke to ende, too long the frute of thought
        My minde hath tasted.

But thou, sure Hope, tickle my leaping heart.
    Comfort, step thou in place of wonted sadnes.
Fore-felt Desire, begin to savour part
        Of comming gladnes.

Let voice of Sighes into cleare musike runne,
    Eyes, let your Teares with gazing now be mended,
In stede of Thought, true pleasure be begunne,
        And never ended.

Fulke Greville, Lord Brooke
1554-1628

From CÆLICA

VIII

Selfe-pitties teares, wherein my hope lyes drown'd,
  Sighs from thoughts fire, where my desires languish,
Despaire by humble love of beauty crown'd,
  Furrowes not worne by time, but weals of anguish;
Dry up, smile, joy, make smooth, and see
Furrowes, despaires, sighes, teares, in beauty be.

Beauty, out of whose clouds my heart teares rained,
  Beauty, whose niggard fire sighs' smoke did nourish,
Beauty in whose eclipse despaires remained,
  Beauty, whose scorching beames make wrinkles florish,
Time hath made free of teares, sighes, and despaire,
Writing in furrowes deep: *she once was faire.*

XXII

I, with whose colors *Myra* drest her head,
  I, that ware posies of her owne hand making,
I, that mine owne name in the chimnies read
  By *Myra* finely wrought ere I was waking:
Must I looke on, in hope time comming may
With change bring backe my turne againe to play?

I, that on Sunday at the Church-stile found,
  A Garland sweet, with true-love knots in flowers,
Which I to weare about mine arme was bound,
  That each of us might know that all was ours:
Must I now lead an idle life in wishes?
And follow *Cupid* for his loaves, and fishes?

I, that did weare the ring her Mother left,
  I, for whose love she gloried to be blamed,
I, with whose eyes her eyes committed theft,
  I, who did make her blush when I was named;
Must I lose ring, flowers, blush, theft and go naked,
Watching with sighs, till dead love be awaked?

I, that when drowsie *Argus* fell asleep,
  Like Jealousie o'rewatched with desire,
Was even warned modestie to keepe,
  While her breath, speaking, kindled Natures fire:
Must I looke on a-cold, while others warme them?
Doe *Vulcans* brothers in such fine nets arme them?

Was it for this that I might *Myra* see
  Washing the water with her beauties white?
Yet would she never write her love to me;
  Thinks wit of change while thoughts are in delight?
Mad Girles must safely love, as they may leave,
No man can print a kisse, lines may deceive.

XXV

Cupid, my pretty Boy, leave off thy crying,
Thou shalt have Bells or Apples; be not peevish;
Kisse me sweet Lad; beshrew her for denying;
Such rude denyalls doe make children theevish.
Did Reason say that Boyes must be restrained?
What was it? Tell: hath cruell Honour chidden?
Or would they have thee from sweet *Myra* weaned?
Are her faire brests made dainty to be hidden?
Tell me (sweet Boy) doth *Myra's* beauty threaten?
Must you say Grace when you would be a playing?
Doth she cause thee make faults, to make thee beaten?
Is Beauties pride in innocents betraying?
  Give me a Bow, let me thy Quiver borrow,
  And she shall play the child with love, or sorrow.

XXXV

Cupid, my little Boy, come home againe,
I doe not blame thee for thy running hence,
Where thou found'st nothing but desires paine,
Jealousie, with selfe-unworthinesse, offence.
Alas, I cannot Sir, I am made lame,
I light no sooner in sweet *Myra's* eyes,
(Whence I thought joy and pleasure tooke their name),
But my right wing of wanton passion dyes.
And I poore child am here in stead of play,
So whip'd and scourg'd with modestie and truth,
As having lost all hope to scape away,
I yet take pleasure to 'tice hither youth:
  That my Schoole-fellowes plagu'd as well as I,
  May not make merry, when they heare me cry.

LII

Away with these selfe-loving Lads,
Whom *Cupids* arrow never glads:
Away poore soules, that sigh and weep,
In love of those that lye asleepe:
For *Cupid* is a meadow-God,
And forceth none to kisse the rod.

Sweet *Cupids* shafts like Destinie
Doe causelesse good or ill decree;
Desert is borne out of his bow,
Reward upon his wing doth goe;
What fooles are they that have not knowne,
That *Love likes no Lawes but his owne.*

My songs they be of *Cynthia's* praise,
I weare her Rings on Holy dayes,
In every Tree I write her name,
And every Day I read the same.
Where Honour *Cupids* rivall is
There miracles are seene of his.

If *Cynthia* crave her Ring of me,
I blot her name out of the Tree,
If doubt doe darken things held deare,
Then well-fare Nothing once a yeare:
For many runne, but one must winne,
Fooles only hedge the Cuckoe in.

The worth that worthinesse should move,
Is *Love,* that is the bow of love,
And *Love* as well thee foster can,
As can the mighty Noble-man.
Sweet Saint 'tis true, you worthy be,
Yet without Love nought worth to me.

Edmund Spenser

1552?-1599

"You will take especial note of the marvellous independence and true imaginative absence of all particular space or time in the Faery Queene. It is in the domain neither of history nor of geography; it is ignorant of all artificial boundary, all material obstacles; it is *truly in land of Faery; that is, of mental space.* The poet has placed you in a dream, a charmed sleep, and you neither wish, nor have the powers, to enquire where you are, or how you got there." So wrote Coleridge in his *Anima Poetae.* That is true, also, though to a lesser degree, of many of Spenser's shorter poems — though not of the *Prothalamion* nor of the *Epithalamion*. It is at once the virtue and the fault of Spenser.

Jean Hélion, writing of a much later artist in a different medium, Cézanne (*The Painter's Object,* edited by Myfanwy Evans), said: "Cézanne appears to me to have caught the Impressionist's mist by handfuls and pressed it, to concentrate it. With him the colour takes back its intensity, its poise, its weight. . . . Out of the mist he once more gets elements, and organises them by degrees on his surface."

Cézanne's mind and spirit are far removed from those of Spenser. Cézanne's was a waking, workaday world. But if you forget the word "Impressionist's," that passage might, I think, have been written of Spenser. He *does* take mist and press it to concentrate it.

From THE SHEPHEARDES CALENDER

From APRILL

Ye dayntye Nymphs, that in this blessed Brooke
    Doe bathe your brest,
Forsake your watry bowres, and hether looke,
    At my request:
And eke you Virgins, that on *Parnasse* dwell,
Whence floweth *Helicon* the learned well,
    Helpe me to blaze
    Her worthy praise,
  Which in her sexe doth all excell.

Of fayre *Elisa* be your silver song,
    That blessed wight:
The flowre of Virgins, may shee florish long,
    In princely plight.

For shee is *Syrinx* daughter without spotte,
Which *Pan,* the shepheards God, of her begot:
    So sprong her grace
    Of heavenly race,
  No mortall blemishe may her blotte.

See, where she sits upon the grassie greene,
    (O seemely sight)
Yclad in Scarlot like a mayden Queene,
    And Ermines white.
Upon her head a Cremosin coronet,
With Damaske roses and Daffadillies set:
    Bayleaves betweene,
    And Primroses greene
  Embellish the sweete Violet.

Tell me, have ye seene her angelick face,
    Like *Phœbe* fayre?
Her heavenly haveour, her princely grace
    Can you well compare?
The Redde rose medled with the White yfere,
In either cheeke depeincten lively chere.
    Her modest eye,
    Her Majestie,
  Where have you seene the like, but there?

I saw *Phœbus* thrust out his golden hedde,
    Upon her to gaze:
But when he sawe, how broade her beames did spredde,
    It did him amaze.
He blusht to see another Sunne belowe,
Ne durst againe his fyrye face out showe:
    Let him, if he dare,
    His brightnesse compare
  With hers, to have the overthrowe.

Shewe thy selfe *Cynthia* with thy silver rayes,
    And be not abasht:
When shee the beames of her beauty displayes,
    O how art thou dasht?
But I will not match her with *Latonaes* seede,
Such follie great sorow to *Niobe* did breede.
    Now she is a stone,
    And makes dayly none,
  Warning all other to take heede.

             cremosin] crimson.

Pan may be proud, that ever he begot
    Such a Bellibone,
And *Syrinx* rejoyse, that ever was her lot
    To beare such an one.
Soone as my younglings cryen for the dam,
To her will I offer a milkwhite Lamb:
    Shee is my goddesse plaine,
    And I her shepherds swayne,
   Albee forswonck and forswatt I am.

I see *Calliope* speede her to the place,
    Where my Goddesse shines:
And after her the other Muses trace,
    With their Violines.
Bene they not Bay braunches, which they doe beare,
All for *Elisa* in her hand to weare?
    So sweetely they play,
    And sing all the way,
   That it a heaven is to heare.

Lo how finely the graces can it foote
    To the Instrument:
They dauncen deffly, and singen soote,
    In their meriment.
Wants not a fourth grace, to make the daunce even?
Let that rowme to my Lady be yeven:
    She shalbe a grace,
    To fyll the fourth place,
   And reigne with the rest in heaven.

And whither rennes this bevie of Ladies bright,
    Raunged in a rowe?
They bene all Ladyes of the lake behight,
    That unto her goe.
Chloris, that is the chiefest Nymph of al,
Of Olive braunches beares a Coronall:
    Olives bene for peace,
    When wars doe surcease:
   Such for a Princesse bene principall.

Ye shepheards daughters, that dwell on the greene,
    Hye you there apace:
Let none come there, but that Virgins bene,
    To adorne her grace.

bellibone] a fair maid.   forswonck] exhausted with labor.   forswatt] covered with sweat.

And when you come, whereas shee is in place,
See, that your rudeness doe not you disgrace:
    Binde your fillets faste,
    And gird in your waste,
For more finesse, with a tawdrie lace.

Bring hether the Pincke and purple Cullambine,
    With Gelliflowres:
Bring Coronations, and Sops in wine,
    Worne of Paramoures.
Strowe me the ground with Daffadowndillies,
And Cowslips, and Kingcups, and loved Lillies:
    The pretie Pawnce,
    And the Chevisaunce,
Shall match with the fayre flowre Delice.

Now ryse up *Elisa,* decked as thou art,
    In royall aray:
And now ye daintie Damsells may depart
    Eche one her way,
I feare, I have troubled your troupes too longe:
Let dame *Eliza* thanke you for her song.
    And if you come hether,
    When Damsines I gether,
I will part them all you among.

a tawdrie lace] a neckerchief of fine silk, originally sold at St. Audrey's fair.

From *NOVEMBER*

Up then *Melpomene* thou mournefulst Muse of nyne,
    Such cause of mourning never hadst afore:
Up grieslie ghostes and up my rufull ryme,
    Matter of myrth now shalt thou have no more.
For dead shee is, that myrth thee made of yore.
    Dido my deare alas is dead,
    Dead and lyeth wrapt in lead:
    O heavie herse,
Let streaming teares be poured out in store:
    O carefull verse.

Shepheards, that by your flocks on Kentish downes abyde,
    Waile ye this wofull waste of natures warke:
Waile we the wight, whose presence was our pryde:
    Waile we the wight, whose absence is our carke.

The sonne of all the world is dimme and darke:
   The earth now lacks her wonted light,
   And all we dwell in deadly night,
     O heavie herse.
Breake we our pypes, that shrild as lowde as Larke,
     O carefull verse.

Why doe we longer live, (ah why live we so long)
   Whose better dayes death hath shut up in woe?
The fayrest floure our gyrlond all emong,
   Is faded quite and into dust ygoe.
Sing now ye shepheards daughters, sing no moe
   The songs that *Colin* made in her prayse,
   But into weeping turne your wanton layes,
     O heavie herse,
Now is time to dye. Nay time was long ygoe,
     O carefull verse.

Whence is it, that the flouret of the field doth fade,
   And lyeth buryed long in Winters bale:
Yet soone as spring his mantle doth displaye,
   It floureth fresh, as it should never fayle?
But thing on earth that is of most availe,
   As vertues braunch and beauties budde,
   Reliven not for any good.
     O heavie herse,
The braunch once dead, the budde eke needes must quaile,
     O carefull verse.

She while she was, (that was, a woful word to sayne)
   For beauties prayse and plesaunce had no pere:
So well she couth the shepherds entertayne,
   With cakes and cracknells and such country chere.
Ne would she scorne the simple shepheards swaine,
   For she would cal hem often heme
   And give hem curds and clouted Creame.
     O heavie herse,
Als *Colin cloute* she would not once disdayne.
     O carefull verse.

But nowe sike happy cheere is turnd to heavie chaunce,
   Such pleasaunce now displast by dolors dint:
All Musick sleepes, where death doth leade the daunce,
   And shepherds wonted solace is extinct.

The blew in black, the greene in gray is tinct,
  The gaudie girlonds deck her grave,
The faded flowres her corse embrave.
    O heavie herse,
Morne nowe my Muse, now morne with tears besprint,
    O carefull verse.

O thou greate shepheard *Lobbin,* how great is thy griefe,
  Where bene the nosegayes that she dight for thee:
The colourd chaplets wrought with a chiefe,
  The knotted rushrings, and gilte Rosemaree?
For shee deemed nothing too deere for thee.
    Ah they bene all yclad in clay,
    One bitter blast blewe all away.
    O heavie herse,
Thereof nought remaynes but the memoree.
    O carefull verse.

Ay me that dreerie death should strike so mortall stroke,
  That can undoe Dame natures kindly course:
The faded lockes fall from the loftie oke,
  The flouds do gaspe, for dryed is theyr sourse,
  And flouds of teares flowe in theyr stead perforse.
    The mantled medowes mourne,
    Theyr sondry colours tourne.
    O heavie herse,
The heavens doe melt in teares without remorse.
    O carefull verse.

The feeble flocks in field refuse their former foode,
  And hang theyr heads, as they would learne to weepe:
The beastes in forest wayle as they were woode,
  Except the Wolves, that chase the wandring sheepe:
  Now she is gon that safely did hem keepe,
    The Turtle on the bared braunch,
    Laments the wound, that death did launch.
    O heavie herse,
And *Philomele* her song with teares doth steepe.
    O carefull verse.

The water Nymphs, that wont with her to sing and daunce,
  And for her girlond Olive braunches beare,
Now balefull boughes of Cypres doen advaunce:
  The Muses, that were wont greene bayes to weare,

woode] crazed.

Now bringen bitter Eldre braunches seare,
　The fatall sisters eke repent,
　　Her vitall threde so soone was spent.
　　　O heavie herse,
Morne now my Muse, now morne with heavie cheare.
　　　O carefull verse.

O trustlesse state of earthly things, and slipper hope
　Of mortal men, that swincke and sweate for nought,
And shooting wide, doe misse the marked scope:
　Now have I learnd (a lesson derely bought)
　That nys on earth assuraunce to be sought:
　　For what might be in earthlie mould,
　　That did her buried body hould,
　　　O heavie herse,
　Yet saw I on the beare when it was brought
　　　O carefull verse.

But maugre death, and dreaded sisters deadly spight,
　And gates of hel, and fyrie furies forse:
She hath the bonds broke of eternall night,
　Her soule unbodied of the burdenous corpse.
　Why then weepes *Lobbin* so without remorse?
　　O *Lobb*, thy losse no longer lament,
　　Dido nis dead, but into heaven hent.
　　　O happye herse,
Cease now my Muse, now cease thy sorrowes sourse,
　　　O joyfull verse.

Why wayle we then? why weary we the Gods with playnts,
　As if some evill were to her betight?
She raignes a goddesse now emong the saintes,
　That whilome was the saynte of shepheards light:
　And is enstalled nowe in heavens hight.
　　I see thee blessed soule, I see,
　　Walke in *Elisian* fieldes so free.
　　　O happy herse,
　Might I once come to thee (O that I might)
　　　O joyfull verse.

Unwise and wretched men to weete whats good or ill,
　We deeme of Death as doome of ill desert:
But knewe we fooles, what it us bringes until,
　Dye would we dayly, once it to expert.

　　　　　swincke] labor.

No daunger there the shepheard can astert:
Fayre fieldes and pleasaunt layes there bene,
The fieldes ay fresh, the grasse ay greene:
O happy herse,
Make hast ye shepheards, thether to revert,
O joyfull verse.

Dido is gone afore (whose turne shall be the next?)
There lives shee with the blessed Gods in blisse,
There drincks she *Nectar* with *Ambrosia* mixt,
And joyes enjoyes, that mortall men doe misse.
The honor now of highest gods she is,
That whilome was poore shepheards pryde,
While here on earth she did abyde.
O happy herse,
Cease now my song, my woe now wasted is.
O joyfull verse.

COMMING TO KISSE HER LYPS

Comming to kisse her lyps, (such grace I found)
Me seemd I smelt a gardin of sweet flowres:
That dainty odours from them threw around
For damzels fit to decke their lovers bowres.
Her lips did smell lyke unto Gillyflowers,
Her ruddy cheekes lyke unto Roses red:
Her snowy browes lyke budded Bellamoures,
Her lovely eyes lyke Pincks but newly spred.
Her goodly bosome lyke a Strawberry bed,
Her neck lyke to a bounch of Cullambynes:
Her brest lyke lyllyes, ere theyr leaves be shed,
Her nipples lyke yong blossomd Jessemynes.
Such fragrant flowres doe give most odorous smell,
But her sweet odour did them all excell.

PROTHALAMION

Calme was the day, and through the trembling ayre,
Sweete breathing *Zephyrus* did softly play
A gentle spirit, that lightly did delay
Hot *Titans* beames, which then did glyster fayre:
When I whom sullein care,
Through discontent of my long fruitlesse stay
In Princes Court, and expectation vayne

Of idle hopes, which still doe flye away,
Like empty shaddowes, did aflict my brayne,
Walkt forth to ease my payne
Along the shoare of silver streaming *Themmes*,
Whose rutty Bancke, the which his River hemmes,
Was paynted all with variable flowers,
And all the meades adornd with daintie gemmes,
Fit to decke maydens bowres,
And crowne their Paramours,
Against the Brydale day, which is not long:
   Sweete *Themmes* runne softly, till I end my Song.

There, in a Meadow, by the Rivers side,
A Flocke of *Nymphes* I chaunced to espy,
All lovely Daughters of the Flood thereby,
With goodly greenish locks all loose untyde,
As each had bene a Bryde,
And each one had a little wicker basket,
Made of fine twigs entrayled curiously,
In which they gathered flowers to fill their flasket:
And with fine Fingers, cropt full feateously
The tender stalkes on hye.
Of every sort, which in that Meadow grew,
They gathered some; the Violet pallid blew,
The little Dazie, that at evening closes,
The virgin Lillie, and the Primrose trew,
With store of vermeil Roses,
To decke their Bridegromes posies,
Against the Brydale day, which was not long:
   Sweete *Themmes* runne softly, till I end my Song.

With that, I saw two Swannes of goodly hewe,
Come softly swimming down along the Lee;
Two fairer Birds I yet did never see:
The snow which doth the top of *Pindus* strew,
Did never whiter shew,
Nor *Jove* himselfe when he a Swan would be
For love of *Leda*, whiter did appeare:
Yet *Leda* was they say as white as he,
Yet not so white as these, nor nothing neare;
So purely white they were,
That even the gentle streame, the which them bare,
Seem'd foule to them, and bade his billowes spare
To wet their silken feathers, lest they might
Soyle their fayre plumes with water not so fayre,
And marre their beauties bright,

That shone as heavens light,
Against their Brydale day, which was not long:
   Sweete *Themmes* runne softly, till I end my Song.

Eftsoones the *Nymphes,* which now had Flowers their fill,
Ran all in haste, to see that silver brood,
As they came floating on the Christal Flood.
Whom when they sawe, they stood amazed still,
Their wondring eyes to fill,
Them seem'd they never saw a sight so fayre,
Of Fowles so lovely, that they sure did deeme
Them heavenly borne, or to be that same payre
Which through the Skie draw *Venus* silver Teeme,
For sure they did not seeme
To be begot of any earthly Seede,
But rather Angels or of Angels breede:
Yet were they bred of *Somers-heat* they say,
In sweetest Season, when each Flower and weede
The earth did fresh aray,
So fresh they seem'd as day,
Even as their Brydale day, which was not long:
   Sweete *Themmes* runne softly, till I end my Song.

Then forth they all out of their baskets drew,
Great store of Flowers, the honour of the field,
That to the sense did fragrant odours yeild,
All which upon those goodly Birds they threw,
And all the Waves did strew,
That like old *Peneus* Waters they did seeme,
When downe along by pleasant *Tempes* shore
Scattred with Flowres, through *Thessaly* they streeme,
That they appeare through Lillies plenteous store,
Like a Brydes Chamber flore:
Two of those *Nymphes,* meane while, two Garlands bound,
Of freshest Flowres which in that Mead they found,
The which presenting all in trim Array,
Their snowie Foreheads therewithall they crownd,
Whil'st one did sing this Lay,
Prepar'd against that Day,
Against their Brydale day, which was not long:
   Sweete *Themmes* runne softly, till I end my Song.

Ye gentle Birdes, the worlds faire ornament,
And heavens glorie, whom this happie hower
Doth leade unto your lovers blisfull bower,
Joy may you have and gentle hearts content

Of your loves couplement:
And let faire *Venus*, that is Queene of love,
With her heart-quelling Sonne upon you smile,
Whose smile they say, hath vertue to remove
All Loves dislike, and friendships faultie guile
For ever to assoile.
Let endlesse Peace your steadfast hearts accord,
And blessed Plentie wait upon your bord,
And let your bed with pleasures chast abound,
That fruitfull issue may to you afford,
Which may your foes confound,
And make your joyes redound,
Upon your Brydale day, which is not long:
    Sweete *Themmes* run softlie, till I end my Song.

So ended she; and all the rest around
To her redoubled that her undersong,
Which said, their bridale daye should not be long.
And gentle Eccho from the neighbour ground,
Their accents did resound.
So forth those joyous Birdes did passe along,
Adowne the Lee, that to them murmurde low,
As he would speake, but that he lackt a tongue
Yet did by signes his glad affection show,
Making his streame run slow.
And all the fowle which in his flood did dwell
Gan flock about these twaine, that did excell
The rest, so far, as *Cynthia* doth shend
The lesser starres. So they enranged well,
Did on those two attend,
And their best service lend,
Against their wedding day, which was not long:
    Sweete *Themmes* run softly, till I end my song.

At length they all to mery *London* came,
To mery London, my most kyndly Nurse,
That to me gave this Lifes first native sourse:
Though from another place I take my name,
An house of auncient fame.
There when they came, whereas those bricky towres,
The which on *Themmes* brode aged backe doe ryde,
Where now the studious Lawyers have their bowers
There whylome wont the Templer Knights to byde,
Till they decayd through pride:

shend] put to shame.

Next whereunto there standes a stately place,
Where oft I gayned giftes and goodly grace
Of that great Lord, which therein wont to dwell,
Whose want too well now feeles my freendles case:
But Ah here fits not well
Olde woes but joyes to tell
Against the bridale daye, which is not long:
   Sweete *Themmes* runne softly, till I end my Song.

Yet therein now doth lodge a noble Peer,
Great *Englands* glory and the Worlds wide wonder,
Whose dreadfull name, late through all *Spaine* did thunder,
And *Hercules* two pillors standing neere,
Did make to quake and feare:
Faire branch of Honor, flower of Chevalrie,
That fillest *England* with thy triumphs fame,
Joy have thou of thy noble victorie,
And endlesse happinesse of thine owne name
That promiseth the same:
That through thy prowesse and victorious armes,
Thy country may be freed from forraine harmes:
And great *Elisaes* glorious name may ring
Through al the world, fil'd with thy wide Alarmes,
Which some brave muse may sing
To ages following,
Upon the Brydale day, which is not long:
   Sweete *Themmes* runne softly, till I end my Song.

From those high Towers, this noble Lord issuing,
Like Radiant *Hesper* when his golden hayre
In th' *Ocean* billowes he hath Bathed fayre,
Descended to the Rivers open vewing,
With a great traine ensuing.
Above the rest were goodly to bee seene
Two gentle Knights of lovely face and feature
Beseeming well the bower of anie Queene,
With gifts of wit and ornaments of nature,
Fit for so goodly stature:
That like the twins of *Jove* they seem'd in sight,
Which decke the Bauldricke of the Heavens bright.
They two forth pacing to the Rivers side,
Received those two faire Brides, their loves delight,
Which at th' appointed tyde,
Each one did make his Bryde,
Against their Brydale day, which is not long:
   Sweet *Themmes* runne softly, till I end my Song.

From EPITHALAMION

Ye learned sisters which have oftentimes
Beene to me ayding, others to adorne:
Whom ye thought worthy of your gracefull rymes,
That even the greatest did not greatly scorne
To heare theyr names sung in your simple layes,
But joyed in theyr prayse.
And when ye list your owne mishaps to mourne,
Which death, or love, or fortunes wreck did rayse,
Your string could soone to sadder tenor turne,
And teach the woods and waters to lament
Your dolefull dreriment.
Now lay those sorrowfull complaints aside,
And having all your heads with girland crownd,
Helpe me mine owne loves prayses to resound,
Ne let the same of any be envide:
So Orpheus did for his owne bride,
So I unto my selfe alone will sing,
The woods shall to me answer and my Eccho ring.

Early before the worlds light giving lampe,
His golden beame upon the hils doth spred,
Having disperst the nights unchearefull dampe,
Doe ye awake, and with fresh lusty hed,
Go to the bowre of my beloved love,
My truest turtle dove,
Bid her awake; for Hymen is awake,
And long since ready forth his maske to move,
With his bright Tead that flames with many a flake,
And many a bachelor to waite on him,
In theyr fresh garments trim.
Bid her awake therefore and soone her dight,
For lo the wished day is come at last,
That shall for al the paynes and sorrowes past,
Pay to her usury of long delight:
And whylest she doth her dight,
Doe ye to her of joy and solace sing,
That all the woods may answer and your eccho ring.

Bring with you all the Nymphes that you can heare
Both of the rivers and the forrests greene:
And of the sea that neighbours to her neare,
Al with gay girlands goodly wel beseene.

tead] torch.

And let them also with them bring in hand,
Another gay girland
For my fayre love of lillyes and of roses,
Bound truelove wize with a blew silke riband.
And let them make great store of bridale poses,
And let them eeke bring store of other flowers
To deck the bridale bowers.
And let the ground whereas her foot shall tread,
For feare the stones her tender foot should wrong
Be strewed with fragrant flowers all along,
And diapred lyke the discolored mead.
Which done, doe at her chamber dore awayt,
For she will waken strayt,
The whiles doe ye this song unto her sing,
The woods shall to you answer and your Eccho ring.

Ye Nymphes of Mulla which with carefull heed,
The silver scaly trouts doe tend full well,
And greedy pikes which use therein to feed,
(Those trouts and pikes all others doo excell)
And ye likewise which keepe the rushy lake,
Where none doo fishes take,
Bynd up the locks the which hang scatterd light,
And in his waters which your mirror make,
Behold your faces as the christall bright,
That when you come whereas my love doth lie,
No blemish she may spie.
And eke ye lightfoot mayds which keepe the deere,
That on the hoary mountayne use to towre,
And the wylde wolves which seeke them to devoure,
With your steele darts doo chace from comming neer
Be also present heere,
To helpe to decke her and to help to sing,
That all the woods may answer and your eccho ring.

Wake, now my love, awake; for it is time,
The rosy Morne long since left Tithones bed,
All ready to her silver coche to clyme,
And Phœbus gins to shew his glorious hed.
Hark how the cheerefull birds do chaunt theyr laies
And carroll of loves praise.
The merry Larke hir mattins sings aloft,
The thrush replyes, the Mavis descant playes,
The Ouzell shrills, the Ruddock warbles soft,
So goodly all agree with sweet consent,
To this dayes merriment.

Ah my deere love why doe ye sleepe thus long,
When meeter were that ye should now awake,
T' awayt the comming of your joyous make,
And hearken to the birds love-learned song,
The deawy leaves among.
For they of joy and pleasance to you sing,
That all the woods them answer and theyr eccho ring.

My love is now awake out of her dreame,
And her fayre eyes like stars that dimmed were
With darksome cloud, now shew theyr goodly beams
More bright then Hesperus his head doth rere.
Come now ye damzels, daughters of delight,
Helpe quickly her to dight,
But first come ye fayre houres which were begot
In loves sweet paradice, of Day and Night,
Which doe the seasons of the yeare allot,
And al that ever in this world is fayre
Doe make and still rapayre.
And ye three handmayds of the Cyprian Queene,
The which doe still adorne her beauties pride,
Helpe to addorne my beautifullest bride:
And as ye her array, still throw betweene
Some graces to be seene,
And as ye use to Venus, to her sing,
The whiles the woods shal answer and your eccho ring.

Now is my love all ready forth to come,
Let all the virgins therefore well awayt,
And ye fresh boyes that tend upon her groome
Prepare your selves; for he is comming strayt.
Set all your things in seemely good aray
Fit for so joyfull day,
The joyfulst day that ever sunne did see.
Faire Sun, shew forth thy favourable ray,
And let thy lifull heat not fervent be
For feare of burning her sunshyny face,
Her beauty to disgrace.
O fayrest Phœbus, father of the Muse,
If ever I did honour thee aright,
Or sing the thing, that mote thy mind delight,
Doe not thy servants simple boone refuse,
But let this day let this one day be myne,
Let all the rest be thine.

> make] mate.   lifull] lifeful, vitalizing.

Then I thy soverayne prayses loud wil sing,
That all the woods shal answer and theyr eccho ring.

Harke how the Minstrels gin to shrill aloud
Their merry Musick that resounds from far,
The pipe, the tabor, and the trembling Croud,
That well agree withouten breach or jar.
But most of all the Damzels doe delite,
When they their tymbrels smyte,
And thereunto doe daunce and carrol sweet,
That all the sences they doe ravish quite,
The whyles the boyes run up and downe the street,
Crying aloud with strong confused noyce,
As if it were one voyce.
Hymen Iö Hymen, Hymen they do shout,
That even to the heavens theyr shouting shrill
Doth reach, and all the firmament doth fill,
To which the people standing all about,
As in approvance doe thereto applaud
And loud advaunce her laud,
And evermore they Hymen Hymen sing,
That al the woods them answer and theyr eccho ring.

Loe where she comes along with portly pace
Lyke Phœbe from her chamber of the East,
Arysing forth to run her mighty race,
Clad all in white, that seemes a virgin best.
So well it her beseemes that ye would weene
Some angell she had beene.
Her long loose yellow locks lyke golden wyre,
Sprinckled with perle, and perling flowres a tweene,
Doe lyke a golden mantle her attyre,
And being crowned with a girland greene,
Seeme lyke some mayden Queene.
Her modest eyes abashed to behold
So many gazers, as on her do stare,
Upon the lowly ground affixed are.
Ne dare lift up her countenance too bold,
But blush to heare her prayses sung so loud,
So farre from being proud.
Nathlesse doe ye still loud her prayses sing.
That all the woods may answer and your eccho ring.

Tell me ye merchants daughters did ye see
So fayre a creature in your towne before,

portly] stately, majestic.

So sweet, so lovely, and so mild as she,
Adornd with beautyes grace and vertues store,
Her goodly eyes lyke Saphyres shining bright,
Her forehead ivory white,
Her cheekes lyke apples which the sun hath rudded,
Her lips lyke cherryes charming men to byte,
Her brest like to a bowle of creame uncrudded,
Her paps lyke lyllies budded,
Her snowie necke lyke to a marbled towre,
And all her body like a pallace fayre,
Ascending uppe with many a stately stayre,
To honors seat and chastities sweet bowre.
Why stand ye still ye virgins in amaze,
Upon her so to gaze,
Whiles ye forget your former lay to sing,
To which the woods did answer and your eccho ring.

From THE FAERIE QUEENE

The waves come rolling, and the billowes rore
Outragiously, as they enraged were,
Or wrathfull *Neptune* did them drive before
His whirling charet, for exceeding feare:
For not one puffe of wind there did appeare,
That all the three thereat woxe much afrayd,
Unweeting, what such horrour straunge did reare.
Eftsoones they saw an hideous hoast arrayd,
Of huge Sea monsters, such as living sence dismayd.

Most ugly shapes, and horrible aspects,
Such as Dame Nature selfe mote feare to see,
Or shame, that ever should so fowle defects
From her most cunning hand escaped bee;
All dreadfull pourtraicts of deformitee:
Spring-headed *Hydraes,* and sea-shouldring Whales,
Great whirlpooles, which all fishes make to flee,
Bright Scolopendraes, arm'd with silver scales,
Mighty *Monoceroses,* with immeasured tayles.

The dreadfull Fish, that hath deserv'd the name
Of Death, and like him lookes in dreadfull hew,
The griesly Wasserman, that makes his game
The flying ships with swiftnesse to pursew,
The horrible Sea-satyre, that doth shew
His fearefull face in time of greatest storme,

Huge *Ziffius,* whom Mariners eschew
No lesse, than rockes, (as travellers informe,)
And greedy Rosmarines with visages deforme.

All these, and thousand thousands many more,
And more deformed Monsters thousand fold,
With dreadfull noise, and hollow rombling rore,
Came rushing in the fomy waves enrold,
Which seem'd to fly for feare, them to behold:
Ne wonder, if these did the knight appall;
For all that here on earth we dreadfull hold,
Be but as bugs to fearen babes withall,
Compared to the creatures in the seas entrall.

Christopher Marlowe
1564-1593

Marlowe is usually unmistakable. He has a walk like that of no other poet (we do not tell the work of a poet, in many cases, so much by the use of imagery, unless the imagery is exceedingly unusual, as by something inimitable in the gait). Marlowe treads the air like the Dauphin's palfrey in Shakespeare's *The Life of Henry the Fifth,* Act III, Scene 7: "He trots the ayre: the Earth sings when he touches it."

None but he seems such a fire in the air. A bird sang in his voice.

One of the signs of Marlowe at his greatest is the *upward* movement with which each line ends. This ending is not, of course, invariable, for that would be monotonous. It does not apply to the ineffable lines about Helen, or the last lines of Faustus. . . . But it is a sign and a portent in *Tamburlaine.* There each line, in passage after passage, seems to soar into the air. Elsewhere the lines end with an extraordinary crispness.

The magnificent and heart-rending scene where Faustus faces his damnation, and certain other lines from the same play, *Hero and Leander,* and the two excerpts given here from *Tamburlaine* are the greatest heights to which Marlowe has attained.

The lines from *Faustus:*

O thou art fairer then the evening aire,
Clad in the beauty of a thousand starres . . .

are amongst the most wonderful in the whole of our poetry. The heavenly loveliness is due, in part, to the softness of the *f* and *v* sounds in the first line (*v* being, to a fraction of a degree, fainter, softer than *f*), and to the fact that the line is prolonged by the echoing double vowels of the assonances "fairer" and "aire" and the long *e* of "evening." Vowels are amongst the most important prolongers of a line. The lingering loveliness of this, soft as the evening air of which it speaks, changes then to the splendor of: "Clad in the beauty of a thousand starres" — a result brought about, as far as technique is concerned, by the bright *c* and *b,* by the *t* of "starres," by the poignant vowels of "beauty" and the brightening vowel sound of the *ou* in "thousand."

The magnificence of the lines where Faustus faces his damnation is entirely one of the spirit.

The vowel music, the movement of *Hero and Leander* is flawless.

All the characters in the *principal* works of Marlowe, excepting Faustus at the moment of his damnation, when he speaks with the agony of a great human soul, are glories of the air, and not beings of the earth in whose hearts the pulse of the spring and of the earth beat. Their gait is a planetary movement, as splendid and as uncaring.

Among the more responsible persons who believe certain lines ascribed to Shakespeare were, in truth, by Marlowe, one critic placed these, from the Second Part of *Henry the Sixth:*

> Ah, barbarous villaines! Hath this lovely face
> Ruled, like a wandering Plannet, over me,
> And could it not inforce them to relent
> That were unworthy to behold the same?

I think it is possible that Marlowe *did* write those lines, but not because, as the critic suggests, the words "wandering Plannet," which occur in Marlowe, figure here, but because of the movement, which has something of the same softness as that of "O thou art fairer than the evening aire," and which is entirely different from the flower-softness, the air, of Perdita's lines at the sheep-shearing.

Books I and II of the *Elegies* are full of beauties. They were first pointed out to me by a gifted young poet, Quentin Stevenson, and they include such lovely lines as these, from Book I, *Elegia 13:*

> The Moone sleepes with Endymion every day.
> Thou art as faire as she, then kisse and play.

And this, about a blush, from Book II, *Elegia 5:*

> Such as a rose mixt with a lilly breedes,
> Or when the Moone travailes with charmed steedes.

In nearly all the works of this time, and indeed, an earlier age, Cupid appears as a little human boy. In *The Tragedie of Dido,* playing with another child, changing places with another child, as human as his playmate, he might be the child in *Dalyaunce* (page 73):

> VENUS. Faire child stay thou with *Dido's* waiting maide.
> Ile give thee Sugar-almonds, sweet Conserves,
> A silver girdle, and a golden purse,
> And this yong Prince shall be thy Play-fellow.
> ASCANIUS. Are you Queene Dido's sonne?
> CUPID. I, and my mother gave me this fine bow.
> ASCANIUS. Shall I have such a quiver and a bow?
> VENUS. Such bow, such quiver, and such golden shafts
> Will Dido give to sweet *Ascanius.*
> For Dido's sake I take thee in my armes,
> And sticke these spangled feathers in thy hat,
> Eate Comfittes in mine armes, and I will sing.

The play contains several wonders, such as these lines of Dido's:

> The man that I doe eye where ere I am,
> Whose amorous face like *Pean* sparkles fire,
> When as he puts his beames on *Floras* bed.
> Prometheus hath put on *Cupid's* shape,
> And I must perish in his twining armes:
> *Æneas,* O *Æneas,* quench these flames.

From HERO AND LEANDER

FIRST SESTIAD

> On *Hellespont* guiltie of True-loves blood,
> In view and opposit two citties stood,
> Seaborderers, disjoin'd by *Neptunes* might:
> The one *Abydos,* the other *Sestos* hight.
> At *Sestos, Hero* dwelt; *Hero* the faire,
> Whom young *Apollo* courted for her haire,
> And offred as a dower his burning throne,
> Where she should sit for men to gaze upon.
> The outside of her garments were of lawne,
> The lining purple silke, with gilt starres drawne,
> Her wide sleeves greene, and bordered with a grove,
> Where *Venus* in her naked glory strove,
> To please the carelesse and disdainfull eies
> Of proud *Adonis* that before her lies.
> Her kirtle blew, wheron was many a staine,
> Made with the blood of wretched Lovers slaine.

Upon her head she ware a myrtle wreath,
From whence her vaile reacht to the ground beneath.
Her vaile was artificiall flowers and leaves,
Whose workmanship both man and beast deceaves.
Many would praise the sweet smell as she past,
When t' was the odour which her breath foorth cast,
And there for honie bees have sought in vaine,
And beat from thence, have lighted there againe.
About her necke hung chaines of peble stone,
Which lightned by her necke, like Diamonds shone.
She ware no gloves, for neither sunne nor wind
Would burne or parch her hands, but to her mind,
Or warme or coole them, for they tooke delite
To play upon those hands, they were so white.
Buskins of shels all silvered used she,
And brancht with blushing corall to the knee;
Where sparrowes pearcht, of hollow pearle and gold,
Such as the world would woonder to behold:
Those with sweet water oft her handmaid fils,
Which as shee went would cherupe through the bils.
Some say, for her the fairest *Cupid* pyn'd,
And looking in her face, was strooken blind.
But this is true, so like was one the other,
As he imagyn'd *Hero* was his mother.
And oftentimes into her bosome flew,
About her naked necke his bare armes threw,
And laid his childish head upon her brest,
And with still panting rockt, there tooke his rest.
So lovely faire was *Hero, Venus* Nun,
As nature wept, thinking she was undone;
Because she tooke more from her than she left,
And of such wondrous beautie her bereft:
Therefore in signe her treasure suffred wracke,
Since *Heroes* time, hath halfe the world been blacke.
Amorous *Leander,* beautifull and young,
(Whose tragedie divine *Musæus* sung)
Dwelt at *Abidus:* since him dwelt there none,
For whom succeeding times make greater mone.
His dangling tresses that were never shorne,
Had they beene cut, and unto *Colchos* borne,
Would have allur'd the vent'rous youth of *Greece*
To hazard more than for the golden Fleece.
Faire *Cinthia* wisht his armes might be her spheare,
Greefe makes her pale, because she mooves not there.
His bodie was as straight as *Circes* wand,
Jove might have sipt out *Nectar* from his hand.

Even as delicious meat is to the tast,
So was his necke in touching, and surpast
The white of *Pelops* shoulder. I could tell ye,
How smooth his brest was, and how white his bellie,
And whose immortall fingars did imprint
That heavenly path, with many a curious dint,
That runs along his backe, but my rude pen
Can hardly blazon foorth the loves of men,
Much lesse of powerfull gods: let it suffise,
That my slacke muse sings of *Leanders* eies,
Those orient cheekes and lippes, exceeding his
That leapt into the water for a kis
Of his owne shadow, and despising many,
Died ere he could enjoy the love of any.
Had wilde *Hippolitus Leander* seene,
Enamoured of his beautie had he beene,
His presence made the rudest paisant melt,
That in the vast uplandish countrie dwelt,
The barbarous *Thratian* soldier moov'd with nought,
Was moov'd with him, and for his favour sought.
Some swore he was a maid in mans attire,
For in his lookes were all that men desire,
A pleasant smiling cheeke, a speaking eye,
A brow for love to banquet roiallye,
And such as knew he was a man would say,
Leander, thou art made for amorous play:
Why art thou not in love, and lov'd of all?
Though thou be faire, yet be not thine owne thrall.
    The men of wealthie *Sestos,* everie yeare,
(For his sake whom their goddesse held so deare,
Rose-cheekt *Adonis*) kept a solemne feast.
Thither resorted many a wandring guest,
To meet their loves; such as had none at all,
Came lovers home from this great festivall.
For everie street like to a Firmament
Glistered with breathing stars, who where they went,
Frighted the melancholie earth, which deem'd
Eternall heaven to burne, for so it seem'd,
As if another *Phaeton* had got
The guidance of the sunnes rich chariot.
But far above the loveliest *Hero* shin'd,
And stole away th' inchaunted gazers mind,
For like Sea-nimphs inveigling harmony,
So was her beautie to the standers by.
Nor that night-wandring pale and watrie starre
(When yawning dragons draw her thirling carre

From *Latmus* mount up to the glomie skie,
Where crown'd with blazing light and majestie,
She proudly sits) more over-rules the flood,
Than she the hearts of those that neere her stood.
Even as, when gawdie Nymphs pursue the chace,
Wretched *Ixions* shaggie footed race,
Incenst with savage heat, gallop amaine
From steepe Pine-bearing mountains to the plaine:
So ran the people foorth to gaze upon her,
And all that view'd her, were enamour'd on her.
And as in furie of a dreadfull fight,
Their fellowes being slaine or put to flight,
Poore soldiers stand with fear of death dead **strooken,**
So at her presence all surpris'd and tooken,
Await the sentence of her scornefull eies:
He whom she favours lives, the other dies.
There might you see one sigh, another rage,
And some (their violent passions to asswage)
Compile sharpe satyrs, but alas too late,
For faithfull love will never turne to hate.
And many seeing great princes were denied,
Pyn'd as they went, and thinking on her died.
On this feast day, O cursed day and hower,
Went *Hero* thorow *Sestos,* from her tower
To *Venus* temple, where unhappilye,
As after chaunc'd, they did each other spye.
So faire a church as this, had *Venus* none,
The wals were of discoloured *Jasper* stone,
Wherein was *Proteus* carved, and o'erhead,
A livelie vine of greene sea agget spread;
Where by one hand, light headed *Bacchus* hung,
And with the other, wine from grapes out wrung.
Of Christall shining faire the pavement was,
The towne of *Sestos* cal'd it *Venus* glasse.
There might you see the gods in sundrie shapes,
Committing headdie ryots, incest, rapes:
For know, that underneath this radiant floure
Was *Danaes* statue in a brazen tower,
Jove slylie stealing from his sisters bed,
To dallie with *Idalian Ganimed,*
And for his love *Europa* bellowing loud,
And tumbling with the Rainbow in a cloud:
Blood-quaffing *Mars* heaving the yron net,
Which limping *Vulcan* and his *Cyclops* set:
Love kindling fire, to burne such townes as *Troy,*
Sylvanus weeping for the lovely boy

That now is turn'd into a *Cypres* tree,
Under whose shade the Wood-gods love to bee.
And in the midst a silver altar stood;
There *Hero* sacrificing turtles blood,
Vaild to the ground, vailing her eie-lids close,
And modestly they opened as she rose:
Thence flew Loves arrow with the golden head,
And thus *Leander* was enamoured.
Stone still he stood, and evermore he gazed,
Till with the fire that from his count'nance blazed,
Relenting *Heroes* gentle heart was strooke,
Such force and vertue hath an amorous looke.
  It lies not in our power to love, or hate,
For will in us is over-rul'd by fate.
When two are stript long ere the course begin,
We wish that one should loose, the other win;
And one especiallie doe we affect
Of two gold Ingots like in each respect.
The reason no man knowes, let it suffise,
What we behold is censur'd by our eies.
Where both deliberat, the love is slight,
Who ever lov'd, that lov'd not at first sight?
  He kneel'd, but unto her devoutly praid;
Chast *Hero* to her selfe thus softly said:
Were I the saint hee worships, I would heare him,
And as shee spake those words, came somewhat nere him.
He started up, she blusht as one asham'd;
Wherewith *Leander* much more was inflam'd.
He toucht her hand, in touching it she trembled,
Love deepely grounded, hardly is dissembled.
These lovers parled by the touch of hands,
True love is mute, and oft amazed stands.
Thus while dum signs their yeelding harts entangled,
The aire with sparkes of living fire was spangled,
And night deepe drencht in mystie *Acheron*
Heav'd up her head, and halfe the world upon
Breath'd darkenesse forth (darke night is *Cupids* day).
And now begins *Leander* to display
Loves holy fire, with words, with sighs and teares,
Which like sweet musicke entred *Heroes* eares,
And yet at everie word shee turn'd aside,
And alwaies cut him off as he replide.
At last, like to a bold sharpe Sophister,
With chearefull hope thus he accosted her.
  Faire creature, let me speake without offence,
I would my rude words had the influence,

To lead thy thoughts as thy faire lookes doe mine,
Then shouldst thou bee his prisoner who is thine.
Be not unkind and faire, mishapen stuffe
Are of behaviour boisterous and ruffe.
O shun me not, but heare me ere you goe,
God knowes I cannot force love, as you doe.
My words shall be as spotlesse as my youth,
Full of simplicitie and naked truth.
This sacrifice (whose sweet perfume descending,
From *Venus* altar to your footsteps bending)
Doth testifie that you exceed her farre,
To whom you offer, and whose Nunne you are.
Why should you worship her? her you surpasse,
As much as sparkling Diamonds flaring glasse.
A Diamond set in lead his worth retaines,
A heavenly Nimph, belov'd of humane swaines,
Receives no blemish, but oft-times more grace,
Which makes me hope, although I am but base,
Base in respect of thee, divine and pure,
Dutifull service may thy love procure,
And I in dutie will excell all other,
As thou in beautie doest exceed loves mother.
Nor heaven, nor thou, were made to gaze upon,
As heaven preserves all things, so save thou one.
A stately builded ship, well rig'd and tall,
The Ocean maketh more majesticall:
Why vowest thou then to live in *Sestos* here,
Who on Loves seas more glorious wouldst appeare?
Like untun'd golden strings all women are,
Which long time lie untoucht, will harshly jarre.
Vessels of Brasse oft handled, brightly shine,
What difference betwixt the richest mine
And basest mold, but use? for both, not us'de,
Are of like worth. Then treasure is abus'de,
When misers keepe it; being put to loane,
In time it will returne us two for one.
Rich robes themselves and others do adorne,
Neither themselves nor others, if not worne.
Who builds a pallace and rams up the gate,
Shall see it ruinous and desolate.
Ah simple *Hero,* learne thy selfe to cherish,
Lone women like to emptie houses perish.
Lesse sinnes the poore rich man that starves himselfe,
In heaping up a masse of drossie pelfe,
Than such as you: his golden earth remains,
Which after his disceasse, some other gains.

But this faire gem, sweet in the losse alone,
When you fleet hence, can be bequeath'd to none.
Or if it could, downe from th' enameld skie
All heaven would come to claime this legacie,
And with intestine broiles the world destroy,
And quite confound natures sweet harmony.
Well therefore by the gods decreed it is,
We humane creatures should enjoy that blisse:
One is no number, mayds are nothing then,
Without the sweet societie of men.
Wilt thou live single still? one shalt thou bee,
Though never-singling *Hymen* couple thee.
Wild savages, that drinke of running springs,
Thinke water farre excels all earthly things:
But they that dayly tast neat wine, despise it.
Virginitie, albeit some highly prise it,
Compar'd with marriage, had you tried them both,
Differs as much as wine and water doth.
Base bullion for the stampes sake we allow,
Even so for mens impression do we you,
By which alone, our reverend fathers say,
Women receave perfection everie way.
This idoll which you terme *Virginitie*,
Is neither essence subject to the eie,
No, nor to any one exterior sence,
Nor hath it any place of residence,
Nor is't of earth or mold celestiall,
Or capable of any forme at all.
Of that which hath no being doe not boast,
Things that are not at all are never lost.
Men foolishly doe call it vertuous,
What vertue is it that is borne with us?
Much lesse can honour bee ascrib'd thereto,
Honour is purchac'd by the deedes wee do.
Beleeve me *Hero,* honour is not wone,
Untill some honourable deed be done.
Seeke you for chastitie, immortall fame,
And know that some have wrong'd *Dianas* name?
Whose name is it, if she be false or not,
So she be faire, but some vile tongues will blot?
But you are faire (aye me) so wondrous faire,
So young, so gentle, and so debonaire,
As *Greece* will thinke, if thus you live alone,
Some one or other keepes you as his owne.
Then *Hero* hate me not, nor from me flie,
To follow swiftly blasting infamie.

Perhaps, thy sacred Priesthood makes thee loath,
Tell me, to whom mad'st thou that heedlesse oath?
  To *Venus,* answered shee, and as shee spake,
Foorth from those two tralucent cesternes brake
A streame of liquid pearle, which downe her face
Made milk-white paths, wheron the gods might trace
To *Joves* high court. Hee thus replide: The rites
In which Loves beauteous Empresse most delites,
Are banquets, Dorick musicke, midnight-revell,
Plaies, maskes, and all that stern age counteth evill.
Thee as a holy Idiot doth she scorne,
For thou in vowing chastitie hast sworne
To rob her name and honour, and thereby
Commit'st a sinne far worse than perjurie,
Even sacrilege against her Deitie,
Through regular and formall puritie.
To expiat which sinne, kisse and shake hands,
Such sacrifice as this *Venus* demands.
  Thereat she smild, and did denie him so,
As put thereby, yet might he hope for mo.
Which makes him quickly re-enforce his speech,
And her in humble manner thus beseech.
  Though neither gods nor men may thee deserve,
Yet for her sake whom you have vow'd to serve,
Abandon fruitlesse cold Virginitie,
The gentle queene of Loves sole enemie.
Then shall you most resemble *Venus* Nun,
When *Venus* sweet rites are perform'd and done.
Flint-brested *Pallas* joies in single life,
But *Pallas* and your mistresse are at strife.
Love *Hero* then, and be not tirannous,
But heale the heart, that thou hast wounded thus,
Nor staine thy youthfull years with avarice,
Faire fooles delight to be accounted nice.
The richest corne dies, if it be not reapt,
Beautie alone is lost, too warily kept.
These arguments he us'de, and many more,
Wherewith she yeelded, that was won before.
Heroes lookes yeelded, but her words made warre,
Women are won when they begin to jarre.
Thus having swallow'd *Cupids* golden hooke,
The more she striv'd, the deeper was she strooke.
Yet evilly faining anger, strove she still,
And would be thought to graunt against her will.
So having paus'd a while, at last shee said:
Who taught thee Rhethoricke to deceive a maid?

Aye me, such words as these should I abhor,
And yet I like them for the Orator.
   With that *Leander* stoopt, to have imbrac'd her,
But from his spreading armes away she cast her,
And thus bespake him: Gentle youth forbeare
To touch the sacred garments which I weare.
Upon a rocke, and underneath a hill,
Far from the towne (where all is whist and still,
Save that the sea playing on yellow sand,
Sends foorth a ratling murmure to the land,
Whose sound allures the golden *Morpheus*
In silence of the night to visite us)
My turret stands, and there God knowes I play
With *Venus* swannes and sparrowes all the day.
A dwarfish beldame beares me companie,
That hops about the chamber where I lie,
And spends the night (that might be better spent)
In vaine discourse, and apish merriment.
Come thither. As she spake this, her tongue tript,
For unawares *Come thither* from her slipt,
And sodainly her former colour chang'd,
And here and there her eies through anger rang'd.
And like a planet, mooving severall waies,
At one selfe instant, she poore soule assaies,
Loving, not to love at all, and everie part
Strove to resist the motions of her hart.
And hands so pure, so innocent, nay such,
As might have made heaven stoope to have a touch,
Did she uphold to *Venus,* and againe
Vow'd spotlesse chastitie, but all in vaine.
Cupid beats downe her praiers with his wings,
Her vowes above the emptie aire he flings:
All deepe enrag'd, his sinowie bow he bent,
And shot a shaft that burning from him went,
Wherewith she strooken look'd so dolefully,
As made Love sigh, to see his tirannie.
And as she wept, her teares to pearle he turn'd,
And wound them on his arme, and for her mourn'd.
Then towards the pallace of the destinies,
Laden with languishment and griefe he flies,
And to those sterne nymphs humblie made request,
Both might enjoy ech other, and be blest.
But with a ghastly dreadfull countenaunce,
Threatning a thousand deaths at everie glaunce,
They answered Love, nor would vouchsafe so much
As one poore word, their hate to him was such.

Harken a while, and I will tell you why:
Heavens winged herrald, *Jove-borne Mercury,*
The selfe-same day that he asleepe had layd
Inchaunted Argus, spied a countrie mayd,
Whose carelesse haire, in stead of pearle t' adorne it,
Glist'red with deaw, as one that seem'd to skorne it:
Her breath as fragrant as the morning rose,
Her mind pure, and her tongue untaught to glose.
Yet prowd she was, (for loftie pride that dwels
In tow'red courts, is oft in sheapheards cels)
And too too well the faire vermilion knew,
And silver tincture of her cheekes, that drew
The love of everie swaine: On her, this god
Enamoured was, and with his snakie rod,
Did charme her nimble feet, and made her stay,
The while upon a hillocke downe he lay,
And sweetly on his pipe began to play,
And with smooth speech her fancie to assay,
Till in his twining armes he lockt her fast,
And then he woo'd with kisses, and at last,
As sheap-heards do, her on the ground hee layd,
And tumbling in the grasse, he often strayd
Beyond the bounds of shame, in being bold
To eie those parts, which no eie should behold.
And like an insolent commaunding lover,
Boasting his parentage, would needs discover
The way to new *Elisium:* but she,
Whose only dower was her chastitie,
Having striv'ne in vaine, was now about to crie,
And crave the helpe of sheap-heards that were nie.
Herewith he stayd his furie, and began
To give her leave to rise: away she ran,
After went *Mercurie,* who us'd such cunning,
As she to heare his tale, left off her running.
Maids are not won by brutish force and might,
But speeches full of pleasure and delight.
And knowing *Hermes* courted her, was glad
That she such lovelinesse and beautie had
As could provoke his liking, yet was mute,
And neither would denie, nor graunt his sute.
Still vowd he love, she wanting no excuse
To feed him with delaies, as women use,
Or thirsting after immortalitie, —
All women are ambitious naturallie, —
Impos'd upon her lover such a taske,
As he ought not performe, nor yet she aske.

A draught of flowing *Nectar* she requested,
Wherewith the king of Gods and men is feasted.
He readie to accomplish what she wil'd,
Stole some from *Hebe* (*Hebe Joves* cup fil'd)
And gave it to his simple rustike love,
Which being knowne (as what is hid from *Jove?*)
He inly storm'd, and waxt more furious
Than for the fire filcht by *Prometheus,*
And thrusts him down from heaven: he wandring here,
In mournfull termes, with sad and heavie cheare
Complaind to *Cupid. Cupid* for his sake,
To be reveng'd on Jove did undertake,
And those on whom heaven, earth, and hell relies,
I mean the Adamantine Destinies,
He wounds with love, and forst them equallie
To dote upon deceitfull *Mercurie.*
They offred him the deadly fatall knife,
That sheares the slender threads of humane life,
At his faire feathered feet the engins layd,
Which th' earth from ougly *Chaos* den up-wayd:
These he regarded not, but did intreat,
That *Jove,* usurper of his fathers seat,
Might presently be banisht into hell,
And aged *Saturne* in *Olympus* dwell.
They granted what he crav'd, and once againe
Saturne and *Ops* began their golden raigne.
Murder, rape, warre, lust and trecherie,
Were with *Jove* clos'd in *Stigian* Emprie.
But long this blessed time continued not:
As soone as he his wished purpose got,
He recklesse of his promise did despise
The love of th' everlasting Destinies.
They seeing it, both Love and him abhor'd,
And *Jupiter* unto his place restor'd.
And but that Learning, in despight of Fate,
Will mount aloft, and enter heaven gate,
And to the seat of *Jove* it selfe advaunce,
Hermes had slept in hell with ignoraunce,
Yet as a punishment they added this,
That he and *Povertie* should alwaies kis.
And to this day is everie scholler poore,
Grosse gold from them runs headlong to the boore.
Likewise the angrie sisters thus deluded,
To venge themselves on *Hermes,* have concluded
That *Midas* brood shall sit in Honors chaire,
To which the *Muses* sonnes are only heire:

And fruitfull wits that in aspiring are,
Shall discontent run into regions farre;
And few great lords in vertuous deeds shall joy,
But be surpris'd with every garish toy;
And still inrich the loftie servile clowne,
Who with incroching guile keepes learning downe:
Then muse not *Cupids* sute no better sped,
Seeing in their loves the Fates were injured.

From SECOND SESTIAD

O *Hero, Hero,* thus he cry'de full oft,
And then he got him to a rocke aloft,
Where having spy'de her tower, long star'd he on't,
And pray'd the narrow toyling *Hellespont*
To part intwaine, that hee might come and go,
But still the rising billowes answered no.
With that hee stript him to the iv'rie skin,
And crying, Love I come, leapt lively in.
Whereat the saphir visag'd god grew prowd,
And made his capring *Triton* sound alowd,
Imagining that *Ganimed* displeas'd,
Had left the heavens; therefore on him hee seaz'd.
Leander striv'd, the waves about him wound,
And puld him to the bottome, where the ground
Was strewd with pearle, and in low corrall groves
Sweet singing Meremaids, sported with their loves
On heapes of heavie gold, and tooke great pleasure
To spurne in carelesse sort the shipwracke treasure
For here the stately azure pallace stood,
Where kingly *Neptune* and his traine abode.

From TAMBURLAINE

ACT V, SCENE 2

TAMBURLAINE. Ah faire *Zenocrate,* divine *Zenocrate,*
Faire is too foule an Epithite for thee,
That in thy passion for thy countries love,
And feare to see thy kingly Fathers harme,
With haire disheveld wip'st thy watery cheeks:
And like to *Flora* in her mornings pride,
Shaking her silver tresses in the aire,
Rain'st on the earth resolved pearle in showers,
And sprinklest Saphyrs on thy shining face,
Wher Beauty, mother to the Muses sits,

And comments vollumes with her Ivory pen:
Taking instructions from thy flowing eies,
Eies when that *Ebena* steps to heaven,
In silence of thy solemn Evenings walk,
Making the mantle of the richest night,
The Moone, the Planets, and the Meteors light.
There Angels in their christal armours fight
A doubtfull battell with my tempted thoughtes,
For Egypts freedom and the Souldans life:
His life that so consumes *Zenocrate,*
Whose sorrowes lay more siege unto my soule,
Than all my Army to *Damascus* walles.
And neither Perseans Soveraign, nor the Turk
Troubled my sences with conceit of foile,
So much by much, as dooth *Zenocrate.*
What is beauty saith my sufferings then?
If all the pens that ever poets held,
Had fed the feeling of their maisters thoughts,
And every sweetnes that inspir'd their harts,
Their minds, and muses on admyred theames:
If all the heavenly Quintessence they still
From their immortall flowers of Poesy,
Wherein as in a myrrour we perceive
The highest reaches of a humaine wit:
If these had made one Poems period
And all combin'd in Beauties worthinesse,
Yet should ther hover in their restlesse heads,
One thought, one grace, one woonder at the least,
Which into words no vertue can digest:
But how unseemly is it for my Sex
My discipline of armes and Chivalrie,
My nature and the terrour of my name,
To harbour thoughts effeminate and faint!
Save onely that in Beauties just applause,
With whose instinct the soule of man is toucht,
And every warriour that is rapt with love,
Of fame, of valour, and of victory
Must needs have beauty beat on his conceites.
I thus conceiving and subduing both
That which hath stoopt the tempest of the Gods,
Even from the fiery spangled vaile of heaven,
To feel the lovely warmth of shepheards flames,
And martch in cottages of strowed weeds,
Shal give the world to note for all my byrth,
That Vertue solely is the sum of glorie,
And fashions men with true nobility.

From TAMBURLAINE: Part 2

ACT II, SCENE 3

TAMBURLAINE. Blacke is the beauty of the brightest day,
The golden balle of heavens eternal fire,
That danc'd with glorie on the silver waves,
Now wants the fewell that enflamde his beames
And all with faintnesse and for foule disgrace,
He bindes his temples with a frowning cloude,
Ready to darken earth with endlesse night:
Zenocrate that gave him light and life,
Whose eies shot fire from their Ivory bowers,
And tempered every soule with lively heat,
Now by the malice of the angry Skies,
Whose jealousie admits no second Mate,
Drawes in the comfort of her latest breath
All dasled with the hellish mists of death.
Now walk the angels on the walles of heaven,
As Centinels to warne th' immortall soules,
To entertaine devine *Zenocrate.*
Apollo, Cynthia, and the ceaselesse lamps
That gently look'd upon this loathsome earth,
Shine downwards now no more, but deck the heavens
To entertaine divine *Zenocrate.*
The christall springs whose taste illuminates
Refined eies with an eternall sight,
Like tried silver runs through Paradice
To entertaine divine *Zenocrate.*
The Cherubins and holy Seraphins
That sing and play before the king of kings,
Use all their voices and their instruments
To entertaine divine *Zenocrate.*
And in this sweet and currious harmony,
The God that tunes this musicke to our soules
Holds out his hand in highest majesty
To entertaine divine *Zenocrate.*
Then let some holy trance convay my thoughts,
Up to the pallace of th' imperiall heaven:
That this my life may be as short to me
As are the daies of sweet *Zenocrate.*

From DOCTOR FAUSTUS

Enter Helen.

FAUSTUS. Was this the face that lancht a thousand shippes?
 And burnt the toplesse Towres of *Ilium?*
 Sweet *Helen,* make me immortall with a kisse: [*Kisses her.*]
 Her lips sucke forth my soule, see where it flies:
 Come *Helen,* come give mee my soule againe.
 Here wil I dwel, for heaven be in these lips,
 And all is drosse that is not *Helena:*
 I wil be *Paris,* and for love of thee,
 Insteede of Troy shal *Wertenberge* be sackt,
 And I wil combate with weake *Menelaus,*
 And weare thy colours on my plumed Crest:
 Yea I wil wound *Achilles* in the heele,
 And then returne to *Helen* for a kisse.
 O thou art fairer then the evening aire,
 Clad in the beauty of a thousand starres,
 Brighter art thou then flaming *Jupiter,*
 When he appeared to haplesse *Semele,*
 More lovely then the monarke of the skie
 In wanton *Arethusaes* azurde armes,
 And none but thou shalt be my paramour. . . .

The clocke strikes eleauen.

FAUSTUS. Ah Faustus,
 Now hast thou but one bare hower to live,
 And then thou must be damnd perpetually:
 Stand stil you ever mooving spheres of heaven,
 That time may cease, and midnight never come:
 Faire Natures eie, rise, rise againe, and make
 Perpetuall day, or let this houre be but
 A yeere, a moneth, a weeke, a naturall day,
 That Faustus may repent, and save his soule.
 O lente, lente currite noctis equi:
 The starres moove stil, time runs, the clocke wil strike,
 The divel wil come, and Faustus must be damnd.
 O Ile leape up to my God: who pulles me downe?
 See see where Christs blood streames in the firmament.
 One drop would save my soule, halfe a drop, ah my Christ.
 Ah rend not my heart for naming of my Christ,
 Yet wil I call on him: oh spare me *Lucifer!*
 Where is it now? tis gone: And see where God
 Stretcheth out his arme, and bends his irefull browes:
 Mountaines and hilles, come, come, and fall on me,

And hide me from the heavy wrath of God.
No, no.
Then wil I headlong runne into the earth:
Earth gape. O no, it wil not harbour me:
You starres that raignd at my nativitie,
Whose influence hath alotted death and hel,
Now draw up Faustus like a foggy mist,
Into the intrailes of yon labring cloude,
That when you vomite foorth into the ayre,
My limbes may issue from your smoaky mouthes,
So that my soule may but ascend to heaven: [*The clocke strikes.*]
Ah, halfe the houre is past:
Twil all be past anone:
Oh, God,
If thou wilt not have mercy on my soule,
Yet for Christs sake, whose bloud hath ransomd me,
Impose some end to my incessant paine.
Let Faustus live in hel a thousand yeeres,
A hundred thousand, and at last be sav'd.
O no end is limited to damned soules,
Why wert thou not a creature wanting soule?
Or, why is this immortall that thou hast?
Ah *Pythagoras metemsucosis,* were that true,
This soule should flie from me, and I be changde
Unto some brutish beast: al beasts are happy,
For when they die,
Their soules are soone dissolvd in elements,
But mine must live still to be plagde in hel:
Curst be the parents that ingendred me:
No Faustus, curse thy selfe, curse *Lucifer,*
That hath deprivde thee of the joyes of heaven.

> *The clocke striketh twelve.*

O it strikes, it strikes: now body turne to ayre,
Or *Lucifer* wil beare thee quicke to hel.

> *Thunder and lightning.*

O soule, be changde into little water drops,
And fal into the *Ocean,* nere be found:
My God, my God, looke not so fierce on me.

> *Enter divels.*

Adders, and Serpents, let me breathe a while:
Ugly hell gape not, come not *Lucifer,*
Ile burne my bookes, ah *Mephastophilis.*   [*Exeunt with him.*]

George Chapman
1559-1634

Swinburne, writing of Chapman's translation of Homer, said: "His fiery and turbid style has in it the action rather of earthquakes and volcanoes than of the oceanic verse. . . . It can show but the huge movement of the heaving earth, inflated and inflamed with unequal and violent life, for the innumerable unity and harmony, the simplicity and equality of passion and of power, the majestic monochord of single sound underlying as it were the multitudinous measures of the epic sea."

"It is said of the incomparable Virgil," said Ben Jonson (*Discoveries*), "that he brought forth his verses like a Beare, and after form'd them with licking."

This might be said of Chapman, although I imagine he bears no other resemblance to Virgil.

"Some words," said Dante (*De vulgari eloquentia*), "are rustic [sylvan], some urban; and of those which we call urban, we feel some to be combed and slippery, some shaggy and rumpled." (*Rebourra, à rebours,* brushed, or growing, the wrong way.) Chapman's words are sometimes sylvan, sometimes urban, but they are, for the most part, shaggy.

Yet he has grandeurs—such as this, from *Ovid's Battle of Sence:*

> She lifts her lightning arms above her head,
> 　And stretcheth a meridian from her blood,
> That slept awake in her Elysian bed.

Or this, from the Third Sestiad of *Hero and Leander:*

> And all the while the red sea of her blood
> Ebd with Leander.

And how great is the opening of the otherwise bathetic long poem *The Amorous Zodiack:*

> I never see the sun, but suddenly
> My soul is moved with spite and jealousy
> Of his high bliss, in his sweet course discern'd.

From HERO AND LEANDER

From the Fifth Sestiad: EPITHALAMION TERATUS

Come, come deare night, Loves Mart of kisses,
Sweet close of his ambitious line,
The fruitfull summer of his blisses,
Loves glorie doth in darknes shine.
O come soft rest of Cares, come night,
Come naked vertues only tire,
The reaped harvest of the light
Bound up in sheaves of sacred fire.
 Love cals to warre,
 Sighs his Alarmes,
 Lips his swords are,
 The field his Armes.
Come Night and lay thy velvet hand
On glorious Dayes outfacing face;
And all the crowned flames command
For Torches to our Nuptiall grace.
 Love cals to warre,
 Sighs his Alarmes,
 Lips his swords are,
 The field his Armes.
No neede have we of factious Day,
To cast in envie of thy peace
Her bals of Discord in thy way:
Here beauties day doth never cease,
Day is abstracted here,
And varied in a triple sphere.
Hero, Alcmane, Mya so outshine thee,
Ere thou come here let *Thetis* thrice refine thee.
 Love cals to warre,
 Sighs his Alarmes,
 Lips his swords are,
 The field his Armes.
The Evening starre I see:
Rise youths, the Evening starre
Helps Love to summon warre,
Both now imbracing bee.
Rise youths, loves right claims more than banquets, rise.
Now the bright Marygolds that deck the skies,
Phoebus celestiall flowers, that (contrarie
To his flowers here) ope when he shuts his eie,

And shuts when he doth open, crowne your sports:
Now love in night, and night in love exhorts
Courtship and Dances: All your parts employ,
And suit nights rich expansure with your joy,
Love paints his longings in sweet virgins eyes:
Rise youths, loves right claims more than banquets, rise. . . .

Herewith the amorous spirit that was so kinde
To *Teras* haire, and combd it downe with winde,
Still as it Comet-like brake from her braine,
Would needes have *Teras* gone, and did refraine
To blow it downe: which staring up, dismaid
The timorous feast, and she no longer staid:
But bowing to the Bridegrome and the Bride,
Did like a shooting exhalation glide
Out of their sights: the turning of her back
Made them all shrieke, it lookt so ghastly black.

From HOMER'S ILIADS

From THE EPISTLE DEDICATORY

A Princes statue, or in Marble carv'd,
Or steele, or gold, and shrin'd (to be preserv'd)
Aloft on Pillars, or Pyramides,
Time into lowest ruines may depresse:
But, drawne with all his vertues in learn'd verse,
Fame shall resound them on Oblivions hearse,
Till graves gaspe with her blasts, and dead men rise.
No gold can follow, where true Poesie flies.
   Then let not this Divinitie in earth
(Deare Prince) be slighted, as she were the birth
Of idle Fancie, since she workes so hie:
Nor let her poore disposer (Learning) lie
Still bed-rid. Both which, being in men defac't,
In men (with them) is Gods bright image rac't.
For, as the Sunne, and Moone, are figures given
Of his refulgent Deitie in Heaven:
So, Learning, and her Lightner, Poesie,
In earth present his fierie Majestie.
Nor are Kings like him, since their Diademes
Thunder, and lighten, and project brave beames;
But since they his cleare vertues emulate,
In Truth and Justice imaging his State,

rac't | marred, torn.

In Bountie, and Humanitie since they shine;
Than which, is nothing (like him) more divine:
Not Fire, not Light; the Sunnes admired course;
The Rise, nor Set of Starres; nor all their force
In us, and all this Cope beneath the Skie;
Nor great *Existence,* term'd his Treasurie.
Since not, for being greatest, he is blest;
But being Just, and in all vertues best.
　　What sets his Justice, and his Truth, best forth,
(Best Prince) then use best; which is Poesies worth.

From BOOK VIII

Hector speaks.

"O that I were as sure to live, immortal, and sustain
No frailties with increasing yeares, but evermore remain
Ador'd like *Pallas,* or the Sun, as all doubts die in me
That heavens next light shall be the last the Greeks shall ever see."
This speech all Trojans did applaud; who from their traces loos'd
Their sweating horse; which severally with headstalls they repos'd,
And fastned by their chariots; when others brought from towne,
Fat sheepe and oxen, instantly; bread, wine; and hewed downe
Huge store of wood: the winds transfer'd, into the friendly skie
Their suppers savour; to the which, they sate delightfully,
And spent all night in open field; fires round about them shin'd;
As when about the silver Moone, when aire is free from wind,
And stars shine cleare; to whose sweete beames, high prospects, **and the
　　brows**
Of all steepe hills and pinnacles, thrust up themselves for showes;
And even the lowly vallies joy, to glitter in their sight,
When the unmeasur'd firmament, bursts to disclose her light,
And all the signes in heaven are seene, that glad the shepheards **heart;**
So many fires disclos'd their beames, made by the Trojan part
Before the face of *Ilion;* and her bright turrets show'd.
A thousand courts of guard kept fires: and every guard allow'd
Fiftie stout men, by whom their horse ate oates and hard white corne,
And all did wilfully expect, the silver-throned morne.

From BOOK XII

Sarpedon speaks.

Nor had great *Hector* and his friends the rampire overrun,
If heavens great Counsellor, high *Jove,* had not inflam'd his son
Sarpedon (like the forest's king when he on oxen flies)
Against the *Grecians;* his round targe he to his arm applies,

Brass-leav'd without, and all within thicke ox-hides quilted hard,
The verge nail'd round with rods of gold; and, with two darts prepar'd,
He leads his people. As ye see a mountaine Lion fare,
Long kept from prey: in forcing which, his high mind makes him dare
Assault upon the whole full fold: though guarded never so
With well-arm'd men, and eager dogs; away he will not go,
But venture on, and either snatch a prey, or be a prey:
So far'd divine *Sarpedons* mind, resolv'd to force his way
Through all the fore-fights, and the wall: yet since he did not see
Others as great as he, in name, as great in mind as he:
He spake to *Glaucus:* "*Glaucus,* say, why are we honor'd more
Than other men of *Lycia,* in place? with greater store
Of meates and cups? with goodlier roofes? delightsome gardens? walks?
More lands, and better? so much wealth, that Court and countrie talks
Of us, and our possessions; and every way we go,
Gaze on us as we were their Gods? this where we dwell, is so:
The shores of *Xanthus* ring of this; and shall not we exceed
As much in merit, as in noise? Come, be we great in deed
As well as looke; shine not in gold, but in the flames of fight;
That so our neat-arm'd *Lycians* may say: See, these are right,
Our kings, our Rulers; these deserve, to eate and drinke the best;
These governe not ingloriously: these, thus exceed the rest,
Do more than they command to do. O friend, if keeping backe
Would keepe backe age from us, and death; and that we might not
     wracke
In this lifes humane sea at all: but that deferring now
We shun'd death ever; nor would I, halfe this vaine valour show,
Nor glorifie a folly so, to wish thee to advance:
But since we must go, though not here; and that, besides the chance
Propos'd now, there are infinite fates, of other sort in death,
Which (neither to be fled nor scap't) a man must sinke beneath:
Come, trie we, if this sort be ours: and either render thus,
Glorie to others, or make them, resigne the like to us."

From THE SHADOW OF NIGHT

HYMNUS IN NOCTEM

Great Goddesse to whose throne in Cynthian fires,
This earthlie Alter endlesse fumes exspires,
Therefore, in fumes of sighes and fires of griefe,
To tearefull chances thou sendst bold reliefe,
Happie, thrise happie, Type and nurse of death,
Who breathlesse, feeds on nothing but our breath,
In whom must vertue and her issue live,
Or dye for ever; now let humor give

Seas to mine eyes, that I may quicklie weepe
The shipwracke of the world: or let soft sleepe
(Binding my sences) loose my working soule,
That in her highest pitch, she may controule
The court of skill, compact of misterie,
Wanting but franchisement and memorie
To reach all secrets: then in blissful trance,
Raise her (deare Night) to that perseverance,
That in my torture, she all earths may sing,
And force to tremble in her trumpeting
Heavens christall temples: in her powrs implant
Skill of my griefs, and she can nothing want.

   Then like fierce bolts, well rammd with heate and cold
In Joves Artillerie, my words unfold,
To breake the labyrinth of everie eare,
And make ech frighted soule come forth and heare;
Let them breake harts, as well as yeelding ayre,
That all mens bosoms (pierst with no affaires,
But gaine of riches) may be lanced wide,
And with the threates of vertue terrified.

   Sorrowes deare soveraigne, and the queene of rest,
That when unlightsome, vast, and indigest
The formelesse matter of this world did lye,
Fildst every place with thy Divinitie,
Why did thy absolute and endlesse sway,
Licence heavens torch, the scepter of the Day,
Distinguisht intercession to thy throne,
That long before, all matchlesse rul'd alone?
Why letst thou order, orderlesse, disperse
The fighting parents of this universe?
When earth, the ayre, and sea, in fire remaind,
When fire, the sea, and earth, the ayre containd,
When ayre, the earth, and fire, the sea enclosde
When sea, fire, ayre, in earth were indisposde,
Nothing, as now, remainde so out of kinde,
All things in grosse, were finer than refinde,
Substance was sound within, and had no being,
Now forme gives being; all our essence seeming.
Chaos had soule without a bodie then,
Now bodies live without the soules of men,
Lumps being digested; monsters, in our pride.

   And as a wealthie fount, that hils did hide,
Let forth by labor of industrious hands,
Powres out her treasure through the fruitefull strands,
Seemely divided to a hundred streames,
Whose bewties shed such profitable beames,

And make such Orphean Musicke in their courses,
That Citties follow their enchanting forces,
Who running farre, at length ech powres her hart
Into the bosome of the gulfie desart,
As much confounded there, and indigest,
As in the chaos of the hills comprest:
So all things now (extract out of the prime)
Are turned to chaos, and confound the time. . . .

And as when hosts of starres attend thy flight,
(Day of deepe students, most contentfull night)
The morning (mounted on the Muses stead)
Ushers the sonne from Vulcans golden bed,
And then from forth their sundrie roofes of rest,
All sorts of men, to sorted taskes addrest,
Spreade this inferiour element: and yeeld
Labour his due: the souldier to the field,
States-men to counsell, Judges to their pleas,
Merchants to commerce, mariners to seas:
All beasts, and birds, the groves and forrests range,
To fill all corners of this round Exchange,
Till thou (deare Night, O goddesse of most worth)
Letst thy sweet seas of golden humor forth
And Eagle-like dost with thy starrie wings,
Beate in the foules, and beasts to Somnus lodgings,
And haughtie Day to the infernall deepe,
Proclaiming silence, studie, ease, and sleepe.
All things before thy forces put in rout,
Retiring where the morning fir'd them out.
   So to the chaos of our first descent,
(All dayes of honor, and of vertue spent)
We basely make retrait, and are no lesse
Then huge impolisht heapes of filthinesse.
Mens faces flitter, and their hearts are blacke,
But thou (great Mistresse of heavens gloomie racke)
Art blacke in face, and glitterst in thy heart,
There is thy glorie, riches, force, and Art.

Of George Peele, Robert Greene
and Thomas Campion

"Poetry should always be running upon pleasant feet, sometimes swift, sometimes slow," said George Puttenham, in *The Art of English Poesie* (1589).

The Elizabethans ran, almost always, upon pleasant feet.

They have been mutilated and dwarfed, their music has been stolen from them and a mortal injury done them by inflicting on them modern spelling. This deprives them entirely of their natural character.

Swinburne said of a poet of a very different age and species * that his line was "as sinuous as water or as light; flexible and penetrative, delicate and rapid, it works on its way without jolt or collapse."

This might have been written of George Peele.

Peele is haunted, in some plays, by the sound of water and by the ghosts of water and by the depth of water (but inland waters, not oceans) — as in these lines from *The Old Wives Tale:*

SACROPANT. How now, fair Delia, where have you been?
   DELIA. At the foote of the rocke for running water and gathering rootes
     for your dinner, Sir.

— could any sound be stranger, more remote than the water-wavering sound of those lines? — and in the exquisite song *Gently dip: but not too deepe* from the same play. Part of the aural beauty of that wonderful song derives from the alliterative dissonances "dip," "deepe," the assonances "feare," "beard," and the long dissonantal o's of "combe" and "smoothe."

The great aural beauties of Bethsabe's song, *Hot sunne, coole fire,* result, I think, from the long pauses, and the fact that "aire" — a word that seems to have more than one syllable — floats onward and outward, and is slightly longer than "fire," which is also a word of apparently more than one syllable, and the movement of which is completely different. It seems to be leaping into the air and then subsiding. The beauty of sound comes, too, from the dissonance of "burning" and "mourning," and from the extreme strangeness of the assonance or false rhyme of "bright eye," "lightly."

David and Bethsabe, the play in which this miraculous beauty appears, though it has no dramatic interest (as I think), contains such splendors as Absalom's:

* D. G. Rossetti.

> At him the thunder shall discharge his bolt,
> And his faire spouse, with bright and fierie wings
> Sit ever burning on his hatefull bones.

— a passage that has been compared with Aeschylus; and "His thunder is intangled in my haire"; and, as well, the delicious:

> God in the whizzing of a pleasant wind
> Shall march upon the tops of mulberrie trees
> To coole all breasts that burne with any griefes.

The man who was capable of these beauties was not, in any true sense, a minor poet.

Leaving aside the exquisite *Sephestia's Song*, with its poignant refrain "When thou art olde, ther's grief inough for thee!" (that does, indeed, sound as if "Teares of bloud fell from [her] hart"), Robert Greene's shining line "Face Rose hued, Cherry red, with a silver taint like a Lilly," with sharp dew glittering on it (brought there by the particular placing of "Rose" and "red") — this wonderful line, even if he had written nothing else, would give him his place among the elect.
And the lines:

> O glorious Sun! imagine me the West,
> Shine in my Arms, and set thou in my Breast.

are scarcely short of what might have been written by the greatest of all English poets; but though the splendor of imagination is there, they have not the utmost splendor of diction, because the *s*'s, and the soft *g* of "imagine" are a little unshaping and sluggish.

"Play secretly under dim sounds, and under the great strings; as though the craft we used should be ashamed if it were taken." *
This might have been said of certain of Campion's poems, as, reflecting on others, we might think this passage from Bacon might apply to them: "There be in music certain figures or tropes almost agreeing with the affections of the mind and other senses. First, the division and quavering, which please so much in music, have an agreement with the glittering of light."
But he has great variety.
"The Apothecaries," said Thomas Campion, in the preface to his *Fourth Book of Ayres*, "have Books of Gold that are so light that they are subject to be shaken with the least breath, yet rightly handled, they serve both for ornament and use. Such are light Ayres."
As Saintsbury † says, "*When to her lute Corinna sings* is rigidly iambic,

---

* Trevisa.
† *The History of English Prosody.*

decasyllabic, and non-redundant; yet Ben himself has left us nothing more beautiful. And *Follow thy fair sun, unhappie shadowe* . . . is even more complicated than it looks — full of reverses, extensions, and contractions of rhythm, yet all most artfully managed. . . . But who that feels the charm of English prosody at all shall speak with measure of *Follow your saint?* Here we have practically everything — audacious and unfailing conjunction of trochee and iamb, bold trisyllabic substitution with incomparable effect, extraordinary variation of pause, and telescoping of lines, all quite miraculous in effect."

"A poet is a light and winged thing, but holy," said Plato. (Were the Bee-Priestesses, the Thriae, in his mind?) Perhaps it was a memory of this that caused Campion, speaking through Orpheus' lips to Entheus (the Poetick Furie) to say:

> . . . thy excelling rapture, ev'n through things
> That seem most light, is borne with sacred wings.

"The world," he said, "is made of symmetry and proportion, and is in that respect compared to music, and music to poetry. . . . What music can there be where no proportion is observed?"

George Peele
1556?-1596?

From DAVID AND BETHSABE

BETHSABE'S SONG

Hot sunne, coole fire, temperd with sweet aire,
Black shade, fair nurse, shadow my white haire,
Shine sun, burne fire, breath aire, and ease mee,
Black shade, fair nurse, shroud me and please me,
Shadow (my sweet nurse) keep me from burning,
Make not my glad cause, cause of mourning.
    Let not my beauties fire,
    Enflame unstaied desire,
    Nor pierce any bright eye,
    That wandreth lightly.

From THE OLD WIVES TALE

THE SONG AT THE WELL

COREBUS. Come wench, are we almost at the well?

ZELANTO. Ay, *Corebus* we are almost at the Well now, ile go fetch some
water: sit downe while I dip my pitcher in.

VOYCE. Gently dip: but not too deepe;
For feare you make the goulden beard to weepe.

*A head comes up with eares of Corne, and she combes them
in her lap.*

Faire maiden white and red,
Combe me smoothe, and stroke my head:
And thou shalt have some cockell bread.
Gently dippe, but not too deepe,
For feare thou make the goulden beard to weep.
Faire maide, white and redde,
Combe me smooth, and stroke my head;
And every haire, a sheave shall be,
And every sheave a goulden tree.

SONG: *WHEN AS THE RIE REACH TO THE CHIN*

When as the Rie reach to the chin
And chopcherrie chopcherrie ripe within,
Strawberries swimming in the creame,
And schoole boyes playing in the streame:
Then O, then O, then O my true love said,
Till that time come againe,
Shee could not live a maid.

From POLYHYMNIA

HIS GOLDEN LOCKES, TIME HATH TO SILVER TURN'D

His Golden lockes, Time hath to Silver turn'd,
O Time too swift, O Swiftnesse never ceasing:
His Youth gainst Time and Age hath ever spurn'd
But spurn'd in vain, Youth waineth by increasing.
Beauty, Strength, Youth, are flowers, but fading seen,
Dutie, Faith, Love, are roots, and ever greene.

His Helmet now, shall make a hive for Bees,
   And Lovers Sonets, turn'd to holy Psalmes:
A man at Armes must now serve on his knees,
   And feede on praiers, which are Age his almes.
But though from Court to Cottage he depart,
His Saint is sure of his unspotted heart.

And when he saddest sits in homely Cell,
   Heele teach his Swaines this Carroll for a Song,
Blest be the heartes that wish my Soveraigne well,
   Curst be the soules that thinke her any wrong.
Goddesse, allow this aged man his right,
To be your Beads-man now, that was your Knight.

Robert Greene
1558?-1592?

From GREENE'S MOURNING GARMENT

IN PRAISE OF ROSAMUND

Oft have I heard my liefe *Coridon* report on a love-day,
When bonny maides doe meete with the Swaines in the vally by *Tempe*,
How bright eyd his *Phillis* was, how lovely they glanced,
When fro th' Aarches Eben black, flew lookes as a lightning,
That set a fire with piercing flames even hearts adamantine:
Face Rose hued, Cherry red, with a silver taint like a Lilly.
Venus pride might abate, might abash with a blush to behold her.
Phoebus wyers compar'd to her haires unworthy the praysing.
Junoes state, and *Pallas* wit disgrac'd with the Graces,
That grac'd her, whom poore *Coridon* did choose for a love-mate:
Ah, but had *Coridon* now seene the starre that *Alexis*
Likes and loves so deare, that he melts to sighs when he sees her.
Did *Coridon* but see those eyes, those amorous eyelids,
From whence fly holy flames of death or life in a moment.
Ah, did he see that face, those haires that *Venus, Apollo*
Basht to behold, and both disgrac'd, did grieve, that a creature
Should exceed in hue, compare both a god and a goddesse:
Ah, had he seene my sweet Paramour the saint of *Alexis*,
Then had he sayd, *Phillis,* sit downe surpassed in all points,
For there is one more faire then thou, beloved of *Alexis*.

liefe] love, sweetheart.

From MENAPHON

SEPHESTIA'S SONG TO HER CHILDE

Weepe not my wanton! smile upon my knee!
When thou art olde, ther's grief inough for thee!
　　Mothers wagge, pretie boy.
　　Fathers sorrow, fathers joy.
　　When thy father first did see
　　Such a boy by him and mee,
　　He was glad, I was woe.
　　Fortune changde made him so,
　　When he left his pretie boy,
　　Last his sorowe, first his joy.

Weepe not my wanton! smile upon my knee!
When thou art olde, ther's griefe inough for thee!
　　Streaming teares that never stint,
　　Like pearle drops from a flint,
　　Fell by course from his eyes,
　　That one anothers place supplies:
　　Thus he grievd in everie part,
　　Teares of bloud fell from his hart,
　　When he left his pretie boy,
　　Fathers sorrow, fathers joy.

Weepe not my wanton! smile upon my knee!
When thou art olde, ther's griefe inough for thee!
　　The wanton smilde, father wept;
　　Mother cride, babie lept:
　　More he crowde, more we cride;
　　Nature could not sorowe hide.
　　He must goe, he must kisse
　　Childe and mother, babie blisse:
　　For he left his pretie boy,
　　Fathers sorowe, fathers joy.

Weepe not my wanton! smile upon my knee!
When thou art olde, ther's grief inough for thee!

DORON'S DESCRIPTION OF SAMELA

Like to *Diana* in her Summer weede
　　Girt with a crimson roabe of brightest die,
　　　　Goes faire *Samela*.

Whiter than be the flockes that straggling feede,
　　When washt by *Arethusa,* faint they lie:
　　　　Is faire *Samela.*
As faire *Aurora* in her morning gray
　　Deckt with the ruddie glister of her love,
　　　　Is faire *Samela.*
Like lovely *Thetis* on a calmed day,
　　When as her brightnesse *Neptunes* fancie move,
　　　　Shines faire *Samela.*
Her tresses gold, her eyes like glassie streames,
　　Her teeth are pearle, the breast of yvorie
　　　　Of faire *Samela.*
Her cheekes like rose and lilly yeeld foorth gleames,
　　Her browes bright arches framde of ebonie:
　　　　Thus faire *Samela.*
Passeth faire *Venus* in her bravest hiew,
　　And *Juno* in the shew of majestie,
　　　　For she is *Samela.*
Pallas in wit, all three if you will view,
　　For beautie, wit, and matchlesse dignitie
　　　　Yeeld to *Samela.*

DORON'S JIGGE

Through the shrubs as I can cracke,
　　For my Lambes pretty ones,
　　Mongst many little ones,
Nymphes I meane, whose haire was blacke,
　　　　As the Crow;
　　　　Like the snow,
Her face and browes shine I weene,
　　I saw a little one,
　　A bonny pretty one,
As bright, buxome, and as sheene,
　　　　As was she
　　　　On her knee,
That lulled the God, whose arrowes warmes,
　　Such merry little ones,
　　Such faire fac'de pretty ones,
As dally in loves chiefest harmes:
　　　　Such was mine,
　　　　Whose gray eyne
Made me love. I gan to woo
　　This sweet little one,
　　This bonny pretty one,

I wooed hard a day or two,
    Till she bad,
    Be not sad,
Woo no more, I am thine owne,
    Thy deerest little one,
    Thy truest pretty one:
Thus was faith and firme love showne,
    As behoves
    Shepheards loves.

From PANDOSTO

IN PRAISE OF HIS LOVING
AND BEST–BELOVED FAWNIA

Ah! were she Pitiful as she is Fair,
    Or but as mild as she is seeming so,
Then were my Hopes greater than my Despair;
    Then all the World were Heaven, nothing Woe.
Ah! were her Heart relenting as her Hand,
    That seems to melt even with the mildest touch,
Then knew I where to seat me in a Land
    Under the wide Heavens, but yet not such:
So as she shews, so seems the budding Rose,
    Yet sweeter far than is an earthly Flower;
Sovereign of Beauty! like the Spray she grows,
    Compass'd she is with Thorns and canker'd Flower:
Yet were she willing to be pluck'd and worn,
She would be gather'd, tho she grew on Thorn.

Ah! when she sings, all Musick else be still,
    For none must be compared to her Note;
Ne'er breath'd such Glee from *Philomela's* Bill,
    Nor from the Morning-singer's swelling Throat:
Ah! when she riseth from her blissful Bed,
    She comforts all the World, as doth the Sun;
And at her sight, the Night's foul Vapour's fled:
    When she is set, the gladsom Day is done:
O glorious Sun! imagine me the West,
Shine in my Arms, and set thou in my Breast.

From NEVER TOO LATE

INFIDA'S SONG

Sweet Adon, darst not glaunce
    thine eye.
  N'oserez vous, mon bel amy?
Upon thy Venus that must die,
  Je vous en prie, pitie me:
N'oserez vous, mon bel, mon bel,
  N'oserez vous, mon bel amy?

See how sad thy Venus lies,
  N'oserez vous, mon bel amy?
Love in heart and teares in eyes,
  Je vous en prie, pitie me:
N'oserez vous, mon bel, mon bel,
  N'oserez vous, mon bel amy?

Thy face as faire as Paphos brookes,
  N'oserez vous, mon bel amy?
Wherein fancie baites her hookes,
  Je vous en prie, pitie me:
N'oserez vous, mon bel, mon bel,
  N'oserez vous, mon bel amy?

Thy cheekes like cherries that
    doo growe,
  N'oserez vous, mon bel amy?
Amongst the Westerne mounts of
    snowe,
  Je vous en prie, pitie me:
N'oserez vous, mon bel, mon bel,
  N'oserez vous, mon bel amy?

Thy lips vermilion, full of love,
  N'oserez vous, mon bel amy?

Thy necke as silver-white as dove,
  Je vous en prie, pitie me:
N'oserez vous, mon bel, mon bel,
  N'oserez vous, mon bel amy?

Thine eyes like flames of holie fires,
  N'oserez vous, mon bel amy?
Burnes all my thoughts with sweet
    desires,
  Je vous en prie, pitie me:
N'oserez vous, mon bel, mon bel,
  N'oserez vous, mon bel amy?

All thy beauties sting my hart,
  N'oserez vous, mon bel amy?
I must die through Cupid's dart,
  Je vous en prie, pitie me:
N'oserez vous, mon bel, mon bel,
  N'oserez vous, mon bel amy?

Wilt thou let thy Venus die?
  N'oserez vous, mon bel amy?
Adon were unkinde, say I,
  Je vous en prie, pitie me:
N'oserez vous, mon bel, mon bel,
  N'oserez vous, mon bel amy?

To let faire Venus die for woe,
  N'oserez vous, mon bel amy?
That doth love sweete Adon so;
  Je vous en prie, pitie me:
N'oserez vous, mon bel, mon bel,
  N'oserez vous, mon bel amy?

Thomas Campion
1567-1620

ROSE-CHEEKT LAURA, COME

Rose-cheekt *Laura*, come
Sing thou smoothly with thy beawties
Silent musick, either other
    Sweetely gracing.

Lovely formes do flowe
From concent devinely framed;
Heav'n is musick, and thy beawties
    Birth is heavenly.

These dull notes we sing
Discords neede for helps to grace them;
Only beawty purely loving
    Knowes no discord,

But still mooves delight,
Like cleare springs renu'd by flowing,
Ever perfet, ever in them-
    selves eternall.

FOLLOWE THY FAIRE SUNNE

Followe thy faire sunne, unhappy shadowe,
  Though thou be blacke as night,
  And she made all of light,
Yet follow thy faire sun, unhappie shadowe.

Follow her whose light thy light depriveth,
  Though here thou liv'st disgrac't,
  And she in heaven is plac't,
Yet follow her whose light the world reviveth.

Follow those pure beames whose beautie burneth,
  That so have scorched thee,
  As thou still blacke must bee,
Til her kind beames thy black to brightnes turneth.

Follow her while yet her glorie shineth:
   There comes a luckles night,
   That will dim all her light;
And this the black unhappie shade devineth.

Follow still since so thy fates ordained;
   The Sunne must have his shade,
   Till both at once doe fade,
The Sun still proud, the shadow still disdained.

KINDE ARE HER ANSWERES

   Kinde are her answeres,
But her performance keeps no day;
   Breaks time, as dancers
From their own Musicke when they stray:
All her free favors and smooth words,
   Wing my hopes in vaine.
   O did ever voice so sweet but only fain?
Can true love yeeld such delay,
   Converting joy to pain?

   Lost is our freedome,
When we submit to women so:
   Why doe wee neede them,
When in their best they worke our woe?
There is no wisedome
   Can alter ends, by Fate prefixt.
   O why is the good of man with evill mixt?
Never were days yet cal'd two,
   But one night went betwixt.

WHEN TO HER LUTE CORINNA SINGS

   When to her lute Corinna sings,
   Her voice revives the leaden stringes,
   And doth in highest noates appeare,
   As any challeng'd eccho cleere;
   But when she doth of mourning speake,
   Ev'n with her sighes the strings do breake.

   And as her lute doth live or die,
   Led by her passion, so must I,

For when of pleasure she doth sing,
My thoughts enjoy a sodaine spring,
But if she doth of sorrow speake,
Ev'n from my hart the strings doe breake.

FOLLOW YOUR SAINT

Follow your Saint, follow with accents sweet;
Haste you, sad noates, fall at her flying feete:
There, wrapt in cloud of sorrowe pitie move,
And tell the ravisher of my soule I perish for her love.
But if she scorns my never-ceasing paine,
Then burst with sighing in her sight and nere returne
    againe.

All that I sung still to her praise did tend,
Still she was first; still she my songs did end.
Yet she my love and Musicke both doeth flie,
The Musicke that her Eccho is and beauties simpathie;
Then let my Noates pursue her scornfull flight:
It shall suffice that they were breath'd and dy'd for
    her delight.

BEAUTY IS BUT A PAINTED HELL

Beauty is but a painted hell:
    Aye me, aye me,
    Shee wounds them that admire it,
    Shee kils them that desire it.
    Give her pride but fuell,
    No fire is more cruell.

Pittie from ev'ry heart is fled:
    Aye me, aye me,
    Since false desire could borrow
    Teares of dissembled sorrow,
    Constant vowes turn truthlesse,
    Love cruele, Beauty ruthlesse.

Sorrow can laugh, and Fury sing:
    Aye me, aye me,
    My raving griefes discover
    I liv'd too true a lover:
    The first step to madnesse
    Is the excesse of sadnesse.

WHEN THOU MUST HOME

When thou must home to shades of under ground,
    And there ariv'd, a newe admired guest,
The beauteous spirits do ingirt thee round,
    White Iope, blith Hellen, and the rest,
To heare the stories of thy finisht love
From that smoothe tongue whose musicke hell can move;

Then wilt thou speake of banqueting delights,
    Of masks and revels which sweete youth did make,
Of Turnies and great challenges of knights,
    And all these triumphes for thy beauties sake:
When thou hast told these honours done to thee,
Then tell, O tell, how thou didst murther me.

NOW WINTER NIGHTS ENLARGE

Now winter nights enlarge
    The number of their houres;
And clouds their stormes discharge
    Upon the ayrie towres.
Let now the chimneys blaze
    And cups o'erflow with wine,
Let well-tun'd words amaze
    With harmonie divine.
Now yellow waxen lights
    Shall waite on honey Love
While youthfull Revels, Masks, and
    Courtly sights,
Sleepes leaden spels remove.

This time doth well dispence
    With lovers long discourse;
Much speech hath some defence,
    Though beauty no remorse.
All doe not all things well;
    Some measures comely tread;
Some knotted Ridles tell;
    Some Poems smoothly read.
The Summer hath his joyes,
    And Winter his delights;
Though Love and all his pleasures
    are but toyes,
They shorten tedious nights.

THRICE TOSSE THESE OAKEN ASHES

Thrice tosse these Oaken ashes in the ayre,
Thrice sit thou mute in this inchanted chayre;
And thrice three times tye up this true loves knot,
And murmur soft, shee will, or shee will not.

Goe burn these poys'nous weedes in yon blew fire,
These Screech-owles fethers and this prickling bryer;
This Cypresse gathered at a dead mans grave;
That all thy feares and cares, an end may have.

Then come, you Fayries, dance with me a round;
Melt her hard heart with your melodious sound:
In vaine are all the charms I can devise:
She hath an Arte to breake them with her eyes.

WHAT FAIRE POMPE

What faire pompe have I spide of glittering Ladies;
  With locks sparckled abroad, and rosie Coronet
On their yvorie browes, trackt to the daintie thies
  With roabs like *Amazons*, blew as Violet,
With gold Aiglets adornd, some in a changeable
Pale; with spangs wavering taught to be moveable.

Then those Knights that a farre off with dolorous viewing
  Cast their eyes hetherward; loe, in an agonie,
All unbrac'd, crie aloud, their heavie state ruing:
  Moyst cheekes with blubbering, painted as *Ebonie*
Blacke; their feltred haire torne with wrathful hand:
And whiles astonied, starke in a maze they stand.

But hearke! what merry sound! what sodaine harmonie!
  Looke looke neere the grove where the Ladies doe tread
With their Knights the measures waide by the melodie.
  Wantons! whose traversing make men enamoured;
Now they faine an honor, now by the slender waist
He must lift hir aloft, and seale a kisse in hast.

Streight downe under a shadow for wearines they lie
  With pleasant daliance, hand knit with arme in arme,
Now close, now set aloof, they gaze with an equall eie,
  Changing kisses alike; streight with a false alarme,
Mocking kisses alike, powt with a lovely lip.
Thus drownd with jollities, their merry daies doe slip.

But stay! now I discerne they gone on a Pilgrimage
  Towards Loves holy land, faire *Paphos* or *Cyprus*.
Such devotion is meete for a blithesome age;
  With sweet youth, it agrees well to be amorous.
Let olde angrie fathers lurke in an Hermitage:
Come, weele associate this jolly Pilgrimage!

JUST BEGUILER

Just beguiler,
Kindest love, yet only chastest,
Royall in thy smooth denyals,
Frowning or demurely smiling,
    Still my pure delight.

    Let me view thee
With thoughts and with eyes affected,
And if then the flames do murmur,
Quench them with thy vertue, charme them
    With thy stormy browes.

    Heav'n so cheerefull
Laughs not ever, hory winter
Knowes his season, even the freshest
Sommer mornes from angry thundre
    Yet not still secure.

THOU ART NOT FAIRE

Thou art not faire for all thy red and white,
    For all those rosie ornaments in thee,
Thou art not sweet, though made of meer delight,
    Nor faire nor sweet, unlesse thou pitie mee.
I will not sooth thy fancies: thou shalt prove
That beauty is no beautie without love.

Yet love not me, nor seeke thou to allure
    My thoughts with beautie, were it more devine,
Thy smiles and kisses I cannot endure,
    I'le not be wrapt up in those armes of thine.
Now shew it, if thou be a woman right, —
Embrace, and kisse, and love me, in despight.

MY SWEETEST LESBIA

My sweetest Lesbia let us live and love,
And though the sager sort our deedes reprove,
Let us not weigh them: heav'ns great lampes doe dive
Into their west, and strait againe revive,
But soone as once set is our little light,
Then must we sleepe one ever-during night.

If all would lead their lives in love like mee,
Then bloudie swords and armour should not be,
No drum nor trumpet peaceful sleepes should move,
Unles alar'me came from the campe of love:
But fooles do live, and wast their little light,
And seeke with paine their ever-during night.

When timely death my life and fortune ends,
Let not my hearse be vext with mourning friends,
But let all lovers rich in triumph come,
And with sweet pastimes grace my happie tombe;
And Lesbia close up thou my little light,
And crowne with love my ever-during night.

THERE IS A GARDEN

There is a Garden in her face,
  Where Roses and white Lillies grow;
A heav'nly paradice is that place,
  Wherein all pleasant fruits doe flow.
There Cherries grow, which none may buy
Till Cherry ripe themselves doe cry.

Those Cherries fayrely doe enclose
  Of Orient Pearle a double row;
Which when her lovely laughter showes,
  They look like Rose-buds fill'd with snow.
Yet them nor Peere nor Prince can buy,
Till Cherry ripe themselves doe cry.

Her Eyes like Angels watch them still;
  Her Browes like bended bowes doe stand,
Threatning with piercing frownes to kill
  All that attempt with eye or hand
Those sacred Cherries to come nigh,
Till Cherry ripe themselves doe cry.

COME, O COME

Come, O come, my lifes delight,
  Let me not in langour pine:
Love loves no delay; thy sight,
  The more enjoy'd, the more
    divine:
O come, and take from mee
The paine of being depriv'd of thee.

Thou all sweetnesse dost enclose,
  Like a little world of blisse.
Beauty guards thy lookes: the
    Rose
  In them pure and eternall is.
Come, then, and make thy flight
As swift to me as heav'nly light.

THERE IS NONE, O NONE BUT YOU

There is none, O none but you,
  That from mee estrange your sight,
Whom mine eyes affect to view
  Or chained eares heare with delight.

Other beauties others move,
  In you I all graces finde;
Such is the effect of love,
  To make them happy that are kinde.

Women in fraile beauty trust,
  Onely seeme you faire to mee;
Yet prove truely kinde and just,
  For that may not dissembled be.

Sweet, afford mee then your sight,
  That, survaying all your lookes,
Endlesse volumes I may write
  And fill the world with envyed bookes:

Which when after ages view,
  All shall wonder and despaire,
Woman to finde man so true,
  Or man a woman halfe so faire.

AUTHOR OF LIGHT

Author of light, revive my dying spright;
Redeeme it from the snares of all-confounding night.
    Lord, light me to thy blessed way:
For blinde with worldly vaine desires, I wander as a stray.
  Sunne and Moone, Starres and underlights I see,
But all their glorious beames are mists and darknes, being
    compar'd to thee.

Fountaine of health, my soules deepe wounds recure,
Sweet showres of pitty raine, wash my uncleannesse pure.
    One drop of thy desired grace
The faint and fading hart can raise, and in joyes bosome place.
  Sinne and Death, Hell and tempting Fiends may rage;
But God his owne will guard, and their sharp paines and
    griefe in time asswage.

Thomas Lodge
1558?-1625

From ROSALYNDE

ROSALYNDE'S MADRIGALL

Love in my bosome like a Bee
    Doth sucke his sweete:
Now with his wings he playes with
    me,
    Now with his feete.
Within mine eyes he makes his nest,
His bed amidst my tender brest,
My kisses are his dayly feast,
And yet he robs me of my rest,
    Ah wanton, will ye?

And if I sleepe, then pearcheth he
    With pretty flight,
And makes his pillow of my knee
    The livelong night.
Strike I my lute, he tunes the
    string,
He musicke playes if so I sing,
He lends me every lovely thing;
Yet cruell he my heart doth sting.
    Whist wanton, still ye.

Else I with Roses every day
    Will whip you hence:
And binde you when you long to
    play,
    For your offence.
Ile shut mine eyes to keep you in,
Ile make you fast it for your sinne,
Ile count your power not worth a
    pinne
And what hereby shall I winne,
    If he gainsay me?

What if I beate the wanton boy
    With many a rod?
He wil repay me with annoy,
    Because a God.
Then sit thou safely on my knee,
And let thy bower my bosome be;
Lurke in mine eies, I like of thee.
O *Cupid* so thou pittie me,
    Spare not but play thee.

MONTANUS' SONNET

Phoebe sate,
Sweet she sate,
Sweet sate Phoebe when I saw her,
White her brow,
Coy her eye;
Brow and eye, how much you please me!
Words I spent,
Sighs I sent,
Sighs and words could never draw her,
Oh my Love,
Thou art lost,
Since no sight could ever ease thee.

Phoebe sat
By a Fount,
Sitting by a Fount I spide her,
Sweet her touch,
Rare her voyce:
Touch and voice, what may distaine you?
As she sung,
I did sigh,
And by sighs whilst that I tride her,
Oh mine eyes
You did lose,
Her first sight whose want did pain you.

Phoebes flockes,
White as wooll,
Yet were Phoebes locks more whiter.
Phoebes eyes,
Dovelike mild,
Dovelike eyes, both mild and cruell.
Montan sweares,
In your lampes
He will die for to delight her,
Phoebe yeeld,
Or I die:
Shall true hearts be fancies fuell?

Thomas Nashe

1567-1601

From SUMMER'S LAST WILL AND TESTAMENT

ADIEU, FAREWELL EARTHS BLISSE

Adieu, farewell earths blisse,
This world uncertaine is,
Fond are lifes lustfull joyes,
Death proves them all but toyes,
None from his darts can flye;
I am sick, I must dye:
  Lord, have mercy on us.

Rich men, trust not in wealth,
Gold cannot buy you health;

Phisick himselfe must fade.
All things to end are made,
The plague full swift goes bye;
I am sick, I must dye:
  Lord, have mercy on us.

Beauty is but a flowre,
Which wrinckles will devoure,
Brightnesse falls from the ayre,
Queenes have died yong and faire,

Dust hath closde *Helens* eye.
I am sick, I must dye:
  Lord, have mercy on us.

Strength stoopes unto the grave,
Wormes feed on *Hector* brave,
Swords may not fight with fate,
Earth still holds ope her gate.
Come, come, the bells do crye.
I am sick, I must dye:
  Lord, have mercy on us.

Wit with his wantonesse
Tasteth deaths bitternesse:

Hells executioner
Hath no eares for to heare
What vaine art can reply.
I am sick, I must dye:
  Lord, have mercy on us.

Haste therefore eche degree,
To welcome destiny:
Heaven is our heritage,
Earth but a players stage,
Mount wee unto the sky.
I am sick, I must dye:
  Lord, have mercy on us.

SPRING

Spring, the sweet spring, is the year's pleasant king;
Then blooms each thing, then maids dance in a ring,
Cold doth not sting, the pretty birds do sing —
  Cuckoo, jug-jug, pu-we, to-witta-woo!

The palm and may make country houses gay,
Lambs frisk and play, the shepherds pipe all day,
And we hear aye birds tune this merry lay —
  Cuckoo, jug-jug, pu-we, to-witta-woo!

The fields breathe sweet, the daisies kiss our feet,
Young lovers meet, old wives a-sunning sit,
In every street these tunes our ears do greet —
  Cuckoo, jug-jug, pu-we, to-witta-woo!
    Spring, the sweet Spring!

Thomas Dekker
1570?-1632?

From THE PLEASANT COMEDIE OF OLD FORTUNATUS

FORTUNE SMILES

Fortune smiles, cry holyday.
  Dimples on her cheekes doe dwell,
Fortune frownes, cry welladay,
  Her love is heaven, her hate is hell:
Since heaven and hell obey her power,
Tremble when her eyes doe lowre,
Since heaven and hell her power obey,
When shee smiles, crie holy day.
  Holy-day with joy we cry
  And bend, and bend, and merily
  Sing Hymnes to Fortunes deitie,
  Sing Hymnes to Fortunes deitie.

ALL. Let us sing merrily, merrily, merrily,
    With our Song let heaven resound,
    Fortunes hands our heads have crown'd,
  Let us sing merrily, merrily, merrily.

O PITTIE

Vertues braunches wither, Vertue pines,
O pittie, pittie, and alacke the time,
Vice doth flourish, Vice in glorie shines,
Her gilded boughes above the Cedar clime.
Vice hath golden cheekes, O pittie, pittie,
She in every land doth monarchize.

Vertue is exilde from every Cittie,
Vertue is a foole, Vice onely wise.
O pittie, pittie, Vertue weeping dies.
Vice laughs to see her faint (alacke the time)
This sinckes: with painted wings the other flies,
Alacke that best should fall, and bad should clime,
O pittie, pittie, pittie, mourne, not sing,
Vice is a Saint, Vertue an Underling.
Vice doth flourish, Vice in glorie shines,
Vertues braunches wither, Vertue pines.

From THE PLEASANT COMEDIE OF PATIENT GRISSILL

O SWEET CONTENT

Art thou poore yet hast thou golden Slumbers?
  O sweet content!
Art thou rich yet in thy mind perplexed?
  O punnishment.
Dost thou laugh to see how fooles are vexed?
To ad to golden numbers, golden numbers.
  O sweet content, O sweet content.

Work apace, apace, apace, apace:
Honest labour beares a lovely face,
Then hey noney, noney: hey noney, noney.

Canst drinke the waters of the Crisped spring,
  O sweet content!
Swim'st thou in wealth, yet sinck'st in thine owne teares,
  O punnishment.
Then hee that patiently want's burden beares,
No burden beares, but is a King, a King.
  O sweet content, O sweet content.

Work apace, apace, apace, apace:
Honest labour beares a lovely face,
Then hey noney, noney: hey noney, noney.

Sir John Davies
1569-1626

From ORCHESTRA

Dauncing (bright Lady) then began to bee,
 When the first seeds whereof the World did spring,
The fire, ayre, earth, and water — did agree,
 By Love's perswasion, — Nature's mighty King, —
 To leave their first disordred combating;
And in a daunce such measure to observe,
As all the world their motion should preserve.

Since when, they still are carried in a round,
  And changing, come one in another's place;
Yet doe they neither mingle nor confound,
  But every one doth keepe the bounded space
  Wherein the Daunce doth bid it turne or trace;
This wondrous myracle did Love devise,
For Dauncing is Love's proper exercise.

Michael Drayton
1563-1631

Saintsbury * said of Drayton: "The Sonnet chose to take him from the second or third even to the seventh heaven of poetry, and let him see and say such things as no one else but Shakespeare ever saw or said."

No poet has more variety — from the tragic magnificence of *Since ther's no helpe* to the quite different strength and control of *To the Virginian Voyage,* a strength and control that is due, in part, to its strongly stopped line ends, all of which seem to take in a fresh breath of air before beginning the next line. There are only two alterations in the strong rhythm (in both cases these are weaknesses): in the slightly flaccid "Quickly aboord bestow you . . . As the winds that blow you," and in the rather inferior fourth verse.

Then there is the very different *Song to Sirena.* In this the poet seems, by his magic, to have changed the waters of the "Silver Trent" into those for which Chloris sighed in the *Fourth Nimphall* — wishing:

  That all the pearle, the seas, or Indias have
  Were well dissolv'd, and thereof made a lake
  Thou there in bathing, and I by to take
  Pleasure to see thee clearer than the wave.

And from this, we move again to the unsurpassable sunny sweetness of the lines beginning thus: "With full-leav'd Lillies I will stick," in which the summer lights seem bees "From lillies gathering honey there," and in which Drayton himself seems to have changed into a bee.

* *The History of English Prosody.*

TO THE VIRGINIAN VOYAGE

You brave Heroique Minds,
  Worthy your Countries Name,
    That Honour still pursue,
    Goe, and subdue,
Whilst loyt'ring Hinds
  Lurke here at home, with shame.

Britans, you stay too long,
  Quickly aboord bestow you,
    And with a merry Gale
    Swell your stretch'd Sayle,
With Vowes as strong,
  As the Winds that blow you.

Your Course securely steere,
  West and by South forth keepe,
    Rocks, Lee-shores, nor Sholes,
    When *Eolus* scowles,
You need not feare,
  So absolute the Deepe.

And cheerefully at Sea,
  Successe you still intice,
    To get the Pearle and Gold,
    And ours to hold,
Virginia,
  Earth's onely Paradise.

Where Nature hath in store
  Fowle, Venison, and Fish,
    And the fruitfull'st Soyle,
    Without your Toyle,
Three Harvests more,
  All greater then your wish.

And the ambitious Vine
  Crownes with his purple Masse,
    The Cedar reaching hie
    To kisse the Sky,
The Cypresse, Pine
  And use-full Sassafras.

To whose, the golden Age
  Still Natures lawes doth give,
    No other Cares that tend,
    But Them to defend
From Winters age,
  That long there doth not live.

When as the Lushious smell
  Of that delicious Land,
    Above the Seas that flowes,
    The cleere Wind throwes,
Your Hearts to swell
  Approaching the deare Strand.

In kenning of the Shore
  (Thanks to God first given,)
    O you the happy'st men,
    Be Frolike then,
Let Cannons roare,
  Frighting the wide Heaven.

And in Regions farre
  Such *Heroes* bring yee foorth,
    As those from whom We came,
    And plant Our name,
Under that Starre
  Not knowne unto our North.

And as there Plenty growes
  Of Lawrell every where,
    Apollo's Sacred tree,
    You it may see,
A Poets Browes
  To crowne, that may sing there.

Thy Voyage attend,
  Industrious *Hackluit,*
    Whose Reading shall inflame
    Men to seeke Fame,
And much commend
  To after-Times thy Wit.

TO THE NEW YEERE

Rich Statue, double-faced,
With Marble Temples graced,
  To rayse thy God-head hyer,
In flames where Altars shining,
Before thy Priests divining,
  Doe od'rous Fumes expire.

Great *Janus,* I thy pleasure,
With all the *Thespian* Treasure,
  Doe seriously pursue;
To th' passed yeere returning,
As though the old adjourning,
  Yet bringing in the new.

Thy ancient Vigils yeerely,
I have observed cleerely,
  Thy Feasts yet smoaking bee;
Since all thy store abroad is,
Give something to my Goddesse,
  As hath been us'd by thee.

Give her th' *Eoan* brightnesse,
Wing'd with that subtill lightnesse,
  That doth trans-pierce the Ayre;
The Roses of the Morning
The rising Heav'n adorning,
  To mesh with flames of Hayre.

Those ceaselesse Sounds, above all,
Made by those Orbes that move all,
  And ever swelling there,
Wrap'd up in Numbers flowing,
Them actually bestowing,
  For Jewels at her Eare.

O Rapture great and holy,
Doe thou transport me wholly,
  So well her forme to vary,
That I aloft may beare her,
Whereas I will insphere her
  In Regions high and starry.

And in my choise Composures,
The soft and easie Closures,
  So amorously shall meet;
That ev'ry lively Ceasure
Shall tread a perfect Measure,
  Set on so equall feet.

That Spray to fame so fertle,
The Lover-crowning Mirtle,
  In Wreaths of mixed Boughes
Within whose shades are dwelling
Those Beauties most excelling,
  Inthron'd upon her Browes.

Those Paralels so even,
Drawne on the face of Heaven,
  That curious Art supposes,
Direct those Gems, whose
    cleerenesse
Farre off amaze by neerenesse,
  Each Globe such fire incloses.

Her Bosome full of Blisses,
By nature made for Kisses,
  So pure and wond'rous cleere,
Whereas a thousand Graces
Behold their lovely Faces,
  As they are bathing there.

O, thou selfe-little blindnesse,
The kindnesse of unkindnesse,
  Yet one of those divine;
Thy Brands to me were lever,
Thy Fascia, and thy Quiver,
  And thou this Quill of mine.

This Heart so freshly bleeding,
Upon it owne selfe feeding,
  Whose wounds still dropping be;
O Love, thy selfe confounding,
Her coldnesse so abounding,
  And yet such heat in me.

ceasure] caesura

Yet if I be inspired,
Ile leave thee so admired,
   To all that shall succeed,
That were they more then many,
'Mongst all, there is not any,
   That Time so oft shall reed.

Nor Adamant ingraved,
That hath been choisely'st saved,
   Idea's Name out-weares;
So large a Dower as this is,
The greatest often misses,
   The Diadem that beares.

TO HIS VALENTINE

Muse, bid the Morne awake,
   Sad Winter now declines,
Each Bird doth chuse a Make,
   This day's Saint *Valentines;*
For that good Bishops sake
      Get up, and let us see,
      What Beautie it shall bee,
   That Fortune us assignes.

But lo, in happy How'r,
   The place wherein she lyes,
In yonder climbing Tow'r,
   Gilt by the glitt'ring Rise;
O *Jove!* that in a Show'r,
      As once that Thund'rer did,
      When he in drops lay hid,
   That I could her surprize.

Her Canopie Ile draw,
   With spangled Plumes bedight,
No Mortall ever saw
   So ravishing a sight;
That it the Gods might awe,
      And pow'rfully trans-pierce
      The Globie Universe,
   Out-shooting ev'ry Light.

My Lips Ile softly lay
   Upon her heav'nly Cheeke,
Dy'd like the dawning Day,
   As polish'd Ivorie sleeke:
And in her Eare Ile say:
      O, thou bright Morning-Starre,
      'Tis I that come so farre,
   My Valentine to seeke.

Each little Bird, this Tyde,
   Doth chuse her loved Pheere,
Which constantly abide
   In Wedlock all the yeere,
As Nature is their Guide:
      So may we two be true,
      This yeere, nor change for new,
   As Turtles coupled were.

The Sparrow, Swan, the Dove,
   Though *Venus* Birds they be,
Yet are they not for Love
   So absolute as we:
For Reason us doth move;
      They but by billing woo:
      Then try what we can doo,
   To whom each sense is free.

Which we have more than they,
   By livelyer Organs sway'd,
Our Appetite each way
   More by our Sense obay'd:
Our Passions to display,
      This Season us doth fit;
      Then let us follow it,
   As Nature us doth lead.

One Kiss in two let's breake,
   Confounded with the touch,
But halfe words let us speake,
   Our Lip's imploy'd so much;
Untill we both grow weake,
      With sweetnesse of thy breath;
      O smother me to death:
   Long let our Joyes be such.

make] mate.   phcere] fere, mate.

Let's laugh at them that chuse
  Their Valentines by lot,
To weare their Names that use,
  Whom idly they have got:

Such poore choise we refuse,
  Saint *Valentine* befriend;
  We thus this Morne may spend,
  Else Muse, awake her not.

From POLY–OLBION

SONG XX

Now are the *Tritons* heard, to *Loving-land* to call,
Which *Neptunes* great commaunds, before them bravely beare,
Commanding all the Nymphs of high account that were. . . .

These Nymphs trick'd up in tyers, the Sea-gods to delight:
Of Corrall of each kind, the blacke, the red, the white;
With many sundry shels, the Scallop large, and faire;
The Cockle small and round, the Periwinkle spare,
The Oyster, wherein oft the pearle is found to breed,
The Mussell, which retaines that daintie Orient seed:
In Chaines and Bracelets made, with linkes of sundry twists,
Some worne about their wasts, their necks, some on the wrists.
Great store of Amber there, and Jet they did not misse;
Their lips they sweetned had with costly Ambergris. . . .

Now thus together com'n, they friendly doe devise,
Some of light toyes, and some of matters grave and wise.
But to breake off their speech, her reed when *Syrinx* sounds,
Some cast themselves in Rings, and fell to Hornepipe rounds:
They ceasing, as againe to others turnes it falls,
They lustie Galiards tread, some others Jiggs, and Braules.
This done, upon the banke together being set,
Proceeding in the cause, for which they thus were met,
In mightie *Neptunes* praise, these Sea-borne Virgins sing:
Let earth, and ayre, say they, with the high praises ring. . . .

Where is there one to him that may compared be,
That both the Poles at once continually doth see;
And Gyant-like with heaven as often maketh warres;
The Ilands (in his power) as numberlesse as Starres,
He washeth at his will, and with his mightie hands,
He makes the even shores, oft mountainous with Sands:
Whose creatures, which observe his wide Emperiall seat,
Like his immeasured selfe, are infinite and great.
  Thus ended they their Song, and off th' assembly brake.

      tyers] attires.   braule] branle (a French dance).

From THE SECOND NIMPHALL

LALUS. With full-leav'd Lillies I will stick
    Thy braded hayre all o'r so thick,
    That from it a Light shall throw
    Like the Sunnes upon the Snow.
    Thy Mantle shall be Violet Leaves,
    With the fin'st the Silkeworme weaves
    As finely Woven; whose rich smell
    The Ayre about thee so shall swell
    That it shall have no power to moove.
    A Ruffe of Pinkes thy Robe above
    About thy necke so neatly set
    That Art it cannot counterfet,
    Which still shall looke so Fresh and new,
    As if upon their Roots they grew:
    And for thy head Ile have a Tyer
    Of netting, made of Strawbery wyer,
    And in each knot that doth compose
    A Mesh, shall stick a halfe-blowne Rose,
    Red, damaske, white, in order set
    About the sides, shall run a Fret
    Of Primroses, the Tyer throughout
    With Thrift and Daysies fringd about;
    All this, faire Nimph, Ile doe for thee,
    So thou'lt leave him and goe with me.

From THE THIRD ECLOGUE

ROWLAND. Stay, *Thames,* to heare my Song, thou great and
        famous Flood,
Beta alone the *Phoenix* is of all thy watry Brood,
    The Queene of Virgins onely Shee,
    The King of Floods allotting Thee
Of all the rest, be joyfull then to see this happy Day,
Thy *Beta* now alone shall be the Subject of my Lay.

With daintie and delightsome straynes of dapper Verilayes:
Come lovely Shepheards, sit by me, to tell our *Beta's* prayse,
    And let us sing so high a Verse,
    Her soveraigne Vertues to rehearse:
That little Birds shall silent sit to heare us Shepheards sing,
Whilst Rivers backward bend their course, and flow up to
        their spring.

Range all thy Swans, faire *Thames,* together on a ranke,
And place them each in their degree upon thy winding Banke,
  And let them set together all,
  Time keeping with the Waters fall:
And crave the tunefull *Nightingale* to helpe them with her
   Lay,
The *Woosell* and the *Throstle-Cocke,* chief musike of our May.

See what a troupe of Nymphs, come leading Hand in Hand,
In such a number that well-neere they take up all the Strand:
  And harke how merrily they sing,
  That makes the Neigh'bring Meddowes ring,
And *Beta* comes before alone, clad in a purple Pall,
And as the Queene of all the rest doth weare a Coronall.

Trim up her golden Tresses with *Apollo's* sacred Tree,
Whose Tutage and especiall care I wish her still to bee,
  That for his Darling hath prepar'd,
  A glorious Crowne as her reward,
Not such a golden Crowne as haughtie *Caesar* weares,
But such a glittering starry one as *Ariadne* beares.

Mayds, get the choycest Flowres, a Garland and entwine,
Nor Pinks nor Pansies let there want, be sure of Eglantine,
  See that there be store of Lillyes,
  (Call'd of Shepheards Daffadillyes)
With Roses Damaske, White, and Red, the dearest Flower-de-
   lice,
The Cowslip of *Jerusalem,* and Clove of *Paradise.*

O thou great Eye of Heaven, the Dayes most dearest Light,
With thy bright Sister *Cynthia,* the Glorie of the Night,
  And those that make yee seven,
  To us the neer'st of Heaven,
And thou, O gorgeous *Iris,* with all thy Colour dy'd,
When shee streames forth her Rayes, then dasht is all your
   pride.

In thee, whilst shee beholds (O Flood) her heavenly Face,
The Sea-Gods in their watry Armes would gladly her imbrace,
  The intising *Syrens* in their layes,
  And *Tritons* doe resound her prayse,
Hasting with all the speed they can unto the spacious Sea,
And through all *Neptunes* Court proclaim our *Beta's* holyday.

O evermore refresh the Roote of the fat Olive Tree,
In whose sweet shaddow ever may thy Banks preserved bee.
    With Bayes that Poets doe adorne,
    And Mirtles of chaste Lovers worne,
That faire may be the Fruit, the Boughes preserv'd by peace,
And let the mournefull Cypres die, and here for ever cease.

Weele strew the Shore with Pearle, where *Beta* walks alone,
And we will pave her Summer Bower with the rich *Indian*
        stone,
    Perfume the Ayre and make it sweet,
    For such a Goddesse as is meet,
For it her Eyes for purity contend with *Titans* Light,
No marvaile then although their Beames doe dazle humane
        sight.

Sound lowde your Trumpets then from *Londons* loftiest
        Towers,
To beate the stormie Tempests back, and calme the raging
        Showers,
    Set the Cornet with the Flute,
    The Orpharion to the Lute,
Tuning the Taber and the Pipe to the sweet Violons,
And mocke the Thunder in the Ayre with the lowd Clarions.

Beta, long may thine Altars smoke with yeerely Sacrifice,
And long thy sacred Temples may their high Dayes solemnize,
    Thy Shepheards watch by Day and Night,
    Thy Mayds attend thy holy Light,
And thy large Empire stretch her Armes from East in to the
        West,
And *Albion* on the *Appenines* advance her conquering Crest.

From THE SHEPHEARDS SIRENA

SONG TO SIRENA

Neare to the Silver *Trent,*
  Sirena dwelleth:
She to whom Nature lent
  All that excelleth:
By which the *Muses* late,
  And the neate *Graces,*
Have for their greater state
  Taken their places:
Twisting an *Anadem,*

Wherewith to Crowne
  her,
As it belong'd to them
  Most to renowne her.
  On thy Bancke,
  In a Rancke,
Let thy Swanes sing her,
  And with their Musick,
Along let them bring her.

Tagus and *Pactolus*
  Are to thee Debter,
Nor for their gold to us
  Are they the better:
Henceforth of all the rest,
  Be thou the River,
Which as the daintiest,
  Puts them downe ever,
For as my precious one,
  O'r thee doth travell,
She to Pearle Parragon
  Turneth thy gravell.
    On thy Bancke, etc.

Our mournefull *Philomell,*
  That rarest Turner,
Henceforth in *Aperill*
  Shall wake the sooner,
And to her shall complaine
  From the thicke Cover,
Redoubling every straine
  Over and over:
For when my Love too long
  Her Chamber keepeth;
As though it suffered wrong,
  The Morning weepeth.

Oft have I seene the Sunne,
  To doe her honour,
Fix himselfe at his noone,
  To looke upon her,
And hath gilt every Grove,
  Every Hill neare her,
With his flames from above,
  Striving to cheere her,
And when shee from his sight
  Hath her selfe turned,
He as it had beene night,
  In Cloudes hath mourned.

The Verdant Meades are seene,
  When she doth view them,
In fresh and gallant Greene,
  Straight to renewe them,
And every little Grasse
  Broad it selfe spreadeth,

Proud that this bonny Lasse
  Upon it treadeth:
Nor flower is so sweete
  In this large Cincture
But it upon her feete
  Leaveth some Tincture.

The Fishes in the Flood,
  When she doth Angle,
For the Hooke strive a good
  Them to intangle;
And leaping on the Land
  From the cleare water,
Their Scales upon the sand
  Lavishly scatter;
Therewith to pave the mould
  Whereon she passes,
So her selfe to behold,
  As in her glasses.

When shee lookes out by night,
  The Starres stand gazing,
Like Commets to our sight
  Fearefully blazing,
As wondring at her eyes,
  With their much brightnesse,
Which so amaze the skies,
  Dimming their lightnesse,
The raging Tempests are Calme,
  When shee speaketh,
Such most delightsome balme,
  From her lips breaketh.

In all our *Brittany,*
  Ther's not a fayrer,
Nor can you fitt any:
  Should you compare her.
Angels her eye-lids keepe
  All hearts surprizing,
Which looke whilst she doth sleepe
  Like the Sunnes rising:
She alone of her kinde
  Knoweth true measure,
And her unmatched mind
  Is Heavens treasure.

a good] heartily.

Fayre *Dove* and *Darwine* cleare
  Boast yee your beauties,
To *Trent* your Mistres here
  Yet pay your duties,
My Love was higher borne
  Tow'rds the full Fountaines,
Yet she doth *Moorland* scorne,
  And the *Peake* Mountaines;
Nor would she none should dreame,
  Where she abideth,
Humble as is the streame,
  Which by her slydeth.

Yet my poore Rusticke *Muse*,
  Nothing can move her,

Nor the meanes I can use,
  Though her true Lover:
Many a long Winters night
  Have I wak'd for her,
Yet this my piteous plight,
  Nothing can stirre her.
All thy Sands silver *Trent*
  Downe to the *Humber,*
The sighes that I have spent
  Never can number.
    On thy Bancke,
    In a Rancke,
  Let thy Swanes sing her,
    And with their Musick,
  Along let them bring her.

From IDEA

SONNET LXI

Since ther's no helpe, Come let us kisse and part,
Nay, I have done: You get no more of Me,
And I am glad, yea glad withall my heart,
That thus so cleanly, I my Selfe can free,
Shake hands for ever, Cancell all our Vowes,
And when We meet at any time againe,
Be it not seene in either of our Browes,
That We one jot of former Love reteyne;
Now at the last gaspe, of Loves latest Breath,
When his Pulse fayling, Passion speechlesse lies,
When Faith is kneeling by his bed of Death,
And Innocence is closing up his Eyes,
  Now if thou would'st, when all have given him over,
  From Death to Life thou might'st him yet recover.

SOE WELL I LOVE THEE
These verses were made by Michael Drayton Esquier
Poett Laureatt the night before hee dyed

Soe well I love thee, as without thee I
Love Nothing; if I might Chuse, I'de rather dye
Than bee one day debarde thy companye.

Since Beasts, and plantes doe growe, and live and move,
Beastes are those men, that such a life approve:
Hee onlye Lives, that Deadly is in Love.

The Corne that in the grownd is sowen first dies
And of one seed doe manye Eares arise:
Love, this worldes Corne, by dying Multiplies.

The seeds of Love first by thy eyes were throwne
Into a grownd untild, a hearte unknowne
To beare such fruitt, tyll by thy hands t'was sowen.

Looke as your Looking glass by Chance may fall
Devyde and breake in manye peyces smale
And yett shewes forth, the selfe same face in all;

Proportions, Features, Graces just the same,
And in the smalest peyce as well the name
Of Fayrest one deserves, as in the richest frame.

Soe all my Thoughts are peyces but of you
Whiche put together makes a Glasse soe true
As I therin noe others face but yours can Viewe.

John Lyly
1553-1606

From ALEXANDER AND CAMPASPE

CUPID AND CAMPASPE

Cupid and my Campaspe playd
At cardes for kisses; Cupid payd:
He stakes his quiver, bow and arrows,
His mothers doves, and teame of sparrows;
Loses them too; then down he throws
The coral of his lippe, the rose
Growing on's cheek (but none knows how);
With these, the crystal of his browe,
And then the dimple of his chinne;
All these did my Campaspe winne.

At last he set her both his eyes:
She won, and Cupid blind did rise.
O Love! has she done this to thee?
What shall, alas! become of mee?

From MYDAS

PAN'S SONG

Pan's Syrinx was a girle indeed,
Though now shee's turn'd into a reed,
From that deare reed Pan's pipe does come,
A pipe that strikes *Apollo* dumbe;
Nor flute, nor lute, nor gitterne can,
So chant it, as the pipe of *Pan;*
Cross-gartred swaines, and dairie girles,
With faces smug, and round as pearles,
When *Pan's* shrill pipe begins to play,
With dancing weare out night and day:
The bag-pipes drone his hum layes by,
When *Pan* sounds up his minstrelsie,
His minstrelsie! O base! This quill
Which at my mouth with winde I fill,
Puts me in minde though her I misse,
That still my *Syrinx* lips I kisse.

smug] fresh, neat.

SONG TO APOLLO

Sing to *Apollo,* god of day,
Whose golden beames with morning play,
And make her eyes so brightly shine
Aurora's face is call'd divine.
Sing to *Phœbus,* and that throne
Of diamonds which he sits upon;
  Iö! pæans let us sing,
  To physicke's, and to poesie's king.

Crowne all his altars with bright fire,
Laurels bind about his lyre,
A *Daphnean* coronet for his head,
The Muses dance about his bed;
When on his ravishing lute he playes,
Strew his temple round with bayes.
  Iö! pæans let us sing,
  To the glittering *Delian* king.

Thomas Watson

1557?-1592

THE MARIGOLD SO LIKES THE LOVELY SUNNE

The Marigold so likes the lovely Sunne,
　That when he settes the other hides her face,
And when he ginnes his morning course to runne,
　She spreads abroad, and showes her greatest grace;
So shuts or sprouts my joy, as doth this flow're,
When my She sunne doth either laugh or lowre.

When she departs my sight, I die for paine,
　In closing up my heart with cloudie care;
And yet when once I view her face againe,
　I streight revive and joye my wonted fare.
Therewith my heart ofte saies, when all is done,
That heav'n and earth have not a brighter sunne.

Tobias Hume

d. 1645

FAIN WOULD I CHANGE THAT NOTE

Fain would I change that note,
　To which fond Love hath
　　charmd me,
Long, long to sing by rote
　Fancying that that harmd me.
Yet when this thought doth come,
Love is the perfect summe
　Of all delight;
I have no other choice
Either for pen or voyce
　To sing or write.

O Love, they wrong thee
　much
　That say thy sweete is bitter;
When thy ripe fruit is such
　As nothing can be sweeter.
Faire house of joy and blisse,
Where truest pleasure is,
　I doe adore thee:
I know thee what thou art,
I serve thee with my heart
　And fall before thee.

Anonymous Songs, Airs and Madrigals

DEARE, IF YOU CHANGE

Deare, if you change, Ile never chuse againe,
    Sweete, if you shrinke, Ile never think of love;
Fayre, if you faile, Ile judge all beauty vaine,
    Wise, if too weake, my wits Ile never prove.
Deare, sweete, fayre, wise; change, shrinke nor be not weake,
And on my faith, my faith shall never breake.

Earth with her flowers shall sooner heav'n adorne,
    Heaven her bright stars through earths dim globe shall move,
Fire heate shall lose and frosts of flames be borne,
    Ayre made to shine as blacke as hell shall prove:
Earth, heaven, fire, ayre, the world transform'd shall view,
E're I prove false to faith, or strange to you.

LACHRIMAE

Flowe, my teares! falle from your springes;
    Exiled for ever, let me mourne
Where Night's blacke birde her sadde infamie singes,
    There, let me live forlorne:
Never maye my woes be relieved, since Pitie is fled;
And teares, and sighes, and groanes, my Wearie Dayes, of all
        Joyes have deprived.

Downe vaine Lightes, shine you no more,
    No Nightes are darke enough for those
That in Despair, their last fortunes deplore.
    Light dothe but Shame disclose:
From the highest spire of Contentment, my Fortune is thrown;
And Feare, and Griefe, and Pain, for my deserts, are my hopes,
        since Hope is gone.

Hark, you Shaddowes! that in Darkenesse dwelle,
    Learn to contemne Light:
Happy! happy they, that in hell,
    Feel not the world's despite.

WEEPE YOU NO MORE, SAD FOUNTAINES

Weepe you no more, sad fountaines,
 What need you flowe so fast?
Looke how the snowie mountaines,
 Heav'ns sunne doth gently waste.
But my sunnes heav'nly eyes
 View not your weeping,
 That nowe lies sleeping:
Softly, now softly lies sleeping.

Sleepe is a reconciling,
 A rest that peace begets:
Doth not the sunne rise smiling,
 When faire at ev'n he sets?
Rest you, then rest sad eyes,
 Melt not in weeping,
 While she lies sleeping:
Softly, now softly lies sleeping.

THE SILVER SWANNE, WHO LIVING HAD NO NOTE

The silver Swanne, who living had no Note,
 When death approacht unlockt her silent throat,
Leaning her breast against the reedie shore,
 Thus sung her first and last, and sung no more:
Farewell all joyes, O death come close mine eyes,
More Geese than Swannes now live, more fooles than wise.

WEEPE O MINE EYES

Weepe O mine eyes,
Weepe O mine eyes, and cease not;
(Alas) these your spring-tides,
Me-thinkes increase not.
O when begin you,
To swell so high that I may drowne me in you?
O when begin you,
To swell so high, that I may drowne me in you?
That I may drowne me in you?

A HA HA HA! THIS WORLD DOTH PASSE

A ha ha ha! this world doth passe,
 Most merily, most merily Ile bee sworne,
For many an honest Indian Asse
 Goes for a unicorne.
  Farra diddle diddle dyno,
  This is idle idle fyno.

Tygh hygh, tygh hygh! O sweet delight,
  He tickles this age that can
Call Tulliæ's Ape a Marmasyte,
  And Ledæ's Goose a swan.
    Farra diddle diddle dyno,
    This is idle idle fyno.

So so so so! fine English dayes,
  For false play is no reproch,
For that he doth the Cochman prayse,
  May safely use the Coch.
    Farra diddle diddle dyno,
    This is idle idle fyno.

BROWN IS MY LOVE, BUT GRACEFULL

Brown is my Love, but gracefull;
And each renowned whiteness
Matched with thy lovely brown loseth its brightnes.

Faire is my love, but scornful;
Yet have I seene despised
Daintie white Lillies, and sad Flowers well prized.

ON A ROSEBUD SENT TO HER LOVER

The tender bud within itselfe doth close
With secret sweetnesse till it prove a Rose;
And then as fit for profit as for pleasure
Yields sweet Contente to him that gaines the treasure:
  So she that sent this, yet a bud unblowne,
  In time may prove a Rose, and be your owne.

Samuel Daniel
1562-1619

From TETHYS FESTIVAL

ARE THEY SHADOWES THAT WE SEE

Are they shadowes that we see?
   And can shadowes pleasure give?
Pleasures onely shadowes bee
   Cast by bodies we conceive,
And are made the thinges we deeme,
In those figures which they seeme.

But these pleasures vanish fast
   Which by shadowes are exprest:
Pleasures are not, if they last:
   In their passing, is their best.
Glory is most bright and gay
In a flash, and so away.

Feed apace then greedy eyes
   On the wonder you behold.
Take it sodaine as it flies
   Though you take it not to hold:
When your eyes have done their part,
Thought must length it in the heart.

From HYMEN'S TRIUMPH

HAD SORROW EVER FITTER PLACE

Had sorrow ever fitter place
   To act his part,
   Than is my heart,
Where it takes up all the space?
   Where is no veine
   To entertaine
A thought that weares another face.

Nor will I sorrow ever have,
   Therein to be,
   But onely thee,
To whom I full possession gave:
   Thou in my name
   Must holde the same,
Untill thou bring it to the grave.

LOVE IS A SICKNESSE FULL OF WOES

Love is a sicknesse full of woes,
  All remedies refusing:
A plant that with most cutting
    growes,
  Most barren with best using.
    Why so?
More we enjoy it, more it dyes,
If not enjoy'd, it sighing cries,
    Hey ho.

Love is a torment of the minde,
  A tempest everlasting;
And Jove hath made it of a
    kinde,
  Not well, nor full nor fasting.
    Why so?
More we enjoy it, more it dies,
If not enjoy'd, it sighing cries,
    Hey ho.

From DELIA

LOOKE DELIA HOW WEE 'STEEME THE HALF–BLOWNE ROSE

Looke *Delia* how wee 'steeme the half-blowne Rose,
The image of thy blush and Summers honor:
Whilst in her tender greene she doth inclose
That pure sweete beautie, Time bestowes uppon her.
No sooner spreades her glorie in the ayre,
But straight her ful-blowne pride is in declyning;
She then is scorn'd that late adorn'd the fayre:
So clowdes thy beautie, after fayrest shining.
No Aprill can revive thy withred flowers,
Whose blooming grace adornes thy glorie now:
Swift speedy Time, feathred with flying howers,
Dissolves the beautie of the fairest brow.
   O let not then such riches waste in vaine;
   But love whilst that thou maist be lov'd againe.

BUT LOVE WHILST THAT THOU MAIST BE LOV'D AGAINE

But love whilst that thou maist be lov'd againe,
Now whilst thy May hath fill'd thy lappe with flowers;
Now whilst thy beautie beares without a staine;
Now use thy Summer smiles ere Winter lowres.
And whilst thou spread'st unto the rysing sunne,
The fairest flowre that ever sawe the light:
Now joye thy time before thy sweete be dunne,
And *Delia,* thinke thy morning must have night.

And that thy brightnes sets at length to West:
When thou wilt close up that which now thou showest:
And thinke the same becomes thy fading best,
Which then shall hide it most, and cover lowest.
    Men doe not weigh the stalke for that it was,
    When once they finde her flowre, her glory passe.

MY CARES DRAW ON MINE EVERLASTING NIGHT

My cares draw on mine everlasting night,
In horrors sable clowdes sets my lives sunne:
My lives sweet sunne, my deerest comforts light,
Will rise no more to me, whose day is dunne.
I goe before unto the Mirtle shades,
To attend the presence of my worlds Deere:
And there prepare her flowres that never fades,
And all things fit against her comming there.
If any aske me why so soone I came,
Ile hide her sinne, and say it was my lot,
In life and death Ile tender her good name,
My life nor death shall never be her blot.
    Although this world may seeme her deede to blame:
    Th' *Elisean* ghosts shall never know the same.

TIME, CRUELL TIME, COME AND SUBDUE THAT BROW

Time, cruell time, come and subdue that Brow
Which conquers all but thee, and thee too staies
As if she were exempt from Syeth or Bow,
From love or yeares unsubject to decaies.
Or art thou growne in league with those faire eies
That they may helpe thee to consume our daies?
Or dost thou spare her for her cruelties,
Being merciles like thee that no man weies?
And yet thou seest thy powre she disobaies,
Cares not for thee, but lets thee waste in vaine,
And prodigall of howers and yeares betraies
Beauty and youth t' opinion and disdaine.
    Yet spare her Time, let her exempted be,
    She may become more kinde to thee or me.

CARE-CHARMER SLEEPE, SONNE OF THE SABLE NIGHT

Care-charmer Sleepe, sonne of the sable night,
Brother to death, in silent darknes borne:
Relieve my languish, and restore the light,
With darke forgetting of my cares returne.
And let the day be time enough to mourne
The shipwracke of my ill-adventred youth:
Let waking eyes suffice to 'waile their scorne,
Without the torment of the nights untruth.
Cease dreames, the Images of day desires,
To modell foorth the passions of the morrow:
Never let rising Sunne approve you liers,
To adde more griefe to aggravate my sorrow.
   Still let me sleepe, imbracing clowdes in vaine;
   And never wake to feele the dayes disdayne.

Lord Herbert of Cherbury
1583-1648

INNUMERABLE BEAUTIES

Innumerable Beauties, thou white haire
Spredde forth like to a Region of the Aire,
  Curld like a sea, and like Ethereall fire
  Dost from thy vitall principles aspire
To bee the highest Element of faire,
  From thy proud heights, thou so commandst desire
That when it would presume, it grows, dispare,
  And from it selfe a Vengeance, doth require,
While absolute in that thy brave command
  Knittinge each haire, into an awfull frowne
Like to an Hoste of Lightninges, thou dost stand
  To ruine all that fall not prostrate doune
  While to the humble like a beamy Croune
Thou seemest wreathed, by some immortall Hande.

ECHO TO A ROCK

Thou heaven-threat'ning Rock, gentler then she!
    Since of my pain
  Thou still more sensible wilt be,
Only when thou giv'st leave but to complain.
      ECHO. Complain.

But thou dost answer too, although in vain
Thou answer'st when thou canst no pity show.
      ECHO. Oh.
What canst thou speak and pity too?
  Then yet a further favour do,
And tell if of my griefs I any end shall know.
      ECHO. No.

Sure she will pity him that loves her so truly.
      ECHO. You ly.
  Vile Rock, thou now grow'st so unruly,
  That had'st thou life as thou hast voice,
    Thou should'st dye at my foot.
      ECHO. Dye at my foot.
  Thou canst not make me do't,
  Unless thou leave it to my choice,
  Who thy hard sentence shall fulfill,
When thou shalt say, I dye to please her only will.
      ECHO. I will.
When she comes hither, then, I pray thee, tell,
Thou art my Monument, and this my last farewell.
      ECHO. Well.

SONNET OF BLACK BEAUTY

Black beauty, which above that common light,
  Whose Power can no colours here renew
  But those which darkness can again subdue,
Do'st still remain unvary'd to the sight,
  And like an object equal to the view,
Art neither chang'd with day, nor hid with night;
When all these colours which the world call bright,
  And which old Poetry doth so persue,
Are with the night so perished and gone,
  That of their being there remains no mark,

Thou still abidest so intirely one,
　　That we may know thy blackness is a spark
Of light inaccessible, and alone
　　Our darkness which can make us think it dark.

LA GIALLETTA GALLANTE

or

THE SUN–BURN'D EXOTIQUE BEAUTY

Child of the Sun, in whom his Rays appear,
Hatch'd to that lustre, as doth make thee wear
Heav'ns livery in thy skin, What need'st thou fear
　　The injury of Air, and change of Clime,
　　When thy exalted form is so sublime,
　　As to transcend all power of change or time?

How proud are they that in their hair but show
Some part of thee, thinking therein they ow
The greatest beauty Nature can bestow!
　　When thou art so much fairer to the sight,
　　As beams each where diffused are more bright
　　Then their deriv'd and secondary light.

But thou art cordial both to sight and taste,
While each rare fruit seems in his time to haste
To ripen in thee, till at length they waste
　　Themselves to inward sweets, from whence again,
　　They, like Elixirs, passing through each vein,
　　An endless circulation do maintain.

How poor are they then, whom if we but greet,
Think that raw juyce, which in their lips we meet,
Enough, to make us hold their Kisses sweet!
　　When that rich odour, which in thee is smelt,
　　Can it self to a balmy liquor melt,
　　And make it to our inward senses felt.

Leave then thy Country Soil, and Mothers home,
Wander a Planet this way, till thou come
To give our Lovers here their fatal doom;
　　While if our beauties scorn to envy thine,
　　It will be just they to a Jaundice pine,
　　And by thy Gold shew like some Copper-mine.

ELEGY OVER A TOMB

Must I then see, alas! eternal night
　　Sitting upon those fairest eyes,
And closing all those beams, which once did rise
　　So radiant and bright,
That light and heat in them to us did prove
　　Knowledge and Love?

Oh, if you did delight no more to stay
　　Upon this low and earthly stage,
But rather chose an endless heritage,
　　Tell us at least, we pray,
Where all the beauties that those ashes ow'd
　　Are now bestow'd?

Doth the Sun now his light with yours renew?
　　Have Waves the curling of your hair?
Did you restore unto the Sky and Air,
　　The red, and white, and blue?
Have you vouchsafed to flowrs since your death
　　That sweetest breath?

Had not Heav'ns Lights else in their houses slept,
　　Or to some private life retir'd?
Must not the Sky and Air have else conspir'd,
　　And in their Regions wept?
Must not each flower else the earth could breed
　　Have been a weed?

But thus enrich'd may we not yield some cause
　　Why they themselves lament no more?
That must have changed the course they held before,
　　And broke their proper Laws,
Had not your beauties giv'n this second birth
　　To Heaven and Earth?

Tell us, for Oracles must still ascend,
　　For those that crave them at your tomb:
Tell us, where are those beauties now become,
　　And what they now intend:
Tell us, alas, that cannot tell our grief,
　　Or hope relief.

TEARS, FLOW NO MORE

Tears, flow no more, or if you needs must flow,
    Fall yet more slow,
      Do not the world invade,
From smaller springs then your rivers have grown,
    And they again a Sea have made,
Brackish like you, and which like you hath flown.

Ebb to my heart, and on the burning fires
    Of my desires,
      O let your torrents fall,
From smaller heate then theirs such sparks arise
    As into flame converting all,
This world might be but my love's sacrifice.

Yet if the tempests of my sighs so blow
    You both must flow,
      And my desires still burn,
Since that in vain all help my love requires,
    Why may not yet their rages turn
To dry those tears, and to blow out those fires?

William Drummond of Hawthornden
1585-1649

REGRET

In this Worlds raging sea
Where many Scillas barke,
Where many Syrens are,
Save, and not cast away,
Hee onlye saves his barge
With too much ware who doth it not o'recharge;
Or when huge stormes arise,
And waves menace the skies,
Gives what he got with no deploring show,
And doth againe in seas his burthen throw.

MADRIGAL: UNHAPPIE LIGHT

Unhappie Light,
Doe not approach to bring the wofull Day,
When I must bid for ay
Farewell to Her, and live in endlesse Plight.
Faire *Moone,* with gentle Beames
The Sight who never marres,
Long cleare Heavens sable Vault, and you bright Starres
Your golden Lockes long glasse in Earths pure Streames,
Let *Phœbus* never rise
To dimme your watchfull Eyes:
   Prolong (alas) prolong my short Delight,
   And if yee can, make an eternall Night.

MADRIGAL: MY THOUGHTS HOLD MORTALL STRIFE

My Thoughts hold mortall Strife,
I doe detest my Life,
And with lamenting Cries
(Peace to my Soule to bring)
Oft calles that Prince which here doth Monarchise,
But Hee grimme-grinning King,
Who Caitiffs scornes, and doth the Blest surprise,
   Late having deckt with *Beauties* Rose his Tombe,
   Disdaines to croppe a Weede, and will not come.

MADRIGAL: THE BEAUTIE, AND THE LIFE

The Beautie, and the Life,
Of *Lifes* and *Beauties* fairest Paragon,
(O Teares! O Griefe!) hang at a feeble thread,
To which pale *Atropos* had set her Knife.
The Soule with many a Grone
Had left each outward Part,
And now did take his last Leave of the Heart,
Nought else did want, save *Death,* even to be dead:
When the affecting Band about her Bed
(Seeing so faire in Lips, Cheekes, Eyes)
Cried, ah! And can *Death enter Paradise?*

IÖLAS' EPITAPH

Here deare *Iölas* lies,
Who whilst hee liv'd in Beautie did surpasse
That Boy, whose heavenly Eyes
Brought *Cypris* from above,
Or him till Death who look'd in watrie Glasse,
Even Judge the God of Love:
And if the Nymphe once held of him so deare,
Dorine the faire, would heere but shed one Teare,
    Thou shouldst (in *Natures* Scorne)
    A purple Flowre see of this Marble borne.

FOR THE MAGDALENE

These Eyes (deare Lord) once Brandons of Desire,
Fraile Scouts betraying what they had to keepe,
Which their owne heart, then others set on fire,
Their traitrous blacke before thee heere out-weepe:
These Lockes, of blushing deedes the faire attire,
Smooth-frizled Waves, sad Shelfes which shadow deepe,
Soule-stinging Serpents in gilt curles which creepe,
To touch thy sacred Feete doe now aspire.
In Seas of Care behold a sinking Barke,
By windes of sharpe Remorse unto thee driven
O let mee not expos'd be Ruines marke,
My faults confest (Lord) say they are forgiven.
    Thus sigh'd to Jesus the Bethananian faire,
    His teare-wet Feet still drying with her Haire.

John Donne
1572?-1631

These great poems, whose generation, like that of lions (according
to Aristotle) was "attended by great heat" — poems whose structure resembles the bones of the lion that are "so hard that if they are rubbed
strongly against each other, they emit sparks like flint stones" — are
yet capable of the melodious wonder of such a line as "A bracelet of
bright haire about the bone"; or of these lines from *Sappho to Philænus:*

> Thou art not soft, and cleare, and faire
>   As *Down,* as *Stars, Cedars,* and *Lillies* are,
> But thy right hand, and cheek, and eye, only
>   Are like thy other hand, and cheek, and eye.

Coleridge, in *Anima Poetæ,* said that "To read Dryden, Pope, etc. you need only count syllables, but to read Donne you must measure Time, and discover the Time of each word by the sense of Passion."

As Baudelaire said in *Mon Cœur Mis à Nu,* "Music gives the idea of space." So it is with the poems of Donne.

In many of these the very air seems dark — not with the darkness of night, but rather as if we had been translated into some different climate: one of heat, but darkness — the same kind of darkness as we find in Baudelaire.

Jean Cocteau, in *Le Secret Professionel,* said, "La nuit de Rimbaud met en valeur son système d'étoiles. Mallarmé, à force de nuit, de carbon pur, arrive au diamant."

Though Rimbaud and Mallarmé are poets of an entirely different order, this might have been said of Donne.

The love poems are, perhaps, the greatest in our language.

In *A Nocturnall upon S. Lucies Day, Being the Shortest Day,* with the sinking of the blood into death of these giant lovers (these "two Chaosses,"), "The worlds whole sap is sunke." Sometimes, in this poem, there is a hissing sound — a sound of the dust arising to overwhelm the lovers, or of the entwining worm, the last paramour, in the last bed of love. These sounds are conveyed by the *s*'s in such lines as:

> For his art did expresse
> A quintessence even from nothingnesse,
> From dull privations, and leane emptinesse:
> He ruin'd mee, and I am re-begot
> Of absence, darknesse, death; things which are not.

With Donne, "Harmony itself is a thing of thought." *

THE GOOD–MORROW

> I wonder by my troth, what thou, and I
>   Did, till we lov'd? were we not wean'd till then?
> But suck'd on countrey pleasures, childishly?
>   Or snorted we in the seaven sleepers den?
> T'was so; But this, all pleasures fancies bee.
> If ever any beauty I did see,
> Which I desir'd, and got, t'was but a dreame of thee.

* Richard Wagner.

And now good morrow to our waking soules,
  Which watch not one another out of feare;
For love, all love of other sights controules,
  And makes one little roome, an every where.
Let sea-discoverers to new worlds have gone,
Let Maps to other, worlds on worlds have showne,
Let us possesse one world, each hath one, and is one.

My face in thine eye, thine in mine appeares,
  And true plaine hearts doe in the faces rest,
Where can we finde two better hemispheares
  Without sharpe North, without declining West?
What ever dyes, was not mixt equally;
If our two loves be one, or, thou and I
Love so alike, that none doe slacken, none can die.

GOE, AND CATCHE A FALLING STARRE

Goe, and catche a falling starre,
  Get with child a mandrake roote,
Tell me, where all past yeares are,
  Or who cleft the Divels foot,
Teach me to heare Mermaides singing,
Or to keep off envies stinging,
    And finde
    What winde
Serves to advance an honest minde.

If thou beest borne to strange sights,
  Things invisible to see,
Ride ten thousand daies and nights,
  Till age snow white haires on thee,
Thou, when thou retorn'st, wilt tell mee
All strange wonders that befell thee,
    And sweare
    No where
Lives a woman true, and faire.

If thou findst one, let mee know,
  Such a Pilgrimage were sweet;
Yet doe not, I would not goe,
  Though at next doore wee might meet,
Though shee were true, when you met her,
And last, till you write your letter,
    Yet shee
    Will bee
False, ere I come, to two, or three.

THE SUNNE RISING

Busie old foole, unruly Sunne,
    Why dost thou thus,
Through windowes, and through curtaines call on us?
Must to thy motions lovers seasons run?
    Sawcy pedantique wretch, goe chide
    Late schoole boyes, and sowre prentices,
  Goe tell Court-huntsmen, that the King will ride,
  Call countrey ants to harvest offices;
Love, all alike, no season knowes, nor clyme,
Nor houres, dayes, moneths, which are the rags of time.

    Thy beames, so reverend, and strong
    Why shouldst thou thinke?
I could eclipse and cloud them with a winke,
But that I would not lose her sight so long:
    If her eyes have not blinded thine,
    Looke, and to morrow late, tell mee,
  Whether both the'India's of spice and Myne
  Be where thou leftst them, or lie here with mee.
Aske for those Kings whom thou saw'st yesterday,
And thou shalt heare, All here in one bed lay.

    She'is all States, and all Princes, I,
    Nothing else is.
Princes doe but play us; compar'd to this,
All honor's mimique; All wealth alchimie.
    Thou sunne art halfe as happy'as wee,
    In that the world's contracted thus;
  Thine age askes ease, and since thy duties bee
  To warme the world, that's done in warming us.
Shine here to us, and thou art every where;
This bed thy center is, these walls, thy spheare.

THE LEGACIE

When I dyed last, and, Deare, I dye
  As often as from thee I goe,
    Though it be but an houre agoe,
And Lovers houres be full eternity,
I can remember yet, that I
    Something did say, and something did bestow;
  Though I be dead, which sent mee, I should be
Mine owne executor and Legacie.

I heard mee say, Tell her anon,
   That my selfe, (that is you, not I,)
   Did kill me, and when I felt mee dye,
I bid mee send my heart, when I was gone,
But I alas could there finde none,
   When I had ripp'd me, 'and search'd where
         hearts did lye;
It kill'd mee agaaine, that I who still was true,
In life, in my last Will should cozen you.

Yet I found something like a heart,
   But colours it, and corners had,
   It was not good, it was not bad,
It was intire to none, and few had part.
As good as could be made by art
   It seem'd; and therefore for our losses sad,
I meant to send this heart in stead of mine,
But oh, no man could hold it, for twas thine.

AIRE AND ANGELLS

Twice or thrice had I loved thee,
   Before I knew thy face or name,
   So in a voice, so in a shapelesse flame,
Angells affect us oft, and worship'd bee;
   Still when, to where thou wert, I came,
Some lovely glorious nothing I did see.
   But since my soule, whose child love is,
Takes limmes of flesh, and else could nothing doe,
   More subtile then the parent is,
Love must not be, but take a body too,
   And therefore what thou wert, and who,
      I bid Love aske, and now
That it assume thy body, I allow,
And fixe it selfe in thy lip, eye, and brow.

Whilst thus to ballast love, I thought,
   And so more steddily to have gone,
   With wares which would sinke admiration,
I saw, I had loves pinnace overfraught,
   Ev'ry thy haire for love to worke upon
Is much too much, some fitter must be sought;
   For, nor in nothing, nor in things
Extreme, and scatt'ring bright, can love inhere;
   Then as an Angell, face, and wings

Of aire, not pure as it, yet pure doth weare,
   So thy love may be my loves spheare;
      Just such disparitie
   As is twixt Aire and Angells puritie,
'Twixt womens love, and mens will ever bee.

A VALEDICTION: OF WEEPING

      Let me powre forth
My teares before thy face, whil'st I stay here,
For thy face coines them, and thy stampe they beare,
And by this Mintage they are something worth,
      For thus they bee
      Pregnant of thee;
Fruits of much griefe they are, emblemes of more,
When a teare falls, that thou falls which it bore,
So thou and I are nothing then, when on a divers shore.

      On a round ball
A workeman that hath copies by, can lay
An Europe, Afrique, and an Asia,
And quickly make that, which was nothing, *All*,
      So doth each teare,
      Which thee doth weare,
A globe, yea world by that impression grow,
Till thy teares mixt with mine doe overflow
This world, by waters sent from thee, my heaven dissolved so.

      O more then Moone,
Draw not up seas to drowne me in thy spheare,
Weepe me not dead, in thine armes, but forbeare
To teach the sea, what it may doe too soone;
      Let not the winde
      Example finde,
To doe me more harme, then it purposeth;
Since thou and I sigh one anothers breath,
Who e'r sighes most, is cruellest, and hastes the others death.

A NOCTURNALL UPON S. LUCIES DAY,
BEING THE SHORTEST DAY

   Tis the yeares midnight, and it is the dayes,
Lucies, who scarce seaven houres herself unmaskes,
   The Sunne is spent, and now his flasks

Send forth light squibs, no constant rayes;
   The worlds whole sap is sunke:
The generall balme th' hydroptique earth hath drunk,
Whither, as to the beds-feet, life is shrunke,
Dead and enterr'd; yet all these seeme to laugh,
Compar'd with mee, who am their Epitaph.

Study me then, you who shall lovers bee
At the next world, that is, at the next Spring:
   For I am every dead thing,
   In whom love wrought new Alchimie.
    For his art did expresse
A quintessence even from nothingnesse,
From dull privations, and leane emptinesse:
He ruin'd mee, and I am re-begot
Of absence, darknesse, death; things which are not.

All others, from all things, draw all that's good,
Life, soule, forme, spirit, whence they beeing have;
   I, by loves limbecke, am the grave
   Of all, that's nothing. Oft a flood
    Have wee two wept, and so
Drownd the whole world, us two; oft did we grow
To be two Chaosses, when we did show
Care to ought else; and often absences
Withdrew our soules, and made us carcasses.

But I am by her death, (which word wrongs her)
Of the first nothing, the Elixer grown;
   Were I a man, that I were one,
   I needs must know; I should preferre,
    If I were any beast,
Some ends, some means; Yea plants, yea stones detest,
And love; All, all some properties invest;
If I an ordinary nothing were,
As shadow, a light, and body must be here.

But I am None; nor will my Sunne renew.
You lovers, for whose sake, the lesser Sunne
   At this time to the Goat is runne
   To fetch new lust, and give it you,
    Enjoy your summer all;
Since shee enjoyes her long nights festivall,
Let mee prepare towards her, and let mee call
This houre her Vigill, and her Eve, since this
Both the yeares, and the dayes deep midnight is.

THE BROKEN HEART

He is starke mad, who ever sayes,
   That he hath beene in love an houre,
Yet not that love so soone decayes,
   But that it can tenne in lesse space devour;
Who will beleeve mee, if I sweare
That I have had the plague a yeare?
    Who would not laugh at mee, if I should say,
    I saw a flaske of *powder burne a day?*

Ah, what a trifle is a heart,
   If once into loves hands it come!
All other griefes allow a part
   To other griefes, and aske themselves but some;
They come to us, but us Love draws,
Hee swallows us, and never chawes:
    By him, as by chain'd shot, whole rankes doe dye,
    He is the tyran Pike, our hearts the Frye.

If 'twere not so, what did become
   Of my heart, when I first saw thee?
I brought a heart into the roome,
   But from the roome, I carried none with me:
If it had gone to thee, I know
Mine would have taught thine heart to show
    More pitty unto mee: but Love, alas,
    At one first blow did shiver it as glasse.

Yet nothing can to nothing fall,
   Nor any place be empty quite,
Therefore I thinke my breast hath all
   Those peeces still, though they be not unite;
And now as broken glasses show
A hundred lesser faces, so
    My ragges of heart can like, wish, and adore,
    But after one such love, can love no more.

THE RELIQUE

   When my grave is broke up againe
   Some second guest to entertaine,
   (For graves have learn'd that woman-head
   To be to more than one a Bed)
    And he that digs it, spies

A bracelet of bright haire about the bone,
  Will he not let'us alone,
And thinke that there a loving couple lies,
Who thought that this device might be some way
To make their soules, at the last busie day,
Meet at this grave, and make a little stay?

  If this fall in a time, or land,
  Where mis-devotion doth command,
  Then, he that digges us up, will bring
  Us, to the Bishop, and the King,
   To make us Reliques; then
Thou shalt be a Mary Magdalen, and I
  A something else thereby;
All women shall adore us, and some men;
And since at such time, miracles are sought,
I would have that age by this paper taught
What miracles wee harmelesse lovers wrought.

  First, we lov'd well and faithfully,
  Yet knew not what wee lov'd, nor why,
  Difference of sex no more wee knew,
  Then our Guardian Angells doe;
   Coming and going, wee
Perchance might kisse, but not between those meales;
  Our hands ne'r toucht the seales,
Which nature, injur'd by late law, sets free:
These miracles wee did; but now alas,
All measure, and all language, I should passe,
Should I tell what a miracle shee was.

THE EXPIRATION

So, so, breake off this last lamenting kisse,
  Which sucks two soules, and vapors Both away,
Turne thou ghost that way, and let mee turne this,
  And let our selves benight our happiest day,
We ask'd none leave to love; nor will we owe
Any, so cheape a death, as saying, Goe;

Goe; and if that word have not quite kil'd thee,
  Ease mee with death, by bidding mee goe too.
Or, if it have, let my word worke on mee,
  And a just office on a murderer doe.
Except it be too late, to kill me so,
Being double dead, going, and bidding, goe.

ELEGIE IX: THE AUTUMNALL

No *Spring,* nor *Summer* Beauty hath such grace,
As I have seen in one *Autumnall* face.
Yong *Beauties* force our love, and that's a *Rape,*
This doth but *counsaile,* yet you cannot scape.
If t'were a *shame* to love, here t'were no *shame,*
Affection here takes *Reverences* name.
Were her first yeares the *Golden Age?* That's true,
But now shee's *gold* oft tried, and never new.
That was her torrid and inflaming time,
This is her tolerable *Tropique clyme.*
Faire eyes, who askes more heate then comes from hence,
He in a fever wishes pestilence.
Call not these wrinkles, *graves;* If *graves* they were,
They were *Loves graves;* for else he is no where.
Yet lies not Love *dead* here, but here doth sit
Vow'd to this trench, like an *Anachorit.*
And here, till hers, which must be his *death,* come,
He doth not digge a *Grave,* but build a *Tombe.*
Here dwells he, though he sojourne ev'ry where,
In *Progresse,* yet his standing house is here.
Here, where still *Evening* is; not *noone,* nor *night;*
Where no *voluptuousnesse,* yet all *delight.*
In all her words, unto all hearers fit,
You may at *Revels,* you at *Counsaile,* sit.
This is loves timber, youth his under-wood;
There he, as wine in *June,* enrages blood,
Which then comes seasonabliest, when our taste
And appetite to other things, is past.
Xerxes strange *Lydian* love, the *Platane* tree,
Was lov'd for age, none being so large as shee,
Or else because, being yong, nature did blesse
Her youth with ages glory, *Barrennesse.*
If we love things sought, *Age* is a thing
Which we are fifty yeares in compassing.
If transitory things, which soone decay,
Age must be lovelyest at the latest day.
But name not *Winter-faces,* whose skin's slacke;
Lanke, as an unthrifts purse; but a soules sacke;
Whose *Eyes* seeke light within, for all here's shade;
Whose *mouthes* are holes, rather worne out, then made;
Whose every tooth to a severall place is gone,
To vexe their soules at *Resurrection;*
Name not these living *Deaths-heads* unto mee,
For these, not *Ancient,* but *Antique* be.

I hate extreames; yet I had rather stay
With *Tombs,* then *Cradles,* to weare out a day.
Since such loves naturall lation is, may still
My love descend, and journey downe the hill,
Not panting after growing beauties, so,
I shall ebbe out with them, who home-ward goe.

AN EPITHALAMION
*Or mariage Song on the Lady Elizabeth, and
Count Palatine being married on St. Valentine's day*

Haile Bishop Valentine, whose day this is,
    All the Aire is thy Diocis,
    And all the chirping Choristers
And other birds are thy Parishioners,
    Thou marryest every yeare
The Lirique Larke, and the grave whispering Dove,
The Sparrow that neglects his life for love,
The household Bird, with the red stomacher,
    Thou mak'st the black bird speed as soone,
As doth the Goldfinch, or the Halcyon;
The husband cocke lookes out, and straight is sped,
And meets his wife, which brings her feather-bed.
This day more cheerfully then ever shine,
This day, which might enflame thy self, Old Valentine.

Till now, Thou warmd'st with multiplying loves
    Two larkes, two sparrowes, or two Doves,
    All that is nothing unto this,
For thou this day couplest two Phœnixes;
    Thou mak'st a Taper see
What the sunne never saw, and what the Arke
(Which was of foules, and beasts, the cage, and park)
Did not containe, one bed containes, through Thee,
    Two Phœnixes, whose joyned breasts
Are unto one another mutuall nests,
Where motion kindles such fires, as shall give
Yong Phœnixes, and yet the old shall live.
Whose love and courage never shall decline,
But make the whole year through, thy day, O Valentine.

Up then faire Phœnix Bride, frustrate the Sunne,
    Thy selfe from thine affection
    Takest warmth enough, and from thine eye
All lesser birds will take their Jollitie.

    lation] locomotion (an astrological term),

Up, up, faire Bride, and call,
Thy starres, from out their severall boxes, take
Thy Rubies, Pearles, and Diamonds forth, and make
Thy selfe a constellation, of them All,
  And by their blazing, signifie,
That a Great Princess falls, but doth not die;
Bee thou a new starre, that to us portends
Ends of much wonder; And be Thou those ends.
Since thou dost this day in new glory shine,
May all men date Records, from this thy Valentine.

Come forth, come forth, and as one glorious flame
  Meeting Another, growes the same,
  So meet thy Fredericke, and so
To an unseparable union growe.
  Since separation
Falls not on such things as are infinite,
Nor things which are but one, can disunite,
You'are twice inseparable, great, and one;
  Goe then to where the Bishop staies,
To make you one, his way, which divers waies
Must be effected; and when all is past,
And that you'are one, by hearts and hands made fast,
You two have one way left, your selves to'entwine,
Besides this Bishops knot, or Bishop Valentine.

But oh, what ailes the Sunne, that here he staies,
  Longer to day, then other daies?
  Staies he new light from these to get?
And finding here such store, is loth to set?
  And why doe you two walke,
So slowly pac'd in this procession?
Is all your care but to be look'd upon,
And be to others spectacle, and talke?
  The feast, with gluttonous delaies,
Is eaten, and too long their meat they praise,
The masquers come too late, and'I thinke, will stay,
Like Fairies, till the Cock crow them away.
Alas, did not Antiquity assigne
A night, as well as day, to thee, O Valentine?

They did, and night is come; and yet wee see
  Formalities retarding thee.
  What meane these Ladies, which (as though
They were to take a clock in peeces) goe

So nicely about the Bride;
A Bride, before a good night could be said,
Should vanish from her cloathes, into her bed,
As Soules from bodies steale, and are not spy'd.
    But now she is laid; What though shee bee?
Yet there are more delayes, For, where is he?
He comes, and passes through Spheare after Spheare,
First her sheetes, then her Armes, then any where.
Let not this day, then, but this night be thine,
Thy day was but the eve to this, O Valentine.

Here lyes a shee Sunne, and a hee Moone here,
    She gives the best light to his Spheare,
    Or each is both, and all, and so
They unto one another nothing owe,
    And yet they doe, but are
So just and rich in that coyne which they pay,
That neither would, nor needs forbeare, nor stay;
Neither desires to be spar'd, nor to spare,
    They quickly pay their debt, and then
Take no acquittances, but pay again;
They pay, they give, they lend, and so let fall
No such occasion to be liberall.
More truth, more courage in these two do shine,
Then all thy turtles have, and sparrows, Valentine.

And by this act of these two Phenixes
    Nature againe restored is,
    For since these two are two no more,
Ther's but one Phenix still, as was before.
    Rest now at last, and wee
As Satyres watch the Sunnes uprise, will stay
Waiting, when your eyes opened, let out day,
Onely desir'd, because your face wee see;
    Others neare you shall whispering speake,
And wagers lay, at which side day will breake,
And win by'observing, then, whose hand it is
That opens first a curtaine, hers or his;
This will be tryed to morrow after nine,
Till which houre, wee thy day enlarge, O Valentine.

THE APPARITION

When by thy scorne, O murdresse I am dead,
   And that thou thinkst thee free
   From all solicitation from mee,
Then shall my ghost come to thy bed,
And thee, fain'd vestall, in worse armes shall see;
Then thy sicke taper will begin to winke,
And he, whose thou art then, being tyr'd before,
Will, if thou stirre, or pinch to wake him, thinke
     Thou call'st for more,
   And in false sleepe will from thee shrinke,
And then poore Aspen wretch, neglected thou
Bath'd in a cold quicksilver sweat wilt lye
     A veryer ghost then I;
What I will say, I will not tell thee now,
Lest that preserve thee'; and since my love is spent,
I'had rather thou shouldst painfully repent,
Then by my threatnings rest still innocent.

A LECTURE UPON THE SHADOW

   Stand still, and I will read to thee
A Lecture, Love, in loves philosophy.
   These three houres that we have spent,
   Walking here, Two shadowes went
Along with us, which we our selves produc'd:
But, now the Sunne is just above our head,
    We doe those shadowes tread;
And to brave clearnesse all things are reduc'd.
   So whilst our infant loves did grow,
   Disguises did, and shadowes, flow,
   From us, and our cares; but, now 'tis not so.

That love hath not attain'd the high'st degree,
Which is still diligent lest others see.

   Except our loves at this noone stay,
We shall new shadowes make the other way.
   As the first were made to blinde
   Others; these which come behinde
Will worke upon our selves, and blind our eyes.

If our loves faint, and westwardly decline;
        To me thou, falsly, thine,
And I to thee mine actions shall disguise.
    The morning shadowes weare away,
        But these grow longer all the day,
        But oh, loves day is short, if love decay.

    Love is a growing, or full constant light;
    And his first minute, after noone, is night.

From HOLY SONNETS

VII

At the round earths imagin'd corners, blow
Your trumpets, Angells, and arise, arise
From death, you numberlesse infinities
Of soules, and to your scattred bodies goe,
All whom the flood did, and fire shall o'erthrow,
All whom warre, dearth, age, agues, tyrannies,
Despaire, law, chance, hath slaine, and you whose eyes,
Shall behold God, and never tast deaths woe.
But let them sleepe, Lord, and mee mourne a space,
For, if above all these, my sinnes abound,
'Tis late to aske abundance of thy grace,
When wee are there; here on this lowly ground,
    Teach mee how to repent; for that's as good
    As if thou'hadst seal'd my pardon, with thy blood.

IX

If poysonous mineralls, and if that tree,
Whose fruit threw death on else immortall us,
If lecherous goats, if serpents envious
Cannot be damn'd; Alas; why should I bee?
Why should intent or reason, borne in mee,
Make sinnes, else equall, in mee more heinous?
And mercy being easie, and glorious
To God; in his sterne wrath, why threatens hee?
But who am I, that dare dispute with thee
O God? Oh! of thine onely worthy blood,
And my teares, make a heavenly Lethean flood,
And drowne in it my sinnes blacke memorie;
    That thou remember them, some claime as debt,
    I thinke it mercy, if thou wilt forget.

X

Death be not proud, though some have called thee
Mighty and dreadfull, for, thou art not soe,
For, those, whom thou think'st, thou dost overthrow,
Die not, poore death, nor yet canst thou kill mee.
From rest and sleepe, which but thy pictures bee,
Much pleasure, then from thee, much more must flow,
And soonest our best men with thee doe goe,
Rest of their bones, and soules deliverie.
Thou art slave to Fate, Chance, kings, and desperate men,
And dost with poyson, warre, and sicknesse dwell,
And poppie, or charmes can make us sleepe as well,
And better then thy stroake; why swell'st thou then?
    One short sleepe past, wee wake eternally,
    And death shall be no more; death, thou shalt die.

GOODFRIDAY, 1613. RIDING WESTWARD

Let mans Soule be a Spheare, and then, in this,
The intelligence that moves, devotion is,
And as the other Spheares, by being growne
Subject to forraigne motions, lose their owne,
And being by others hurried every day,
Scarce in a yeare their naturall forme obey:
Pleasure or businesse, so, our Soules admit
For their first mover, and are whirld by it.
Hence is't, that I am carryed towards the West
This day, when my Soules forme bends toward the East.
There I should see a Sunne, by rising set,
And by that setting endlesse day beget;
But that Christ on this Crosse, did rise and fall,
Sinne had eternally benighted all.
Yet dare I'almost be glad, I do not see
That spectacle of too much weight for mee.
Who sees Gods face, that is selfe life, must dye;
What a death were it then to see God dye?
It made his owne Lieutenant Nature shrinke,
It made his footstoole crack, and the Sunne winke.
Could I behold those hands which span the Poles,
And turne all spheares at once, peirc'd with those holes?
Could I behold that endlesse height which is
Zenith to us, and our Antipodes,
Humbled below us? or that blood which is
The seat of all our Soules, if not of his,

Made dirt of dust, or that flesh which was worne
By God, for his apparell, ragg'd, and torne?
If on these things I durst not looke, durst I
Upon his miserable mother cast mine eye,
Who was Gods partner here, and furnish'd thus
Halfe of that Sacrifice, which ransom'd us?
Though these things, as I ride, be from mine eye,
They'are present yet unto my memory,
For that looks towards them; and thou look'st towards mee,
O Saviour, as thou hang'st upon the tree;
I turne my backe to thee, but to receive
Corrections, till thy mercies bid thee leave.
O thinke mee worth thine anger, punish mee,
Burne off my rusts, and my deformity,
Restore thine Image, so much, by thy grace,
That thou may'st know mee, and I'll turne my face.

HYMNE TO GOD MY GOD, IN MY SICKNESSE

Since I am comming to that Holy roome,
　　Where, with thy Quire of Saints for evermore,
I shall be made thy Musique; As I come
　　I tune the Instrument here at the dore,
　　And what I must doe then, thinke here before.

Whilst my Physitians by their love are growne
　　Cosmographers, and I their Mapp, who lie
Flat on this bed, that by them may be showne
　　That this is my South-west discoverie
　　Per fretum febris, by these streights to die,

I joy, that in these straits, I see my West;
　　For, though theire currents yeeld returne to none,
What shall my West hurt me? As West and East
　　In all flatt Maps (and I am one) are one,
　　So death doth touch the Resurrection.

Is the Pacifique Sea my home? Or are
　　The Easterne riches? Is *Jerusalem?*
Anyan, and *Magellan,* and *Gibraltare,*
　　All streights, and none but streights, are wayes to them,
　　Whether where *Japhet* dwelt, or *Cham,* or *Sem.*

We thinke that *Paradise* and *Calvarie,*
　　Christs Crosse, and *Adams* tree, stood in one place;

Looke Lord, and finde both *Adams* met in me;
As the first *Adams* sweat surrounds my face,
May the last *Adams* blood my soule embrace.

So, in his purple wrapp'd receive mee Lord,
By these his thornes give me his other Crowne;
And as to others soules I preach'd thy word,
Be this my Text, my Sermon to mine owne,
Therfore that he may raise the Lord throws down.

A HYMNE TO GOD THE FATHER

Wilt thou forgive that sinne where I begunne,
Which was my sin, though it were done before?
Wilt thou forgive that sinne; through which I runne,
And do run still: though still I do deplore?
When thou hast done, thou hast not done,
For, I have more.

Wilt thou forgive that sinne which I have wonne
Others to sinne? and, made my sinne their doore?
Wilt thou forgive that sinne which I did shunne
A yeare, or two: but wallowed in, a score?
When thou hast done, thou hast not done,
For I have more.

I have a sinne of feare, that when I have spunne
My last thred, I shall perish on the shore;
But sweare by thy selfe, that at my death thy sonne
Shall shine as he shines now, and heretofore;
And, having done that, Thou hast done,
I feare no more.

THE LITANIE

THE FATHER
Father of Heaven, and him, by whom
It, and us for it, and all else, for us
Thou madest, and govern'st ever, come
And re-create mee, now growne ruinous:
My heart is by dejection, clay,
And by selfe-murder, red.

From this red earth, O Father, purge away
All vicious tinctures, that new fashioned
I may rise up from death, before I'am dead.

THE SONNE

O Sonne of God, who seeing two things,
Sinne, and death crept in, which were never made,
By bearing one, tryed'st with what stings
The other could thine heritage invade;
 O be thou nail'd unto my heart,
  And crucified againe,
Part not from it, though it from thee would part,
But let it be, by applying so thy paine,
Drown'd in thy blood, and in thy passion slaine.

THE HOLY GHOST

O Holy Ghost, whose temple I
Am, but of mudde walls, and condensed dust,
 And being sacrilegiously
Halfe wasted with youths fires, of pride and lust,
 Must with new stormes be weatherbeat;
  Double in my heart thy flame,
Which let devout sad teares intend; and let
(Though this glasse lanthorne, flesh, do suffer maime)
Fire, Sacrifice, Priest, Altar be the same.

THE TRINITY

O Blessed glorious Trinity,
Bones to Philosophy, but milke to faith,
 Which, as wise serpents, diversly
Most slipperinesse, yet most entanglings hath,
 As you distinguish'd undistinct
  By power, love, knowledge bee,
Give mee a such selfe different instinct
Of these; let all mee elemented bee,
Of power, to love, to know, you unnumbered three.

THE VIRGIN MARY

For that faire blessed Mother-maid,
Whose flesh redeem'd us; That she-Cherubin,
 Which unlock'd Paradise, and made
One claime for innocence, and disseiz'd sinne,
 Whose wombe was a strange heav'n, for there
  God cloath'd himselfe, and grew,

Our zealous thankes wee poure. As her deeds were
Our helpes, so are her prayers; nor can she sue
In vaine, who hath such titles unto you.

THE ANGELS

And since this life our nonage is,
And wee in Wardship to thine Angels be,
Native in heavens faire Palaces,
Where we shall be but denizen'd by thee,
As th' earth conceiving by the Sunne,
Yeelds faire diversitie,
Yet never knowes which course that light doth run,
So let mee study, that mine actions bee
Worthy their sight, though blinde in how they see.

THE PATRIARCHES

And let thy Patriarches Desire
(Those great Grandfathers of thy Church, which saw
More in the cloud, then wee in fire,
Whom Nature clear'd more, then us Grace and Law,
And now in Heaven still pray, that wee
May use our new helpes right)
Be satisfy'd, and fructifie in mee;
Let not my minde be blinder by more light
Nor Faith, by Reason added, lose her sight.

THE PROPHETS

Thy Eagle-sighted Prophets too,
Which were thy Churches Organs, and did sound
That harmony, which made of two
One law, and did unite, but not confound;
Those heavenly Poets which did see
Thy will, and it expresse
In rythmique feet, in common pray for mee,
That I by them excuse not my excesse
In seeking secrets, or Poetiquenesse.

THE APOSTLES

And thy illustrious Zodiacke
Of twelve Apostles, which ingirt this All,
(From whom whosoever do not take
Their light, to darke deep pits, throw downe, and fall)
As through their prayers, thou'hast let mee know
That their bookes are divine;

May they pray still, and be heard, that I goe
Th'old broad way in applying; O decline
Mee, when my comment would make thy word mine.

THE MARTYRS

And since thou so desirously
Did'st long to die, that long before thou could'st,
And long since thou no more couldst dye,
Thou in thy scatter'd mystique body wouldst
    In Abel dye, and ever since
        In thine; let their blood come
To begge for us, a discreet patience
Of death, or of worse life: for Oh, to some
Not to be Martyrs, is a martyrdome.

THE CONFESSORS

Therefore with thee triumpheth there
A Virgin Squadron of white Confessors,
    Whose bloods betroth'd, not marryed were,
Tender'd, not taken by those Ravishers:
    They know, and pray, that wee may know,
        In every Christian
Hourly tempestuous persecutions grow;
Tentations martyr us alive; A man
Is to himselfe a Dioclesian.

THE VIRGINS

The cold white snowie Nunnery,
Which, as thy mother, their high Abbesse, sent
    Their bodies backe againe to thee,
As thou hadst lent them, cleane and innocent,
    Though they have not obtain'd of thee,
        That or thy Church, or I,
Should keep, as they, our first integrity;
Divorce thou sinne in us, or bid it die,
And call chast widowhead Virginitie.

THE DOCTORS

Thy sacred Academie above
Of Doctors, whose paines have unclasp'd, and taught
    Both bookes of life to us (for love
To know thy Scriptures tells us, we are wrote
    In thy other booke) pray for us there
        That what they have misdone

Or mis-said, wee to that may not adhere;
Their zeale may be our sinne. Lord let us runne
Meane waies, and call them stars, but not the Sunne.

    And whil'st this universall Quire,
That Church in triumph, this is warfare here,
    Warm'd with one all-partaking fire
Of love, that none be lost, which cost thee deare,
      Prayes ceaslesly,'and thou hearken too,
        (Since to be gratious
Our taske is treble, to pray, beare, and doe)
Heare this prayer Lord: O Lord deliver us
From trusting in those prayers, though powr'd out thus.

    From being anxious, or secure,
Dead clods of sadnesse, or light squibs of mirth,
    From thinking, that great courts immure
All, or no happinesse, or that this earth
      Is only for our prison fram'd,
        Or that thou art covetous
To them whom thou lovest, or that they are maim'd
From reaching this worlds sweet, who seek thee thus,
With all their might, Good Lord deliver us.

    From needing danger, to bee good,
From owing thee yesterdaies teares to day,
    From trusting so much to thy blood,
That in that hope, wee wound our soule away,
      From bribing thee with Almes, to excuse
        Some sinne more burdenous,
From light affecting, in religion, newes,
From thinking us all soule, neglecting thus
Our mutuall duties, Lord deliver us.

    From tempting Satan to tempt us,
By our connivence, or slack companie,
    From measuring ill by vitious,
Neglecting to choake sins spawne, Vanitie,
      From indiscreet humilitie,
        Which might be scandalous,
And cast reproach on Christianitie,
From being spies, or to spies pervious,
From thirst, or scorne of fame, deliver us.

Deliver us for thy descent
Into the Virgin, whose wombe was a place
  Of middle kind; and thou being sent
To'ungratious us, staid'st at her full of grace;
      And through thy poore birth, where first thou
          Glorifiedst Povertie,
And yet soone after riches didst allow,
By accepting Kings gifts in the Epiphanie,
Deliver, and make us, to both waies free.

And through that bitter agonie,
Which is still the agonie of pious wits,
  Disputing what distorted thee,
And interrupted evennesse, with fits;
      And through thy free confession
          Though thereby they were then
Made blind, so that thou might'st from them have gone,
Good Lord deliver us, and teach us when
Wee may not, and we may blinde unjust men.

Through thy submitting all, to blowes
Thy face, thy clothes to spoile; thy fame to scorne,
  All waies, which rage, or Justice knowes,
And by which thou could'st shew, that thou wast born;
      And through thy gallant humblenesse
          Which thou in death did'st shew,
Dying before thy soule they could expresse,
Deliver us from death, by dying so,
To this world, ere this world doe bid us goe.

When senses, which thy souldiers are,
Wee arme against thee, and they fight for sinne,
  When want, sent but to tame, doth warre
And worke despaire a breach to enter in,
      When plenty, Gods image, and seale
          Makes us Idolatrous,
And love it, not him, whom it should reveale,
When wee are mov'd to seeme religious
Only to vent wit, Lord deliver us.

In Churches, when the'infirmitie
Of him which speakes, diminishes the Word,
  When Magistrates doe mis-apply
To us, as we judge, lay or ghostly sword,

When plague, which is thine Angell, raignes,
   Or wars, thy Champions, swaie,
When Heresie, thy second deluge, gaines;
In th'houre of death, the'Eve of last judgement day,
Deliver us from the sinister way.

   Heare us, O heare us Lord; to thee
A sinner is more musique, when he prayes,
   Then spheares, or Angels praises bee,
In Panegyrique Allelujaes;
    Heare us, for till thou heare us, Lord
     We know not what to say;
Thine eare to'our sighes, teares, thoughts gives voice and word.
O Thou who Satan heard'st in Jobs sicke day,
Heare thy selfe now, for thou in us dost pray.

   That wee may change to evennesse
This intermitting aguish Pietie;
   That snatching cramps of wickednesse
And Apoplexies of fast sin, may die;
    That musique of thy promises,
     Not threats in Thunder may
Awaken us to our just offices;
What in thy booke, thou dost, or creatures say,
That we may heare, Lord heare us, when wee pray.

   That our eares sicknesse wee may cure,
And rectifie those Labyrinths aright;
   That wee, by harkning, not procure
Our praise, nor others dispraise so invite;
    That wee get not a slipperinesse
     And senslesly decline,
From hearing bold wits jeast at Kings excesse,
To'admit the like of majestie divine;
That we may locke our eares, Lord open thine.

   That living law, the Magistrate,
Which to give us, and make us physicke, doth
   Our vices often aggravate,
That Preachers taxing sinne, before her growth,
    That Satan, and invenom'd men
     Which well, if we starve, dine,
When they doe most accuse us, may see then
Us, to amendment, heare them; thee decline:
That we may open our eares, Lord lock thine.

That learning, thine Ambassador,
From thine allegeance wee never tempt,
  That beauty, paradises flower
For physicke made, from poyson be exempt,
    That wit, borne apt high good to doe,
        By dwelling lazily
On Natures nothing, be not nothing too,
That our affections kill us not, nor dye,
Heare us, weake ecchoes, O thou eare, and cry.

  Sonne of God heare us, and since thou
By taking our blood, owest it us againe,
  Gaine to thy self, or us allow;
And let not both us and thy selfe be slaine;
    O Lambe of God, which took'st our sinne
        Which could not stick to thee,
O let it not returne to us againe,
But Patient and Physition being free,
As sinne is nothing, let it no where be.

Henry King
1592-1669

THE DOUBLE ROCK

Since thou hast view'd some Gorgon, and art grown
        A solid stone:
To bring again to softness thy hard heart
        Is past my art.
Ice may relent to water in a thaw;
But stone made flesh Loves Chymistry ne're saw.

Therefore, by thinking on thy hardness, I
        Will petrify;
And so within our double Quarryes Wombe,
        Dig our Loves Tombe.

Thus strangely will our differences agree;
And, with our selves, amaze the world, to see
How both Revenge and Sympathy consent
To make two Rocks each others Monument.

THE EXEQUY

Accept thou Shrine of my dead Saint,
Insteed of Dirges this complaint;
And for sweet flowres to crown thy hearse,
Receive a strew of weeping verse
From thy griev'd friend, whom thou might'st see
Quite melted into tears for thee.

   Dear loss! since thy untimely fate
My task hath been to meditate
On thee, on thee: thou art the book,
The library whereon I look
Though almost blind. For thee (lov'd clay)
I languish out not live the day,
Using no other exercise
But what I practise with mine eyes:
By which wet glasses I find out
How lazily time creeps about
To one that mourns: this, onely this
My exercise and bus'ness is:
So I compute the weary houres
With sighs dissolved into showres.

   Nor wonder if my time go thus
Backward and most preposterous;
Thou hast benighted me, thy set
This Eve of blackness did beget,
Who was't my day, (though overcast
Before thou had'st thy Noon-tide past)
And I remember must in tears,
Thou scarce had'st seen so many years
As Day tells houres. By thy cleer Sun
My love and fortune first did run;
But thou wilt never more appear
Folded within my Hemisphear,
Since both thy light and motion
Like a fled Star is fall'n and gon,
And twixt me and my soules dear wish
The earth now interposed is,
With such a strange eclipse doth make
As ne're was read in Almanake.

I could allow thee for a time
To darken me and my sad Clime,
Were it a month, a year, or ten,
I would they exile live till then;
And all that space my mirth adjourn,
So thou wouldst promise to return;
And putting off thy ashy shrowd
At length disperse this sorrows cloud.

But woe is me! the longest date
Too narrow is to calculate
These empty hopes: never shall I
Be so much blest as to descry
A glimpse of thee, till that day come
Which shall the earth to cinder doome,
And a fierce Feaver must calcine
The body of this world like thine,
(My little World!) that fit of fire
Once off, our bodies shall aspire
To our soules bliss: then we shall rise,
And view our selves with cleerer eyes
In that calm Region, where no night
Can hide us from each others sight.

Mean time, thou hast her, earth: much
       good
May my harm do thee. Since it stood
With Heavens will I might not call
Her longer mine, I give thee all
My short-liv'd right and interest
In her, whom living I lov'd best:
With a most free and bounteous grief,
I give thee what I could not keep.
Be kind to her, and prethee look
Thou write into thy Dooms-day book
Each parcell of this Rarity
Which in thy Casket shrin'd doth ly:
See that thou make thy reck'ning streight,
And yield her back again by weight;
For thou must audit on thy trust
Each graine and atome of this dust,
As thou wilt answer *Him* that lent,
Not gave thee my dear Monument.

So close the ground, and 'bout her shade
Black curtains draw, my *Bride* is laid.

Sleep on, my *Love,* in thy cold bed
Never to be disquieted!
My last good night! Thou wilt not wake
Till I thy fate shall overtake:
Till age, or grief, or sickness must
Marry my body to that dust
It so much loves; and fill the room
My heart keeps empty in thy Tomb.
Stay for me there; I will not faile
To meet thee in that hallow Vale.
And think not much of my delay;
I am already on the way,
And follow thee with all the speed
Desire can make, or sorrows breed.
Each minute is a short degree,
And ev'ry houre a step towards thee.
At night when I betake to rest,
Next morn I rise neerer my West
Of life, almost by eight houres saile,
Than when sleep breath'd his drowsie gale.

Thus from the Sun my Bottom stears,
And my dayes Compass downward bears:
Nor labour I to stemme the tide
Through which to *Thee* I swiftly glide.

'Tis true, with shame and grief I yield,
Thou like the *Vann* first took'st the field,
And gotten hast the victory
In thus adventuring to dy
Before me, whose more years might crave
A just precedence in the grave.
But heark! My pulse like a soft Drum
Beats my approach, tells *Thee* I come;
And slow howere my marches be,
I shall at last sit down by *Thee.*

The thought of this bids me go on,
And wait my dissolution
With hope and comfort. *Dear* (forgive
The crime) I am content to live
Divided, with but half a heart,
Till we shall meet and never part.

James Shirley
1596-1666

O FLY MY SOUL

O fly my soul, what hangs upon
    Thy drooping wings,
      And weighs them down,
With love of gaudy mortall things?
The Sun is now i' th' East, each shade
    As he doth rise,
      Is shorter made,
That Earth may lessen to our eyes:
Oh be not careless then, and play
    Until the Star of peace
Hide all his beames in dark recess;
Poor Pilgrims needs must lose their way,
When all the shadows do increase.

John Webster
1580?-1625?

From THE DEVIL'S LAW–CASE

ACT III, SCENE 3

ROMELIO. Oh heere's my mother: I ha strange newes for you —
  My sister is with child.
LEONORA.   I doe looke now
  For some great misfortunes to follow: for indeed mischiefes
  Are like the Visits of Franciscan Fryers,
  They never come to pray upon us single.
  In what estate left you *Contarino?*
ROMELIO.   Strange, that you
  Can skip from the former sorrow to such a question!
  Ile tell you — in the absence of his Surgeon,
  My charitie did that for him in a trice,
  They would have done at leasure, and been paid for 't.
  I have killed him.

LEONORA.   I am twentie yeares elder
    Since you last opened your lips.
ROMELIO.   Ha?
LEONORA. You have given him the wound you speake of
    Quite thorow your mothers heart.
ROMELIO. I will heale it presently mother: for this sorrow
    Belongs to your errour: you would have him live,
    Because you thinke hee's father of the child;
    But *Jolenta* vowes by all the rights of Truth,
    Tis *Ercole's:* it makes me smile to thinke,
    How cunningly my sister could be drawen
    To the Contract, and yet how familiarly
    To his bed. Doves never couple without
    A kind of murmur.
LEONORA.   Oh, I am very sicke.
ROMELIO. Your old disease — when you are griev'd, you are troubled
    With the Mother.
LEONORA [*aside*].   I am rapt with the Mother indeed,
    That I ever bore such a sonne.
ROMELIO.   Pray tend my sister,
    I am infinitely full of businesse.
LEONORA.   Stay, you will mourne
    For *Contarino?*
ROMELIO.   Oh by all meanes, tis fit —
    My sister is his heire.   [*Exit.*]
LEONORA. I will make you chiefe mourner, beleeve it.
    Never was woe like mine: oh that my care,
    And absolute study to preserve his life,
    Should be his absolute ruine! Is he gone then?
    There is no plague i' th world can be compared
    To impossible desire, for they are plagued
    In the desire it selfe: never, oh never
    Shall I behold him living, in whose life
    I lived farre sweetlier then in mine owne.
    A precise curiositie has undone me; why did I not
    Make my love knowne directly? 't had not been
    Beyond example, for a Matron to affect
    I' th honourable way of Marriage,
    So youthfull a person: oh I shall runne mad,
    For as we love our youngest children best:
    So the last fruit of our affection,
    Where ever we bestow it, is most strong,
    Most violent, most unresistable,
    Since tis indeed our latest Harvest-home,

mother] hysteria.

Last merryment fore Winter; and we widdowes,
As men report of our best Picture-makers,
We love the piece we are in hand with better,
Then all the excellent worke we have done before —
And my sonne has depriv'd me of all this.
Ha my sonne! —
Ile be a fury to him — like an Amazon Lady,
Ide cut off this right pap, that gave him sucke,
To shoot him dead. Ile no more tender him,
Then had a Wolfe stolne to my teat i' th night,
And robb'd me of my milke: nay, such a creature
I should love better farre. — Ha, ha, what say you?
I doe talke to somewhat, me thinks; it may be
My evill Genius. Doe not the Bells ring?
I have a strange noyse in my head: oh, fly in pieces! —
Come age, and wither me into the malice
Of those that have been happy; let me have
One propertie more then the Devill of Hell,
Let me envy the pleasure of youth heartily,
Let me in this life feare no kinde of ill,
That have no good to hope for: let me dye
In the distraction of that worthy Princesse,
Who loathed food, and sleepe, and ceremony,
For thought of losing that brave Gentleman,
She would faine have saved, had not a false convayance
Exprest him stubborne-hearted. Let me sinke,
Where neither man, nor memory may ever find me.

Falls downe. Enter Capuchin and Ercole.

CAPUCHIN. This is a private way which I command,
  As her Confessor. I would not have you seene yet,
  Till I prepare her. [*Ercole withdraws.*] Peace to you Lady.
LEONORA.   Ha?
CAPUCHIN. You are wel imployd, I hope; the best pillow i' th world
  For this your contemplation, is the earth,
  And the best object heaven.
LEONORA. I am whispering to a dead friend.

ACT V, SCENE 4

All the Flowers of the Spring
Meet to perfume our burying:
These have but their growing prime,
And man does flourish but his time.
Survey our progresse from our birth,
We are set, we grow, we turne to earth.

Courts adieu, and all delights,
All bewitching appetites;
Sweetest Breath, and clearest eye,
Like perfumes goe out and dye;
And consequently this is done,
As shadowes wait upon the Sunne.
Vaine the ambition of Kings,
Who seeke by trophies and dead things,
To leave a living name behind,
And weave but nets to catch the wind.

From THE WHITE DIVEL

ACT I, SCENE 1

LODOVICO. Banisht!
ANTONELLI.   It greev'd me much to heare the sentence.
LODOVICO. Ha, Ha, O *Democritus* thy Gods
  That governe the whole world! Courtly reward
  And punishment. Fortun's a right whore.
  If she give ought, she deales it in smal percels,
  That she may take away all at one swope.
  This tis to have great enemies, God quite them:
  Your woolfe no longer seemes to be a woolfe
  Then when shees hungry.
GASPARO.   You terme those enemies
  Are men of Princely ranke.
LODOVICO.   Oh I pray for them.
  The violent thunder is adored by those
  Are pasht in peeces by it.
ANTONELLI.   Come my Lord,
  You are justly doom'd; looke but a little backe
  Into your former life: you have in three yeares
  Ruin'd the noblest Earldome.
GASPARO.   Your followers
  Have swallowed you like Mummia, and being sicke
  With such unnaturall and horrid Phisicke
  Vomit you up ith kennell.
ANTONELLI.   All the damnable degrees
  Of drinkings have you staggerd through — one Cittizen
  Is Lord of two faire Manors cald you master,
  Only for Caviare.
GASPARO.   Those noblemen
  Which were invited to your prodigall feastes,
  Wherein the Phænix scarce could scape your throtes,
  Laugh at your misery, as fore-deeminge you

An idle Meteor which drawne forth the earth
Would bee soone lost ith aire.
ANTONELLI.   Jeast upon you,
And say you were begotten in an Earthquake,
You have ruin'd such faire Lordships.

ACT I, SCENE 2

CAMILLO. Indeede I am studying Alcumye.
FLAMINEO. Thou shalt lye in a bed stuft with turtles feathers, swoone in
perfumed lynnen like the fellow was smothered in roses — so perfect
shall be thy happinesse, that as men at Sea thinke land and trees and
shippes go that way they go, so both heaven and earth shall seeme to go
your voyage. Shalt meete him, tis fixt with nayles of dyamonds to inevitable necessitie.

ACT III, SCENE 2

FRANCISCO. How now my Noble cossin — what in blacke!
GIOVANNI. Yes, Unckle, I was taught to imitate you
In vertue, and you must imitate mee
In couloures for your garments — my sweete mother
Is —
FRANCISCO. How? Where?
GIOVANNI. Is there — no yonder — indeed sir I'le not tell you,
For I shall make you weepe.
FRANCISCO.   Is dead?
GIOVANNI.   Do not blame me now,
I did not tell you so.
LODOVICO.   She's dead my Lord.
FRANCISCO.   Dead?
MONTICELSO. Blessed Lady; thou art now above thy woes —
Wilt please your Lordships to with-draw a little?
GIOVANNI. What do the dead do, uncle? do they eate,
Heare musicke, goe a-hunting, and bee merrie,
As wee that live?
FRANCISCO. No, cose; they sleepe.
GIOVANNI.   Lord, Lord, that I were dead,
I have not slept these six nights. When doe they wake?
FRANCISCO. When God shall please.
GIOVANNI.   Good God let her sleepe ever.
For I have knowne her wake an hundreth nights,
When all the pillow, where shee laid her head,
Was brine-wet with her teares. I am to complaine to you Sir.
Ile tell you how they have used her now shees dead:
They wrapt her in a cruell fould of lead,
And would not let mee kisse her.
FRANCISCO.   Thou didst love her?

GIOVANNI. I have often heard her say shee gave mee sucke,
  And it should seeme by that shee deerely lov'd mee,
  Since Princes seldome doe it.

ACT V, SCENE 3

BRACHIANO. O thou soft naturall death, thou art joint-twin
  To sweetest slumber: no rough-bearded Comet,
  Stares on thy milde departure: the dull Owle
  Beates not against thy casement: the hoarse wolfe
  Scents not thy carion. Pitty windes thy corse,
  Whilst horrour waights on Princes.

ACT V, SCENE 4

CORNELIA. Call for the Robin-Red-brest and the wren,
  Since ore shadie groves they hover,
  And with leaves and flowers doe cover
  The friendlesse bodies of unburied men.
  Call unto his funerall Dole
  The Ante, the field-mouse, and the mole
  To reare him hillockes, that shall keepe him warme,
  And (when gay tombes are robb'd) sustaine no harme,
  But keepe the wolfe far thence, that's foe to men,
  For with his nailes hee'l dig them up agen.

ACT V, SCENE 6

FLAMINEO. Then here's an end of me: fare-well day-light
  And O contemtible Physike! that dost take
  So long a study, onely to preserve
  So short a life, I take my leave of thee.
  These are two cupping-glasses [*shewing the pistols*], that shall draw
  All my infected bloud out — Are you ready?
VITTORIA AND ZANCHE [*together*]. Ready.
FLAMINEO. Whither shall I go now? O *Lucian* thy ridiculous Purgatory
  — to finde *Alexander* the Great cobling shooes, *Pompey* tagging
  points, and *Julius Cæsar* making haire buttons, *Haniball* selling black-
  ing, and *Augustus* crying garlike, *Charlemaigne* selling lists by the
  dozen, and King *Pippin* crying Apples in a cart drawn with one horse!
  Whether I resolve to Fire, Earth, water, Aire,
  Or all the Elements by scruples; I know not
  Nor greatly care, — Shoote, shoote,
  Of all deaths the violent death is best,
  For from our selves it steales our selves so fast
  The paine once apprehended is quite past.

  They shoot and run to him and tread upon him.

VITTORIA. What, are you drop't?

FLAMINEO. I am mixt with Earth already. As you are Noble
Performe your vowes, and bravely follow mee.

VITTORIA. Whither — to hell?

ZANCHE.   To most assured damnation.

VITTORIA. O thou most cursed devill.

ZANCHE.   Thou art caught —

VITTORIA. In thine owne Engine, I tread the fire out
That would have bene my ruine.

FLAMINEO. Will you be perjur'd? what a religious oath was Stix that the
Gods never durst sweare by and violate! O that wee had such an oath
to minister, and to be so well kept in our Courts of Justice.

VITTORIA. Thinke whither thou art going.

ZANCHE.   And remember
What villanies thou hast acted.

VITTORIA.   This thy death
Shall make me like a blazing ominous starre,
Looke up and tremble.

FLAMINEO.   O I am caught with a springe!

VITTORIA. You see the Fox comes many times short home,
'Tis here prov'd true.

FLAMINEO.   Kild with a couple of braches.

VITTORIA. No fitter offring for the infernall furies
Then one in whom they raign'd while hee was living.

FLAMINEO. O the waies darke and horrid! I cannot see,
Shall I have no company?

VITTORIA.   O yes thy sinnes
Do runne before thee to fetch fire from hell,
To light thee thither.

FLAMINEO.   O I smell soote,
Most stinking soote, the chimne is a-fire,
My liver's purboil'd like scotch holly-bread;
There's a plumber laying pipes in my guts, it scalds;
Wilt thou out-live mee?

ZANCHE.   Yes, and drive a stake
Thorough thy body; for we'le give it out,
Thou didst this violence upon thy selfe.

FLAMINEO. O cunning Devils! now I have tri'd your love,
And doubled all your reaches. I am not wounded: [*Flamineo riseth.*]
The pistols held no bullets: 'twas a plot
To prove your kindnesse to mee; and I live
To punish your ingratitude — I knew
One time or other you would finde a way
To give me a strong potion — O Men
That lye upon your death-beds, and are haunted
With howling wives, neere trust them, they'le re-marry

Ere the worme peirce your winding sheete: ere the Spider
Make a thinne curtaine for your Epitaphes.
How cunning you were to discharge! Do you practise at the Artillery
yard? Trust a woman? never, never; *Brachiano* bee my precedent: we
lay our soules to pawne to the Devill for a little pleasure, and a woman
makes the bill of sale. That ever man should marry! For one
Hypermnestra that sav'd her Lord and husband, forty nine of her
sisters cut their husbands throates all in one night. There was a shole
of vertuous horse-leeches.   [*Enter Lodovico, Gasparo, disguised.*]
Here are two other Instruments.

VITTORIA.   Helpe, helpe!

FLAMINEO. What noise is that? hah? falce keies i' th Court.

LODOVICO. We have brought you a Maske.

FLAMINEO.   A matachine it seemes,
By your drawne swords. Church-men turn'd revellers!

GASPARO. *Isabella, Isabella!*

LODOVICO. Doe you know us now?

FLAMINEO.   *Lodovico* and *Gasparo!*

LODOVICO. Yes and that Moore the Duke gave pention to
Was the great Duke of Florence.

VITTORIA.   O wee are lost.

FLAMINEO. You shall not take Justice from forth my hands,
O let me kill her. — Ile cut my safety
Through your coates of steele: Fate's a Spaniell,
Wee cannot beat it from us: what remaines now?
Let all that doe ill, take this precedent:
Man may his Fate foresee, but not prevent.
And of all Axiomes this shall winne the prise,
'Tis better to be fortunate then wise.

GASPARO. Bind him to the pillar.

VITTORIA.   O your gentle pitty:
I have seene a black-bird that would sooner fly
To a mans bosome, then to stay the gripe
Of the feirce Sparrow-hawke.

GASPARO.   Your hope deceives you.

VITTORIA. If Florence be ith Court, would hee would kill mee!

GASPARO. Foole! Princes give rewards with their owne hands,
But death or punishment by the handes of others.

LODOVICO. Sirha you once did strike mee, Ile strike you
Into the Center.

FLAMINEO. Thou'lt doe it like a hangeman; a base hangman;
Not like a noble fellow, for thou seest
I cannot strike againe.

LODOVICO.   Dost laugh?

FLAMINEO. Wouldst have me dye, as I was borne, in whining?

GASPARO. Recommend your selfe to heaven.

FLAMINEO. Noe I will carry mine owne commendations thither.

LODOVICO. Oh could I kill you forty times a day
And use't foure yeere together; 'tweare too little:
Nought greev's but that you are too few to feede
The famine of our vengeance. What dost thinke on?

FLAMINEO. Nothing; of nothing: leave thy idle questions,
I am ith way to study a long silence,
To prate were idle, I remember nothing.
Thers nothing of so infinit vexation
As mans owne thoughts.

LODOVICO.   O thou glorious strumpet,
Could I devide thy breath from this pure aire
When't leaves thy body, I would sucke it up
And breath't upon some dunghill.

VITTORIA.   You, my Deathsman!
Me thinkes thou doest not looke horrid enough,
Thou hast too good a face to be a hang-man,
If thou be, doe thy office in right forme;
Fall downe upon thy knees and aske forgivenesse.

LODOVICO. O thou hast bin a most prodigious comet,
But Ile cut off your traine: kill the Moore first.

VITTORIA. You shall not kill her first, behould my breast,
I will be waited on in death; my servant
Shall never go before mee.

GASPARO.   Are you so brave?

VITTORIA. Yes I shall wellcome death
As Princes doe some great Embassadors;
Ile meete thy weapon halfe way.

LODOVICO.   Thou dost tremble,
Mee thinkes feare should dissolve thee into ayre.

VITTORIA. O thou art deceiv'd, I am too true a woman:
Conceit can never kill me: Ile tell thee what,
I will not in my death shed one base teare,
Or if looke pale, for want of blood, not feare.

GASPARO. Thou art my taske, blacke fury.

ZANCHE.   I have blood
As red as either of theirs; wilt drinke some?
'Tis good for the falling sicknesse: I am proud
Death cannot alter my complexion,
For I shall neere looke pale.

LODOVICO.   Strike, strike,
With a Joint motion.

From THE DUTCHESSE OF MALFY

ACT IV, SCENE 2

DUCHESS. What hideous noyse was that?

CARIOLA.   'Tis the wild consort
Of Mad-men (Lady) which your Tyrant brother
Hath plac'd about your lodging: This tyranny,
I thinke was never practis'd till this howre.

DUCHESS. Indeed I thanke him: nothing but noyce, and folly
Can keepe me in my right wits, whereas reason
And silence, make me starke mad: Sit downe,
Discourse to me some dismall Tragedy.

CARIOLA. O 'twill encrease your mellancholly.

DUCHESS.   Thou art deceiv'd,
To heare of greater griefe, would lessen mine —
This is a prison?

CARIOLA.   Yes, but you shall live
To shake this durance off.

DUCHESS.   Thou art a foole,
The Robin red-brest, and the Nightingale,
Never live long in cages.

CARIOLA.   Pray drie your eyes.
What thinke you of, Madam?

DUCHESS.   Of nothing:
When I muse thus, I sleepe.

CARIOLA. Like a mad-man, with your eyes open?

DUCHESS. Do'st thou thinke we shall know one another,
In th' other world?

CARIOLA.   Yes, out of question.

DUCHESS. O that it were possible we might
But hold some two dayes conference with the dead,
From them, I should learne somewhat, I am sure
I never shall know here: I'll tell thee a miracle —
I am not mad yet, to my cause of sorrow.
Th' heaven ore my head, seemes made of molten brasse,
The earth of flaming sulphure, yet I am not mad:
I am acquainted with sad misery,
As the tann'd galley-slave is with his Oare,
Necessity makes me suffer constantly,
And custome makes it easie — who do I looke like now?

CARIOLA. Like to your picture in the gallery,
A deale of life in shew, but none in practise:
Or rather like some reverend monument
Whose ruines are even pittied.

DUCHESS. Very proper:
And Fortune seemes onely to have her eie-sight,
To behold my Tragedy: How now, what noyce is that? [*Enter Servant.*]
SERVANT. I am come to tell you,
Your brother hath entended you some sport:
A great Physitian, when the Pope was sicke
Of a deepe mellancholly, presented him
With severall sorts of mad-men, which wilde object
(Being full of change, and sport,) forc'd him to laugh,
And so th' impost-hume broke: the selfe same cure,
The Duke intends on you.
DUCHESS. Let them come in.
SERVANT. There's a mad Lawyer, and a secular Priest,
A Doctor that hath forfeited his wits
By jealousie: an Astrologian,
That in his workes, sayd such a day o' th' moneth
Should be the day of doome; and fayling of't,
Ran mad: an English Taylor, crais'd i' th' braine,
With the studdy of new fashion: a gentleman usher
Quite beside himselfe, with care to keepe in minde,
The number of his Ladies salutations,
Or "how do you," she employ'd him in each morning:
A Farmer too, (an excellent knave in graine)
Mad, 'cause he was hindred transportation,
And let one Broaker (that's mad) loose to these,
You'ld thinke the divell were among them.
DUCHESS. Sit *Cariola:* let them loose when you please,
For I am chain'd to endure all your tyranny. [*Enter Madmen.*]

*Here (by a Mad-man) this song is sung, to a dismall kind
of Musique.*

O let us howle, some heavy note,
   Some deadly-dogged howle,
Sounding, as from the threatning throat,
   Of beastes, and fatall fowle.
As Ravens, Schrich-owles, Bulls, and Beares,
   We'll bell, and bawle our parts,
Till irksome noyce have cloy'd your eares,
   And corasiv'd your hearts.
At last when as our quire wants breath,
   Our bodies being blest,
We'll sing like Swans, to welcome death,
   And die in love and rest.

FIRST MAD-MAN (ASTROLOGER). Doomes-day not come yet? I'll draw it neerer by a perspective, or make a glasse, that shall set all the world on fire upon an instant: I cannot sleepe, my pillow is stuff't with a littour of Porcupines.

SECOND MAD-MAN (LAWYER). Hell is a meere glasse-house, where the divells are continually blowing up womens soules, on hollow yrons, and the fire never goes out.

THIRD MAD-MAN (PRIEST). I will lie with every woman in my parish the tenth night: I will tithe them over, like hay-cockes.

FOURTH MAD-MAN (DOCTOR). Shall my Pothecary out-go me, because I am a Cuck-old? I have found out his roguery: he makes allom of his wives urin, and sells it to Puritaines, that have sore throates with over-strayning.

FIRST MAD-MAN. I have skill in Harroldry.

SECOND MAD-MAN. Hast?

FIRST MAD-MAN. You do give for your creast a wood-cockes head, with the Braines pickt out on't, you are a very ancient Gentleman.

THIRD MAD-MAN. Greeke is turn'd Turke, we are onely to be sav'd by the Helvetian translation.

FIRST MAD-MAN. Come on Sir, I will lay the law to you.

SECOND MAD-MAN. Oh, rather lay a corazive — the law will eate to the bone.

THIRD MAD-MAN. He that drinkes but to satisfie nature is damn'd.

FOURTH MAD-MAN. If I had my glasse here, I would shew a sight should make all the women here call me mad Doctor.

FIRST MAD-MAN. What's he, a rope-maker? [*Pointing at the Priest.*]

SECOND MAD-MAN. No, no, no, a snufling knave, that while he shewes the tombes, will have his hand in a wenches placket.

THIRD MAD-MAN. Woe to the Caroach, that brought home my wife from the Masque, at three a clocke in the morning, it had a large Feather-bed in it.

FOURTH MAD-MAN. I have paired the divells nayles forty times, roasted them in Ravens egges, and cur'd agues with them.

THIRD MAD-MAN. Get me three hundred milch bats, to make possets, to procure sleepe.

FOURTH MAD-MAN. All the Colledge may throw their caps at me, I have made a Soape-boyler costive, it was my master-peece.

Here the Daunce consisting of 8 Mad-men, with musicke answerable thereunto, after which, Bosola (like an old man) enters.

DUCHESS. Is he mad too?

SERVANT.   'Pray question him: I'll leave you.

                                 [*Exeunt Servant and Madmen.*]

BOSOLA. I am come to make thy tombe.

DUCHESS.   Hah, my tombe?
Thou speak'st, as if I lay upon my death bed,
  Gasping for breath: do'st thou perceive me sicke?

BOSOLA. Yes, and the more dangerously, since thy sicknesse is insensible.

DUCHESS. Thou art not mad sure, do'st know me?

BOSOLA.   Yes.

DUCHESS.   Who am I?

BOSOLA. Thou art a box of worme-seede, at best, but a salvatory of greene
  mummey: what's this flesh? a little curded milke, phantasticall puffe-
  paste: our bodies are weaker than those paper prisons boyes use to
  keepe flies in: more contemptible: since ours is to preserve earth-
  wormes: didst thou ever see a Larke in a cage? such is the soule in the
  body: this world is like her little turfe of grasse, and the Heaven ore
  our heades, like her looking glasse, onely gives us a misearable knowledge of the small compasse of our prison.

DUCHESS. Am not I, thy Duchesse?

BOSOLA. Thou art some great woman sure, for riot begins to sit on thy
  fore-head (clad in gray haires) twenty yeares sooner, then on a merry
  milkemaydes. Thou sleep'st worse, then if a mouse should be forc'd
  to take up her lodging in a cats eare: a little infant, that breedes it's
  teeth, should it lie with thee, would crie out, as if thou wert the more
  unquiet bed-fellow.

DUCHESS. I am Duchesse of *Malfy* still.

BOSOLA. That makes thy sleepes so broken:
  "Glories (like glow-wormes) afarre off, shine bright,
  But look'd to neere, have neither heate, nor light."

DUCHESS. Thou art very plaine.

BOSOLA. My trade is to flatter the dead, not the living —
  I am a tombemaker.

DUCHESS. And thou com'st to make my tombe?

BOSOLA. Yes.

DUCHESS. Let me be a little merry —
  Of what stuffe wilt thou make it?

BOSOLA. Nay, resolve me first, of what fashion?

DUCHESS. Why, do we grow phantasticall in our death-bed?
  Do we affect fashion in the grave?

BOSOLA. Most ambitiously: Princes images on their tombes
  Do not lie, as they were wont, seeming to pray
  Up to heaven: but with their hands under their cheekes,
  (As if they died of the tooth-ache) — they are not carved
  With their eies fix'd upon the starres; but as
  Their mindes were wholy bent upon the world,
  The selfe-same way they seeme to turne their faces.

DUCHESS. Let me know fully therefore the effect
  Of this thy dismall preparation,

This talke, fit for a charnell!

BOSOLA. Now, I shall —

Enter Executioners with a Coffin, Cords, and a Bell.

Here is a present from your Princely brothers,
And may it arrive wel-come, for it brings
Last benefit, last sorrow.

DUCHESS. Let me see it —
I have so much obedience, in my blood,
I wish it in ther veines, to do them good.

BOSOLA. This is your last presence Chamber.

CARIOLA. O my sweete Lady.

DUCHESS. Peace, it affrights not me.

BOSOLA. I am the common Bell-man,
[*Takes up the Bell.*]
That usually is sent to condemn'd persons
The Night before they suffer:

DUCHESS. Even now thou said'st,
Thou wast a tombe-maker?

BOSOLA. 'Twas to bring you
By degrees to mortification: Listen. [*Rings his bell.*]

> *Hearke, now every thing is still —*
> *The Schritch-Owle, and the whistler shrill,*
> *Call upon our Dame, aloud,*
> *And bid her quickly don her shrowd:*
> *Much you had of Land and rent,*
> *Your length in clay's now competent.*
> *A long war disturb'd your minde,*
> *Here your perfect peace is sign'd —*
> *Of what is't fooles make such vaine keeping?*
> *Sin their conception, their birth, weeping:*
> *Their life, a generall mist of error,*
> *Their death, a hideous storme of terror —*
> *Strew your haire, with powders sweete:*
> *Don cleane linnen, bath your feete,*
> *And (the foule feend more to checke)*
> *A crucifixe let blesse your necke,*
> *'Tis now full tide, 'tweene night, and day,*
> *End your groane, and come away.*

CARIOLA. Hence villaines, tyrants, murderers: alas!
What will you do with my Lady? call for helpe.

DUCHESS. To whom, to our next neighbours? they are mad-folkes.

BOSOLA. Remoove that noyse.

DUCHESS.   Farwell *Cariola*,
  In my last will, I have not much to give —
  A many hungry guests have fed upon me,
  Thine will be a poore reversion.
CARIOLA.   I will die with her.
DUCHESS. I pray-thee looke thou giv'st my little boy
  Some sirrop, for his cold, and let the girle
  Say her prayers, ere she sleepe. [*Cariola is forced off.*] Now what you
    please,
  What death?
BOSOLA.   Strangling, here are your Executioners.
DUCHESS. I forgive them:
  The apoplexie, cathar, or cough o' th' lungs,
  Would do as much as they do.
BOSOLA. Doth not death fright you?
DUCHESS.   Who would be afraid on't?
  Knowing to meete such excellent company
  In th' other world.
BOSOLA.   Yet, me thinkes,
  The manner of your death should much afflict you,
  This cord should terrifie you!
DUCHESS.   Not a whit —
  What would it pleasure me, to have my throate cut
  With diamonds? or to be smothered
  With Cassia? or to be shot to death, with pearles?
  I know death hath ten thousand severall doores
  For men, to take their *Exits:* and 'tis found
  They go on such strange geometricall hinges,
  You may open them both wayes: any way, (for heaven sake)
  So I were out of your whispering: Tell my brothers,
  That I perceive death, (now I am well awake)
  Best guift is, they can give, or I can take —
  I would faine put off my last womans-fault,
  I'ld not be tedious to you.
EXECUTIONER.   We are ready.
DUCHESS. Dispose my breath, how please you, but my body
  Bestow upon my women, will you?
EXECUTIONER.   Yes.
DUCHESS. Pull, and pull strongly, for your able strength,
  Must pull downe heaven upon me:
  Yet stay, heaven gates are not so highly arch'd
  As Princes pallaces — they that enter there
  Must go upon their knees: Come violent death,   [*She kneels.*]
  Serve for *Mandragora*, to make me sleepe;
  Go tell my brothers, when I am laid out,
  They then may feede in quiet.   [*They strangle her.*]

ACT V, SCENE 3

*Enter Antonio and Delio. There is an Eccho, (from the
Dutchesse Grave.)*

DELIO. Yond's the Cardinall's window: This fortification
  Grew from the ruines of an auncient Abbey:
  And to yond side o' th' river, lies a wall
  (Peece of a Cloyster) which in my opinion
  Gives the best Eccho, that you ever heard;
  So hollow, and so dismall, and withall
  So plaine in the destinction of our words,
  That many have supposde it is a Spirit
  That answeres.
ANTONIO.   I doe love these auncient ruynes:
  We never tread upon them, but we set
  Our foote upon some reverend History.
  And questionles, here in this open Court
  (Which lies naked to the injuries
  Of stormy weather) some men lye interr'd
  Lov'd the Church so well, and gave so largely to't,
  They thought it should have canopide their Bones
  Till Doombes-day: But all things have their end:
  Churches, and Citties (which have diseases like to men)
  Must have like death that we have.
ECCHO.   *Like death that we have.*
DELIO. Now the *Eccho* hath caught you.
ANTONIO.   It groan'd (me thought) and gave
  A very deadly Accent.
ECCHO.   *Deadly Accent.*
DELIO. I told you 'twas a pretty one: You may make it
  A Huntes-man, or a Faulconer, a Musitian,
  Or a Thing of Sorrow.
ECCHO.   *A Thing of Sorrow.*
ANTONIO. Ay sure: that suites it best.
ECCHO.   *That suites it best.*
ANTONIO. 'Tis very like my wifes voyce.
ECCHO.   *Ay, wifes-voyce.*
DELIO. Come: let's walke farther from't.
  I would not have you go
  To th' *Cardinalls* to-night: Doe not.
ECCHO.   *Doe not.*
DELIO. Wisdome doth not more moderate wasting Sorrow
  Then time: take time for't: be mindfull of thy safety.
ECCHO. *Be mindfull of thy safety.*

ANTONIO.   Necessitie compells me:
  Make scruteny throughout the passages
  Of your owne life; you'll find it impossible
  To flye your fate.
ECCHO.   *O flye your fate.*
DELIO. Harke: the dead stones seeme to have pitty on you
  And give you good counsell.
ANTONIO. *Eccho,* I will not talke with thee;
  For thou art a dead Thing.
ECCHO.   *Thou art a dead Thing.*
ANTONIO. My Dutchesse is asleepe now.
  And her litle-Ones, I hope sweetly: oh Heaven
  Shall I never see her more?
ECCHO.   *Never see her more.*
ANTONIO. I mark'd not one repetition of the *Eccho*
  But that: and on the sudden, a cleare light
  Presented me a face folded in sorrow.
DELIO. Your fancy; meerely.

Cyril Tourneur
1575?-1626

From THE ATHEIST'S TRAGEDY

ACT V, SCENE 1

D'AMVILLE. Cease that harsh musick; we are not pleas'd with it.
                                    [*He handles the gold.*]
  Here sounds a musicke whose melodious touch
  Like angels' voices ravishes the sense.
  Behold, thou ignorant astronomer
  Whose wandering Speculation seekes among
  The Planets for Mens fortunes, with amazement
  Behold their Error and be Planet-strucke.
  These are the Starres whose operations make
  The fortunes and the destinies of men.
  Your lesser eies of Heaven (like subjects raised
  Unto their lofty houses, when their Prince
  Rides underneath the ambition of their loves)
  Are mounted only to behold the face
  Of your more rich imperious Eminence
  With unprevented sighte. Unmask, faire queene.   [*Unpurses the gold.*]
  Vouchsafe their expectations may enjoye

The gracious favour they admire to see.
These are the Starres, the ministers of Fate,
And Man's high wisedome the superior power
To which their forces are subordinate.

From THE REVENGER'S TRAGEDY

ACT I, SCENE 3

VINDICE.   O hour of incest!
  Any kin now, next to the ruin o' th' sister,
  Is men's meate in these dayes; and in the morning,
  When they are up and dressed; and their maske on,
  Who can perceive this, save that eternall Eie
  That sees through flesh and all? Well, if anything be damned
  It will be twelve o'clock at Nyght; that twelve
  Will never scape:
  It is the Judas of the houres, wherein
  Honest Salvation is betrayed to sin.
LUSSORIOSO. In truth, it is true; but let this talk glide.
  It is our blood to err, though hell gape wide.

ACT II, SCENE 2

LUSSORIOSO. Ravish me in thine answere; art thou rare,
  Hast thou beguiled her of salvation,
  And rubb'd hell o'er with honey?

ACT III, SCENE 5

  Enter Vindice, with the skull of his love drest up in
  Cloths.

VINDICE. Madame, his grace will not be absent long.
  Secret? nere doubt us Madame! twill be worth
  Three velvet gownes to your Ladyship — knowne?
  Few Ladies respect that disgrace, a poore thin shell,
  Tis the best grace you have to do it well,
  Ile save your hand that labour, ile unmaske you!
HIPPOLITO. Why brother, brother.
VINDICE. Art thou beguild now? tut, a Lady can,
  As such all hid, beguile a wiser man;
  Have I not fitted the old surfetter
  With a quaint piece of beauty? Age and bare bone
  Are ere allied in action; here's an eye,
  Able to tempt a great man — so serve God,
  A prety hanging lip, that has forgot how to dissemble.

Me thinkes this mouth should make a swearer tremble,
A drunckard claspe his teeth, and not undo 'em.
Heres a cheeke keepes her colour let the wind go whistle,
Spout Raine, we feare thee not, be hot or cold
Alls one with us; and is not he absurd,
Whose fortunes are upon their faces set,
That fear no other God but winde and wet.
HIPPOLITO. Brother y'ave spoke that right,
  Is this the forme that living shone so bright?
VINDICE. The very same,
  And now me thinkes I could e'en chide my selfe,
  For doating on her beauty, tho her death
  Shall be revenged after no common action;
  Dos the Silke-worme expend her yellow labours
  For thee? for thee dos she undoe herselfe?
  Are Lord-ships sold to maintaine Lady-ships
  For the poore benefit of a bewitching minute?
  Why dos yon fellow falsify hie-waies
  And put his life betweene the Judges lippes,
  To refine such a thing, keepes horse and men
  To beate their valours for her?
  Surely wee're all mad people, and they
  Whome we thinke are, are not, we mistake those,
  Tis we are mad in sense, they but in clothes.
HIPPOLITO. Faith and in clothes too we, give us our due.
VINDICE. Dos every proud and selfe-affecting Dame
  Camphire her face for this? and grieve her Maker
  In sinfull baths of milke, — when many an infant starves,
  For her superfluous out-side, all for this?
  Who now bids twenty pound a night, prepares
  Musick, perfumes, and sweete-meates, all are husht,
  Thou maist lie chast now! it were fine me thinkes
  To have thee seene at Revells, forgetfull feasts,
  And uncleane Brothells; sure twould fright the sinner
  And make him a good coward, put a Reveller,
  Out of his Antick amble
  And cloye an Epicure with empty dishes!
  Here might a scornefull and ambitious woman,
  Looke through and through her selfe — see Ladies, with false formes
  You deceive men, but cannot deceive wormes.
  Now to my tragick businesse, looke you brother,
  I have not fashiond this only for show
  And useless property, no, it shall beare a part
  E'en in its owne Revenge. This very skull,
  Whose Mistris the Duke poysoned, with this drug
  The mortall curse of the earth, shall be revengd

In the like straine, and kiss his lippes to death,
As much as the dumbe thing can, he shall feele:
What fayles in poyson, weele supply in steele.

HIPPOLITO. Brother I do applaud thy constant vengeance,
The quaintnesse of thy malice above thought.

VINDICE. So tis layde on: now come and welcome Duke,
I have her for thee, I protest it brother:
Me thinkes she makes almost as faire a fine
As some old gentlewoman in a Periwig!
Hide thy face now for shame, thou hadst neede have a Maske now
Tis vaine when beauty flowes, but when it fleetes
This would become graves better then the streetes.

HIPPOLITO. You have my voice in that; harke, the Duke's come.

VINDICE. Peace, let's observe what company he brings,
And how he dos absent 'em, for you knowe
Heele wish all private, — brother fall you back a little,
With the bony Lady.

HIPPOLITO.   That I will.

VINDICE.   So, so, —
Now nine years vengeance crowde into a minute!

Thomas Middleton

1570-1627

From BLURT: MASTER CONSTABLE

SONG: *LOVE IS LIKE A LAMB*

Love is like a lamb, and love is like a lion;
Fly from love, he fights; fight, then does he fly on;
Love is all on fire, and yet is ever freezing,
Love is much in winning, yet is more in leesing;
Love is ever sick, and yet is never dying,
Love is ever true, and yet is ever lying;
Love does doat in liking, and is mad in loathing,
Love indeed is any thing, yet indeed is nothing.

From THE CHANGELING

ACT III, SCENE 4

DEFLORES. What makes your lip so strange?
This must not be betwixt us.

BEATRICE. The man talks wildly.

DEFLORES. Come kisse me with a zeal now.

BEATRICE. Heaven I doubt him.

DEFLORES. I will not stand so long to beg 'em shortly.

BEATRICE. Take heed *Deflores* of forgetfulness,
    'Twill soon betray us.

DEFLORES. Take you heed first;
    Faith y'are grown much forgetfull, y'are to blame in't.

BEATRICE. He's bold, and I am blam'd for't.

DEFLORES. I have eas'd you
    Of your trouble. Think on't, I'me in pain,
    And must be eas'd of you; 'tis a charity,
    Justice invites your blood to understand me.

BEATRICE. I dare not.

DEFLORES. Quickly.

BEATRICE. Oh I never shall,
    Speak it yet further off that I may lose
    What has been spoken, and no sound remain on't.
    I would not hear so much offence again
    For such another deed.

DEFLORES. Soft, Lady, soft;
    The last is not yet paid for, oh this act
    Has put me into spirit; I was as greedy on't
    As the parcht earth of moisture, when the clouds weep.
    Did you not mark, I wrought my self into't.
    Nay sued, and kneel'd for't: Why was all that pains took?
    You see I have thrown contempt upon your gold,
    Not that I want it not, for I doe piteously,
    In order I will come unto't, and make use on't,
    But 'twas not held so pretious to begin with;
    For I place wealth after the heels of pleasure,
    And were I not resolv'd in my belief
    That thy virginity were perfect in thee,
    I should but take my recompence with grudging,
    As if I had but halfe my hopes I agreed for.

BEATRICE. Why 'tis impossible thou canst be so wicked,
    Or shelter such a cunning cruelty,
    To make his death the murderer of my honor.
    Thy language is so bold and vitious,
    I cannot see which way I can forgive it
    With any modesty.

DEFLORES. Push, you forget your selfe,
    A woman dipt in blood, and talk of modesty.

BEATRICE. O misery of sin! would I had been bound
    Perpetually unto my living hate

push] pish, pshaw.

In that *Piracquo,* then to hear these words.
Think but upon the distance that Creation
Set 'twixt thy blood and mine, and keep thee there.
DEFLORES. Look but into your conscience, read me there,
'Tis a true Book, you'l find me there your equall:
Push, flye not to your birth, but settle you
In what the act has made you, y'are no more now,
You must forget your parentage to me,
Y'are the deeds creature, by that name
You lost your first condition, and I challenge you,
As peace and innocency has turn'd you out,
And made you one with me.
BEATRICE.   With thee, foul villain?
DEFLORES. Yes, my fair murdress; Do you urge me?
Though thou writ'st maid, thou whore in thy affection,
'Twas chang'd from thy first love, and that's a kind
Of whoredome in thy heart, and he's chang'd now,
To bring thy second on thy *Alsemero,*
Whom by all sweets that ever darkness tasted,
If I enjoy thee not thou ne're enjoyst,
I'le blast the hopes and joyes of marriage,
I'le confess all, my life I rate at nothing.
BEATRICE. *Deflores.*
DEFLORES.   I shall rest from all lovers plagues then,
I live in pain now: that shooting eye
Will burn my heart to cinders.
BEATRICE.   O sir, hear me.
DEFLORES. She that in life and love refuses me,
In death and shame my partner she shall be.
BEATRICE. Stay, hear me once for all, I make thee master
Of all the wealth I have in gold and jewels,
Let me go poor unto my bed with honor,
And I am rich in all things.
DEFLORES.   Let this silence thee,
The wealth of all *Valentia* shall not buy my pleasure from me,
Can you weep Fate from its determin'd purpose?
So soon may you weep me.
BEATRICE.   Vengeance begins;
Murder I see is followed by more sins.
Was my creation in the womb so curst,
It must ingender with a Viper first?
DEFLORES. Come, rise, and shrowd your blushes in my bosome,
Silence is one of pleasures best receipts:
Thy peace is wrought for ever in this yeelding.
'Las, how the Turtle pants! Thou'lt love anon,
What thou so fear'st, and faintst to venture on.   [*Exeunt.*]

ACT V, SCENE 3

Enter Deflores bringing in Beatrice.

DEFLORES. Here we are, if you have any more
　To say to us, speak quickly, I shall not
　Give you the hearing else, I am so stout yet,
　And so I think that broken rib of mankind.
VERMANDERO. An Host of enemies entred my Citadell,
　Could not amaze like this, *Joanna, Beatrice, Joanna.*
BEATRICE. O come not neer me sir, I shall defile you,
　I am that of your blood was taken from you
　For your better health, look no more upon't,
　But cast it to the ground regardlessly,
　Let the common sewer take it from distinction,
　Beneath the starres, upon yon Meteor
　Ever hang my fate, 'mongst things corruptible,
　I ne're could pluck it from him, my loathing
　Was Prophet to the rest, but ne're believ'd:
　Mine honour fell with him, and now my life.
　Alsemero, I am a stranger to your bed,
　Your bed was coz'ned on the nuptiall night,
　For which your false-bride died.
ALSEMERO.　　　　　　　　　　　　*Diaphanta?*
DEFLORES. Yes, and the while I coupled with your mate
　At barly-break; now we are left in hell.
VERMANDERO. We are all there, it circumscribes here.
DEFLORES. I lov'd this woman in spite of her heart,
　Her love I earn'd out of *Piracquos* murder.
TOMASO. Ha, my brothers murtherer.
DEFLORES.　　　　　　　　　　　Yes, and her honors prize
　Was my reward, I thank life for nothing
　But that pleasure, it was so sweet to me,
　That I have drunk up all, left none behinde,
　For any man to pledge me.

William Shakespeare
1564-1616

In these gigantic works, there are the differences in nature, in matter,
in light, in darkness, in movement, that we find in the universe.
　Sometimes the identities of which the world is composed belong, as it
were, to the different grades in the series of existence — to the mineral

kingdom, the vegetable kingdom, the brute creation. Or they are one of the elements: Water: Hamlet. Air: Romeo and Juliet. Fire: Lear. (Goethe said that "Time is an element." Time may be said to be the other element in Lear — Coleridge said of the play that "old age is a character." But in *King Lear* the character is more than old age: it is Time itself. Time is the essence of Lear's being, the space in which that being exists.) The fourth element, Earth, is always present.

Characters such as Falstaffe are "lumps of the world," are "still alive from the roots, a part not yet cut off from universal nature," and they have a gross physical enormity of sensation which approaches a kind of physical godhead.

Shakespeare is like "the sun, that common-kissing Titan, having a passion for matter, pure and impure, an energy beyond good and evil, an immense benevolence creating without choice or preference, out of the need of giving birth to life. Never was there such a homage to light, to light and the principle of life." *

Poor Pompey, the bawd's tapster in *Measure for Measure,* excuses himself to his judge by saying: "Truly, sir, I am a poor fellow that would live." And Shakespeare, if no one else, forgives him, for to Shakespeare life is holy, and Pompey, Mrs. Quickly, and other earthy characters, of this as of every other kind, hold in them the principle, and the love, of life. These, and Nilus' slime, are worthy in his eyes of the light and heat of the sun.

"None does offend, none, I say, none," said the old mad King upon the dark moor. And so said his loving creator. The terrible storms of the most gigantic tragedies ever born from the heart of Man, though they are vast as the upheavals of Nature, are not blind as these. It is no fault of the sun if we wreck our world. . . . In *King Lear,* in *Timon of Athens,* the diatribes are only the reverse side of love.

"There's sap in it yet," says Antony to his Queen before darkness falls. Sap in the event, sap in the heart of Man.

Only that which is too cold for Hell (as was, perhaps, Iago) is condemned. Only the hard heart offends. But this, too, though it is more inflexible than marble or than the cold of death, must be investigated.

"Then let them Anatomize *Regan,*" said the old outcast King: "See what breeds about her heart. Is there any cause in Nature that makes these hard-hearts."

In these hymns to life, the very blood of the beings, the animate heat, is spirit † — "Not fire, it does not take its origin from fire, but derives from the solar ray. . . . The blood acquires remarkable and most excellent powers, and is analogous to the stars. . . ." In beings like Othello, the blood "is spirit. It is celestial, something analogous to heaven, vicarious of heaven . . . the innate heat, the sun of the microcosm, the

---

* This was said by Arthur Symons of a still great, though infinitely lesser artist than Shakespeare, and an artist in a different medium — Edouard Manet.

† William Harvey, *On Generation.*

fire of Plato. . . ." In such beings as Juliet's nurse, "in so far as it is spirit, it is the hearth, the Vesta, the household divinity."

Such plays as *King Henry the Fourth* (Parts I and II) and *King Henry the Fifth* are hymns to the physical glory of Life, and the characters seem "the animalisation of God." ". . . banish plumpe Jacke, and banish all the World." * (That round berry the world, with its sweetness . . . the world with its earthiness and juice; the old happy laughing world that forgets it must die.)

"Music," said Wagner, "blots out our entire civilization, as sunshine does lamplight." This is true of the harmonies of Shakespeare. In another kind, his poetry is a sun whose light does not blot out a civilization, but fuses it into a single being.

In the Comedies, the Sun forgives and remakes the shape of evil, dances, laughing and loving the world, over stupidity. We see the nettle-dull Dogberry and Verges. Shakespeare reduces their sheer nonsense, their incomprehension and rustic fears, into Chaos; and then from Chaos he produces a dancing star. "Foolery, sir, does walke about the Orbe like the Sunne; it shines every where," said Feste. And all the characters of the Fools have "dimensions that are half-way between those of an atom and those of a star."

When John Ray, the great seventeenth-century naturalist, was asked, "What is the use of butterflies?" he replied, "To adorn the world and delight the eyes of men, to brighten the countryside, serving like so many golden spangles, to decorate the fields." And he added, "Who can contemplate their exquisite beauty and not acknowledge and adore the traces of divine art upon them?"

Watteau's Pierrot is of this kind . . . *"Je vécus, étincelle d'or de la lumière nature"* . . . a simple creature adorning the world, and soon to die. The Fool in *King Lear* was once such a being.

"All is indiscriminately stamped with grandeur," as Fuseli said of Michael Angelo. "A beggar rose from his hand the patriarch of poverty; the hump of his dwarf is impressed with dignity. . . . The hump and withered arm of Richard the Third are engines of terror and persuasion in Shakespeare" as "the crook-back of Michael Angelo strikes with awe."

In the Tragedies the theme is the struggle of Man against the gigantic forces of Nature, or Man brought face to face with the eternal truths. . . . The King made equal with the beggar at the feast of the worm, the King whose will had never been combated, finding that his hand "smelles of Mortality."

"It is great morning." So says Paris in the opening of the third scene of the fourth act of *Troilus and Cressida*. And, by the light of that great morning, even the beings whom we see passing in the common street are transformed for us, forevermore, into the epitome of all beauty, or all sorrow. We ask: "Who were those went by?" And the answer comes: "Queen Hecuba and Helen."

* *King Henry the Fourth (Part I).*

From *the* SONNETS

1

From fairest creatures we desire increase,
That thereby beauties *Rose* might never die,
But as the riper should by time decease,
His tender heire might beare his memory:
But thou contracted to thine owne bright eyes,
Feed'st thy lights flame with selfe substantiall fewell,
Making a famine where aboundance lies,
Thy selfe thy foe, to thy sweet selfe too cruell:
Thou that art now the worlds fresh ornament,
And only herauld to the gaudy spring,
Within thine owne bud buriest thy content,
And tender chorle makst wast in niggarding:
   Pitty the world, or else this glutton be,
    To eate the worlds due, by the grave and thee.

18

Shall I compare thee to a Summers day?
Thou art more lovely and more temperate:
Rough windes do shake the darling buds of Maie,
And Sommers lease hath all too short a date:
Sometime too hot the eye of heaven shines,
And often is his gold complexion dimm'd,
And every faire from faire some-time declines,
By chance, or natures changing course untrim'd:
But thy eternall Sommer shall not fade,
Nor lose possession of that faire thou ow'st,
Nor shall death brag thou wandr'st in his shade,
When in eternall lines to time thou grow'st,
   So long as men can breath or eyes can see,
    So long lives this, and this gives life to thee.

19

Devouring time blunt thou the Lyons pawes,
And make the earth devoure her owne sweet brood,
Plucke the keene teeth from the fierce Tygers jawes,
And burne the long liv'd Phænix in her blood,
Make glad and sorry seasons as thou fleet'st,
And do what ere thou wilt swift-footed time
To the wide world and all her fading sweets:

But I forbid thee one most hainous crime,
O carve not with thy howers my loves faire brow,
Nor draw noe lines there with thine antique pen,
Him in thy course untainted doe allow,
For beauties patterne to succeeding men.
 Yet doe thy worst ould Time: dispight thy wrong,
 My Love shall in my verse ever live young.

29

When in disgrace with Fortune and mens eyes,
I all alone beweepe my out-cast state,
And trouble deafe heaven with my bootlesse cries,
And looke upon my selfe and curse my fate,
Wishing me like to one more rich in hope,
Featur'd like him, like him with friends possest,
Desiring this mans art, and that mans skope,
With what I most injoy contented least,
Yet in these thoughts my selfe almost despising,
Haplye I thinke on thee, and then my state,
(Like to the Larke at breake of daye arising)
From sullen earth sings himns at Heavens gate,
 For thy sweet love remembred such welth brings,
 That then I skorne to change my state with Kings.

53

What is your substance, whereof are you made,
That millions of strange shaddowes on you tend?
Since every one, hath every one, one shade,
And you but one, can every shaddow lend:
Describe *Adonis* and the counterfet,
Is poorely immitated after you,
On *Hellens* cheeke all art of beautie set,
And you in *Grecian* tires are painted new:
Speake of the spring, and foison of the yeare,
The one doth shaddow of your beautie show,
The other as your bountie doth appeare,
And you in every blessed shape we know.
 In all externall grace you have some part,
 But you like none, none you, for constant heart.

65

Since brasse, nor stone, nor earth, nor boundlesse sea,
But sad mortallity ore-swaies their power,
How with this rage shall beautie hold a plea,

Whose action is no stronger then a flower?
O how shall summers honey breath hold out,
Against the wrackfull siedge of battring dayes,
When rocks impregnable are not so stoute,
Nor gates of steele so strong but time decayes?
O fearefull meditation, where alack,
Shall times best Jewell from times chest lie hid?
Or what strong hand can hold his swift foote back,
Or who his spoile of beautie can forbid?
   O none, unlesse this miracle have might,
   That in black inck my love may still shine bright.

146

Poore soule the center of my sinfull earth,
Thrall to these rebbell powres that thee array,
Why dost thou pine within and suffer dearth
Painting thy outward walls so costlie gay?
Why so large cost having so short a lease,
Dost thou upon thy fading mansion spend?
Shall wormes inheritors of this excesse
Eate up thy charge? is this thy bodies end?
Then soule live thou upon thy servants losse,
And let that pine to aggravat thy store;
Buy tearmes divine in selling houres of drosse:
Within be fed, without be rich no more,
   So shalt thou feed on death, that feeds on men,
   And death once dead, ther's no more dying then.

From A MIDSOMMER NIGHTS DREAME

ACT II, SCENE 1

ROBIN. How now spirit, whether wander you?
FAIRIE. Over hil, over dale, through bush, through briar,
   Over parke, over pale, through flood, through fire,
   I do wander everie where, swifter then the Moons sphere;
   And I serve the Fairy Queene, to dew her orbs upon the green.
   The Cowslips tall, her pensioners bee,
   In their gold coats, spots you see,
   Those be Rubies, Fairie favors,
   In those freckles, live their savors,
   I must go seeke some dew drops heere,
   And hang a pearle in every cowslips eare.
   Farewell thou Lob of spirits, Ile be gon,
   Our Queene and all her Elves come heere anon.

ROBIN. The King doth keepe his Revels here to night,
Take heed the Queene come not within his sight,
For *Oberon* is passing fell and wrath,
Because that she, as her attendant, hath
A lovely boy stolne from an Indian King,
She never had so sweet a changeling,
And jealous *Oberon* would have the childe
Knight of his traine, to trace the Forrests wilde.
But she (perforce) with-holds the loved boy,
Crownes him with flowers, and makes him all her joy.
And now they never meete in grove, or greene,
By fountaine cleere, or spangled star-light sheene,
But they do square, that all their Elves for feare
Creepe into Acorne cups and hide them there.

FAIRIE. Either I mistake your shape and making quite,
Or else you are that shrew'd and knavish sprite
Cal'd Robin Good-fellow. Are you not hee,
That frights the maidens of the Villageree,
Skim milke, and sometimes labour in the querne,
And bootlesse make the breathlesse huswife cherne,
And sometime make the drinke to beare no barme,
Misleade night-wanderers, laughing at their harme?
Those that Hobgoblin call you, and sweet Pucke,
You do their worke, and they shall have good lucke.
Are not you he?

ROBIN.   Thou speak'st aright;
I am that merrie wanderer of the night:
I jest to *Oberon,* and make him smile,
When I a fat and beane-fed horse beguile,
Neighing in likenesse of a filly foale,
And sometime lurke I in a Gossips bole,
In very likenesse of a roasted crab:
And when she drinkes, against her lips I bob,
And on her withered dewlop poure the Ale.
The wisest Aunt telling the saddest tale,
Sometime for three-foot stoole, mistaketh me,
Then slip I from her bum, downe topples she,
And tailour cries, and fals into a coffe.
And then the whole quire hold their hips, and loffe,
And waxen in their mirth, and neeze, and sweare,
A merrier houre was never wasted there.
But roome Fairy, here comes *Oberon.*

FAIRIE. And heere my Mistris: Would that he were gone.

Enter the King of Fairies at one doore with his traine,
and the Queene at another with hers.

OBERON. Ill met by Moone-light, proud *Tytania*.
QUEENE. What, jealous *Oberon?* Fairy skip hence.
  I have forsworne his bed and companie.
OBERON. Tarrie rash Wanton; am not I thy Lord?
QUEENE. Then I must be thy Lady: but I know
  When thou hast stolne away from Fairy Land,
  And in the shape of *Corin,* sate all day,
  Playing on pipes of Corne, and versing love
  To amorous Phillida. Why art thou heere
  Come from the farthest steppe of *India?*
  But that forsooth the bouncing *Amazon*
  Your buskin'd Mistresse, and your Warrior love,
  To *Theseus* must be Wedded; and you come,
  To give their bed joy and prosperitie.
OBERON. How canst thou thus for shame *Tytania,*
  Glance at my credite, with *Hippolita?*
  Knowing I know thy love to *Theseus?*
  Didst thou not leade him through the glimmering night
  From *Peregenia,* whom he ravished?
  And make him with faire Eagles breake his faith
  With *Ariadne,* and *Antiopa?*
QUEENE. These are the forgeries of jealousie,
  And never since the middle Summers spring
  Met we on hil, in dale, forrest, or mead,
  By paved fountaine, or by rushie brooke,
  Or in the beached margent of the sea,
  To dance our ringlets to the whistling Winde,
  But with thy braules thou hast disturb'd our sport.
  Therefore the Windes, piping to us in vaine,
  As in revenge, have suck'd up from the sea
  Contagious fogges: Which falling in the Land,
  Hath everie petty River made so proud,
  That they have over-borne their Continents.
  The Oxe hath therefore stretch'd his yoake in vaine,
  The Ploughman lost his sweat, and the greene Corne
  Hath rotted, ere his youth attain'd a beard:
  The fold stands empty in the drowned field,
  And Crowes are fatted with the murrion flocke,
  The nine mens Morris is fild up with mud,
  And the queint Mazes in the wanton greene,
  For lacke of tread are undistinguishable.
  The human mortals want their winter heere,
  No night is now with hymne or caroll blest;
  Therefore the Moone (the governesse of floods)
  Pale in her anger, washes all the aire;
  That Rheumaticke diseases doe abound.

And thorough this distemperature, we see
The seasons alter; hoary headed frosts
Fall in the fresh lap of the crimson Rose,
And on old *Hyems* chinne and Icie crowne,
An odorous Chaplet of sweet Sommer buds
Is as in mockry set. The Spring, the Sommer,
The childing Autumne, angry Winter change
Their wonted Liveries, and the mazed world,
By their increase, now knowes not which is which;
And this same progeny of evills, comes
From our debate, from our dissention,
We are their parents and originall.
OBERON. Do you amend it then, it lies in you,
Why should *Titania* crosse her *Oberon?*
I do but beg a little changeling boy,
To be my Henchman.
QUEENE.   Set your heart at rest,
The Fairy land buyes not the childe of me.
His mother was a Votresse of my Order,
And in the spiced *Indian* aire, by night
Full often hath she gossipt by my side,
And sat with me on *Neptunes* yellow sands,
Marking th' embarked traders on the flood,
When we have laught to see the sailes conceive,
And grow big bellied with the wanton winde:
Which she with pretty and with swimming gate,
Following (her wombe then rich with my yong squire)
Would imitate, and saile upon the Land,
To fetch me trifles, and returne againe,
As from a voyage, rich with merchandize.
But she being mortall, of that boy did die,
And for her sake I doe reare up her boy,
And for her sake I will not part with him.
OBERON. How long within this wood intend you stay?
QUEENE. Perchance till after *Theseus* wedding day.
If you will patiently dance in our Round,
And see our Moone-light revels, goe with us;
If not, shun me and I will spare your haunts.
OBERON. Give me that boy, and I will goe with thee.
QUEENE. Not for thy Fairy Kingdome. Fairies away:
We shall chide downe right, if I longer stay.

ACT V, SCENE 1

PUCK. Now the hungry Lyon rores,
And the Wolfe behowls the Moone:

Whilest the heavy ploughman snores,
All with weary taske fore-done.
Now the wasted brands doe glow,
Whil'st the scritch-owle, scritching loud,
Puts the wretch that lies in woe,
In remembrance of a shrowd.
Now it is the time of night,
That the graves, all gaping wide,
Every one lets forth his spright,
In the Church-way paths to glide.
And we Fairies, that do runne,
By the triple *Hecates* teame,
From the presence of the Sunne,
Following darkenesse like a dreame,
Now are frollicke; not a Mouse
Shall disturbe this hallowed house.
I am sent with broome before,
To sweep the dust behinde the doore.

Enter King and Queene of Fairies, with their traine.

OBERON. Through the house give glimmering light,
    By the dead and drowsie fier,
    Everie Elfe and Fairie spright,
    Hop as light as bird from brier,
    And this Ditty after me,
    Sing and dance it trippinglie.
QUEENE. First rehearse this song by roate,
    To each word a warbling note.
    Hand in hand, with Fairie grace,
    Will we sing and blesse this place.

THE SONG

Now untill the breake of day,
Through this house each Fairy stray.
To the best Bride-bed will we,
Which by us shall blessed be:
And the issue there create,
Ever shall be fortunate:
So shall all the couples three,
Ever true in loving be:
And the blots of Natures hand,
Shall not in their issue stand.
Never mole, harelip, nor scarre,
Nor marke prodigious, such as are

Despised in Nativitie,
Shall upon their children be.
With this field dew consecrate,
Every Fairy take his gate,
And each severall chamber blesse,
Through this Pallace with sweet peace,
Ever shall in safety rest,
And the owner of it blest.
Trip away, make no stay;
Meet me all by breake of day.

From ROMEO AND JULIET

ACT V, SCENE 3

ROMEO. How oft when men are at the point of death,
Have they beene merrie? Which their Keepers call
A lightning before death: Oh how may I
Call this a lightning? O my Love, my Wife,
Death that hath suckt the honey of thy breath,
Hath had no power yet upon thy Beautie:
Thou art not conquer'd: Beauties ensigne yet
Is Crymson in thy lips, and in thy cheekes,
And Deaths pale flag is not advanced there.
Tybalt, ly'st thou there in thy bloudy sheet?
O what more favour can I do to thee,
Then with that hand that cut thy youth in twaine,
To sunder his that was thy enemie?
Forgive me Cozen. Ah deare *Juliet:*
Why art thou yet so faire? Shall I beleeve,
That unsubstantiall death is amorous?
And that the leane abhorred Monster keepes
Thee here in darke to be his Paramour?
For feare of that, I still will stay with thee,
And never from this Pallace of dym night
Depart againe: come lie thou in my armes,
Heere's to thy health, where ere thou tumblest in.
Depart againe; here, here will I remaine,
With Wormes that are thy Chambermaides: O here
Will I set up my everlasting rest:
And shake the yoke of inauspicious starres
From this world-wearied flesh: Eyes looke your last:
Armes take your last embrace: And lips, O you
The doores of breath, seale with a righteous kisse
A datelesse bargaine to ingrossing death:

Come bitter conduct, come unsavoury guide,
Thou desperate Pilot, now at once run on
The dashing Rocks, thy Sea-sicke wearie Barke:
Heere's to my Love. O true Appothecary:
Thy drugs are quicke. Thus with a kisse I die.

From KING LEAR

ACT II, SCENE 4

Enter Cornewall, Regan, Gloucester, Servants.

LEAR. Good morrow to you both.
CORNEWALL.   Haile to your Grace.
                              [*Kent here set at liberty.*]
REGAN. I am glad to see your Highnesse.
LEAR. *Regan,* I thinke you are. I know what reason
  I have to thinke so, if thou should'st not be glad,
  I would divorce me from thy Mothers Tombe,
  Sepulchring an Adultresse. [*To Kent.*] O are you free?
  Some other time for that. Beloved *Regan,*
  Thy Sisters naught: oh *Regan,* she hath tied
  Sharpe-tooth'd unkindnesse, like a vulture heere,
  I can scarce speake to thee, thou'lt not beleeve
  With how deprav'd a quality. Oh *Regan.*
REGAN. I pray you Sir, take patience, I have hope
  You lesse know how to value her desert,
  Then she to scant her dutie.
LEAR.   Say? How is that?
REGAN. I cannot thinke my Sister in the least
  Would faile her Obligation. If Sir perchance
  She have restrained the Riots of your Followres,
  'Tis on such ground, and to such wholesome end,
  As cleeres her from all blame.
LEAR. My curses on her.
REGAN.   O Sir, you are old,
  Nature in you stands on the very Verge
  Of his confine: you should be rul'd, and led
  By some discretion, that discernes your state
  Better then you your selfe: therefore I pray you,
  That to our Sister, you do make returne,
  Say you have wrong'd her.
LEAR.   Aske her forgivenesse?
  Do you but marke how this becomes the house?
  "Deere daughter, I confesse that I am old;
  Age is unnecessary: on my knees I begge,

That you'l vouchsafe me Rayment, Bed, and Food."
REGAN. Good Sir, no more: these are unsightly trickes:
 Returne you to my Sister.
LEAR.   Never *Regan:*
 She hath abated me of halfe my Traine;
 Look'd blacke upon me, strooke me with her Tongue
 Most Serpent-like, upon the very Heart.
 All the stor'd Vengeances of Heaven, fall
 On her ingratefull top: strike her yong bones
 You taking Ayres, with Lamenesse.
CORNEWALL.   Fye sir, fie.
LEAR. You nimble Lightnings, dart your blinding flames
 Into her scornfull eyes: Infect her Beauty,
 You Fen-suck'd Fogges, drawne by the powrfull Sunne,
 To fall, and blister.
REGAN.   O the blest Gods!
 So will you wish on me, when the rash moode is on.
LEAR. No *Regan,* thou shalt never have my curse:
 Thy tender-hefted Nature shall not give
 Thee o're to harshnesse: Her eyes are fierce, but thine
 Do comfort, and not burne. 'Tis not in thee
 To grudge my pleasures, to cut off my Traine,
 To bandy hasty words, to scant my sizes,
 And in conclusion, to oppose the bolt
 Against my comming in. Thou better know'st
 The Offices of Nature, bond of Childhood,
 Effects of Curtesie, dues of Gratitude:
 Thy halfe o' th' Kingdome hast thou not forgot,
 Wherein I thee endow'd.
REGAN.   Good Sir, to th' purpose.
            [Tucket within.]
LEAR. Who put my man i' th' Stockes?
            [Enter Steward.]
CORNEWALL.   What Trumpet's that?
REGAN. I know't, my Sisters: this approves her Letter,
 That she would soone be heere. Is your Lady come?
LEAR. This is a Slave, whose easie borrowed pride
 Dwels in the fickly grace of her he followes.
 Out Varlet, from my sight.
CORNEWALL.   What meanes your Grace?
           [Enter Gonerill.]
LEAR. Who stockt my Servant? *Regan,* I have good hope
 Thou did'st not know on't. Who comes here? O Heavens!
 If you do love old men; if your sweet sway
 Allow Obedience; if you your selves are old,
 Make it your cause: Send downe, and take my part.

Art not asham'd to looke upon this Beard?
O *Regan,* will you take her by the hand?

GONERILL. Why not by th' hand Sir? How have I offended?
All's not offence that indiscretion findes,
And dotage termes so.

LEAR.   O sides, you are too tough!
Will you yet hold? How came my man i' th' Stockes?

CORNEWALL. I set him there, Sir: but his owne Disorders
Deserv'd much lesse advancement.

LEAR.   You? Did you?

REGAN. I pray you Father being weake, seeme so.
If till the expiration of your Moneth
You will returne and sojourne with my Sister,
Dismissing halfe your traine, come then to me,
I am now from home, and out of that provision
Which shall be needfull for your entertainement.

LEAR. Returne to her? and fifty men dismiss'd?
No, rather I abjure all roofes, and chuse
To wage against the enmity o' th' ayre,
To be a Comrade with the Wolfe, and Owle,
Necessities sharpe pinch. Returne with her?
Why the hot-bloodied *France,* that dowerlesse tooke
Our youngest borne, I could as well be brought
To knee his Throne, and Squire-like pension beg,
To keepe base life a foote; returne with her?
Perswade me rather to be slave and sumpter
To this detested groome.

GONERILL.   At your choice Sir.

LEAR. I prythee Daughter do not make me mad,
I will not trouble thee my Child: farewell:
Wee'l no more meete, no more see one another.
But yet thou art my flesh, my blood, my Daughter,
Or rather a disease that's in my flesh,
Which I must needs call mine. Thou art a Byle,
A plague sore, or imbossed Carbuncle
In my corrupted blood. But Ile not chide thee,
Let shame come when it will, I do not call it,
I do not bid the Thunder-bearer shoote,
Nor tell tales of thee to high-judging *Jove,*
Mend when thou can'st, be better at thy leisure,
I can be patient, I can stay with *Regan,*
I and my hundred Knights.

REGAN.   Not altogether so,
I look'd not for you yet, nor am provided
For your fit welcome, give eare Sir to my Sister,
For those that mingle reason with your passion,

Must be content to thinke you old, and so,
But she knowes what she doe's.

LEAR.   Is this well spoken?

REGAN. I dare avouch it Sir, what fifty Followers?
Is it not well? What should you need of more?
Yea, or so many? Sith that both charge and danger,
Speake 'gainst so great a number? How in one house
Should many people, under two commands
Hold amity? 'Tis hard, almost impossible.

GONERILL. Why might not you my Lord, receive attendance
From those that she cals Servants, or from mine?

REGAN. Why not my Lord? If then they chanc'd to slacke ye,
We could comptroll them; if you will come to me,
(For now I spie a danger) I entreate you
To bring but five and twentie, to no more
Will I give place or notice.

LEAR. I gave you all.

REGAN.   And in good time you gave it.

LEAR. Made you my Guardians, my Depositaries,
But kept a reservation to be followed
With such a number. What, must I come to you
With five and twenty? *Regan,* said you so?

REGAN. And speak't againe my Lord, no more with me.

LEAR. Those wicked Creatures yet do look wel favor'd
When others are more wicked, not being the worst
Stands in some ranke of praise. Ile go with thee,
Thy fifty yet doth double five and twenty,
And thou art twice her Love.

GONERILL.   Heare me my Lord;
What need you five and twenty? Ten? Or five?
To follow in a house, where twice so many
Have a command to tend you?

REGAN.   What need one?

LEAR. O reason not the need: our basest Beggers
Are in the poorest thing superfluous,
Allow not Nature, more then Nature needs:
Mans life is cheape as Beastes. Thou art a Lady;
If onely to go warme were gorgeous,
Why Nature needs not what thou gorgeous wear'st,
Which scarcely keepes thee warme, but for true need:
You Heavens, give me that patience, patience I need,
You see me heere (you Gods) a poore old man,
As full of griefe as age, wretched in both,
If it be you that stirres these Daughters hearts
Against their Father, foole me not so much,
To beare it tamely: touch me with Noble anger,

And let not womens weapons, water drops,
Staine my mans cheekes. No you unnaturall Hags,
I will have such revenges on you both,
That all the world shall — I will do such things,
What they are yet, I know not, but they shal be
The terrors of the earth. You thinke Ile weepe,
No, Ile not weepe, I have full cause of weeping, [*Storme and Tempest.*]
But this heart shal break into a hundred thousand flawes
Or ere Ile weepe; O Foole, I shall go mad.   [*Exeunt.*]

ACT III, SCENE 2

LEAR. Blow windes, and crack your cheeks; Rage, blow
    You Cataracts, and Hyrricano's spout,
    Till you have drench'd our Steeples, drown the Cockes.
    You Sulph'rous and Thought-executing Fires,
    Vaunt-curriors of Oake-cleaving Thunder-bolts,
    Sindge my white head. And thou all-shaking Thunder,
    Strike flat the thicke Rotundity o' th' world,
    Cracke Natures moulds, all germes spill at once
    That make ingratefull Man.
FOOLE. O Nunkle, Court holy-water in a dry house, is better then this
    Rain-water out o' doore. Good Nunkle, in, aske thy Daughters bless-
    ing, heere's a night pitties neither Wisemen, nor Fooles.
LEAR. Rumble thy belly full: spit Fire, spowt Raine:
    Nor Raine, Winde, Thunder, Fire are my Daughters;
    I taxe not you, you Elements with unkindnesse.
    I never gave you Kingdome, call'd you Children;
    You owe me no subscription. Then let fall
    Your horrible pleasure. Heere I stand your Slave,
    A poore, infirme, weake, and dispis'd old man:
    But yet I call you Servile Ministers,
    That will with two pernicious Daughters joyne
    Your high-engender'd Battailes, 'gainst a head
    So old, and white as this. O, ho! 'tis foule.
FOOLE. He that has a house to put's head in, has a good Head-peece:
    The Codpiece that will house, before the head has any;
    The Head, and he shall Lowse: so Beggers marry many.
    The man that makes his Toe, what he his Hart shold make,
    Shall of a Corne cry woe, and turne his sleepe to wake.
For there was never yet faire woman, but shee made mouthes in a
    glasse.
                                        [*Enter Kent.*]

LEAR. No, I will be the patterne of all patience,
    I will say nothing.
KENT. Who's there?

FOOLE. Marry here's Grace, and a Codpiece, that's a Wiseman, and a
Foole.

KENT. Alas Sir are you here? Things that love night,
Love not such nights as these: The wrathfull Skies
Gallow the very wanderers of the darke
And make them keepe their Caves: Since I was man,
Such sheets of Fire, such bursts of horrid Thunder,
Such groanes of roaring Winde, and Raine, I never
Remember to have heard. Mans Nature cannot carry
Th' affliction, nor the feare.

LEAR.   Let the great Goddes
That keepe this dreadfull Powther o're our heads,
Finde out their enemies now. Tremble thou Wretch,
That hast within thee undivulged Crimes
Unwhipt of Justice. Hide thee, thou Bloudy hand;
Thou Perjur'd, and thou Simular of Vertue
That art Incestuous. Caytiffe, to peeces shake
That under covert, and convenient seeming
Ha's pratcis'd on mans life. Close pent-up guilts,
Rive your concealing Continents, and cry
These dreadfull Summoners grace. I am a man,
More sinn'd against, then sinning.

KENT.   Alacke, bare-headed?
Gracious my Lord, hard by heere is a Hovell,
Some friendship will it lend you 'gainst the Tempest:
Repose you there, while I to this hard house,
(More harder then the stones wherof 'tis rais'd,
Which even but now, demanding after you,
Deny'd me to come in) returne, and force
Their scanted curtesie.

LEAR.   My wits begin to turne.
Come on my boy. How dost my boy? Art cold?
I am cold my selfe. Where is this straw, my Fellow?
The Art of our Necessities is strange,
And can make vile things precious. Come, your Hovel;
Poore Foole, and Knave, I have one part in my heart
That's sorry yet for thee.

FOOLE.   He that has and a little tiny wit,
                 With heigh-ho, the Winde and the Raine,
                 Must make content with his Fortunes fit,
                 Though the Raine it raineth every day.

LEAR. True Boy: Come bring us to this Hovell.   [*Exit.*]

ACT III, SCENE 4

Enter Lear, Kent, and Foole.

KENT. Here is the place my Lord, good my Lord enter,
   The tirrany of the open night's too rough
   For Nature to endure.   *[Storme still.]*

LEAR.   Let me alone.

KENT. Good my Lord enter heere.

LEAR.   Wilt breake my heart?

KENT. I had rather breake mine owne, Good my Lord enter.

LEAR. Thou think'st 'tis much that this contentious storme
   Invades us to the skin so: 'tis to thee,
   But where the greater malady is fixt,
   The lesser is scarce felt. Thou'dst shun a Beare,
   But if thy flight lay toward the roaring Sea,
   Thou'dst meete the Bear i' th' mouth. When the mind's free,
   The bodies delicate: the tempest in my mind,
   Doth from my sences take all feeling else,
   Save what beates there, Filliall ingratitude,
   Is it not as this mouth should teare this hand
   For lifting food to it? But I will punish home;
   No, I will weepe no more; in such a night,
   To shut me out! Poure on, I will endure:
   In such a night as this! O *Regan, Gonerill,*
   Your old kind Father, whose franke heart gave all,
   O that way madnesse lies, let me shun that:
   No more of that.

KENT.   Good my Lord enter here.

LEAR. Prythee go in thy selfe, seeke thine owne ease,
   This tempest will not give me leave to ponder
   On things would hurt me more, but Ile goe in,
   In Boy, go first. You houselesse povertie,
   Nay get thee in; Ile pray, and then Ile sleepe.   *[Exit Foole.]*
   Poore naked wretches, where so ere you are
   That bide the pelting of this pittilesse storme,
   How shall your House-lesse heads, and unfed sides,
   Your loopt and window'd raggednesse defend you
   From seasons such as these? O I have ta'en
   Too little care of this: Take Physicke, Pompe,
   Expose thy selfe to feele what wretches feele,
   That thou maist shake the superflux to them,
   And shew the Heavens more just.

                    [Enter Edgar, and Foole.]

EDGAR. Fathom, and halfe, Fathom and halfe; poore *Tom.*

FOOLE. Come not in heere Nuncle, here's a spirit, helpe me, helpe me.

KENT. Give me thy hand, who's there?

FOOLE. A spirite, a spirite, he sayes his name's poore *Tom*.

KENT. What art thou that dost grumble there i' th' straw? Come forth.

EDGAR. Away, the foule Fiend followes me, through the sharpe Hauthorne blow the windes. Humh, goe to thy bed and warme thee.

LEAR. Did'st thou give all to thy Daughters? And art thou come to this?

EDGAR. Who gives any thing to poore *Tom?* Whom the foule fiend hath led through Fire, and through Flame, through Sword, and Whirle-Poole, o're Bog, and Quagmire, that hath laid Knives under his Pillow, and Halters in his Pue, set Rats-bane by his Porredge, made him Proud of heart, to ride on a Bay trotting Horse, over foure incht Bridges, to course his owne shadow for a Traitor. Blisse thy five Wits, *Toms* a cold. O do, de, do, de, do de, blisse thee from Whirle-Windes, Starre-blasting, and taking, do poore *Tom* some charitie, whom the foule Fiend vexes. There could I have him now, and there, and there againe, and there. [*Storme still.*]

LEAR. Ha's his Daughters brought him to this passe?
Could'st thou save nothing? Would'st thou give 'em all?

FOOLE. Nay, he reserv'd a Blanket, else we had bin all sham'd.

LEAR. Now all the plagues that in the pendulous ayre
Hang fated o're mens faults, light on thy Daughters.

KENT. He hath no Daughters Sir.

LEAR. Death Traitor, nothing could have subdu'd Nature
To such a lownesse, but his unkind Daughters.
Is it the fashion, that discarded Fathers,
Should have thus little mercy on their flesh:
Judicious punishment, 'twas this flesh begot
Those Pelicane Daughters.

EDGAR. Pillicock sat on Pillicock hill, alow: alow, loo, loo.

FOOLE. This cold night will turne us all to Fooles, and Madmen.

EDGAR. Take heed o' th' foule Fiend, obey thy Parents, keepe thy words Justice, sweare not, commit not, with mans sworne Spouse; set not thy Sweet-heart on proud array. *Tom's* a cold.

LEAR. What has thou bin?

EDGAR. A Servingman. Proud in heart, and minde; that curl'd my haire, wore Gloves in my cap; serv'd the Lust of my Mistris heart, and did the acte of darkenesse with her. Swore as many Oathes, as I spake words, and broke them in the sweet face of Heaven. One that slept in the contriving of Lust, and wak'd to doe it. Wine lov'd I deerely, Dice deerely; and in Woman, out-Paramour'd the Turke. False of heart, light of eare, bloody of hand; Hog in sloth, Foxe in stealth, Wolfe in greedinesse, Dog in madnes, Lyon in prey. Let not the creaking of shooes, Nor the rustling of Silkes, betray thy poore heart to woman. Keepe thy foote out of Brothels, thy hand out of Plackets, thy pen from Lenders Bookes, and defye the foule Fiend. Still through the Hauthorne blowes the cold winde: Sayes suum, mun, nonny, Dolphin my Boy, Boy *Sesey:* let him trot by.   [*Storme still.*]

LEAR. Thou wert better in a Grave, then to answere with thy uncover'd body, this extremitie of the Skies. Is man no more then this? Consider him well. Thou ow'st the Worme no Silke; the Beast, no Hide; the Sheepe, no Wooll; the Cat, no perfume. Ha! Here's three on's are sophisticated. Thou art the thing it selfe; unaccommodated man, is no more but such a poore, bare, forked Animall as thou art. Off, off you Lendings: Come, unbutton heere.

[*Enter Gloucester, with a Torch.*]

FOOLE. Prythee Nunckle be contented, 'tis a naughtie night to swimme in. Now a little fire in a wilde Field, were like an old Letchers heart, a small spark, all the rest on's body, cold: Looke, heere comes a walking fire.

EDGAR. This is the foule Flibbertigibbet; hee begins at Curfew, and walkes at first Cocke: Hee gives the Web and the Pin, squints the eye, and makes the Hare-lippe; Mildewes the white Wheate, and hurts the poore Creature of earth.
> *Swithold* footed thrice the old,
> He met the Night-Mare, and her nine-fold;
> Bid her a-light, and her troth-plight,
> And aroynt thee Witch, aroynt thee.

KENT. How fares your Grace?

LEAR. What's he?

KENT. Who's there? What is't you seeke?

GLOUCESTER. What are you there? Your Names?

EDGAR. Poore Tom, that eates the swimming Frog, the Toad, the Todpole, the wall-Neut, and the water: that in the furie of his heart, when the foule Fiend rages, eats Cow-dung for Sallets; swallowes the old Rat, and the ditch-Dogge; drinkes the green Mantle of the standing Poole: who is whipt from Tything to Tything, and stockt, punish'd, and imprison'd: who hath three Suites to his backe, six shirts to his body:
> Horse to ride, and weapon to weare:
> But Mice, and Rats, and such small Deer,
> Have bin Toms food, for seven long yeare:

Beware my Follower. Peace Smulkin, peace thou Fiend.

GLOUCESTER. What, hath your Grace no better company?

EDGAR. The Prince of Darkenesse is a Gentleman.
Modo he's call'd, and *Mahu.*

GLOUCESTER. Our flesh and blood, my Lord, is growne so vile,
That it doth hate what gets it.

EDGAR.   Poore Tom's a cold.

GLOUCESTER. Go in with me; my duty cannot suffer
T'obey in all your daughters hard commands:
Though their Injunction be to barre my doores,
And let this Tyrannous night take hold upon you,

Yet have I ventured to come seeke you out,
  And bring you where both fire, and food is ready.
LEAR. First let me talke with this Philosopher,
  What is the cause of Thunder?
KENT. Good my Lord take his offer, Go into th' house.
LEAR. Ile talke a word with this same lerned Theban:
  What is your study?
EDGAR. How to prevent the Fiend, and to kill Vermine.
LEAR. Let me aske you one word in private.
KENT. Importune him once more to go my Lord,
  His wits begin t'unsettle.   [*Storme still.*]
GLOUCESTER.   Canst thou blame him?
  His Daughters seeke his death: Ah, that good Kent,
  He said it would be thus: poore banish'd man:
  Thou sayest the King growes mad, Ile tell thee Friend
  I am almost mad my selfe. I had a Sonne,
  Now out-law'd from my blood: he sought my life
  But lately: very late: I lov'd him (Friend)
  No Father his Sonne deerer: true to tell thee,
  The greefe hath craz'd my wits. What a night's this?
  I do beseech your grace.
LEAR.   O cry you mercy, Sir:
  Noble Philosopher, your company.
EDGAR. Tom's a cold.
GLOUCESTER. In fellow there, into th' Hovel; keep thee warm.
LEAR. Come, let's in all.
KENT.   This way, my Lord.
LEAR.   With him;
  I will keepe still with my Philosopher.
KENT. Good my Lord, sooth him: Let him take the Fellow.
GLOUCESTER. Take him you on.
KENT. Sirra, come on: go along with us.
LEAR. Come, good Athenian.
GLOUCESTER.   No words, no words, hush.
EDGAR. Childe *Rowland* to the darke Tower came,
  His word was still, fie, foh, and fumme,
  I smell the blood of a Brittish man.   [*Exeunt.*]

ACT III, SCENE 6

Enter Kent, and Gloucester.

GLOUCESTER. Heere is better then the open ayre, take it thankfully: I will
  peece out the comfort with what addition I can: I will not be long
  from you.   [*Exit.*]

KENT. All the powre of his wits, have given way to his impatience: the
Gods reward your kindnesse.

[Enter Lear, Edgar, and Foole.]

EDGAR. *Fraterretto* cals me, and tells me *Nero* is an Angler in the Lake of
Darknesse: pray Innocent, and beware the foule Fiend.

FOOLE. Prythee Nunkle tell me, whether a madman be a Gentleman, or
a Yeoman.

LEAR. A King, a King.

FOOLE. No, he's a Yeoman, that ha's a Gentleman to his Sonne: for hee's
a mad Yeoman that sees his Sonne a Gentleman before him.

LEAR. To have a thousand with red burning spits
Come hizzing in upon 'em.

EDGAR. Blesse thy five wits.

KENT. O pitty: Sir, where is the patience now
That you so oft have boasted to retaine?

EDGAR. My teares begin to take his part so much,
They marre my counterfetting.

LEAR. The little dogges, and all;
Trey, Blanch, and Sweet-heart: see, they barke at me.

EDGAR. Tom, will throw his head at them: Avaunt you Curres,
Be thy mouth or blacke or white:
Tooth that poysons if it bite:
Mastiffe, Grey-hound, Mongrill, Grim,
Hound or Spaniell, Brache, or Hym:
Or Bobtaile tight, or Troudle taile,
Tom will make him weepe and waile,
For with throwing thus my head;
Dogs leapt the hatch, and all are fled.
Do, de, de, de, sese: Come, march to Wakes and Fayres, and Market
Townes: poore Tom thy horne is dry.

LEAR. Then let them Anatomize *Regan:* See what breeds about her heart.
Is there any cause in Nature that makes these hard-hearts? You Sir, I
entertaine for one of my hundred; only, I do not like the fashion of
your garments. You will say they are Persian, but let them bee chang'd.

[Enter Gloucester.]

KENT. Now good my Lord, lye heere, and rest awhile.

LEAR. Make no noise, make no noise, draw the Curtaines: so, so, wee'l go
to Supper i' th' morning.

FOOLE. And Ile go to bed at noone.

GLOUCESTER. Come hither Friend: Where is the King my Master?

KENT. Here Sir, but trouble him not, his wits are gon.

GLOUCESTER. Good friend, I prythee take him in thy armes;
I have ore-heard a plot of death upon him:
There is a Litter ready, lay him in't,
And drive toward Dover friend, where thou shalt meete

Both welcome, and protection. Take up thy Master,
If thou should'st dally halfe an houre, his life
With thine, and all that offer to defend him,
Stand in assured losse. Take up, take up,
And follow me, that will to some provision
Give thee quicke conduct. Come, come, away.   [*Exeunt.*]

ACT IV, SCENE 6

LEAR. No, they cannot touch me for coyning. I am the King himselfe.

EDGAR. O thou side-piercing sight!

LEAR. Nature's above Art, in that respect. Ther's your Presse-money. That
fellow handles his bow, like a Crow-keeper: draw mee a Cloathiers
yard. Looke, looke, a Mouse: peace, peace, this peece of toasted Cheese
will doo't. There's my Gauntlet, Ile prove it on a Gyant. Bring up the
browne Billes. O well flowne Bird: i' th' clout, i' th' clout: Hewgh. Give
the word.

EDGAR. Sweet Marjorum.

LEAR. Passe.

GLOUCESTER. I know that voice.

LEAR. Ha! *Gonerill* with a white beard? They flatter'd me like a Dogge,
and told mee I had the white hayres in my Beard, ere the blacke ones
were there. To say ay, and no, to every thing that I said: ay, and no
too, was no good Divinity. When the raine came to wet me once, and
the winde to make me chatter: when the Thunder would not peace at
my bidding, there I found 'em, there I smelt 'em out. Go too, they are
not men o' their words; they told me, I was every thing: 'Tis a Lye, I
am not Agu-proofe.

GLOUCESTER. The tricke of that voyce, I do well remember:
Is't not the King?

LEAR.   Ay, every inch a King.
When I do stare, see how the Subject quakes.
I pardon that mans life. What was thy cause?
Adultery? thou shalt not dye: dye for Adultery?
No, the Wren goes too't, and the small gilded Fly
Do's letcher in my sight! Let Copulation thrive:
For Gloucesters bastard Son was kinder to his Father,
Then my Daughters got 'tweene the lawfull sheets.
Too't Luxury pell-mell, for I lacke Souldiers.
Behold yond simpring Dame, whose face betweene her
Forkes presages Snow; that minces Vertue,
And do's shake the head to heare of pleasures name.
The Fitchew, nor the soyled Horse goes too't
With a more riotous appetite: Downe from the waste
They are Centaures, though Women all above: but to the Girdle
Do the Gods inherit, beneath is all the Fiends.

There's hell, there's darkenes, there is the sulphurous pit;
Burning scalding, stench, consumption: Fye, fie, fie; pah, pah: Give me
an Ounce of Civet; good Apothecary sweeten my immagination:
There's money for thee.

GLOUCESTER. O let me kisse that hand.

LEAR. Let me wipe it first, It smelles of Mortality.

GLOUCESTER. O ruin'd peece of Nature, this great world
Shall so weare out to naught. Do'st thou know me?

LEAR. I remember thine eyes well enough: dost thou squiny at me? No,
doe thy worst blinde Cupid, Ile not love. Reade thou this Challenge,
marke but the penning of it.

GLOUCESTER. Were all thy Letters Sunnes, I could not see.

EDGAR. I would not take this from report, It is,
And my heart breakes at it.

LEAR. Read.

GLOUCESTER. What with the Case of eyes?

LEAR. Oh ho, are you there with me? No eies in your head, nor no mony
in your purse? Your eyes are in a heavy case, your purse in a light, yet
you see how this world goes.

GLOUCESTER. I see it feelingly.

LEAR. What, art mad? A man may see how this world goes, with no eyes.
Looke with thine eares: See how yond Justice railes upon yond simple
theefe. Hearke in thine eare: Change places, and handy-dandy, which
is the Justice, which is the theefe: Thou hast seene a Farmers dogge
barke at a Beggar?

GLOUCESTER. Ay Sir.

LEAR. And the Creature run from the Cur: there thou might'st behold
the great image of Authoritie, a Dogg's obey'd in Office.
Thou, Rascall Beadle, hold thy bloody hand:
Why dost thou lash that Whore? Strip thy owne backe,
Thou hotly lusts to use her in that kind,
For which thou whip'st her. The Usurer hangs the Cozener.
Thorough tatter'd cloathes great Vices do appeare:
Robes, and Furr'd gownes hide all. Plate sinnes with Gold,
And the strong Lance of Justice, hurtlesse breakes:
Arme it in ragges, a Pigmies straw do's pierce it.
None do's offend, none, I say none, Ile able 'em;
Take that of me my Friend, who have the power
To seale th' accusers lips. Get thee glasse-eyes,
And like a scurvy Politician, seeme
To see the things thou dost not. Now, now, now, now.
Pull off my Bootes: harder, harder, so.

EDGAR. O matter, and impertinency mixt,
Reason in Madnesse.

LEAR. If thou wilt weepe my Fortunes, take my eyes.
I know thee well enough, thy name is Gloucester:

Thou must be patient; we came crying hither:
Thou know'st, the first time that we smell the Ayre
We wawle, and cry. I will preach to thee: Marke.

GLOUCESTER. Alacke, alacke the day.

LEAR. When we are borne, we cry that we are come
To this great stage of Fooles. This a good blocke:
It were a delicate stratagem to shoo
A Troope of Horse with Felt: Ile put't in proofe,
And when I have stolne upon these Sonnes in Lawe,
Then kill, kill, kill, kill, kill, kill.

[Enter a Gentleman.]

GENTLEMAN. Oh heere he is: lay hand upon him. Sir,
Your most deere Daughter —

LEAR. No rescue? What, a Prisoner? I am even
The Naturall Foole of Fortune. Use me well,
You shall have ransome. Let me have Surgeons,
I am cut to th' Braines.

GENTLEMAN.　　　　　You shall have any thing.

LEAR. No Seconds? All my selfe?
Why, this would make a man, a man of Salt
To use his eyes for Garden water-pots. I wil die bravely,
Like a smugge Bridegroome. What? I will be Joviall:
Come, come, I am a King, Masters, know you that?

ACT V, SCENE 3

LEAR. Howle, howle, howle, howle: O you are men of stones,
Had I your tongues and eyes, Il'd use them so,
That Heavens vault should crack: she's gone for ever.
I know when one is dead, and when one lives,
She's dead as earth: Lend me a Looking-glasse,
If that her breath will mist or staine the stone,
Why then she lives.

KENT.　　　　　Is this the promis'd end?

EDGAR. Or image of that horror.

ALBANY.　　　　　Fall and cease.

LEAR. This feather stirs, she lives: if it be so,
It is a chance which do's redeeme all sorrowes
That ever I have felt.

KENT.　　　　　O my good Master.

LEAR. Prythee away.

EDGAR.　　　　　'Tis Noble *Kent* your Friend.

LEAR. A plague upon you Murderors, Traitors all,
I might have sav'd her, now she's gone for ever:
Cordelia, Cordelia, stay a little. Ha:
What is't thou saist? Her voice was ever soft,

Gentle, and low, an excellent thing in woman.
I kill'd the Slave that was a hanging thee.
GENTLEMAN. 'Tis true (my Lords) he did.
LEAR.   Did I not fellow?
I have seene the day, with my good biting Faulchion
I would have made him skip: I am old now,
And these same crosses spoile me. Who are you?
Mine eyes are not o' th' best, Ile tell you straight.
KENT. If Fortune brag of two, she lov'd and hated,
One of them we behold.
LEAR. This is a dull sight, are you not *Kent?*
KENT.   The same:
Your Servant *Kent.* Where is your Servant *Caius?*
LEAR. He's a good fellow, I can tell you that,
He'le strike and quickly too, he's dead and rotten.
KENT. No my good Lord, I am the very man.
LEAR. Ile see that straight.
KENT. That from your first of difference and decay,
Have follow'd your sad steps.
LEAR.   You are welcome hither.
KENT. Nor no man else: All's cheerlesse, darke, and deadly,
Your eldest Daughters have fore-done themselves,
And desperately are dead.
LEAR.   Ay so I thinke.
ALBANY. He knowes not what he saies, and vaine is it
That we present us to him.

                                   [*Enter a Messenger.*]
EDGAR.   Very bootlesse.
MESSENGER. *Edmund* is dead my Lord.
ALBANY.   That's but a trifle heere:
You Lords and Noble Friends, know our intent,
What comfort to this great decay may come,
Shall be appli'd. For us we will resigne,
During the life of this old Majesty
To him our absolute power, you to your rights,
With boote, and such addition as your Honours
Have more then merited. All Friends shall taste
The wages of their vertue, and all Foes
The cup of their deservings: O see, see.
LEAR. And my poore Foole is hang'd: no, no, no life?
Why should a Dog, a Horse, a Rat have life,
And thou no breath at all? Thou'lt come no more,
Never, never, never, never, never.
Pray you undo this Button. Thanke you Sir,
Do you see this? Looke on her. Looke her lips,
Looke there, looke there.   [*He dies.*]

EDGAR. He faints, my Lord, my Lord.

KENT. Breake heart, I prythee breake.

EDGAR. Looke up my Lord.

KENT. Vex not his ghost, O let him passe, he hates him,
That would upon the wracke of this tough world
Stretch him out longer.

EDGAR. He is gon indeed.

KENT. The wonder is, he hath endur'd so long,
He but usurpt his life.

ALBANY. Beare them from hence, our present businesse
Is generall woe: Friends of my soule, you twaine,
Rule in this Realme, and the gor'd state sustaine.

KENT. I have a journey Sir, shortly to go,
My Master calls me, I must not say no.

EDGAR. The waight of this sad time we must obey,
Speake what we feele, not what we ought to say:
The oldest hath borne most, we that are yong,
Shall never see so much, nor live so long.

[*Exeunt with a dead March.*]

From MACBETH

ACT 1, SCENE 5

Enter Macbeths Wife alone with a Letter.

LADY. *They met me in the day of successe: and I have learn'd by the perfect'st report, they have more in them, then mortall knowledge. When I burnt in desire to question them further, they made themselves Ayre, into which they vanish'd. Whiles I stood rapt in the wonder of it, came Missives from the King, who all-hail'd me Thane of Cawdor, by which Title before, these weyward Sisters saluted me, and referr'd me to the coming on of time, with haile King that shalt be. This have I thought good to deliver thee (my dearest Partner of Greatnesse) that thou might'st not lose the dues of rejoycing by being ignorant of what Greatnesse is promis'd thee. Lay it to thy heart and farewell.*
Glamys thou art, and Cawdor, and shalt be
What thou art promis'd: yet doe I feare thy Nature,
It is too full o' th' Milke of human kindnesse,
To catch the neerest way. Thou would'st be great,
Art not without Ambition, but without
The illnesse should attend it. What thou would'st highly,
That would'st thou holily: would'st not play false,
And yet would'st wrongly winne. Thould'st have, great Glamys,
That which cryes, Thus thou must doe, if thou have it;
And that which rather thou do'st feare to doe,

Then wishest should be undone. High thee hither,
That I may powre my Spirits in thine Eare,
And chastise with the valour of my Tongue
All that impeides thee from the Golden Round,
Which Fate and Metaphysicall ayde doth seeme
To have thee crown'd withall.   [*Enter Messenger.*]
                              What is your tidings?
MESSENGER. The King comes here to Night.
LADY.   Thou'rt mad to say it.
Is not thy Master with him? who, wer't so,
Would have inform'd for preparation.
MESSENGER. So please you, it is true: our *Thane* is comming:
One of my fellowes had the speed of him;
Who almost dead for breath, had scarcely more
Then would make up his Message.
LADY.   Give him tending,
He brings great newes.
                              [*Exit Messenger.*]
                    The Raven himselfe is hoarse,
That croakes the fatall entrance of *Duncan*
Under my Battlements. Come you Spirits,
That tend on mortall thoughts, unsex me here,
And fill me from the Crowne to the Toe, top-full
Of direst Crueltie: make thick my blood,
Stop up th' accesse, and passage to Remorse,
That no compunctious visitings of Nature,
Shake my fell purpose, nor keepe peace betweene
Th' effect, and it. Come to my Womans Brests,
And take my Milke for Gall, you murth'ring Ministers,
Where-ever, in your sightlesse substances,
You wait on Natures Mischiefe. Come thick Night,
And pall thee in the dunnest smoake of Hell,
That my keene Knife see not the Wound it makes,
Nor Heaven peepe through the Blanket of the darke,
To cry, hold, hold.   [*Enter Macbeth.*]
                    Great Glamys, worthy Cawdor,
Greater then both, by the all-haile hereafter,
Thy Letters have transported me beyond
This ignorant present, and I feele now
The future in the instant.
MACBETH.   My dearest Love,
Duncan comes here to Night.
LADY.   And when goes hence?
MACBETH. To morrow, as he purposes.
LADY.   O never,
Shall Sunne that Morrow see.

Your Face, my Thane, is as a Booke, where men
May reade strange matters. To beguile the time,
Looke like the time, beare welcome in your Eye,
Your Hand, your Tongue: looke like th' innocent flower,
But be the Serpent under't. He that's comming,
Must be provided for: and you shall put
This Nights great Businesse into my dispatch,
Which shall to all our Nights, and Dayes to come,
Give solely soveraigne sway, and Masterdome.

MACBETH. We will speake further.

LADY.   Only looke up cleare:
To alter favor, ever is to feare:
Leave all the rest to me.   [*Exeunt.*]

ACT II, SCENE 2

LADY. That which hath made them drunk, hath made me bold:
What hath quench'd them, hath given me fire. Hearke, peace:
It was the Owle that shriek'd, the fatall Bell-man,
Which gives the stern'st good-night. He is about it,
The Doores are open: and the surfeted Groomes
Doe mock their charge with Snores. I have drugg'd their Possets,
That Death and Nature doe contend about them,
Whether they live, or dye.

MACBETH [*within.*]   Who's there? what hoa?

LADY. Alack, I am afraid they have awak'd,
And 'tis not done: th' attempt, and not the deed,
Confounds us: hearke: I lay'd their Daggers ready,
He could not misse 'em. Had he not resembled
My Father as he slept, I had done't.   [*Enter Macbeth.*]
                                        My husband?

MACBETH. I have done the deed: Didst thou not heare a noyse?

LADY. I heard the Owle schreame, and the Crickets cry.
Did you not speake?

MACBETH.   When?

LADY.   Now.

MACBETH.   As I descended?

LADY. Ay.

MACBETH. Hearke, who lyes i' th' second Chamber?

LADY. *Donalbaine.*

MACBETH.   This is a sorry sight.

LADY. A foolish thought, to say a sorry sight.

MACBETH. There's one did laugh in's sleepe, and one cry'd Murther,
That they did wake each other: I stood, and heard them:
But they did say their Prayers, and addrest them
Againe to sleepe.

LADY.   There are two lodg'd together.

MACBETH. One cry'd God blesse us, and Amen the other,
 As they had seene me with these Hangmans hands:
 Listning their feare, I could not say Amen,
 When they did say God blesse us.

LADY.   Consider it not so deepely.

MACBETH. But wherefore could not I pronounce Amen?
 I had most need of Blessing, and Amen
 Stuck in my throat.

LADY.   These deeds must not be thought
 After these wayes: so, it will make us mad.

MACBETH. Me thought I heard a voyce cry, Sleep no more:
 Macbeth does murther Sleepe, the innocent Sleepe,
 Sleepe that knits up the ravel'd Sleeve of Care,
 The death of each dayes Life, sore Labors Bath,
 Balme of hurt Mindes, great Natures second Course,
 Chiefe nourisher in Life's Feast.

LADY.   What doe you meane?

MACBETH. Still it cry'd, Sleepe no more to all the House:
 Glamis hath murther'd Sleepe, and therefore *Cawdor*
 Shall sleepe no more: *Macbeth* shall sleepe no more.

LADY. Who was it, that thus cry'd? why worthy *Thane,*
 You doe unbend your Noble strength, to thinke
 So braine-sickly of things: Goe get some Water,
 And wash this filthie Witnesse from your Hand.
 Why did you bring these Daggers from the place?
 They must lye there: goe carry them, and smeare
 The sleepie Groomes with blood.

MACBETH.   Ile goe no more:
 I am afraid, to thinke what I have done:
 Looke on't againe, I dare not.

LADY.   Infirme of purpose:
 Give me the Daggers: the sleeping, and the dead,
 Are but as Pictures: 'tis the Eye of Child-hood,
 That feares a painted Devill. If he doe bleed,
 Ile guild the Faces of the Groomes withall,
 For it must seeme their Guilt.   [*Exit. Knocke within.*]

MACBETH.   Whence is that knocking?
 How is't with me, when every noyse appalls me?
 What Hands are here? hah: they pluck out mine Eyes.
 Will all great *Neptunes* Ocean wash this blood
 Cleane from my Hand? no: this my Hand will rather
 The multitudinous Seas incarnardine,
 Making the Greene one, Red.

           [*Enter Lady.*]

LADY. My Hands are of your colour: but I shame

To weare a Heart so white. [*Knocke.*] I heare a knocking
At the South entry: Retyre we to our Chamber:
A little Water cleares us of this deed.
How easie is it then! your Constancie
Hath left you unattended. [*Knocke.*] Hearke, more knocking.
Get on your Night-Gowne, lest occasion call us,
And shew us to be Watchers: be not lost
So poorely in your thoughts.
MACBETH.   To know my deed,
'Twere best not know my selfe.   [*Knocke.*]
Wake *Duncan* with thy knocking: I would thou could'st.   [*Exeunt.*]

ACT II, SCENE 3

Enter a Porter. Knocking within.

PORTER. Here's a knocking indeede: if a man were Porter of Hell Gate,
hee should have old turning the Key. [*Knock.*] Knock, Knock, Knock.
Who's there i' th' name of *Belzebub?* Here's a Farmer, that hang'd
himselfe on th' expectation of Plentie: Come in time, have Napkins
enow about you, here you'le sweat for't. [*Knock.*] Knock, Knock. Who's
there in th' other Devils Name? Faith here's an Equivocator, that could
sweare in both the Scales against eyther Scale, who committed Treason
enough for Gods sake, yet could not equivocate to Heaven: oh come
in, Equivocator. [*Knock.*] Knock, Knock, Knock. Who's there? 'Faith
here's an English Taylor come hither, for stealing out of a French
Hose: Come in Taylor, here you may rost your Goose. [*Knock.*] Knock,
Knock. Never at quiet: What are you? but this place is too cold for
Hell. Ile Devill-Porter it no further: I had thought to have let in some
of all Professions, that goe the Primrose way to th' everlasting Bonfire.
[*Knock.*] Anon, anon, I pray you remember the Porter.

ACT III, SCENE 2

MACBETH. We have scotch'd the Snake, not kill'd it:
Shee'le close, and be her selfe, whilest our poore Mallice
Remaines in danger of her former Tooth.
But let the frame of things dis-joynt, both the Worlds suffer,
Ere we will eate our Meale in feare, and sleepe
In the affliction of these terrible Dreames,
That shake us Nightly: Better be with the dead,
Whom we, to gayne our peace, have sent to peace,
Then on the torture of the Minde to lye
In restlesse extasie. *Duncane* is in his Grave:
After Lifes fitfull Fever, he sleepes well,
Treason ha's done his worst: nor Steele, nor Poyson,

Mallice domestique, forraine Levie, nothing,
Can touch him further.
LADY.   Come on:
Gentle my Lord, sleeke o're your rugged Lookes,
Be bright and Joviall among your Guests to Night.
MACBETH. So shall I Love, and so I pray be you:
Let your remembrance apply to *Banquo,*
Present him Eminence, both with Eye and Tongue:
Unsafe the while, that wee must lave
Our Honors in these flattering streames,
And make our Faces Vizards to our Hearts,
Disguising what they are.
LADY.   You must leave this.
MACBETH. O, full of Scorpions is my Minde, deare Wife:
Thou know'st, that *Banquo* and his *Fleans* lives.
LADY. But in them, Natures Coppie's not eterne.
MACBETH. There's comfort yet, they are assaileable,
Then be thou jocund: ere the Bat hath flowne
His Cloyster'd flight, ere to black *Heccats* summons
The shard-borne Beetle, with his drowsie hums,
Hath rung Nights yawning Peale, there shall be done
A deed of dreadfull note.
LADY.   What's to be done?
MACBETH. Be innocent of the knowledge, dearest chuck,
Till thou applaud the deed: Come, seeling Night,
Skarfe up the tender Eye of pittifull Day,
And with thy bloodie and invisible Hand
Cancell and teare to pieces that great Bond,
Which keepes me pale. Light thickens, and the Crow
Makes Wing to th' Rookie Wood:
Good things of Day begin to droope, and drowse,
Whiles Nights black Agents to their Prey's doe rowse.
Thou marvell'st at my words: but hold thee still,
Things bad begun, make strong themselves by ill:
So prythee goe with me.

From HAMLET

ACT I, SCENE 5

GHOST. I am thy Fathers Spirit,
Doom'd for a certaine terme to walke the night;
And for the day confin'd to fast in Fiers,
Till the foule crimes done in my dayes of Nature
Are burnt and purg'd away. But that I am forbid
To tell the secrets of my Prison-House,

I could a Tale unfold, whose lightest word
Would harrow up thy soule, freeze thy young blood,
Make thy two eyes like Starres, start from their Spheres,
Thy knotty and combined locks to part,
And each particular haire to stand an end,
Like Quilles upon the fretfull Porpentine:
But this eternall blason must not be
To eares of flesh and bloud; list *Hamlet,* oh list,
If thou didst ever thy deare Father love.

HAMLET. Oh Heaven!

GHOST. Revenge his foule and most unnaturall Murther.

HAMLET. Murther?

GHOST. Murther most foule, as in the best it is;
But this most foule, strange, and unnaturall.

HAMLET. Haste, haste me to know it, that with wings as swift
As meditation, or the thoughts of Love,
May sweepe to my Revenge.

GHOST.   I finde thee apt,
And duller should'st thou be then the fat weede
That rots it selfe in ease, on Lethe Wharfe,
Would'st thou not stirre in this. Now *Hamlet* heare:
It's given out, that sleeping in mine Orchard,
A Serpent stung me: so the whole eare of Denmarke,
Is by a forged processe of my death
Rankly abus'd: But know thou Noble youth,
The Serpent that did sting thy Fathers life,
Now weares his Crowne.

ACT II, SCENE 2

Enter Hamlet reading on a Booke.

QUEENE. But looke where sadly the poore wretch comes reading.

POLONIUS. Away I do beseech you, both away,
Ile boord him presently.   [*Exit King and Queen.*]
                        Oh give me leave.
How does my good Lord *Hamlet?*

HAMLET. Well, God-a-mercy.

POLONIUS. Do you know me, my Lord?

HAMLET. Excellent, excellent well: y'are a Fishmonger.

POLONIUS. Not I my Lord.

HAMLET. Then I would you were so honest a man.

POLONIUS. Honest, my Lord?

HAMLET. Ay, sir, to be honest as this world goes, is to bee one man pick'd
out of two thousand.

POLONIUS. That's very true, my Lord.

HAMLET. For if the Sun breed Magots in a dead dogge, being a good kissing Carrion — Have you a daughter?

POLONIUS. I have my Lord.

HAMLET. Let her not walke i' th' Sunne: Conception is a blessing, but not as your daughter may conceive. Friend looke to't.

POLONIUS. How say you by that? Still harping on my daughter: yet he knew me not at first; he said I was a Fishmonger: he is farre gone, farre gone: and truly in my youth, I suffred much extreamity for love: very neere this. Ile speake to him againe. What do you read my Lord?

HAMLET. Words, words, words.

POLONIUS. What is the matter, my Lord?

HAMLET. Betweene who?

POLONIUS. I meane the matter that you read, my Lord.

HAMLET. Slanders Sir: for the Satyricall slave saies here, that old men have gray Beards; that their faces are wrinkled: their eyes purging thicke Amber, or Plum-Tree Gumme: and that they have a plentifull lacke of Wit, together with weake Hammes. All which Sir, though I most powerfully, and potently beleeve, yet I holde it not Honestie to have it thus set downe: For you your selfe Sir, should be old as I am, if like a Crab you could go backward.

POLONIUS. Though this be madnesse, yet there is Method in't: will you walke out of the ayre my Lord?

HAMLET. Into my Grave?

POLONIUS. Indeed that is out o' th' Ayre: How pregnant (sometimes) his Replies are. A happinesse, that often Madnesse hits on, which Reason and Sanitie could not so prosperously be deliver'd of. I will leave him, and sodainely contrive the meanes of meeting between him, and my daughter. My Honourable Lord, I will most humbly take my leave of you.

HAMLET. You cannot Sir take from me any thing, that I will more willingly part withall, except my life, my life.

POLONIUS. Fare you well my Lord. [*Going.*]

HAMLET. These tedious old fooles. . . .

[*Enter Rosincrance and Guildensterne.*]

HAMLET. What's the newes?

ROSINCRANCE. None my Lord; but that the World's growne honest.

HAMLET. Then is Doomesday neere: But your newes is not true. Let me question more in particular: what have you my good friends, deserved at the hands of Fortune, that she sends you to Prison hither?

GUILDENSTERNE. Prison, my Lord?

HAMLET. Denmark's a Prison.

ROSINCRANCE. Then is the World one.

HAMLET. A goodly one, in which there are many Confines, Wards, and Dungeons; *Denmarke* being one o' th' worst.

ROSINCRANCE. We thinke not so my Lord.

HAMLET. Why then 'tis none to you; for there is nothing either good or bad, but thinking makes it so: to me it is a prison.

ROSINCRANCE. Why then your Ambition makes it one: 'tis too narrow for your minde.

HAMLET. O God, I could be bounded in a nutshell, and count my selfe a King of infinite space; were it not that I have bad dreames.

GUILDENSTERNE. Which dreames indeed are Ambition: for the very substance of the Ambitious, is meerely the shadow of a Dreame.

HAMLET. A dreame it selfe is but a shadow.

ROSINCRANCE. Truely, and I hold Ambition of so ayry and light a quality, that it is but a shadowes shadow.

HAMLET. Then are our Beggers bodies; and our Monarchs and out-strecht Heroes the Beggers Shadowes: shall wee to th' Court? for, by my fey I cannot reason.

ACT III, SCENE 1

HAMLET. To be, or not to be, that is the Question:
Whether 'tis Nobler in the minde to suffer
The Slings and Arrowes of outragious Fortune,
Or to take Armes against a Sea of troubles,
And by opposing end them: to dye, to sleepe
No more; and by a sleepe, to say we end
The Heart-ake, and the thousand Naturall shockes
That Flesh is heyre to. 'Tis a consummation
Devoutly to be wish'd. To dye to sleepe,
To sleepe, perchance to Dreame; ay, there's the rub,
For in that sleepe of death, what dreames may come,
When we have shufflel'd off this mortall coile,
Must give us pawse. There's the respect
That makes Calamity of so long life:
For who would beare the Whips and Scornes of time,
The Oppressors wrong, the poore mans Contumely,
The pangs of dispriz'd Love, the Lawes delay,
The insolence of Office, and the Spurnes
That patient merit of the unworthy takes,
When he himselfe might his *Quietus* make
With a bare Bodkin? Who would these Fardles beare
To grunt and sweat under a weary life,
But that the dread of something after death,
The undiscovered Countrey, from whose Borne
No Traveller returnes, Puzels the will,
And makes us rather beare those illes we have,
Then flye to others that we know not of.
Thus Conscience does make Cowards of us all,
And thus the Native hew of Resolution

Is sicklied o're, with the pale cast of Thought,
And enterprizes of great pith and moment,
With this regard their Currants turne away,
And lose the name of Action.

ACT IV, SCENE 3

KING. Now *Hamlet*, where's *Polonius*?

HAMLET. At Supper.

KING. At Supper? Where?

HAMLET. Not where he eats, but where he is eaten, a certaine convocation
of politick wormes are e'ne at him. Your worm is your only Emperor for
diet. We fat all creatures else to fat us, and we fat our selfe for Magots.
Your fat King, and your leane Begger is but variable service, two
dishes, but to one Table that's the end.

KING. What dost thou meane by this?

HAMLET. Nothing but to shew you how a King may go a Progresse
through the guts of a Begger.

KING. Where is *Polonius*?

HAMLET. In heaven, send thither to see. If your Messenger finde him not
there, seeke him i' th' other place your selfe: but indeed, if you finde
him not this moneth, you shall nose him as you go up the staires into
the Lobby.

KING [*to servants*]. Go seeke him there.

HAMLET. He will stay till ye come.

ACT IV, SCENE 5

Enter Ophelia distracted.

OPHELIA. Where is the beauteous Majesty of Denmark?

QUEENE. How now *Ophelia*?

OPHELIA.　　*How should I your true love know*
　　　　　　From another one?
　　　　　　By his Cockle hat and staffe,
　　　　　　And his Sandal shoone.

QUEENE. Alas sweet Lady: what imports this Song?

OPHELIA. Say you? Nay pray you marke.
　　　　　　He is dead and gone Lady,
　　　　　　He is dead and gone,
　　　　　　At his head a grasse-green Turfe,
　　　　　　At his heeles a stone.

　　　　　　　　　　　　　　　　　　　[*Enter King.*]

QUEENE. Nay but *Ophelia*.

OPHELIA. Pray you marke.
　　　　White his Shrow'd as the Mountaine Snow —

QUEENE. Alas, looke heere my Lord.

OPHELIA.   *Larded with sweet flowers:*
            Which bewept to the grave did go,
            With true-love showres.

KING. How do ye, pretty Lady?

OPHELIA. Well, God dil'd you. They say the Owle was a Bakers daughter. Lord, wee know what we are, but know not what we may be. God be at your Table.

KING. Conceit upon her Father.

OPHELIA. Pray you let's have no words of this: but when they aske you what it meanes, say you this:

        To morrow is Saint Valentines day,
          All in the morning betime,
          And I a Maid at your Window,
          To be your Valentine.
        Then up he rose, and don'd his clothes,
          And dupt the chamber dore,
        Let in the Maid, that out a Maid,
          Never departed more.

KING. Pretty *Ophelia.*

OPHELIA. Indeed la? without an oath Ile make an end on't.

        By gis, and by Saint Charity,
          Alacke, and fie for shame:
        Yong men wil doo't, if they come too't,
          By Cocke they are to blame.
        Quoth she: Before you tumbled me,
          You promis'd me to Wed:
        So would I ha done by yonder Sunne,
          And thou hadst not come to my bed.

KING. How long hath she bin thus?

OPHELIA. I hope all will be well. We must bee patient, but I cannot choose but weepe, to thinke they should lay him i' th' cold ground: My brother shall knowe of it, and so I thanke you for your good counsell. Come, my Coach: Goodnight Ladies: Goodnight sweet Ladies: Goodnight, goodnight.

ACT IV, SCENE 5

LAERTES. How now? what noise is that?   *[Enter Ophelia.]*
Oh heate drie up my Braines, teares seven times salt,
Burne out the Sence and Vertue of mine eye.
By Heaven, thy madnesse shall be payed by waight,
Till our Scale turnes the beame. Oh Rose of May,
Deere Maid, kinde Sister, sweet *Ophelia:*
Oh Heavens, is't possible, a yong Maids wits,
Should be as mortall as an old mans life?
Nature is fine in Love, and where 'tis fine,

It sends some precious instance of it selfe
After the thing it loves.
OPHELIA. *They bore him bare fac'd on the Beer,*
Hey non nony, nony, hey nony:
And on his grave raines many a teare,
Fare you well my Dove.
LAERTES. Had'st thou thy wits, and did'st perswade Revenge,
It could not move thus.
OPHELIA. You must sing downe a-downe, and you call him a-downe-a. Oh,
how the wheele becomes it! It is the false Steward that stole his mas-
ters daughter.
LAERTES. This nothings more then matter.
OPHELIA. There's Rosemary, that's for Remembraunce. Pray love remem-
ber: and there is Pancies, that's for Thoughts.
LAERTES. A document in madnesse, thoughts and remembrance fitted.
OPHELIA. There's Fennell for you, and Columbines: ther's Rew for you,
and heere's some for me. Wee may call it Herbe-Grace a Sundaies: Oh
you must weare your Rew with a difference. There's a Daysie, I would
give you some Violets, but they wither'd all when my Father dyed:
They say, he made a good end;
For bonny sweet Robin is all my joy.
LAERTES. Thought, and Affliction, Passion, Hell it selfe:
She turnes to Favour, and to prettinesse.
OPHELIA. *And will he not come againe,*
And will he not come againe:
No, no, he is dead,
Go to thy Death-bed,
He never wil come againe.
His Beard as white as Snow,
All Flaxen was his Pole:
He is gone, he is gone,
And we cast away mone,
Gramercy on his Soule.
And of all Christian Soules, I pray God. God buy ye.   *[Exit.]*

ACT V, SCENE 1

Enter two Clownes.

CLOWN. Is she to bee buried in Christian buriall, that wilfully seekes her
owne salvation?
OTHER. I tell thee she is, and therefore make her Grave straight, the
Crowner hath sate on her, and finds it Christian buriall.
CLOWN. How can that be, unlesse she drowned her selfe in her owne de-
fence?
OTHER. Why 'tis found so.

CLOWN. It must be *Se offendendo,* it cannot bee else: for heere lies the point: If I drowne my selfe wittingly, it argues an Act: and an Act hath three branches. It is an Act to doe and to performe; argall, she drown'd her selfe wittingly.

OTHER. Nay but heare you Goodman Delver.

CLOWN. Give me leave; heere lies the water; good: heere stands the man; good: If the man goe to this water and drowne himsele; it is will he nill he, he goes; marke you that? But if the water come to him and drowne him; hee drownes not himselfe. Argall, hee that is not guilty of his owne death, shortens not his owne life.

OTHER. But is this law?

CLOWN. Ay marry is't, Crowners Quest Law.

OTHER. Will you ha the truth on't? If this had not beene a Gentlewoman, shee should have beene buried out of Christian Buriall.

CLOWN. Why there thou say'st. And the more pitty that great folke should have countenance in this world to drowne or hang themselves, more then their even Christian. Come, my Spade; there is no ancient Gentlemen, but Gardiners, Ditchers and Grave-makers; they hold up *Adams* Profession.

OTHER. Was he a Gentleman?

CLOWN. He was the first that ever bore Armes.

OTHER. Why he had none.

CLOWN. What, ar't a Heathen? how dost thou understand the Scripture? the Scripture sayes *Adam* dig'd; could hee digge without Armes? Ile put another question to thee; if thou answerest me not to the purpose, confesse thy selfe —

OTHER. Go to.

CLOWN. What is he that builds stronger then either the Mason, the Shipwright, or the Carpenter?

OTHER. The Gallowes maker; for that Frame outlives a thousand Tenants.

CLOWN. I like thy wit well in good faith, the Gallowes does well; but how does it well? it does well to those that doe ill: now, thou dost ill to say the Gallowes is built stronger then the Church: Argall, the Gallowes may doe well to thee. To't againe, Come.

OTHER. Who builds stronger then a Mason, a Shipwright, or a Carpenter?

CLOWN. Ay, tell me that, and unyoake.

OTHER. Marry, now I can tell.

CLOWN. To't.

OTHER. Masse, I cannot tell.   [*Enter Hamlet and Horatio a farre off.*]

CLOWN. Cudgell thy braines no more about it; for your dull Asse will not mend his pace with beating; and when you are ask't this question next, say a Grave-maker: the Houses that he makes, lasts till Doomesday: go, get thee to *Yaughan,* fetch me a stoupe of Liquor. [*Exit Other.*]

[*Sings.*]

In youth when I did love, did love,
Me thought it was very sweete:

> *To contract, O, the time for, ah, my behove,*
> *O me thought there was nothing meete.*

HAMLET. Ha's this fellow no feeling of his businesse, that he sings at Grave-making?

HORATIO. Custome hath made it in him a property of easinesse.

HAMLET. 'Tis ee'n so; the hand of little Imployment hath the daintier sense.

CLOWN.   *But Age with his stealing steps*
> *Hath caught me in his clutch:*
> *And hath shipped me intill the Land,*
> *As if I had never beene such.*

HAMLET. That Scull had a tongue in it, and could sing once: how the knave jowles it to th' grownd, as if it were *Caines* Jaw-bone, that did the first murther: It might be the Pate of a Polititian which this Asse o're Offices: one that could circumvent God, might it not?

HORATIO. It might, my Lord.

HAMLET. Or of a Courtier, which could say, Good Morrow sweet Lord: how dost thou, good Lord? this might be my Lord such a one, that prais'd my Lord such a ones Horse, when he meant to begge it; might it not?

HORATIO. Ay, my Lord.

HAMLET. Why ee'n so: and now my Lady Worme's, Chaplesse, and knockt about the Mazard with a Sextons Spade; heere's fine Revolution, if wee had the tricke to see't. Did these bones cost no more the breeding, but to play at Loggets with 'em? mine ake to thinke on't.

CLOWN.   *A Pickhaxe and a Spade, a Spade,*
> *For and a shrowding-Sheete:*
> *O, a Pit of Clay for to be made,*
> *For such a Guest is meete.*

HAMLET. There's another: why might not that bee the Scull of a Lawyer? where be his Quiddities now? his Quillets? his Cases? his Tenures, and his Tricks? Why doe's he suffer this rude knave now to knocke him about the Sconce with a dirty Shovell, and will not tell him of his Action of Battery? hum. This fellow might be in's time a great buyer of Land, with his Statutes, his Recognizances, his Fines, his double Vouchers, his Recoveries: Is this the fine of his Fines, and the recovery of his Recoveries, to have his fine Pate full of fine Dirt? will his Vouchers vouch him no more of his Purchases, and double ones too, then the length and breadth of a paire of Indentures? the very Conveyances of his Lands will hardly lye in this Boxe; and must the Inheritor himselfe have no more? ha?

HORATIO. Not a jot more, my Lord.

HAMLET. Is not Parchment made of Sheep-skinnes?

HORATIO. Ay my Lord, and of Calve-skinnes too.

HAMLET. They are Sheepe and Calves that seek out assurance in that. I will speake to this fellow: whose Grave's this Sir?

CLOWN. Mine Sir:

> *O, a Pit of Clay for to be made,*
> *For such a Guest is meete.*

HAMLET. I thinke it be thine indeed: for thou liest in't.

CLOWN. You lye out on't Sir, and therefore it is not yours: for my part, I doe not lye in't; and yet it is mine.

HAMLET. Thou dost lye in't, to be in't and say 'tis thine: 'tis for the dead, not for the quicke, therefore thou lyest.

CLOWN. 'Tis a quicke lye Sir, 'twill away againe from me to you.

HAMLET. What man dost thou digge it for?

CLOWN. For no man Sir.

HAMLET. What woman then?

CLOWN. For none neither.

HAMLET. Who is to be buried in't?

CLOWN. One that was a woman Sir; but rest her Soule, shee's dead.

HAMLET. How absolute the knave is! wee must speake by the Carde, or equivocation will undoe us: by the Lord *Horatio*, these three yeares I have taken note of it, the Age is growne so picked, that the toe of the Pesant comes so neere the heeles of our Courtier, hee galls his Kibe. How long hast thou been a Grave-maker?

CLOWN. Of all the dayes i' th' yeare, I came to't that day that our last King *Hamlet* o'recame *Fortinbras.*

HAMLET. How long is that since?

CLOWN. Cannot you tell that? every foole can tell that: It was the very day, that young *Hamlet* was borne, hee that was mad, and sent into England.

HAMLET. Ay marry, why was he sent into England?

CLOWN. Why, because he was mad; hee shall recover his wits there; or if he do not, its no great matter there.

HAMLET. Why?

CLOWN. 'Twill not be seene in him, there the men are as mad as he.

HAMLET. How came he mad?

CLOWN. Very strangely they say.

HAMLET. How strangely?

CLOWN. Faith e'ene with losing his wits.

HAMLET. Upon what ground?

CLOWN. Why heere in Denmarke: I have bin Sexton heere, man and Boy thirty yeares.

HAMLET. How long will a man lie i' th' earth ere he rot?

CLOWN. Ifaith, if he be not rotten before he die (as we have many pocky Corses now adaies, that will scarce hold the laying in) he will last you some eight yeare, or nine yeare. A Tanner will last you nine yeare.

HAMLET. Why he, more than another?

CLOWN. Why sir, his hide is so tan'd with his Trade, that he will keepe out water a great while. And your water, is a sore Decayer of your whoreson dead body. Heres a Scull now: this Scul, has laine in the earth three and twenty years.

HAMLET. Whose was it?

CLOWN. A whoreson mad Fellowes it was; Whose doe you thinke it was?

HAMLET. Nay, I know not.

CLOWN. A pestilence on him for a mad Rogue, a pour'd a Flaggon of Renish on my head once. This same Scull Sir, this same Scull sir, was *Yoricks* Scull, the Kings Jester.

HAMLET. This?

CLOWN. E'ene that.

HAMLET. Let me see. Alas poore *Yorick,* I knew him *Horatio,* a fellow of infinite Jest; of most excellent fancy, he hath borne me on his backe a thousand times: And now how abhorred in my Imagination it is, my gorge rises at it. Heere hung those lipps, that I have kist I know not how oft. Where be your Jibes now? Your Gambals? Your Songs? Your flashes of Merriment that were wont to set the Table on a Rore? No one now to mock your own Jeering? Quite chopfalne? Now get you to my Ladies Chamber, and tell her, let her paint an inch thicke, to this favour she must come. Make her laugh at that: prythee *Horatio* tell me one thing.

HORATIO. What's that my Lord?

HAMLET. Dost thou thinke *Alexander* look't o' this fashion i' th' earth?

HORATIO. E'ene so.

HAMLET. And smelt so? Puh.

HORATIO. E'ene so, my Lord.

HAMLET. To what base uses we may returne *Horatio.* Why may not Imagination trace the Noble dust of *Alexander,* till he find it stopping a bunghole?

HORATIO. 'Twere to consider too curiously to consider so.

HAMLET. No faith, not a jot. But to follow him thether with modestie enough, and likeliehood to lead it; as thus: *Alexander* died: *Alexander* was buried: *Alexander* returneth into dust; the dust is earth; of earth we make Lome, and why of that Lome (whereto he was converted) might they not stopp a Beere-barrell?

> Imperiall *Cæsar,* dead and turn'd to clay,
> Might stop a hole to keepe the winde away.
> Oh, that that earth, which kept the world in awe,
> Should patch a Wall, t'expell the winters flaw.

But soft, but soft, aside; heere comes the King.

From ANTHONIE AND CLEOPATRA

ACT IV, SCENE 15

CLEOPATRA.   Oh Sunne,
Burne the great Sphere thou mov'st in, darkling stand
The varrying shore o' th' world. O *Antony,*
Antony, Antony. Helpe *Charmian,* helpe *Iras* helpe:
Helpe Friends below, let's draw him hither.

ANTONY. Peace,
Not *Cæsars* Valour hath o'erthrowne *Anthony*,
But *Anthonie's* hath Triumpht on it selfe.
CLEOPATRA. So it should be, that none but *Anthony*
Should conquer *Anthony*, but woe 'tis so.
ANTONY. I am dying Egypt, dying; only
I heere importune death a-while, untill
Of many thousand kisses, the poore last
I lay upon thy lippes.
CLEOPATRA. I dare not Deere,
Deere my Lord pardon: I dare not,
Lest I be taken: not th' Imperious shew
Of the full-Fortun'd *Cæsar*, ever shall
Be brooch'd with me, if Knife, Drugges, Serpents have
Edge, sting, or operation. I am safe:
Your Wife *Octavia*, with her modest eyes,
And still Conclusion, shall acquire no Honour
Demuring upon me: but come, come *Anthony*,
Helpe me my women, we must draw thee up:
Assist good Friends.
ANTONY. Oh quicke, or I am gone.
CLEOPATRA. Heere's sport indeede: How heavy weighes my Lord!
Our strength is all gone into heavinesse,
That makes the waight. Had I great *Juno's* power,
The strong wing'd Mercury should fetch thee up,
And set thee by Joves side. Yet come a little,
Wishers were ever Fooles. Oh come, come, come,
                    [*They heave Anthony aloft to Cleopatra.*]
And welcome, welcome. Dye when thou hast liv'd,
Quicken with kissing: had my lippes that power,
Thus would I weare them out.
ALL. A heavy sight.
ANTONY. I am dying Egypt, dying.
Give me some Wine, and let me speake a little.
CLEOPATRA. No, let me speake, and let me rayle so hye,
That the false Huswife Fortune, breake her Wheele,
Provok'd by my offence.
ANTONY. One word (sweet Queene)
Of *Cæsar* seeke your Honour, with your safety. Oh.
CLEOPATRA. They do not go together.
ANTONY. Gentle heare me,
None about *Cæsar* trust, but *Proculeius*.
CLEOPATRA. My Resolution, and my hands, Ile trust,
None about *Cæsar*.
ANTONY. The miserable change now at my end,
Lament nor sorrow at: but please your thoughts

In feeding them with those my former Fortunes
Wherein I lived. The greatest Prince o' th' world,
The Noblest: and do now not basely dye,
Not Cowardly put off my Helmet to
My Countreyman. A Roman, by a Roman
Valiantly vanquish'd. Now my Spirit is going,
I can no more.

CLEOPATRA.   Noblest of men, woo't dye?
Hast thou no care of me, shall I abide
In this dull world, which in thy absence is
No better then a Stye? Oh see, my women:
The Crowne o' th' earth doth melt. My Lord!
Oh wither'd is the Garland of the Warre,
The Souldiers pole is falne: young Boyes and Gyrles
Are levell now with men: The oddes is gone,
And there is nothing left remarkeable
Beneath the visiting Moone.

CHARMIAN.   O quietnesse, Lady.

ACT V, SCENE 2

CLEOPATRA. Give me my Robe, put on my Crowne, I have
Immortall longings in me. Now no more
The juyce of Egypts Grape shall moyst this lip.
Yare, yare, good *Iras;* quicke: Me thinkes I heare
Anthony call: I see him rowse himselfe
To praise my Noble Act. I heare him mock
The lucke of *Cæsar,* which the Gods give men
To excuse their after wrath. Husband, I come:
Now to that name, my Courage prove my Title.
I am Fire, and Ayre; my other Elements
I give to baser life. So, have you done?
Come then, and take the last warmth of my Lippes.
Farewell kinde *Charmian, Iras,* long farewell.
Have I the Aspicke in my lippes? Dost fall?
If thou, and Nature can so gently part,
The stroke of death is as a Lovers pinch,
Which hurts, and is desir'd. Dost thou lye still?
If thus thou vanishest, thou tell'st the world,
It is not worth leave-taking.

CHARMIAN. Dissolve thicke clowde, and Raine, that I may say
The Gods themselves do weepe.

CLEOPATRA.   This proves me base:
If she first meete the Curled *Anthony,*
Hee'l make demand of her, and spend that kisse
Which is my heaven to have. Come thou mortal wretch,

With thy sharpe teeth this knot intrinsicate,
Of life at once untye: Poore venomous Foole,
Be angry, and dispatch. Oh could'st thou speake,
That I might heare thee call great *Cæsar* Asse,
Unpolicied.
CHARMIAN.   Oh Easterne Starre.
CLEOPATRA.   Peace, peace:
Dost thou not see my Baby at my breast,
That suckes the Nurse asleepe.
CHARMIAN.   O breake! O breake!
CLEOPATRA. As sweet as Balme, as soft as Ayre, as gentle.
O *Anthony!* Nay I will take thee too.
What should I stay —   [*Dyes.*]
CHARMIAN. In this vile World? So fare thee well:
Now boast thee Death, in thy possession lyes
A Lasse unparalell'd. Downie Windowes cloze,
And golden Phœbus, never be beheld
Of eyes againe so Royall: your Crownes awry,
Ile mend it, and then play.

From OTHELLO

ACT IV, SCENE 3

ÆMELIA. I have laied these Sheetes you bad me on the bed.
DESDEMONA. All's one: good Father, how foolish are our minds?
If I do die before thee, prythee shrow'd me
In one of these same Sheetes.
ÆMILIA.   Come, come: you talke.
DESDEMONA. My Mother had a Maid call'd *Barbarie*,
She was in love: and he she lov'd prov'd mad,
And did forsake her. She had a Song of Willough,
An old thing 'twas: but it express'd her Fortune,
And she dy'd singing it. That Song to night,
Will not go from my mind: I have much to do,
But to go hang my head all at one side
And sing it like poore *Barbarie:* prythee dispatch.
ÆMILIA. Shall I go fetch your Night-gowne?
DESDEMONA.   No, un-pin me here,
This *Lodovico* is a proper man.
ÆMILIA. A very handsome man.
DESDEMONA. He speakes well.
ÆMILIA. I know a Lady in Venice would have walk'd barefoot to Palestine
for a touch of his nether lip.
DESDEMONA. *The poore Soule set sighing, by a Sicamour tree.*
    Sing all a greene Willough:

Her hand on her bosome, her head on her knee,
   Sing Willough, Willough, Willough.
The fresh Streames ran by her, and murmur'd her moanes
   Sing Willough, Willough, Willough.
Her salt teares fell from her, and softned the stones,
   Sing Willough, Willough, Willough.
(Lay by these)
   Willough, Willough.
(Prythee high thee: he'le come anon)
   Sing all a greene Willough must be my Garland.
   Let no body blame him, his scorne I approve.
(Nay that's not next. Harke, who is't that knocks?)

ÆMILIA. It's the wind.

DESDEMONA. *I call'd my Love false Love: but what said he then?*
   Sing Willough, Willough, Willough.
   If I court mo women, you'le couch with mo men.
So get thee gone, good night: mine eyes do itch:
Doth that boade weeping?

ACT V, SCENE 2

Enter Othello. Desdemona in her bed.

OTHELLO. It is the Cause, it is the Cause (my Soule)
   Let me not name it to you, you chaste Starres,
   It is the Cause. Yet Ile not shed her blood,
   Nor scarre that whiter skins of hers than Snow,
   And smooth as Monumentall Alabaster:
   Yet she must dye, else shee'l betray more men:
   Put out the Light, and then put out the Light:
   If I quench thee, thou flaming Minister,
   I can againe thy former light restore,
   Should I repent me. But once put out thy Light,
   Thou cunning'st Patterne of excelling Nature,
   I know not where is that *Promethœan* heate
   That can thy Light re-Lume. When I have pluck'd thy Rose,
   I cannot give it vitall growth againe,
   It needs must wither. Ile smell thee on the Tree.
   Oh Balmy breath, that dost almost perswade
   Justice to breake her Sword. One more, one more:
   Be thus when thou art dead, and I will kill thee,
   And love thee after. One more, and that's the last.
   So sweet, was ne're so fatall. I must weepe,
   But they are cruell Teares: This sorrow's heavenly,
   It strikes, where it doth love. She wakes.

DESDEMONA.   Who's there?
   Othello?

OTHELLO. Ay *Desdemona.*

DESDEMONA. Will you come to bed,
My Lord?

OTHELLO. Have you pray'd to night, *Desdemon?*

DESDEMONA. Ay my Lord.

OTHELLO. If you bethinke your selfe of any Crime
Unreconcil'd as yet to Heaven, and Grace,
Solicite for it straight.

DESDEMONA. Alacke, my Lord, what may you meane by that?

OTHELLO. Well, do it, and be breefe, I will walke by:
I would not kill thy unprepared Spirit,
No, Heavens fore-fend! I would not kill thy Soule.

DESDEMONA. Talke you of killing?

OTHELLO. Ay, I do.

DESDEMONA. Then Heaven
Have mercy on mee.

OTHELLO. Amen, with all my heart.

DESDEMONA. If you say so, I hope you will not kill me.

OTHELLO. Humh.

DESDEMONA. And yet I feare you: for you're fatall then
When your eyes rowle so. Why I should feare, I know not,
Since guiltinesse I know not: But yet I feele I feare.

OTHELLO. Thinke on thy sinnes.

DESDEMONA. They are Loves I beare to you.

OTHELLO. Ay, and for that thou dy'st.

DESDEMONA. That death's unnaturall, that kils for loving.
Alas, why gnaw you so your nether-lip?
Some blood passion shakes your very Frame:
These are portents: but yet I hope, I hope,
They do not point on me.

OTHELLO. Peace, and be still.

DESDEMONA. I will so: What's the matter?

OTHELLO. That Handkerchiefe
Which I so lov'd, and gave thee, thou gav'st to *Cassio.*

DESDEMONA. No by my Life, and Soule: send for the man,
And aske him.

OTHELLO. Sweet Soule, take heed, take heed of Perjury,
Thou art on thy death-bed.

DESDEMONA. Ay, but not yet to dye.

OTHELLO. Presently.
Therefore confesse thee freely of thy sinne:
For to deny each Article with Oath,
Cannot remove, nor choake the strong Conception
That I do grone withall. Thou art to dye.

DESDEMONA. O Heaven have mercy on me.

OTHELLO. I say, Amen.

DESDEMONA. And have you mercy too. I never did
 Offend you in my life: never lov'd *Cassio*,
 But with such generall warrantie of Heaven,
 As I might love. I never gave him Token.
OTHELLO. By Heaven I saw my Handkerchiefe in's hand.
 O perjur'd woman, thou do'st stone my heart,
 And makes me call, what I intend to do,
 A Murther, which I thought a Sacrifice.
 I saw the Handkerchiefe.
DESDEMONA.   He found it then:
 I never gave it him: Send for him hither:
 Let him confesse a truth.
OTHELLO.   He hath confest.
DESDEMONA. What, my Lord?
OTHELLO.   That he hath us'd thee.
DESDEMONA.   How? unlawfully?
OTHELLO. Ay.
DESDEMONA. He will not say so.
OTHELLO.   No: his mouth is stopp'd:
 Honest *Iago* hath tane order for't.
DESDEMONA. Oh, my feare interprets. What is he dead?
OTHELLO. Had all his haires been lives, my great Revenge
 Had stomacke for them all.
DESDEMONA. Alas, he is betray'd,
 And I undone.
OTHELLO.   Out Strumpet: weep'st thou for him
 To my face?
DESDEMONA. O banish me, my Lord, but kill me not.
OTHELLO. Downe Strumpet.
DESDEMONA.   Kill me to morrow, let me live to night.
OTHELLO. Nay, if you strive.
DESDEMONA.   But halfe an houre.
OTHELLO.   Being done,
 There is no pawse.
DESDEMONA.   But while I say one prayer.
OTHELLO. It is too late.   *[Smothers her.]*

ACT V, SCENE 2

ÆMILIA. What did thy Song boad Lady?
 Hearke, canst thou heare me? I will play the Swan,
 And dye in Musicke: *Willough, Willough, Willough.*
 Moor, she was chaste: She lov'd thee, cruell Moor,
 So come my Soule to blisse, as I speake true:
 So speaking as I thinke, alas, I dye.   *[She dies.]*
OTHELLO. I have another weapon in this Chamber,

It was a Sword of Spaine, the Ice brookes temper:
  Oh heere it is: Unkle I must come forth.
GRATIANO. If thou attempt it, it will cost thee deere;
  Thou hast no weapon, and perforce must suffer.
OTHELLO. Looke in upon me then, and speake with me,
  Or naked as I am I will assault thee.
GRATIANO. What is the matter?
OTHELLO.   Behold, I have a weapon:
  A better never did it selfe sustaine
  Upon a Soldiers Thigh. I have seene the day,
  That with this little Arme, and this good Sword,
  I have made my way through more impediments
  Then twenty times your stop. But (oh vaine boast)
  Who can controll his Fate? 'Tis not so now.
  Be not affraid, though you do see me weapon'd:
  Heere is my journies end, heere is my butt
  And verie Sea-marke of my utmost Saile.
  Do you go backe dismaid? 'Tis a lost feare:
  Man but a Rush against *Othello's* brest,
  And he retires. Where should *Othello* go?
  Now: how dost thou looke now? Oh ill-Starr'd wench,
  Pale as thy Smocke: when we shall meete at compt,
  This looke of thine will hurle my Soule from Heaven,
  And Fiends will snatch at it. Cold, cold, my Girle?
  Even like thy Chastity.
  O cursed, cursed Slave! Whip me ye Divels,
  From the possession of this Heavenly sight:
  Blow me about in windes, roast me in Sulphure,
  Wash me in steepe-downe gulfes of Liquid fire.
  Oh *Desdemon!* dead *Desdemon:* dead. Oh, oh!

    Enter Lodovico, Cassio, Montano, and Iago, with Officers.

LODOVICO. Where is this rash, and most unfortunate man?
OTHELLO. That's he that was *Othello:* heere I am.
LODOVICO. Where is that Viper? Bring the Villaine forth.
OTHELLO. I look down towards his feet; but that's a Fable,
  If that thou bee'st a Divell, I cannot kill thee.   [*Wounds Iago.*]
LODOVICO. Wrench his Sword from him.
IAGO.   I bleed Sir, but not kill'd.
OTHELLO. I am not sorry neither, Il'd have thee live:
  For in my sense, 'tis happinesse to die.
LODOVICO. Oh thou *Othello,* that was once so good,
  Falne in the practise of a cursed Slave,
  What shall be saide to thee.
OTHELLO.   Why any thing:

An honourable Murderer, if you will:
For nought I did in hate, but all in Honour.

LODOVICO. This wretch hath part confest his Villany:
Did you and he consent in *Cassio's* death?

OTHELLO. Ay.

CASSIO.   Deere Generall, I never gave you cause.

OTHELLO. I do beleeve it, and I aske your pardon:
Will you, I pray, demand that demy-Divell,
Why he hath thus ensnar'd my Soule and Body.

IAGO. Demand me nothing: what you know, you know:
From this time forth, I never will speake word.

LODOVICO. What? not to pray?

GRATIANO.   Torments will ope your lips.

OTHELLO. Well, thou dost best.

LODOVICO. Sir, you shall understand what hath befalne,
(Which, as I thinke, you know not) heere is a Letter
Found in the pocket of the slaine *Rodorigo,*
And heere another, the one of them imports
The death of *Cassio,* to be undertooke
By *Rodorigo.*

OTHELLO.   O Villaine!

CASSIO.   Most Heathenish, and most grosse.

LODOVICO. Now, heere's another discontented paper
Found in his pocket too: and this it seemes
Rodorigo meant t'have sent this damned villaine:
But that (belike) *Iago* in the interim
Came in, and satisfi'd him.

OTHELLO.   Oh thou pernitious Caitiffe;
How came you, *Cassio,* by that Handkerchiefe
That was my wives?

CASSIO.   I found it in my Chamber:
And he himselfe confest it but even now,
That there he dropt it for a speciall purpose,
Which wrought to his desire.

OTHELLO.   O Foole, foole, foole!

CASSIO. There is besides, in *Rodorigo's* Letter,
How he upbraides *Iago,* that he made him
Brave me upon the Watch: whereon it came
That I was cast: and even but now he spake
(After long seeming dead) *Iago* hurt him,
Iago set him on.

LODOVICO. You must forsake this roome, and go with us:
Your Power, and your Command is taken off,
And *Cassio* rules in Cyprus. For this Slave,
If there be any cunning Crueltie,
That can torment him much, and hold him long,

It shall be his. You shall close Prisoner rest,
Till that the Nature of your fault be knowne
To the Venetian State. Come, bring away.
OTHELLO. Soft you; a word or two before you goe:
I have done the State some service, and they know't:
No more of that. I pray you in your Letters,
When you shall these unluckie deeds relate,
Speake of me, as I am. Nothing extenuate,
Nor set downe ought in malice. Then must you speake,
Of one that lov'd not wisely, but too well:
Of one, not easily Jealious, but being wrought,
Perplexed in the extreame: Of one, whose hand
(Like the base Indian) threw a Pearle away
Richer then all his Tribe: Of one, whose subdu'd Eyes,
Albeit un-used to the melting moode,
Drops teares as fast as the Arabian Trees
Their Medicinable gumme. Set you downe this:
And say besides, that in *Aleppo* once,
Where a malignant, and a Turbond-Turke
Beate a Venetian, and traduc'd the State,
I tooke by th' throat the circumcised Dogge,
And smoate him, thus.   [*Stabs himself.*]
LODOVICO. Oh bloody period.
GRATIANO.   All that is spoke, is marr'd.
OTHELLO. I kist thee, ere I kill'd thee: No way but this,
Killing my selfe, to dye upon a kisse.   [*Dyes.*]
CASSIO. This did I feare, but thought he had no weapon:
For he was great of heart.
LODOVICO [*to Iago*].   Oh Sparton Dogge:
More fell than Anguish, Hunger, or the Sea:
Looke on the Tragicke Loading of this bed:
This is thy worke: The Object poysons Sight,
Let it be hid. *Gratiano,* keepe the house,
And seize upon the Fortunes of the Moor,
For they succeede on you. To you, Lord Governor,
Remaines the Censure of this hellish villaine:
The Time, the Place, the Torture, oh inforce it:
My selfe will straight aboord, and to the State,
This heavie Act, with heavie heart relate.

From CYMBELINE

ACT II, SCENE 2

IACHIMO. The Crickets sing, and mans ore-labor'd sense
Repaires it selfe by rest: Our *Tarquine* thus

Did softly presse the Rushes, ere he waken'd
The Chastitie he wounded. *Cytherea,*
How bravely thou becom'st thy Bed; fresh Lilly,
And whiter then the Sheetes: that I might touch,
But kisse, one kisse. Rubies unparagon'd,
How deerely they doo't: 'Tis her breathing that
Perfumes the Chamber thus: the Flame o' th' Taper
Bowes toward her, and would under-peepe her lids
To see th' inclosed Lights, now Canopied
Under these windowes, White and Azure lac'd
With Blew of Heavens owne tinct. But my designe:
To note the Chamber, I will write all downe,
Such, and such pictures: There the window, such
Th' adornement of her Bed; the Arras, Figures,
Why such, and such: and the Contents o' th' Story.
Ah, but some naturall notes about her Body,
Above ten thousand meaner Moveables
Would testifie, t'enrich mine Inventorie.
O sleepe, thou Ape of death, lye dull upon her,
And be her Sense but as a Monument,
Thus in a Chappell lying.   [*Taking off her bracelet.*]
    Come off, come off;
As slippery as the Gordian-knot was hard.
'Tis mine, and this will witnesse outwardly,
As strongly as the Conscience do's within:
To th' madding of her Lord. On her left brest
A mole Cinque-spotted: Like the Crimson drops
I' th' bottome of a Cowslippe. Heere's a Voucher,
Stronger then ever Law could make; this Secret
Will force him thinke I have pick'd the lock, and ta'en
The treasure of her Honour. No more: to what end?
Why should I write this downe, that's riveted,
Screw'd to my memorie. She hath bin reading late,
The Tale of *Tereus,* heere the leaffe's turn'd downe
Where *Philomele* gave up. I have enough,
To th' Truncke againe, and shut the spring of it.
Swift, swift, you Dragons of the night, that dawning
May bare the Ravens eye: I lodge in feare,
Though this a heavenly Angell: hell is heere.

     Clocke strikes.

One, two, three: time, time.   [*Exit.*]

ACT II, SCENE 3

Hearke, hearke, the Larke at Heavens gate sings,
  And Phœbus gins arise,
His Steeds to water at those Springs
  On chalic'd Flowres that lyes:
And winking Mary-buds begin
  To ope their Golden eyes:
With every thing that pretty is,
  My Lady sweet arise:
    Arise, arise.

ACT IV, SCENE 2

GUIDERIUS. Feare no more the heate o' th' Sun,
  Nor the furious Winters rages,
Thou thy worldly task hast don,
  Home art gon, and tane thy wages.
Golden Lads, and Girles all must,
As Chimney-Sweepers come to dust.

ARVIRAGUS. Feare no more the frowne o' th' Great,
  Thou art past the Tirants stroake,
Care no more to cloath and eate,
  To thee the Reede is as the Oake:
The Scepter, Learning, Physicke must,
All follow this and come to dust.

GUIDERIUS. Feare no more the Lightning flash.
ARVIRAGUS. Nor th' all-dreaded Thunderstone.
GUIDERIUS. Feare not Slander, Censure rash.
ARVIRAGUS. Thou hast finish'd Joy and mone.
BOTH. All Lovers young, all Lovers must,
Consigne to thee and come to dust.

GUIDERIUS. No Exorcisor harme thee,
ARVIRAGUS. Nor no witch-craft charme thee.
GUIDERIUS. Ghost unlaid forbeare thee.
ARVIRAGUS. Nothing ill come neere thee.
BOTH. Quiet consumation have,
And renowned be thy grave.

From THE TEMPEST

ACT I, SCENE 2

Come unto these yellow sands,
 And then take hands:
Curtsied when you have, and kist
 The wilde waves whist:
Foote it featly heere, and there, and sweete Sprights
   the burthen beare.
  Harke, harke: *bowgh wawgh:*
  The watch-Dogges barke: *bowgh-wawgh.*
Hark, hark, I heare, the straine of strutting Chanticlere:
  Cry cockadidle-dowe.

ACT I, SCENE 2

Full fadom five thy Father lies,
 Of his bones are Corrall made:
Those are pearles that were his eies,
 Nothing of him that doth fade,
But doth suffer a Sea-change
Into something rich, and strange:
Sea-Nimphs hourly ring his knell.
   [BURTHEN:] *Ding dong.*
Harke now I heare them, ding-dong bell.

ACT III, SCENE 2

CALIBAN. Be not affeard, the Isle is full of noyses,
 Sounds, and sweet aires, that give delight and hurt not:
 Sometimes a thousand twangling Instruments
 Will hum about mine eares; and sometime voices,
 That if I then had wak'd after long sleepe,
 Will make me sleepe againe, and then in dreaming,
 The clouds methought would open, and shew riches
 Ready to drop upon me, that when I wak'd
 I cri'de to dreame againe.

ACT IV, SCENE 1

IRIS. *Ceres,* most bounteous Lady, thy rich Leas
 Of Wheate, Rye, Barley, Vetches, Oates and Pease;
 Thy turfy Mountaines, where live nibling Sheepe,

And flat Medes thetchd with Stover, them to keepe:
Thy bankes with pioned, and twilled brims
Which spungie *Aprill,* at thy hest betrims;
To make cold Nymphes chast crownes; and thy broome-groves;
Whose shadow the dismissed Batchelor loves,
Being lasse-lorne: thy pole-clipt vineyard,
And thy Sea-marge sterile, and rockey-hard,
Where thou thy selfe do'st ayre, the Queene o' th' Skie,
Whos watry Arch, and messenger, am I,
Bids thee leave these, and with her soveraigne grace,   *[Juno descends.]*
Here on this grasse-plot, in this very place
To come, and sport: here Peacocks flye amaine:
Approach, rich *Ceres,* her to entertaine.   *[Enter Ceres.]*
CERES. Haile, many-coloured Messenger, that nere
Do'st disobey the wife of *Jupiter:*
Who, with thy saffron wings, upon my flowres
Diffusest hony drops, refreshing showres,
And with each end of thy blew bowe do'st crowne
My boskie acres, and my unshrubd downe,
Rich scarph to my proud earth: why hath thy Queene
Summond me hither, to this short gras'd Greene?
IRIS. A contract of true Love, to celebrate,
And some donation freely to estate
On the bles'd Lovers.

From THE WINTER'S TALE

ACT IV, SCENE 3

PERDITA.   Sir, welcome:
It is my Fathers will, I should take on mee
The Hostesseship o' th' day: you're welcome sir.
Give me those Flowres there, *Dorcas.* Reverend Sirs,
For you, there's Rosemary, and Rue, these keepe
Seeming, and savour all the Winter long:
Grace, and Remembrance be to you both,
And welcome to our Shearing.
POLIXENES.   Shepherdesse,
(A faire one are you:) well you fit our ages
With flowres of Winter.
PERDITA.   Sir, the yeare growing ancient,
Not yet on summers death, nor on the birth
Of trembling winter, the fayrest flowres o' th' season
Are our Carnations, and streak'd Gilly-vors,
(Which some call Natures bastards): of that kind

Our rusticke Garden's barren, and I care not
To get slips of them.
POLIXENES.　　　　　　Wherefore (gentle Maiden)
Do you neglect them?
PERDITA.　　　　　　For I have heard it said,
There is an Art, which in their pidenesse shares
With great creating-Nature.
POLIXENES.　　　　　　Say there be:
Yet Nature is made better by no meane,
But Nature makes that Meane: so over that Art,
(Which you say addes to Nature) is an Art
That Nature makes: you see (sweet Maid) we marry
A gentler Scion, to the wildest Stocke,
And make conceyve a barke of baser kinde
By bud of Nobler race. This is an Art
Which do's mend Nature: change it rather, but
The Art it selfe, is Nature.
PERDITA.　　　　　　So it is.
POLIXENES. Then make your Garden rich in Gilly'vors,
And do not call them bastards.
PERDITA.　　　　　　　　Ile not put
The Dible in earth, to set one slip of them:
No more then were I painted, I would wish
This youth should say 'twer well: and onely therefore
Desire to breed by me. Here's flowres for you:
Hot Lavender, Mints, Savory, Marjorum,
The Mary-gold, that goes to bed wi' th' Sun,
And with him rises, weeping: These are flowres
Of middle summer, and I thinke they are given
To men of middle age. Y'are very welcome.
CAMILLO. I should leave grasing, were I of your flocke,
And onely live by gazing.
PERDITA.　　　　　　Out alas:
You'ld be so leane, that blasts of January
Would blow you through and through. Now, my fairst Friend,
I would I had some Flowres o' th' Spring, that might
Become your time of day: and yours, and yours,
That weare upon your Virgin-branches yet
Your Maiden-heads growing: *O Proserpina,*
For the Flowres now, that (frighted) thou let'st fall
From *Dis's* Waggon: Daffadils,
That come before the Swallow dares, and take
The windes of March with beauty: Violets (dim,
But sweeter then the lids of *Juno's* eyes,
Or *Cytherea's* breath) pale Prime-roses,
That dye unmarried, ere they can behold

Bright Phœbus in his strength (a Maladie
Most incident to Maids:) bold Oxlips, and
The Crowne Imperiall: Lillies of all kinds,
(The Flowre-de-Luce being one.) O, these I lacke,
To make you Garlands of, and my sweet friend,
To strew him o're, and ore.
FLORIZELL.   What? like a Corse?
PERDITA. No, like a banke, for Love to lye, and play on:
Not like a Corse: or if: not to be buried,
But quicke, and in mine armes. Come, take your flowrs,
Me thinkes I play as I have seene them do
In Whitson-Pastorals: Sure this Robe of mine
Do's change my disposition:
FLORIZELL.   What you do,
Still betters what is done. When you speake (Sweet)
I'ld have you do it ever: When you sing,
I'ld have you buy, and sell so: so give Almes,
Pray so: and for the ord'ring your Affayres,
To sing them too. When you do dance, I wish you
A wave o' th' Sea, that you might ever do
Nothing but that: move still, still so:
And owne no other Function. Each your doing,
(So singular, in each particular)
Crownes what you are doing, in the present deeds,
That all your Actes, are Queenes.

From MEASURE FOR MEASURE

ACT IV, SCENE 1

Enter Mariana, and Boy singing.

Take, oh take those lips away,
    That so sweetly were forsworne,
And those eyes: the breake of day
    Lights that doe mislead the Morne;
But my kisses bring againe, bring againe,
Seales of love, but seal'd in vaine, seal'd in vaine.

From TWELFE NIGHT

ACT II, SCENE 4

Come away, come away death,
    And in sad cypresse let me be laide.
Fly away, fly away breath,

I am slaine by a faire cruell maide:
My shrowd of white, stuck all with Yew,
    O prepare it.
My part of death no one so true
    Did share it.

Not a flower, not a flower sweete
  On my blacke coffin, let there be strewne:
Not a friend, not a friend greet
  My poore corpes, where my bones shall be throwne:
A thousand thousand sighes to save,
    Lay me o where
Sad true lover never find my grave,
    To weepe there.

ACT V, SCENE 1

When that I was and a little tiny boy,
  With hey, ho, the winde and the raine:
A foolish thing was but a toy,
  For the raine it raineth every day.

But when I came to mans estate,
  With hey, ho, the winde and the raine:
Gainst Knaves and Theeves men shut their gate,
  For the raine it raineth every day.

But when I came alas to wive,
  With hey, ho, the winde and the raine:
By swaggering could I never thrive,
  For the raine it raineth every day.

But when I came unto my beds,
  With hey, ho, the winde and the raine:
With tospottes still had drunken heades,
  For the raine it raineth every day.

A great while ago the world begon,
  With hey, ho, the winde and the raine:
But that's all one, our Play is done,
  And wee'l strive to please you every day.

From THE MERCHANT OF VENICE

ACT III, SCENE 2

Tell me where is fancie bred,
Or in the heart, or in the head:
How begot, how nourished?
　　　Replie, replie.
It is engendred in the eyes,
With gazing fed, and Fancie dies,
In the cradle where it lies:
Let us all ring Fancies knell.
Ile begin it: Ding, dong, bell.
ALL. Ding, dong, bell.

From THE TWO NOBLE KINSMEN *

FUNERAL SONG

Urns and Odours, bring away,
Vapors, sighs, darken the day;
　　Our dole more deadly looks, than dying
Balmes, and Gumms, and heavy cheers,
Sacred vials fill'd with tears,
　　And clamors, through the wild air flying:

Come all sad and solemn Shows,
That are quick-ey'd pleasures foes;
We convent nought else but woes.
　　We convent nought else but woes.

From HENRY THE EIGHTH †

ORPHEUS WITH HIS LUTE MADE TREES

Orpheus with his Lute made Trees,
And the Mountaine tops that freeze,
　　Bow themselves when he did sing.
To his Musicke, Plants and Flowers
Ever sprung; as Sunne and Showers,
　　There had made a lasting Spring.

---

* This play is of doubtful authorship — possibly by John Fletcher. Shakespeare is assumed to have had a share in it.
† Possibly written from a draft by John Fletcher.

Every thing that heard him play,
Even the Billowes of the Sea,
    Hung their heads, and then lay by.
In sweet Musicke is such Art,
Killing care, and griefe of heart,
    Fall asleepe, or hearing dye.

Ben Jonson
1572-1637

From CYNTHIA'S REVELS

SONG: SLOW, SLOW, FRESH FOUNT

Slow, slow, fresh fount, keepe time with my salt teares;
    Yet slower, yet, O faintly gentle springs:
List to the heavy part the musique beares,
    "Woe weepes out her division, when shee sings.
        Droupe hearbs, and flowres;
        Fall griefe in showres;
        Our beauties are not ours":
            O, I could still
(Like melting snow upon some craggie hill,)
        Drop, drop, drop, drop,
Since natures pride is, now, a wither'd daffodill.

THE HYMNE

Queene, and *Huntress*, chaste, and faire,
    Now the Sunne is laid to sleepe,
Seated in thy silver chaire,
    State in wonted manner keepe:
        Hesperus intreats thy light,
        Goddesse, excellently bright.

Earth, let not thy envious shade
    Dare it selfe to interpose;
Cynthias shining orbe was made
    Heaven to cleere, when day did close:
        Blesse us then with wished sight,
        Goddesse, excellently bright.

Lay thy bow of pearle apart,
  And thy cristall-shining quiver;
Give unto the flying hart
  Space to breathe, how short soever:
    Thou that mak'st a day of night,
    Goddesse, excellently bright.

From THE FORREST

SONG: TO CELIA

Drinke to me, onely, with thine eyes,
  And I will pledge with mine;
Or leave a kisse but in the cup,
  And Ile not looke for wine.
The thirst, that from the soule doth rise,
  Doth aske a drinke divine:
But might I of JOVE's *Nectar* sup,
  I would not change for thine.

I sent thee, late, a rosie wreath,
  Not so much honoring thee,
As giving it a hope, that there
  It could not withered bee.
But thou thereon did'st onely breath,
  And sent'st it backe to mee:
Since when it growes, and smells, I sweare,
  Not of it selfe, but thee.

TO PENSHURST

Thou art not, PENSHURST, built to envious show,
Of touch, or marble; nor canst boast a row
Of polish'd pillars, or a roofe of gold:
Thou hast no lantherne, whereof tales are told;
Or stayre, or courts; but stand'st an ancient pile,
And these grudg'd at, art reverenc'd the while.
Thou joy'st in better markes, of soyle, of ayre,
Of wood, of water: therein thou art faire.
Thou hast thy walkes for health, as well as sport:
Thy *Mount,* to which the *Dryads* doe resort,
Where PAN and BACCHUS their high feasts have made,
Beneath the broad beech, and the chest-nut shade;
That taller tree, which of a nut was set,
At his great birth, where all the *Muses* met.
There, in the writhed barke, are cut the names

Of many a SYLVANE, taken with his flames.
And thence, the ruddy *Satyres* oft provoke
The lighter *Faunes,* to reach thy *Ladies oke.*
Thy copp's, too, nam'd of GAMAGE, thou hast there,
That never failes to serve thee season'd deere,
When thou would'st feast, or exercise thy friends.
The lower land, that to the river bends,
Thy sheepe, thy bullocks, kine, and calves doe feed:
The middle grounds thy, and horses breed.
Each banke doth yeeld thee conies; and the tops
Fertile of WOOD, ASHORE, and SYDNEY's copp's,
To crowne thy open table, doth provide
The purpled pheasant, with the speckled side:
The painted partrich lyes in every field,
And, for thy messe, is willing to be kill'd.
And if the high-swolne Medway faile thy dish,
Thou hast thy ponds, that pay thee tribute fish,
Fat, aged carps, that runne into thy net.
And pikes, now weary their owne kinde to eat,
As loth, the second draught or cast to stay,
Officiously, at first, themselves betray.
Bright eeles, that emulate them, and leape on land,
Before the fisher, or into his hand.
Then hath thy orchard fruit, thy garden flowers,
Fresh as the ayre, and new as are the houres.
The early cherry, with the later plum,
Fig, grape, and quince, each in his time doth come;
The blushing apricot, and woolly peach
Hang on thy walls, that every child may reach.
And though thy walls be of the countrey stone,
They'are rear'd with no mans ruine, no mans grone,
There's none, that dwell about them, wish them downe;
But all come in, the farmer, and the clowne:
And no one empty-handed, to salute
Thy lord, and lady, though they have no sute.
Some bring a capon, some a rurall cake,
Some nuts, some apples; some that thinke they make
The better cheeses, bring 'hem; or else send
By their ripe daughters, whom they would commend
This way to husbands; and whose baskets beare
An embleme of themselves, in plum, or peare.
But what can this (more than expresse their love)
Adde to thy free provisions, farre above
The neede of such? whose liberall boord doth flow,
With all that hospitalitie doth know!
Where comes no guest, but is allow'd to eate,

Without his feare, and of thy Lords owne meate:
Where the same beere, and bread, and selfe-same **wine**,
That is his Lordships, shall be also mine.
And I not faine to sit (as some, this day,
At great mens tables) and yet dine away.
Here no man tells my cups; nor, standing by,
A waiter doth my gluttony envy:
But gives me what I call, and lets me eate;
He knowes, below, he shall finde plentie of meate,
Thy tables hoord not up for the next day.
Nor, when I take my lodging, need I pray
For fire, or lights, or livorie: all is there;
As if thou, then, wert mine, or I raign'd here:
There's nothing I can wish, for which I stay.
That found King JAMES, when hunting late this way,
With his brave sonne, the Prince, they saw thy fires
Shine bright on every harth as the desires
Of thy *Penates* had been set on flame,
To entertayne them; or the country came,
With all their zeale, to warme their welcome here.
What (great, I will not say, but) sodayne cheare
Did'st thou, then, make 'em! and what praise was heap'd
On thy good lady, then! who, therein, reap'd
The just reward of her high huswifery;
To have her linnen, plate, and all things nigh,
When shee was farre: and not a roome, but drest,
As if it had expected such a guest!
These, PENSHURST, are thy praise, and yet not all.
Thy lady's noble, fruitfull, chaste withall.
His children thy great lord may call his owne:
A fortune in this age but rarely knowne.
They are, and have beene taught religion: Thence
Their gentler spirits have suck'd innocence.
Each morne, and even, they are taught to pray,
With the whole houshold, and may, every day,
Reade, in their vertuous parents noble parts,
The mysteries of manners, armes, and arts.
Now, PENSHURST, they that will proportion thee
With other edifices, when they see
Those proud, ambitious heaps, and nothing else,
May say, their lords have built, but thy lord dwells.

THAT WOMEN ARE BUT MENS SHADDOWES

Follow a shaddow, it still flies you;
Seeme to flye it, it will pursue:

So court a mistris, shee denyes you;
   Let her alone, shee will court you.
Say, are not women truely, then,
Styl'd but the shaddowes of us men?

At morne, and even, shades are longest;
   At noone, they are or short, or none:
So men at weakest, they are strongest,
   But grant us perfect, they're not knowne.
Say, are not women truely, then,
Styl'd but the shaddowes of us men?

From EPIGRAMS

ON MY FIRST SONNE

Farewell, thou child of my right hand, and joy;
My sinne was too much hope of thee, lov'd boy,
Seven yeeres tho' wert lent to me, and I thee pay,
Exacted by thy fate, on the just day.
O, could I lose all father, now. For why
Will man lament the state he should envie?
To have so soone scap'd worlds and fleshes rage,
And, if no other miserie, yet age.
Rest in soft peace, and, ask'd, say here doth lye
BEN. JONSON his best piece of *poetrie*.
For whose sake, hence-forth, all his vowes be such,
As what he loves may never like too much.

From THE MASQUE OF THE GYPSIES

THE JACKMAN'S SONG

The faiery beame upon you,
The starres to glister on you;
   A Moone of light,
   In the Noone of night,
Till the Fire-Drake hath o're-gone you.

The Wheele of fortune guide you,
The Boy with the Bow beside you,
   Runne aye in the way,
   Till the Bird of day,
And the luckyer lot betide you.

From A CELEBRATION OF CHARIS

From HOW HE SAW HER

I beheld her, on a Day,
When her looke out-flourisht May:
And her dressing did out-brave
All the Pride the fields then have.

HER TRIUMPH

See the Chariot at hand here of Love,
    Wherein my Lady rideth!
Each that drawes, is a Swan, or a Dove,
    And well the Carre Love guideth.
As she goes, all hearts doe duty
      Unto her beauty;
And enamour'd, doe wish, so they might
      But enjoy such a sight,
That they still were to run by her side,
Thorough Swords, thorough Seas, whither she would ride.

Doe but looke on her eyes, they doe light
    All that Loves world compriseth!
Doe but looke on her Haire, it is bright
    As Loves starre when it riseth!
Doe but marke, her forehead's smoother
      Then words that sooth her!
And from her arched browes, such a grace
      Sheds it selfe through the face,
As alone there triumphs to the life
All the Gaine, all the Good, of the Elements strife.

Have you seene but a bright Lillie grow,
    Before rude hands have touch'd it?
Ha' you mark'd but the fall o' the Snow
    Before the soyle hath smutch'd it?
Ha' you felt the wooll o' the Bever?
      Or Swans Downe ever?
Or have smelt o' the bud o' the Brier?
      Or the Nard in the fire?
Or have tasted the bag o' the Bee?
O so white! O so soft! O so sweet is she!

THE KISS

For *Loves*-sake, kisse me once againe,
I long, and should not beg in vaine,
 Here's none to spie, or see;
  Why do you doubt, or stay?
I'le taste as lightly as the Bee,
That doth but touch his flower, and flies away.

Once more, and (faith) I will be gone,
Can he that loves, aske lesse than one?
 Nay, you may erre in this,
  And all your bountie wrong:
This could be call'd but halfe a kisse.
What w'are but once to doe, we should doe long.

I will but mend the last, and tell
Where, how it would have relish'd well;
 Joyne lip to lip, and try:
  Each suck others breath.
And whilst our tongues perplexed lie,
Let who will thinke us dead, or wish our death.

HER MAN DESCRIBED BY HER OWN DICTAMEN

Of your trouble, *Ben,* to ease me,
I will tell what man would please
 me.
I would have him if I could,
Noble; or of greater Blood:
Titles, I confesse, do take me.
And a woman, God did make me.
French to boote, at least in fashion,
And his Manners of that Nation.
 Young Il'd have him too, and
  faire,
Yet a man; with crisped haire
Cast in thousand snares, or rings
For *Loves* fingers, or his wings:
Chestnut colour, or more slack
Gold, upon a ground of black.
Venus, or *Minerva's* eyes,
For he must look wanton-wise.
 Eye-brows bent like Cupid's bow,

Front, an ample field of snow;
Even nose, and cheeke (withall)
Smooth as is the Billiard Ball:
Chin, as woolly as the Peach;
And his lip should kissing teach,
Till he cherish'd too much beard,
And made *Love* or me afeard.
 He would have a hand as soft
As the Downe, and shew it oft;
Skin as smooth as any rush,
And so thin to see a blush
Rising through it e're it came:
All his blood should be a flame,
Quickly fir'd as in beginners
In love's schoole, and yet no sinners.
 'Twere too long to speak of all,
What we harmonie doe call
In a body should be there.
Well he should his clothes to weare;

Yet no Taylor help to make him
Drest, you still for man should take
  him;
And not think h' had eat a stake,
Or were set up in a Brake.
  Valiant he should be as fire,
Shewing danger more than ire.
Bounteous as the clouds to earth;
And as honest as his Birth.
All his actions to be such,
As to doe no thing too much.

Nor o're-praise, nor yet condemne;
Nor out-valew, nor contemne;
Nor doe wrongs, nor wrongs
  receave;
Nor tie knots, nor knots unweave;
And from baseness to be free,
As he durst love Truth and me.
  Such a man, with every part,
I could give my very heart,
But of one, if short he came,
I can rest me where I am.

From UNDERWOODS

AN ODE; TO HIMSELF

Where do'st Thou carelesse lie
    Buried in ease and sloth?
Knowledge, that sleepes, doth die;
And this securitie,
    It is the common moath,
That eats on wits, and Arts, and destroyes them both.

Are all th' *Aonian* springs
    Dri'd up? Lyes Thespia wast?
Doth *Clarius* Harp want strings,
That not a Nymph now sings:
    Or droop they as disgrac't,
To see their Seats and Bowers by chattring Pies defac't?

If hence thy silence be,
    As 'tis too just a cause;
Let this thought quicken thee,
Minds that are great and free,
    Should not on fortune pause,
'Tis crowne enough to vertue still, her owne applause.

What though the greedie Frie
    Be taken with false Baytes
Of worded Balladrie,
And thinke it Poesie?
    They die with their conceits,
And only pitious scorne, upon their folly waites.

Then take in hand thy Lyre,
    Strike in thy proper straine,

With *Japhets* line, aspire
Sols Chariot for new fire,
   To give the world againe:
Who aided him, will thee, the issue of *Joves* braine.

And since our Daintie age,
   Cannot endure reproofe,
Make not thy selfe a Page
To that strumpet the Stage,
   But sing high and aloofe,
Safe from the wolves black jaw, and the dull Asses hoofe.

From THE SAD SHEPHERD

KAROLIN'S SONG

Though I am young, and cannot tell,
Either what Death, or Love is well,
Yet I have heard, they both beare darts,
And both doe ayme at humane hearts:
And then againe, I have beene told
Love wounds with heat, as Death with cold;
So that I feare, they doe but bring
Extreames to touch, and meane one thing.

As in a ruine, we it call
One thing to be blowne up, or fall;
Or to our end, like way may have,
By a flash of lightning, or a wave:
So Loves inflamed shaft, or brand,
May kill as soone as Deaths cold hand;
Except Loves fires the vertue have
To fright the frost out of the grave.

From VOLPONE

ACT I, SCENE 1

VOLPONE. Good morning to the day; and, next, my gold:
Open the shrine, that I may see my *saint*.
Haile the worlds soule, and mine. More glad then is
The teeming earth, to see the long'd-for sunne
Peepe through the hornes of the celestiall *ram,*
Am I, to view thy splendor, darkening his:
That, lying here, amongst my other hoords,
Shew'st like a flame, by night; or like the day

Struck out of *chaos*, when all darknesse fled
Unto the center. O, thou sonne of SOL,
(But brighter then thy father) let me kisse,
With adoration, thee, and every relique
Of sacred treasure, in this blessed roome.
Well did wise Poets, by thy glorious name,
Title that age, which they would have the best;
Thou being the best of things: and far transcending
All stile of joy, in children, parents, friends,
Or any other waking dreame on earth.
Thy lookes, when they to VENUS did ascribe,
They should have giv'n her twentie thousand CUPIDS;
Such are thy beauties, and our loves! Deare *saint*,
Riches, the dumbe god, that giv'st all men tongues:
That canst doe nought, and yet mak'st men doe all things;
The price of soules; even hell, with thee to boot,
Is made worth heaven! Thou art vertue, fame,
Honour, and all things else! Who can get thee,
He shall be noble, valiant, honest, wise —
MOSCA. And what he will, sir. Riches are in fortune
A greater good, then wisedome is in nature.

ACT III, SCENE 7

SONG

Come, my CELIA, let us prove,
While we can, the sports of love;
Time will not be ours, for ever,
He, at length, our good will sever;
Spend not then his gifts, in vaine.
Sunnes, that set, may rise againe:
But if, once, we lose this light,
'Tis with us perpetuall night.
Why should wee deferre our joyes?
Fame, and rumor are but toies.
Cannot we delude the eyes
Of a few poore houshold-spies?
Or his easier eares beguile,
Thus remooved, by our wile?
'Tis no sinne, loves fruits to steale;
But the sweet thefts to reveale:
To be taken, to be seene
These have crimes accounted beene.

CELIA. Some *serene* blast me, or dire lightning strike
This my offending face.

VOLPONE.   Why droopes my CELIA?
  Thou hast in place of a base husband, found
  A worthy lover: use thy fortune well,
  With secrecie, and pleasure. See, behold,
  What thou art queene of; not in expectation,
  As I feed others: but possess'd, and crown'd.
  See, here, a rope of pearle; and each, more orient
  Then that the brave *Ægyptian* queene carrous'd:
  Dissolve, and drinke 'hem. See, a carbuncle,
  May put out both the eyes of our St. MARKE;
  A diamant, would have bought LOLLIA PAVLINA,
  When she came in, like star-light hid with jewels,
  That were the spoiles of provinces; take these,
  And weare, and lose 'hem: yet remaines an eare-ring
  To purchase them againe, and this whole state.
  A gem, but worth a private patrimony,
  Is nothing: we will eate such at a meale.
  The heads of parrats, tongues of nightingales,
  The braines of peacoks, and of estriches
  Shall be our food: and, could we get the phœnix,
  (Though nature lost her kind) shee were our dish.
CELIA. Good sir, these things might move a minde affected
  With such delights; but I, whose innocence
  Is all I can thinke wealthy, or worth th'enjoying,
  And which once lost, I have nought to lose beyond it,
  Cannot be taken with these sensuall baites:
  If you have conscience ——
VOLPONE.   'Tis the beggers vertue,
  If thou hast wisdome, heare me, CELIA.
  Thy bathes shall be the juyce of july-flowres,
  Spirit of roses, and of violets,
  The milke of unicornes, and panthers breath
  Gather'd in bagges, and mixt with *Cretan* wines.
  Our drinke shall be prepared gold, and amber;
  Which we will take, untill my roofe whirle round
  With the *vertigo:* and my dwarfe shall dance,
  My eunuch sing, my foole make up the antique.
  Whil'st we, in changed shapes, act OVIDS tales,
  Thou, like EUROPA now, and I like JOVE,
  Then I like MARS, and thou like ERYCINE,
  So, of the rest, till we have quite run through
  And weary'd all the fables of the gods.
  Then will I have thee in more moderne formes,
  Attired like some sprightly dame of *France*,
  Brave *Tuscan* lady, or proud *Spanish* beauty;
  Sometimes, unto the *Persian Sophies* wife;

Or the grand-*Signiors* mistresse; and, for change,
To one of our most art-full courtizans,
Or some quick *Negro,* or cold *Russian;*
And I will meet thee, in as many shapes:
Where we may, so, trans-fuse our wandring soules,
Out at our lippes, and score up summes of pleasures,
   That the curious shall not know,
   How to tell them, as they flow;
   And the envious, when they find
   What their number is, be pin'd.

From THE ALCHEMIST

ACT II, SCENES 1, 2

MAMMON. Come on, sir. Now, you set your foot on shore
   In *novo orbe;* Here's the rich *Peru:*
   And there within, sir, are the golden mines,
   Great *Salomon's Ophir!* He was sayling to't,
   Three yeeres, but we have reach't it in ten months.
   This is the day, wherein, to all my friends,
   I will pronounce the happy Word, *Be rich.*
   This day, you shall be *spectatissimi.*
   You shall no more deale with the hollow die,
   Or the fraile card. No more be at charge of keeping
   The livery-punke, for the young heire, that must
   Seale, at all houres, in his shirt. No more
   If he denie, ha' him beaten to't, as he is
   That brings him the commoditie. No more
   Shall thirst of satten, or the covetous hunger
   Of velvet entrailes, for a rude-spun cloke,
   To be displaid at *Madame Augusta's,* make
   The sonnes of *sword,* and *hazzard* fall before
   The golden calfe, and on their knees, whole nights,
   Commit idolatrie with wine, and trumpets:
   Or goe a feasting, after drum and ensigne.
   No more of this. You shall start up yong *Vice-royes,*
   And have your punques, and punquettees, my *Surly.*
   And unto thee, I speake it first, *Be rich.*
   Where is my *Subtle,* there? Within ho!
FACE [*within*].   Sir,
   Hee'll come to you, by and by.
MAMMON.   That's his fire-drake,
   His lungs, his *Zephyrus,* he that puffes his coales,
   Till he firke nature up, in her owne center.

You are not faithfull, sir. This night, I'll change
All, that is mettall, in thy house, to gold.
And, early in the morning, will I send
To all the plumbers, and the pewterers,
And buy their tin, and lead up: and to *Lothbury*,
For all the copper.

SURLY. What, and turne that too?

MAMMON. Yes, and I'll purchase *Devonshire*, and *Cornwaile*,
And make them perfect *Indies!* You admire now?

SURLY. No, faith.

MAMMON. But when you see th' effects of the great med'cine!
Of which one part projected on a hundred
Of *Mercurie*, or *Venus*, or the *Moone*,
Shall turne it, to as many of the *Sunne;*
Nay, to a thousand, so *ad infinitum:*
You will beleeve me.

SURLY. Yes, when I see't, I will.
But, if my eyes doe cossen me so (and I
Giving 'hem no occasion) sure, I'll have
A whore, shall pisse 'hem out, next day.

MAMMON. Ha! Why?
Doe you thinke, I fable with you? I assure you,
He that has once the *flower of the sunne*,
The perfect *ruby*, which we call *elixir*,
Not onely can doe that, but by it's vertue,
Can confer honour, love, respect, long life,
Give safetie, valour: yea, and victorie,
To whom he will. In eight and twentie dayes,
I'll make an old man, of fourescore, a childe.

SURLY. No doubt, hee's that alreadie.

MAMMON. Nay, I meane,
Restore his yeeres, renew him, like an eagle,
To the fifth age; make him get sonnes, and daughters,
Yong giants; as our *Philosophers* have done
(The antient *Patriarkes* afore the floud)
But taking, once a weeke, on a knives point,
The quantitie of a graine of mustard, of it:
Become stout *Marses*, and beget young *Cupids*.

SURLY. The decay'd *Vestall's* of *Pickt-hatch* would thanke you.
That keepe the fire a-live, there.

MAMMON. 'Tis the secret
Of nature, naturiz'd 'gainst all infections,
Cures all diseases, comming of all causes,
A month's griefe, in a day; a yeeres, in twelve:
And, of what age soever, in a month.
Past all the doses, of your drugging Doctors.

I'll undertake, withall, to fright the plague
Out o' the kingdome, in three months.

SURLY.   And I'll
Be bound, the players shall sing your praises, then
Without their poets.

MAMMON.   Sir, I'll doo't. Meanetime,
I'll give away so much, unto my man,
Shall serve th' whole citie, with preservative,
Weekely, each house his dose, and at the rate —

SURLY. As he that built the water-worke, do's with water?

MAMMON. You are incredulous.

SURLY.   Faith, I have a humor,
I would not willingly be gull'd. Your *stone*
Cannot transmute me.

MAMMON.   *Pertinax, my Surly,*
Will you beleeve antiquitie? recordes?
I'll shew you a booke, where *Moses,* and his sister,
And *Salomon* have written, of the art;
Ay, and a treatise penn'd by Adam.

SURLY.   How!

MAMMON. O' the *Philosophers stone,* and in high-*Dutch.*

SURLY. Did *Adam* write, sir, in high-*Dutch?*

MAMMON.   He did:
Which proves it was the primitive tongue.

SURLY.   What paper?

MAMMON. On cedar board.

SURLY.   O that, indeed (they say)
Will last 'gainst wormes.

MAMMON.   'Tis like your *Irish* wood,
'Gainst cob-webs. I have a peece of *Jasons* fleece, too,
Which was no other, then a booke of *alchemie,*
Writ in large sheepe-skin, a good fat ram-vellam.
Such was *Pythagoras'* thigh, *Pandora's* tub;
And, all that fable of *Medeas* charmes,
The manner of our worke: The Bulls, our fornace,
Still breathing fire; our *argent-vive,* the Dragon:
The Dragons teeth, *mercury* sublimate,
That keepes the whitenesse, hardnesse, and the biting;
And they are gather'd, into *Jason's* helme,
(Th' *alembeke*) and then sow'd in *Mars* his field,
And, thence, sublim'd so often, till they are fix'd.
Both this, th' *Hesperian* garden, *Cadmus* storie,
Jove's shower, the boone of *Midas, Argus* eyes,
Boccace his *Demogorgon,* thousands more,
All abstract riddles of our *stone.*

                                                        [*Enter Face.*]

How now?
Doe wee succeed? Is our day come? and hold's it?

FACE. The evening will set red, upon you, sir;
You have colour for it, crimson: the red *ferment*
Has done his office. Three houres hence, prepare you
To see projection.

MAMMON. *Pertinax,* my *Surly,*
Againe, I say to thee, aloud: *be rich.*
This day, thou shalt have ingots: and, to morrow,
Give lords th' affront. Is it, my *Zephyrus,* right?
Blushes the *bolts-head?*

FACE. Like a wench with child, sir,
That were, but now, discover'd to her master.

MAMMON. Excellent wittie *Lungs!* My onely care is,
Where to get stuffe, inough now, to project on,
This towne will not halfe serve me.

FACE. No, sir? Buy
The covering off o' churches.

MAMMON. That's true.

FACE. Yes.
Let 'hem stand bare, as doe their auditorie.
Or cap 'hem, new, with shingles.

MAMMON. No, good thatch:
Thatch will lie light upo' the rafters, *Lungs.*
Lungs, I will manumit thee, from the fornace;
I will restore thee thy complexion, *Puffe,*
Lost in the embers; and repaire this braine,
Hurt wi' the fume o' the mettalls.

FACE. I have blowne, sir,
Hard, for your worship; throwne by many a coale,
When 'twas not beech; weigh'd those I put in, just,
To keepe your heat, still even; These bleard-eyes
Have wak'd, to reade your severall colours, sir,
Of the *pale citron,* the *greene lyon,* the *crow,*
The *peacocks taile,* the *plumed swan.*

MAMMON. And, lastly,
Thou hast descryed the *flower,* the *sanguis agni?*

FACE. Yes, sir.

MAMMON. Where's master?

FACE. At's praiers, sir, he,
Good man, hee's doing his devotions,
For his successe.

MAMMON. *Lungs,* I will set a period,
To all thy labours: Thou shalt be the master
Of my *seraglia.*

FACE. Good, sir.

MAMMON. But doe you heare?
I'll geld you, *Lungs.*
FACE. Yes, sir.
MAMMON. For I doe meane
To have a list of wives, and concubines,
Equall with *Salomon;* who had the *stone*
Alike, with me: and I will make me, a back
With the *elixir,* that shall be as tough
As *Hercules,* to encounter fiftie a night.
Th'art, thou saw'st it *bloud?*
FACE. Both *bloud,* and *spirit,* sir.
MAMMON. I will have all my beds, blowne up; not stuft:
Downe is too hard. And then, mine oval roome,
Fill'd with such pictures, as *Tiberius* tooke
From *Elephantis:* and dull *Aretine*
But coldly imitated. Then, my glasses,
Cut in more subtill angles, to disperse
And multiply the figures, as I walke
Naked between my *succubæ.* My mists
I'le have of perfume, vapor'd 'bout the roome,
To lose our selves in; and my baths, like pits
To fall into: from whence, we will come forth,
And rowle us drie in gossamour, and roses.
(Is it arriv'd at *ruby?*) — Where I spie
A wealthy citizen, or rich lawyer,
Have a sublim'd pure wife, unto that fellow
I'll send a thousand pound, to be my cuckold.
FACE. And I shall carry it?
MAMMON. No. I'll ha' no bawds,
But fathers, and mothers. They will doe it best.
Best of all others. And, my flatterers
Shall be the pure, and gravest of Divines,
That I can get for money. My mere fooles,
Eloquent burgesses, and then my poets
The same that writ so subtly of the *fart,*
Whom I will entertaine, still, for that subject.
The few, that would give out themselves, to be
Court and towne-stallions, and, each where, belye
Ladies, who are knowne most innocent, for them;
Those will I begge, to make me *eunuchs* of:
And they shall fan me with ten estrich tailes
A piece, made in a plume, to gather wind.
We will be brave, *Puffe,* now we ha' the *med'cine.*
My meat, shall all come in, in *Indian* shells,
Dishes of agate, set in gold, and studded
With emeralds, saphyres, hiacynths, and rubies.

The tongues of carpes, dormice, and camels heeles,
Boil'd i' the spirit of *Sol,* and dissolv'd pearle,
(*Apicius* diet, 'gainst the *epilepsie*)
And I will eate these broaths, with spoones of amber,
Headed with diamant, and carbuncle.
My foot-boy shall eate phesants, calverd salmons,
Knots, godwits, lamprey's: I my selfe will have
The beards of barbels, serv'd, in stead of sallades;
Oild mushromes; and the swelling unctuous paps
Of a fat pregnant sow, newly cut off,
Drest with an exquisite, and poynant sauce;
For which, Ile say unto my cooke: There's gold,
Goe forth, and be a knight.

FACE.   Sir, I'll goe looke
A little, how it heightens.

MAMMON.   Doe. My shirts
I'll have of taffata-sarsnet, soft, and light
As cob-webs; and for all my other rayment
It shall be such, as might provoke the *Persian,*
Were he to teach the world riot anew.
My gloves of fishes, and birds-skins, perfum'd
With gummes of *paradise,* and easterne aire —

SURLY. And do you thinke, to have the *stone,* with this?
MAMMON. No, I doe thinke, t'have all this, with the *stone.*

John Fletcher
1579-1625

From THE QUEEN OF CORINTH

WEEP NO MORE

Weep no more, nor sigh nor groan,
Sorrow call no time that's gone:
Violets pluck'd, the sweetest rain
Makes not fresh, nor grow again;
Trim thy locks, look chearfully,
Fate's hidden ends eyes cannot see.
Joys as winged dreams fly fast,
Why should sadness longer last?
Grief is but a wound to woe;
Gentlest fair, mourn, mourn no moe.

From THE ELDER BROTHER

BEAUTY CLEERE AND FAIR

Beauty cleere and fair,
   Where the Aire
Rather like a perfume dwells,
   Where the Violet and the Rose
   The blew Veines in blush disclose,
And come to honour nothing else.

Where to live neere,
   And planted there,
Is to live, and still live new;
   Where to gain a favour is
   More than light, perpetual blisse;
Make me live by serving you.

Deare again, backe recall
   To this light,
A stranger to himselfe and all;
   Both the wonder and the story
   Shall be yours, and eke the Glory;
I am your servant, and your thrall.

From THE BLOODY BROTHER

TAKE, OH TAKE THOSE LIPS AWAY

Take, oh take those Lips away
   That so sweetly were forsworn,
And those Eyes, like break of day,
   Lights that do mislead the Morn.
But my Kisses bring again,
Seals of Love, though seal'd in vain.

Hide, oh hide those hills of Snow,
   Which thy frozen Bosom bears,
On whose tops the Pinks that grow
   Are of those that *April* wears,
But first set my poor Heart free,
Bound in those Ivy Chains by thee.

From LOVE'S CURE

TURN, TURN THY BEAUTEOUS FACE AWAY

Turn, turn thy beauteous face away,
How pale and sickly looks the day,
   In emulation of thy brighter beams!
Oh envious light, fly, fly, begone,

Come night, and piece two breasts as one;
  When what love does, we will repeat in dreams.
Yet (thy eyes open) who can day hence fright,
Let but their lids fall, and it will be night.

From THE TRAGEDY OF VALENTINIAN

CARE–CHARMING SLEEP, THOU EASER OF ALL WOES

Care-charming sleep, thou easer of all woes,
Brother to death, sweetly thy self dispose
On this afflicted Prince, fall like a Cloud
In gentle showres, give nothing that is lowd,
Or painfull to his slumbers; easie, sweet,
And as a purling stream, thou son of night,
Passe by his troubled senses; sing his pain
Like hollow murmuring Winde, or silver Raine.
Into this Prince gently, Oh, gently slide,
And kisse him into slumbers like a Bride.

From THE KNIGHT OF THE BURNING PESTLE

COME YOU WHOSE LOVES ARE DEAD

Come you whose loves are dead,
  And whiles I sing
  Weepe and wring
Every hand and every head,
Bind with Cipres, and sad Yew,
Ribands blacke and candles blew,
For him that was of men most
    true.

Come with heavy moaning,
  And on his grave
  Let him have
Sacrifice of sighes and groaning,
Let him have faire flowers enow,
White and purple, greene and
    yellow,
For him that was of men most true.

From THE MAIDE'S TRAGEDY

LAY A GARLAND ON MY HEARSE

Lay a garland on my hearse
  Of the dismall Yew,
Maidens willow branches beare,
  Say I died true.

My love was false, but I was firme,
  From my houre of birth,
Upon my buried body lay
  Lightly gentle earth.

From THE NICE VALOUR

HENCE ALL YOU VAINE DELIGHTS

Hence all you vaine Delights,
As short as are the nights,
  Wherein you spend your folly,
Ther's nought in this life, sweet,
If man were wise to see't,
  But only Melancholy,
  Oh sweetest Melancholy.
Welcome folded Armes, and fixed Eyes,
A sigh that piercing mortifies,
A look that's fast'ned to the ground,
A tongue chain'd up without a sound.

Fountaine heads, and pathlesse Groves,
  Places which pale passion loves:
Moon-light walkes, when all the fowles
Are warmly hous'd, save Bats and Owles;
  A mid-night Bell, a parting groane,
  These are the sounds we feed upon;
Then stretch our bones in a still gloomy valley,
Nothing so daintie sweet, as lovely Melancholy.

John Marston
1575?-1634

O LOVE, HOW STRANGELY SWEET

O Love, how strangely sweet
  Are thy weak passions,
That love and joye should meet
  In self-same fashions!
Oh, who can tell
  The cause why this should move?
But onely this,
  No reason aske of Love.

John Ford
1586?-1640?

From THE BROKEN HEART

OH NO MORE, NO MORE, TOO LATE

Oh no more, no more, too late
  Sighes are spent; the burning
     Tapers
Of a life as chast as Fate,
  Pure as are unwritten papers,
Are burnt out: no heat, no light
Now remaines, 'tis ever night.

Love is dead, let lovers eyes,
Lock'd in endlesse dreames,
Th' extremes of all extremes,
Ope' no more, for now Love dyes,
Now Love dyes, implying
Loves Martyrs must be ever, ever
  dying.

CAN YOU PAINT A THOUGHT

Can you paint a thought? or number
Every fancy in a slumber?
Can you count soft minutes roving
From a dyals point by moving?
Can you graspe a sigh? or lastly,
Rob a Virgins honour chastly?

No, O no; yet you may
  Sooner doe both that and this,
  This and that, and never misse,
Then by any praise display
  Beauties beauty, such a glory
  As beyond all Fate, all Story,
    All armes, all arts,
    All loves, all hearts,
  Greater then those, or they,
  Doe, shall, and must obey.

Robert Herrick
1591-1674

The spirit of Herrick might have been the "apparition" seen anno 1670, near Cirencester, of whom John Aubrey tells us in his *Miscellanies:* "Being demanded whether a good spirit or a bad, returned no answer, but disappeared with a curious perfume and a most melodious Twang. Mr. W. Lilly believes it was a Fairie."

The poems are as subtle, and as delicate, as the breaths of air and perfume wafting through the branches of a flowering tree, or the stillness of a sweet night.

In the flawlessly beautiful *Lovers how they come and part,* the only emphasis is in the shapes of the pear and plum, the only color that which steals into them.

To these shapes of the fruit the *p*'s give body — the first shape being longer and more delicate, tapering down from the roundness, through the long double vowels, to the fading *r;* the second rounder, and with more body, because of the enclosing *pl* and *m.* ". . . So silently," with the alliterative *s*'s, the rising vowels, gives another, but fainter, embodiment; "clouds" melts into "come," "come" fades into "colours." "Peare or Plum" has the faintest echo in the *p* and the *pl* of "parting place." There is the slightest possible lengthening of line — a lengthening so faint as to be hardly perceptible — that comes from the wavering movement of the double-vowelled "Peare" and "Aire" (with that hardly perceptible flutter caused by the *r*), and the echo of these in "Where e're." "Beare" has not the same wavering movement, because the *b,* which begins the word, concentrates it.

These wavering airs, these faint rills of air that come and go, as with the subtle dropping sound of "dew" and the wavering sound of "haire" in the poem *Upon Julia's Haire Fill'd with Dew* — the faint sharpening sound of "dew" softening to the warmer *ju* sound in "Julia" and the sound of "too"; the points of light given by the long assonantal *e*'s of "Leaves," "Beames," "Streames"; the dewy *l*'s — these subtleties are like the bloom upon the poem, the differences in the glitter of that dew on leaves and hair.

To him, death, and life, and the business of life, were a sweet scent, intangible but rich, like the uncorrupted fame of which he wrote in his epigram *To His Honoured Kinsman, Sir William Soame* — a fame that:

> Casts forth a light like to a Virgin flame:
> And as it shines, it throwes a scent about,
> As when a Rain-bow in perfumes goes out.

THE ARGUMENT OF HIS BOOK

> I sing of *Brooks,* of *Blossomes, Birds,* and *Bowers:*
> Of *April, May,* of *June,* and *July*-Flowers.
> I sing of *May-poles, Hock-carts, Wassails, Wakes,*
> Of *Bride-grooms, Brides,* and of their *Bridall-cakes.*

I write of *Youth*, of *Love*, and have Accesse
By these, to sing of cleanly-*Wantonnesse*.
I sing of *Dewes*, of *Raines*, and piece by piece
Of *Balme*, of *Oyle*, of *Spice*, and *Amber-Greece*.
I sing of *Times trans-shifting*; and I write
How *Roses* first came *Red*, and *Lillies White*.
I write of *Groves*, of *Twilights*, and I sing
The Court of *Mab*, and of the *Fairie-King*.
I write of *Hell*; I sing (and ever shall)
Of *Heaven*, and hope to have it after all.

UPON JULIA'S HAIRE FILL'D WITH DEW

Dew sate on *Julia's* haire,
And spangled too,
Like Leaves that laden are
With trembling Dew:
Or glitter'd to my sight,
As when the Beames
Have their reflected light,
Daunc't by the Streames.

UPON JULIA'S CLOTHES

When as in silks my *Julia* goes,
Then, then (me thinks) how sweetly flowes
That liquefaction of her clothes.

Next, when I cast mine eyes and see
That brave Vibration each way free;
O how that glittering taketh me!

LOVERS HOW THEY COME AND PART

A *Gyges* Ring they beare about them still,
To be, and not seen when and where they will.
They tread on clouds, and though they sometimes fall,
They fall like dew, but make no noise at all.
So silently they one to th' other come,
As colours steale into the Peare or Plum,
And Aire-like, leave no pression to be seen
Where e're they met, or parting place has been.

THE NIGHT-PIECE, TO JULIA

Her Eyes the Glow-worme lend thee,
The Shooting Starres attend thee
    And the Elves also,
    Whose little eyes glow,
Like the sparks of fire, befriend thee.

No *Will-o'-th'-Wispe* mis-light thee;
Nor Snake, or Slow-worme bite thee:
    But on, on thy way
    Not making a stay,
Since Ghost ther's none to affright thee.

Let not the darke thee cumber;
What though the Moon do's slumber?
    The Starres of the night
    Will lend thee their light,
Like Tapers cleare without number.

Then *Julia* let me wooe thee,
Thus, thus to come unto me:
    And when I shall meet
    Thy silv'ry feet,
My soule Ile poure into thee.

A CONJURATION, TO ELECTRA

By those soft Tods of wooll
With which the aire is full:
By all those Tinctures there,
That paint the *Hemisphere:*
By Dewes and drisling Raine,
That swell the Golden Graine:
By all those sweets that be
I' th' flowrie Nunnerie:
By silent Nights, and the
Three Formes of *Heccate:*

By all Aspects that blesse
The sober *Sorceresse,*
While juice she straines, and pith
To make her Philters with:
By Time, that hastens on
Things to perfection:
And by your self, the best
Conjuration of the rest:
O my *Electra!* be
In love with none, but me.

THE LILLY IN A CHRISTAL

You have beheld a smiling *Rose*
  When Virgins hands have drawn
  O'r it a Cobweb-Lawne:
And here, you see, this Lilly shows,
  Tomb'd in a *Christal* stone,
More faire in this transparent case,
  Then when it grew alone;
  And had but single grace.

You see how *Creame* but naked is;
  Nor daunces in the eye
  Without a Strawberrie:
Or some fine tincture, like to this,
  Which draws the sight thereto,
More by that wantoning with it;
  Then when the paler hieu
  No mixture did admit.

You see how *Amber* through the
    streams
  More gently stroaks the sight, ·
  With some conceal'd delight;
Then when he darts his radiant
    beames
  Into the boundlesse aire:
Where either too much light his
    worth
  Doth all at once impaire,
  Or set it little forth.

Put Purple Grapes, or Cherries in-
  To Glasse, and they will send
  More beauty to commend
Them, from that cleane and subtile
  skin,

Then if they naked stood,
  And had no other pride at all,
  But their own flesh and blood,
  And tinctures naturall.

Thus Lillie, Rose, Grape, Cherry,
    Creame,
  And Straw-berry do stir
  More love, when they transfer
A weak, a soft, a broken beame;
  Then if they sho'd discover
At full their proper excellence;
  Without some Scean cast over,
  To juggle with the sense.

Thus let this *Christal'd Lillie* be
  A Rule, how far to teach,
  Your nakednesse must reach:
And that, no further, then we see
  Those glaring colours laid
By Arts wise hand, but to this
    end
  They sho'd obey a shade;
  Lest they too far extend.

So though y'are white as Swan, or
    Snow,
  And have the power to move
  A world of men to love:
Yet, when your Lawns and Silks shal
    flow;
  And that white cloud divide
Into a doubtful Twi-light; then,
  Then will your hidden Pride
  Raise greater fires in men.

UPON JULIA'S RECOVERY

Droop, droop no more, or hang the head
Ye *Roses* almost withered;
Now strength, and newer Purple get,
Each here declining *Violet*.

O *Primroses!* let this day be
A Resurrection unto ye;
And to all flowers ally'd in blood,
Or sworn to that sweet Sister-hood:
For Health on *Julia's* cheek hath shed
Clarret, and Creame commingled.
And those her lips doe now appeare
As beames of *Corrall,* but more cleare.

THE WEEPING CHERRY

I saw a *Cherry* weep, and why?
Why wept it? but for shame,
Because my *Julia's* lip was by,
And did out-red the same.
But pretty Fondling, let not fall
A teare at all for that:
Which *Rubies, Corralls, Scarlets,* all
For tincture, wonder at.

UPON JULIA'S VOICE

So smooth, so sweet, so silv'ry is thy voice,
As, could they hear, the Damn'd would make no noise,
But listen to thee (walking in thy chamber)
Melting melodious words, to Lutes of Amber.

TO HIS HONOURED KINSMAN SIR WILLIAM SOAME

I can but name thee, and methinks I call
All that have been, or are canonicall
For love and bountie, to come neare, and see,
Their many vertues volum'd up in thee;
In thee Brave Man! Whose incorrupted fame,
Casts forth a light like to a Virgin flame:
And as it shines, it throwes a scent about,
As when a Rain-bow in perfumes goes out.
So vanish hence, but leave a name, as sweet,
As *Benjamin,* and *Storax,* when they meet.

TO THE MOST FAIR AND LOVELY MISTRIS, ANNE SOAME, NOW LADY ABDIE

So smell those odours that do rise
From out the wealthy spiceries:
So smels the flowre of *blooming Clove;*
Or *Roses* smother'd in the stove:
So smells the Aire of spiced wine;
Or *Essences* of *Jessimine:*
So smells the Breath about the hives,
When well the work of hony thrives;
And all the *busie Factours* come
Laden with wax and hony home:
So smell those neat and woven Bowers,
All over-archt with *Oringe flowers;*
And *Almond blossoms,* that do mix
To make rich these *Aromatikes:*
So smell those bracelets, and those bands
Of *Amber* chaf't between the hands,
When thus enkindled they transpire
A noble perfume from the fire.
The wine of cherries, and to these,
The cooling breath of Respasses;
The smell of mornings milk, and cream;
Butter of *Cowslips* mixt with them;
Of rosted warden, or bak'd peare,
These are not to be reckon'd here;
When as the meanest part of her,
Smells like the maiden-Pomander.
Thus sweet she smells, or what can be
More lik'd by her, or lov'd by mee.

respasses] raspberries.   warden] a variety of pear.

TO MEDDOWES

Ye have been fresh and green,
  Ye have been fill'd with flowers:
And ye the Walks have been
  Where Maids have spent their
    houres.

You have beheld, how they
  With *Wicker Arks* did
    come
To kisse, and beare away
  The richer Couslips home.

Y'ave heard them sweetly sing,
 And seen them in a Round:
Each Virgin, like a Spring,
 With Hony-succles crown'd.

But now, we see, none here,
 Whose silv'rie feet did tread,
And with dishevell'd Haire,
 Adorn'd this smoother Mead.

Like Unthrifts, having spent,
 Your stock, and needy grown,
Y'are left here to lament
 Your poore estates, alone.

TO DAFFADILLS

Faire Daffadills, we weep to see
 You haste away so soone:
As yet the early-rising Sun
 Has not attain'd his Noone.
  Stay, stay,
 Untill the hasting day
  Has run
 But to the Even-song;
And, having pray'd together, we
 Will goe with you along.

We have short time to stay, as you,
 We have as short a Spring;
As quick a growth to meet Decay,
 As you, or any thing.
  We die,
 As your hours doe, and drie
  Away,
 Like to the Summers raine;
Or as the pearles of Mornings dew
 Ne'r to be found againe.

TO DAISIES, NOT TO SHUT SO SOONE

Shut not so soon; the dull-ey'd night
 Ha's not as yet begunne
To make a seisure on the light,
 Or to seale up the Sun.

No Marigolds yet closed are;
 No shadowes great appeare;
Nor doth the early Shepheards Starre
 Shine like a spangle here.

Stay but till my *Julia* close
 Her life-begetting eye;
And let the whole world then dispose
 It selfe to live or dye.

A NUPTIALL SONG, OR EPITHALMIE
On Sir Clipseby Crew and His Lady

What's that we see from far? the spring of Day
Bloom'd from the East, or faire Injewel'd May
    Blowne out of April; or some New-
    Star fill'd with glory to our view,
        Reaching at heaven,
To adde a nobler Planet to the seven?
    Say, or doe we not descrie
Some Goddesse, in a cloud of Tiffanie
      To move, or rather the
    Emergent *Venus* from the Sea?

'Tis she! 'tis she! or else some more Divine
Enlightned substance; mark how from the Shrine
    Of holy Saints she paces on,
    Treading upon *Vermilion*
        And *Amber;* Spice-
ing the Chaste Aire with fumes of Paradise.
    Then come on, come on, and yeeld
A savour like unto a blessed field,
      When the bedabled Morne
    Washes the golden eares of corne.

See where she comes; and smell how all the street
Breathes Vine-yards and Pomgranats: O how sweet!
    As a fir'd Altar, is each stone,
    Perspiring pounded Cynamon.
      The Phenix nest,
Built up of odours, burneth in her breast.
    Who therein wo'd not consume
His soule to Ash-heaps in that rich perfume?
      Bestroaking Fate the while
    He burnes to Embers on the Pile.

Himen, O Himen! Tread the sacred ground;
Shew thy white feet, and head with Marjoram crown'd:
    Mount up thy flames, and let thy Torch
    Display the Bridegroom in the porch,
      In his desires
More towring, more disparkling then thy fires:
    Shew her how his eyes do turne
And roule about, and in their motions burne
      Their balls to Cindars: haste,
    Or else to ashes he will waste.

Glide by the banks of Virgins then, and passe
The Shewers of Roses, lucky-foure-leav'd grasse:
   The while the cloud of younglings sing,
   And drown yee with a flowrie Spring:
     While some repeat
Your praise, and bless you, sprinkling you with Wheat:
   While that others doe divine;
Blest is the Bride, on whom the Sun doth shine;
    And thousands gladly wish
    You multiply, as doth a Fish.

And beautious Bride we do confess y'are wise,
In dealing forth these bashfull jealousies:
   In Lov's name do so; and a price
   Set on your selfe, by being nice:
     But yet take heed;
What now you seem, be not the same indeed,
   And turne *Apostate:* Love will
Part of the way be met: or sit stone-still.
    On them, and though you slow-
    ly go, yet, howsoever, go.

And now y'are enter'd; see the Codled Cook
Runs from his *Torrid Zone,* to prie, and look,
   And blesse his dainty Mistresse: see,
   The Aged point out, This is she,
     Who now must sway
The House (Love shield her) with Yea and Nay:
   And the smirk Butler thinks it
Sin, in 's Nap'rie, not to express his wit;
    Each striving to devise
    Some gin, wherewith to catch your eyes.

To bed, to bed, kind Turtles, now, and write
This the short'st day, and this the longest night;
   But yet too short for you: 'tis we,
   Who count this night as long as three,
     Lying alone,
Telling the Clock strike Ten, Eleven, Twelve, One.
   Quickly, quickly, then prepare;
And let the Young-men and the Bride-maids share
    Your Garters; and their joynts
    Encircle with the Bride-grooms Points.

By the Brides eyes, and by the teeming life
Of her green hopes, we charge ye, that no strife,
   (Farther then Gentlenes tends) gets place
     Among ye, striving for her lace:
        O doe not fall
Foule in these noble pastimes, lest ye call
     Discord in, and so divide
The youthfull Bride-groom, and the fragrant Bride:
     Which Love fore-fend; but spoken
     Be 't to your praise, no peace was broken.

Strip her of Spring-time, tender-whimpring-maids,
Now *Autumne's* come, when all those flowrie aids
   Of her Delayes must end; Dispose
     That *Lady-smock,* that *Pansie,* and that *Rose*
        Neatly apart;
But for *Prick-madam,* and for *Gentle-heart;*
     And soft-*Maidens-blush,* the Bride
Makes holy these, all others lay aside:
     Then strip her, or unto her
     Let him come, who dares undo her.

And to enchant yee more, see every where
About the Roofe a *Syren* in a Sphere;
   (As we think) singing to the dinne
     Of many a warbling *Cherubim:*
        O marke yee how
The soule of Nature melts in numbers: now
     See, a thousand *Cupids* flye,
To light their Tapers at the Brides bright eye.
     To Bed; or her they'l tire,
     Were she an Element of fire.

And to your more bewitching, see, the proud
Plumpe Bed beare up, and swelling like a cloud,
   Tempting the two too modest; can
     You see it brusle like a Swan,
        And you be cold
To meet it, when it woo's and seemes to fold
     The Armes to hugge it? throw, throw
Your selves into the mighty over-flow
     Of that white Pride, and Drowne
     The night, with you, in floods of Downe.

The bed is ready, and the maze of Love
Lookes for the treaders; every where is wove
   Wit and new misterie; read, and
   Put in practise, to understand
     And know each wile,
Each hieroglyphick of a kisse or smile;
   And do it to the full; reach
High in your own conceipt, and some way teach
     Nature and Art, one more
   Play then they ever knew before.

If needs we must for Ceremonies-sake,
Blesse a *Sack-posset;* Luck go with it; take
   The Night-Charme quickly; you have spells,
   And magicks for to end, and hells,
     To passe; but such
And of such Torture as no one would grutch
   To live therein for ever: Frie
And consume, and grow again to die,
     And live, and in that case,
   Love the confusion of the place.

But since It must be done, dispatch, and sowe
Up in a sheet your Bride, and what if so
   It be with Rock, or walles of Brasse,
   Ye Towre her up, as *Danae* was;
     Thinke you that this,
Or hell it selfe a powerfull Bulwarke is?
   I tell yee no; but like a
Bold bolt of thunder he will make his way,
     And rend the cloud, and throw
   The sheet about, like flakes of snow.

All now is husht in silence; *Midwife-moone,*
With all her *Owle-ey'd* issue begs a boon
   Which you must grant; that's entrance; with
   Which extract, all we can call pith
     And quintiscence
Of Planetary bodies; so commence
   All faire *Constellations*
Looking upon yee, That two Nations
     Springing from two such Fires,
   May blaze the vertue of their Sires.

TO PERILLA

Ah my *Perilla!* do'st thou grieve to see
Me, day by day, to steale away from thee?
Age calls me hence, and my gray haires bid come,
And haste away to mine eternal home;
'Twill not be long (*Perilla*) after this,
That I must give thee the *supremest* kisse;
Dead when I am, first cast in salt, and bring
Part of the creame from that *Religious Spring;*
With which (*Perilla*) wash my hands and feet;
That done, then wind me in that very sheet
Which wrapt thy smooth limbs (when thou didst implore
The Gods protection, but the night before),
Follow me weeping to my Turfe, and there
Let fall a *Primrose,* and with it a teare:
Then lastly, let some weekly-strewings be
Devoted to the memory of me:
Then shall my *Ghost* not walk about, but keep
Still in the coole, and silent shades of sleep.

CORINNA'S GOING A MAYING

Get up, get up for shame, the Blooming Morne
Upon her wings presents the god unshorne.
   See how *Aurora* throwes her faire
   Fresh-quilted colours through the aire:
   Get up, sweet-Slug-a-bed, and see
   The Dew-bespangling Herbe and Tree.
Each Flower has wept, and bow'd toward the East,
Above an houre since; yet you not drest,
   Nay! not so much as out of bed?
   When all the Birds have Mattens seyd,
   And sung their thankfull Hymnes: 'tis sin,
   Nay, profanation to keep in,
When as a thousand Virgins on this day,
Spring, sooner than the Lark, to fetch in May.

Rise; and put on your Foliage, and be seene
To come forth, like the Spring-time, fresh and greene;
   And sweet as *Flora.* Take no care
   For Jewels for your Gowne, or Haire:
   Feare not; the leaves will strew
   Gemms in abundance upon you:

Besides, the childhood of the Day has kept,
Against you come, some *Orient Pearls* unwept:
    Come, and receive them while the light
    Hangs on the Dew-locks of the night:
    And *Titan* on the Eastern hill
    Retires himselfe, or else stands still
Till you come forth. Wash, dresse, be briefe in praying:
Few Beads are best, when once we goe a Maying.

Come, my *Corinna,* come; and comming, marke
How each field turns a street; each street a Parke
    Made green, and trimm'd with trees: see how
    Devotion gives each House a Bough,
    Or Branch: Each Porch, each doore, ere this,
    An Arke a Tabernacle is
Made up of white-thorn neatly enterwove;
As if here were those cooler shades of love.
    Can such delights be in the street,
    And open fields, and we not see 't?
    Come, we'll abroad; and let's obay
    The Proclamation made for May:
And sin no more, as we have done, by staying;
But my *Corinna,* come, let's goe a Maying.

There's not a budding Boy, or Girle, this day,
But is got up, and gone to bring in May.
    A deale of Youth, ere this, is come
    Back, and with *White-thorn* laden home.
    Some have dispatcht their Cakes and Creame,
    Before that we have left to dreame:
And some have wept, and woo'd, and plighted Troth,
And chose their Priest, ere we can cast off sloth:
    Many a green-gown has been given;
    Many a kisse, both odde and even:
    Many a glance too has been sent
    From out the eye, Loves Firmament:
Many a jest told of the Keyes betraying
This night, and Locks pickt, yet w'are not a Maying.

Come, let us goe, while we are in our prime;
And take the harmlesse follie of the time.
    We shall grow old apace, and die
    Before we know our liberty.
    Our life is short; and our dayes run
    As fast away as do's the Sunne:
And as a vapour, or a drop of raine

Once lost, can ne'r be found againe:
    So when or you or I are made
    A fable, song, or fleeting shade;
    All love, all liking, all delight
    Lies drown'd with us in endlesse night.
Then while time serves, and we are but decaying;
Come, my *Corinna,* come, let's goe a Maying.

THE COMMING OF GOOD LUCK

So Good-luck came, and on my roofe did light,
Like noyse-lesse Snow; or as the dew of night:
Not all at once, but gently, as the trees
Are, by the Sun-beams, tickel'd by degrees.

George Herbert
1593-1633

THE COLLAR

    I struck the board, and cry'd, No more.
        I will abroad.
    What? shall I ever sigh and pine?
My lines and life are free; free as the roade,
    Loose as the winde, as large as store.
        Shall I be still in suit?
    Have I no harvest but a thorn
    To let me bloud, and not restore
What I have lost with cordiall fruit?
        Sure there was wine
Before my sighs did drie it: there was corn
    Before my tears did drown it.
    Is the yeare onely lost to me?
    Have I no bayes to crown it?
No flowers, no garlands gay? all blasted?
        All wasted?
    Not so, my heart: but there is fruit,
        And thou hast hands.
    Recover all thy sigh-blown age
On double pleasures: leave thy cold dispute
Of what is fit, and not. Forsake thy cage,
        Thy rope of sands,

Which pettie thoughts have made, and made to thee
Good cable, to enforce and draw,
And be thy law,
While thou didst wink and wouldst not see.
Away; take heed:
I will abroad.
Call in thy deaths head there: tie up thy fears.
He that forbears
To suit and serve his need,
Deserves his load.
But as I rav'd and grew more fierce and wilde
At every word,
Me thought I heard one calling, *Child!*
And I reply'd, *My Lord.*

PRAYER

Of what an easie quick accesse,
My blessed Lord, art thou! how suddenly
May our requests thine eare invade!
To shew that state dislikes not easinesse,
If I but lift mine eyes, my suit is made:
Thou canst no more not heare, than thou canst die.

Of what supreme almightie power
Is thy great arm, which spans the east and west,
And tacks the centre to the sphere!
By it do all things live their measur'd houre:
We cannot ask the thing, which is not there,
Blaming the shallownesse of our request.

Of what unmeasurable love
Art thou possest, who, when thou couldst not die,
Wert fain to take our flesh and curse,
And for our sakes in person sinne reprove,
That by destroying that which ty'd thy purse,
Thou mightst make way for liberalitie!

Since then these three wait on thy throne,
Ease, Power, and *Love;* I value prayer so,
That were I to leave all but one,
Wealth, fame, endowments, vertues, all should go;
I and deare prayer would together dwell,
And quickly gain, for each inch lost, an ell.

THE TEMPER

How should I praise thee, Lord! how should my rymes
    Gladly engrave thy love in steel,
    If what my soul doth feel sometimes,
        My soul might ever feel!

Although there were some fourtie heav'ns, or more,
    Sometimes I peere above them all;
    Sometimes I hardly reach a score,
        Sometimes to hell I fall.

O rack me not to such a vast extent;
    Those distances belong to thee:
    The world's too little for thy tent,
        A grave too big for me.

Wilt thou meet arms with man, that thou dost stretch
    A crumme of dust from heav'n to hell?
    Will great God measure with a wretch?
        Shall he thy stature spell?

O let me, when thy roof my soul hath hid,
    O let me roost and nestle there:
    Then of a sinner thou art rid,
        And I of hope and fear.

Yet take thy way; for sure thy way is best:
    Stretch or contract me, thy poore debter:
    This is but tuning of my breast,
        To make the musick better.

Whether I flie with angels, fall with dust,
    Thy hands made both, and I am there:
    Thy power and love, my love and trust
        Make one place ev'ry where.

EMPLOYMENT

    If as a flowre doth spread and die,
    Thou wouldst extend me to some good,
Before I were by frosts extremitie
        Nipt in the bud;

The sweetnesse and the praise were thine;
But the extension and the room,
Which in thy garland I should fill, were mine
At thy great doom.

For as thou dost impart thy grace,
The greater shall our glorie be.
The measure of our joyes is in this place,
The stuffe with thee.

Let me not languish then, and spend
A life as barren to thy praise,
As is the dust, to which that life doth tend,
But with delaies.

All things are busie; onely I
Neither bring hony with the bees,
Nor flowres to make that, nor the husbandrie
To water these.

I am no link of thy great chain,
But all my companie is a weed.
Lord place me in thy consort; give one strain
To my poore reed.

From EASTER

I got me flowers to straw thy way;
I got me boughs off many a tree:
But thou wast up by break of day,
And brought'st thy sweets along with thee.

The Sunne arising in the East,
Though he give light, and th' East perfume;
If they should offer to contest
With thy arising, they presume.

Can there be any day but this,
Though many sunnes to shine endeavour?
We count three hundred, but we misse:
There is but one, and that one ever.

THE FLOWER

How fresh, O Lord, how sweet and clean
Are thy returns! ev'n as the flowers in spring;
  To which, besides their own demean,
The late-past frosts tributes of pleasure bring.
          Grief melts away
          Like snow in May,
    As if there were no such cold thing.

Who would have thought my shrivel'd heart
Could have recover'd greennesse? It was gone
  Quite under ground; as flowers depart
To see their mother-root, when they have blown;
          Where they together
          All the hard weather,
    Dead to the world, keep house unknown.

These are thy wonders, Lord of power,
Killing and quickning, bringing down to hell
  And up to heaven in an houre;
Making a chiming of a passing-bell.
          We say amisse,
          This or that is:
    Thy word is all, if we could spell.

O that I once past changing were,
Fast in thy Paradise, where no flower can wither!
  Many a spring I shoot up fair,
Offring at heav'n, growing and groning thither:
          Nor doth my flower
          Want a spring-showre,
    My sinnes and I joining together.

But while I grow in a straight line,
Still upwards bent, as if heav'n were mine own,
  Thy anger comes, and I decline:
What frost to that? what pole is not the zone,
          Where all things burn,
          When thou dost turn,
    And the least frown of thine is shown?

And now in age I bud again,
After so many deaths I live and write;
  I once more smell the dew and rain,

And relish versing: O my onely light,
   It cannot be
   That I am he
 On whom thy tempests fell all night.

  These are thy wonders, Lord of love,
To make us see we are but flowers that glide:
  Which when we once can finde and prove,
Thou hast a garden for us, where to bide.
   Who would be more,
   Swelling through store,
Forfeit their Paradise by their pride.

SIGHS AND GRONES

   O do not use me
After my sinnes! look not on my desert,
 But on thy glorie! then thou wilt reform
And not refuse me: for thou onely art
  The mightie God, but I a sillie worm;
   O do not bruise me!

   O do not urge me!
For what account can thy ill steward make?
 I have abus'd thy stock, destroy'd thy woods,
Suckt all thy magazens: my head did ake,
  Till it found out how to consume thy goods:
   O do not scourge me!

   O do not blinde me!
I have deserv'd that an Egyptian night
 Should thicken all my powers; because my lust
Hath still sow'd fig-leaves to exclude thy light:
  But I am frailtie, and already dust;
   O do not grinde me!

   O do not fill me
With the turn'd viall of thy bitter wrath!
 For thou hast other vessels full of bloud,
A part whereof my Saviour empti'd hath,
  Ev'n unto death: since he di'd for my good,
   O do not kill me!

But O reprieve me!
For thou hast life and death at thy command;
   Thou art both *Judge* and *Saviour, feast* and *rod,*
Cordiall and *Corrosive:* put not thy hand
   Into the bitter box; but O my God,
      My God, relieve me!

WHITSUNDAY

Listen sweet Dove unto my song,
  And spread thy golden wings in me;
Hatching my tender heart so long,
Till it get wing, and flie away with thee.

Where is that fire which once descended
  On thy Apostles? thou didst then
Keep open house, richly attended,
Feasting all comers by twelve chosen men.

Such glorious gifts thou didst bestow,
  That th' earth did like a heav'n appeare;
The starres were coming down to know
If they might mend their wages, and serve here.

The sunne, which once did shine alone,
  Hung down his head, and wisht for night,
When he beheld twelve sunnes for one
Going about the world, and giving light.

But since those pipes of gold, which brought
  That cordiall water to our ground,
Were cut and martyr'd by the fault
Of those, who did themselves through their side wound,

Thou shutt'st the doore, and keep'st within;
  Scarce a good joy creeps through the chink:
And if the braves of conqu'ring sinne
Did not excite thee, we should wholly sink.

Lord, though we change, thou art the same;
  The same sweet God of love and light:
Restore this day, for thy great name,
Unto his ancient and miraculous right.

THE STARRE

Bright spark, shot from a brighter place,
Where beams surround my Saviours face,
    Canst thou be any where
      So well as there?

Yet, if thou wilt from thence depart,
Take a bad lodging in my heart;
    For thou canst make a debter,
      And make it better.

First with thy fire-work burn to dust
Folly, and worse then folly, lust:
    Then with thy light refine,
      And make it shine:

So disengag'd from sinne and sicknesse,
Touch it with thy celestiall quicknesse,
    That it may hang and move
      After thy love.

Then with our trinitie of light,
Motion, and heat, let's take our flight
    Unto the place where thou
      Before didst bow.

Get me a standing there, and place
Among the beams, which crown the face
    Of him, who dy'd to part
      Sinne and my heart:

That so among the rest I may
Glitter, and curle, and winde as they:
    That winding is their fashion
      Of adoration.

Sure thou wilt joy, by gaining me
To flie home like a laden bee
    Unto that hive of beams
      And garland-streams.

VERTUE

Sweet day, so cool, so calm, so bright,
The bridall of the earth and skie:
The dew shall weep thy fall to night;
      For thou must die.

Sweet rose, whose hue angrie and brave
Bids the rash gazer wipe his eye:
Thy root is ever in its grave,
      And thou must die.

Sweet spring, full of sweet dayes and roses,
A box where sweets compacted lie;
My musick shows ye have your closes,
      And all must die.

Onely a sweet and vertuous soul,
Like season'd timber, never gives;
But though the whole world turn to coal,
      Then chiefly lives.

THE ROSE

Presse me not to take more pleasure
  In this world of sugred lies,
And to use a larger measure
  Then my strict, yet welcome size.

First, there is no pleasure here:
  Colour'd griefs indeed there
     are,
Blushing woes, that look as cleare
  As if they could beautie spare.

Or if such deceits there be,
  Such delights I meant to say;
There are no such things to me,
  Who have pass'd my right away.

But I will not much oppose
  Unto what you now advise:
Onely take this gentle rose,
  And therein my answer lies.

What is fairer then a rose?
  What is sweeter? yet it purgeth.
Purgings enmitie disclose,
  Enmitie forbearance urgeth.

If then all that worldlings prize
  Be contracted to a rose;
Sweetly there indeed it lies,
  But it biteth in the close.

So this flower doth judge and
    sentence
  Worldly joyes to be a scourge:
For they all produce repentance,
  And repentance is a purge.

But I health, not physick choose:
  Onely though I you oppose,
Say that fairly I refuse,
  For my answer is a rose.

THE SACRIFICE

Oh all ye, who passe by, whose eyes and minde
To worldly things are sharp, but to me blinde;
To me, who took eyes that I might you finde:
    Was ever grief like mine?

The Princes of my people make a head
Against their Maker: they do wish me dead,
Who cannot wish, except I give them bread:
    Was ever grief like mine?

Without me each one, who doth now me brave,
Had to this day been an Egyptian slave.
They use that power against me, which I gave:
    Was ever grief like mine?

Mine own Apostle, who the bag did beare,
Though he had all I had, did not forbeare
To sell me also, and to put me there:
    Was ever grief like mine?

For thirtie pence he did my death devise,
Who at three hundred did the ointment prize,
Not half so sweet as my sweet sacrifice:
    Was ever grief like mine?

Therefore my soul melts, and my hearts deare treasure
Drops bloud (the onely beads) my words to measure:
O let this cup passe, if it be thy pleasure:
    Was ever grief like mine?

These drops being temper'd with a sinners tears
A Balsome are for both the Hemispheres:
Curing all wounds, but mine; all, but my fears:
    Was ever grief like mine?

Yet my Disciples sleep: I cannot gain
One houre of watching; but their drowsie brain
Comforts not me, and doth my doctrine stain:
    Was ever grief like mine?

Arise, arise, they come. Look how they runne!
Alas! what haste they make to be undone!
How with their lanterns do they seek the sunne!
    Was ever grief like mine?

With clubs and staves they seek me, as a thief,
Who am the Way and Truth, the true relief;
Most true to those, who are my greatest grief:
   Was ever grief like mine?

Judas, dost thou betray me with a kisse?
Canst thou finde hell about my lips? and misse
Of life, just at the gates of life and blisse?
   Was ever grief like mine?

See, they lay hold on me, not with the hands
Of faith, but furie: yet at their commands
I suffer binding, who have loos'd their bands:
   Was ever grief like mine?

All my Disciples flie; fear put a barre
Betwixt my friends and me. They leave the starre,
That brought the wise men of the East from farre.
   Was ever grief like mine?

Then from one ruler to another bound
They leade me; urging, that it was not sound
What I taught: Comments would the text confound.
   Was ever grief like mine?

The Priest and rulers all false witnesse seek
'Gainst him, who seeks not life, but is the meek
And readie Paschal Lambe of this great week:
   Was ever grief like mine?

Then they accuse me of great blasphemie,
That I did thrust into the Deitie,
Who never thought that any robberie:
   Was ever grief like mine?

Some said, that I the Temple to the floore
In three dayes raz'd, and raised as before.
Why, he that built the world can do much more:
   Was ever grief like mine?

Then they condemne me all with that same breath,
Which I do give them daily, unto death.
Thus *Adam* my first breathing rendereth:
   Was ever grief like mine?

They binde, and leade me unto *Herod:* he
Sends me to *Pilate*. This makes them agree;
But yet their friendship is my enmitie:
     Was ever grief like mine?

Herod and all his bands do set me light,
Who teach all hands to warre, fingers to fight,
And onely am the Lord of Hosts and might:
     Was ever grief like mine?

Herod in judgement sits, while I do stand;
Examines me with a censorious hand:
I him obey, who all things else command:
     Was ever grief like mine?

The *Jews* accuse me with despitefulnesse;
And vying malice with my gentlenesse,
Pick quarrels with their onely happinesse:
     Was ever grief like mine?

I answer nothing, but with patience prove
If stonie hearts will melt with gentle love.
But who does hawk at eagles with a dove?
     Was ever grief like mine?

My silence rather doth augment their crie;
My dove doth back into my bosome flie,
Because the raging waters still are high:
     Was ever grief like mine?

Heark how they crie aloud still, *Crucifie:*
It is not fit he live a day, they crie,
Who cannot live lesse then eternally:
     Was ever grief like mine?

Pilate, a stranger, holdeth off; but they,
Mine owne deare people, cry, *Away, away,*
With noises confused frighting the day:
     Was ever grief like mine?

Yet still they shout, and crie, and stop their eares,
Putting my life among their sinnes and fears,
And therefore wish *my bloud on them and theirs:*
     Was ever grief like mine?

See how spite cankers things. These words aright
Used, and wished, are the whole worlds light:
But hony is their gall, brightnesse their night:
     Was ever grief like mine?

They choose a murderer, and all agree
In him to do themselves a courtesie:
For it was their own case who killed me:
     Was ever grief like mine?

And a seditious murderer he was:
But I the Prince of peace; peace that doth passe
All understanding, more then heav'n doth glasse:
     Was ever grief like mine?

Why, Cæsar is their onely King, not I:
He clave the stonie rock, when they were drie;
But surely not their hearts, as I well trie:
     Was ever grief like mine?

Ah! how thy scourge me! yet my tendernesse
Doubles each lash: and yet their bitternesse
Windes up my grief to a mysteriousnesse:
     Was ever grief like mine?

They buffet him, and box him as they list,
Who grasps the earth and heaven with his fist,
And never yet, whom he would punish, miss'd:
     Was ever grief like mine?

Behold, they spit on me in scornfull wise,
Who by my spittle gave the blinde man eies,
Leaving his blindnesse to my enemies:
     Was ever grief like mine?

My face they cover, though it be divine.
As *Moses* face was vailed, so is mine,
Lest on their double-dark souls either shine:
     Was ever grief like mine?

Servants and abjects flout me; they are wittie:
Now prophesie who strikes thee, is their dittie.
So they in me denie themselves all pitie:
     Was ever grief like mine?

And now I am deliver'd unto death,
Which each one calls for so with utmost breath,
That he before me well nigh suffereth:
　　　　Was ever grief like mine?

Weep not, deare friends, since I for both have wept
When all my tears were bloud, the while you slept:
Your tears for your own fortunes should be kept:
　　　　Was ever grief like mine?

The souldiers lead me to the Common Hall;
There they deride me, they abuse me all:
Yet for twelve heav'nly legions I could call:
　　　　Was ever grief like mine?

Then with a scarlet robe they me array;
Which shews my bloud to be the onely way
And cordiall left to repair mans decay:
　　　　Was ever grief like mine?

Then on my head a crown of thorns I wear:
For these are all the grapes *Sion* doth bear,
Though I my vine planted and watred there:
　　　　Was ever grief like mine?

So sits the earths great curse in *Adams* fall
Upon my head: so I remove it all
From th' earth unto my brows, and bear the thrall:
　　　　Was ever grief like mine?

Then with the reed they gave to me before,
They strike my head, the rock from whence all store
Of heav'nly blessings issue evermore:
　　　　Was ever grief like mine?

They bow their knees to me, and cry, *Hail king:*
What ever scoffes and scornfulnesse can bring,
I am the floore, the sink, where they it fling:
　　　　Was ever grief like mine?

Yet since mans scepters are as frail as reeds,
And thorny all their crowns, bloudie their weeds;
I, who am Truth, turn into truth their deeds:
　　　　Was ever grief like mine?

The souldiers also spit upon that face,
Which Angels did desire to have the grace,
And Prophets, once to see, but found no place:
        Was ever grief like mine?

Thus trimmed, forth they bring me to the rout,
Who *Crucifie him,* crie with one strong shout.
God holds his peace at man, and man cries out:
        Was ever grief like mine?

They leade me in once more, and putting then
Mine own clothes on, they leade me out agen.
Whom devils flie, thus is he toss'd of men:
        Was ever grief like mine?

And now wearie of sport, glad to ingrosse
All spite in one, counting my life their losse,
They carrie me to my most bitter crosse:
        Was ever grief like mine?

My crosse I bear my self, untill I faint:
Then Simon bears it for me by constraint,
The decreed burden of each mortall Saint:
        Was ever grief like mine?

O all ye who passe by, behold and see;
Man stole the fruit, but I must climbe the tree;
The tree of life to all, but onely me:
        Was ever grief like mine?

Lo, here I hang, charg'd with a world of sinne,
The greater world o' th' two; for that came in
By words, but this by sorrow I must win:
        Was ever grief like mine?

Such sorrow as, if sinfull man could feel,
Or feel his part, he would not cease to kneel,
Till all were melted, though he were all steel:
        Was ever grief like mine?

But, *O my God, my God!* why leav'st thou me,
The sonne, in whom thou dost delight to be?
My God, my God —
        Never was grief like mine.

Shame tears my soul, my bodie many a wound;
Sharp nails pierce this, but sharper that confound;
Reproches, which are free, while I am bound.
      Was ever grief like mine?

Now heal thy self, Physician; now come down.
Alas! I did so, when I left my crown
And fathers smile for you, to feel his frown:
      Was ever grief like mine?

In healing not my self, there doth consist
All that salvation, which ye now resist;
Your safetie in my sicknesse doth subsist:
      Was ever grief like mine?

Betwixt two theeves I spend my utmost breath,
As he that for some robberie suffereth.
Alas! what have I stollen from you? Death.
      Was ever grief like mine?

A king my title is, prefixt on high;
Yet by my subjects am condemn'd to die
A servile death in servile companie:
      Was ever grief like mine?

They give me vineger mingled with gall,
But more with malice; yet, when they did call,
With Manna, Angels food, I fed them all:
      Was ever grief like mine?

They part my garments, and by lot dispose
My coat, the type of love, which once cur'd those
Who sought for help, never malicious foes:
      Was ever grief like mine?

Nay, after death their spite shall further go;
For they will pierce my side, I full well know;
That as sinne came, so Sacraments might flow:
      Was ever grief like mine?

But now I die; now all is finished.
My wo, mans weal: and now I bow my head.
Onely let others say, when I am dead,
      Never was grief like mine.

THE PULLEY

When God at first made man,
Having a glasse of blessings standing by;
Let us (said he) poure on him all we can:
Let the worlds riches, which dispersed lie,
　　Contract into a span.

So strength first made a way;
Then beautie flow'd, then wisdome, honour, pleasure:
When almost all was out, God made a stay,
Perceiving that alone of all his treasure
　　Rest in the bottome lay.

For if I should (said he)
Bestow this jewell also on my creature,
He would adore my gifts in stead of me,
And rest in Nature, not the God of Nature:
　　So both should losers be.

Yet let him keep the rest,
But keep them with repining restlesnesse:
Let him be rich and wearie, that at least,
If goodnesse leade him not, yet wearinesse
　　May tosse him to my breast.

Thomas Carew
1595?-1639?

SONG: ASKE ME NO MORE WHERE JOVE BESTOWES

Aske me no more where Jove bestowes,
When June is past, the fading rose:
For in your beautie's orient deepe,
These flowers, as in their causes, sleepe.

Aske me no more whither doth stray
The golden Atomes of the day:
For in pure love heaven did prepare
Those powders to inrich your haire.

Aske me no more whither doth haste
The Nightingale when May is past:
For in your sweet dividing throat
She winters and keepes warme her note.

Aske me no more where those starres light,
That downewards fall in dead of night:
For in your eyes they sit, and there
Fixed become as in their sphere.

Aske me no more if East or West
The Phenix builds her spicy nest:
For unto you at last shee flies,
And in your fragrant bosome dyes.

From UNFADING BEAUTY

Hee that loves a Rosie cheeke,
 Or a corall lip admires,
Or from star-like eyes doth seeke
 Fuell to maintaine his fires;
As old *Time* makes these decay,
So his flames must waste away.

But a smooth and stedfast mind,
 Gentle thoughts, and calme desires,
Hearts with equall love combind
 Kindle never-dying fires:
Where these are not I despise
Lovely cheekes, or lips, or eyes.

Sir John Suckling
1609-1642

SONG: NO, NO, FAIR HERETICK

No, no, fair Heretick, it needs must be
 But an ill love in me,
  And worse for Thee;
 For were it in my power,
 To love thee now this hower
  More than I did the last;

    I would then so fall
    I might not love at all;
Love that can flow, and can admit increase,
Admits as well an ebbe, and may grow lesse.

True Love is still the same; the Torrid Zones,
    And those more frigid ones
      It must not know:
    For love grown cold or hot,
    Is lust, or friendship, not
      The thing we have.
    For that's a flame would dye
    Held down, or up too high:
Then think I love more than I can expresse,
And would love more could I but love thee lesse.

A BALLAD UPON A WEDDING

I tell thee *Dick* where I have been,
Where I the rarest things have seen;
    Oh things without compare!
Such sights again cannot be found
In any place on English ground,
    Be it at Wake, or Fair.

At *Charing-Crosse,* hard by the way
Where we (thou know'st) do sell our Hay,
    There is a house with stairs;
And there did I see coming down
Such folk as are not in our Town,
    Forty at least, in Pairs.

Amongst the rest, one Pest'lent fine,
(His beard no bigger though than thine)
    Walkt on before the rest:
Our Landlord looks like nothing to him:
The King (God bless him) 'twould undo him,
    Should he go still so drest.

At Course-a-Park, without all doubt,
He should have just been taken out
    By all the Maids i' th' Town:
Though lusty *Roger* there had been,
Or little *George* upon the Green,
    Or *Vincent* of the Crown.

But wot you what? the youth was going
To make an end of all his wooing;
    The Parson for him staid;
Yet by his leave (for all his haste)
He did not so much wish all past
    (Perchance) as did the maid.

The maid (and thereby hangs a tale)
For such a maid no Whitsun-ale
    Could ever yet produce:
No Grape that's kindly ripe, could be
So sound, so plump, so soft as she,
    Nor half so full of Juice.

Her finger was so small, the Ring
Would not stay on, which they did bring,
    It was too wide a Peck;
And to say truth (for out it must)
It lookt like a great Collar (just)
    About our young Colts neck.

Her feet beneath her Petticoat
Like little mice stole in and out,
    As if they fear'd the light:
But oh! she dances such a way
No Sun upon an Easter day
    Is half so fine a sight.

He would have kist her once or twice,
But she would not, she was so nice,
    She would not do't in sight,
And then she lookt as who should say
I will do what I list to day;
    And you shall do't at night.

Her Cheeks so rare a white was on,
No Dazy makes comparison,
    (Who sees them is undone)
For streaks of red were mingled there,
Such as are on a Katherine Pear,
    (The side that's next the Sun.)

Her lips were red, and one was thin,
Compar'd to that was next her chin;
    (Some Bee had stung it newly.)

But (*Dick*) her eyes so guard her face;
I durst no more upon them gaze,
   Than on the Sun in *July*.

Her mouth so small when she does speak,
Thou'dst swear her teeth her words did break,
   That they might passage get,
But she so handled still the matter,
They came as good as ours, or better,
   And are not spent a whit.

If wishing should be any sin,
The Parson himself had guilty bin;
   (She lookt that day so purely,)
And did the youth so oft the feat
At night, as some did in conceit,
   It would have spoil'd him, surely.

Just in the nick the Cook knockt thrice,
And all the waiters in a trice
   His summons did obey,
Each serving man with dish in hand,
Marcht boldly up, like our Train'd Band,
   Presented, and away.

When all the meat was on the Table,
What man of knife, or teeth, was able
   To stay to be intreated?
And this the very reason was,
Before the Parson could say Grace,
   The Company was seated.

The bus'nesse of the Kitchin's great,
For it is fit that men should eat;
   Nor was it there deni'd:
Passion o' me! How I run on!
There's that that would be thought upon,
   (I trow) besides the Bride.

Now hats fly off, and youths carouse;
Healths first go round, and then the house,
   The Bride's came thick and thick;
And when 'twas nam'd anothers health,
Perhaps he made it hers by stealth.
   (And who could help it, *Dick?*)

O' th' sudden up and they rise and dance;
Then sit again and sigh, and glance:
   Then dance again and kisse:
Thus sev'ral waies the time did passe,
Till ev'ry Woman wisht her place,
   And ev'ry Man wisht his.

By this time all were stoln aside
To counsel and undresse the Bride;
   But that he must not know:
But yet 'twas thought he guess'd her mind,
And did not mean to stay behind
   Above an hour or so.

When in he came (*Dick*) there she lay
Like new-faln snow melting away
   ('Twas time I trow to part)
Kisses were now the only stay,
Which soon she gave, as who would say,
   Good Boy! with all my heart.

But just as heav'ns would have to cross it,
In came the Bridesmaids with the Posset:
   The Bridegroom eat in spight;
For had he left the Women to't
It would have cost two hours to do't,
   Which were too much that night.

At length the candles out and out,
All that they had not done, they do't:
   What that is, who can tell?
But I believe it was no more
Than thou and I have done before
   With *Bridget,* and with *Nell.*

Richard Lovelace

1618-1658

TO LUCASTA, GOING BEYOND THE SEAS

If to be absent were to be
   Away from thee;
   Or that when I am gone,

You or I were alone;
Then my *Lucasta* might I crave
Pity from blustring winde or swallowing wave.

But I'le not sigh one blast or gale
    To swell my saile,
    Or pay a teare to swage
    The foaming blew-Gods rage;
For whether he will let me passe
Or no, I'm still as happy as I was.

Though Seas and Land betwixt us both,
    Our Faith and Troth,
    Like separated soules,
    All time and space controules:
Above the highest sphere wee meet
Unseene, unknowne, and greet as Angels greet.

So then we doe anticipate
    Our after-fate,
    And are alive i' th' skies,
    If thus our lips and eyes
Can speake like spirits unconfin'd
In Heav'n, their earthy bodies left behind.

TO LUCASTA, GOING TO THE WARRES

Tell me not (Sweet) I am unkinde,
    That from the Nunnerie
Of thy chaste breast, and quiet minde,
    To Warre and Armes I flie.

True; a new Mistresse now I chase,
    The first Foe in the Field;
And with a stronger Faith imbrace
    A Sword, a Horse, a Shield.

Yet this Inconstancy is such,
    As you too shall adore;
I could not love thee (Deare) so much,
    Lov'd I not Honour more.

THE SNAYL

Wise Emblem of our Politick World,
Sage Snayl, within thine own self curl'd;
Instruct me softly to make hast,
Whilst these my Feet go slowly fast.
    Compendious Snayl! thou seem'st to me
Large *Euclids* strickt Epitome;
And in each Diagram, dost Fling
Thee from the point unto the Ring.
A Figure now Triangulare,
An Oval now, and now a Square;
And then a Serpentine dost crawl
Now a straight Line, now crook'd, now all.
    Preventing Rival of the Day,
Th'art up and openest thy Ray,
And ere the Morn cradles the Moon,
Th'art broke into a Beauteous Noon.
Then when the Sun sups in the Deep,
Thy Silver Horns e're *Cinthia's* peep;
And thou from thine own liquid Bed
New *Phoebus* heav'st thy pleasant Head.
    Who shall a Name for thee create,
Deep Riddle of Mysterious State?
Bold Nature, that gives common Birth
To all products of Seas and Earth,
Of thee, as Earth-quakes, is affraid,
Nor will thy dire Deliv'ry aid.
    Thou thine own daughter then, and Sire,
That Son and Mother art intire,
That big still with thy self dost go,
And liv'st an aged Embrio;
That like the Cubbs of *India,*
Thou from thy self a while dost play:
But frighted with a Dog or Gun,
In thine own Belly thou dost run,
And as thy House was thine own womb,
So thine own womb concludes thy tomb.
    But now I must (analys'd King)
Thy Œconomick Virtues sing:
Thou great stay'd Husband still within,
Thou, thee, that's thine dost Discipline;
And when thou art to progress bent,
Thou mov'st thy self and tenement,

As Warlike *Scythians* travayl'd, you
Remove your Men and City too;
Then after a sad Dearth and Rain,
Thou scatterest thy Silver Train;
And when the Trees grow nak'd and old,
Thou cloathest them with Cloth of Gold,
Which from thy Bowels thou dost spin,
And draw from the rich Mines within.
  Now hast thou chang'd thee Saint; and made
Thy self a Fane that's cupula'd;
And in thy wreathed Cloister thou
Walkest thine own Gray fryer too;
Strickt, and lock'd up, th'art Hood all ore
And ne'r Eliminat'st thy Dore.
On Sallads thou dost feed severe,
And 'stead of Beads thou drop'st a tear.
And when to rest, each calls the Bell,
Thou sleep'st within thy Marble Cell;
Where in dark contemplation plac'd,
The sweets of Nature thou dost tast;
Who now with Time thy days resolve,
And in a Jelly thee dissolve.
Like a shot Star, which doth repair
Upward, and Rarifie the Air.

ANOTHER

The Centaur, Syren, I foregoe,
Those have been sung, and lowdly too;
Nor of the mixed Sphynx Ile write,
Nor the renown'd Hermaphrodite:
Behold, this Huddle doth appear
Of Horses, Coach, and Charioteer;
That moveth him by traverse Law,
And doth himself both drive and draw;
Then when the Sun the South doth winne,
He baits him hot in his own Inne.
I heard a grave and austere Clark,
Resolv'd him Pilot both and Barque;
That like the fam'd Ship of *Trevere*,
Did on the Shore himself Lavere:
Yet the Authentick do beleeve,
Who keep their Judgement in their Sleeve,

lavere] tack.

That he is his own Double man,
And sick, still carries his Sedan:
Or that like Dames i' th' Land of Luyck,
He wears his everlasting Huyck:
But banisht, I admire his fate
Since neither Ostracisme of State,
Nor a perpetual exile,
Can force this Virtue change his Soyl;
For wheresoever he doth go,
He wanders with his Country too.

THE GRASSE–HOPPER

O thou that swing'st upon the waving haire
    Of some well-filled Oaten Beard,
Drunke ev'ry night with a Delicious teare
    Dropt thee from Heav'n, where now th'art reard.

The Joyes of Earth and Ayre are thine intire,
    That with thy feet and wings dost hop and flye;
And when thy Poppy workes thou dost retire
    To thy Carv'd Acorn-bed to lye.

Up with the Day, the Sun thou welcomst then,
    Sportst in the guilt-plats of his Beames,
And all these merry dayes mak'st merry men,
    Thy selfe, and Melancholy streames.

But ah the Sickle! Golden Eares are Cropt;
    Ceres and *Bacchus* bid good night;
Sharpe frosty fingers all your Flow'rs have topt,
    And what sithes spar'd, Winds shave off quite.

Poore verdant foole! and now green Ice! thy Joys
    Large and as lasting, as thy Perch of Grasse,
Bid us lay in 'gainst Winter, Raine, and poize
    Their flouds, with an o'reflowing glasse.

Thou best of *Men* and *Friends!* we will create
    A Genuine Summer in each others breast;
And spite of this cold Time and frosen Fate
    Thaw us a warme seate to our rest.

Luyck] Liége.   huyck] huke, a long head veil.

Our sacred harthes shall burne eternally
    As Vestall Flames, the North-wind, he
Shall strike his frost-stretch'd Winges, dissolve and flye
    This *Ætna* in Epitome.

Dropping *December* shall come weeping in,
    Bewayle th' usurping of his Raigne;
But when in show'rs of old Greeke we beginne,
    Shall crie, he hath his Crowne againe!

Night as cleare *Hesper* shall our Tapers whip
    From the light Casements where we play,
And the darke Hagge from her black mantle strip,
    And sticke there everlasting Day.

Thus richer then untempted Kings are we,
    That asking nothing, nothing need:
Though Lord of all what Seas imbrace; yet he
    That wants himselfe, is poore indeed.

LA BELLA BONA ROBA

I cannot tell who loves the Skeleton
Of a poor Marmoset, nought but boan, boan.
Give me a nakednesse with her cloath's on.

Such whose white-sattin upper coat of skin,
Cuts upon Velvet rich Incarnadin,
Ha's yet a Body (and of Flesh) within.

Sure it is meant good Husbandry in men,
Who do incorporate with Aëry leane,
T' repair their sides, and get their Ribb agen.

Hard hap unto that Huntsman that Decrees
Fat joys for all his swet, when as he sees,
After his 'Say, nought but his Keepers Fees.

Then Love I beg, when next thou tak'st thy Bow,
Thy angry shafts, and dost Heart-chasing go,
Passe *Rascal Deare,* strike me the largest Doe.

Edmund Waller
1606-1687

SONG: GO LOVELY ROSE

Go lovely Rose,
Tell her that wastes her time and me,
That now she knows
When I resemble her to thee,
How sweet and faire she seems to be.

Tell her that's young,
And shuns to have her Graces spy'd,
That hadst thou sprung
In Desarts, where no men abide,
Thou must have uncommended dy'd.

Small is the worth
Of Beauty from the light retir'd;
Bid her come forth,
Suffer her self to be desir'd,
And not blush so to be admir'd.

Then die, that she,
The common fate of all things rare,
May read in thee
How small a part of time they share,
That are so wondrous sweet and fair.

Richard Crashaw
1613?-1649

HYMN OF THE NATIVITY
Sung as by the Shepheards

CHORUS.   Come we shepheards whose blest Sight
Hath met love's Noon in Nature's night;
Come lift we up our loftyer Song
And wake the SUN that lyes too long.

To all our world of well-stoln joy
 He slept; and dream't of no such thing;
While we found out Heavn's fairer eye
 And Kiss'd the Cradle of our KING.
Tell him He rises now, too late
To show us ought worth looking at.

Tell him we now can show Him more
 Then He e'er show'd to mortall Sight;
Then he Himselfe e'er saw before;
 Which to be seen needes not His light.
Tell him, Tityrus, where th'hast been,
Tell him, Thyrsis, what th'hast seen.

TITYRUS. Gloomy night embrac't the Place
  Where The Noble Infant lay.
The BABE look't up and shew'd his Face;
  In spite of Darkness, it was DAY.
It was THY day, SWEET! and did rise
Not from the EAST, but from thine EYES.

CHORUS. It was THY day, SWEET, &c.

THYRSIS. WINTER chidde aloud; and sent
  The angry North to wage his warres.
The North forgot his fierce Intent;
  And left perfumes in stead of scarres.
By those sweet eyes persuasive powrs
Where he mean't frost, he scatter'd flowrs.

CHORUS. By those sweet eyes, &c.

BOTH. We saw thee in thy baulmy Nest,
  Young dawn of our æternall DAY!
We saw thine eyes break from their EAST
  And chase the trembling shades away.
We saw thee; and we blest the sight,
We saw thee by thine own sweet light.

TITYRUS. Poor WORLD (said I) what wilt thou doe
  To entertain this starry STRANGER?
Is this the best thou canst bestow?
  A cold, and not too cleanly, manger?
Contend ye powres of heav'n and earth
To fit a bed for this huge birthe.

CHORUS. Contend ye powers, &c.

THYRSIS. Proud world, said I; cease your contest,
 And let the MIGHTY BABE alone.
 The Phænix builds the Phænix' nest.
  Love's architecture is his own.
 The BABE whose birth embraves this morn,
 Made his own bed ere he was born.

CHORUS. The BABE whose, &c.

TITYRUS. I saw the curl'd drops, soft and slow,
  Come hovering o'er the place's head;
 Offring their whitest sheets of snow
  To furnish the fair INFANT's bed:
 Forbear, said I; be not too bold.
 Your fleece is white, But 'tis too cold.

CHORUS. Forbear, said I, &c.

THYRSIS. I saw the obsequious SERAPHINS
  Their rosy fleece of fire bestow,
 For well they now can spare their wings,
  Since HEAVN it self lyes here below.
 Well done, said I: but are you sure
 Your down so warm, will passe for pure?

CHORUS. Well done, said I, &c.

TITYRUS. No no, your KING's not yet to seeke
  Where to repose his Royall HEAD,
 See see, how soon his new-bloom'd CHEEK
  Twixt's mother's breasts is gone to bed.
 Sweet choise, said we! no way but so
 Not to lye cold, yet sleep in snow.

CHORUS. Sweet choise, said we, &c.

BOTH. We saw thee in thy baulmy nest,
  Bright dawn of our æternall Day!
 We saw thine eyes break from their EAST
  And chase the trembling shades away.
 We saw thee: and we blest the sight.
 We saw thee by thine own sweet light.

CHORUS. We saw thee, &c.

| FULL | Wellcome, all WONDERS in one sight! |
| CHORUS. | Æternity shut in a span. |

Sommer in Winter. Day in Night.
Heaven in earth, and GOD in MAN.
Great little one! whose all-embracing birth
Lifts earth to heaven, stoopes heav'n to earth.

WELLCOME. Though nor to gold nor silk,
 To more than Cæsar's birth right is;
Two sister-seas of Virgin-Milk,
 With many a rarely-temper'd kisse
That breathes at once both MAID and MOTHER,
Warmes in the one, cooles in the other.

Shee sings thy Teares asleepe, and dips
 Her Kisses in thy weeping Eye,
She spreads the red leaves of thy Lips
 That in their Buds yet blushing lye,
 She 'gainst those Mother-Diamonds tryes
The points of her young Eagles Eyes.

WELLCOME, though not to those gay flyes
 Gilded ith' Beames of earthly kings;
Slippery soules in smiling eyes;
 But to poor Shepherds, home-spun things:
Whose Wealth's their flock; whose wit, to be
Well read in their simplicity.

Yet when young April's husband showrs
 Shall blesse the fruitfull Maia's bed,
We'll bring the First-born of her flowrs
 To kisse thy FEET and crown thy HEAD.
To thee, dread Lamb! whose love must keep
The shepheards, more than they the sheep.

To THEE, meek Majesty! soft KING
 Of simple GRACES and sweet LOVES.
Each of us his lamb will bring
 Each his pair of sylver Doves;
 Till burnt at last in fire of Thy fair eyes,
Our selves become our own best SACRIFICE.

From THE FLAMING HEART

UPON THE BOOK AND PICTURE OF THE SERAPHICALL SAINT TERESA
(*As She is usually expressed with a Seraphim beside her*)

Live here, great HEART; and love and dy and kill;
And bleed and wound; and yeild and conquer still.
Let this immortall life where'er it comes
Walk in a crowd of loves and MARTYRDOMES.
Let mystick DEATHS wait on't; and wise soules be
The love-slain witnesses of this life of thee.
O sweet incendiary! shew here thy art,
Upon this carcase of a hard, cold, heart;
Let all thy scatter'd shafts of light, that play
Among the leaves of thy large Books of day,
Combin'd against this BREST at once break in
And take away from me my self and sin;
This gratious Robbery shall thy bounty be;
And my best fortunes such fair spoiles of me.
O thou undaunted daughter of desires!
By all thy dow'r of LIGHTS and FIRES;
By all the eagle in thee, all the dove;
By all thy lives and deaths of love;
By thy large draughts of intellectuall day,
And by thy thirsts of love more large than they;
By all thy brim-fill'd Bowles of fierce desire
By thy last Morning's draught of liquid fire;
By the full kingdome of that finall kisse
That seiz'd thy parting Soul, and seal'd thee his;
By all the heav'ns thou hast in him
(Fair sister of the SERAPHIM)
By all of HIM we have in THEE;
Leave nothing of my SELF in me.
Let me so read thy life, that I
Unto all life of mine may dy.

SAINT MARY MAGDALENE
or
THE WEEPER

Hail, sister springs!
   Parents of sylver-footed rills!
Ever bubling things!

Thawing crystall! snowy hills,
Still spending, never spent! I mean
Thy fair eyes, sweet MAGDALENE!

Heavens thy fair eyes be;
   Heavens of ever-falling starres.
'Tis seed-time still with thee
   And starres thou sow'st, whose harvest dares
Promise the earth to counter shine
Whatever makes heavn's forhead fine.

But we'are deceived all.
   Starres indeed they are too true;
For they but seem to fall,
   As Heavn's other spangles doe.
It is not for our earth and us
To shine in Things so pretious.

Upwards thou dost weep.
   Heavn's bosome drinks the gentle stream,
Where th' milky rivers creep,
   Thine floates above; and is the cream.
Waters above th' Heavns, what they be
We'are taught best by thy TEARES and thee.

Every morn from hence
   A brisk Cherub somthing sippes
Whose sacred influence
   Addes sweetnes to his sweetest Lippes,
Then to his musick. And his song
Tasts of this Breakfast all day long.

Not in the evening's eyes
   When they Red with weeping are
For the Sun that dyes,
   Sitts sorrow with a face so fair,
No where but here did ever meet
Sweetnesse so sad, sadnesse so sweet.

When sorrow would be seen
   In her brightest majesty
(For she is a Queen)
   Then is she drest by none but thee.
Then, and only then, she weares
Her proudest pearles; I mean, thy TEARES.

The deaw no more will weep
  The primrose's pale cheek to deck,
The deaw no more will sleep
  Nuzzel'd in the lilly's neck;
Much rather would it be thy TEAR,
And leave them Both to tremble here.

There's no need at all
  That the balsom-sweating bough
So coyly should let fall
  His med-cinable teares; for now
Nature hath learn't to'extract a deaw
More soveraign and sweet from you.

Yet let the poore drops weep
  (Weeping is the ease of woe)
Softly let them creep,
  Sad that they are vanquish't so.
They, though to others no releife,
Balsom maybe, for their own greife.

Such the maiden gemme
  By the purpling vine put on,
Peeps from her parent stemme
  And blushes at the bridegroomes sun.
This watry Blossom of thy eyn,
Ripe, will make the richer wine.

When some new bright Guest
  Takes up among the starres a room,
And Heavn will make a feast,
  Angels with crystall violls come
And draw from these full eyes of thine
Their master's water: their own Wine.

Golden though he be,
  Golden Tagus murmures tho;
Were his way by thee,
  Content and quiet he would goe.
So much more rich would he esteem
Thy sylver, then his golden stream.

Well does the May that lyes
  Smiling in thy cheeks, confesse
The April in thine eyes.

Mutuall sweetnesse they expresse.
No April ere lent kinder showres,
Nor May return'd more faithfull flowres.

O cheeks! Bedds of chast loves
   By your own showres seasonably dash't.
Eyes! nests of milky doves
   In your own wells decently washt.
O wit of love! that thus could place
Fountain and Garden in one face.

O sweet Contest; of woes
   With loves, of teares with smiles disputing!
O fair, and Freindly Foes,
   Each other kissing and confuting!
While rain and sunshine, Cheekes and Eyes
Close in kind contrarietyes.

But can these fair Flouds be
   Freinds with the bosom fires that fill thee!
Can so great flames agree
   Æternall Teares should thus distill thee!
O flouds, O fires! O suns, O showres!
Mixt and made freinds by love's sweet powres.

Twas his well-pointed dart
   That digg'd these wells, and drest this Vine;
And taught the wounded HEART
   The way into these weeping Eyn.
Vain loves avant! bold hands forbear!
The lamb hath dipp't his white foot here.

And now where're he strayes,
   Among the Galilean mountaines,
Or more unwellcome wayes,
   He's followed by two faithfull fountaines;
Two walking baths; two weeping motions;
Portable, and compendious oceans.

O Thou, thy lord's fair store!
   In thy so rich and rare expenses,
Even when he show'd most poor,
   He might provoke the wealth of Princes.
What Prince's wanton'st pride e're could
Wash with Sylver, wipe with Gold?

Who is that King, but he
   Who call'st his Crown to be call'd thine,
That thus can boast to be
   Waited on by a wandring mine,
A voluntary mint, that strowes
Warm sylver shoures where're he goes!

O pretious Prodigall!
   Fair spend-thrift of thy self! thy measure
(Mercilesse love!) is all.
   Even to the last Pearle in thy treasure.
All places, Times, and objects be
Thy teare's sweet opportunity.

Does the day-starre rise?
   Still thy starres doe fall and fall;
Does day close his eyes?
   Still the FOUNTAIN weeps for all.
Let night or day doe what they will,
Thou hast thy task; thou weepest still.

Does thy song lull the air?
   Thy falling teares keep faith full time.
Does thy sweet-breath'd prayer
   Up in clouds of incense climb?
Still at each sigh, that is, each stop,
A bead, that is, A TEAR, does drop.

At these thy weeping gates,
   (Watching their watry motion)
Each winged moment waits,
   Takes his TEAR, and gets him gone.
By thine Ey's tinct enobled thus
Time layes him up; he's pretious.

Not, so long she lived,
   Shall thy tomb report of thee;
But, so long she greived,
   Thus must we date thy memory.
Others by moments, months, and yeares
Measure their ages; thou, by TEARES.

So doe perfumes expire.
   So sigh tormented sweets, opprest
With proud unpitying fires.

Such Teares the suffring Rose that's vext
With ungentle flames does shed,
Sweating in a too warm bed.

Say, ye bright brothers,
    The fugitive sons of those fair Eyes
Your fruitfull mothers!
    What make you here? what hopes can tice
You to be born? what cause can borrow
You from those nests of noble sorrow?

Whither away so fast?
    For sure the sordid earth
Your Sweetnes cannot tast
    Nor does the dust deserve your birth.
Sweet, whither hast you then? O say
Why you trip so fast away?

We goe not to seek
    The darlings of Auroras bed,
The rose's modest Cheek
    Nor the violet's humble head.
Though the Feild's eyes too WEEPERS be
Because they want such TEARES as we.

Much lesse mean we to trace
    The Fortune of inferior gemmes,
Preferr'd to some proud face
    Or pertch't upon fear'd Diadems.
Crown'd Heads are toyes. We woe to meet
A worthy object, our Lord's FEET.

TO A YOUNG GENTLE–WOMAN, COUNCEL CONCERNING HER CHOICE

Dear, heavn-designed SOUL!
    Amongst the rest
Of suitors that besiege your Maiden brest,
    Why may not I
    My fortune try
    And venture to speak one good word
Not for my self alas, but for my dearer LORD?
You've seen already, in this lower sphear
Of froth and bubbles, what to look for here.

Say, gentle soul, what can you find
      But painted shapes,
      Peacocks and Apes,
      Illustrious flyes,
    Gilded dunghills, glorious LYES,
      Goodly surmises
      And deep disguises,
    Oathes of water, words of wind?
TRUTH biddes me say, 'tis time you cease to trust
    Your soul to any son of dust.
'Tis time you listen to a braver love,
      Which from above
      Calls you up higher
      And biddes you come
      And choose your roome
    Among his own fair sonnes of fire,
      Where you among
      The golden throng
    That watches at his palace doores
      May passe along
And follow those faire starres of yours;
Starrs much too fair and pure to wait upon
The false smiles of a sublunary sun.
Sweet, let me prophesy that at last 'twill prove
      Your wary love
Layes up his purer and more pretious vowes,
And meanes them for a farre more worthy SPOUSE
    Than this world of Lyes can give ye,
    Ev'n for Him with whom nor cost,
    Nor love, nor labour can be lost;
    Him who never will deceive ye.
    Let not my lord, the Mighty lover
    Of soules, disdain that I discover
      The hidden art
Of his high stratagem to win your heart,
      It was his heavnly art
      Kindly to crosse you
      In your mistaken love,
      That, at the next remove
      Thence he might tosse you
    And strike your troubled heart
Home to himself; to hide it in his brest
    The bright ambrosiall nest,
Of love, of life, and everlasting rest.
      Happy Mistake!
    That thus shall wake

Your wise soul, never to be won
Now with a love below the sun.
Your first choyce failes, O when you choose agen
May it not be amongst the sons of Men.

Abraham Cowley
1618-1667

HYMN, TO LIGHT

First born of *Chaos,* who so fair didst come
    From the old *Negro's* darksome womb!
    Which when it saw the lovely Child,
The melancholly Mass put on kind looks and smil'd.

Thou Tide of Glory which no Rest dost know,
    But ever Ebb, and ever Flow!
    Thou Golden shower of a true *Jove!*
Who does in thee descend, and Heav'n to Earth make Love!

Hail active Natures watchful Life and Health!
    Her Joy, her Ornament, and Wealth!
    Hail to thy Husband Heat, and Thee!
Thou the worlds beauteous Bride, the lusty Bridegroom He!

Say from what Golden Quivers of the Sky,
    Do all thy winged Arrows fly?
    Swiftness and Power by Birth are thine:
From thy Great Sire they came, thy Sire the word Divine.

'Tis, I believe, this Archery to show,
    That so much cost in Colours thou,
    And skill in Painting dost bestow,
Upon thy ancient Arms, the Gawdy Heav'nly Bow.

Swift as light Thoughts their empty Carriere run,
    Thy Race is finisht, when begun,
    Let a Post-Angel start with Thee,
And Thou the Goal of Earth shalt reach as soon as He:

Thou in the Moons bright Chariot proud and gay,
  Dost thy bright wood of Stars survey;
  And all the year dost with thee bring
Of thousand flowry Lights thine own Nocturnal Spring.

Thou *Scythian*-like dost round thy Lands above
  The Suns gilt Tent for ever move,
  And still as thou in pomp dost go
The shining Pageants of the World attend thy show.

Nor amidst all these Triumphs dost thou scorn
  The humble Glow-worms to adorn,
  And with those living spangles gild,
(O Greatness without Pride!) the Bushes of the Field.

Night, and her ugly Subjects thou dost fright,
  And sleep, the lazy Owl of Night;
  Asham'd and fearful to appear
They skreen their horrid shapes with the black Hemisphere.

With 'em there hastes, and wildly takes the Alarm,
  Of painted Dreams, a busie swarm,
  At the first opening of thine eye,
The various Clusters break, the antick Atomes fly.

The guilty Serpents, and obscener Beasts
  Creep conscious to their secret rests:
  Nature to thee does reverence pay,
Ill omens, and ill Sights remove out of thy way.

At thy appearance, Grief it self is said,
  To shake his Wings, and rowse his Head.
  And cloudy care has often took
A gentle beamy Smile reflected from thy Look.

At thy appearance, Fear it self grows bold;
  Thy Sun-shine melts away his Cold.
  Encourag'd at the sight of Thee,
To the cheek Colour comes, and firmness to the knee.

Even Lust the Master of a hardned Face,
  Blushes if thou beest in the place,
  To darkness' Curtains he retires,
In Sympathizing Night he rowls his smoaky Fires.

When, Goddess, thou liftst up thy wakened Head,
    Out of the Mornings purple bed,
    Thy Quire of Birds about thee play,
And all the joyful world salutes the rising day.

The Ghosts, and Monster Spirits, that did presume
    A Bodies Priv'lege to assume,
    Vanish again invisibly,
And Bodies gain agen their visibility.

All the Worlds bravery that delights our Eyes
    Is but thy sev'ral Liveries,
    Thou thy Rich Dy on them bestow'st,
Thy nimble Pencil Paints this Landskape as thou go'st.

A Crimson Garment in the Rose thou wear'st;
    A Crown of studded Gold thou bear'st,
    The Virgin Lillies in their White,
Are clad but with the Lawn of almost Naked Light.

The Violet, springs little Infant, stands,
    Girt in thy purple Swadling-bands:
    On the fair Tulip thou dost dote;
Thou cloath'st it in a gay and party-colour'd Coat.

With Flame condenst thou dost the Jewels fix,
    And solid Colours in it mix:
    Flora her self envyes to see
Flowers fairer then her own, and durable as she.

Ah, Goddess! would thou could'st thy hand withhold,
    And be less Liberall to Gold;
    Didst thou less value to it give,
Of how much care (alas) might'st thou poor Man relieve!

To me the Sun is more delightful far,
    And all fair Dayes much fairer are.
    But few, ah wondrous few there be,
Who do not Gold preferr, O Goddess, ev'n to Thee.

Through the soft wayes of Heaven, and Air, and Sea,
    Which open all their Pores to Thee;
    Like a cleer River thou dost glide,
And with thy Living Stream through the close Channels slide.

But where firm Bodies thy free course oppose,
Gently thy source the Land o'erflowes;
Takes there possession, and does make,
Of Colours mingled, Light, a thick and standing Lake.

But the vast Ocean of unbounded Day
In th' Empyræan Heaven does stay.
Thy Rivers, Lakes, and Springs below
From thence took first their Rise, thither at last must Flow.

John Milton
1608-1674

Milton had the sense of the difference between height and depth in texture more than any other poet, if we except Pope, who arrived at his heights and depths by different means. Milton has not the same feeling as Pope for the difference in texture between apple-cheek and peach-cheek. (I said in my book *Alexander Pope* that his feeling for texture was so phenomenally sensitive that had the verses been transformed into flowers, he could have told lily from rose, buttercup from cowslip, in no matter how starless and moonless a night, merely by touching one petal.) Milton's differences are more enormous, though of a lesser energy. In one passage he can give us the fall from the heights of Heaven into the depths of Hell, and this not only through the powers of inspiration that his genius gives to describe, but through the heaving and falling powers of the actual technical line.

Take Milton's control of alliteration in the hymn to light (*Paradise Lost*).

The use of the aspirates in the first line — "Hail holy light, ofspring of Heav'n first-born" — gives the effect of an immense, once sleeping force, taking again its life-breath, and casting away the dull earth-cloths of its sleep. In the vast swinging movement of "May I express thee unblam'd? Since God is light," there is the impression of the universe surrounded by all the airs and light of eternity. This line, with any other poet, would have fallen into irregularity, owing to the extra syllable coming in the middle of the line — an amazing technical feat. Again, the long *a* in the final, and rising, foot makes the line seem even longer than its eleven syllables — yet there is no irregularity. The prosody of all this huge and primeval passage is unexpected. Milton can actually end two lines with the word "light" without producing any feeling of monotony. In fact, it adds to the beauty.

And how wonderful is the line "Bright effluence of bright essence increate," with the peacefulness created by the balance of "effluence," "essence" — a sound which makes one think of matter resolving itself into spirit.

The song *Nymphs and Shepherds* from *Arcades* is another proof of Milton's supreme power over rhetoric added to imagination — his mastery over sound is controlled and variable, the variation taking many forms, being produced sometimes by heightening the middle of the line by the use of long vowels, or by his miraculous power of spreading a comparatively short line into a succeeding long one, which again shrinks into a short line, so that the sound and movement are like that of waves spreading, advancing, and retreating. Here the longer line seems to bring us round the corner of a sea cave, into the sight of a vast sea horizon. The effect of lengthening and widening is helped, too, in the first three lines, by the drone sound of the *l*'s. In the third line the word "old" prolongs the sound, succeeded by the strange and drowsy sound of "Lycœus" — though the line, in spite of this prolongation of the early part of it, is perfectly and magically balanced.

The song *Sabrina Fair* from *Comus,* another of the miracles of English poetry, is an added example of Milton's power over rhetoric. (Rhetoric is not — or should not be — a foreign body which has somehow transformed the *outside* of the poem; it should be a fire breaking from the poem as from a volcano. Sometimes it is smooth, sometimes it is fierce; but the principle is the same. The idea of "decoration" in poetry is foolish and all wrong. Either the physical beauty has grown from the poem, or it does not exist.)

In *Sabrina Fair* as in *Nymphs and Shepherds,* part of the waterlike beauty and inspiration of the sound is gained by the *l* pattern used throughout the first verse. The effect is also helped by the rich pattern of *s*'s, which in this case seems to give depth to the water.

In the line "On old *Lycœus* or *Cyllene* hoar" (*Nymphs and Shepherds*) the lovely, opening, waving sound, like that of the airs coming from some enchanted sea, produced by the length of "Lycœus" and "Cyllene" explains a little — but how little — of the beauty and strangeness of those two lines. But "By hoary Nereus wrincled look" (*Sabrina Fair*) does not open, it does not wave; it is secretive, like something shining beneath the water in a deep and glittering sea cave.

The sound of the first verse in *Sabrina Fair* varies from sea air to sea air, from wave to wave, as its beauty lengthens and runs back again. This perpetual variation, followed by the sea-cave secretiveness of part of the second verse, varied by the feeling of a wide sea strand, or of waves marching, the result (apart from the magical inspiration of it) to some degree of alliteration, produces its beauty.

Lycidas, though a rhymed poem, begins, strangely enough, with a line to which there is no rhyme, and the sound of which gives the impression of a dark and mournful air: "Yet once more, O ye Laurels, and once more." I cannot recall another rhymed poem which *begins* with an unrhymed line.

This is followed, in the next line, by a dissonance.

There is a strange subtlety about the darkness and depth of the line "Yet once more, O ye Laurels, and once more," followed by the pallor of the last word (the dissonance to "more") of "Ye Myrtles brown, with Ivy never-sear." How subtle is this scheme, wherein those lines which are *not* rhymed immediately are in any case related in sound, changing from light to dark, then lightening again as the rhyme comes.

ON THE MORNING OF CHRISTS NATIVITY

This is the Month, and this the happy morn
Wherin the Son of Heav'ns eternal King,
Of wedded Maid, and Virgin Mother born,
Our great redemption from above did bring;
For so the holy sages once did sing,
   That he our deadly forfeit should release,
And with his Father work us a perpetual peace.

That glorious Form, that Light unsufferable,
And that far-beaming blaze of Majesty,
Wherwith he wont at Heav'ns high Councel-Table,
To sit the midst of Trinal Unity,
He laid aside; and here with us to be,
   Forsook the Courts of everlasting Day,
And chose with us a darksom House of mortal Clay.

Say Heav'nly Muse, shall not thy sacred vein
Afford a present to the Infant God?
Hast thou no verse, no hymn, or solemn strein,
To welcom him to this his new abode,
Now while the Heav'n by the Suns team untrod,
   Hath took no print of the approaching light,
And all the spangled host keep watch in squadrons bright?

See how from far upon the Eastern rode
The Star-led Wisards haste with odours sweet:
O run, prevent them with thy humble ode,
And lay it lowly at his blessed feet;
Have thou the honour first, thy Lord to greet,
   And joyn thy voice unto the Angel Quire,
From out his secret Altar toucht with hallow'd fire.

THE HYMN

It was the Winter wilde,
While the Heav'n-born-childe,
    All meanly wrapt in the rude manger lies;
Nature in awe to him
Had doff't her gawdy trim,
    With her great Master so to sympathize:
It was no season then for her
To wanton with the Sun her lusty Paramour.

Only with speeches fair
She woo's the gentle Air
    To hide her guilty front with innocent Snow,
And on her naked shame,
Pollute with sinfull blame,
    The Saintly Vail of Maiden white to throw,
Confounded, that her Makers eyes
Should look so neer upon her foul deformities.

But he her fears to cease,
Sent down the meek-eyd Peace,
    She crown'd with Olive green, came softly sliding
Down through the turning sphear
His ready Harbinger,
    With Turtle wing the amorous clouds dividing,
And waving wide her mirtle wand,
She strikes a universall Peace through Sea and Land.

No War, or Battails sound
Was heard the World around,
    The idle spear and shield were high up hung;
The hooked Chariot stood
Unstain'd with hostile blood,
    The Trumpet spake not to the armed throng,
And Kings sate still with awfull eye,
As if they surely knew their sovran Lord was by.

But peacefull was the night
Wherin the Prince of Light
    His raign of peace upon the earth began:
The Windes with wonder whist,
Smoothly the waters kist,
    Whispering new joyes to the milde Ocean,
Who now hath quite forgot to rave,
While Birds of Calm sit brooding on the charmed wave.

The Stars with deep amaze
Stand fixt in stedfast gaze,
   Bending one way their pretious influence,
And will not take their flight,
For all the morning light,
   Or *Lucifer* that often warn'd them thence;
But in their glimmering Orbs did glow,
Untill their Lord himself bespake, and bid them go.

And though the shady gloom
Had given day her room,
   The Sun himself with-held his wonted speed,
And hid his head for shame,
As his inferiour flame,
   The new-enlightn'd world no more should need;
He saw a greater Sun appear
Then his bright Throne, or burning Axletree could bear.

The Shepherds on the Lawn,
Or e're the point of dawn,
   Sate simply chatting in a rustick row;
Full little thought they than,
That the mighty *Pan*
   Was kindly com to live with them below;
Perhaps their loves, or else their sheep,
Was all that did their silly thoughts so busie keep.

When such musick sweet
Their hearts and ears did greet,
   As never was by mortall finger strook,
Divinely-warbled voice
Answering the stringed noise,
   As all their souls in blisfull rapture took:
The Air such pleasure loth to lose,
With thousand echo's still prolongs each heav'nly close.

Nature that heard such sound
Beneath the hollow round
   Of *Cynthia's* seat, the Airy region thrilling,
Now was almost won
To think her part was done,
   And that her raign had here its last fulfilling;
She knew such harmony alone
Could hold all Heav'n and Earth in happier union.

At last surrounds their sight
A Globe of circular light,
   That with long beams the shame-fac't night array'd,
The helmed Cherubim
And sworded Seraphim,
   Are seen in glittering ranks with wings displaid,
Harping in loud and solemn quire,
With unexpressive notes to Heav'ns new-born Heir.

Such Musick (as 'tis said)
Before was never made,
   But when of old the sons of morning sung,
While the Creator great
His constellations set,
   And the well-ballanc't world on hinges hung,
And cast the dark foundations deep,
And bid the weltring waves their oozy channel keep.

Ring out ye Crystall sphears,
Once bless our human ears,
   (If ye have power to touch our senses so)
And let your silver chime
Move in melodious time;
   And let the Base of Heav'ns deep Organ blow,
And with your ninefold harmony
Make up full consort to th' Angelike symphony.

For if such holy Song
Enwrap our fancy long,
   Time will run back, and fetch the age of gold,
And speckl'd vanity
Will sicken soon and die,
   And leprous sin will melt from earthly mould,
And Hell it self will pass away,
And leave her dolorous mansions to the peering day.

Yea Truth, and Justice then
Will down return to men,
   Th' enameld *Arras* of the Rain-bow wearing,
And Mercy set between,
Thron'd in Celestiall sheen,
   With radiant feet the tissued clouds down stearing,
And Heav'n as at som festivall,
Will open wide the Gates of her high Palace Hall.

But wisest Fate sayes no,
This must not yet be so,
   The Babe lies yet in smiling Infancy,
That on the bitter cross
Must redeem our loss;
   So both himself and us to glorifie:
Yet first to those ychain'd in sleep,
The wakeful trump of doom must thunder through the deep.

With such a horrid clang
As on mount *Sinai* rang
   While the red fire, and smouldring clouds out brake:
The aged Earth agast
With terrour of that blast,
   Shall from the surface to the center shake;
When at the worlds last session,
The dreadfull Judge in middle Air shall spread his throne.

And then at last our bliss
Full and perfect is,
   But now begins; for from this happy day
Th' old Dragon under ground
In straiter limits bound,
   Not half so far casts his usurped sway,
And wrath to see his Kingdom fail,
Swindges the scaly Horrour of his foulded tail.

The Oracles are dumm,
No voice or hideous humm
   Runs through the arched roof in words deceiving.
Apollo from his shrine
Can no more divine,
   With hollow shreik the steep of *Delphos* leaving.
No nightly trance, or breathed spell,
Inspire's the pale-ey'd Priest from the prophetic cell.

The lonely mountains o're,
And the resounding shore,
   A voice of weeping heard, and loud lament;
From haunted spring, and dale
Edg'd with poplar pale,
   The parting Genius is with sighing sent,
With flowre-inwov'n tresses torn
The Nimphs in twilight shade of tangled thickets mourn.

In consecrated Earth,
And on the holy Hearth,
    The *Lars*, and *Lemures* moan with midnight plaint,
In Urns, and Altars round,
A drear, and dying sound
    Affrights the *Flamins* at their service quaint;
And the chill Marble seems to sweat,
While each peculiar power forgoes his wonted seat.

Peor, and *Baalim*,
Forsake their Temples dim,
    With that twise-batter'd god of *Palestine*,
And mooned *Ashtaroth*,
Heav'ns Queen and Mother both,
    Now sits not girt with Tapers holy shine,
The Libyc *Hammon* shrinks his horn,
In vain the *Tyrian* Maids their wounded *Thamuz* mourn.

And sullen *Moloch* fled,
Hath left in shadows dred,
    His burning Idol all of blackest hue,
In vain with Cymbals ring,
They call the grisly king,
    In dismall dance about the furnace blue;
The brutish gods of *Nile* as fast,
Isis and *Orus*, and the Dog *Anubis* hast.

Nor is *Osiris* seen
In *Memphian* Grove, or Green,
    Trampling the unshowr'd Grasse with lowings loud:
Nor can he be at rest
Within his sacred chest,
    Naught but profoundest Hell can be his shroud;
In vain with Timbrel'd Anthems dark
The sable-stoled Sorcerers bear his worshipt Ark.

He feels from *Juda's* Land
The dredded Infants hand
    The rayes of *Bethlehem* blind his dusky eyn;
Nor all the gods beside,
Longer dare abide,
    Not *Typhon* huge ending in snaky twine:
Our Babe to shew his Godhead true,
Can in his swadling hands controul the damned crew.

So when the Sun in bed,
Curtain'd with cloudy red,
 Pillows his chin upon an Orient wave,
The flocking shadows pale,
Troop to th ' infernall jail,
 Each fetter'd Ghost slips to his severall grave,
And the yellow-skirted *Fayes,*
Fly after the Night-steeds, leaving their Moon-lov'd maze.

But see the Virgin blest,
Hath laid her Babe to rest.
 Time is our tedious Song should here have ending,
Heav'ns youngest teemed Star,
Hath fixt her polisht Car,
 Her sleeping Lord with Handmaid Lamp attending:
And all about the Courtly Stable,
Bright-harnest Angels sit in order serviceable.

LYCIDAS

Yet once more, O ye Laurels, and once more
Ye Myrtles brown, with Ivy never-sear,
I come to pluck your Berries harsh and crude,
And with forc'd fingers rude,
Shatter your leaves before the mellowing year.
Bitter constraint, and sad occasion dear,
Compels me to disturb your season due:
For *Lycidas* is dead, dead ere his prime
Young *Lycidas,* and hath not left his peer:
Who would not sing for *Lycidas?* he knew
Himself to sing, and build the lofty rhyme.
He must not flote upon his watry bear
Unwept, and welter to the parching wind,
Without the meed of some melodious tear.
 Begin then, Sisters of the sacred well,
That from beneath the seat of *Jove* doth spring,
Begin, and somewhat loudly sweep the string.
Hence with denial vain, and coy excuse,
So may some gentle Muse
With lucky words favour my destin'd Urn,
And as he passes turn,
And bid fair peace be to my sable shrowd.
For we were nurst upon the self-same hill,
Fed the same flock, by fountain, shade, and rill.
 Together both, ere the high Lawns appear'd

Under the opening eye-lids of the morn,
We drove a field, and both together heard
What time the Gray-fly winds her sultry horn,
Batt'ning our flocks with the fresh dews of night,
Oft till the Star that rose, at Ev'ning, bright
Toward Heav'ns descent had slop'd his westering wheel.
Mean while the Rural ditties were not mute,
Temper'd to th' Oaten Flute;
Rough *Satyrs* danc'd, and *Fauns* with clov'n heel,
From the glad sound would not be absent long,
And old *Damœtus* lov'd to hear our song.

   But O the heavy change, now thou art gon,
Now thou art gon, and never must return!
Thee Shepherd, thee the Woods, and desert Caves,
With wilde Thyme and the gadding Vine o'regrown,
And all their echoes mourn.
The Willows, and the Hazle Copses green,
Shall now no more be seen,
Fanning their joyous Leaves to thy soft layes.
As killing as the Canker to the Rose,
Or Taint-worm to the weanling Herds that graze,
Or Frost to Flowers, that their gay wardrop wear,
When first the White thorn blows;
Such, *Lycidas,* thy loss to Shepherds ear.

   Where were ye Nymphs when the remorseless deep
Clos'd o're the head of your lov'd *Lycidas?*
For neither were ye playing on the steep,
Where your old *Bards,* the famous *Druids* ly,
Nor on the shaggy top of *Mona* high,
Nor yet where *Deva* spreads her wisard stream:
Ay me, I fondly dream!
Had ye bin there — for what could that have done?
What could the Muse her self that *Orpheus* bore,
The Muse her self, for her inchanting son
Whom Universal nature did lament,
When by the rout that made the hideous roar,
His goary visage down the stream was sent,
Down the swift *Hebrus* to the *Lesbian* shore.

   Alas! What boots it with uncessant care
To tend the homely slighted Shepherds trade,
And strictly meditate the thankles Muse!
Were it not better done as others use,
To sport with *Amaryllis* in the shade,
Or with the tangles of *Neœra's* hair?
Fame is the spur that the clear spirit doth raise
(That last infirmity of Noble mind)

To scorn delights, and live laborious dayes;
But the fair Guerdon when we hope to find,
And think to burst out into sudden blaze,
Comes the blind *Fury* with th' abhorred shears,
And slits the thin spun life. But not the praise,
Phœbus repli'd, and touch'd my trembling ears;
Fame is no plant that grows on mortal soil,
Nor in the glistering foil
Set off to th' world, nor in broad rumour lies,
But lives and spreds aloft by those pure eyes,
And perfet witnes of all judging *Jove*;
As he pronounces lastly on each deed,
Of so much fame in Heav'n except thy meed.

  O Fountain *Arethuse,* and thou honour'd floud,
Smooth-sliding *Mincius,* crown'd with vocall reeds,
That strain I heard was of a higher mood:
But now my Oate proceeds,
And listens to the Herald of the Sea
That came in *Neptune's* plea:
He ask'd the Waves, and ask'd the Fellon winds,
What hard mishap hath doom'd this gentle swain?
And question'd every gust of rugged wings
That blows from off each beaked Promontory;
They knew not of his story,
And sage *Hippotades* their answer brings,
That not a blast was from his dungeon stray'd,
The Ayr was calm, and on the level brine,
Sleek *Panope* with all her sisters play'd.
It was that fatall and perfidious Bark
Built in th' eclipse, and rigg'd with curses dark,
That sunk so low that sacred head of thine.

  Next *Camus,* reverend Sire, went footing slow,
His Mantle hairy, and his Bonnet sedge,
Inwrought with figures dim, and on the edge
Like to that sanguine flower inscrib'd with woe.
Ah; Who hath reft (quoth he) my dearest pledge?
Last came, and last did go,
The Pilot of the *Galilean* lake,
Two massy Keyes he bore of metals twain,
(The Golden opes, the Iron shuts amain)
He shook his Miter'd locks, and stern bespake,
How well could I have spar'd for thee, young swain,
Anow of such as for their bellies sake,
Creep and intrude, and climb into the fold?
Of other care they little reck'ning make,
Then how to scramble at the shearers feast,

And shove away the worthy bidden guest.
Blind mouthes! that scare themselves know how to hold
A Sheep-hook, or have learn'd ought else the least
That to the faithfull Herdmans art belongs!
What recks it them? What need they? They are sped;
And when they list, their lean and flashy songs
Grate on their scrannel Pipes of wretched straw,
The hungry Sheep look up, and are not fed,
But swoln with wind, and the rank mist they draw,
Rot inwardly, and foul contagion spread:
Besides what the grim Woolf with privy paw
Daily devours apace, and nothing sed,
But that two-handed engine at the door,
Stands ready to smite once, and smite no more.
  Return *Alpheus*, the dread voice is past,
That shrunk thy streams; Return *Sicilian* Muse,
And call the Vales, and bid them hither cast
Their Bels, and Flourets of a thousand hues.
Ye valleys low where the milde whispers use,
Of shades and wanton winds, and gushing brooks
On whose fresh lap the swart Star sparely looks,
Throw hither all your quaint enameld eyes,
That on the green terf suck the honied showres,
And purple all the ground with vernal flowres.
Bring the rathe Primrose that forsaken dies.
The tufted Crow-toe, and pale Gessamine,
The white Pink, and the Pansie freakt with jeat,
The glowing Violet.
The Musk-rose, and the well attir'd Woodbine.
With Cowslips wan that hang the pensive hed,
And every flower that sad embroidery wears:
Bid *Amaranthus* all his beauty shed,
And Daffadillies fill their cups with tears,
To strew the Laureat Herse where *Lycid* lies.
For so to interpose a little ease,
Let our frail thoughts dally with false surmise.
Ay me! Whilst thee the shores, and sounding Seas
Wash far away, where ere thy bones are hurld,
Whether beyond the stormy *Hebrides*,
Where thou perhaps under the whelming tide
Visit'st the bottom of the monstrous world;
Or whether thou to our moist vows deny'd,
Sleep'st by the fable of *Bellerus* old,
Where the great vision of the guarded Mount
Looks toward *Namancos* and *Bayona's* hold;
Look homeward Angel now, and melt with ruth.

And, O ye *Dolphins,* waft the haples youth.
   Weep no more, woful Shepherds weep no more,
For *Lycidas* your sorrow is not dead,
Sunk though he be beneath the watry floar;
So sinks the day-star in the Ocean bed,
And yet anon repairs his drooping head,
And tricks his beams, and with new spangled Ore,
Flames in the forehead of the morning sky:
So *Lycidas* sunk low, but mounted high,
Through the dear might of him that walk'd the waves
Where other groves, and other streams along,
With *Nectar* pure his oozy Lock's he laves,
And hears the unexpressive nuptiall Song,
In the blest Kingdoms meek of joy and love.
There entertain him all the Saints above,
In solemn troops, and sweet Societies
That sing, and singing in their glory move,
And wipe the tears for ever from his eyes.
Now *Lycidas* the Shepherds weep no more;
Hence forth thou art the Genius of the shore,
In thy large recompense, and shalt be good
To all that wander in that perilous flood.
   Thus sang the uncouth Swain to th' Okes and rills,
While the still morn went out with Sandals gray,
He touch'd the tender stops of various Quills,
With eager thought warbling his *Dorick* lay:
And now the Sun had stretch'd out all the hills,
And now was dropt into the Western bay;
At last he rose, and twitch'd his Mantle blew:
To morrow to fresh Woods, and Pastures new.

Songs from ARCADES

O'RE THE SMOOTH ENAMELD GREEN

    O're the smooth enameld green
    Where no print of step hath been,
      Follow me as I sing,
      And touch the warbled string.
    Under the shady roof
    Of branching Elm Star-proof,
      Follow me,
    I will bring you where she sits
    Clad in splendor as befits
      Her deity.
    Such a rural Queen
    All *Arcadia* hath not seen.

NYMPHS AND SHEPHERDS DANCE NO MORE

Nymphs and Shepherds dance no more
    By sandy *Ladons* Lillied banks.
On old *Lycæus* or *Cyllene* hoar,
    Trip no more in twilight ranks,
Though *Erymanth* your loss deplore,
    A better soyl shall give ye thanks.
From the stony *Mœnalus*,
Bring your Flocks, and live with us,
Here ye shall have greater grace,
To serve the Lady of this place.
        Though *Syrinx* your *Pans* Mistres were
        Yet *Syrinx* well might wait on her.
            Such a rural Queen
        All *Arcadia* hath not seen.

From COMUS

SWEET ECHO

Sweet Echo, sweetest Nymph that liv'st unseen
        Within thy airy shell
        By slow Meander's margent green,
And in the violet imbroider'd vale
    Where the love-lorn Nightingale
Nightly to thee her sad Song mourneth well.
Canst thou not tell me of a gentle Pair
        That likest thy Narcissus are?
            O if thou have
        Hid them in some flowry Cave,
            Tell me but where
Sweet Queen of Parly, Daughter of the Sphear,
So maist thou be translated to the skies,
And give resounding grace to all Heav'ns Harmonies.

COMUS. Can any mortal mixture of Earths mould
    Breath such Divine inchanting ravishment?
    Sure something holy lodges in that brest,
    And with these raptures moves the vocal air
    To testifie his hidd'n residence;
    How sweetly did they float upon the wings
    Of silence, through the empty-vaulted night
    At every fall smoothing the Raven doune
    Of darknes till it smil'd: I have oft heard

My mother *Circe* with the Sirens three,
Amid'st the flowry-kirtl'd *Naiades*
Culling their Potent hearbs, and balefull drugs,
Who as they sung, would take the prison'd soul,
And lap it in *Elysium, Scylla* wept,
And chid her barking waves into attention,
And fell *Charybdis* murmur'd soft applause:
Yet they in pleasing slumber lull'd the sense,
And in sweet madnes rob'd it of it self,
But such a sacred, and home-felt delight,
Such sober certainty of waking bliss
I never heard till now. Ile speak to her
And she shall be my Queen. Hail forren wonder
Whom certain these rough shades did never breed
Unlesse the Goddes that in rurall shrine
Dwell'st here with *Pan,* or *Silvan,* by blest Song
Forbidding every bleak unkindly Fog
To touch the prosperous growth of this tall Wood.

O FOOLISHNES OF MEN

COMUS. O foolishnes of men! that lend their ears
To those budge doctors of the *Stoick* Furr,
And fetch their precepts from the *Cynick* Tub,
Praising the lean and sallow Abstinence.
Wherefore did Nature powre her bounties forth,
With such a full and unwithdrawing hand,
Covering the earth with odours, fruits, and flocks,
Thronging the Seas with spawn innumerable,
But all to please, and sate the curious taste?
And set to work millions of spinning Worms,
That in their green shops weave the smooth-hair'd silk
To deck her Sons, and that no corner might
Be vacant of her plenty, in her own loyns
She hutch't th' all-worshipt ore, and precious gems
To store her children with; if all the world
Should in a pet of temperance feed on Pulse,
Drink the clear stream, and nothing wear but Freize,
Th' all-giver would be unthank't, would be unprais'd,
Not half his riches known, and yet despis'd,
And we should serve him as a grudging master,
As a penurious niggard of his wealth,
And live like Natures bastards, not her sons,
Who would be quite surcharged with her own weight,
And strangl'd with her waste fertility;
Th' earth cumber'd, and the wing'd air dark't with plumes,

The herds would over-multitude their Lords,
The Sea o'refraught would swell, and th' unsought diamonds
Would so emblaze the forhead of the Deep,
And so bestudd with Stars, that they below
Would grow inur'd to light, and come at last
To gaze upon the Sun with shameless brows.
List Lady be not coy, and be not cosen'd
With that same vaunted name Virginity,
Beauty is natures coyn, must not be hoorded,
But must be currant, and the good thereof
Consists in mutual and partak'n bliss,
Unsavoury in th' injoyment of it self
If you let slip time, like a neglected rose
It withers on the stalk with languish't head.
Beauty is natures brag, and must be shown
In courts, at feasts, and high solemnities
Where most may wonder at the workmanship;
It is for homely features to keep home,
They had their name thence; course complexions
And cheeks of sorry grain will serve to ply
The sampler, and to teize the huswifes wooll.
What need a vermeil-tinctured lip for that
Love-darting eyes, or tresses like the Morn?
There was another meaning in these gifts,
Think what, and be adviz'd, you are but young yet.

SABRINA FAIR

Sabrina fair
      Listen where thou art sitting
Under the glassie, cool, translucent wave,
      In twisted braids of Lillies knitting
The loose train of thy amber-dropping hair,
      Listen for dear honour's sake,
      Goddess of the silver lake,
            Listen and save.

Listen and appear to us
In name of great *Oceanus*,
By the earth-shaking *Neptune's* mace,
And *Tethys* grave majestick pace,
By hoary *Nereus* wrincled look,
And the *Carpathian* wisards hook,
By scaly *Tritons* winding shell,
And old sooth-saying *Glaucus* spell,

By *Leucothea's* lovely hands,
And her son that rules the strands,
By *Thetis* tinsel-slipper'd feet,
And the Songs of *Sirens* sweet,
By dead *Parthenope's* dear tomb,
And fair *Ligea's* golden comb,
Wherwith she sits on diamond rocks
Sleeking her soft alluring locks,
By all the *Nymphs* that nightly dance
Upon thy streams with wily glance,
Rise, rise, and heave thy rosie head
From thy coral-pav'n bed,
And bridle in thy headlong wave,
Till thou our summons answered have.
                Listen and save.

Sabrina rises, attended by water-Nymphes, and sings.

    By the rushy-fringed bank,
Where grows the Willow and the Osier dank,
        My sliding Chariot stayes,
Thick set with Agat, and the azurn sheen
    Of Turkis blew, and Emrauld green
        That in the channell strayes,
    Whilst from off the waters fleet
    Thus I set my printless feet
    O're the Cowslips Velvet head,
        That bends not as I tread,
    Gentle swain at thy request
            I am here.

SPIRIT. Goddess dear
    We implore thy powerful hand
    To undo the charmed band
    Of true Virgin here distrest,
    Through the force, and through the wile
    Of unblest inchanter vile.

SABRINA. Shepherd 'tis my office best
    To help insnared chastity;
    Brightest Lady look on me,
    Thus I sprinkle on thy brest
    Drops that from my fountain pure,
    I have kept of pretious cure,
    Thrice upon thy fingers tip,
    Thrice upon thy rubied lip,

Next this marble venom'd seat
Smear'd with gumms of glutenous heat
I touch with chaste palms moist and cold,
Now the spell hath lost his hold;
And I must haste ere morning hour
To wait in *Amphitrite's* bowr.

TO THE OCEAN NOW I FLY

The dances ended, the Spirit Epiloguizes.

SPIRIT. To the Ocean now I fly,
  And those happy climes that ly
  Where day never shuts his eye,
  Up in the broad fields of the sky:
  There I suck the liquid ayr
  All amidst the Gardens fair
  Of *Hesperus,* and his daughters three
  That sing about the golden tree:
  Along the crisped shades and bowres
  Revels the spruce and jocond Spring,
  The Graces, and the rosie-boosom'd Howres,
  Thither all their bounties bring,
  That there eternal Summer dwels,
  And West winds, with musky wing
  About the cedar'n alleys fling
  Nard, and *Cassia's* balmy smels.
  Iris there with humid bow,
  Waters the odorous banks that blow
  Flowers of more mingled hew
  Then her purfl'd scarf can shew,
  And drenches with *Elysian* dew
  (List mortals, if your ears be true)
  Beds of *Hyacinth,* and roses
  Where young *Adonis* oft reposes,
  Waxing well of his deep wound
  In slumber soft, and on the ground
  Sadly sits th' *Assyrian* Queen;
  But far above in spangled sheen
  Celestial *Cupid* her fam'd son advanc't,
  Holds his dear *Psyche* sweet intranc't
  After her wandring labours long,
  Till free consent the gods among
  Make her his eternal Bride,
  And from her fair unspotted side

Two blissful twins are to be born,
Youth and Joy; so *Jove* hath sworn.
  But now my task is smoothly done,
I can fly, or I can run
Quickly to the green earths end,
Where the bow'd welkin slow doth bend,
And from thence can soar as soon
To the corners of the Moon.
  Mortals that would follow me,
Love vertue, she alone is free,
She can teach ye how to clime
Higher then the Spheary chime;
Or if Vertue feeble were,
Heav'n it self would stoop to her.

From PARADISE LOST

BOOK II

  High on a Throne of Royal State, which far
Outshon the wealth of *Ormus* and of *Ind,*
Or where the gorgeous East with richest hand
Showrs on her Kings *Barbaric* Pearl and Gold,
Satan exalted sat, by merit rais'd
To that bad eminence; and from despair
Thus high uplifted beyond hope, aspires
Beyond thus high, insatiate to pursue
Vain Warr with Heav'n, and by success untaught
His proud imaginations thus displaid.
  Powers and Dominions, Deities of Heav'n,
For since no deep within her gulf can hold
Immortal vigor, though opprest and fall'n,
I give not Heav'n for lost. From this descent
Celestial vertues rising, will appear
More glorious and more dread then from no fall,
And trust themselves to fear no second fate:
Mee though just right, and the fixt Laws of Heav'n
Did first create your Leader, next, free choice,
With what besides, in Counsel or in Fight,
Hath bin achievd of merit, yet this loss
Thus farr at least recover'd, hath much more
Establisht in a safe unenvied Throne
Yielded with full consent. The happier state
In Heav'n, which follows dignity, might draw
Envy from each inferior; but who here
Will envy whom the highest place exposes

Formost to stand against the Thunderers aime
Your bulwark, and condemns to greatest share
Of endless pain? where there is then no good
For which to strive, no strife can grow up there
From Faction; for none sure will claim in hell
Precedence, none, whose portion is so small
Of present pain, that with ambitious mind
Will covet more. With this advantage then
To union, and firm Faith, and firm accord,
More then can be in Heav'n, we now return
To claim our just inheritance of old,
Surer to prosper then prosperity
Could have assur'd us; and by what best way,
Whether of open Warr or covert guile,
We now debate; who can advise, may speak.
   He ceas'd, and next him *Moloc,* Scepter'd **King**
Stood up, the strongest and the fiercest Spirit
That fought in Heav'n; now fiercer by despair:
His trust was with th' Eternal to be deem'd
Equal in strength, and rather then be less
Car'd not to be at all; with that care lost
Went all his fear: of God, or Hell, or worse
He reckd not, and these words thereafter spake.
   My sentence is for open Warr: Of Wiles,
More unexpert, I boast not: them let those
Contrive who need, or when they need, not now.
For while they sit contriving, shall the rest,
Millions that stand in Arms, and longing wait
The Signal to ascend, sit lingring here
Heav'ns fugitives, and for thir dwelling place
Accept this dark opprobrious Den of shame,
The Prison of his Tyranny who Reigns
By our delay? no, let us rather choose
Arm'd with Hell flames and fury all at once
O're Heav'ns high Towrs to force resistless way,
Turning our Tortures into horrid Arms
Against the Torturer; when to meet the noise
Of his Almighty Engin he shall hear
Infernal Thunder, and for Lightning see
Black fire and horror shot with equal rage
Among his Angels; and his Throne it self
Mixt with *Tartarean* Sulphur, and strange fire,
His own invented Torments. But perhaps
The way seems difficult and steep to scale
With upright wing against a higher foe.
Let such bethink them, if the sleepy drench

Of that forgetful Lake benumme not still,
That in our proper motion we ascend
Up to our native seat: descent and fall
To us is adverse. Who but felt of late
When the fierce Foe hung on our brok'n Rear
Insulting, and pursu'd us through the Deep,
With what compulsion and laborious flight
We sunk thus low? Th' ascent is easie then;
Th' event is fear'd; should we again provoke
Our stronger, some worse way his wrath may find
To our destruction: if there be in Hell
Fear to be worse destroy'd: what can be worse
Then to dwell here, driv'n out from bliss, condemn'd
In this abhorred deep to utter woe;
Where pain of unextinguishable fire
Must exercise us without hope of end
The Vassals of his anger, when the Scourge
Inexorably, and the torturing houre
Calls us to Penance? More destroy'd then thus
We should be quite abolisht and expire.
What fear we then? what doubt we to incense
His utmost ire? which to the highth enrag'd,
Will either quite consume us, and reduce
To nothing this essential, happier farr
Then miserable to have eternal being:
Or if our substance be indeed Divine,
And cannot cease to be, we are at worst
On this side nothing; and by proof we feel
Our power sufficient to disturb his Heav'n,
And with perpetual inrodes to Allarme,
Though inaccessible, his fatal Throne:
Which if not Victory is yet Revenge. . . .

    The *Stygian* Councel thus dissolv'd; and forth
In order came the grand infernal Peers,
Midst came thir mighty Paramount, and seemd
Alone th' Antagonist of Heav'n, nor less
Then Hells dread Emperour with pomp Supream,
And God-like imitated State; him round
A Globe of fierie Seraphim inclos'd
With bright imblazonrie, and horrent Arms.
Then of thir Session ended they bid cry
With Trumpets regal sound the great result:
Toward the four winds four speedy Cherubim
Put to thir mouths the sounding Alchymie
By Haralds voice explain'd: the hollow Abyss

Heard farr and wide, and all the host of Hell
With deafning shout, return'd them loud acclaim.
Thence more at ease thir minds and somwhat rais'd
By false presumptuous hope, the ranged powers
Disband, and wandring, each his several way
Pursues, as inclination or sad choice
Leads him perplext, where he may likeliest find
Truce to his restless thoughts, and entertain
The irksome hours, till his great Chief return.
Part on the Plain, or in the Air sublime
Upon the wing, or in swift race contend,
As at th' Olympian Games or *Pythian* fields;
Part curb thir fierie Steeds, or shun the Goal
With rapid wheels, or fronted Brigads form.
As when to warn proud Cities warr appears
Wag'd in the troubl'd Skie, and Armies rush
To Battel in the Clouds, before each Van
Pric forth the Aerie Knights, and couch thir spears
Till thickest Legions close; with feats of Arms
From either end of Heav'n the welkin burns.
Others with vast *Typhœan* rage more fell
Rend up both Rocks and Hills, and ride the Air
In whirlwind; Hell scarce holds the wilde uproar.
As when *Alcides* from *Oechalia* Crown'd
With conquest, felt th' envenom'd robe, and tore
Through pain up by the roots *Thessalian* Pines,
And *Lichas* from the top of *Oeta* threw
Into th' *Euboic* Sea. Others more milde,
Retreated in a silent valley, sing
With notes Angelical to many a Harp
Thir own Heroic deeds and hapless fall
By doom of Battel; and complain that Fate
Free Vertue should enthrall to Force or Chance.
Thir song was partial, but the harmony
(What could it less when Spirits immortal sing?)
Suspended Hell, and took with ravishment
The thronging audience. In discourse more sweet
(For Eloquence the Soul, Song charms the Sense,)
Others apart sat on a Hill retir'd,
In thoughts more elevate, and reason'd high
Of Providence, Foreknowledge, Will, and Fate,
Fixt Fate, free will, foreknowledge absolute,
And found no end, in wandring mazes lost.
Of good and evil much they argu'd then,
Of happiness and final misery,
Passion and Apathie, and glory and shame,

Vain wisdom all, and false Philosophie:
Yet with a pleasing sorcerie could charm
Pain for a while or anguish, and excite
Fallacious hope, or arm th' obdured brest
With stubborn patience as with triple steel.
Another part in Squadrons and gross Bands
On bold adventure to discover wide
The dismal World, if any Clime perhaps
Might yeild them easier habitation, bend
Four ways thir flying March, along the Banks
Of four infernal Rivers that disgorge
Into the burning Lake thir baleful streams;
Abhorred *Styx* the flood of deadly hate,
Sad *Acheron* of Sorrow, black and deep;
Cocytus, nam'd of lamentation loud
Heard on the ruful stream; fierce *Phlegeton*
Whose waves of torrent fire inflame with rage.
Farr off from these a slow and silent stream,
Lethe the River of Oblivion roules
Her watrie Labyrinth, whereof who drinks,
Forthwith his former state and being forgets,
Forgets both joy and grief, pleasure and pain.
Beyond this flood a frozen Continent
Lies dark and wilde, beat with perpetual storms
Of Whirlwind and dire Hail, which on firm land
Thaws not, but gathers heap, and ruin seems
Of ancient pile; all else deep snow and ice,
A gulf profound as that *Serbonian* Bog
Betwixt *Damiata* and mount *Casius* old,
Where Armies whole have sunk: the parching Air
Burns frore, and cold performs th' effect of Fire.
Thither by harpy-footed Furies hail'd,
At certain revolutions all the damn'd
Are brought: and feel by turns the bitter change
Of fierce extreams, extreams by change more fierce,
From Beds of raging Fire to starve in Ice
Thir soft Ethereal warmth, and there to pine
Immovable, infixt, and frozen round,
Periods of time, thence hurried back to fire.
They ferry over this *Lethean* Sound
Both to and fro, thir sorrow to augment,
And wish and struggle, as they pass, to reach
The tempting stream, with one small drop to loose
In sweet forgetfulness all pain and woe,
All in one moment, and so neer the brink;
But fate withstands, and to oppose th' attempt
Medusa with *Gorgonian* terror guards

The Ford, and of it self the water flies
All taste of living wight, as once it fled
The lip of *Tantalus*. Thus roving on
In confus'd march forlorn, th' adventrous Bands
With shuddring horror pale, and eyes agast
View'd first thir lamentable lot, and found
No rest: through many a dark and drearie Vaile
They pass'd, and many a Region dolorous,
O're many a Frozen, many a Fierie Alpe,
Rocks, Caves, Lakes, Fens, Bogs, Dens, and shades of
    death,
A Universe of death, which God by curse
Created evil, for evil only good,
Where all life dies, death lives, and nature breeds,
Perverse, all monstrous, all prodigious things.
Abominable, inutterable, and worse
Then Fables yet have feign'd, or fear conceiv'd,
Gorgons and *Hydra's*, and *Chimera's* dire.

BOOK III

Hail holy light, ofspring of Heav'n first-born,
Or of th' Eternal Coeternal beam,
May I express thee unblam'd? since God is light,
And never but in unapproached light
Dwelt from Eternitie, dwelt then in thee,
Bright effluence of bright essence increate.
Or hear'st thou rather pure Ethereal stream,
Whose Fountain who shall tell? before the Sun,
Before the Heavens thou wert, and at the voice
Of God, as with a Mantle didst invest
The rising world of waters dark and deep,
Won from the void and formless infinite.
Thee I revisit now with bolder wing,
Escap't the *Stygian* Pool, though long detain'd
In that obscure sojourn, while in my flight
Through utter and through middle darkness borne
With other notes then to th' *Orphean* Lyre
I sung of *Chaos* and *Eternal Night*,
Taught by the Heav'nly Muse to venture down
The dark descent, and up to reascend,
Though hard and rare: thee I revisit safe,
And feel thy sovran vital Lamp; but thou
Revisit'st not these eyes, that rowle in vain
To find thy piercing ray, and find no dawn;
So thick a drop serene hath quencht thir Orbs,

Or dim suffusion veild. Yet not the more
Cease I to wander where the Muses haunt
Cleer Spring, or shadie Grove, or Sunnie Hill,
Smit with the love of sacred song; but chief
Thee *Sion* and the flowrie Brooks beneath
That wash thy hallowd feet, and warbling flow,
Nightly I visit: nor somtimes forget
Those other two equal'd with me in Fate,
So were I equal'd with them in renown,
Blind *Thamyris* and blind *Mæonides,*
And *Tiresias* and *Phineus* Prophets old.
Then feed on thoughts, that voluntarie move
Harmonious numbers; as the wakeful Bird
Sings darkling, and in shadiest Covert hid
Tunes her nocturnal Note. Thus with the Year
Seasons return, but not to me returns
Day, or the sweet approach of Ev'n or Morn,
Or sight of vernal bloom, or Summers Rose,
Or flocks, or herds, or human face divine;
But cloud in stead, and ever-during dark
Surrounds me, from the chearful waies of men
Cut off, and for the Book of knowledge fair
Presented with a Universal blanc
Of Natures works to mee expung'd and ras'd,
And wisdome at one entrance quite shut out.
So much the rather thou Celestial light
Shine inward, and the mind through all her powers
Irradiate, there plant eyes, all mist from thence
Purge and disperse, that I may see and tell
Of things invisible to mortal sight.

From SAMSON AGONISTES

SAMSON. A little onward lend thy guiding hand
    To these dark steps, a little further on;
    For yonder bank hath choice of Sun or shade,
    There I am wont to sit, when any chance
    Relieves me from my task of servile toyl,
    Daily in the common Prison else enjoyn'd me,
    Where I a Prisoner chain'd, scarce freely draw
    The air imprison'd also, close and damp,
    Unwholsom draught: but here I feel amends,
    The breath of Heav'n fresh-blowing, pure and sweet,
    With day-spring born; here leave me to respire.
    This day a solemn Feast the people hold

To *Dagon* thir Sea-Idol, and forbid
Laborious works, unwillingly this rest
Thir Superstition yields me; hence with leave
Retiring from the popular noise, I seek
This unfrequented place to find some ease,
Ease to the body some, none to the mind
From restless thoughts, that like a deadly swarm
Of Hornets arm'd, no sooner found alone,
But rush upon me thronging, and present
Times past, what once I was, and what am now.
O wherefore was my birth from Heaven foretold
Twice by an Angel, who at last in sight
Of both my Parents all in flames ascended
From off the Altar, where an Off'ring burn'd,
As in a fiery column charioting
His Godlike presence, and from some great act
Or benefit reveal'd to *Abraham's* race?
Why was my breeding order'd and prescrib'd
As of a person separate to God,
Design'd for great exploits; if I must dye
Betray'd, Captiv'd, and both my Eyes put out,
Made of my Enemies the scorn and gaze;
To grind in Brazen Fetters under task
With this Heav'n-gifted strength? O glorious strength
Put to the labour of a Beast, debas't
Lower then bondslave! Promise was that I
Should *Israel* from *Philistian* yoke deliver;
Ask for this great Deliverer now, and find him
Eyeless in *Gaza* at the Mill with slaves,
Himself in bonds under *Philistian* yoke;
Yet stay, let me not rashly call in doubt
Divine Prediction; what if all foretold
Had been fulfilld but through mine own default,
Whom have I to complain of but my self?
Who this high gift of strength committed to me,
In what part lodg'd, how easily bereft me,
Under the Seal of silence could not keep,
But weakly to a woman must reveal it
O'recome with importunity and tears.
O impotence of mind, in body strong!
But what is strength without a double share
Of wisdom, vast, unwieldy, burdensom,
Proudly secure, yet liable to fall
By weakest suttleties, not made to rule,
But to subserve where wisdom bears command.
God, when he gave me strength, to shew withal

How slight the gift was, hung it in my Hair.
But peace, I must not quarrel with the will
Of highest dispensation, which herein
Happ'ly had ends above my reach to know:
Suffices that to me strength is my bane,
And proves the sourse of all my miseries;
So many, and so huge, that each apart
Would ask a life to wail, but chief of all,
O loss of sight, of thee I most complain!
Blind among enemies, O worse then chains,
Dungeon, or beggery, or decrepit age!
Light the prime work of God to me is extinct,
And all her various objects of delight
Annull'd, which might in part my grief have eas'd,
Inferiour to the vilest now become
Of man or worm; the vilest here excel me,
They creep, yet see, I dark in light expos'd
To daily fraud, contempt, abuse and wrong,
Within doors, or without, still as a fool,
In power of others, never in my own;
Scarce half I seem to live, dead more then half.
O dark, dark, dark, amid the blaze of noon,
Irrecoverably dark, total Eclipse
Without all hope of day!
O first created Beam, and thou great Word,
Let there be light, and light was over all;
Why am I thus bereav'd thy prime decree?
The Sun to me is dark
And silent as the Moon,
When she deserts the night
Hid in her vacant interlunar cave.
Since light so necessary is to life,
And almost life itself, if it be true
That light is in the Soul,
She all in every part; why was the sight
To such a tender ball as th' eye confin'd?
So obvious and so easie to be quench't,
And not as feeling through all parts diffus'd,
That she might look at will through every pore?
Then had I not been thus exil'd from light;
As in the land of darkness yet in light,
To live a life half dead, a living death,
And buried; but O yet more miserable!
My self, my Sepulcher, a moving Grave,
Buried, yet not exempt
By priviledge of death and burial

From worst of other evils, pains and wrongs,
But made hereby obnoxious more
To all the miseries of life,
Life in captivity
Among inhuman foes.
But who are these? for with joint pace I hear
The tread of many feet stearing this way;
Perhaps my enemies who come to stare
At my affliction, and perhaps to insult,
Thir daily practice to afflict me more.

CHORUS. This, this is he; softly a while,
Let us not break in upon him;
O change beyond report, thought, or belief!
See how he lies at random, carelessly diffus'd,
With languish't head unpropt,
As one past hope, abandon'd
And by himself given over;
In slavish habit, ill-fitted weeds
O're worn and soild;
Or do my eyes misrepresent? Can this be hee,
That Heroic, that Renown'd,
Irresistible *Samson?* whom unarm'd
No strength of man, or fiercest wild beast could withstand;
Who tore the Lion, as the Lion tears the Kid,
Ran on embattelld Armies clad in Iron,
And weaponless himself,
Made Arms ridiculous, useless the forgery
Of brazen shield and spear, the hammer'd Cuirass,
Chalybean temper'd steel, and frock of mail
Adamantean Proof;
But safest he who stood aloof,
When insupportably his foot advanc't,
In scorn of thir proud arms and warlike tools,
Spurn'd them to death by Troops. The bold *Ascalonite*
Fled from his Lion ramp, old Warriors turn'd
Thir plated backs under his heel;
Or grovling soild thir crested helmets in the dust.
Then with what trivial weapon came to hand,
The Jaw of a dead Ass, his sword of bone,
A thousand fore-skins fell, the flower of *Palestin*
In *Ramath-lechi* famous to this day:
Then by main force pull'd up, and on his shoulders bore
The Gates of *Azza*, Post, and massie Bar
Up to the Hill by *Hebron,* seat of Giants old,
No journey of a Sabbath day, and loaded so;
Like whom the Gentiles feign to bear up Heav'n.

Which shall I first bewail,
Thy Bondage or lost Sight,
Prison within Prison
Inseparably dark?
Thou art become (O worst imprisonment!)
The Dungeon of thy self; thy Soul
(Which Men enjoying sight oft without cause complain)
Imprison'd now indeed,
In real darkness of the body dwells,
Shut up from outward light
To incorporate with gloomy night;
For inward light alas
Puts forth no visual beam.
O mirror of our fickle state,
Since man on earth unparallel'd!
The rarer thy example stands,
By how much from the top of wondrous glory,
Strongest of mortal men,
To lowest pitch of abject fortune thou art fall'n.
For him I reckon not in high estate
Whom long descent of birth
Or the sphear of fortune raises;
But thee whose strength, while vertue was her mate
Might have subdu'd the Earth,
Universally crown'd with highest praises.

Samuel Butler
1612-1680

From HUDIBRAS

PORTRAIT OF HUDIBRAS

He was in *Logick* a great Critick,
Profoundly skill'd in Analytick.
He could distinguish, and divide
A Hair 'twixt South and South-West side:
On either which he would dispute,
Confute, change hands, and still confute.
He'd undertake to prove by force
Of Argument, a Man's no Horse.
He'd prove a Buzard is no Fowl,
And that a *Lord* may be an Owl;

A Calf an *Alderman,* a Goose a *Justice,*
And Rooks *Committee-men* and *Trustees;*
He'd run in Debt by Disputation,
And pay with Ratiocination.
All this by Syllogism, true
In Mood and Figure, he would do.

For *Rhetorick,* he could not ope
His mouth, but out there flew a Trope:
And when he hapned to break off
I' th' middle of his speech, or cough,
H' had hard words, ready to shew why,
And tell what Rules he did it by.
Else when with greatest Art he spoke,
You'd think he talk'd like other folk.
For all a Rhetoricians Rules
Teach nothing but to name his Tools,
His ordinary Rate of Speech
In loftiness of sound was rich,
A *Babylonish* dialect,
Which learned Pedants much affect.
It was a parti-colour'd dress
Of patch'd and Pyball'd Languages:
'Twas *English* cut on *Greek* and *Latin,*
Like Fustian heretofore on Sattin.
It had an odd promiscuous Tone,
As if h' had talk'd three parts in one.
Which made some think when he did gabble,
Th' had heard three Labourers of *Babel;*
Or *Cerberus* himself pronounce
A Leash of Languages at once.
This he as volubly would vent,
As if his stock would ne'r be spent.
And truly to support that charge
He had supplies as vast and large.
For he could coyn or counterfeit
New words with little or no wit:
Words so debas'd and hard, no stone
Was hard enough to touch them on.
And when with hasty noise he spoke 'em,
The Ignorant for currant took 'em.
That had the Orator who once,
Did fill his Mouth with Pibble stones
When he harangu'd, but known his Phrase
He would have us'd no other ways.

In *Mathematicks* he was greater
Then *Tycho Brahe,* or *Erra Pater:*
For he by *Geometrick* seale
Could take the size of *Pots of Ale;*
Resolve by Signs and Tangents straight,
If *Bread* or *Butter* wanted weight;
And wisely tell what hour o' th' day
The Clock does strike, by *Algebra.*

Beside he was a shrewd *Philosopher;*
And had read every Text and gloss over:
What e're the crabbed'st Author hath
He understood b' implicit Faith,
What ever *Sceptick* could inquire for;
For every *why* he had a *wherefore:*
Knew more then forty of them do,
As far as words and terms could go.
All which he understood by Rote,
And as occasion serv'd, would quote;
No matter whether right or wrong:
They might be either said or sung.
His Notions fitted things so well,
That which was which he could not tell;
But oftentimes mistook the one
For th' other, as Great Clerks have done.
He could reduce all things to Acts,
And knew their Natures by Abstracts,
Where Entity and Quiddity
The Ghosts of defunct Bodies flie;
Where Truth in Person does appear,
Like words congeal'd in Northern Air.
He knew *what's what,* and that's as high
As *Metaphysick* Wit can fly.
In *School Divinity* as able
As he that hight *Irrefragable;*
Profound in all the Nominal
And real ways beyond them all,
And with as delicate a Hand
Could twist as tough a Rope of Sand,
And weave fine Cobwebs, fit for Skull
That's empty when the Moon is full;
Such as take Lodgings in a Head
That's to be lett unfurnished.
He could raise Scruples dark and nice,
And after solve 'em in a trice:

As if Divinity had catch'd
The Itch, of purpose to be scratch'd;
Or, like a Mountebank, did wound
And stab her self with doubts profound,
Only to shew with how small pain
The sores of faith are cur'd again,
Although by woful proof we find,
They always leave a Scar behind.
He knew the Seat of Paradise,
Could tell in what degree it lies:
And, as he was dispos'd, could prove it,
Below the Moon, or else above it:
What *Adam* dreamt of when his Bride
Came from her Closet in his side:
Whether the Devil tempted her
By a *High Dutch* Interpreter:
If either of them had a Navel;
Who first made Musick malleable:
Whether the Serpent at the fall
Had cloven Feet, or none at all.
All this without a Gloss or Comment,
He would unriddle in a moment
In proper terms, such as men smatter
When they throw out and miss the matter.

For his *Religion* it was fit
To match his Learning and his Wit:
'Twas *Presbyterian* true blew,
For he was of that stubborn Crew
Of Errant Saints, whom all men grant
To be the true Church *Militant:*
Such as do build their Faith upon
The holy Text of *Pike* and *Gun;*
Decide all Controversies by
Infallible *Artillery;*
And prove their Doctrine Orthodox
By Apostolick *Blows* and *Knocks;*
Call Fire and Sword and Desolation,
A *godly-thorough-Reformation,*
Which always must be carry'd on,
And still be doing, never done:
As if Religion were intended
For nothing else but to be mended.
A Sect, whose chief Devotion lies
In odd perverse Antipathies;

In falling out with that or this,
And finding somewhat still amiss:
More peevish, cross, and spleenatick
Then Dog distract, or Monky sick.
That with more care keep Holy-day
The wrong, then others the right way:
Compound for Sins, they are inclin'd to,
By damning those they have no mind to;
Still so perverse and opposite,
As if they worshipp'd God for spight,
The self-same thing they will abhor
One way, and long another for.
Free-will they one way disavow,
Another, nothing else allow.

Andrew Marvell
1621-1678

BERMUDAS

Where the remote Bermudas ride,
In th' ocean's bosome unespy'd,
From a small boat, that row'd along,
The list'ning winds receiv'd this song:
    "What should we do but sing His praise,
That led us through the wat'ry maze,
Unto an isle so long unknown,
And yet far kinder than our own?
Where he the huge sea-monsters wracks,
That lift the deep upon their backs;
He lands us on a grassy stage,
Safe from the storms, and prelat's rage.
He gave us this eternal Spring,
Which here enamells every thing;
And sends the fowls to us in care,
On daily visits through the air;
He hangs in shades the orange bright,
Like golden lamps in a green night;
And does in the pomegranates close,
Jewels more rich than Ormus shows;
He makes the figs our mouths to meet,
And throws the melons at our feet;

But apples, plants of such a price,
No tree could ever bear them twice;
With cedars, chosen by His hand,
From Lebanon, He stores the land;
And makes the hollow seas, that roar,
Proclaim the ambergris on shoar.
He cast (of which we rather boast)
The Gospel's pearl upon our coast,
And in these rocks for us did frame
A temple, where to sound His name.
Oh! let our voice His praise exalt,
'Till it arrive at Heaven's vault;
Which, thence (perhaps) rebounding, may
Eccho beyond the Mexique Bay."
   Thus sung they, in the English boat,
An holy and a chearful note,
And all the way, to guide their chime,
With falling oars they kept the time.

THE GARDEN

How vainly men themselves amaze,
To win the palm, the oak, or bayes;
And their uncessant labours see
Crown'd from some single herb or tree,
Whose short and narrow-verged shade
Does prudently their toyles upbraid;
While all the flow'rs and trees do close,
To weave the garlands of repose.

Fair Quiet, have I found thee here,
And Innocence, thy sister dear!
Mistaken long, I sought you then
In busie companies of men.
Your sacred plants, if here below,
Only among the plants will grow;
Society is all but rude
To this delicious solitude.

No white nor red was ever seen
So am'rous as this lovely green.
Fond lovers, cruel as their flame,
Cut in these trees their mistress' name:

Little, alas! they know or heed,
How far these beauties her's exceed!
Fair trees! wheres'eer your barkes I wound,
No name shall but your own be found.

When we have run our passions' heat,
Love hither makes his best retreat.
The gods, who mortal beauty chase,
Still in a tree did end their race;
Apollo hunted Daphne so,
Only that she might laurel grow;
And Pan did after Syrinx speed,
Not as a nymph, but for a reed.

What wond'rous life is this I lead!
Ripe apples drop about my head;
The luscious clusters of the vine
Upon my mouth do crush their wine;
The nectaren and curious peach,
Into my hands themselves do reach;
Stumbling on melons, as I pass,
Insnar'd with flow'rs, I fall on grass.

Meanwhile the mind, from pleasure less,
Withdraws into its happiness:
The mind, that ocean where each kind
Does straight its own resemblance find;
Yet it creates — transcending these —
Far other worlds and other seas;
Annihilating all that's made
To a green thought in a green shade.

Here at the fountain's sliding foot,
Or at some fruit-tree's mossy root,
Casting the bodie's vest aside,
My soul into the boughs does glide:
There, like a bird it sits, and sings,
Then whets and claps its silver wings;
And, till prepar'd for longer flight,
Waves in its plumes the various light.

Such was that happy garden-state,
While man there walk'd without a mate:
After a place so pure and sweet,
What other help could yet be meet!

But 'twas beyond a mortal's share
To wander solitary there:
Two paradises 'twere in one,
To live in paradise alone.

How well the skilful gardner drew
Of flow'rs and herbs this dial new;
Where, from above, the milder sun
Does through a fragrant zodiack run,
And, as it works, th' industrious bee
Computes its time as well as we!
How could such sweet and wholsome hours
Be reckon'd but with herbs and flow'rs!

THE NYMPH COMPLAINING FOR THE DEATH OF HER FAWN

The wanton troopers riding by
Have shot my faun, and it will dye.
Ungentle men! they cannot thrive
Who killed thee. Thou neer didst alive
Them any harm: alas! nor cou'd
Thy death yet do them any good.
I'me sure I never wisht them ill;
Nor do I for all this, nor will:
But, if my simple pray'rs may yet
Prevail with heaven to forget
Thy murder, I will joyn my tears,
Rather then fail. But, O my fears!
It cannot dye so. Heaven's king
Keeps register of every thing;
And nothing may we use in vain:
Even beasts must be with justice slain;
Else men are made their deodands.
Though they should wash their guilty hands
In this warm life-blood, which doth part
From thine, and wound me to the heart,
Yet could they not be clean; their stain
Is dy'd in such a purple grain.
There is not such another in
The world, to offer for their sin.
    Inconstant SYLVIO, when yet
I had not found him counterfeit,
One morning (I remember well),
Ty'd in this silver chain and bell,

Gave it to me: nay, and I know
What he said then; I'me sure I do:
Said he, "Look how your huntsman here
Hath taught a faunt to hunt his dear."
But SYLVIO soon had me beguil'd;
This waxed tame, while he grew wild,
And quite regardless of my smart,
Left me his faun, but took his heart.

  Thenceforth I set my self to play
My solitary time away,
With this; and, very well content,
Could so mine idle life have spent;
For it was full of sport, and light
Of foot and heart; and did invite
Me to its game: it seem'd to bless
It self in me; how could I less
Than love it? O, I cannot be
Unkind t' a beast that loveth me.

  Had it liv'd long, I do not know
Whether it too might have done so
As SYLVIO did; his gifts might be
Perhaps as false, or more, than he;
But I am sure, for aught that I
Could in so short a time espie,
Thy love was far more better then
The love of false and cruel men.

  With sweetest milk and sugar, first
I it at my own fingers nurst;
And as it grew, so every day
It wax'd more white and sweet than they.
It had so sweet a breath! And oft
I blusht to see its foot more soft,
And white (shall I say then my hand?)
Nay, any ladie's of the Land.

  It is a wond'rous thing how fleet
'Twas on those little silver feet;
With what a pretty skipping grace
It oft would challenge me the race;
And when 't had left me far away,
'Twould stay, and run again, and stay;
For it was nimbler much than hindes,
And trod as if on the four winds.

  I have a garden of my own,
But so with roses overgrown,
And lillies, that you would it guess

To be a little wilderness;
And all the Spring time of the year
It onely loved to be there.
Among the beds of lillyes, I
Have sought it oft, where it should lye,
Yet could not, till it self would rise,
Find it, although before mine eyes;
For, in the flaxen lillies' shade,
It like a bank of lillies laid.
Upon the roses it would feed,
Until its lips ev'n seem'd to bleed;
And then to me 'twould boldly trip,
And print those roses on my lip.
But all its chief delight was still
On roses thus it self to fill,
And its pure virgin limbs to fold
In whitest sheets of lillies cold:
Had it liv'd long, it would have been
Lillies without, roses within.
    O help! O help! I see it faint
And dye as calmly as a saint:
See how it weeps! the tears do come
Sad, slowly dropping, like a gumme.
So weeps the wounded balsome; so
The holy frankincense doth flow;
The brotherless Heliades
Melt in such amber tears as these.
    I in a golden vial will
Keep these two crystal tears; and fill
It till it doth o'reflow with mine;
Then place it in DIANA's shrine.
    Now my sweet faun is vanish'd to
Whether the swans and turtles go;
In fair Elizium to endure,
With milk-white lambs, and ermins pure.
O do not run too fast: for I
Will but bespeak thy grave, and dye.
    First, my unhappy statue shall
Be cut in marble; and withal,
Let it be weeping too; but there
The engraver sure his art may spare;
For I so truly thee bemoane,
That I shall weep, though I be stone,
Until my tears, still dropping, wear
My breast, themselves engraving there;

Then at my feet shalt thou be laid,
Of purest alabaster made;
For I would have thine image be
White as I can, though not as thee.

THE MOWER TO THE GLOW–WORMS

Ye living lamps, by whose dear light
The nightingale does sit so late,
And studying all the Summer-night,
Her matchless songs does meditate;

Ye country comets, that portend
No war nor prince's funeral,
Shining unto no higher end
Then to presage the grass's fall;

Ye glow-worms, whose officious flame
To wandring mowers shows the way,
That in the night have lost their aim,
And after foolish fires do stray;

Your courteous lights in vain you wast,
Since Juliana here is come;
For she my mind hath so displac'd,
That I shall never find my home.

From APPLETON HOUSE

And now to the abbyss I pass
Of that unfathomable grass,
Where men like grasshoppers appear,
But grasshoppers are gyants there:
They, in their squeaking laugh, contemn
Us as we walk more low then them,
And from the precipices tall
Of the green spires, to us do call.
To see men through this meadow dive,
We wonder how they rise alive;
As, under water, none does know
Whether he fall through it or go,
But, as the marriners that sound,
And show upon their lead the ground,

They bring up flow'rs so to be seen,
And prove they've at the bottom been.
No scene, that turns with engines strange,
Does oftner then these meadows change;
For when the sun the grass hath vext,
The tawny mowers enter next;
Who seem like Israelites to be,
Walking on foot through a green sea.
To them the grassy deeps divide,
And crowd a lane to either side.
With whistling sithe and elbow strong
These massacre the grass along . . . .

THE KINGFISHER

So when the Shadows laid asleep
From underneath these Banks do creep,
And on the River as it flows
With *Eben Shuts* begin to close;
The modest *Halcyon* comes in sight,
Flying betwixt the Day and Night;
And such an horror calm and dumb,
Admiring Nature does benum.

The viscous Air, wheres'ere She fly,
Follows and sucks her Azure dy;
The gellying Stream compacts below,
If it might fix her shadow so;
The stupid Fishes hang, as plain
As *Flies* in *Chrystal* overt'ane;
And Men the silent *Scene* assist,
Charm'd with the *Saphir-winged Mist*.

TO HIS COY MISTRESS

Had we but world enough, and time,
This coyness, lady, were no crime.
We would sit down, and think which way
To walk, and pass our long love's day.
Thou by the Indian Ganges' side
Should'st rubies find: I by the tide
Of Humber would complain. I would
Love you ten years before the Flood,

And you should, if you please, refuse
Till the conversion of the Jews;
My vegetable love should grow
Vaster then empires and more slow;
An hundred years should go to praise
Thine eyes, and on thy forehead gaze;
Two hundred to adore each breast,
But thirty thousand to the rest;
An age at least to every part,
And the last age should show your heart.
For, lady, you deserve this state,
Nor would I love at lower rate.
   But at my back I alwaies hear
Time's winged charriot hurrying near;
And yonder all before us lye
Desarts of vast Eternity.
Thy beauty shall no more be found,
Nor, in thy marble vault, shall sound
My ecchoing song; then, worms shall try
That long preserv'd virginity;
And your quaint honour turn to dust,
And into ashes all my lust:
The grave's a fine and private place,
But none, I think, do there embrace.
   Now therefore, while the youthful hew
Sits on thy skin like morning dew,
And while thy willing soul transpires
At every pore with instant fires,
Now let us sport us while we may,
And now, like am'rous birds of prey,
Rather at once our time devour,
Than languish in his slow-chapt pow'r.
Let us roll all our strength, and all
Our sweetness up into one ball;
And tear our pleasures with rough strife,
Thorough the iron gates of life;
Thus, though we cannot make our sun
Stand still, yet we will make him run.

Henry Vaughan

1622-1695

UNPROFITABLENES

How rich, O Lord! how fresh thy visits are!
'Twas but Just now my bleak leaves hopeles hung
    Sullyed with dust and mud;
Each snarling blast shot through me, and did share
Their Youth, and beauty, Cold showres nipt, and wrung
    Their spiciness, and bloud;
But since thou didst in one sweet glance survey
Their sad decays, I flourish, and once more
    Breath all perfumes, and spice;
I smell a dew like *Myrrh,* and all the day
Wear in my bosome a full Sun; such store
    Hath one beame from thy Eys.
But, ah, my God! what fruit hast thou of this?
What one poor leaf did ever I let fall
    To wait upon thy wreath?
Thus thou all day a thankless weed doest dress,
And when th' hast done, a stench, or fog is all
    The odour I bequeath.

CHRIST'S NATIVITY

I

Awake, glad heart! get up, and Sing,
It is the Birth-day of thy King,
    Awake! awake!
    The Sun doth shake
Light from his locks, and all the way
Breathing Perfumes, doth spice the day.

Awake, awake! heark, how th' *wood* rings,
Winds whisper, and the busie *springs*
    A Consort make;
    Awake, awake!
Man is their high-priest, and should rise
To offer up the sacrifice.

I would I were some *Bird,* or Star,
Flutt'ring in woods, or lifted far
    Above this *Inne*
    And Rode of sin!
Then either Star, or *Bird,* should be
Shining, or singing still to thee.

I would I had in my best part
Fit Roomes for thee! or that my heart
    Were so clean as
    Thy manger was!
But I am all filth, and obscene,
Yet, if thou wilt, thou canst make clean.

Sweet Jesu! will then; Let no more
This Leper haunt, and soyl thy door,
    Cure him, Ease him
    O release him!
And let once more by mystick birth
The Lord of life be borne in Earth.

II

How kind is heav'n to man! If here
    One sinner doth amend
Strait there is Joy, and ev'ry sphere
    In musick doth Contend;
And shall we then no voices lift?
    Are mercy, and salvation
Not worth our thanks? Is life a gift
    Of no more acceptation?
Shal he that did come down from thence,
    And here for us was slain,
Shal he be now cast off? no sense
    Of all his woes remain?
Can neither Love, nor suff'rings bind?
    Are we all stone, and Earth?
Neither his bloudy passions mind,
    Nor one day blesse his birth?
  Alas, my God! Thy birth now here
  Must not be numbred in the year.

SON–DAYES

Bright shadows of true Rest! some shoots of blisse,
      Heaven once a week;
The next worlds gladnes prepossest in this;
      A day to seek
Eternity in time; the steps by which
  We Climb above all ages; Lamps that light
Man through his heap of dark days; and the rich,
  And full redemption of the whole weeks flight.

The Pulleys unto headlong man; times bower;
      The narrow way;
Transplanted Paradise; Gods walking houre;
      The Cool o' th' day;
The Creatures *Jubile;* Gods parle with dust;
  Heaven here; Man on those hills of Myrrh, and flowres;
Angels descending; the Returns of Trust;
  A Gleam of glory, after six-days-showres.

The Churches love-feasts; Times Prerogative,
      And Interest
Deducted from the whole; The Combs, and hive,
      And home of rest.
The milky way Chalkt out with Suns; a Clue
  That guides through erring hours; and in full story
A taste of Heav'n on earth; the pledge, and Cue
  Of a full feast; And the Out Courts of glory.

COCK–CROWING

Father of lights! what Sunnie seed,
  What glance of day hast thou confin'd
Into this bird? To all the breed
  This busie Ray thou hast assign'd;
Their magnetisme works all night,
And dreams of Paradise and light.

Their eyes watch for the morning hue,
  Their little grain expelling night
So shines and sings, as if it knew
  The path unto the house of light.
It seems their candle, howe'r done,
Was tinn'd and lighted at the sunne.

If such a tincture, such a touch,
  So firm a longing can impowre
Shall thy own image think it much
  To watch for thy appearing hour?
If a meer blast so fill the sail,
Shall not the breath of God prevail?

O thou immortall light and heat!
  Whose hand so shines through all this frame,
That by the beauty of the seat,
  We plainly see, who made the same.
Seeing thy seed abides in me,
Dwell thou in it, and I in thee.

To sleep without thee, is to die;
  Yea, 'tis a death partakes of hell:
For where thou dost not close the eye
  It never opens, I can tell.
In such a dark, Ægyptian border,
The shades of death dwell and disorder.

If joyes, and hopes, and earnest throws,
  And hearts, whose Pulse beats still for light
Are given to birds; who, but thee, knows
  A love-sick souls exalted flight?
Can souls be track'd by any eye
But his, who gave them wings to flie?

Onely this Veyle which thou hast broke,
  And must be broken yet in me,
This veyle, I say, is all the cloke
  And cloud which shadows thee from me.
This veyle thy full-ey'd love denies,
And onely gleams and fractions spies.

O take it off! make no delay,
  But brush me with thy light, that I
May shine unto a perfect day,
  And warme me at thy glorious Eye!
O take it off! or till it flee,
Though with no Lilie, stay with me!

THE RETREATE

Happy those early dayes! when I
Shin'd in my Angell-infancy.
Before I understood this place
Appointed for my second race,
Or taught my soul to fancy ought
But a white, Celestiall thought,
When yet I had not walkt above
A mile, or two, from my first love,
And looking back (at that short space,)
Could see a glimpse of his bright-face;
When on some *gilded Cloud,* or *flowre*
My gazing soul would dwell an houre,
And in those weaker glories spy
Some shadows of eternity;
Before I taught my tongue to wound
My Conscience with a sinfull sound,
Or had the black art to dispence
A sev'rall sinne to ev'ry sence,
But felt through all this fleshly dresse
Bright *shootes* of everlastingnesse.
  O how I long to travell back
And tread again that ancient track!
That I might once more reach that plaine,
Where first I left my glorious traine,
From whence th' Inlightned spirit sees
That shady City of Palme trees;
But (ah!) my soul with too much stay
Is drunk, and staggers in the way.
Some men a forward motion love,
But I by backward steps would move,
And when this dust falls to the urn
In that state I came return.

IDLE VERSE

Go, go, queint folies, sugred sin,
  Shadow no more my door;
I will no longer Cobwebs spin,
  I'm too much on the score.

For since amidst my youth, and night,
  My great preserver smiles,
Wee'l make a Match, my only light,
  And Joyn against their wiles;

Blind, desp'rate *fits,* that study how
  To dresse, and trim our shame,
That gild rank poyson, and allow
  Vice in a fairer name;

The Purles of youthfull bloud, and
    bowles,
  Lust in the Robes of Love,
The idle talk of feav'rish souls
  Sick with a scarf, or glove;

Let it suffice my warmer days
  Simper'd, and shin'd on you,
Twist not my Cypresse with your
    Bays,
  Or Roses with my Yewgh;

Go, go, seek out some greener thing,
  It snows, and freezeth here;
Let Nightingales attend the spring,
  Winter is all my year.

THE BIRD

Hither thou com'st: the busie wind all night
Blew through thy lodging, where thy own warm wing
Thy pillow was. Many a sullen storm
(For which course man seems much the fitter born,)
    Rain'd on thy bed
    And harmless head.

And now as fresh and chearful as the light
Thy little heart in early hymns doth sing
Unto that *Providence,* whose unseen arm
Curb'd them, and cloath'd thee well and warm.
    All things that be, praise him; and had
    Their lesson taught them, when first made.

So hills and valleys into singing break,
And though poor stones have neither speech nor tongue,
While active winds and streams both run and speak,
Yet stones are deep in admiration.
Thus Praise and Prayer here beneath the Sun
Make lesser mornings, when the great are done.

For each inclosed Spirit is a star
    Inlightning his own little sphære,
Whose light, though fetcht and borrowed from far,
    Both mornings makes, and evenings there.

But as these Birds of light make a land glad,
    Chirping their solemn Matins on each tree:
    So in the shades of night some dark fowls be,
    Whose heavy notes make all that hear them, sad.

The Turtle then in Palm-trees mourns,
　　While Owls and Satyrs howl;
The pleasant Land to brimstone turns
　　And all her streams grow foul.

Brightness and mirth, and love and faith, all flye,
Till the Day-spring breaks forth again from high.

PALM–SUNDAY

Come, drop your branches, strow the way
　　Plants of the day!
Whom sufferings make most green and gay.

The King of grief, the man of sorrow
Weeping still, like the wet morrow,
Your shades and freshness comes to borrow.

Put on, put on your best array;
Let the joy'd rode make holy-day,
And flowers that into fields do stray,
Or secret groves, keep the high-way.

Trees, flowers and herbs; birds, beasts and stones,
That since man fell, expect with groans
To see the lamb, which all at once,
Lift up your heads and leave your moans!
　　For here comes he
　　Whose death will be
Mans life, and your full liberty.

Hark! how the children shril and high
　　Hosanna cry,
Their joys provoke the distant skie,
Where thrones and Seraphins reply,
And their own Angels shine and sing
　　In a bright ring:
　　Such yong, sweet mirth
　　Makes heaven and earth
Joyn in a joyful Symphony,

The harmless, yong and happy Ass,
Seen long before this came to pass,
Is in these joys an high partaker
Ordain'd, and made to bear his Maker.

Dear feast of Palms, of Flowers and Dew!
  Whose fruitful dawn sheds hopes and lights;
Thy bright solemnities did shew,
  The third glad day through two sad nights.

I'le get me up before the Sun,
  I'le cut me boughs off many a tree,
And all alone full early run
  To gather flowers to wellcome thee.

Then like the *Palm,* though wrong, I'le bear,
  I will be still a childe, still meek
As the poor Ass, which the proud jear,
  And onely my dear *Jesus* seek.

If I lose all, and must endure
  The proverb'd griefs of holy *Job,*
I care not, so I may secure
  But one *green Branch* and a *white robe.*

THE SHOWER

Waters above! Eternal springs!
The dew that silvers the Dove's wings!
O welcom, welcom to the sad:
Give dry dust drink, drink that makes glad!
Many fair ev'nings, many flow'rs
Sweetened with rich and gentle showers,
Have I enjoyed, and down have run
Many a fine and shining sun;
But never, till this happy hour,
Was blest with such an evening-shower!

THE WORLD

I saw Eternity the other night,
Like a great *Ring* of pure and endless light,
    All calm, as it was bright;
And round beneath it, Time in hours, days, years,
    Driv'n by the spheres
Like a vast shadow mov'd, In which the world
    And all her train were hurl'd.
The doting Lover in his queintest strain
    Did their Complain;

Neer him, his Lute, his fancy, and his flights,
    Wits sour delights;
With gloves, and knots the silly snares of pleasure,
    Yet his dear Treasure
All scatter'd lay, while he his eys did pour
    Upon a flowr.

The darksome States-man hung with weights and woe
Like a thick midnight-fog mov'd there so slow
    He did nor stay, nor go;
Condemning thoughts (like sad Ecclipses) scowl
    Upon his soul,
And Clouds of crying witnesses without
    Pursued him with one shout.
Yet dig'd the Mole, and lest his ways be found,
    Workt under ground,
Where he did Clutch his prey; but one did see
    That policie,
Churches and altars fed him, Perjuries
    Were gnats and flies,
It rain'd about him bloud and tears, but he
    Drank them as free.

The fearfull miser on a heap of rust
Sate pining all his life there, did scarce trust
    His own hands with the dust,
Yet would not place one peece above, but lives
    In feare of theeves.
Thousands there were as frantick as himself
    And hug'd each one his pelf,
The down-right Epicure plac'd heav'n in sense
    And scornd pretence
While others, slipt into a wide Excesse
    Said little lesse;
The weaker sort slight, triviall wares Inslave
    Who think them brave;
And poor, despised truth sate Counting by
    Their victory.

Yet some, who all this while did weep and sing,
And sing, and weep, soar'd up into the *Ring*,
    But most would use no wing.
O fools (said I,) thus to prefer dark night
    Before true light,
To live in grots, and caves, and hate the day
    Because it shews the way,

The way which from this dead and dark abode
　　　Leads up to God,
A way where you might tread the Sun, and be
　　　More bright than he.
But as I did their madnes so discusse
　　　One whisper'd thus,
This Ring the Bride-groome did for none provide
　　　But for his bride.

I JOHN II,16,17

*All that is in the world, the lust of the flesh, the lust of the Eyes, and
the pride of life, is not of the father, but is of the world.*

*And the world passeth away, and the lusts thereof; but he that doth
the will of God abideth for ever.*

Thomas Traherne

1637?-1674

WONDER

How like an Angel came I down!
　　　How bright are all things here!
When first among his Works I did appear
　　　O how their Glory did me crown!
The World resembled his ETERNITY,
　　　In which my Soul did walk;
　　　And evry thing that I did see
　　　　　Did with me talk.

The Skies in their Magnificence,
　　　The lovly lively Air,
Oh how divine, how soft, how sweet, how fair!
　　　The Stars did entertain my Sense;
And all the Works of God so bright and pure,
　　　So rich and great, did seem,
　　　As if they ever must endure
　　　　　In my Esteem.

A Native Health and Innocence
　　　Within my Bones did grow,
And while my God did all his Glories show
　　　I felt a vigor in my Sense

That was all SPIRIT: I within did flow
    With Seas of Life like Wine;
  I nothing in the World did know
    But 'twas Divine.

   Harsh rugged Objects were conceal'd,
    Oppressions, Tears, and Cries,
Sins, Griefs, Complaints, Dissentions, weeping Eys,
    Were hid: And only things reveal'd
Which hevenly Spirits and the Angels prize:
    The State of Innocence
  And Bliss, not Trades and Poverties,
    Did fill my Sense.

   The Streets seem'd paved with golden Stones,
    The Boys and Girls all mine;
To me how did their lovly faces shine!
    The Sons of men all Holy ones,
In Joy and Beauty, then appear'd to me;
    And evry Thing I found
  (While like an Angel I did see)
    Adorn'd the Ground.

   Rich Diamonds, and Pearl, and Gold
    Might evry where be seen;
Rare Colors, yellow, blew, red, white, and green
    Mine Eys on evry side behold:
All that I saw, a Wonder did appear,
    Amazement was my Bliss:
  That and my Wealth met evry where,
    No Joy to this!

   Curs'd, ill-devis'd Proprieties
    With Envy, Avarice,
And Fraud, (those Fiends that spoil ev'n Paradise)
    Were not the Object of mine Eys;
Nor Hedges, Ditches, Limits, narrow Bounds:
    I dreamt not ought of those,
  But in surveying all mens Grounds
    I found Repose.

   For Property its self was mine,
    And Hedges, Ornaments:
Walls, Houses, Coffers, and their rich Contents,
    To make me Rich combine.

Cloaths, costly Jewels, Laces, I esteem'd
My Wealth by others worn,
For me they all to wear them seem'd,
When I was born.

SHADOWS IN THE WATER

In inexperienc'd Infancy
Many a sweet Mistake doth ly:
Mistake tho false, intending true;
A *Seeming* somewhat more than View,
That doth instruct the Mind,
In things that lie behind,
And many Secrets to us show
Which afterwards we come to know.

Thus did I by the Water's brink
Another World beneath me think;
And while the lofty spacious Skies
Reversed there abus'd mine Eyes,
I fancy'd other Feet
Came mine to touch or meet;
As by some Puddle I did play
Another World within it lay.

Beneath the Water People drown'd,
Yet with Another Heav'n crown'd,
In spacious Regions seem'd to go
As freely, moving to and fro:
In bright and open Space
I saw their very face;
Eyes, Hands, and Feet they had like mine;
Another Sun did with them shine.

'Twas strange that People there should walk,
And yet I could not hear them talk:
That through a little wat'ry Chink,
Which one day Ox or Horse might drink,
We other Worlds should see,
Yet not admitted be;
And other Confines there behold
Of Light and Darkness, Heat and Cold.

I call'd them oft, but call'd in vain;
No Speeches we could entertain:
Yet did I there expect to find
Some other World, to please my Mind.
    I plainly saw by these
      A new *Antipodes,*
Whom, tho they were so plainly seen,
A Film kept off that stood between.

By walking Man's reversed Feet
I chanc'd another World to meet;
Tho it did not to View exceed.
A Phantasm, 'tis a World indeed,
    Whose Skies beneath us shine,
    And Earth by Art divine
Another face presents below
Where People's feet against ours go.

Within the Regions of the Air,
Compass'd about with Heav'ns fair,
Great Tracts of Land there may be found
Enricht with Fields and fertile Ground;
    Where many num'rous Hosts,
    In those far-distant Coasts,
For other great and glorious Ends,
Inhabit, my yet unknown Friends.

O ye that stand upon the Brink,
Whom I so near me, through the Chink,
With Wonder see: What Faces there,
Whose Feet, whose Bodies do ye wear?
    I my Companions see
    In You, another Me.
They seemed others, but are We;
Our second Selves those Shadows be.

Look how far off those lower Skies
Extend themselves, scarce with mine Eyes
I can them reach, O ye my Friends,
What *Secret* borders on those Ends?
    Are lofty Heavens hurl'd
    'Bout your inferior World?
Are ye the Representatives
Of other People's distant Lives?

Of all the Play-mates which I knew
That here I do the Image view
In other Selves; what can it mean?
But that below the purling Stream
    Some unknown Joys there be
    Laid up in Store for me;
To which I shall, when that thin Skin
Is broken, be admitted in.

THE SALUTATION

    These little Limbs,
  These Eyes and Hands which here I find,
This panting Heart wherewith my Life begins;
    Where have ye been? Behind
What Curtain were ye from me hid so long?
Where was, in what Abyss, my new-made Tongue?

    When silent I
  So many thousand thousand years
Beneath the Dust did in a *Chaos* lie,
    How could I *Smiles,* or *Tears,*
Or *Lips,* or *Hands* or *Eyes,* or *Ears* perceive?
Welcome ye Treasures which I now receive.

    I that so long
  Was *Nothing* from Eternity,
Did little think such Joys as Ear and Tongue
    To celebrate or see:
Such Sounds to hear, such Hands to feel, such Feet,
Such Eyes and Objects, on the Ground to meet.

    New burnisht Joys!
  Which finest Gold and Pearl excell!
Such sacred Treasures are the Limbs of Boys
    In which a Soul doth dwell:
Their organised Joints and azure veins
More Wealth include than the dead World contains.

    From Dust I rise
  And out of Nothing now awake;
These brighter Regions which salute mine Eyes
    A Gift from God I take:
The Earth, the Stars, the Light, the lofty Skies,
The Sun and Stars are mine; if these I prize.

A Stranger here
Strange things doth meet, strange Glory see;
Strange Treasures lodg'd in this fair World appear,
Strange all and New to me:
But that they *mine* should be who Nothing was,
That Strangest is of all, yet brought to pass.

ON LEAPING OVER THE MOON

I saw new Worlds beneath the Water ly,
New Peeple; yea, another Sky,
And Sun, which seen by Day
Might things more clear display.
Just such another
Of late my Brother
Did in his Travel see, and saw by Night,
A much more strange and wondrous Sight:
Nor could the World exhibit such another,
So Great a Sight, but in a Brother.

Adventure strange! No such in Story we
New or old, true or feigned, see.
On Earth he seem'd to move
Yet Heven went above;
Up in the Skies
His Body flies
In open, visible, yet Magick, sort:
As he along the Way did sport,
Over the Flood he takes his nimble Cours
Without the help of feigned Horse.

As he went tripping o'r the King's high-way,
A little pearly River lay
O'r which, without a Wing
Or Oar, he dar'd to swim,
Swim throu the Air
On Body fair;
He would not use nor trust Icarian Wings
Lest they should prove deceitful things;
For had he faln, it had been wondrous high,
Not from, but from above, the Sky:

He might have dropt throu that thin Element
Into a fathomless Descent;

Unto the nether Sky
    That did beneath him ly,
        And there might tell
        What Wonders dwell
On Earth above. Yet doth he briskly run,
    And bold the Danger overcome;
Who, as he leapt, with Joy related soon
    How *happy he* o'r-leapt the Moon.

What wondrous things upon the Earth are done
    Beneath, and yet above, the Sun?
        Deeds all appear again
        In higher Spheres; remain
            In Clouds as yet:
            But there they get
Another Light, and in another way
    Themselves to us *above* display.
The Skies themselves this earthly Globe surround;
    W'are even here within them found.

On hev'nly Ground within the Skies we walk,
  ·   And in this middle Center talk:
        Did we but wisely move,
        On Earth in Hev'n above,
            Then soon should we
            Exalted be
Above the Sky: from whence whoever falls,
    Through a long dismall Precipice,
Sinks to the deep Abyss where Satan crawls
    Where horrid Death and Despair lies.

As much as others thought themselves to ly
    Beneath the Moon, so much more high
        Himself he thought to fly
        Above the starry Sky,
            As that he spy'd
            Below the Tide.
Thus did he yield me in the shady Night
    A wondrous and instructive Light,
Which taught me that under our Feet there is,
    As o'r our Heads, a place of Bliss.

John Wilmot, Earl of Rochester
1647-1680

From THE MISTRESS

An Age in her Embraces past,
  Would seem a Winter's Day;
Where Life and Light, with
    envious haste,
  Are torn and snatch'd away.

But, oh! how slowly Minutes roul,
  When absent from her Eyes,
That fed my Love, which is my
    Soul;
  It languishes and dies.

For then no more a Soul but Shade,
  It mournfully does move;
And haunts my Breast, by Absence
    made
  The living Tomb of Love.

You wiser Men despise me not;
  Whose Love-sick Fancy raves,
On Shades of Souls, and Heav'n
    knows what;
  Short Ages live in Graves.

    Whene'er those wounding Eyes, so
        full
      Of Sweetness, you did see;
    Had you not been profoundly dull,
      You had gone mad like me.

UPON NOTHING

Nothing! thou Elder Brother ev'n to Shade,
Thou hadst a being ere the World was made,
And (well fixt) art alone of Ending not afraid.

Ere Time and Place were, Time and Place were not,
When Primitive *Nothing* something streight begot,
Then all proceeded from the great united — What.

Something, the gen'ral Attribute of all,
Sever'd from thee, its sole Original,
Into thy boundless self must undistinguish'd fall.

Yet Something did thy mighty Pow'r command,
And from thy fruitful Emptiness's Hand,
Snatch'd Men, Beasts, Birds, Fire, Air, and Land.

Matter, the wickedest Off-spring of thy Race,
By Form assisted, flew from thy Embrace,
And Rebel Light obscur'd thy reverend dusky Face.

With Form and Matter, Time and Place did join;
Body, thy Foe, with thee did Leagues combine,
To spoil thy peaceful Realm, and ruin all thy Line.

But Turn-Coat Time assists the Foe in vain,
And, brib'd by thee, assists thy short-liv'd Reign,
And to thy hungry Womb drives back thy Slaves again.

Tho' Mysteries are barr'd from Laick Eyes,
And the Divine alone, with Warrant, pries
Into thy Bosom, where the Truth in private lies:

Yet this of thee the Wise may freely say,
Thou from the Virtuous nothing tak'st away,
And to be part with thee the Wicked wisely pray.

Great Negative, how vainly wou'd the Wise
Enquire, define, distinguish, teach, devise?
Didst thou not stand to point their dull Philosophies.

Is, or *is not,* the Two great Ends of Fate,
And, true or false, the Subject of Debate,
That perfect, or destroy, the vast Designs of Fate;

When they have rack'd the *Politician's* Breast,
Within thy Bosom most securely rest,
And, when reduc'd to thee, are least unsafe and best.

But *Nothing,* why does *Something* still permit,
That Sacred Monarchs should at Council sit,
With Persons highly thought at best for nothing fit.

Whilst weighty *Something* modestly abstains
From Princes' Coffers, and from Statesmen's Brains,
And Nothing there like stately *Nothing* reigns.

Nothing, who dwell's with Fools in grave Disguise,
For whom they reverend Shapes, and Forms devise,
Lawn Sleeves, and Furrs, and Gowns, when they like thee look wise.

French Truth, *Dutch* Prowess, *British* Policy,
Hibernian Learning, *Scotch* Civility,
Spaniards' Dispatch, *Danes'* Wit, are mainly seen in thee.

The Great Man's Gratitude to his best Friend,
Kings' Promises, Whores' Vows, towards thee they bend,
Flow swiftly into thee, and in thee ever end.

Aphra Behn
1640-1689

SONG: LOVE IN FANTASTIQUE TRIUMPH SATT

Love in Fantastique Triumph satt,
 Whilst Bleeding Hearts around him flow'd,
For whom Fresh paines he did Create,
 And strange Tyranick power he show'd;
From thy Bright Eyes he took his fire,
 Which round about, in sport he hurl'd;
But 'twas from mine he took desire,
 Enough to undo the Amorous World.

From me he took his sighs and tears,
 From thee his Pride and Crueltie;
From me his Languishments and Feares,
 And every Killing Dart from thee;
Thus thou and I, the God have arm'd,
 And set him up a Deity;
But my poor Heart alone is harm'd,
 Whilst thine the Victor is, and free.

William Congreve
1670-1729

SONG: AH STAY

Ah stay! ah turn! ah whither would you fly,
 Too charming, too relentless Maid?
I follow not to Conquer, but to Die;
 You of the fearful are afraid.

In vain I call; for she like fleeting Air,
 When prest by some tempestuous Wind,
Flies swifter from the Voice of my Despair,
 Nor casts one pitying Look behind.

Edward Taylor

1644-1729

From SACRAMENTAL MEDITATIONS

MEDITATION SIX

CANTICLES II,1. *I am . . . the lily of the valleys.*

Am I thy Gold? Or Purse, Lord, for thy Wealth;
    Whether in mine or mint refinde for thee?
Ime counted so, but count me o're thyselfe,
    Lest Gold washt face, and brass in Heart I bee.
I feare my Touchstone touches when I try
Mee, and my Counted Gold too overly.

Am I new-minted by thy Stamp indeed?
    Mine Eyes are dim; I cannot clearly see.
Be thou my Spectacles that I may read
    Thine Image and Inscription stampt on mee.
If thy bright Image do upon me stand
I am a Golden Angell in thy hand.

Lord, make my Soule thy Plate: thine Image bright
    Within the Circle of the same enfoile,
And on its brims in golden Letters write
    Thy Superscription in an Holy style.
Then I shall be thy Money, thou my Hord:
Let me thy Angell bee, bee thou my Lord.

MEDITATION EIGHT

JOHN VI,51. *I am the living bread.*

I kenning through Astronomy Divine
    The Worlds bright Battlement, wherein I spy
A Golden Path my Pensill cannot line
    From that bright Throne unto my Threshold ly.
And while my puzzled thoughts about it pore,
I find the Bread of Life in't at my doore.

When that this Bird of Paradise put in
    This Wicker Cage (my Corps) to tweedle praise

Had peckt the Fruite forbid: and so did fling
    Away its Food, and lost its golden dayes,
It fell into Celestiall Famine sore,
And never could attain a morsell more.

Alas! alas! Poore Bird, what wilt thou doe?
    This Creatures field no food for Souls e're gave:
And if thou knock at Angells dores, they show
    An Empty Barrell: they no soul bread have.
Alas! Poore Bird, the Worlds White Loafe is done,
And cannot yield thee here the smallest Crumb.

In this sad state, Gods Tender Bowells run
    Out streams of Grace: And he to end all strife,
The Purest Wheate in Heaven, his deare-dear Son
    Grinds, and kneads up into this Bread of Life:
Which Bread of Life from Heaven down came and stands
Disht in thy Table up by Angells Hands.

Did God mould up this Bread in Heaven, and bake,
    Which from his Table came, and to thine goeth?
Doth he bespeake thee thus: This Soule Bread take;
    Come, Eate thy fill of this, thy Gods White Loafe?
Its Food too fine for Angells; yet come, take
And Eate thy fill! Its Heavens Sugar Cake.

What Grace is this knead in this Loafe? This thing
    Souls are but petty things it to admire.
Yee Angells, help: This fill would to the brim
    Heav'ns whelm'd-down Chrystall meele Bowle, yea and
        higher.
This Bread of Life dropt in thy mouth doth Cry:
Eate, Eate me, Soul, and thou shalt never dy.

MEDITATION THIRTY-THREE

I CORINTHIANS III,22. *Whether Paul, or Apollos, or Cephas,
or the world, or life, or death, or things present, or things
to come; all are yours.*

    My Lord, my Life, can Envy ever bee
        A Golden Vertue? Then would God I were
    Top full thereof untill it colours mee
        With yellow streaks for thy Deare sake most Deare;
    Till I be Envious made by't at myselfe:
    As scarcely loving thee, my Life, my Health.

Oh! what strange Charm encrampt my Heart with spite,
    Making my Love gleame out upon a Toy?
Lay out Cart Loads of Love upon a mite?
    Scarce lay a mite of Love on thee, my Joy?
Oh! Lovely thou! Shalt not thou loved bee?
Shall I ashame thee thus? Oh! shame for mee!

Nature's amaz'de. Oh, monstrous thing, Quoth shee,
    Not Love my life? What Violence doth split
True Love and Life, that they should sunder'd bee?
    She doth not lay such Eggs, nor on them sit.
How do I sever then my Heart with all
Its Powers whose Love scarce to my Life doth crawle.

Glory lin'de out a Paradise in Power
    Where e'ry seed a Royall Coach became
For Life to ride in, to each shining Flower.
    And made mans Flower with glory all ore flame.
Hells Inkfac'de Elfe black Venom spat upon
The same, and kill'd it. So that Life is gone.

Life thus abus'de fled to the golden Arke,
    Lay lockt up there in Mercie's seate inclosde:
Which did incorporate it whence its Sparke
    Enlivens all things in this Arke inclos'de.
Oh, glorious Arke! Life's Store-House full of Glee!
Shall not my Love safe lockt up ly in thee?

Lord, arke my Soule safe in thyselfe, whereby
    I and my Life again may joyned bee.
That I may finde what once I did destroy
    Again Confer'de upon my soul in thee.
Thou art this Golden Ark, this Living Tree,
Where life lies treasurde up for all in thee.

Oh! Graft me in this Tree of Life within
    The Paradise of God, that I may live.
Thy Life make live in mee; I'le then begin
    To beare thy Living Fruits, and them forth give.
Give mee my Life this way; and I'le bestow
My Love on thee, my Life. And it shall grow.

UPON A WASP CHILLED WITH COLD

The Bear that breaths the Northern blast
Did numb, Torpedo-like, a Wasp
Whose stiffend limbs encrampt, lay bathing
In Sol's warm breath and shine as saving,
Which with her hands she chafes and slams
Rubbing her Legs, Shanks, Thighs, and hands.
Her petty toes, and fingers ends
Nipt with this breath, she out extends
Unto the sun, in greate desire
To warm her digits at that fire:
Doth hold her Temples in this state
Where pulse doth beate, and head doth ake:
Doth turn and stretch her body small,
Doth comb her velvet capitall
As if her little brain-pan were
A Volume of choice precepts cleare:
As if her sattin jacket hot
Contained Apothecaries Shop
Of Natures recepts, that prevails
To remedy all her sad ailes,
As if her velvet helmet high
Did turret rationality.
She fans her wing up to the winde
As if her Pettycoate were lin'de
With reasons fleece, and hoises saile
And humming flies in thankfull gaile
Unto her dun curld palace Hall,
Her warm thanks offering for all.

Lord, cleare my misted sight that I
May hence view thy Divinity,
Some sparkes whereof thou up dost hasp
Within this little downy Wasp,
In whose small Corporation wee
A school and a schoolmaster see:
Where we may learn, and easily finde
A nimble Spirit, bravely minde
Her worke in ev'ry limb: and lace
It up neate with a vitall grace,
Acting each part though ne'er so small,
Here of this fustian animall,

Till I enravisht climb into
The Godhead on this ladder doe:
Where all my pipes inspir'de upraise
An Heavenly musick, furr'd with praise.

THE REFLEXION

CANTICLES II,1. *I am the rose of Sharon.*

Lord, art thou at the Table head above
　Meat, Med'cine, Sweetness, sparkling Beauties, to
Enamour Souls with Flaming Flakes of Love,
　And not my Trencher, nor my Cup o'reflow?
Ben't I a bidden guest? Oh! sweat mine Eye:
O're flow with Teares: Oh! draw thy fountains dry.

Shall I not smell thy sweet, oh! Sharons Rose?
　Shall not mine Eye salute thy Beauty? Why?
Shall thy sweet leaves their Beauteous sweets upclose?
　As halfe ashamde my sight should on them ly?
Woe's me! For this my sighs shall be in grain
Offer'd on Sorrows Altar for the same.

Had not my Soule's, thy Conduit, Pipes stopt bin
　With mud, what Ravishment wouldst thou convey?
Let Graces Golden Spade dig till the Spring
　Of tears arise, and cleare this filth away.
Lord, let thy Spirit raise my sighings till
These Pipes my soule do with thy sweetness fill.

Earth once was Paradise of Heaven below,
　Till inkefac'd sin had it with poyson stockt;
And Chast this Paradise away into
　Heavn's upmost Loft, and it in Glory Lockt.
But thou, sweet Lord, hast with thy golden key
Unlockt the Doore, and made a golden day.

Once at thy Feast, I saw thee Pearle-like stand
　'Tween Heaven and Earth, where Heavens Bright glory all
In streams fell on thee as a floodgate and
　Like Sun Beams through thee on the World to Fall.
Oh! Sugar sweet then! My Deare sweet Lord, I see
Saints Heaven-lost Happiness restor'd by thee.

Shall Heaven and Earth's bright glory all up lie,
　Like Sun Beams bundled in the sun in thee?
Dost thou sit Rose at Table Head, where I

Do sit, and Carv'st the morsell sweet for mee?
So much before, so little now! Sprindge, Lord,
Thy Rosie Leaves, and me their Glee afford.

Shall not thy Rose my Garden fresh perfume?
 Shall not thy Beauty my dull Heart assaile?
Shall not thy golden gleams run through this gloom?
 Shall my black Velvet Mask thy fair Face Vaile?
Pass o're my Faults: shine forth, bright sun, arise!
Enthrone thy Rosy-selfe within mine Eyes.

John Dryden
1631-1700

As an example of Dryden's variation, we can turn from the water-depths of certain passages in *Annus Mirabilis* to the exquisite lightness and tenderness of the *Song of the Zambra Dance* in *The Conquest of Granada*.

The softness and tenderness of this, due to the apparently wavering, yet completely controlled length of the lines, still contains, within it, the sharpness of flames, and this is owing to the elaborate scheme of *a*'s in the first verse, and of mixed *i*'s in the second verse. The two schemes are brought together in the third verse.

The satires are thick, gross, terrible, and blind as stupidity itself. *Absalom and Achitophel* is a very great poem. Dryden's victims are not so much impaled (as are Pope's) in an everlasting, moving, heaving hell of lava as made into a thick and world-wide mud pudding (the supreme epitome of soulless matter), or buried alive beneath an immense rumbling fall of mountains. Dryden seems not so much to rear himself to a world's height and crash down on his victims from the very heavens (like Pope), as to be in the state of Goya's *Giant Dancing*. He treads on these insects, and they are gone. He has been at no effort to obliterate them.

A SONG FOR ST. CECILIA'S DAY
November 22, 1687

From Harmony, from heav'nly Harmony
 This universal Frame began;
 When Nature underneath a heap
  Of jarring Atomes lay,
 And cou'd not heave her Head,

The tuneful Voice was heard from high,
  Arise, ye more than dead.
Then cold and hot and moist and dry
  In order to their Stations leap,
    And MUSICK's pow'r obey.
From Harmony, from heavenly Harmony
  This universal Frame began:
  From Harmony to Harmony
Through all the Compass of the Notes it ran,
The Diapason closing full in Man.

What Passion cannot MUSICK raise and quell?
  When *Jubal* struck the corded Shell,
  His listening Brethren stood around,
    And, wond'ring, on their Faces fell
  To worship that Celestial Sound:
Less than a God they thought there could not dwell
    Within the hollow of that Shell,
    That spoke so sweetly, and so well.
What Passion cannot MUSICK raise and quell?

    The TRUMPETS loud Clangor
      Excites us to Arms
    With shrill Notes of Anger
      And mortal Alarms.
    The double double double beat
      Of the thund'ring DRUM
      Cryes, heark the Foes come;
  Charge, Charge, 'tis too late to retreat.

    The soft complaining FLUTE
    In dying Notes discovers
    The Woes of hopeless Lovers,
  Whose Dirge is whisper'd by the warbling LUTE.

    Sharp VIOLINS proclaim
  Their jealous Pangs and Desperation,
  Fury, frantick Indignation,
  Depth of Pains and Height of Passion,
    For the fair, disdainful Dame.

    But oh! what Art can teach
    What human Voice can reach
      The sacred ORGANS Praise?
    Notes inspiring holy Love,
  Notes that wing their heavenly Ways
    To mend the Choires above.

Orpheus cou'd lead the savage race,
And Trees unrooted left their Place,
    Sequacious of the Lyre;
But bright CECILIA rais'd the Wonder high'r;
When to her Organ vocal Breath was given,
An Angel heard, and straight appear'd
    Mistaking Earth for Heav'n.

GRAND CHORUS

As from the Pow'r of Sacred Lays
    The Spheres began to move,
And sung the great Creator's Praise
    To all the bless'd above;
So, when the last and dreadful Hour
This crumbling Pageant shall devour,
The TRUMPET *shall be heard on high,*
The dead shall live, the living die.
And MUSICK *shall untune the Sky.*

AN ODE
To the Pious Memory of the Accomplisht Young Lady
Mrs. Anne Killigrew
Excellent in the Two Sister-Arts of Poesie and Painting

Thou youngest Virgin-Daughter of the Skies,
    Made in the last Promotion of the *Blest;*
Whose Palms, new pluckt from Paradise,
In spreading *Branches* more sublimely rise,
    Rich with Immortal Green above the rest:
Whether, adopted to some Neighbouring Star,
Thou rol'st above us in thy wand'ring Race,
    Or, in Procession fixt and regular,
Mov'd with the Heavens Majestick pace;
    Or, call'd to more Superior *Bliss,*
Thou tread'st, with Seraphims, the vast *Abyss:*
Whatever happy region is thy place,
Cease thy Celestial Song a little space;
(Thou wilt have time enough for Hymns Divine,
Since Heav'ns Eternal Year is thine.)
Hear then a Mortal Muse thy praise rehearse
    In no ignoble Verse;
But such as thy own voice did practise here,
When thy first Fruits of Poesie were given,
To make thyself a welcome Inmate there;
    While yet a young Probationer,
        And Candidate of Heav'n.

If by Traduction came thy Mind,
  Our Wonder is the less to find
A Soul so charming from a Stock so good;
Thy Father was transfus'd into thy *Blood*:
So wert thou born into the tuneful strain,
  (An early, rich, and inexhausted Vein.)
  But if thy Præ-existing Soul
Was form'd, at first, with Myriads more,
  It did through all the Mighty Poets roul
Who *Greek* or *Latine* Laurels wore,
And was that *Sappho* last, which once it was before.
  If so, then cease thy flight, *O Heav'n-born Mind!*
Thou hast no *Dross* to purge from thy Rich Ore:
  Nor can thy Soul a fairer Mansion find
  Than was the *Beauteous* Frame she left behind:
Return, to fill or mend the Quire of thy Celestial kind.

  May we presume to say, that at thy *Birth,*
New joy was sprung in HEAV'N as well as here on *Earth?*
For sure the Milder Planets did combine
On thy *Auspicious* Horoscope to shine,
And ev'n the most Malicious were in Trine.
Thy *Brother-Angels* at thy *Birth*
  Strung each his Lyre, and tun'd it high,
  That all the People of the Skie
Might know a Poetess was born on Earth.
  And then if ever, Mortal Ears
  Had heard the Musick of the Spheres!
  And if no clust'ring Swarm of *Bees*
On thy sweet Mouth distill'd their golden Dew,
  'Twas that, such vulgar Miracles
  Heav'n had not Leasure to renew:
  For all the *Blest* Fraternity of Love
Solemniz'd there thy *Birth,* and kept thy Holyday above.

  O Gracious God! How far have we
Prophan'd thy Heav'nly Gift of Poesy!
Made prostitute and profligate the Muse,
Debas'd to each obscene and impious use,
Whose Harmony was first ordain'd *Above,*
  For Tongues of *Angels* and for *Hymns* of *Love!*
Oh wretched We! why were we hurry'd down
  This lubrique and adult'rate age,
(Nay, added fat Pollutions of our own)
  T' increase the steaming Ordures of the Stage?

What can we say t' excuse our *Second Fall?*
Let this thy *Vestal,* Heav'n, atone for all:
Her *Arethusian* Stream remains unsoil'd,
Unmixt with Forreign Filth and undefil'd,
Her Wit was more than Man, her Innocence a Child.

Art she had none, yet wanted none,
    For Nature did that Want supply:
So rich in Treasures of her Own,
    She might our boasted Stores defy:
Such Noble Vigour did her Verse adorn,
That it seem'd borrow'd, where 'twas only born.
Her Morals too were in her *Bosom* bred
    By great Examples daily fed,
What in the best of *Books,* her Father's Life, she read.
    And to be read her self she need not fear;
    Each Test, and ev'ry Light, her Muse will bear,
    Though *Epictetus* with his Lamp were there.
    Ev'n Love (for Love sometimes her Muse exprest),
Was but a Lambent-flame which play'd about her *Breast:*
    Light as the Vapours of a Morning Dream,
    So cold herself, whilst she such Warmth exprest,
      'Twas *Cupid* bathing in *Diana's* Stream.

Born to the Spacious Empire of the Nine,
One wou'd have thought, she should have been content
To manage well that Mighty Government;
But what can young ambitious Souls confine?
    To the next Realm she stretcht her Sway,
    For *Painture* near adjoyning lay,
A plenteous Province, and alluring Prey.
A *Chamber of Dependences* was fram'd,
(As Conquerors will never want Pretence,
    When arm'd, to justifie th' Offence),
And the whole Fief, in right of Poetry she claim'd.
    The Country open lay without Defence;
For Poets frequent In-rodes there had made,
    And perfectly cou'd represent
    The Shape, the Face, with ev'ry Lineament;
And all the large Demains which the Dumb-sister sway'd;
    All bow'd beneath her Government,
    Receiv'd in Triumph wheresoe're she went.
Her Pencil drew whate're her Soul design'd
And oft the *happy Draught* surpass'd the *Image* in her *Mind.*
    The *Sylvan* Scenes of Herds and Flocks
    And fruitful Plains and barren Rocks,

Of shallow *Brooks* that flow'd so clear,
The bottom did the top appear;
Of deeper too and ampler Floods
Which as in Mirrors, shew'd the Woods;
Of lofty Trees, with Sacred Shades
And Perspectives of pleasant Glades,
Where Nymphs of brightest Form appear,
And shaggy Satyrs standing near,
Which them at once admire and fear.
The Ruines too of some Majestick Piece,
Boasting the Pow'r of ancient *Rome* or *Greece,*
Whose Statues, Freezes, Columns, broken lie,
And, tho' defac'd, the Wonder of the Eye;
What *Nature, Art,* bold *Fiction,* e're durst frame,
Her forming Hand gave Feature to the Name.
So strange a Concourse ne're was seen before,
But when the peopl'd *Ark* the whole Creation bore.

The Scene then chang'd; with bold Erected Look
Our Martial King the sight with Reverence strook:
For, not content t' express his Outward Part,
Her hand call'd out the Image of his Heart,
His Warlike Mind, his Soul devoid of Fear,
His High-designing *Thoughts* were figur'd there,
As when, by Magick, Ghosts are made appear.
Our Phenix queen was portrai'd too so bright,
Beauty alone cou'd *Beauty* take so right:
Her Dress, her Shape, her matchless Grace,
Were all observ'd, as well as heav'nly Face.
With such a Peerless Majesty she stands,
As in that Day she took the Crown from Sacred hands:
Before a Train of Heroins was seen,
In *Beauty* foremost, as in Rank, the Queen!
Thus nothing to her Genius was deny'd,
But like a *Ball* of Fire, the farther thrown,
Still with a greater *Blaze* she shone,
And her bright Soul broke out on ev'ry side.
What next she had design'd, Heaven only knows:
To such Immod'rate Growth her Conquest rose
That Fate alone its Progress cou'd oppose.

Now all those Charms, that blooming Grace,
The well-proportion'd Shape and beauteous Face,
Shall never more be seen by Mortal Eyes;
In Earth the much-lamented Virgin lies!

Not Wit nor Piety cou'd Fate prevent;
Nor was the cruel *Destiny* content
To finish all the Murder at a blow,
To sweep at once her *Life* and *Beauty* too;
But, like a hardn'd Fellon, took a pride
To work more Mischievously slow,
And plunder'd first, and then destroy'd.
O double Sacriledge on things Divine,
To rob the Relique, and deface the Shrine!
But thus *Orinda* dy'd:
Heav'n, by the same Disease, did both translate,
As equal were their Souls, so equal was their fate.

Mean time, her *Warlike Brother* on the Seas
His waving Streamers to the Winds displays,
And vows for his Return, with vain Devotion, pays.
Ah, Generous Youth! that Wish forbear,
The Winds too soon will waft thee here!
Slack all thy Sails, and fear to come,
Alas, thou know'st not, thou art wreck'd at home!
No more shalt thou behold thy Sister's Face,
Thou hast already had her last Embrace.
But look aloft, and if thou ken'st from far,
Among the *Pleiad's,* a New-kindl'd star,
If any sparkles, than the rest, more bright,
'Tis she that shines in that propitious Light.

When in mid-Air the Golden Trump shall sound,
To raise the Nations under ground;
When in the Valley of *Jehosaphat*
The Judging God shall close the book of Fate;
And there the last *Assizes* keep
For those who Wake and those who Sleep;
When ratling *Bones* together fly
From the four Corners of the Skie,
When Sinews o're the Skeletons are spread,
Those cloath'd with Flesh, and Life inspires the Dead;
The Sacred Poets first shall hear the Sound,
And formost from the Tomb shall bound:
For they are cover'd with the lightest ground;
And streight, with in-born Vigour, on the Wing,
Like mounting Larks, to the New Morning sing.
There *Thou,* sweet Saint, before the Quire shalt go,
As Harbinger of Heav'n, the Way to show,
The Way which thou so well hast learn'd below.

From THE FABLE OF ACIS, POLYPHEMUS
AND GALATEA

Translated from the Thirteenth Book of Ovid's Metamorphoses

I HEARD THE RUFFIAN–SHEPHERD RUDELY BLOW

I heard the Ruffian-Shepherd rudely blow,
Where, in a hollow Cave, I sat below;
On *Acis* bosom I my head reclin'd:
And still preserve the Poem in my mind.
   Oh lovely *Galatea*, whiter far
Than falling Snows, and rising Lillies are;
More flowry than the Meads, as Crystal bright;
Erect as Alders, and of equal height:
More wanton than a Kid, more sleek thy Skin
Than Orient Shells, that on the Shores are seen:
Than Apples fairer, when the boughs they lade;
Pleasing, as Winter Suns or Summer Shade:
More grateful to the sight, than goodly Planes;
And softer to the touch, than down of Swans,
Or Curds new turn'd; and sweeter to the taste
Than swelling Grapes, that to the Vintage haste:
More clear than Ice, or running Streams, that stray
Through Garden Plots, but ah more swift than they.
   Yet, *Galatea,* harder to be broke
Than Bullocks, unreclaim'd to bear the Yoke,
And far more stubborn than the knotted Oak:
Like sliding Streams, impossible to hold;
Like them fallacious; like their Fountains, cold:
More warping than the Willow, to decline
My warm Embrace, more brittle than the Vine;
Immoveable, and fixt in thy disdain;
Rough, as these Rocks, and of a harder grain.
More violent than is the rising Flood:
And the prais'd Peacock is not half so proud.
Fierce as the Fire, and sharp as Thistles are;
And more outragious than a Mother-Bear:
Deaf as the Billows to the Vows I make;
And more revengeful, than a trodden Snake.
In swiftness fleeter than the flying Hind,
Or driven Tempests, or the driving Wind.
All other faults with patience I can bear;
But swiftness is the Vice I only fear.

From ALL FOR LOVE; *or,* THE WORLD WELL LOST

ACT I. SCENE 1

The Temple of Isis. Enter Serapion, Myris, Priests of Isis.

SERAPION. Portents and Prodigies are grown so frequent
    That they have lost their Name. Our fruitfull Nile
    Flow'd ere the wonted Season, with a Torrent
    So unexpected, and so wondrous fierce,
    That the wild Deluge overtook the haste
    Ev'n of the Hinds that watch'd it: Men and Beasts
    Were borne above the tops of Trees, that grew
    On th' utmost Margin of the Water-mark.
    Then, with so swift an Ebb, the Floud drove backward
    It slipt from underneath the Scaly Herd:
    Here monstrous Phocæ panted on the Shore;
    Forsaken Dolphins there, with their broad tails,
    Lay lashing the departing Waves: Hard by 'em,
    Sea-Horses flound'ring in the slimy mud,
    Toss'd up their heads, and dash'd the ooze about 'em.
MYRIS. Avert these Omens, Heav'n.
SERAPION. Last night, between the hours of Twelve and One,
    In a lone aisle o' th' Temple while I walk'd,
    A Whirl-wind rose, that, with a violent blast,
    Shook all the Dome: the Doors around me clapt,
    The Iron Wicket, that defends the Vault,
    Burst open, and disclos'd the mighty dead.
    From out each Monument, in order plac'd,
    An Armed Ghost starts up: the Boy-King last
    Rear'd his inglorious head. A peal of groans
    Then follow'd, and a lamentable voice
    Cry'd, Ægypt is no more.

From THE CONQUEST OF GRANADA

SONG OF THE ZAMBRA DANCE

Beneath a Myrtle shade
Which Love for none but happy Lovers made,
I slept, and straight my Love before me brought
Phillis the object of my waking thought;
Undres'd she came my flames to meet,
While Love strow'd flow'rs beneath her feet:
Flow'rs, which so press'd by her, became more sweet.

From the bright Visions Head
A careless vail of Lawn was loosely spread:
From her white temples fell her shaded hair,
Like cloudy sunshine not too brown nor fair:
Her hands, her lips did love inspire;
Her ev'ry grace my heart did fire:
But most her eyes which languish'd with desire.

Ah, charming Fair, said I,
How long can you my bliss and yours deny?
By Nature and by love this lonely shade
Was for revenge of suffring Lovers made:
Silence and shades with love agree:
Both shelter you and favour me;
You cannot blush because I cannot see.

No, let me dye, she said,
Rather than lose the spotless name of Maid;
Faintly methought she spoke, for all the while
She bid me not believe her, with a smile.
Then dye, said I, she still deny'd:
And is it thus, thus, thus she cry'd
You use a harmless Maid, and so she dy'd!

I wak'd, and straight I knew
I lov'd so well it made my dream prove true:
Fancy, the kinder Mistress of the two,
Fancy had done what *Phillis* wou'd not do!
Ah, Cruel Nymph, cease your disdain,
While I can dream you scorn in vain;
Asleep or waking you must ease my pain.

From THE INDIAN QUEEN

SONG OF AERIAL SPIRITS

Poor Mortals that are clog'd with Earth below
   Sink under Love and Care,
   While we that dwell in Air
Such heavy Passions never know.
   Why then shou'd Mortals be
   Unwilling to be free
   From Blood, that sullen Cloud
   Which shining Souls does shroud?

Then they'll shew bright,
And like us light,
When leaving Bodies with their Care
They slide to us and Air.

From CLEOMENES

NO, NO, POOR SUFF'RING HEART

No, no, poor suff'ring Heart, no Change endeavour,
Choose to sustain the smart, rather than leave her;
My ravish'd Eyes behold such Charms about her,
I can dye with her, but not live without her.
One tender Sigh of hers to see me Languish,
Will more than pay the price of my past Anguish:
Beware, O cruel Fair, how you smile on me,
'Twas a kind look of yours that has undone me.

Love has in store for me one happy Minute,
And She will end my pain who did begin it;
Then no day void of Bliss, or Pleasure leaving,
Ages shall slide away without perceiving:
Cupid shall guard the Door the more to please us,
And keep out Time and Death, when they would seize us:
Time and Death shall depart, and say in flying,
Love has found out a way to Live by Dying.

From ABSALOM AND ACHITOPHEL

From PART I

Of these the false *Achitophel* was first,
A Name to all succeeding Ages curst.
For close Designs and crooked Counsels fit,
Sagacious, Bold, and Turbulent of wit,
Restless, unfixt in Principles and Place,
In Pow'r unpleased, impatient of Disgrace;
A fiery Soul, which working out its way,
Fretted the Pigmy Body to decay:
And o'r informed the Tenement of Clay.
A daring Pilot in extremity;
Pleas'd with the Danger, when the Waves went high
He sought the Storms; but, for a Calm unfit,
Would Steer too nigh the Sands to boast his Wit.
Great Wits are sure to Madness near alli'd
And thin Partitions do their Bounds divide;

Else, why should he, with Wealth and Honour blest,
Refuse his Age the needful hours of Rest?
Punish a Body which he cou'd not please,
Bankrupt of Life, yet Prodigal of Ease?
And all to leave what with his Toil he won
To that unfeather'd two-legg'd thing, a Son:
Got, while his Soul did huddled Notions trie;
And born a shapeless Lump, like Anarchy.
In Friendship false, implacable in Hate,
Resolv'd to Ruine or to Rule the State.
To Compass this the Triple Bond he broke;
The Pillars of the Publick Safety shook:
And fitted *Israel* for a Foreign Yoke.
Then, seiz'd with Fear, yet still affecting Fame,
Usurp'd a Patriot's All-attoning Name.
So easie still it proves in Factious Times
With publick Zeal to cancel private Crimes:
How safe is Treason and how sacred ill,
Where none can sin against the Peoples Will,
Where Crouds can wink; and no offence be known,
Since in anothers guilt they find their own. . . .

A numerous Host of dreaming Saints succeed;
Of the true old Enthusiastick Breed:
'Gainst Form and Order they their Pow'r imploy.
Nothing to Build, and all things to Destroy.
But far more numerous was the Herd of such,
Who think too little, and who talk too much.
These, out of meer instinct, they knew not why,
Adored their Fathers' God, and Property:
And, by the same blind Benefit of Fate,
The Devil and the *Jebusite* did hate:
Born to be sav'd, even in their own despight;
Because they could not help believing right.
Such were the Tools; but a whole Hydra more
Remains, of sprouting heads too long to score.
Some of their Chiefs were Princes of the Land;
In the first Rank of these did *Zimri* stand:
A man so various, that he seem'd to be
Not one, but all Mankind's Epitome.
Stiff in Opinions, always in the wrong;
Was Everything by starts, and Nothing long:
But, in the course of one revolving Moon,
Was Chymist, Fidler, States-man, and Buffoon;
Then all for Women, Painting, Rhiming, Drinking,

Besides ten thousand Freaks that died in thinking.
Blest Madman, who coud every hour employ,
With something New to wish, or to enjoy!
Railing and praising were his usual Theams;
And both (to shew his Judgment) in Extreams:
So over Violent, or over Civil,
That every Man, with him, was God or Devil.
In squandring Wealth was his peculiar Art:
Nothing went unrewarded, but Desert.
Begger'd by fools, whom still he found too late:
He had his Jest, and they had his Estate.

From *PART II*

Levi, thou art a load, I'll lay thee down,
And shew Rebellion bare, without a Gown;
Poor Slaves in metre, dull and adle-pated,
Who Rhime below ev'n *David's* Psalms translated.
Some in my Speedy pace I must outrun,
As lame *Mephibosheth* the Wisard's Son;
To make quick way I'll Leap o'er heavy blocks,
Shun rotten *Uzza* as I woud the Pox;
And hasten *Og* and *Doeg* to rehearse,
Two Fools that Crutch their Feeble sense on Verse,
Who by my Muse, to all succeeding times
Shall live in spight of their own Dogrell Rhimes.
Doeg, though without knowing how or why,
Made still a blund'ring kind of Melody;
Spurd boldly on, and Dash'd through Thick and Thin,
Through Sense and Non-sense, never out nor in;
Free from all meaning, whether good or bad,
And in one word, Heroically mad,
He was too warm on Picking-work to dwell,
But Faggotted his Notions as they fell,
And, if they Rhim'd and Rattl'd, all was well.
Spightfull he was not, though he wrote a Satyr,
For still there goes some *thinking* to ill-Nature:
He needs no more than Birds and Beasts to think,
All his occasions are to eat and drink.
If he call Rogue and Rascal from a Garrat,
He means you no more Mischief than a Parat:
The words for Friend and Foe alike were made,
To Fetter 'em in Verse is all his Trade.
For Almonds he'll cry Whore to his own Mother:
And call young *Absalom* King *David's* Brother.

Let him be Gallows-Free by my consent,
And nothing suffer, since he nothing meant:
Hanging Supposes humane Soul and reason,
This Animal's below committing Treason.
Shall he be hang'd who never cou'd Rebell?
That's a preferment for *Achitophel*. . . .

Now stop your noses, Readers, all and some,
For here's a tun of Midnight work to come,
Og from a Treason Tavern rowling home.
Round as a Globe, and Liquored ev'ry chink,
Goodly and Great he Sayls behind his Link;
With all this Bulk there's nothing lost in *Og*,
For ev'ry inch that is not Fool is Rogue:
A Monstrous mass of foul corrupted matter,
As all the Devils had spew'd to make the batter.
When wine has given him courage to Blaspheme,
He curses God, but God before Curst him;
And if man cou'd have reason, none has more,
That made his Paunch so rich and him so poor.
With wealth he was not trusted, for Heav'n knew
What 'twas of Old to pamper up a *Jew;*
To what would he on Quail and Pheasant swell,
That ev'n on Tripe and Carrion cou'd rebell?
But though Heaven made him poor, (with rev'rence speaking,)
He never was a Poet of God's making;
The Midwife laid her hand on his Thick Skull,
With this Prophetick blessing — *Be thou Dull;*
Drink, Swear, and Roar, forbear no lew'd delight
Fit for thy Bulk, doe anything but write.

From MAC FLECKNOE

All humane things are subject to decay,
And, when Fate summons, Monarchs must obey:
This *Fleckno* found, who, like *Augustus,* young
Was call'd to Empire and had govern'd long:
In Prose and Verse was own'd, without dispute
Through all the realms of Non-sense, absolute.
This aged Prince now flourishing in Peace,
And blest with issue of a large increase,
Worn out with business, did at length debate
To settle the Succession of the State;

And pond'ring which of all his Sons was fit
To Reign, and wage immortal War with Wit,
Cry'd, 'tis resolv'd; for Nature pleads that He
Should onely rule, who most resembles me:
Sh —— alone my perfect image bears,
Mature in dullness from his tender years;
Sh —— alone of all my Sons is he
Who stands confirm'd in full stupidity.
The rest to some faint meaning make pretence,
But *Sh* —— never deviates into sense.
Some Beams of Wit on other souls may fall,
Strike through and make a lucid intervall;
But *Sh* —— 's genuine night admits no ray,
His rising Fogs prevail upon the Day:
Besides, his goodly Fabrick fills the eye,
And seems design'd for thoughtless Majesty:
Thoughtless as Monarch Oakes that shade the plain,
And, spread in solemn state, supinely reign.
Heywood and *Shirley* were but Types of thee,
Thou last great Prophet of Tautology:
Even I, a dunce of more renown than they,
Was sent before but to prepare thy way:
And coarsely clad in *Norwich* Drugget came
To teach the Nations in thy greater name.

John Gay
1685-1732

From THE BEGGAR'S OPERA

WERE I LAID ON GREENLAND'S COAST

Were I laid on *Greenland's* Coast,
   And in my Arms embrac'd my Lass;
Warm amidst eternal Frost,
   Too soon the Half Year's Night would pass.
Were I sold on *Indian* Soil,
   Soon as the burning Day was clos'd,
I could mock the sultry Toil,
   When on my Charmer's Breast repos'd.
And I would love you all the Day,
Every Night would kiss and play,
If with me you'd fondly stray
Over the Hills and far away.

Traditional Songs and Light Ballads

MY HANDSOME GILDEROY

Gilderoy was a bonnie boy,
  Had roses tull his shoone,
His stockings were of silken soy,
  Wi' garters hanging doune:
It was, I weene, a comelie sight,
  To see sae trim a boy;
He was my joy and heart's delight,
  My handsome Gilderoy.

Oh! sike twe charming een he had,
  A breath as sweet as rose;
He never ware a Highland plaid,
  But costly silken clothes.
He gained the luve of ladies gay,
  Nane eir tull him was coy,
Ah! wae is mee! I mourn the day,
  For my dear Gilderoy.

My Gilderoy and I were born
  Baith in one toun together;
We scant were seven years beforn
  We gan to luve each other;
Our daddies and our mammies thay
  Were fill'd wi' mickle joy,
To think upon the bridal day
  'Twixt me and Gilderoy.

For Gilderoy, that luve of mine,
  Gude faith! I freely bought
A wedding sark of Holland fine
  Wi' silken flowers wrought:
And he gied me a wedding ring,
  Which I received with joy,
Nae lad nor lassie eir could sing
  Like me and Gilderoy.

Wi' mickle joy we spent our prime,
  Till we were baith sixteen,

And aft we past the langsome time
  Among the leaves sae green:
Aft on the banks we'd sit us
    thair,
  And sweetly kiss and toy;
Wi' garlands gay wad deck my hair
  My handsome Gilderoy.

Oh! that he still had been content
  Wi' me to lead his life;
But, ah! his manfu' heart was bent
  To stir in feats of strife.
And he in many a venturous deed
  His courage bauld wad try;
And now this gars mine heart to
    bleed
  For my dear Gilderoy.

And when of me his leave he tuik,
  The tears they wet mine ee;
I gave tull him a parting luik,
  "My benison gang wi' thee!
God speed thee weil, mine ain dear
    heart,
  For gane is all my joy;
My heart is rent, sith we maunt
    part,
  My handsome Gilderoy!"

My Gilderoy, baith far and near,
  Was feared in ev'ry toun,
And bauldly bare away the gear
  Of many a lowland loun:
Nane eir durst meet him man to
    man,
  He was sae brave a boy;
At length wi' numbers he was tane,
  My winsome Gilderoy.

tull] to.   sike twe] such two.   scant] scarce.   gars] makes.

Wae worth the loun that made the
  laws,
  To hang a man for gear,
To reave of life for ox or ass,
  For sheep, or horse, or mare:
Had not their laws been made sae
  strick,
  I neir had lost my joy;
Wi' sorrow neir had wat my cheek
  For my dear Gilderoy.

Giff Gilderoy had done amisse,
  He mought hae banisht been,
Ah, what fair cruelty is this,
  To hang sike handsome men!
To hang the flower o' Scottish
  land,
  Sae sweet and fair a boy;
Nae lady had so white a hand
  As thee, my Gilderoy.

Of Gilderoy sae fraid they were,
  They bound him mickle strong,
Tull Edenburrow they led him
  thair,
  And on a gallows hung:
They hung him high aboon the rest
  He was so trim a boy:
Thair dyed the youth whom I lued
  best,
  My handsome Gilderoy.

Thus having yielded up his breath,
  I bare his corpse away;
Wi' teares, that trickled for his
  death,
  I washt his comely clay;
And siker in a grave sae deep
  I laid the dear-lued boy,
And now for evir maun I weep
  My winsome Gilderoy.

    giff] if.   siker] safely.

CAM' YE BY

Cam' ye by the salmon fishers?
  Cam' ye by the roperee?
Saw ye a sailor laddie
  Waiting on the coast for me?

I ken fahr I'm gyain,
  I ken fahs gyain wi' me;
I ha'e a lad o' my ain,
  Ye daurna tack 'im frae me.

Stockings of blue silk,
  Shoes of patent leather,
Kid to tie them up,
  And gold rings on his finger.

Oh for six o'clock!
  Oh for seven I weary!
Oh for eight o'clock!
  And then I'll see my dearie.

    fahr] where.   gyain] going.   fahs] who's.

IRISH SONG: I KNOW WHERE I'M GOING

I know where I'm going
  And I know who's going with me:
I know who I love,
  But the dear knows who I'll marry.

I have stockings of silk,
  Shoes of fine green leather,
Combs to buckle my hair,
  And a ring for every finger.

Some say he's black,
 But I say he's bonny,
The fairest of them all,
 My handsome winsome Johnny.

Feather beds are soft,
 And painted rooms are bonny,
But I would leave them all
 To go with my love Johnny.

 I know where I'm going,
  And I know who's going with me:
 I know who I love,
  But the dear knows who I'll marry.

I GAVE HER CAKES
Song set to music by Henry Purcell

I gave her cakes; I gave her ale,
 I gave her sack and sherry;
I kissed her once, I kissed her twice,
 And we were wondrous merry.

I gave her beads and bracelets fine,
 And I gave her gold down derry;
I thought she was afeard till she stroked my beard,
 And we were wondrous merry.

Merry my heart, merry my cocks, merry my sprights,
 Merry my hey down derry;
I kissed her once and I kissed her twice,
 And we were wondrous merry.

THREE KNIGHTS FROM SPAIN

We are three Brethren come from Spain,
 All in French garlands;
We are come to court your daughter Jane,
 And adieu to you, my darlings.

My daughter Jane! — she is too young,
 All in French garlands;
She cannot bide your flattering tongue,
 And adieu to you, my darlings.

Be she young, or be she old,
 All in French garlands;
'Tis for a bride she must be sold,
 And adieu to you, my darlings.

A bride, a bride, she shall not be
  All in French garlands;
Till she go through this world with me,
  And adieu to you, my darlings.

Then shall you keep your daughter Jane,
  All in French garlands;
Come once, we come not here again,
  And adieu to you, my darlings.

Turn back, turn back, you Spanish Knights,
  All in French garlands;
Scour, scour your spurs, till they be bright,
  And adieu to you, my darlings.

Sharp shine our spurs, all richly wrought,
  All in French garlands;
In towns afar our spurs were bought,
  And adieu to you, my darlings.

Smell my lilies, smell my roses,
  All in French garlands;
Which of my maidens do you choose?
  And adieu to you, my darlings.

Not she. Not she. Thy youngest, Jane!
  All in French garlands;
We ride — and ride not back again,
  And adieu to you, my darlings.

In every pocket a thousand pound,
  All in French garlands;
On every finger a gay gold ring,
  And adieu to you, my darlings.
  And adieu to you, my darlings.

A NEW YEAR CAROL

Here we bring new water
  From the well so clear,
For to worship God with,
  This happy New Year.

Sing levy dew, sing levy dew,
  The water and the wine;
The seven bright gold wires
  And the bugles that do shine.

Sing reign of Fair Maid,
  With gold upon her toe —
Open you the West Door,
  And turn the Old Year go.

Sing reign of Fair Maid
  With gold upon her chin —

Open you the East Door,
  And let the New Year in.
Sing levy dew, sing levy dew,
  The water and the wine;
The seven bright gold wires
  And the bugles they do
    shine.

LILY BRIGHT AND SHINE–A

"Here comes a lusty wooer,
  My a dildin, my a daldin;
Here comes a lusty wooer,
  Lily bright and shine-a."

"Pray who do you woo?
  My a dildin, my a daldin;
Pray who do you woo?
  Lily bright and shine-a."

"Woo! Your fairest daughter!
  My a dildin, my a daldin;
Woo! your fairest daughter!
  Lily bright and shine-a."

"There! there! she is for you,
  My a dildin, my a daldin;
There! there! she is for you,
  Lily bright and shine-a."

JOHNNY FAA, THE GYPSY LADDIE

The gypsies they came to lord Cassilis' gate,
  And O but they sang bonnie!
They sang so sweet and so complete
  Till down came our fair ladie.

She came tripping down the stairs
  And all her maids before her;
As soon as they saw her weel-far'd face
  They cast the glamowrie owre her.

She gave them the good wheat bread,
  And they gave her the ginger;
But she gave them a far better thing,
  The gold rings of her finger.

"Will you go with me, my hinny and my heart?
  Will you go with me, my dearie?
And I will swear, by the hilt of my spear,
  That your lord shall no more come near thee."

It was late in the night when the lord came home
  Enquiring for his lady.
His servant made a sure reply:
  "She's gone with the gipsum laddie" —
    Rattle tum a gipsum gipsum
    Rattle tum a gipsum laddie.

"O go catch up my milk-white steed,
  The black one's not so speedy,
I'll ride all night till broad daylight,
  Or overtake my lady."

He rode and he rode till he came to the town,
  He rode till he came to Barley.
The tears came rolling down his cheeks,
  And then he spied his lady.

"It's come go back, my dearest dear,
  Come go back, my honey;
It's come go back, my dearest dear,
  And you never shall lack for money."

"I won't go back, my dearest dear,
  I won't go back, my honey:
For I wouldn't give a kiss from gipsum's lips
  For you and all your money."

"It's go pull off those snow-white gloves,
  A-made of Spanish leather,
And give to me your lily-white hand,
  And bid farewell for ever."

It's she pulled off those snow-white gloves,
  A-made of Spanish leather,
And gave to him her lily-white hand
  And bade farewell for ever.

She soon ran through her gay clothing,
  Her velvet shoes and stockings;
Her gold ring off her finger's gone,
  And the gold plate off her bosom.

"O once I had a house and land,
  Feather-bed and money;
But now I've come to an old straw pad
  With the gypsies dancing round me."

Refrain from THE BROOMFIELD HILL

BROME, BROME ON HILL

Brome, brome on hill,
The gentle brome on hill, hill,
Brome, brome on Hive hill,
The gentle brome on Hive hill,
The brome stands on Hive hill-a.

THE FALSE KNIGHT UPON THE ROAD

"O whare are ye gaun?"
Quo' the fause knicht upon the road:
"I'm gaun to the scule."
Quo' the wee boy, and still he stude.

"What is that upon your back?"
Quo' the fause knicht upon the road:
"Atweel it is my bukes."
Quo' the wee boy, and still he stude.

"What's that ye've got in your arm?"
Quo' the fause knicht upon the road:
"Atweel it is my peit."
Quo' the wee boy, and still he stude.

"Wha's aucht they sheep?"
Quo' the fause knicht upon the road:
"They're mine and my mither's."
Quo' the wee boy, and still he stude.

"How monie o' them are mine?"
Quo' the fause knicht upon the road:
"A' they that hae blue tails."
Quo' the wee boy, and still he stude.

"I wiss ye were on yon tree."
Quo' the fause knicht upon the road:
"And a gude ladder under me."
Quo' the wee boy, and still he stude.

atweel] why, sure.   peit] peat for school fire.   wha's aucht] who owns.

"And the ladder for to break."
  Quo' the fause knicht upon the road:
"And *you* for to fa' down."
  Quo' the wee boy, and still he stude.

"I wiss ye were in yon sie."
  Quo' the fause knicht upon the road:
"And a gude bottom under me."
  Quo' the wee boy, and still he stude.

"And the bottom for to break."
  Quo' the fause knicht upon the road:
"And *ye* to be drowned."
  Quo' the wee boy, and still he stude.

bottom] vessel, ship.

THE RIDDLING KNIGHT

There was a knicht riding frae the east,
  Jennifer gentle an' rosemaree.
Who had been wooing at monie a place,
  As the doo flies owre the mulberry tree.

He cam' unto a widow's door,
  Jennifer gentle an' rosemaree.
And speird whare her three dochters were,
  As the doo flies owre the mulberry tree.

"The auldest ane's to a washing gane,
  Jennifer gentle an' rosemaree.
The second's to a baking gane,
  As the doo flies owre the mulberry tree.

"The youngest ane's to a wedding gane,
  Jennifer gentle an' rosemaree.
And it will be nicht or she be hame,"
  As the doo flies owre the mulberry tree.

He sat him doun upon a stane,
  Jennifer gentle an' rosemaree.
Till thir three lasses cam' tripping hame,
  As the doo flies owre the mulberry tree.

doo] dove.   speird] asked.   or] ere.

The auldest ane she let him in,
Jennifer gentle an' rosemaree.
And pinned the door wi' a siller pin,
As the doo flies owre the mulberry tree.

The second ane she made his bed,
Jennifer gentle an' rosemaree.
And laid saft pillows unto his head,
As the doo flies owre the mulberry tree.

The youngest ane was bauld and bricht,
Jennifer gentle an' rosemaree.
And she tarried for words wi' this unco knicht,
As the doo flies owre the mulberry tree.

"Gin ye will answer me questions ten,
Jennifer gentle an' rosemaree.
The morn ye sall be made my ain: —
As the doo flies owre the mulberry tree.

"O what is higher nor the tree?
Jennifer gentle an' rosemaree.
And what is deeper nor the sea?
As the doo flies owre the mulberry tree.

"Or what is heavier nor the lead?
Jennifer gentle an' rosemaree.
And what is better nor the bread?
As the doo flies owre the mulberry tree.

"Or what is whiter nor the milk?
Jennifer gentle an' rosemaree.
Or what is safter nor the silk?
As the doo flies owre the mulberry tree.

"Or what is sharper nor a thorn?
Jennifer gentle an' rosemaree.
Or what is louder nor a horn?
As the doo flies owre the mulberry tree.

"Or what is greener nor the grass?
Jennifer gentle an' rosemaree.
Or what is waur nor a woman was?"
As the doo flies owre the mulberry tree.

bauld] bold.   nor] than.   waur] worse.

"O heaven is higher nor the tree,
  Jennifer gentle an' rosemaree.
And hell is deeper nor the sea,
  As the doo flies owre the mulberry tree.

"O sin is heavier nor the lead,
  Jennifer gentle an' rosemaree.
The blessing's better nor the bread,
  As the doo flies owre the mulberry tree.

"The snaw is whiter nor the milk,
  Jennifer gentle an' rosemaree.
And the down is safter nor the silk,
  As the doo flies owre the mulberry tree.

"Hunger is sharper nor a thorn,
  Jennifer gentle an' rosemaree.
And shame is louder nor a horn,
  As the doo flies owre the mulberry tree.

"The pies are greener nor the grass,
  Jennifer gentle an' rosemaree.
And Clootie's waur nor a woman was,"
  As the doo flies owre the mulberry tree.

As sune as she the fiend did name,
  Jennifer gentle an' rosemaree,
He flew awa' in a blazing flame,
  As the doo flies owre the mulberry tree.

Clootie] Scotch dialect for the devil.

OLD MAY SONG

All in this pleasant evening, together come are we,
  For the summer springs so fresh, green, and gay;
We tell you of a blossoming and buds on every tree,
  Drawing near unto the merry month of May.

Rise up, the master of this house, put on your charm of gold,
  For the summer springs so fresh, green, and gay;
Be not in pride offended with your name we make so bold,
  Drawing near unto the merry month of May.

Rise up, the mistress of this house, with gold along your breast;
For the summer springs so fresh, green, and gay;
And if your body be asleep, we hope your soul's at rest,
Drawing near unto the merry month of May.

Rise up, the children of this house, all in your rich attire,
For the summer springs so fresh, green, and gay;
And every hair upon your heads shines like the silver wire,
Drawing near unto the merry month of May.

God bless this house and arbour, your riches and your store,
For the summer springs so fresh, green, and gay;
We hope the Lord will prosper you, both now and evermore,
Drawing near unto the merry month of May.

And now comes we must leave you, in peace and plenty here,
For the summer springs so fresh, green, and gay;
We shall not sing you May again until another year,
To draw you these cold winters away.

FLOWERS IN THE VALLEY

O there was a woman, and she was a widow,
Fair are the flowers in the valley.
With a daughter as fair as a fresh sunny meadow.
The Red, the Green, and the Yellow.
The Harp, the Lute, the Pipe, the Flute, the Cymbal,
Sweet goes the treble Violin.
The maid so rare and the flowers so fair
Together they grew in the valley.

There came a Knight all clothed in red,
Fair are the flowers in the valley.
"I would thou wert my bride," he said.
The Red, the Green, and the Yellow.
The Harp, the Lute, the Pipe, the Flute, the Cymbal,
Sweet goes the treble Violin.
"I would," she sighed, "ne'er wins a bride!"
Fair are the flowers in the valley.

There came a Knight all clothed in green,
Fair are the flowers in the valley.
"This maid so sweet might be my queen."
The Red, the Green, and the Yellow.

The Harp, the Lute, the Pipe, the Flute, the Cymbal,
    Sweet goes the treble Violin.
"Might be," sighed she, "will ne'er win me!"
    Fair are the flowers in the valley.

There came a Knight, in yellow was he,
    Fair are the flowers in the valley.
"My bride, my queen, thou must with me!"
    The Red, the Green, and the Yellow.
The Harp, the Lute, the Pipe, the Flute, the Cymbal,
    Sweet goes the treble Violin.
With blushes red, "I come," she said;
    "Farewell to the flowers in the valley."

MY MASTER HATH A GARDEN

My master hath a garden, full-filled with divers flowers,
Where thou may'st gather posies gay, all times and hours,
        Here nought is heard
        But paradise-bird,
        Harp, dulcimer, and lute,
            With cymbal,
            And timbrel,
        And the gentle sounding flute.

Oh! Jesus, Lord, my heal and weal, my bliss complete,
Make thou my heart thy garden-plot, true, fair and neat,
        That I may hear
        This music clear,
        Harp, dulcimer, and lute,
            With cymbal,
            And timbrel,
        And the gentle sounding flute.

Alexander Pope
1688-1744

With Pope, we return again to the question of the heroic couplet.

The heroic couplet, which is kept strictly within the limits of its outward structure, is as variable within those limits as waves, as the air
with its light variations of wind, indeed as variable as the earth itself,
with its mountains and plains, its snows and gardens, towers, and gulfs.

The reason why, to an insensitive ear, the heroic couplet seems monotonous is that structure alone, and not texture, has been regarded as the
maker of rhythm. In reality, both are the parents of rhythm in poetry;
and variations in speed are certainly the result not only of structure, but
also of texture.

How did the thin, glittering, airy, ever-varying texture of that miracle
of poetry *The Rape of the Lock* come into being?

The ineffably subtle and exquisite changes in the movement of the
lines about the sylphs is caused by the particular arrangement of one-
syllable and two-syllable words with others that have the slightest possible fragment of an extra syllable, casting a tiny shadow, or, when
placed close together, producing a faint stretching pause — as with "their
airy" (here, of course, the fact, that the words "their airy" are assonances
adds to this effect). The changes in the movement are caused, also, by
softening assonances, such as "some," "sun," placed in a certain arrangement with assonances that change from softness to poignancy: "insect-
wings," "Thin glitt'ring" — (the poignancy of the *g* in "wings" lengthens
the line very slightly). The changes in the movement are caused, also,
by an incredibly subtle and ever-changing arrangement of alliteration
and of vowel schemes — these latter stretching the line, making it wave
in the air, heightening it or letting it sink.

It has been the fashion to regard only the tempests of fury and not the
strange murky Tartarean beauty of *The Dunciad,* although it is one of
the greatest poems in our language. Yet it is just as beautiful in its way,
and just as strange, as *The Ancient Mariner.*

How enormous are the opening lines, with the thick muffled dull thud
of the alliterating *m*'s:

> The Mighty Mother, and her Son, who brings
> The Smithfield Muses to the ear of Kings.

As with certain passages in Dryden's *Absalom and Achitophel,* the
sound is thick, gross, and blind as stupidity itself.

He gets a kind of dull drone-insistence in the rhythm, by the alliterating *d*'s of the first syllable in each line of this couplet:

> Dulness o'er all possess'd her ancient right,
> Daughter of Chaos and eternal Night . . .

— the deepest drone being in the second line, followed by:

> Fate in their dotage this fair Idiot gave,
> Gross as her sire, and as her mother grave,
> Laborious, heavy, busy, bold, and blind,
> She rul'd, in native Anarchy, the mind.

The wandering sloth of the first line in this (caused by the fat *f* sounds) is followed by the designedly unwieldy lumbering gait of the second line (caused by the *g* sounds in the first and last words), a gait indicative of the subject; the next line, with its appalling deafening blows caused by the alliterative *b*'s placed so close together, has an overwhelming effect of power.

The lengthening of the last line of the next couplet, by means of alliteration — "For, born a Goddess, Dulness never dies . . ." — gives the feeling of a hopeless eternity of boredom. All is a world of thick nothingness. The empty hour, that drone-sound striking, is struck by Dulness alone.

THE RAPE OF THE LOCK

CANTO I

What dire Offence from am'rous Causes springs,
What mighty Contests rise from trivial Things,
I sing — This Verse to *Caryll*, Muse! is due;
This, ev'n *Belinda* may vouchsafe to view:
Slight is the Subject, but not so the Praise,
If She inspire, and He approve my Lays.
    Say what strange Motive, Goddess! cou'd compel
A well-bred *Lord* t' assault a gentle *Belle?*
Oh say what stranger Cause, yet unexplor'd,
Cou'd make a gentle *Belle* reject a *Lord?*
In Tasks so bold, can Little Men engage,
And in soft Bosoms, dwells such mighty Rage?
    Sol thro' white Curtains shot a tim'rous ray,
And op'd those Eyes that must eclipse the Day:
Now Lap-dogs give themselves the rousing Shake,
And sleepless Lovers, just at Twelve, awake:
Thrice rung the Bell, the Slipper knock'd the Ground,
And the press'd Watch return'd a silver Sound.
Belinda still her downy Pillow press'd,
Her Guardian Sylph prolong'd the balmy Rest.
'Twas he had summon'd to her silent Bed
The Morning Dream that hover'd o'er her Head,
A Youth more glitt'ring than a *Birth-night Beau,*
(That ev'n in Slumber caus'd her Cheek to glow)
Seem'd to her Ear his winning Lips to lay,
And thus in Whispers said, or seem'd to say.
    "Fairest of Mortals, thou distinguish'd Care
Of thousand bright Inhabitants of Air!
If e'er one Vision touch'd thy infant Thought,
Of all the Nurse and all the Priest have taught,

Of airy Elves by Moonlight Shadows seen,
The silver Token, and the circled Green,
Or Virgins visited by Angel-Pow'rs,
With Golden Crowns and Wreaths of heav'nly Flow'rs,
Hear and believe! thy own Importance know,
Nor bound thy narrow Views to Things below.
Some secret Truths, from Learned Pride conceal'd,
To Maids alone and Children are reveal'd:
What tho' no Credit doubting Wits may give?
The Fair and Innocent shall still believe.
Know then, unnumber'd Spirits round thee fly,
The light *Militia* of the lower Sky:
These, tho' unseen, are ever on the Wing,
Hang o'er the *Box*, and hover round the *Ring*.
Think what an Equipage thou hast in Air,
And view with scorn *Two Pages* and a *Chair*.
As now your own, our Beings were of old,
And once inclos'd in Woman's beauteous Mould;
Thence, by a soft Transition, we repair
From earthly Vehicles to these of Air.
Think not, when Woman's transient Breath is fled,
That all her Vanities at once are dead:
Succeeding Vanities she still regards,
And tho' she plays no more, o'erlooks the Cards.
Her Joy in gilded Chariots, when alive,
And Love of *Ombre*, after Death survive.
For when the Fair in all their Pride expire,
To their first Elements their Souls retire:
The Sprites of fiery Termagants in Flame
Mount up, and take a *Salamander's* Name.
Soft yielding Minds to Water glide away,
And sip, with *Nymphs*, their Elemental Tea.
The graver Prude sinks downward to a *Gnome*,
In search of Mischief still on Earth to roam.
The light Coquettes in *Sylphs* aloft repair,
And sport and flutter in the Fields of Air.
    "Know further yet; Whoever fair and chaste
Rejects Mankind, is by some *Sylph* embrac'd:
For Spirits, freed from mortal Laws, with ease
Assume what Sexes and what Shapes they please.
What guards the Purity of melting Maids,
In Courtly Balls, and Midnight Masquerades,
Safe from the treach'rous Friend, the daring Spark,
The Glance by Day, the Whisper in the Dark;
When kind Occasion prompts their warm Desires,
When Musick softens, and when Dancing fires?

'Tis but their *Sylph,* the wise Celestials know,
Tho' *Honour* is the Word with Men below.
 "Some Nymphs there are, too conscious of their Face,
For Life predestin'd to the *Gnomes'* Embrace.
These swell their Prospects and exalt their Pride,
When Offers are disdain'd, and Love deny'd:
Then gay Ideas crowd the vacant Brain;
While Peers and Dukes, and all their sweeping Train,
And Garters, Stars, and Coronets appear,
And in soft Sounds, '*Your Grace*' salutes their Ear.
'Tis these that early taint the Female Soul,
Instruct the Eyes of young *Coquettes* to roll,
Teach Infant-Cheeks a bidden Blush to know,
And little Hearts to flutter at a *Beau.*
 "Oft, when the World imagine Women stray,
The *Sylphs* thro' mystick Mazes guide their Way,
Thro' all the giddy Circle they pursue,
And old Impertinence expel by new.
What tender Maid but must a Victim fall
To one Man's Treat, but for another's Ball?
When *Florio* speaks, what Virgin could withstand,
If gentle *Damon* did not squeeze her Hand?
With varying Vanities, from ev'ry Part,
They shift the moving Toyshop of their Heart;
Where Wigs with Wigs, with Sword-knots Sword-knots strive,
Beaus banish Beaus, and Coaches Coaches drive.
This erring Mortals Levity may call,
Oh blind to Truth! the *Sylphs* contrive it all.
 "Of these am I, who thy Protection claim,
A watchful Sprite, and *Ariel* is my Name.
Late, as I rang'd the Crystal Wilds of Air,
In the clear Mirror of thy ruling *Star*
I saw, alas! some dread Event impend,
Ere to the Main this Morning Sun descend.
But Heav'n reveals not what, or how, or where:
Warn'd by the *Sylph,* oh Pious Maid, beware!
This to disclose is all thy Guardian can.
Beware of all, but most beware of Man!"
 He said; when *Shock,* who thought she slept too long,
Leapt up, and wak'd his Mistress with his Tongue.
'Twas then, *Belinda!* if Report say true,
Thy Eyes first open'd on a *Billet-doux;*
Wounds, Charms, and *Ardours,* were no sooner read,
But all the Vision vanish'd from thy Head.
 And now, unveil'd, the *Toilet* stands display'd,
Each Silver Vase in mystic Order laid.

First, rob'd in White, the Nymph intent adores,
With Head uncover'd, the *Cosmetic* Pow'rs.
A heav'nly Image in the Glass appears,
To that she bends, to that her Eyes she rears;
Th' inferior Priestess, at her Altar's side,
Trembling begins the sacred Rites of Pride.
Unnumber'd Treasures ope at once, and here
The various Off'rings of the World appear;
From each she nicely culls with curious Toil,
And decks the Goddess with the glitt'ring Spoil.
This Casket *India's* glowing Gems unlocks,
And all *Arabia* breathes from yonder Box.
The Tortoise here and Elephant unite,
Transform'd to *Combs*, the speckled, and the white.
Here Files of Pins extend their shining Rows,
Puffs, Powders, Patches, Bibles, Billets-doux.
Now awful Beauty puts on all its Arms;
The Fair each moment rises in her Charms,
Repairs her Smiles, awakens ev'ry Grace,
And calls forth all the Wonders of her Face;
Sees by Degrees a purer Blush arise,
And keener Lightnings quicken in her eyes.
The busy *Sylphs* surround their darling Care;
These set the Head, and those divide the Hair,
Some fold the Sleeve, whilst others plait the Gown;
And *Betty's* prais'd for Labours not her own.

CANTO II

Not with more Glories, in th' Ethereal Plain,
The Sun first rises o'er the purpled Main,
Than, issuing forth, the Rival of his Beams
Launch'd on the Bosom of the silver *Thames*.
Fair Nymphs, and well-dress'd Youths around her shone,
But ev'ry Eye was fix'd on her alone.
On her white Breast a sparkling Cross she wore,
Which *Jews* might kiss, and Infidels adore.
Her lively Looks a sprightly Mind disclose,
Quick as her Eyes, and as unfix'd as those:
Favours to none, to all she Smiles extends,
Oft she rejects, but never once offends.
Bright as the Sun, her Eyes the Gazers strike,
And, like the Sun, they shine on all alike.
Yet graceful Ease, and Sweetness void of Pride,
Might hide her Faults, if *Belles* had Faults to hide:

If to her share some Female Errors fall,
Look on her Face, and you'll forget 'em all.
    This Nymph, to the Destruction of Mankind,
Nourish'd two Locks, which graceful hung behind
In equal Curls, and well conspir'd to deck,
With shining Ringlets, the smooth Iv'ry Neck.
Love in these Labyrinths his Slaves detains,
And mighty Hearts are held in slender Chains.
With hairy Springes we the Birds betray,
Slight Lines of Hair surprize the Finny Prey,
Fair Tresses Man's Imperial Race insnare,
And Beauty draws us with a single Hair.
    Th' Advent'rous *Baron* the bright Locks admir'd,
He saw, he wish'd, and to the Prize aspir'd:
Resolv'd to win, he meditates the way,
By Force to ravish, or by Fraud betray;
For when Success a Lover's Toil attends,
Few ask, if Fraud or Force attain'd his Ends.
    For this, ere *Phœbus* rose, he had implor'd
Propitious Heav'n, and ev'ry Pow'r ador'd,
But chiefly *Love* — to *Love* an Altar built,
Of twelve vast *French* Romances, neatly gilt.
There lay three Garters, half a Pair of Gloves;
And all the Trophies of his former Loves;
With tender *Billets-doux* he lights the Pyre,
And breathes three am'rous Sighs to raise the Fire.
Then prostrate falls, and begs with ardent Eyes
Soon to obtain, and long possess the Prize:
The Pow'rs gave Ear, and granted half his Pray'r,
The rest, the Winds dispers'd in empty Air.
    But now secure the painted Vessel glides,
The Sun-beams trembling on the floating Tides:
While melting Musick steals upon the Sky,
And soften'd Sounds along the Waters die;
Smooth flow the Waves, the Zephyrs gently play,
Belinda smil'd, and all the World was gay.
All but the *Sylph* — With careful Thoughts oppress'd,
Th' impending Woe sat heavy on his Breast.
He summons straight his Denizens of Air;
The lucid Squadrons round the Sails repair:
Soft o'er the Shrouds Aërial Whispers breathe,
That seem'd but *Zephyrs* to the Train beneath.
Some to the Sun their Insect-Wings unfold,
Waft on the Breeze, or sink in Clouds of Gold;
Transparent Forms, too fine for mortal sight,
Their fluid Bodies half dissolv'd in Light.

Loose to the Wind their airy Garments flew,
Thin glitt'ring Textures of the filmy Dew;
Dipp'd in the richest Tincture of the Skies,
Where Light disports in ever-mingling Dyes,
While ev'ry Beam new transient Colours flings,
Colours that change whene'er they wave their Wings.
Amid the Circle, on the gilded Mast,
Superior by the Head, was *Ariel* plac'd;
His Purple Pinions op'ning to the Sun,
He rais'd his Azure Wand, and thus begun.
   "Ye *Sylphs* and *Sylphids,* to your Chief give Ear,
Fays, Fairies, Genii, Elves, and *Demons,* hear!
Ye know the Spheres, and various Tasks assign'd
By Laws Eternal to th' Aërial Kind.
Some in the Fields of purest *Æther* play,
And bask and whiten in the Blaze of Day.
Some guide the Course of wand'ring Orbs on high,
Or roll the Planets thro' the boundless Sky.
Some less refin'd, beneath the Moon's pale Light
Pursue the Stars that shoot athwart the Night,
Or suck the Mists in grosser Air below,
Or dip their Pinions in the painted Bow,
Or brew fierce Tempests on the wintry Main,
Or o'er the Glebe distill the kindly Rain.
Others on Earth o'er human Race preside,
Watch all their Ways, and all their Actions guide:
Of these the Chief the Care of Nations own,
And guard with Arms Divine the *British Throne.*
   "Our humbler Province is to tend the Fair,
Not a less pleasing, tho' less glorious Care.
To save the Powder from too rude a Gale,
Nor let th' imprison'd Essences exhale;
To draw fresh Colours from the vernal Flow'rs;
To steal from Rainbows ere they drop in Show'rs
A brighter Wash; to curl their waving Hairs,
Assist their Blushes, and inspire their Airs;
Nay oft, in Dreams, Invention we bestow,
To change a *Flounce,* or add a *Furbelow.*
   "This Day, black Omens threat the brightest Fair
That e'er deserv'd a watchful Spirit's Care;
Some dire Disaster, or by Force, or Slight,
But what, or where, the Fates have wrapp'd in Night.
Whether the Nymph shall break *Diana's* Law,
Or some frail *China* Jar receive a Flaw;
Or stain her Honour, or her new Brocade,
Forget her Pray'rs, or miss a Masquerade,

Or lose her Heart, or Necklace, at a Ball;
Or whether Heav'n has doom'd that *Shock* must fall.
Haste then, ye Spirits! to your Charge repair:
The flutt'ring Fan be *Zephyretta's* Care;
The Drops to thee, *Brillante,* we consign;
And, *Momentilla,* let the Watch be thine;
Do thou, *Crispissa,* tend her fav'rite Lock;
Ariel himself shall be the Guard of *Shock.*
  "To Fifty chosen *Sylphs,* of special Note,
We trust th' important Charge, the *Petticoat:*
Oft have we known that seven-fold Fence to fail,
Tho' stiff with Hoops, and arm'd with Ribs of Whale;
Form a strong Line about the Silver Bound,
And guard the wide Circumference around.
  "Whatever Spirit, careless of his Charge,
His Post neglects, or leaves the Fair at large,
Shall feel sharp Vengeance soon o'ertake his Sins,
Be stopp'd in *Vials,* or transfix'd with *Pins;*
Or plung'd in Lakes of bitter *Washes* lie,
Or wedg'd whole Ages in a *Bodkin's Eye:*
Gums and *Pomatums* shall his Flight restrain,
While clogg'd he beats his silken Wings in vain;
Or Alum *Styptics* with contracting Pow'r
Shrink his thin Essence like a rivell'd Flow'r.
Or, as *Ixion* fix'd, the Wretch shall feel
The giddy Motion of the whirling Mill,
In Fumes of burning Chocolate shall glow,
And tremble at the Sea that froths below!"
  He spoke; the Spirits from the Sails descend;
Some, Orb in Orb, around the Nymph extend,
Some thrid the mazy Ringlets of her Hair,
Some hang upon the Pendants of her Ear;
With beating Hearts the dire Event they wait,
Anxious, and trembling for the Birth of Fate.

CANTO III

Close by those Meads for ever crown'd with Flow'rs,
Where *Thames* with Pride surveys his rising Tow'rs,
There stands a Structure of Majestick Frame,
Which from the neighb'ring *Hampton* takes its Name.
Here *Britain's* Statesmen oft the Fall foredoom
Of Foreign Tyrants, and of Nymphs at home;
Here Thou, great *Anna!* whom three Realms *obey,*
Dost sometimes Counsel take — and sometimes *Tea.*

Hither the Heroes and the Nymphs resort,
To taste awhile the Pleasures of a Court;
In various Talk th' instructive hours they pass'd,
Who gave the *Ball,* or paid the *Visit* last:
One speaks the Glory of the *British Queen,*
And one describes a charming *Indian Screen;*
A third interprets Motions, Looks, and Eyes;
At ev'ry Word a Reputation dies.
Snuff, or the *Fan,* supply each Pause of Chat,
With singing, laughing, ogling, and all that.
    Meanwhile, declining from the Noon of Day,
The Sun obliquely shoots his burning Ray;
The hungry Judges soon the Sentence sign,
And Wretches hang that Jury-men may Dine;
The Merchant from th' *Exchange* returns in Peace,
And the long Labours of the *Toilet* cease.
Belinda now, whom Thirst of Fame invites,
Burns to encounter two advent'rous Knights,
At *Ombre* singly to decide their Doom;
And swells her Breast with Conquests yet to come.
Straight the three Bands prepare in Arms to join,
Each Band the number of the Sacred Nine.
Soon as she spreads her Hand, th' Aërial Guard
Descend, and sit on each important Card:
First *Ariel* perch'd upon a *Matadore,*
Then each, according to the Rank they bore;
For *Sylphs,* yet mindful of their ancient Race,
Are, as when Women, wondrous fond of Place.
    Behold, four *Kings* in Majesty rever'd,
With hoary Whiskers and a forky Beard;
And four fair *Queens* whose hands sustain a Flow'r,
Th' expressive Emblem of their softer Pow'r;
Four *Knaves* in Garbs succint, a trusty Band,
Caps on their heads, and Halberds in their hand;
And Particolour'd Troops, a shining Train,
Draw forth to Combat on the Velvet Plain.
    The skilful Nymph reviews her Force with Care:
Let Spades be Trumps, she said, and Trumps they were.
    Now move to War her Sable *Matadores,*
In Show like Leaders of the swarthy *Moors.*
Spadillio first, unconquerable Lord!
Led off two captive Trumps, and swept the Board.
As many more *Manillio* forc'd to yield,
And march'd a Victor from the verdant Field.
Him *Basto* follow'd, but his Fate more hard
Gain'd but one Trump and one *Plebeian* Card.

With his broad Sabre next, a Chief in Years,
The hoary Majesty of *Spades* appears;
Puts forth one manly Leg, to sight reveal'd,
The rest, his many-colour'd Robe conceal'd.
The Rebel *Knave,* who dares his Prince engage,
Proves the just Victim of his Royal Rage.
Ev'n mighty *Pam,* that Kings and Queens o'erthrew,
And mow'd down Armies in the Fights of *Lu,*
Sad Chance of War! now destitute of Aid,
Falls undistinguish'd by the Victor *Spade!*

    Thus far both Armies to *Belinda* yield;
Now to the *Baron* Fate inclines the Field.
His warlike *Amazon* her Host invades,
Th' Imperial Consort of the Crown of *Spades*.
The *Club's* black Tyrant first her Victim dy'd,
Spite of his haughty Mien, and barb'rous Pride:
What boots the Regal Circle on his Head,
His Giant Limbs, in State unwieldy spread;
That long behind he trails his pompous Robe,
And of all Monarchs only grasps the Globe?

    The *Baron* now his *Diamonds* pours apace;
Th' embroider'd *King* who shows but half his Face,
And his refulgent *Queen,* with Pow'rs combin'd,
Of broken Troops an easy Conquest find.
Clubs, Diamonds, Hearts, in wild Disorder seen,
With Throngs promiscuous strow the level Green.
Thus when dispers'd a routed Army runs,
Of *Asia's* Troops, and *Africk's* Sable Sons,
With like Confusion different Nations fly,
Of various Habit, and of various Dye,
The pierc'd Battalions dis-united fall,
In Heaps on Heaps; one Fate o'erwhelms them all.

    The *Knave* of *Diamonds* tries his wily Arts,
And wins (oh shameful Chance!) the *Queen* of *Hearts*.
At this, the Blood the Virgin's Cheek forsook,
A livid Paleness spreads o'er all her Look;
She sees, and trembles at th' approaching Ill,
Just in the Jaws of Ruin, and *Codille*.
And now (as oft in some distemper'd State)
On one nice *Trick* depends the gen'ral Fate.
An *Ace* of *Hearts* steps forth: the *King* unseen
Lurk'd in her Hand, and mourn'd his captive *Queen*.
He springs to Vengeance with an eager pace,
And falls like Thunder on the prostrate *Ace*.
The Nymph exulting fills with Shouts the Sky,
The Walls, the Woods, and long Canals reply.

Oh thoughtless Mortals! ever blind to Fate,
Too soon dejected, and too soon elate.
Sudden these Honours shall be snatch'd away,
And curs'd for ever this Victorious Day.
    For lo! the Board with Cups and Spoons is crown'd,
The Berries crackle, and the Mill turns round.
On shining Altars of *Japan* they raise
The silver Lamp; the fiery Spirits blaze.
From silver Spouts the grateful Liquors glide,
While *China's* Earth receives the smoking Tide:
At once they gratify their Scent and Taste,
And frequent Cups prolong the rich Repaste.
Straight hover round the Fair her Airy Band;
Some, as she sipp'd, the fuming Liquor fann'd,
Some o'er her Lap their careful Plumes display'd,
Trembling, and conscious of the rich Brocade.
Coffee (which makes the Politician wise,
And see thro' all things with his half-shut Eyes)
Sent up in Vapours to the *Baron's* Brain
New Stratagems, the radiant Lock to gain.
Ah cease, rash Youth! desist ere 'tis too late,
Fear the just Gods, and think of *Scylla's* Fate!
Chang'd to a Bird, and sent to flit in Air,
She dearly pays for *Nisus'* injur'd Hair!
    But when to Mischief Mortals bend their Will,
How soon they find fit Instruments of Ill!
Just then, *Clarissa* drew with tempting Grace
A two-edg'd Weapon from her shining Case;
So Ladies in Romance assist their Knight,
Present the Spear, and arm him for the Fight.
He takes the Gift with rev'rence, and extends
The little Engine on his Fingers' Ends;
This just behind *Belinda's* Neck he spread,
As o'er the fragrant Steams she bends her Head:
Swift to the Lock a thousand Sprites repair,
A thousand Wings, by turns, blow back the Hair,
And thrice they twitch'd the Diamond in her Ear;
Thrice she look'd back, and thrice the Foe drew near.
Just in that instant, anxious *Ariel* sought
The close Recesses of the Virgin's Thought;
As on the Nosegay in her Breast reclin'd,
He watch'd th' Ideas rising in her Mind,
Sudden he view'd, in spite of all her Art,
An Earthly Lover lurking at her Heart.
Amaz'd, confus'd, he found his Pow'r expir'd,
Resign'd to Fate, and with a Sigh retir'd.

The Peer now spreads the glitt'ring *Forfex* wide,
T' inclose the Lock; now joins it, to divide.
Ev'n then, before the fatal Engine clos'd,
A wretched *Sylph* too fondly interpos'd;
Fate urg'd the Shears, and cut the *Sylph* in twain,
(But Airy Substance soon unites again,)
The meeting Points the sacred Hair dissever
From the fair Head, for ever, and for ever!
  Then flash'd the living Lightning from her Eyes,
And Screams of Horror rend th' affrighted Skies.
Not louder Shrieks to pitying Heav'n are cast,
When Husbands or when Lap-dogs breathe their last,
Or when rich *China* Vessels, fall'n from high,
In glitt'ring Dust and painted Fragments lie!
  "Let Wreaths of Triumph now my Temples twine,"
(The Victor cry'd,) "the glorious Prize is mine!
While Fish in Streams, or Birds delight in Air,
Or in a Coach and Six the *British* Fair,
As long as *Atalantis* shall be read,
Or the small Pillow grace a Lady's Bed,
While *Visits* shall be paid on solemn Days,
When num'rous Wax-lights in bright Order blaze,
While Nymphs take Treats, or Assignations give,
So long my Honour, Name, and Praise shall live!"
  What Time wou'd spare, from Steel receives its date,
And Monuments, like Men, submit to Fate!
Steel cou'd the Labour of the Gods destroy,
And strike to Dust th' Imperial Tow'rs of *Troy;*
Steel cou'd the Works of mortal Pride confound,
And hew Triumphal Arches to the Ground.
What Wonder then, fair Nymph! thy Hairs shou'd feel
The conqu'ring Force of unresisted Steel?

CANTO IV

But anxious Cares the pensive Nymph oppress'd,
And secret Passions labour'd in her Breast.
Not youthful Kings in Battle seiz'd alive,
Not scornful Virgins who their Charms survive,
Not ardent Lovers robb'd of all their Bliss,
Not ancient Ladies when refus'd a Kiss,
Not Tyrants fierce that unrepenting die,
Not *Cynthia* when her *Manteau's* pinn'd awry,
E'er felt such Rage, Resentment, and Despair,
As Thou, sad Virgin! for thy ravish'd Hair.

For, that sad moment, when the *Sylphs* withdrew,
And *Ariel* weeping from *Belinda* flew,
Umbriel, a dusky, melancholy Sprite,
As ever sully'd the fair face of Light,
Down to the Central Earth, his proper Scene,
Repair'd to search the gloomy Cave of *Spleen.*
   Swift on his sooty Pinions flits the *Gnome,*
And in a Vapour reach'd the dismal Dome.
No cheerful Breeze this sullen Region knows,
The dreaded *East* is all the Wind that blows.
Here, in a Grotto, shelt'red close from Air,
And screen'd in Shades from Day's detested Glare,
She sighs for ever on her pensive Bed,
Pain at her Side, and *Megrim* at her Head.
   Two Handmaids wait the Throne: alike in Place,
But diff'ring far in Figure and in Face.
Here stood *Ill-nature* like an *ancient Maid,*
Her wrinkled Form in *Black* and *White* array'd;
With store of Pray'rs, for Mornings, Nights, and Noons,
Her Hand is fill'd; her Bosom with Lampoons.
   There *Affectation* with a Sickly Mien
Shows in her Cheek the Roses of Eighteen,
Practis'd to Lisp, and hang the Head aside,
Faints into Airs, and languishes with Pride;
On the rich Quilt sinks with becoming Woe,
Wrapp'd in a Gown, for Sickness, and for Show.
The Fair-ones feel such Maladies as these,
When each new Night-Dress gives a new Disease.
   A constant *Vapour* o'er the Palace flies;
Strange Phantoms rising as the Mists arise;
Dreadful, as Hermits' Dreams in haunted Shades,
Or bright, as Visions of expiring Maids.
Now glaring Fiends, and Snakes on rolling Spires,
Pale Spectres, gaping Tombs, and purple Fires:
Now Lakes of liquid Gold, *Elysian* Scenes,
And Crystal Domes, and Angels in Machines.
   Unnumber'd Throngs on ev'ry side are seen,
Of Bodies chang'd to various Forms by *Spleen.*
Here living *Teapots* stand, one Arm held out,
One bent; the Handle this, and that the Spout:
A Pipkin there, like *Homer's Tripod* walks;
Here sighs a Jar, and there a Goose-pye talks;
Men prove with Child, as pow'rful Fancy works,
And Maids turn'd Bottles, call aloud for Corks.
   Safe pass'd the *Gnome* thro' this fantastick Band,
A Branch of healing *Spleenwort* in his hand.

Then thus address'd the Pow'r — "Hail, wayward **Queen!**
Who rule the Sex to Fifty from Fifteen,
Parent of Vapours and of Female Wit,
Who give th' *Hysteric,* or *Poetic* Fit,
On various Tempers act by various ways,
Make some take Physick, others scribble Plays;
Who cause the Proud their Visits to delay,
And send the Godly in a Pet to pray.
A Nymph there is, that all thy Pow'r disdains,
And thousands more in equal Mirth maintains.
But oh! if e'er thy *Gnome* could spoil a Grace,
Or raise a Pimple on a beauteous Face,
Like Citron-Waters Matrons' Cheeks inflame,
Or change Complexions at a losing Game;
If e'er with airy Horns I planted Heads,
Or rumpled Petticoats, or tumbled Beds,
Or caus'd Suspicion when no Soul was rude,
Or discompos'd the Head-dress of a Prude,
Or e'er to costive Lap-Dog gave Disease,
Which not the Tears of brightest Eyes could ease:
Hear me, and touch *Belinda* with Chagrin,
That single Act gives half the World the Spleen."
    The Goddess with a discontented Air
Seems to reject him, tho' she grants his Pray'r.
A wondrous Bag with both her Hands she binds,
Like that where once *Ulysses* held the Winds;
There she collects the Force of Female Lungs,
Sighs, Sobs, and Passions, and the War of Tongues.
A Vial next she fills with fainting Fears,
Soft Sorrows, melting Griefs, and flowing Tears.
The *Gnome* rejoicing bears her Gifts away,
Spreads his black Wings, and slowly mounts to Day.
    Sunk in *Thalestris'* Arms the Nymph he found,
Her Eyes dejected, and her Hair unbound.
Full o'er their Heads the swelling Bag he rent,
And all the Furies issu'd at the Vent.
Belinda burns with more than mortal Ire,
And fierce *Thalestris* fans the rising Fire.
"O wretched maid!" she spread her hands, and cry'd,
(While *Hampton's* echoes, "Wretched Maid!" reply'd)
"Was it for this you took such constant Care
The *Bodkin, Comb,* and *Essence* to prepare;
For this your Locks in Paper Durance bound,
For this with tort'ring Irons wreath'd around?
For this with Fillets strain'd your tender Head,
And bravely bore the double Loads of Lead?

Gods! shall the Ravisher display your Hair,
While the Fops envy, and the Ladies stare!
Honour forbid! at whose unrival'd Shrine
Ease, Pleasure, Virtue, All our Sex resign.
Methinks already I your Tears survey,
Already hear the horrid things they say,
Already see you a degraded Toast,
And all your Honour in a Whisper lost!
How shall I, then, your helpless Fame defend?
'Twill then be Infamy to seem your Friend!
And shall this Prize, th' inestimable Prize,
Expos'd thro' Crystal to the gazing Eyes,
And heighten'd by the Diamond's circling Rays,
On that Rapacious Hand for ever blaze?
Sooner shall Grass in *Hyde-Park Circus* grow,
And Wits take Lodgings in the Sound of *Bow;*
Sooner let Earth, Air, Sea, to *Chaos* fall,
Men, Monkeys, Lap-Dogs, Parrots, perish all!"
　　She said; then raging to *Sir Plume* repairs,
And bids her *Beau* demand the precious Hairs:
(*Sir Plume,* of *Amber Snuff-box* justly vain,
And the nice Conduct of a *clouded Cane*)
With earnest Eyes, and round unthinking Face,
He first the Snuff-box open'd, then the Case,
And thus broke out — "My Lord, why, what the Devil?
Zounds! damn the Lock! 'fore Gad, you must be civil!
Plague on't! 'tis past a Jest — nay prithee, Pox!
Give her the Hair" — he spoke, and rapp'd his Box.
　　"It grieves me much," reply'd the Peer again,
"Who speaks so well shou'd ever speak in vain.
But by this Lock, this sacred Lock I swear,
(Which never more shall join its parted Hair;
Which never more its Honours shall renew,
Clipp'd from the lovely Head where late it grew)
That while my Nostrils draw the vital Air,
This Hand, which won it, shall for ever wear."
He spoke, and speaking, in proud Triumph spread
The long-contended Honours of her Head.
　　But *Umbriel,* hateful *Gnome!* forbears not so;
He breaks the Vial whence the Sorrows flow.
Then see! the *Nymph* in beauteous Grief appears,
Her Eyes half languishing, half drown'd in Tears;
On her heav'd Bosom hung her drooping Head,
Which, with a Sigh, she rais'd; and thus she said.
　　"For ever curs'd be this detested Day,
Which snatch'd my best, my fav'rite Curl away!

Happy! ah ten times happy, had I been,
If *Hampton-Court* these Eyes had never seen!
Yet am not I the first mistaken Maid,
By Love of *Courts* to num'rous Ills betray'd.
Oh had I rather un-admir'd remain'd
In some lone Isle, or distant *Northern* Land;
Where the gilt *Chariot* never marks the Way,
Where none learn *Ombre,* none e'er taste *Bohea!*
There kept my Charms conceal'd from mortal Eye,
Like Roses, that in Desarts bloom and die.
What mov'd my Mind with youthful Lords to roam?
O had I stay'd, and said my Pray'rs at home!
'Twas this, the Morning *Omens* seem'd to tell;
Thrice from my trembling hand the *Patch-box* fell;
The tott'ring *China* shook without a Wind,
Nay, *Poll* sat mute, and *Shock* was most Unkind!
A *Sylph* too warn'd me of the Threats of Fate,
In mystic Visions, now believ'd too late!
See the poor Remnants of these slighted Hairs!
My Hands shall rend what ev'n thy Rapine spares:
These, in two sable Ringlets taught to break,
Once gave new Beauties to the snowie Neck.
The Sister-Lock now sits uncouth, alone,
And in its Fellow's Fate foresees its own;
Uncurl'd it hangs, the fatal Sheers demands;
And tempts, once more, thy sacrilegious Hands.
Oh hadst thou, Cruel! been content to seize
Hairs less in sight, or any Hairs but these!"

CANTO V

She said: the pitying Audience melt in Tears,
But *Fate* and *Jove* had stopp'd the *Baron's* Ears.
In vain *Thalestris* with Reproach assails,
For who can move when fair *Belinda* fails?
Not half so fix'd the *Trojan* cou'd remain,
While *Anna* begg'd and *Dido* rag'd in vain.
Then grave *Clarissa* graceful wav'd her Fan;
Silence ensu'd, and thus the Nymph began.
    "Say why are Beauties prais'd and honour'd most,
The wise Man's Passion, and the vain Man's Toast?
Why deck'd with all that Land and Sea afford,
Why Angels call'd, and Angel-like ador'd?
Why round our Coaches crowd the white-glov'd Beaus,
Why bows the Side-box from its inmost Rows?

How vain are all these Glories, all our Pains,
Unless good Sense preserve what Beauty gains:
That Men may say, when we the Front-box grace,
'Behold the first in Virtue, as in Face!'
Oh! if to dance all Night, and dress all Day,
Charm'd the Smallpox, or chas'd old Age away;
Who would not scorn what Housewifes' Cares produce,
Or who would learn one earthly Thing of Use?
To patch, nay ogle, might become a Saint,
Nor could it sure be such a Sin to paint.
But since, alas! frail Beauty must decay,
Curl'd or uncurl'd, since Locks will turn to grey;
Since painted, or not painted, all shall fade,
And she who scorns a Man, must die a Maid;
What then remains, but well our Pow'r to use,
And keep good Humour still whate'er we lose?
And trust me, Dear! good Humour can prevail,
When Airs, and Flights, and Screams, and Scolding fail.
Beauties in vain their pretty Eyes may roll;
Charms strike the Sight, but Merit wins the Soul."

So spoke the Dame, but no Applause ensu'd;
Belinda frown'd, *Thalestris* call'd her Prude.
To Arms, to Arms! the fierce Virago cries,
And swift as Lightning to the Combat flies.
All side in Parties, and begin th' Attack;
Fans clap, Silks rustle, and tough Whalebones crack;
Heroes' and Heroines' Shouts confus'dly rise,
And base and treble Voices strike the Skies.
No common Weapons in their Hands are found,
Like Gods they fight, nor dread a mortal Wound.

So when bold *Homer* makes the Gods engage,
And heav'nly Breasts with human Passions rage;
'Gainst *Pallas, Mars; Latona, Hermes* Arms;
And all *Olympus* rings with loud Alarms:
Jove's Thunder roars, Heav'n trembles all around,
Blue *Neptune* storms, the bellowing Deeps resound;
Earth shakes her nodding Tow'rs, the Ground gives way;
And the pale Ghosts start at the Flash of Day!

Triumphant *Umbriel* on a Sconce's Height
Clapp'd his glad Wings, and sate to view the Fight.
Propp'd on their Bodkin Speares, the Sprites survey
The growing Combat, or assist the Fray.

While thro' the Press enrag'd *Thalestris* flies,
And scatters Death around from both her Eyes,
A *Beau* and *Witling* perish'd in the Throng,
One dy'd in *Metaphor,* and one in *Song.*

"*O cruel Nymph! a living Death I bear,*"
Cry'd *Dapperwit,* and sunk beside his Chair.
A mournful Glance Sir *Fopling* upwards cast,
"*Those Eyes are made so killing*" — was his last:
Thus on *Meander's* flow'ry Margin lies
Th' expiring Swan, and as he sings he dies.

When bold *Sir Plume* had drawn *Clarissa* down,
Chloe stepp'd in, and kill'd him with a Frown;
She smil'd to see the doughty Hero slain,
But, at her Smile, the Beau reviv'd again.

Now *Jove* suspends his golden Scales in Air,
Weighs the Men's Wits against the Lady's Hair;
The doubtful Beam long nods from side to side;
At length the Wits mount up, the Hairs subside.

See fierce *Belinda* on the *Baron* flies,
With more than usual Lightning in her Eyes;
Nor fear'd the Chief th' unequal Fight to try,
Who sought no more than on his Foe to die.
But this bold Lord with manly Strength indu'd,
She with one Finger and a Thumb subdu'd:
Just where the Breath of Life his Nostrils drew,
A Charge of *Snuff* the wily Virgin threw;
The *Gnomes* direct, to ev'ry Atom just,
The pungent Grains of titillating Dust.
Sudden, with starting Tears each Eye o'erflows,
And the high Dome re-echoes to his Nose.

"Now meet thy Fate," incens'd *Belinda* cry'd,
And drew a deadly *Bodkin* from her Side.
(The same, his ancient Personage to deck,
Her great great Grandsire wore about his Neck,
In three *Seal-Rings;* which after, melted down,
Form'd a vast *Buckle* for his Widow's Gown:
Her infant Grandame's *Whistle* next it grew,
The *Bell* she jingled, and the *Whistle* blew;
Then in a *Bodkin* grac'd her Mother's Hairs,
Which long she wore, and now *Belinda* wears.)

"Boast not my Fall," he cry'd, "insulting Foe!
Thou by some other shalt be laid as low.
Nor think, to die dejects my lofty Mind;
All that I dread, is leaving you behind!
Rather than so, ah let me still survive,
And burn in *Cupid's* Flames — but burn alive."

"*Restore the Lock!*" she cries; and all around
"*Restore the Lock!*" the vaulted Roofs rebound.
Not fierce *Othello* in so loud a Strain
Roar'd for the Handkerchief that caus'd his Pain.

But see how oft Ambitious Aims are cross'd,
And Chiefs contend till all the Prize is lost!
The Lock, obtain'd with Guilt, and kept with Pain,
In ev'ry place is sought, but sought in vain:
With such a Prize no Mortal must be blest,
So Heav'n decrees! with Heav'n who can contest?

Some thought it mounted to the Lunar Sphere,
Since all things lost on Earth are treasur'd there.
There Heroes' Wits are kept in pond'rous Vases,
And Beaus' in *Snuff-boxes* and *Tweezer-cases*.
There broken Vows, and Death-bed Alms are found,
And Lovers' Hearts with Ends of Riband bound,
The Courtier's Promises, and Sick Man's Pray'rs,
The Smiles of Harlots, and the Tears of Heirs,
Cages for Gnats, and Chains to Yoke a Flea,
Dry'd Butterflies, and Tomes of Casuistry.

But trust the Muse — she saw it upward rise,
Tho' mark'd by none but quick, Poetic Eyes:
(So *Rome's* great Founder to the Heav'ns withdrew,
To *Proculus* alone confess'd in view.)
A sudden Star, it shot thro' liquid Air,
And drew behind a radiant *Trail of Hair*.
Not *Berenice's* Locks first rose so bright,
The Heav'ns bespangling with dishevel'd Light.
The *Sylphs* behold it kindling as it flies,
And pleas'd pursue its Progress thro' the Skies.

This the *Beau-monde* shall from the *Mall* survey,
And hail with Musick its propitious Ray.
This the bless'd Lover shall from *Venus* take,
And send up Vows from *Rosamonda's* Lake.
This *Partridge* soon shall view in cloudless Skies,
When next he looks thro' *Galileo's* Eyes;
And hence th' Egregious Wizard shall foredoom
The Fate of *Louis,* and the Fall of *Rome.*

Then cease, bright Nymph! to mourn thy ravish'd Hair
Which adds new Glory to the shining Sphere!
Not all the Tresses that fair Head can boast
Shall draw such Envy as the Lock you lost.
For, after all the Murders of your Eye,
When, after Millions slain, yourself shall die;
When those fair Suns shall set, as set they must,
And all those Tresses shall be laid in Dust;
This Lock, the Muse shall consecrate to Fame,
And 'midst the Stars inscribe *Belinda's* Name.

From THE DUNCIAD

From BOOK THE FIRST

The Mighty Mother, and her Son, who brings
The Smithfield Muses to the ear of Kings,
I sing. Say you, her instruments the Great!
Call'd to this work by Dulness, Jove, and Fate:
You by whose care, in vain decry'd, and curst,
Still Dunce the second reigns like Dunce the first;
Say, how the Goddess bade Britannia sleep,
And pour'd her Spirit o'er the land and deep.

In eldest time, ere mortals writ or read,
Ere Pallas issu'd from the Thund'rer's head,
Dulness o'er all possess'd her ancient right,
Daughter of Chaos and eternal Night:
Fate in their dotage this fair Idiot gave,
Gross as her sire, and as her mother grave,
Laborious, heavy, busy, bold, and blind,
She rul'd, in native Anarchy, the mind.

Still her old Empire to restore she tries,
For, born a Goddess, Dulness never dies.

O Thou! whatever title please thine ear,
Dean, Drapier, Bickerstaff, or Gulliver!
Whether thou choose Cervantes' serious air,
Or laugh and shake in Rab'lais' easy chair,
Or praise the Court, or magnify Mankind,
Or thy griev'd Country's copper chains unbind;
From thy Bœtia tho' her Pow'r retires,
Mourn not, my SWIFT! at ought our Realm acquires.
Here pleas'd behold her mighty wings outspread
To hatch a new Saturnian age of Lead.

Close to those walls where Folly holds her throne,
And laughs to think Monroe would take her down,
Where o'er the gates, by his fam'd father's hand,
Great Cibber's brazen, brainless brothers stand;
One cell there is, conceal'd from vulgar eye,
The Cave of Poverty and Poetry.
Keen, hollow winds howl thro' the bleak recess,
Emblem of Music caus'd by Emptiness.
Hence Bards, like Proteus long in vain ty'd down,
Escape in Monsters, and amaze the town.
Hence Miscellanies spring, the weekly boast
Of Curl's chaste press, and Lintot's rubric post:
Hence hymning Tyburn's elegiac lines,
Hence Journals, Medleys, Merc'ries, MAGAZINES;

Sepulchral Lies, our holy walls to grace,
And New-year Odes, and all the Grub-street race.
    In clouded Majesty here Dulness shone;
Four guardian Virtues, round, support her throne:
Fierce champion Fortitude, that knows no fears
Of hisses, blows, or want, or loss of ears:
Calm Temperance, whose blessings those partake
Who hunger and who thirst for scribbling sake:
Prudence, whose glass presents th' approaching jail:
Poetic Justice, with her lifted scale,
Where, in nice balance, truth with gold she weighs,
And solid pudding against empty praise.
    Here she beholds the Chaos dark and deep,
Where nameless Somethings in their causes sleep,
Till genial Jacob, or a warm Third day,
Call forth each mass, a Poem, or a Play:
How hints, like spawn, scarce quick in embryo lie,
How new-born nonsense first is taught to cry,
Maggots half-form'd in rhyme exactly meet,
And learn to crawl upon poetic feet.
Here one poor word an hundred clenches makes,
And ductile Dulness new meanders takes;
There motley Images her fancy strike,
Figures ill pair'd, and Similes unlike.
She sees a Mob of Metaphors advance,
Pleas'd with the madness of the mazy dance!
How Tragedy and Comedy embrace;
How Farce and Epic get a jumbled race;
How Time himself stands still at her command,
Realms shift their place, and Ocean turns to land.
Here gay Description Egypt glads with show'rs,
Or gives to Zembla fruits, to Barca flow'rs;
Glitt'ring with ice here hoary hills are seen,
There painted valleys of eternal green,
In cold December fragrant chaplets blow,
And heavy harvests nod beneath the snow.
    All these, and more, the cloud-compelling Queen
Beholds thro' fogs, that magnify the scene.
She, tinsel'd o'er in robes of varying hues,
With self-applause her wild creation views;
Sees momentary monsters rise and fall,
And with her own fools-colours gilds them all.
    'Twas on the day, when Thorold rich and grave,
Like Cimon, triumph'd both on land and wave:
(Pomps without guilt, of bloodless swords and maces,
Glad chains, warm furs, broad banners, and broad faces)

Now Night descending, the proud scene was o'er,
But liv'd, in Settle's numbers, one day more.
Now May'rs and Shrieves all hush'd and satiate lay,
Yet eat, in dreams, the custard of the day;
While pensive Poets painful vigils keep,
Sleepless themselves to give their readers sleep.
Much to the mindful Queen the feast recalls
What City Swans once sung within their walls;
Much she revolves their arts, their ancient praise,
And sure succession down from Heywood's days.
She saw, with joy, the line immortal run,
Each sire imprest, and glaring in his son:
So watchful Bruin forms, with plastic care,
Each growing lump, and brings it to a Bear.
She saw old Pryn in restless Daniel shine,
And Eusden eke out Blackmore's endless line;
She saw slow Philips creep like Tate's poor page,
And all the mighty Mad in Dennis rage.
In each she marks her Image full exprest,
But chief in BAYS' monster-breeding breast;
Bays, form'd by nature Stage and Town to bless,
And act, and be, a Coxcomb with success.
Dulness, with transport eyes the lively Dunce,
Rememb'ring she herself was Pertness once.
Now (shame to Fortune!) an ill Run at Play
Blank'd his bold visage, and a thin Third day:
Swearing and supperless the Hero sate,
Blasphem'd his Gods, the Dice, and damn'd his Fate.
Then gnaw'd his pen, then dash'd it on the ground,
Sinking from thought to thought, a vast profound!
Plung'd for his sense, but found no bottom there,
Yet wrote and flounder'd on, in mere despair.
Round him much Embryo, much Abortion lay,
Much future Ode, and abdicated Play;
Nonsense precipitate, like running Lead,
That slip'd thro' Cracks and Zig-zags of the Head;
All that on Folly Frenzy could beget,
Fruits of dull Heat, and Sooterkins of Wit.

From *BOOK THE SECOND*

High on a gorgeous seat, that far out-shone
Henley's gilt tub, or Fleckno's Irish throne,
Or that where on her Curls the Public pours,
All-bounteous, fragrant Grains and Golden show'rs.

Great Cibber sate: The proud Parnassian sneer,
The conscious simper, and the jealous leer,
Mix on his look: All eyes direct their rays
On him, and crowds turn Coxcombs as they gaze.
His peers shine round him with reflected grace,
New edge their dulness, and new bronze their face.
So from the Sun's broad beam, in shallow urns
Heav'n's twinkling Sparks draw light, and point their horns.
    Not with more glee, with hands Pontific crown'd,
With scarlet hats wide-waving circled round,
Rome in her Capitol saw Querno sit,
Throned on seven hills, the Antichrist of wit.
    And now the Queen, to glad her sons, proclaims
By herald Hawkers, high heroic Games.
They summon all her Race: an endless band
Pours forth, and leaves unpeopled half the land.
A motley mixture! in long wigs, in bags,
In silks, in crapes, in Garters, and in rags,
From drawing-rooms, from colleges, from garrets,
On horse, on foot, in hacks, and gilded chariots:
All who true Dunces in her cause appear'd,
And all who knew those Dunces to reward.
    Amid that area wide they took their stand,
Where the tall May-pole once o'erlook'd the Strand,
But now (so ANNE and Piety ordain)
A Church collects the saints of Drury-lane.
    With Authors, Stationers obey'd the call
(The field of glory is a field for all).
Glory, and gain, th' industrious tribe provoke;
And gentle Dulness ever loves a joke.
A Poet's form she plac'd before their eyes,
And bade the nimblest racer seize the prize;
No meagre, muse-rid mope, adust and thin,
In a dun night-gown of his own loose skin;
But such a bulk as no twelve bards could raise,
Twelve starv'ling bards of these degen'rate days.
All as a partridge plump, full-fed, and fair,
She form'd this image of well-body'd air;
With pert flat eyes she window'd well its head;
A brain of feathers, and a heart of lead;
And empty words she gave, and sounding strain,
But senseless, lifeless! idol void and vain!
Never was dash'd out, at one lucky hit,
A fool, so just a copy of a wit;
So like, that critics said, and courtiers swore,
A Wit it was, and call'd the phantom More. . . .

"Now turn to diff'rent sports," (the Goddess cries)
"And learn, my sons, the wond'rous power of Noise.
To move, to raise, to ravish ev'ry heart,
With Shakespear's nature, or with Jonson's art,
Let others aim: 'tis yours to shake the soul
With Thunder rumbling from the mustard-bowl,
With horns and trumpets now to madness swell,
Now sink in sorrows with a tolling bell;
Such happy arts attention can command,
When fancy flags, and sense is at a stand.
Improve we these. Three Cat-calls be the bribe
Of him, whose chatt'ring shames the monkey-tribe;
And his this Drum, whose hoarse heroic bass
Drowns the loud clarion of the braying Ass."
    Now thousand tongues are heard in one loud din:
The monkey-mimics rush discordant in;
'Twas chatt'ring, grinning, mouthing, jabb'ring all,
And Noise and Norton, Brangling and Breval,
Dennis and Dissonance, and captious Art,
And Snip-snap short, and Interruption smart,
And Demonstration thin, and Theses thick,
And Major, Minor, and Conclusion quick.
"Hold!" (cry'd the Queen), "a Cat-call each shall win.
Equal your merits! equal is your din!
But that this well-disputed game may end,
Sound forth, my Brayers, and the welkin rend."

From BOOK THE FOURTH

Yet, yet a moment, one dim Ray of Light
Indulge, dread Chaos, and eternal Night!
Of darkness visible so much be lent,
As half to shew, half veil the deep Intent.
Ye Pow'rs! whose Mysteries restor'd I sing,
To whom Time bears me on his rapid wing,
Suspend a while your Force inertly strong,
Then take at once the Poet and the Song. . . .

    In vain, in vain — the all-composing Hour
Resistless falls: The Muse obeys the Pow'r.
She comes! she comes! the sable Throne behold
Of *Night* primæval and of *Chaos* old!
Before her, *Fancy's* gilded clouds decay,
And all its varying Rain-bows die away.

Wit shoots in vain its momentary fires,
The meteor drops, and in a flash expires.
As one by one, at dread Medea's strain,
The sick'ning stars fade off th' ethereal plain;
As Argus' eyes, by Hermes' wand opprest,
Clos'd one by one to everlasting rest;
Thus at her felt approach, and secret might,
Art after *art* goes out, and all is Night.
See skulking *Truth* to her old cavern fled,
Mountains of Casuistry heap'd o'er her head!
Philosophy, that lean'd on Heav'n before,
Shrinks to her second cause, and is no more.
Physic of *Metaphysic* begs defence,
And *Metaphysic* calls for aid on *Sense!*
See *Mystery* to *Mathematics* fly!
In vain! they gaze, turn giddy, rave, and die.
Religion blushing veils her sacred fires,
And unawares *Morality* expires.
Nor *public* Flame, nor *private,* dares to shine;
Nor *human* Spark is left, nor Glimpse *divine!*
Lo! thy dread Empire, CHAOS! is restor'd;
Light dies before thy uncreating word:
Thy hand, great Anarch! lets the curtain fall;
And universal Darkness buries All.

NOTE: The targets of Pope's satire are:

Book the First. Genial Jacob: the bookseller Jacob Tonson. *Thorold:* Sir George Thorold, Lord Mayor of London, 1720. *Settle:* last official city poet. *Heywood:* John Heywood, interlude writer. *Pryn:* W. Prynne. *Daniel:* Daniel Defoe. *Eusden:* Lawrence Eusden, Poet Laureate. *Blackmore:* Sir Richard Blackmore. *Philips:* Ambrose Philips. *Tate:* Nahum Tate. *Dennis:* John Dennis, who persecuted Pope from his youth. *Bays:* Colley Cibber, Poet Laureate.

Book the Second. Henley's gilt tub: "The pulpit of a dissenter is usually called a tub; but that of Mr. Orator Henley was covered with velvet, and adorned with gold. He had also a fair altar and over it this extraordinary inscription, 'The Primitive Eucharist.' " — POPE, *Notes Variorum,* James Sutherland, ed. *Fleckno's Irish Throne:* "Richard Fleckno was an Irish priest, but had laid aside (as himself expressed it,) the mechanic side of priesthood. He printed some plays, poems, letters and travels." — POPE. *Curl:* Edmund Curl sat in the pillory at Charing Cross. *Camille Querno* was of Apulia, who, hearing the great encouragement which Leo X gave to poets, travelled to Rome with a harp in his hand, and sang to it twenty thousand verses of a poem called *Alexias.* — WARBURTON. *The phantom More:* Curl, in his *Key to the Dunciad,* affirmed this to be James Moore Smythe. He wrote *The Rival Modes,* an unsuccessful play.

James Thomson
1700-1748

From THE SEASONS

LO! FROM THE LIVID EAST

Lo! from the livid East, or piercing North,
Thick Clouds ascend, in whose capacious Womb,
A vapoury Deluge lies, to Snow congeal'd:
Heavy, they roll their fleecy World along;
And the Sky saddens with th' impending Storm.
Thro' the hush'd Air, the whitening Shower descends,
At first, thin-wavering; till at last, the Flakes
Fall broad, and wide, and fast, dimming the Day,
With a continual Flow. See! sudden, hoar'd,
The Woods beneath the stainless Burden bow,
Blackning, along the mazy Stream it melts;
Earth's universal Face, deep-hid, and chill,
Is all one, dazzling, Waste. The Labourer-Ox
Stands cover'd o'er with Snow, and then demands
The Fruit of all his Toil. The Fowls of Heaven,
Tam'd by the cruel Season, croud around
The winnowing Store, and claim the little Boon,
That *Providence* allows. The foodless Wilds
Pour forth their brown *Inhabitants;* the Hare,
Tho' timorous of Heart, and hard beset
By Death, in various Forms, dark Snares, and Dogs,
And more unpitying Men, the Garden seeks,
Urg'd on by *fearless* Want. The bleating Kind
Eye the bleak Heavens, and next, the glistening Earth,
With Looks of dumb Despair; then sad, dispers'd
Dig, for the wither'd Herb, thro' Heaps of Snow.

Clear Frost succeeds, and thro' the blew Serene
For Sight too fine, th' Ætherial Nitre flies,
To bake the Glebe, and bind the slip'ry Flood.
This of the wintry Season is the Prime;
Pure are the Days, and lustrous are the Nights,
Brighten'd with starry Worlds, till then unseen.
Mean while, the Orient, darkly red, breathes forth
An Icy Gale, that, in its mid Career,
Arrests the bickering Stream. The nightly Sky,

And all her glowing Constellations pour
Their rigid Influence down: It freezes on
Till Morn, late-rising, o'er the drooping World,
Lifts her pale Eye, unjoyous: then appears
The various Labour of the silent Night,
The pendant Isicle, the Frost-Work fair,
Where thousand Figures rise, the crusted Snow,
Tho' white, made whiter, by the fining North.
On blithsome Frolics bent, the youthful Swains,
While every Work of Man is laid at Rest,
Rush o'er the watry Plains, and, shuddering, view
The fearful Deeps below: or with the Gun,
And faithful Spaniel, range the ravag'd Fields,
And, adding to the Ruins of the Year,
Distress the Feathery, or the Footed *Game.*

But hark! the nightly Winds, with hollow Voice,
Blow, blustering, from the South — the Frost subdu'd,
Gradual, resolves into a weeping Thaw.
Spotted, the Mountains shine: loose Sleet descends,
And floods the Country round: the Rivers swell,
Impatient for the Day. — Those sullen Seas,
That wash th' ungenial Pole, will rest no more,
Beneath the Shackles of the mighty North;
But, rousing all their Waves, resistless heave, —
And hark! — the length'ning Roar, continuous, runs
Athwart the rifted Main; at once, it bursts,
And piles a thousand Mountains to the Clouds!
Ill fares the Bark, the Wretches' last Resort,
That, lost amid the floating Fragments, moors
Beneath the Shelter of an Icy Isle;
While Night o'erwhelms the Sea, and Horror looks
More horrible. Can human Hearts endure
Th' assembled *Mischiefs,* that besiege them round:
Unlist'ning *Hunger,* fainting *Weariness,*
The *Roar* of Winds, and Waves, the *Crush* of Ice,
Now, ceasing, now, renew'd, with louder Rage,
And bellowing round the Main: Nations remote,
Shook from their Midnight-Slumbers, deem they hear
Portentous Thunder, in the troubled Sky.
More to embroil the Deep, Leviathan,
And his unweildy Train, in horrid Sport,
Tempest the loosen'd Brine; while, thro' the Gloom,
Far, from the dire, unhospitable Shore,
The Lyon's Rage, the Wolf's sad Howl is heard,
And all the fell Society of Night.

SPRING FLOWERS

Along the blushing Borders, bright with Dew,
And in yon mingled Wilderness of Flowers,
Fair-handed Spring unbosoms every Grace:
Throws out the Snow-drop, and the Crocus first;
The Daisy, Primrose, Violet darkly blue,
And Polyanthus of unnumber'd Dyes;
The yellow Wall-Flower, stain'd with iron Brown;
And lavish Stock that scents the Garden round:
From the soft Wing of vernal Breezes shed,
Anemonies; Auriculas, enrich'd
With shining Meal o'er all their velvet Leaves;
And full Renunculas, of glowing Red.
Then comes the Tulip-Race, where Beauty plays
Her idle Freaks: from Family diffus'd
To Family, as flies the Father-Dust,
The varied Colours run; and while they *break*
On the charm'd Eye, th' exulting Florist marks,
With secret Pride, the Wonders of his Hand.
No gradual Bloom is wanting; from the Bud,
First-born of Spring, to Summer's musky Tribes:
Nor Hyacinths, deep-purpled; nor Jonquils,
Of potent Fragrance; nor Narcissus fair,
As o'er the fabled Fountain hanging still;
Nor broad Carnations; nor gay-spotted Pinks;
Nor, shower'd from every Bush, the Damask-rose:
Infinite Numbers, Delicacies, Smells,
With Hues on Hues Expression cannot paint,
The Breath of Nature, and her endless Bloom.

Thomas Gray
1716-1771

ELEGY WRITTEN IN A COUNTRY CHURCH–YARD

The Curfew tolls the knell of parting day,
  The lowing herd wind slowly o'er the lea,
The plowman homeward plods his weary way,
  And leaves the world to darkness and to me.

Now fades the glimmering landscape on the sight,
    And all the air a solemn stillness holds,
Save where the beetle wheels his droning flight,
    And drowsy tinklings lull the distant folds;

Save that from yonder ivy-mantled tow'r
    The mopeing owl does to the moon complain
Of such, as wand'ring near her secret bow'r,
    Molest her ancient solitary reign.

Beneath those rugged elms, that yew-tree's shade,
    Where heaves the turf in many a mould'ring heap,
Each in his narrow cell for ever laid,
    The rude Forefathers of the hamlet sleep.

The breezy call of incense-breathing Morn,
    The swallow twitt'ring from the straw-built shed,
The cock's shrill clarion, or the echoing horn,
    No more shall rouse them from their lowly bed.

For them no more the blazing hearth shall burn,
    Or busy housewife ply her evening care:
No children run to lisp their sire's return,
    Or climb his knees the envied kiss to share.

Oft did the harvest to their sickle yield,
    Their furrow oft the stubborn glebe has broke;
How jocund did they drive their team afield!
    How bow'd the woods beneath their sturdy stroke!

Let not Ambition mock their useful toil,
    Their homely joys, and destiny obscure;
Nor Grandeur hear with a disdainful smile,
    The short and simple annals of the poor.

The boast of heraldry, the pomp of pow'r,
    And all that beauty, all that wealth e'er gave,
Awaits alike th' inevitable hour.
    The paths of glory lead but to the grave.

Nor you, ye Proud, impute to These the fault,
    If Mem'ry o'er their Tomb no Trophies raise,
Where thro' the long-drawn isle and fretted vault
    The pealing anthem swells the note of praise.

Can storied urn or animated bust
    Back to its mansion call the fleeting breath?
Can Honour's voice provoke the silent dust,
    Or Flatt'ry sooth the dull cold ear of Death?

Perhaps in this neglected spot is laid
    Some heart once pregnant with celestial fire;
Hands, that the rod of empire might have sway'd,
    Or wak'd to extasy the living lyre.

But Knowledge to their eyes her ample page
    Rich with the spoils of time did ne'er unroll;
Chill Penury repress'd their noble rage,
    And froze the genial current of the soul.

Full many a gem of purest ray serene,
    The dark unfathom'd caves of ocean bear:
Full many a flower is born to blush unseen,
    And waste its sweetness on the desert air.

Some village-Hampden, that with dauntless breast
    The little Tyrant of his fields withstood;
Some mute inglorious Milton here may rest,
    Some Cromwell guiltless of his country's blood.

Th' applause of list'ning senates to command,
    The threats of pain and ruin to despise,
To scatter plenty o'er a smiling land,
    And read their hist'ry in a nation's eyes,

Their lot forbad: nor circumscrib'd alone
    Their growing virtues, but their crimes confin'd;
Forbad to wade through slaughter to a throne,
    And shut the gates of mercy on mankind,

The struggling pangs of conscious truth to hide,
    To quench the blushes of ingenuous shame,
Or heap the shrine of Luxury and Pride
    With incense kindled at the Muse's flame.

Far from the madding crowd's ignoble strife,
    Their sober wishes never learn'd to stray;
Along the cool sequester'd vale of life
    They kept the noiseless tenor of their way.

Yet ev'n these bones from insult to protect
　　Some frail memorial still erected high,
With uncouth rhimes and shapeless sculpture deck'd,
　　Implores the passing tribute of a sigh.

Their name, their years, spelt by th' unletter'd muse,
　　The place of fame and elegy supply:
And many a holy text around she strews,
　　That teach the rustic moralist to die.

For who to dumb Forgetfulness a prey,
　　This pleasing anxious being e'er resign'd,
Left the warm precincts of the chearful day,
　　Nor cast one longing ling'ring look behind?

On some fond breast the parting soul relies,
　　Some pious drops the closing eye requires;
Ev'n from the tomb the voice of Nature cries,
　　Ev'n in our Ashes live their wonted Fires.

For thee, who mindful of th' unhonour'd Dead
　　Dost in these lines their artless tale relate;
If chance, by lonely contemplation led,
　　Some kindred Spirit shall inquire thy fate,

Haply some hoary-headed Swain may say,
　　"Oft have we seen him at the peep of dawn
Brushing with hasty steps the dews away
　　To meet the sun upon the upland lawn.

"There at the foot of yonder nodding beech
　　That wreathes its old fantastic roots so high,
His listless length at noontide would he stretch,
　　And pore upon the brook that babbles by.

"Hard by yon wood, now smiling as in scorn,
　　Mutt'ring his wayward fancies he would rove,
Now drooping, woeful wan, like one forlorn,
　　Or craz'd with care, or cross'd in hopeless love.

"One morn I miss'd him on the custom'd hill,
　　Along the heath and near his fav'rite tree;
Another came; nor yet beside the rill,
　　Nor up the lawn, nor at the wood was he;

"The next with dirges due in sad array
  Slow thro' the church-way path we saw him born.
Approach and read (for thou can'st read) the lay,
  Grav'd on the stone beneath yon aged thorn."

THE EPITAPH

Here rests his head upon the lap of Earth
  A Youth to Fortune and to Fame unknown.
Fair Science frown'd not on his humble birth,
  And Melancholy mark'd him for her own.

Large was his bounty, and his soul sincere,
  Heav'n did a recompence as largely send:
He gave to Mis'ry all he had, a tear,
  He gain'd from Heav'n ('twas all he wish'd) a friend.

No farther seek his merits to disclose,
  Or draw his frailties from their dread abode,
(There they alike in trembling hope repose,)
  The bosom of his Father and his God.

William Collins

1721-1759

TO EVENING

If aught of oaten stop or pastoral song
May hope, O pensive Eve, to soothe thine ear,
    Like thy own brawling springs,
    Thy springs, and dying gales;
O Nymph reserved, while now the bright-hair'd sun
Sits in yon western tent, whose cloudy skirts
    With brede ethereal wove
    O'erhang his wavy bed;
Now air is hush'd, save where the weak-ey'd bat
With short shrill shriek flits by on leathern wing,
    Or where the beetle winds
    His small but sullen horn,
As oft he rises 'midst the twilight path,
Against the pilgrim borne in heedless hum:
    Now teach me, maid composed,

To breathe some soften'd strain,
Whose numbers, stealing through thy dark'ning vale,
May not unseemly with its stillness suit;
    As musing slow I hail
    Thy genial loved return.
For when thy folding-star arising shows
His paly circlet, at his warning lamp
    The fragrant Hours, and Elves
    Who slept in buds the day,
And many a Nymph who wreathes her brow with sedge
And sheds the freshening dew, and lovelier still
    The pensive Pleasures sweet,
    Prepare thy shadowy car.
Then let me rove some wild and heathy scene;
Or find some ruin midst its dreary dells,
    Whose walls more awful nod
    By thy religious gleams.
Or if chill blustering winds or driving rain
Prevent my willing feet, be mine the hut
    That, from the mountain's side,
    Views wilds and swelling floods,
And hamlets brown, and dim-discover'd spires;
And hears their simple bell; and marks o'er all
    Thy dewy fingers draw
    The gradual dusky veil.
While Spring shall pour his showers, as oft he wont,
And bathe thy breathing tresses, meekest Eve!
    While Summer loves to sport
    Beneath thy lingering light;
While sallow Autumn fills thy lap with leaves;
Or Winter, yelling through the troublous air,
    Affrights thy shrinking train
    And rudely rends thy robes;
So long, regardful of thy quiet rule,
Shall Fancy, Friendship, Science, smiling Peace,
    Thy gentlest influence own,
    And love thy favourite name!

Christopher Smart

1722-1771

A SONG TO DAVID

O Thou, that sit'st upon a throne,
With harp of high majestic tone,
  To praise the King of kings:
And voice of heav'n-ascending swell,
Which, while its deeper notes excel,
  Clear, as a clarion, rings:

To bless each valley, grove, and
    coast,
And charm the cherubs to the post
  Of gratitude in throngs;
To keep the days on Zion's Mount
And send the year to his account,
  With dances and with songs:

O Servant of God's holiest charge,
The minister of praise at large,
  Which thou mayst now receive;
From thy blest mansion hail and
    hear,
From topmost eminence appear
  To this the wreath I weave.

Great, valiant, pious, good, and
    clean,
Sublime, contemplative, serene,
  Strong, constant, pleasant, wise!
Bright effluence of exceeding grace;
Best man! — the swiftness and the
    race,
  The peril, and the prize!

Great — from the lustre of his
    crown,
From Samuel's horn, and God's
    renown,
  Which is the people's voice;

For all the host, from rear to van,
Applauded and embrac'd the
    man —
  The man of God's own choice.

Valiant — the word, and up he
    rose —
The fight — he triumph'd o'er the
    foes,
  Whom God's just laws abhor;
And arm'd in gallant faith, he took
Against the boaster, from the brook,
  The weapons of the war.

Pious — magnificent and grand;
'Twas he the famous temple
    plann'd:
  (The seraph in his soul)
Foremost to give his Lord his dues,
Foremost to bless the welcome news,
  And foremost to condole.

Good — from Jehudah's genuine
    vein,
From God's best nature good in
    grain,
  His aspect and his heart;
To pity, to forgive, to save,
Witness En-gedi's conscious cave,
  And Shimei's blunted dart.

Clean — if perpetual prayer be
    pure,
And love, which could itself inure
  To fasting and to fear —
Clean in his gestures, hands, and
    feet,

To smite the lyre, the dance
            complete,
To play the sword and spear.

Sublime — invention ever young,
Of vast conception, tow'ring tongue,
    To God th' eternal theme;
Notes from yon exaltations caught,
Unrival'd royalty of thought,
    O'er meaner strains supreme.

Contemplative — on God to fix
His musings, and above the six
    The sabbath-day he blest;
'Twas then his thoughts self-
            conquest prun'd,
And heav'nly melancholy tun'd,
    To bless and bear the rest.

Serene — to sow the seeds of peace,
Rememb'ring, when he watch'd the
            fleece,
    How sweetly Kidron purl'd —
To further knowledge, silence vice,
And plant perpetual paradise
    When God had calm'd the world.

Strong — in the Lord, who could
            defy
Satan, and all his powers that lie
    In sempiternal night;
And hell, and horror, and despair
Were as the lion and the bear
    To his undaunted might.

Constant — in love to God THE
            TRUTH,
Age, manhood, infancy, and
            youth —
    To Jonathan his friend
Constant, beyond the verge of death;
And Ziba and Mephibosheth,
    His endless fame attend.

Pleasant — and various as the year;
Man, soul, and angel, without peer,
    Priest, champion, sage and boy;

In armour, or in ephod clad,
His pomp, his piety was glad;
    Majestic was his joy.

Wise — in recovery from his fall,
Whence rose his eminence o'er all,
    Of all the most revil'd;
The light of Israel in his ways,
Wise are his precepts, pray'r and
            praise,
    And counsel to his child.

His muse, bright angel of his verse,
Gives balm for all the thorns that
            pierce,
    For all the pangs that rage;
Blest light, still gaining on the
            gloom,
The more than Michal of his bloom,
    Th' Abishag of his age.

He sung of God — the mighty
            source
Of all things — the stupendous
            force
    On which all strength depends;
From whose right arm, beneath
            whose eyes,
All period, pow'r, and enterprize
    Commences, reigns, and ends.

Angels — their ministry and meed,
Which to and fro with blessings
            speed,
    Or with their citterns wait;
Where Michael with his millions
            bows,
Where dwells the seraph and his
            spouse,
    The cherub and her mate.

Of man — the semblance and effect
Of God and Love — the Saint elect
    For infinite applause —
To rule the land, and briny broad,
To be laborious in his laud,
    And heroes in his cause.

The world — the clust'ring spheres
  he made,
The glorious light, the soothing
    shade,
  Dale, champaign, grove, and hill;
The multitudinous abyss,
Where secrecy remains in bliss,
  And wisdom hides her skill.

Trees, plants, and flow'rs — of
  virtuous root;
Gem yielding blossom, yielding fruit,
  Choice gums and precious balm;
Bless ye the nosegay in the vale,
And with the sweet'ners of the gale
  Enrich the thankful psalm.

Of fowl — e'en ev'ry beak and wing
Which cheer the winter, hail the
    spring,
  That live in peace or prey;
They that make music, or that mock,
The quail, the brave domestic cock,
  The raven, swan, and jay.

Of fishes — ev'ry size and shape,
Which Nature frames of light escape,
  Devouring man to shun:
The shells are in the wealthy deep,
The shoals upon the surface leap,
  And love the glancing sun.

Of beasts — the beaver plods his
  task;
While the sleek tigers roll and bask,
  Nor yet the shades arouse;
Her cave the mining coney scoops;
Where o'er the mead the mountain
    stoops,
  The kids exult and brouse.

Of gems — their virtue and their
  price,
Which hid in earth from man's
    device,
  Their darts of lustre sheathe;

The jasper of the master's stamp,
The topaz blazing like a lamp
  Among the mines beneath.

Blest was the tenderness he felt
When to his graceful harp he knelt,
  And did for audience call;
When satan with his hand he
    quell'd,
And in serene suspense he held
  The frantic throes of Saul.

His furious foes no more malign'd
As he such melody divin'd,
  And sense and soul detain'd;
Now striking strong, now soothing
    soft,
He sent the godly sounds aloft,
  Or in delight refrain'd.

When up to heav'n his thoughts he
    pil'd,
From fervent lips fair Michal smil'd,
  As blush to blush she stood;
And chose herself the queen, and
    gave
Her utmost from her heart, "so
    brave,
  And plays his hymns so good."

The pillars of the Lord are seven,
Which stand from earth to topmost
    heav'n;
  His wisdom drew the plan;
His WORD accomplish'd the design,
From brightest gem to deepest mine,
  From CHRIST enthron'd to man.

Alpha, the cause of causes, first
In station, fountain, whence the
    burst
  Of light, and blaze of day;
Whence bold attempt, and brave
    advance,
Have motion, life, and ordinance,
  And heav'n itself its stay.

Gamma supports the glorious arch
On which angelic legions march,
    And is with sapphires pav'd;
Thence the fleet clouds are sent
        adrift,
And thence the painted folds, that
        lift
    The crimson veil, are wav'd.

Eta with living sculpture breathes,
With verdant carvings, flow'ry
        wreathes
    Of never-wasting bloom;
In strong relief his goodly base
All instruments of labour grace,
    The trowel, spade, and loom.

Next Theta stands to the
        Supreme —
Who form'd, in number, sign, and
        scheme,
    Th' illustrious lights that are;
And one address'd his saffron robe,
And one, clad in a silver globe,
    Held rule with ev'ry star.

Iota's tun'd to choral hymns
Of those that fly, while he that
        swims
    In thankful safety lurks;
And foot, and chapitre, and niche,
The various histories enrich
    Of God's recorded works.

Sigma presents the social droves,
With him that solitary roves,
    And man of all the chief;
Fair on whose face, and stately
        frame,
Did God impress his hallow'd
        name,
    For ocular belief.

OMEGA! GREATEST and the BEST,
Stands sacred to the day of rest,
    For gratitude and thought;

Which bless'd the world upon his
        pole,
And gave the universe his goal,
    And clos'd th' infernal draught.

O DAVID, scholar of the Lord!
Such is thy science, whence reward
    And infinite degree;
O strength, O sweetness, lasting ripe!
God's harp thy symbol, and thy type
    The lion and the bee!

There is but One who ne'er rebell'd,
But One by passion unimpell'd,
    By pleasures unentic't;
He from himself his semblance sent,
Grand object of his own content,
    And saw the God in CHRIST.

Tell them I Am, JEHOVAH said
To MOSES; while earth heard in
        dread,
    And smitten to the heart,
At once above, beneath, around,
All Nature, without voice or sound,
    Replied, O Lord, THOU ART.

Thou art — to give and to confirm,
For each his talent and his term;
    All flesh thy bounties share:
Thou shalt not call thy brother fool;
The porches of the Christian school
    Are meekness, peace, and pray'r.

Open, and naked of offense,
Man's made of mercy, soul, and
        sense;
    God arm'd the snail and wilk;
Be good to him that pulls thy
        plough;
Due food and care, due rest, allow
    For her that yields thee milk.

Rise up before the hoary head,
And God's benign commandment
        dread,

Which says thou shalt not die:
"Not as I will, but as thou wilt,"
Pray'd He whose conscience knew
    no guilt;
  With whose bless'd pattern vie.

Use all thy passions! — love is thine,
And joy, and jealousy divine;
  Thine hope's eternal fort,
And care thy leisure to disturb,
With fear concupiscence to curb,
  And rapture to transport.

Act simply, as occasion asks;
Put mellow wine in season'd casks;
  Till not with ass and bull:
Remember thy baptismal bond;
Keep from commixtures foul and
    fond,
  Nor work thy flax with wool.

Distribute: pay the Lord his tithe,
And make the widow's heart-
    strings blithe;
  Resort with those that weep:
As you from all and each expect,
For all and each thy love direct,
  And render as you reap.

The slander and its bearer spurn,
And propagating praise sojourn
  To make thy welcome last;
Turn from old Adam to the New;
By hope futurity pursue;
  Look upwards to the past.

Control thine eye, salute success,
Honour the wiser, happier bless,
  And for thy neighbour feel;
Grutch not of mammon and his
    leaven,
Work emulation up to heaven
  By knowledge and by zeal.

O David, highest in the list
Of worthies, on God's ways insist,

The genuine word repeat.
Vain are the documents of men,
And vain the flourish of the pen
  That keeps the fool's conceit.

Praise above all — for praise
    prevails;
Heap up the measure, load the
    scales,
  And good to goodness add:
The gen'rous soul her Saviour aids,
But peevish obloquy degrades;
  The Lord is great and glad.

For ADORATION all the ranks
Of angels yield eternal thanks,
  And DAVID in the midst;
With God's good poor, which, last
    and least
In man's esteem, thou to thy feast,
  O blessed bridegroom, bid'st.

For ADORATION seasons change,
And order, truth, and beauty range,
  Adjust, attract, and fill:
The grass the polyanthus cheques;
And polish'd porphyry reflects,
  By the descending rill.

Rich almonds colour to the prime
For ADORATION; tendrils climb,
  And fruit-trees pledge their gems;
And Ivis with her gorgeous vest
Builds for her eggs her cunning nest,
  And bell-flow'rs bow their stems.

With vinous syrup cedars spout;
From rocks pure honey gushing out,
  For ADORATION springs:
All scenes of painting crowd the map
Of nature; to the mermaid's pap
  The scalèd infant clings.

The spotted ounce and playsome
    cubs
Run rustling 'mongst the flow'ring
    shrubs,

And lizards feed the moss;
For ADORATION beasts embark,
While waves upholding halcyon's
  ark
No longer roar and toss.

While Israel sits beneath his fig,
With coral root and amber sprig,
  The wean'd advent'rer sports;
Where to the palm the jasmin
  cleaves,
For ADORATION 'mongst the leaves
  The gale his peace reports.

Increasing days their reign exalt,
Nor in the pink and mottled vault
  Th' opposing spirits tilt;
And, by the coasting reader spy'd,
The silverlings and crusions glide
  For ADORATION gilt.

For ADORATION, rip'ning canes
And cocoa's purest milk detains
  The western pilgrim's staff;
Where rain in clasping boughs
  inclos'd,
And vines with oranges dispos'd,
  Embow'r the social laugh.

Now labour his reward receives,
For ADORATION counts his sheaves
  To peace, her bounteous prince;
The nectarine his strong tint
  imbibes,
And apples of ten thousand tribes,
  And quick peculiar quince.

The wealthy crops of whit'ning rice
'Mongst thyine woods and groves of
  spice
  For ADORATION grow;
And, marshall'd in the fencèd land,
The peaches and pomegranates
  stand;
  Where wild carnations blow.

The laurels with the winter strive,
The crocus burnishes alive
  Upon the snow-clad earth.
For ADORATION myrtles stay
To keep the garden from dismay,
  And bless the sight from dearth.

The pheasant shows his pompous
  neck;
And ermine, jealous of a speck,
  With fear eludes offense:
The sable, with his glossy pride,
For ADORATION is descried,
  Where frosts the wave condense.

The cheerful holly, pensive yew,
And holy thorn, their trim renew;
  The squirrel hoards his nuts:
All creatures batten o'er their stores,
And careful Nature all her doors
  For ADORATION shuts.

For ADORATION, David's psalms
Lift up the heart to deeds of alms;
  And he, who kneels and chants,
Prevails his passions to control,
Finds meat and med'cine to the soul
  Which for translation pants.

For ADORATION, beyond match,
The scholar bullfinch aims to catch
  The soft flute's ivory touch;
And, careless on the hazel spray,
The daring redbreast keeps at bay
  The damsel's greedy clutch.

For ADORATION, in the skies,
The Lord's philosopher espies
  The Dog, the Ram, and Rose;
The planet's ring, Orion's sword;
Nor is his greatness less ador'd
  In the vile worm that glows.

For ADORATION, on the strings
The western breezes work their
    wings,
  The captive ear to soothe.
Hark! 'tis a voice — how still, and
    small —
That makes the cataracts to fall,
  Or bids the sea be smooth!

For ADORATION, incense comes
From bezoar, and Arabian gums;
  And on the civet's furr.
But as for pray'r, or ere it faints,
Far better is the breath of saints
  Than galbanum and myrrh.

For ADORATION, from the down
Of dam'sins to th' anana's crown,
  God sends to tempt the taste;
And while the luscious zest invites,
The sense, that in the scene delights,
  Commands desire be chaste.

For ADORATION, all the paths
Of grace are open, all the baths
  Of purity refresh;
And all the rays of glory beam
To deck the man of God's esteem,
  Who triumphs o'er the flesh.

For ADORATION, in the dome
Of Christ the sparrows find an
    home;
  And on his olives perch:
The swallow also dwells with thee,
O man of God's humility,
  Within his Saviour's CHURCH.

Sweet is the dew that falls betimes,
And drops upon the leafy limes;
  Sweet Hermon's fragrant air:
Sweet is the lily's silver bell,
And sweet the wakeful tapers smell
  That watch for early pray'r.

Sweet the young nurse with love
    intense,
Which smiles o'er sleeping
    innocence;
  Sweet when the lost arrive:
Sweet the musician's ardour beats,
While his vague mind's in quest of
    sweets,
  The choicest flow'rs to hive.

Sweeter in all the strains of love
The language of thy turtle dove
  Pair'd to thy swelling chord;
Sweeter with ev'ry grace endu'd
The glory of thy gratitude,
  Respir'd unto the Lord.

Strong is the horse upon his speed;
Strong in pursuit the rapid glede,
  Which makes at once his game;
Strong the tall ostrich on the
    ground;
Strong through the turbulent
    profound
  Shoots xiphias to his aim.

Strong is the lion — like a coal
His eyeball — like a bastion's mole
  His chest against the foes:
Strong, the gier-eagle on his sail,
Strong against tide, th' enormous
    whale
  Emerges as he goes.

But stronger still, in earth and air,
And in the sea, the man of pray'r,
  And far beneath the tide;
And in the seat to faith assign'd,
Where ask is have, where seek is find,
  Where knock is open wide.

Beauteous the fleet before the gale;
Beauteous the multitudes in mail,
  Rank'd arms and crested heads:

Beauteous the garden's umbrage
mild,
Walk, water, meditated wild,
And all the bloomy beds.

Beauteous the moon full on the
lawn;
And beauteous, when the veil's
withdrawn,
The virgin to her spouse:
Beauteous the temple deck'd and
fill'd,
When to the heav'n of heav'ns
they build
Their heart-directed vows.

Beauteous, yea beauteous more
than these,
The shepherd king upon his knees,
For his momentous trust;
With wish of infinite conceit,
For man, beast, mute, the small
and great,
And prostrate dust to dust.

Precious the bounteous widow's
mite;
And precious, for extreme delight,
The largess from the churl:
Precious the ruby's blushing blaze,
And alba's blest imperial rays,
And pure cerulean pearl.

Precious the penitential tear;
And precious is the sigh sincere,
Acceptable to God:

And precious are the winning
flow'rs,
In gladsome Israel's feast of bow'rs,
Bound on the hallow'd sod.

More precious that diviner part
Of David, ev'n the Lord's own heart,
Great, beautiful, and new:
In all things where it was intent,
In all extremes, in each event,
Proof — answ'ring true to true.

Glorious the sun in mid career;
Glorious th' assembled fires appear;
Glorious the comet's train:
Glorious the trumpet and alarm;
Glorious th' almighty stretch'd-out
arm;
Glorious th' enraptur'd main:

Glorious the northern lights
a-stream;
Glorious the song, when God's the
theme;
Glorious the thunder's roar;
Glorious hosannah from the den;
Glorious the catholic amen;
Glorious the martyr's gore:

Glorious — more glorious, is the
crown
Of Him that brought salvation down
By meekness, call'd thy Son;
Thou that stupendous truth believ'd,
And now the matchless deed's
achiev'd,
DETERMIN'D, DAR'D, *and* DONE.

From JUBILATE AGNO

REJOICE IN GOD

Rejoice in God, O ye Tongues; give the glory to the Lord, and the Lamb.

Nations, and languages, and every Creature, in which is the breath of Life.

Let man and beast appear before him, and magnify his name together. . . .

LET LOTAN REJOICE WITH SAUTERELLE

Let Lotan rejoice with Sauterelle. Blessed be the name of the Lord from the Lote-tree to the Palm.

For I pray God to bless improvements in gardening till London be a city of palm-trees.

Let Dishon rejoice with the Landrail, God give his grace to the society for preserving the game.

For I pray to give his grace to the poor of England, that Charity be not offended and that benevolence may increase.

Let Hushim rejoice with the King's Fisher, who is of royal beauty, tho' plebeian size.

For in my nature I quested for beauty, but God, God hath sent me to sea for pearls. . . .

Let Mizbar rejoice with the Cadess, as is their number, so are their names, blessed be the Lord Jesus for them all.

For the names and number of animals are as the names and number of the stars. . . .

Let Ahimaaz rejoice with the Silver-Worm who is a living mineral.

For there is silver in my mines and I bless God that it is rather there than in my coffers. . . .

Let Maacah rejoice with Dryophyte who was blessed of the Lord in the valley.

For the Lord Jesus made him a nosegay and blessed it and he blessed the inhabitants of flowers. . . .

Let Cherub rejoice with the Cherub who is a bird and a blessed Angel.

For I bless God for every feather from the wren in the sedge to the CHERUBS and their MATES. . . .

LET PETER REJOICE WITH THE MOON FISH

LET PETER rejoice with the MOON FISH who keeps up the life in the waters
by night.

FOR I pray the Lord JESUS that cured the LUNATICK to be merciful to all
my brethren and sisters in these houses.

Let Andrew rejoice with the Whale, who is arrayd in beauteous blue and
is a combination of bulk and activity.

For they work me with their harping-irons, which is a barbarous instrument, because I am more unguarded than others.

Let James rejoice with the Skuttle-Fish, who foils his foe by the effusion
of his ink.

For the blessing of God hath been on my epistles, which I have written
for the benefit of others.

Let John rejoice with Nautilus who spreads his sail and plies his oar, and
the Lord is his pilot.

For I bless God that the CHURCH of ENGLAND is one of the SEVEN evn the
candlestick of the Lord.

Let Philip rejoice with Boca, which is a fish that can speak.

For the ENGLISH TONGUE shall be the language of the WEST.

Let Bartholomew rejoice with the Eel, who is pure in proportion to
where he is found and how he is used.

For I pray Almighty CHRIST to bless the MAGDALEN HOUSE * and to forward a National purification.

Let Thomas rejoice with the Sword-Fish, whose aim is perpetual and
strength insuperable.

For I have the blessing of God in the three POINTS of manhood, of the
pen, of the sword, and of chivalry.

Let Matthew rejoice with Uranoscopus, whose eyes are lifted up to God.

For I am inquisitive in the Lord, and defend the philosophy of the scripture against vain deceit.

Let James the less, rejoice with the Haddock, who brought the piece of
money for the Lord and Peter.

For the nets come down from the eyes of the Lord to fish up men to their
salvation.

Let Jude bless with the Bream, who is of melancholy from his depth and
serenity.

For I have a greater compass both of mirth and melancholy than another.

Let Simon rejoice with the Sprat, who is pure and innumerable.

For I bless the Lord JESUS in the innumerables, and for ever and ever.

Let Matthias rejoice with the Flying-Fish, who has a part with the birds,
and is sublimity in his conceit.

For I am redoubted, and redoubtable in the Lord, as is THOMAS BECKET
my father.

* *Magdalen House,* an asylum for prostitutes. — W. F. STEAD.

Let Stephen rejoice with Remora — The Lord remove all obstacles to his
    glory.
For I have had the grace to GO BACK, which is my blessing unto prosperity.
Let Paul rejoice with the Seale, who is pleasant and faithfull, like God's
    good ENGLISHMAN.
For I paid for my seat in St PAUL's, when I was six years old, and took pos-
    session against the evil day. . . .

FOR THE LETTER ל WHICH SIGNIFIES GOD

For the letter ל which signifies God * by himself is on the fibre of some
    leaf in every Tree. . . .

For ל is upon the Sapphire Vault.
For the doubling of flowers is the improvement of the gardners talent.
For the flowers are great blessings.
For the Lord made a Nosegay in the medow with his disciples and
    preached upon the lily.
For the angels of God took it out of his hand and carried it to the
    Height. . . .

For there is no Height in which there are not flowers.
For flowers have great virtues for all the senses.
For the flower glorifies God and the root parries the adversary.
For the flowers have their angels even the words of God's Creation.
For the warp and woof of flowers are worked by perpetual moving spirits.
For flowers are good both for the living and the dead.
For there is a language of flowers.
For there is a sound reasoning upon all flowers.
For elegant phrases are nothing but flowers.
For flowers are peculiarly the poetry of Christ.
For flowers are medicinal.
For flowers are musical in ocular harmony.
For the right names of flowers are yet in heaven. God make gardners bet-
    ter nomenclators.
For the Poorman's nosegay is an introduction to a Prince. . . .

FOR I WILL CONSIDER MY CAT JEOFFRY

For I will consider my Cat Jeoffry.
For he is the servant of the Living God, duly and daily serving him.
For at the first glance of the glory of God in the East he worships in his
    way.

* *The letter* ל *which signifies God.* Smart has rightly taken the Hebrew letter Lamed
as the equivalent of the English letter L, but he then takes this as the equivalent of
the Hebrew word *'el* (actually a pun); *'el,* but not Lamed, stands for God, as in Elohim
and at the end of the names of the Archangels, Gabriel and Raphael. — W. F. STEAD.

For is this done by wreathing his body seven times round with elegant
quickness.

For then he leaps up to catch the musk, which is the blessing of God
upon his prayer.

For he rolls upon prank to work it in.

For having done duty and received blessing he begins to consider himself.

For this he performs in ten degrees.

For first he looks upon his fore-paws to see if they are clean.

For secondly he kicks up behind to clear away there.

For thirdly he works it upon stretch with the fore-paws extended.

For fourthly he sharpens his paws by wood.

For fifthly he washes himself.

For sixthly he rolls upon wash.

For seventhly he fleas himself, that he may not be interrupted upon the
beat.

For eighthly he rubs himself against a post.

For ninthly he looks up for his instructions.

For tenthly he goes in quest of food.

For having consider'd God and himself he will consider his neighbour.

For if he meets another cat he will kiss her in kindness.

For when he takes his prey he plays with it to give it a chance.

For one mouse in seven escapes by his dallying.

For when his day's work is done his business more properly begins.

For he keeps the Lord's watch in the night against the adversary.

For he counteracts the powers of darkness by his electrical skin and glaring eyes.

For he counteracts the Devil, who is death, by brisking about the life.

For in his morning orisons he loves the sun and the sun loves him.

For he is of the tribe of Tiger.

For the Cherub Cat is a term of the Angel Tiger.

For he has the subtlety and hissing of a serpent, which in goodness he
suppresses.

For he will not do destruction, if he is well-fed, neither will he spit without provocation.

For he purrs in thankfulness, when God tells him he's a good Cat.

For he is an instrument for the children to learn benevolence upon.

For every house is incompleat without him and a blessing is lacking in
the spirit. . . .

For he is the cleanest in the use of his fore-paws of any quadrupede.

For the dexterity of his defence is an instance of the love of God to him
exceedingly.

For he is the quickest to his mark of any creature.

For he is tenacious of his point.

For he is a mixture of gravity and waggery.
For he knows that God is his Saviour.
For there is nothing sweeter than his peace when at rest.
For there is nothing brisker than his life when in motion. . . .

For the divine spirit comes about his body to sustain it in compleat cat.
For his tongue is exceeding pure so that it has in purity what it wants in
    musick. . . .

For by stroaking of him I have found out electricity.
For I perceived God's light about him both wax and fire. . . .

For God has blessed him in the variety of his movements.
For, tho he cannot fly, he is an excellent clamberer. . . .

William Cowper
1731-1800

LIGHT SHINING OUT OF DARKNESS

God moves in a mysterious way
  His wonders to perform;
He plants his footsteps in the sea,
  And rides upon the storm.

Deep in unfathomable mines
  Of never-failing skill,
He treasures up his bright designs,
  And works his sovereign will.

Ye fearful saints, fresh courage take,
  The clouds ye so much dread
Are big with mercy, and shall break
  In blessings on your head.

Judge not the Lord by feeble sense,
  But trust him for his grace;
Behind a frowning providence
  He hides a smiling face.

His purposes will ripen fast,
  Unfolding every hour;
The bud may have a bitter taste,
  But sweet will be the flower.

Blind unbelief is sure to err,
  And scan his work in vain:
God is his own interpreter,
  And He will make it plain.

THE CASTAWAY

Obscurest night involv'd the sky,
  Th' Atlantic billows roar'd,
When such a destin'd wretch as I,
  Wash'd headlong from on board,
Of friends, of hope, of all bereft,
His floating home forever left.

No braver chief could Albion boast
  Than he with whom he went,
Nor ever ship left Albion's coast,
  With warmer wishes sent.
He lov'd them both, but both in
    vain,
Nor him beheld, nor her again.

Not long beneath the whelming
    brine,
  Expert to swim, he lay;
Nor soon he felt his strength
    decline,
  Or courage die away;
But wag'd with death a lasting
    strife,
Supported by despair of life.

He shouted; nor his friends had
    fail'd
  To check the vessel's course,
But so the furious blast prevail'd
  That, pitiless perforce,
They left their outcast mate behind,
And scudded still before the wind.

Some succour yet they could afford;
  And, such as storms allow,
The cask, the coop, the floated cord,
  Delay'd not to bestow.
But he (they knew) nor ship nor
    shore,
Whate'er they gave, should visit
    more.

Nor, cruel as it seem'd, could he
  Their haste himself condemn,

Aware that flight, in such a sea,
  Alone could rescue them;
Yet bitter felt it still to die
Deserted, and his friends so nigh.

He long survives, who lives an hour
  In ocean, self-upheld;
And so long he, with unspent pow'r,
  His destiny repell'd;
And ever, as the minutes flew,
Entreated help, or cried —
    "Adieu!"

At length, his transient respite past,
  His comrades, who before
Had heard his voice in ev'ry blast,
  Could catch the sound no more;
For then, by toil subdu'd, he drank
The stifling wave, and then he sank.

No poet wept him; but the page
  Of narrative sincere,
That tells his name, his worth, his
    age,
  Is wet with Anson's tear:
And tears by bards or heroes shed
Alike immortalize the dead.

I therefore purpose not, or dream,
  Descanting on his fate,
To give the melancholy theme
  A more enduring date;
But misery still delights to trace
Its semblance in another's case.

No voice divine the storm allay'd,
  No light propitious shone;
When, snatch'd from all effectual
    aid,
  We perish'd, each alone;
But I beneath a rougher sea,
And whelm'd in deeper gulfs than
  he.

LINES WRITTEN
UNDER THE INFLUENCE OF DELIRIUM

Hatred and vengeance, my eternal portion,
Scarce can endure delay of execution,
Wait with impatient readiness to seize my
Soul in a moment.

Damned below Judas; more abhorred than he was,
Who for a few pence sold his holy Master!
Twice-betrayed Jesus me, the last delinquent,
Deems the profanest.

Man disavows, and Deity disowns me,
Hell might afford my miseries a shelter;
Therefore Hell keeps her ever-hungry mouths all
Bolted against me.

Hard lot! encompass'd with a thousand dangers;
Weary, faint, trembling with a thousand terrors,
I'm called, if vanquish'd, to receive a sentence
Worse than Abiram's.

Him the vindictive rod of angry justice
Sent quick and howling to the centre headlong;
I, fed with judgment, in a fleshy tomb, am
Buried above ground.

William Blake
1757-1827

Schopenhauer, in *The World As Will and Idea*, spoke of "the naïveté
with which every plant expresses and lays open its whole character in its
mere form, reveals its whole being and will. . . . The plant reveals its
whole being at the first glance, and with complete innocence. . . . This
innocence in the plant results from its complete want of knowledge.
. . . Every plant speaks to us, first of all, of its home, of the climate, and
the nature of the ground in which it has grown. . . . Besides this, however, every plant expresses the special will of its species, and says something that cannot be uttered in any other tongue."
Blake had the innocence of the flower, and his innocence did not come

from ignorance, but from wisdom. The extreme poles, innocence and wisdom, are alike. And wisdom, both heavenly and infernal, was his.

The Spirit told him, as it told Caedmon, to "sing the Beginning of Created Things," and these opened to him their essential nature.

He pierced down to what Wagner called "the essence of phenomena" and printed some of his works "in the infernal method, by corrosives, which in Hell are salutary and medicinal, melting apparent surfaces away, and displaying the infinite which was hid." *

In *The Tyger* Blake produces miracles by his varying use of the caesura, and by the way in which he lengthens the line by the use of words containing rather thick consonants (soft, like the fur of the tiger), and by words (sometimes two to a line) with vowels followed by a long harsh animal-purring *r*.

In the first line (to take the use of the caesura first) — "Tyger! Tyger! burning bright" — the punctuation lengthens it, and acts as the natural caesura acts.

The place of the caesura is shifted — time and again; sometimes it hardly exists. In the first and second stanzas, excepting for the line I have mentioned, it is very slight in every case. The occasional lengthening of the pause-syllables is due to the use of texture, as in "*Burnt the fire of thine eyes*" and:

> On what *wings dare* he as*pire?*
> What the *hand dare* seize the *fire?*

In these lines, the shadow of an additional length is given by the elaborate arrangement of *n*'s and *r*'s in the middle of words.

Sometimes the line, owing to the varying height or depth of the vowel sounds, moves like the sinuous length of the tiger, as in the line: "*In what distant deeps or skies.*" The change from the last line of the first quatrain: "Could frame thy fearful symmetry?" — with the love-soft, yet animal-crouching "could" — to the last line of the last quatrain: "Dare frame thy fearful symmetry?" — with its lengthened, uncombatable sound, due to the lengthened, animal-purring *r* in "dare," followed by the higher-keyed *a* with that high fierce animal-purring *r* preceding it, in the word "frame" — this produces one of the most magnificent effects of any poem in our language.

The word "dare" lengthens the line; "frame" lifts the line up; the "fear" in "fearful," being a dissonance to "dare," makes it sink again, and all this gives to the line an extraordinary feeling of length, sinuosity and rippling muscles.

A friend, writing to me on the subject of "The Tyger," said:

"Take the first two lines of the first quatrain, where the broad vowels flame between and beyond all the supple bars of their restraining and

* Blake, *The Marriage of Heaven and Hell.*

supporting consonants, till Space itself seems filled with the fire of the archetypal tiger; and then watch the gradual approach to physical shape and outline through the shortening vowels, into the closed vowel sounds in the word 'symmetry,' which ends the first quatrain.

"There, in four immortal lines, we get what Schopenhauer calls the IDEA of the tiger — Fire and Symmetry."

Blake had the Augustans' supreme mastery over pauses, over the caesura, but these, in his case, do not give so much variety as when used by Dryden and Pope. That is to say, Blake's caesuras have an effect more upon the rhythm than upon the texture, whereas Dryden's and Pope's caesuras affected both. Blake's pauses give, in nearly every case, a feeling of a long stretch of shadow rather than the difference between height and depth. These stretches of shadow, coming in varying places in the line, do, of course, affect the movement of the line.

From MILTON

AND DID THOSE FEET IN ANCIENT TIME

And did those feet in ancient time
   Walk upon England's mountains green?
And was the holy Lamb of God
   On England's pleasant pastures seen?

And did the Countenance Divine
   Shine forth upon our clouded hills?
And was Jerusalem builded here
   Among these dark Satanic Mills?

Bring me my Bow of burning gold:
   Bring me my Arrows of desire:
Bring me my Spear: O clouds, unfold!
   Bring me my Chariot of fire.

I will not cease from Mental Fight,
   Nor shall my Sword sleep in my hand
Till we have built Jerusalem
   In England's green and pleasant Land.

AUGURIES OF INNOCENCE

To see a World in a Grain of Sand
And a Heaven in a Wild Flower,
Hold Infinity in the palm of your hand
And Eternity in an hour.

A Robin Red breast in a Cage
Puts all Heaven in a Rage.
A dove house fill'd with doves and Pigeons
Shudders Hell thro' all its regions.
A dog starv'd at his Master's Gate
Predicts the ruin of the State.
A Horse misus'd upon the Road
Calls to Heaven for Human blood.
Each outcry of the hunted Hare
A fibre from the Brain does tear.
A Skylark wounded in the wing,
A Cherubim does cease to sing.
The Game Cock clip'd and arm'd for fight
Does the Rising Sun affright.
Every Wolf's and Lion's howl
Raises from Hell a Human Soul.
The wild deer, wand'ring here and there,
Keeps the Human Soul from Care.
The Lamb misus'd breeds Public strife
And yet forgives the Butcher's Knife.
The Bat that flits at close of Eve
Has left the Brain that won't Believe.
The Owl that calls upon the Night
Speaks the Unbeliever's fright.
He who shall hurt the little Wren
Shall never be belov'd by Men.
He who the Ox to wrath has mov'd
Shall never be by Woman lov'd.
The wanton Boy that kills the Fly
Shall feel the Spider's enmity.
He who torments the Chafer's sprite
Weaves a Bower in endless Night.
The Catterpiller on the Leaf
Repeats to thee thy Mother's grief.
Kill not the Moth nor Butterfly,
For the Last Judgment draweth nigh.
He who shall train the Horse to War
Shall never pass the Polar Bar.
The Beggar's Dog and Widow's Cat,
Feed them and thou wilt grow fat.
The Gnat that sings his Summer's song
Poison gets from Slander's tongue.
The poison of the Snake and Newt
Is the sweat of Envy's Foot.
The Poison of the Honey Bee
Is the Artist's Jealousy.

The Prince's Robes and Beggar's Rags
Are Toadstools on the Miser's Bags.
A truth that's told with bad intent
Beats all the Lies you can invent.
It is right it should be so;
Man was made for Joy and Woe;
And when this we rightly know
Thro' the World we safely go,
Joy and Woe are woven fine,
A Clothing for the Soul divine;
Under every grief and pine
Runs a joy with silken twine.
The Babe is more than swadling Bands;
Throughout all these Human Lands
Tools were made, and Born were hands,
Every Farmer Understands.
Every Tear from Every Eye
Becomes a Babe in Eternity;
This is caught by Females bright
And return'd to its own delight.
The Bleat, the Bark, Bellow and Roar
Are Waves that Beat on Heaven's Shore.
The Babe that weeps the Rod beneath
Writes Revenge in realms of death.
The Beggar's Rags, fluttering in Air,
Does to Rags the Heavens tear.
The Soldier, arm'd with Sword and Gun,
Palsied strikes the Summer's Sun.
The poor Man's Farthing is worth more
Than all the Gold on Afric's Shore.
One Mite wrung from the Labrer's hands
Shall buy and sell the Miser's Lands:
Or, if protected from on high,
Does that whole Nation sell and buy.
He who mocks the Infant's Faith
Shall be mock'd in Age and Death.
He who shall teach the Child to Doubt
The rotting Grave shall ne'er get out.
He who respects the Infant's faith
Triumphs over Hell and Death.
The Child's Toys and the Old Man's Reasons
Are the Fruits of the Two seasons.
The Questioner, who sits so sly,
Shall never know how to Reply.
He who replies to words of Doubt
Doth put the Light of Knowledge out.

The Strongest Poison ever known
Came from Caesar's Laurel Crown.
Nought can deform the Human Race
Like to the Armour's iron brace.
When Gold and Gems adorn the Plow
To peaceful Arts shall Envy Bow.
A Riddle or the Cricket's Cry
Is to Doubt a fit Reply.
The Emmet's Inch and Eagle's Mile
Make Lame Philosophy to smile.
He who Doubts from what he sees
Will ne'er Believe, do what you Please.
If the Sun and Moon should doubt,
They'd immediately Go out.
To be in a Passion you Good may do,
But no good if a Passion is in you.
The Whore and Gambler, by the State
Licenc'd, build that Nation's Fate.
The Harlot's cry from Street to Street
Shall weave Old England's winding Sheet.
The Winner's Shout, the Loser's Curse,
Dance before dead England's Hearse.
Every Night and every Morn
Some to Misery are Born.
Every Morn and every Night
Some are Born to sweet delight.
Some are Born to sweet delight,
Some are Born to Endless Night.
We are led to Believe a Lie
When we see not Thro' the Eye
Which was Born in a Night to perish in a Night
When the Soul Slept in Beams of Light.
God Appears and God is Light
To those poor Souls who dwell in Night,
But does a Human Form Display
To those who Dwell in Realms of day.

THE TYGER

Tyger! Tyger! burning bright
In the forests of the night,
What immortal hand or eye
Could frame thy fearful symmetry?

In what distant deeps or skies
Burnt the fire of thine eyes?
On what wings dare he aspire?
What the hand dare seize the fire?

And what shoulder and what art
Could twist the sinews of thy heart?
And when thy heart began to beat,
What dread hand? and what dread feet?

What the hammer? what the chain?
In what furnace was thy brain?
What the anvil? What dread grasp
Dare its deadly terrors clasp?

When the stars threw down their spears,
And water'd heaven with their tears,
Did he smile his work to see?
Did he who made the lamb make thee?

Tyger! Tyger! burning bright
In the forests of the night,
What immortal hand or eye
Dare frame thy fearful symmetry?

THE CHIMNEY SWEEPER (I)

When my mother died I was very young,
And my father sold me while yet my tongue
Could scarcely cry " 'weep! 'weep! 'weep! 'weep!"
So your chimneys I sweep, and in soot I sleep.

There's little Tom Dacre, who cried when his head,
That curl'd like a lamb's back, was shav'd: so I said
"Hush, Tom! never mind it, for when your head's bare
"You know that the soot cannot spoil your white hair."

And so he was quiet, and that very night,
As Tom was a-sleeping, he had such a sight!
That thousands of sweepers, Dick, Joe, Ned, and Jack,
Were all of them lock'd up in coffins of black.

And by came an Angel who had a bright key,
And he open'd the coffins and set them all free;
Then down a green plain leaping, laughing, they run,
And wash in a river, and shine in the Sun.

Then naked and white, all their bags left behind,
They rise upon clouds and sport in the wind;
And the Angel told Tom, if he'd be a good boy,
He'd have God for his father, and never want joy.

And so Tom awoke; and we rose in the dark,
And got with our bags and our brushes to work.
Tho' the morning was cold, Tom was happy and warm;
So if all do their duty they need not fear harm.

THE CHIMNEY SWEEPER (II)

A little black thing among the snow,
Crying " 'weep! 'weep!" in notes of woe!
"Where are thy father and mother? say?"
"They are both gone up to the church to pray.

"Because I was happy upon the heath,
"And smil'd among the winter's snow,
"They clothed me in the clothes of death,
"And taught me to sing the notes of woe.

"And because I am happy and dance and sing,
"They think they have done me no injury,
"And are gone to praise God and his Priest and King,
"Who make up a heaven of our misery."

THE LITTLE BLACK BOY

My mother bore me in the southern wild,
And I am black, but O! my soul is white;
White as an angel is the English child,
But I am black, as if bereav'd of light.

My mother taught me underneath a tree,
And sitting down before the heat of day,
She took me on her lap and kissed me,
And pointing to the east, began to say:

"Look on the rising sun: there God does live,
  "And gives his light, and gives his heat away;
"And flowers and trees and beasts and men receive
  "Comfort in morning, joy in the noonday.

"And we are put on earth a little space,
  "That we may learn to bear the beams of love;
"And these black bodies and this sunburnt face
  "Is but a cloud, and like a shady grove.

"For when our souls have learn'd the heat to bear,
  "The cloud will vanish; we shall hear his voice,
"Saying: 'Come out from the grove, my love and care,
  " 'And round my golden tent like lambs rejoice.' "
Thus did my mother say, and kissed me;
  And thus I say to little English boy:
When I from black and he from white cloud free,
  And round the tent of God like lambs we joy,

I'll shade him from the heat, till he can bear
  To lean in joy upon our father's knee;
And then I'll stand and stroke his silver hair,
  And be like him, and he will then love me.

LONDON

I wander thro' each charter'd street,
  Near where the charter'd Thames does flow,
And mark in every face I meet
  Marks of weakness, marks of woe.

In every cry of every Man,
  In every Infant's cry of fear,
In every voice, in every ban,
  The mind-forg'd manacles I hear.

How the Chimney-sweeper's cry
  Every black'ning Church appalls;
And the hapless Soldier's sigh
  Runs in blood down Palace walls.

But most thro' midnight streets I hear
  How the youthful Harlot's curse
Blasts the new born Infant's tear,
  And blights with plagues the Marriage hearse.

SOFT SNOW

I walked abroad in a snowy day:
I ask'd the soft snow with me to play:
She play'd and she melted in all her prime,
And the winter call'd it a dreadful crime.

THE SICK ROSE

O Rose, thou art sick!   Has found out thy bed
  The invisible worm   Of crimson joy,
That flies in the night,   And his dark secret love
  In the howling storm,   Does thy life destroy.

AH, SUN–FLOWER

Ah, Sun-flower! weary of time,
  Who countest the steps of the Sun,
Seeking after that sweet golden clime
  Where the traveller's journey is done:

Where the Youth pined away with desire,
  And the pale Virgin shrouded in snow
Arise from their graves, and aspire
  Where my Sun-flower wishes to go.

MOCK ON

Mock on, Mock on Voltaire, Rousseau:
Mock on, Mock on: 'tis all in vain!
You throw the sand against the wind,
And the wind blows it back again.

And every sand becomes a Gem
Reflected in the beams divine;
Blown back they blind the mocking Eye,
But still in Israel's paths they shine.

The Atoms of Democritus
And Newton's Particles of light
Are sands upon the Red sea shore,
Where Israel's tents do shine so bright.

A DIVINE IMAGE

Cruelty has a Human Heart,
  And Jealousy a Human Face;
Terror the Human Form
    Divine,
  And Secrecy the Human Dress.

The Human Dress is forged Iron,
  The Human Form a fiery Forge,
The Human Face a Furnace seal'd,
  The Human Heart its hungry
    Gorge.

PROVERBS OF HELL

In seed time learn, in harvest teach, in winter enjoy.
Drive your cart and your plow over the bones of the dead.
The road of excess leads to the palace of wisdom.
Prudence is a rich, ugly old maid courted by Incapacity.
He who desires but acts not, breeds pestilence.
The cut worm forgives the plow.
Dip him in the river who loves water.
A fool sees not the same tree that a wise man sees.
He whose face gives no light, shall never become a star.
Eternity is in love with the productions of time.
The busy bee has no time for sorrow.
The hours of folly are measur'd by the clock; but of wisdom, no clock
can measure.
All wholesome food is caught without a net or a trap.
Bring out number, weight and measure in a year of dearth.
No bird soars too high, if he soars with his own wings.
A dead body revenges not injuries.
The most sublime act is to set another before you.
If the fool would persist in his folly he would become wise.
Folly is the cloke of knavery.
Shame is Pride's cloke.
Prisons are built with stones of Law, Brothels with bricks of Religon.
The pride of the peacock is the glory of God.
The lust of the goat is the bounty of God.
The wrath of the lion is the wisdom of God.
The nakedness of woman is the work of God.
Excess of sorrow laughs. Excess of joy weeps.
The roaring of lions, the howling of wolves, the raging of the stormy
sea, and the destructive sword, are portions of eternity, too great for the
eye of man.
The fox condemns the trap, not himself.
Joys impregnate. Sorrows bring forth.
Let man wear the fell of the lion, woman the fleece of the sheep.
The bird a nest, the spider a web, man friendship.

The selfish, smiling fool, and the sullen, frowning fool shall be both thought wise, that they may be a rod.

What is now proved was once only imagin'd.

The rat, the mouse, the fox, the rabbet watch the roots; the lion, the tyger, the horse, the elephant watch the fruits.

The cistern contains: the fountain overflows.

One thought fills immensity.

Always be ready to speak your mind, and a base man will avoid you.

Every thing possible to be believ'd is an image of truth.

The eagle never lost so much time as when he submitted to learn of the crow.

The fox provides for himself, but God provides for the lion.

Think in the morning. Act in the noon. Eat in the evening. Sleep in the night.

He who has suffer'd you to impose on him, knows you.

As the plow follows words, so God rewards prayers.

The tygers of wrath are wiser than the horses of instruction.

Expect poison from the standing water.

You never know what is enough unless you know what is more than enough.

Listen to the fool's reproach! it is a kingly title!

The eyes of fire, the nostrils of air, the mouth of water, the beard of earth.

The weak in courage is strong in cunning.

The apple tree never asks the beech how he shall grow; nor the lion, the horse, how he shall take his prey.

The thankful receiver bears a plentiful harvest.

If others had not been foolish, we should be so.

The soul of sweet delight can never be defil'd.

When thou seest an Eagle, thou seest a portion of Genius; lift up thy head!

As the caterpiller chooses the fairest leaves to lay her eggs on, so the priest lays his curse on the fairest joys.

To create a little flower is the labour of ages.

Damn braces. Bless relaxes.

The best wine is the oldest, the best water the newest.

Prayers plow not! Praises reap not!

Joys laugh not! Sorrows weep not!

The head Sublime, the heart Pathos, the genitals Beauty, the hands and feet Proportion.

As the air to a bird or the sea to a fish, so is contempt to the contemptible.

The crow wish'd every thing was black, the owl that every thing was white.

Exuberance is Beauty.

If the lion was advised by the fox, he would be cunning.

Improvement makes strait roads; but the crooked roads without Improvement are roads of Genius.

Sooner murder an infant in its cradle than nurse unacted desires.

Where man is not, nature is barren.

Truth can never be told so as to be understood, and not be believ'd.

Enough! or Too much.

NIGHT

The sun descending in the west,
The evening star does shine;
The birds are silent in their nest,
And I must seek for mine.
The moon like a flower
In heaven's high bower,
With silent delight
Sits and smiles on the night.

Farewell, green fields and happy
groves,
Where flocks have took delight.
Where lambs have nibbled, silent
moves
The feet of angels bright;
Unseen they pour blessing
And joy without ceasing,
On each bud and blossom,
And each sleeping bosom.

They look in every thoughtless
nest,
Where birds are cover'd warm;
They visit caves of every beast,
To keep them all from harm.
If they see any weeping
That should have been sleeping,
They pour sleep on their head,
And sit down by their bed.

When wolves and tygers howl for
prey,
They pitying stand and weep;
Seeking to drive their thirst away,
And keep them from the sheep;
But if they rush dreadful,
The angels, most heedful,
Receive each mild spirit,
New worlds to inherit.

And there the lion's ruddy eyes
Shall flow with tears of gold,
And pitying the tender cries,
And walking round the fold,
Saying "Wrath, by his meekness,
"And by his health, sickness
"Is driven away
"From our immortal day.

"And now beside thee, bleating
lamb,
"I can lie down and sleep;
"Or think on him who bore thy
name,
"Graze after thee and weep.
"For, wash'd in life's river,
"My brighter mane for ever
"Shall shine like the gold
"As I guard o'er the fold."

SONG: HOW SWEET I ROAM'D

How sweet I roam'd from field to field,
And tasted all the summer's pride,
'Till I the prince of love beheld,
Who in the sunny beams did glide!

He shew'd me lillies for my hair,
    And blushing roses for my brow;
He led me through his gardens fair,
    Where all his golden pleasures grow.

With sweet May dews my wings were wet,
    And Phœbus fir'd my vocal rage;
He caught me in his silken net,
    And shut me in his golden cage.

He loves to sit and hear me sing,
    Then, laughing, sports and plays with me;
Then stretches out my golden wing,
    And mocks my loss of liberty.

From VISIONS OF THE DAUGHTERS OF ALBION

THE MARIGOLD

And thus she spoke to the bright Marygold of Leutha's vale:

"Art thou a flower? art thou a nymph? I see thee now a flower,
"Now a nymph! I dare not pluck thee from thy dewy bed!"

The Golden nymph replied: "Pluck thou my flower, Oothoon the mild!
"Another flower shall spring, because the soul of sweet delight
"Can never pass away." She ceas'd, and clos'd her golden shrine.

Then Oothoon pluck'd the flower, saying: "I pluck thee from thy bed,
"Sweet flower, and put thee here to glow between my breasts,
"And thus I turn my face to where my whole soul seeks."

Over the waves she went in wing'd exulting swift delight,
And over Theotormon's reign took her impetuous course.

William Wordsworth

1770-1850

To Wordsworth "the lights of faith and of nature are subordinate John Baptists." He was, indeed, more of the nature of the disciples than, like Shelley, of an order of being like the archangels.

On the levels of his life, he knew light, but it was the light of Reason rather than the innermost secret Flame. He brought to his poetry all "the household stuffe of Heaven on earth."

It is a poetry more of the reason than of the intellect . . . a reason which is Life.

Wordsworth, at his highest, approached the tranquillity, the activity, of the saints, the "perfect stillness, perfect fecundity," of which Rusbroeck wrote.*

Reason and Tranquillity were the companion Angels of Wordsworth as he walked through an everyday world made splendid by the light of a genius which illuminated but did not transform. Common speech and common experience were here, but all made radiant and unforgettable by inspiration. There were poems — *Intimations of Immortality from Recollections of Early Childhood* was such a poem — when the Pentecostal Flames came to our common speech. The ordinary objects of life became supernatural. The common celandine was still the common celandine, but it was also a star. For Wordsworth had the warmth of the earth and of the human heart; and that genius which was of the heart rather than of the soul had taken all the chill from Reason, till Reason had the pulse of a human, yet a holy, heart.

For his poems are ineffably holy. In the note to that ode which was the mountain on which he and his angels spoke with God (*Intimations of Immortality from Recollections of Early Childhood*) he said, speaking of his early years: "I was often unable to think of eternal things as having external existence, and I communed with all that I saw as something not apart from, but inherent in, my own immaterial nature. Many times while going to school have I grasped at a wall or a tree to recall myself from this abyss of idealism to the reality."

Yet to him, as to Tauler, "the nobler things are, the commoner they are. Love is noble, because it is universal." He knew that "God is an angel in an angel, and a stone in a stone, and a straw in a straw." †

The kernel of all his poems — even when we have to cut to that kernel through an unnecessary husk furred with earth, has a singular purity and fidelity. Matthew Arnold said of him: "It might seem that Nature not only gave him the matter for his poem, but wrote his poem for him."

MY HEART LEAPS UP

My heart leaps up when I behold
    A rainbow in the sky:
So was it when my life began;
So is it now I am a man;
So be it when I shall grow old,
    Or let me die!
The Child is father of the Man;
    And I could wish my days to be
Bound each to each by natural piety.

* Jan van Rusbroeck *De Vera Contemplatione.*
† John Donne.

I WANDERED LONELY AS A CLOUD

I wandered lonely as a cloud
   That floats on high o'er vales and hills,
When all at once I saw a crowd,
   A host, of golden daffodils;
Beside the lake, beneath the trees,
Fluttering and dancing in the breeze.

Continuous as the stars that shine
   And twinkle on the milky way,
They stretched in never-ending line
   Along the margin of a bay:
Ten thousand saw I at a glance,
Tossing their heads in sprightly dance.

The waves beside them danced; but they
   Out-did the sparkling waves in glee:
A poet could not but be gay,
   In such a jocund company:
I gazed — and gazed — but little thought
What wealth the show to me had brought:

For oft, when on my couch I lie
   In vacant or in pensive mood,
They flash upon that inward eye
   Which is the bliss of solitude;
And then my heart with pleasure fills,
And dances with the daffodils.

THREE YEARS SHE GREW

Three years she grew in sun and shower,
Then Nature said, "A lovelier flower
   On earth was never sown;
This Child I to myself will take;
She shall be mine, and I will make
   A Lady of my own.

"Myself will to my darling be
Both law and impulse: and with me
   The girl, in rock and plain,
In earth and heaven, in glade and bower,
Shall feel an overseeing power
   To kindle or restrain.

"She shall be sportive as the fawn
That wild with glee across the lawn
  Or up the mountain springs;
And her's shall be the breathing balm,
And her's the silence and the calm
  Of mute insensate things.

"The floating clouds their state shall lend
To her; for her the willow bend;
  Nor shall she fail to see
Even in the motions of the Storm
Grace that shall mould the Maiden's form
  By silent sympathy.

"The stars of midnight shall be dear
To her; and she shall lean her ear
  In many a secret place
Where rivulets dance their wayward round,
And beauty born of murmuring sound
  Shall pass into her face.

"And vital feelings of delight
Shall rear her form to stately height,
  Her virgin bosom swell;
Such thoughts to Lucy I will give
While she and I together live
  Here in this happy dell."

Thus Nature spake — The work was done —
How soon my Lucy's race was run!
  She died, and left to me
This heath, this calm, and quiet scene;
The memory of what has been,
  And never more will be.

THE SOLITARY REAPER

Behold her, single in the field,
  Yon solitary Highland Lass!
Reaping and singing by herself;
  Stop here, or gently pass!
Alone she cuts and binds the grain,
And sings a melancholy strain;
O listen! for the Vale profound
Is overflowing with the sound.

No Nightingale did ever chaunt
  More welcome notes to weary bands
Of travellers in some shady haunt,
  Among Arabian sands:
A voice so thrilling ne'er was heard
In spring-time from the Cuckoo-bird,
Breaking the silence of the seas
Among the farthest Hebrides.

Will no one tell me what she sings? —
  Perhaps the plaintive numbers flow
For old, unhappy, far-off things,
  And battles long ago:
Or is it some more humble lay,
Familiar matter of to-day?
Some natural sorrow, loss, or pain,
That has been, and may be again!

Whate'er the theme, the Maiden sang
  As if her song could have no ending;
I saw her singing at her work,
  And o'er the sickle bending; —
I listened, motionless and still;
And, as I mounted up the hill,
The music in my heart I bore,
Long after it was heard no more.

O NIGHTINGALE

O Nightingale! thou surely art
A creature of a "fiery heart": —
These notes of thine — they pierce and pierce;
Tumultuous harmony and fierce!
Thou sing'st as if the God of wine
Had helped thee to a Valentine;
A song in mockery and despite
Of shades, and dews, and silent night;
And steady bliss, and all the loves
Now sleeping in these peaceful groves.

I heard a Stock-dove sing or say
His homely tale, this very day;
His voice was buried among trees,
Yet to be come-at by the breeze:

He did not cease; but cooed — and cooed;
And somewhat pensively he wooed:
He sang of love, with quiet blending,
Slow to begin, and never ending;
Of serious faith, and inward glee;
That was the song — the song for me!

THE GREEN LINNET

Beneath these fruit-tree boughs that shed
Their snow-white blossoms on my head,
With brightest sunshine round me spread
    Of spring's unclouded weather,
In this sequestered nook how sweet
To sit upon my orchard-seat!
And birds and flowers once more to greet,
    My last year's friends together.

One have I marked, the happiest guest
In all this covert of the blest:
Hail to Thee, far above the rest
    In joy of voice and pinion!
Thou, Linnet! in thy green array,
Presiding Spirit here to-day,
Dost lead the revels of the May;
    And this is thy dominion.

While birds, and butterflies, and flowers,
Make all one band of paramours,
Thou, ranging up and down the bowers,
    Art sole in thy employment:
A Life, a Presence like the Air,
Scattering thy gladness without care,
Too blest with any one to pair;
    Thyself thy own enjoyment.

Amid yon tuft of hazel trees,
That twinkle to the gusty breeze,
Behold him perched in ecstacies,
    Yet seeming still to hover;
There! where the flutter of his wings
Upon his back and body flings
Shadows and sunny glimmerings,
    That cover him all over.

My dazzled sight he oft deceives,
A Brother of the dancing leaves;
Then flits, and from the cottage-eaves
   Pours forth his song in gushes;
As if by that exulting strain
He mocked and treated with disdain
The voiceless Form he chose to feign,
   While fluttering in the bushes.

ODE ON THE INTIMATIONS OF IMMORTALITY FROM RECOLLECTIONS OF EARLY CHILDHOOD

There was a time when meadow, grove, and stream,
The earth, and every common sight,
     To me did seem
    Apparelled in celestial light,
The glory and the freshness of a dream.
It is not now as it hath been of yore; —
    Turn wheresoe'er I may,
     By night or day,
The things which I have seen I now can see no more.

    The Rainbow comes and goes,
    And lovely is the Rose,
    The Moon doth with delight
Look round her when the heavens are bare,
    Waters on a starry night
    Are beautiful and fair;
   The sunshine is a glorious birth;
   But yet I know, where'er I go,
That there hath past away a glory from the earth.

Now, while the birds thus sing a joyous song,
    And while the young lambs bound
    As to the tabor's sound,
To me alone there came a thought of grief:
A timely utterance gave that thought relief,
    And I again am strong:
The cataracts blow their trumpets from the steep;
  No more shall grief of mine the season wrong;
  I hear the Echoes through the mountains throng,
The Winds come to me from the fields of sleep,
    And all the earth is gay;
     Land and sea
    Give themselves up to jollity,

And with the heart of May
Doth every Beast keep holiday; —
Thou Child of Joy,
Shout round me, let me hear thy shouts, thou happy
Shepherd-boy!

Ye blessed Creatures, I have heard the call
Ye to each other make; I see
The heavens laugh with you in your jubilee;
My heart is at your festival,
My head hath its coronal,
The fulness of your bliss, I feel — I feel it all.
O evil day! if I were sullen
While Earth herself is adorning,
This sweet May-morning,
And the Children are culling
On every side,
In a thousand valleys far and wide,
Fresh flowers; while the sun shines warm,
And the Babe leaps up on his Mother's arm: —
I hear, I hear, with joy I hear!
— But there's a Tree, of many, one,
A single Field which I have looked upon,
Both of them speak of something that is gone:
The Pansy at my feet
Doth the same tale repeat:
Whither is fled the visionary gleam?
Where is it now, the glory and the dream?

Our birth is but a sleep and a forgetting:
The Soul that rises with us, our life's Star,
Hath had elsewhere its setting,
And cometh from afar:
Not in entire forgetfulness,
And not in utter nakedness,
But trailing clouds of glory do we come
From God, who is our home:
Heaven lies about us in our infancy!
Shades of the prison-house begin to close
Upon the growing Boy,
But He beholds the light, and whence it flows,
He sees it in his joy;
The Youth, who daily farther from the east
Must travel, still is Nature's Priest,
And by the vision splendid
Is on his way attended;

At length the Man perceives it die away,
And fade into the light of common day.

Earth fills her lap with pleasures of her own;
    Yearnings she hath in her own natural kind,
    And, even with something of a Mother's mind,
        And no unworthy aim,
    The homely Nurse doth all she can
To make her Foster-child, her Inmate Man,
    Forget the glories he hath known,
And that imperial palace whence he came.

Behold the Child among his new-born blisses,
A six years' Darling of a pigmy size!
See, where 'mid work of his own hand he lies,
Fretted by sallies of his mother's kisses,
With light upon him from his father's eyes!
See, at his feet, some little plan or chart,
Some fragment from his dream of human life,
Shaped by himself with newly-learned art;
        A wedding or a festival,
        A mourning or a funeral;
            And this hath now his heart,
        And unto this he frames his song:
            Then will he fit his tongue
To dialogues of business, love, or strife;
            But it will not be long
            Ere this be thrown aside,
            And with new joy and pride
The little Actor cons another part;
Filling from time to time his "humorous stage"
With all the Persons, down to palsied Age,
That Life brings with her in her equipage;
            As if his whole vocation
            Were endless imitation.

Thou, whose exterior semblance doth belie
    Thy Soul's immensity;
Thou best Philosopher, who yet dost keep
Thy heritage, thou Eye among the blind,
That, deaf and silent, read'st the eternal deep,
Haunted for ever by the eternal mind,—
        Mighty Prophet! Seer blest!
        On whom those truths do rest,
Which we are toiling all our lives to find,
In darkness lost, the darkness of the grave;

Thou, over whom thy Immortality
Broods like the Day, a Master o'er a Slave,
A Presence which is not to be put by;
Thou little Child, yet glorious in the might
Of heaven-born freedom on thy being's height,
Why with such earnest pains dost thou provoke
The years to bring the inevitable yoke,
Thus blindly with thy blessedness at strife?
Full soon thy Soul shall have her earthly freight,
And custom lie upon thee with a weight,
Heavy as frost, and deep almost as life!

O joy! that in our embers
Is something that doth live,
That nature yet remembers
What was so fugitive!
The thought of our past years in me doth breed
Perpetual benediction: not indeed
For that which is most worthy to be blest —
Delight and liberty, the simple creed
Of Childhood, whether busy or at rest,
With new-fledged hope still fluttering in his breast: —
Not for these I raise
The song of thanks and praise;
But for those obstinate questionings
Of sense and outward things,
Fallings from us, vanishings;
Blank misgivings of a Creature
Moving about in worlds not realised,
High instincts before which our mortal Nature
Did tremble like a guilty Thing surprised:
But for those first affections,
Those shadowy recollections,
Which, be they what they may,
Are yet the fountain light of all our day,
Are yet a master light of all our seeing;
Uphold us, cherish, and have power to make
Our noisy years seem moments in the being
Of the eternal Silence: truths that wake,
To perish never;
Which neither listlessness, nor mad endeavour,
Nor Man nor Boy,
Nor all that is at enmity with joy,
Can utterly abolish or destroy!
Hence in a season of calm weather
Though inland far we be,

Our Souls have sight of that immortal sea
          Which brought us hither,
       Can in a moment travel thither,
And see the Children sport upon the shore,
And hear the mighty waters rolling evermore.

Then sing, ye Birds, sing, sing a joyous song!
          And let the young Lambs bound
          As to the tabor's sound!
We in thought will join your throng,
       Ye that pipe and ye that play,
       Ye that through your hearts to-day
       Feel the gladness of the May!
What though the radiance which was once so bright
Be now for ever taken from my sight,
       Though nothing can bring back the hour
Of splendour in the grass, of glory in the flower;
       We will grieve not, rather find
       Strength in what remains behind;
       In the primal sympathy
       Which having been must ever be;
       In the soothing thoughts that spring
       Out of human suffering;
       In the faith that looks through death,
   In years that bring the philosophic mind.

And O, ye Fountains, Meadows, Hills, and Groves,
Forebode not any severing of our loves!
Yet in my heart of hearts I feel your might;
I only have relinquished one delight
To live beneath your more habitual sway.
I love the Brooks which down their channels fret,
Even more than when I tripped lightly as they;
The innocent brightness of a new-born Day
          Is lovely yet;
The Clouds that gather round the setting sun
Do take a sober colouring from an eye
That hath kept watch o'er man's mortality;
Another race hath been, and other palms are won.
Thanks to the human heart by which we live,
Thanks to its tenderness, its joys, and fears,
To me the meanest flower that blows can give
Thoughts that do often lie too deep for tears.

From THE PRELUDE

FAIR SEED–TIME HAD MY SOUL

Fair seed-time had my soul, and I grew up
Fostered alike by beauty and by fear:
Much favoured in my birth-place, and no less
In that beloved Vale to which erelong
We were transplanted; — there were we let loose
For sports of wider range. Ere I had told
Ten birth-days, when among the mountain slopes
Frost, and the breath of frosty wind, had snapped
The last autumnal crocus, 'twas my joy
With store of springes o'er my shoulder hung
To range the open heights where woodcocks run
Along the smooth green turf. Through half the night,
Scudding away from snare to snare, I plied
That anxious visitation; — moon and stars
Were shining o'er my head. I was alone,
And seemed to be a trouble to the peace
That dwelt among them. Sometimes it befell
In these night wanderings, that a strong desire
O'erpowered my better reason, and the bird
Which was the captive of another's toil
Became my prey; and when the deed was done
I heard among the solitary hills
Low breathing coming after me, and sounds
Of undistinguishable motion, steps
Almost as silent as the turf they trod.

Nor less, when spring had warmed the cultured Vale,
Roved we as plunderers where the mother-bird
Had in high places built her lodge; though mean
Our object and inglorious, yet the end
Was not ignoble. Oh! when I have hung
Above the raven's nest, by knots of grass
And half-inch fissures in the slippery rock
But ill sustained, and almost (so it seemed)
Suspended by the blast that blew amain,
Shouldering the naked crag, oh, at that time
While on the perilous ridge I hung alone,
With what strange utterance did the loud dry wind
Blow through my ear! the sky seemed not a sky
Of earth — and with what motion moved the clouds!

Dust as we are, the immortal spirit grows
Like harmony in music; there is a dark
Inscrutable workmanship that reconciles
Discordant elements, makes them cling together
In one society. How strange, that all
The terrors, pains, and early miseries,
Regrets, vexations, lassitudes interfused
Within my mind, should e'er have borne a part,
And that a needful part, in making up
The calm existence that is mine when I
Am worthy of myself! Praise to the end!
Thanks to the means which Nature deigned to employ;
Whether her fearless visitings, or those
That came with soft alarm, like hurtless light
Opening the peaceful clouds; or she would use
Severer interventions, ministry
More palpable, as best might suit her aim.

WISDOM AND SPIRIT OF THE UNIVERSE

Wisdom and Spirit of the universe!
Thou Soul that art the eternity of thought,
That givest to forms and images a breath
And everlasting motion, not in vain
By day or star-light thus from my first dawn
Of childhood didst thou intertwine for me
The passions that build up our human soul;
Not with the mean and vulgar works of man,
But with high objects, with enduring things —
With life and nature — purifying thus
The elements of feeling and of thought,
And sanctifying, by such discipline,
Both pain and fear, until we recognise
A grandeur in the beatings of the heart.
Nor was this fellowship vouchsafed to me
With stinted kindness. In November days,
When vapours rolling down the valley made
A lonely scene more lonesome, among woods,
At noon and 'mid the calm of summer nights,
When, by the margin of the trembling lake,
Beneath the gloomy hills homeward I went
In solitude, such intercourse was mine;
Mine was it in the fields both day and night,
And by the waters, all the summer long.

And in the frosty season, when the sun
Was set, and visible for many a mile

The cottage windows blazed through twilight gloom,
I heeded not their summons: happy time
It was indeed for all of us — for me
It was a time of rapture! Clear and loud
The village clock tolled six, — I wheeled about,
Proud and exulting like an untired horse
That cares not for his home. All shod with steel,
We hissed along the polished ice in games
Confederate, imitative of the chase
And woodland pleasures, — the resounding horn,
The pack loud chiming, and the hunted hare.
So through the darkness and the cold we flew,
And not a voice was idle; with the din
Smitten, the precipices rang aloud;
The leafless trees and every icy crag
Tinkled like iron; while far distant hills
Into the tumult sent an alien sound
Of melancholy not unnoticed, while the stars
Eastward were sparkling clear, and in the west
The orange sky of evening died away.
Not seldom from the uproar I retired
Into a silent bay, or sportively
Glanced sideway, leaving the tumultuous throng,
To cut across the reflex of a star
That fled, and, flying still before me, gleamed
Upon the glassy plain; and oftentimes,
When we had given our bodies to the wind,
And all the shadowy banks on either side
Came sweeping through the darkness, spinning still
The rapid line of motion, then at once
Have I, reclining back upon my heels,
Stopped short; yet still the solitary cliffs
Wheeled by me — even as if the earth had rolled
With visible motion her diurnal round!
Behind me did they stretch in solemn train,
Feebler and feebler, and I stood and watched
Till all was tranquil as a dreamless sleep.

Ye Presences of Nature in the sky
And on the earth! Ye Visions of the hills!
And Souls of lonely places! can I think
A vulgar hope was yours when ye employed
Such ministry, when ye, through many a year
Haunting me thus among my boyish sports,
On caves and trees, upon the woods and hills,
Impressed, upon all forms, the characters

Of danger or desire; and thus did make
The surface of the universal earth,
With triumph and delight, with hope and fear,
Work like a sea?
        Not uselessly employed,
Might I pursue this theme through every change
Of exercise and play, to which the year
Did summon us in his delightful round.

BLEST THE INFANT BABE

      Blest the infant Babe,
(For with my best conjecture I would trace
Our Being's earthly progress,) blest the Babe,
Nursed in his Mother's arms, who sinks to sleep
Rocked on his Mother's breast; who with his soul
Drinks in the feelings of his Mother's eye!
For him, in one dear Presence, there exists
A virtue which irradiates and exalts
Objects through widest intercourse of sense.
No outcast he, bewildered and depressed:
Along his infant veins are interfused
The gravitation and the filial bond
Of nature that connect him with the world.
Is there a flower, to which he points with hand
Too weak to gather it, already love
Drawn from love's purest earthly fount for him
Hath beautified that flower; already shades
Of pity cast from inward tenderness
Do fall around him upon aught that bears
Unsightly marks of violence or harm.
Emphatically such a Being lives,
Frail creature as he is, helpless as frail,
An inmate of this active universe:
For feeling has to him imparted power
That through the growing faculties of sense
Doth like an agent of the one great Mind
Create, creator and receiver both,
Working but in alliance with the works
Which it beholds. — Such, verily, is the first
Poetic spirit of our human life,
By uniform control of after years,
In most, abated or suppressed; in some,
Through every change of growth and of decay,
Pre-eminent till death.

'TWERE LONG TO TELL

'Twere long to tell
What spring and autumn, what the winter snows,
And what the summer shade, what day and night,
Evening and morning, sleep and waking, thought
From sources inexhaustible, poured forth
To feed the spirit of religious love
In which I walked with Nature. But let this
Be not forgotten, that I still retained
My first creative sensibility;
That by the regular action of the world
My soul was unsubdued. A plastic power
Abode with me; a forming hand, at times
Rebellious, acting in a devious mood;
A local spirit of his own, at war
With general tendency, but, for the most,
Subservient strictly to external things
With which it communed. An auxiliar light
Came from my mind, which on the setting sun
Bestowed new splendour; the melodious birds,
The fluttering breezes, fountains that run on
Murmuring so sweetly in themselves, obeyed
A like dominion, and the midnight storm
Grew darker in the presence of my eye:
Hence my obeisance, my devotion hence,
And hence my transport.
                    Nor should this, perchance,
Pass unrecorded, that I still had loved
The exercise and produce of a toil,
Than analytic industry to me
More pleasing, and whose character I deem
Is more poetic as resembling more
Creative agency. The song would speak
Of that interminable building reared
By observation of affinities
In objects where no brotherhood exists
To passive minds. My seventeenth year was come,
And, whether from this habit, rooted now
So deeply in my mind, or from excess
In the great social principle of life
Coercing all things into sympathy,
To unorganic natures were transferred
My own enjoyments; or the power of truth
Coming in revelation, did converse

With things that really are; I, at this time,
Saw blessings spread around me like a sea.
Thus while the days flew by, and years passed on,
From Nature and her overflowing soul,
I had received so much, that all my thoughts
Were steeped in feeling; I was only then
Contented, when with bliss ineffable
I felt the sentiment of Being spread
O'er all that moves and all that seemeth still;
O'er all that, lost beyond the reach of thought
And human knowledge, to the human eye
Invisible, yet liveth to the heart;
O'er all that leaps and runs, and shouts and sings,
Or beats the gladsome air; o'er all that glides
Beneath the wave, yea, in the wave itself,
And mighty depth of waters. Wonder not
If high the transport, great the joy I felt,
Communing in this sort through earth and heaven
With every form of creature, as it looked
Towards the Uncreated with a countenance
Of adoration, with an eye of love.
One song they sang, and it was audible,
Most audible, then, when the fleshly ear,
O'ercome by humblest prelude of that strain,
Forgot her functions, and slept undisturbed.

AS IF AWAKENED, SUMMONED

As if awakened, summoned, roused, constrained,
I looked for universal things; perused
The common countenance of earth and sky:
Earth, nowhere unembellished by some trace
Of that first Paradise whence man was driven;
And sky, whose beauty and bounty are expressed
By the proud name she bears — the name of Heaven.
I called on both to teach me what they might;
Or, turning the mind in upon herself,
Pored, watched, expected, listened, spread my thoughts
And spread them with a wider creeping; felt
Incumbencies more awful, visitings
Of the Upholder of the tranquil soul,
That tolerates the indignities of Time,
And, from the centre of Eternity
All finite motions overruling, lives
In glory immutable. But peace! enough

Here to record that I was mounting now
To such community with highest truth —
A track pursuing, not untrod before,
From strict analogies by thought supplied
Or consciousness not to be subdued.
To every natural form, rock, fruits, or flower,
Even the loose stones that cover the highway,
I gave a moral life: I saw them feel,
Or linked them to some feeling: the great mass
Lay bedded in a quickening soul, and all
That I beheld respired with inward meaning.
Add that whate'er of Terror or of Love
Or Beauty, Nature's daily face put on
From transitory passion, unto this
I was as sensitive as waters are
To the sky's influence in a kindred mood
Of passion; was obedient as a lute
That waits upon the touches of the wind.
Unknown, unthought of, yet I was most rich —
I had a world about me — 'twas my own;
I made it, for it only lived to me,
And to the God who sees into the heart.

OH, BLANK CONFUSION

Oh, blank confusion! true epitome
Of what the mighty City is herself,
To thousands upon thousands of her sons,
Living amid the same perpetual whirl
Of trivial objects, melted and reduced
To one identity, by differences
That have no law, no meaning, and no end —
Oppression, under which even highest minds
Must labour, whence the strongest are not free.
But though the picture weary out the eye,
By nature an unmanageable sight,
It is not wholly so to him who looks
In steadiness, who hath among least things
An under-sense of greatest; sees the parts
As parts, but with a feeling of the whole.
This, of all acquisitions, first awaits
On sundry and most widely different modes
Of education, nor with least delight
On that through which I passed. Attention springs,
And comprehensiveness and memory flow,

From early converse with the works of God
Among all regions; chiefly where appear
Most obviously simplicity and power.
Think, how the everlasting streams and woods,
Stretched and still stretching far and wide, exalt
The roving Indian, on his desert sands:
What grandeur not unfelt, what pregnant show
Of beauty, meets the sun-burnt Arab's eye:
And, as the sea propels, from zone to zone,
Its currents; magnifies its shoals of life
Beyond all compass; spreads, and sends aloft
Armies of clouds, — even so, its power and aspects
Shape for mankind, by principles as fixed,
The views and aspirations of the soul
To majesty. Like virtue have the forms
Perennial of the ancient hills; nor less
The changeful language of their countenances
Quickens the slumbering mind, and aids the thoughts,
However multitudinous, to move
With order and relation. This, if still,
As hitherto, in freedom I may speak,
Not violating any just restraint,
As may be hoped, of real modesty, —
This did I feel, in London's vast domain.
The Spirit of Nature was upon me there;
The soul of Beauty and enduring Life
Vouchsafed her inspiration, and diffused,
Through meagre lines and colours, and the press
Of self-destroying, transitory things,
Composure, and ennobling Harmony.

ENOUGH OF HUMBLE ARGUMENTS

Enough of humble arguments; recall,
My Song! those high emotions which thy voice
Has heretofore made known; that bursting forth
Of sympathy, inspiring and inspired,
When everywhere a vital pulse was felt,
And all the several frames of things, like stars,
Through every magnitude distinguishable,
Shone mutually indebted, or half lost
Each in the other's blaze, a galaxy
Of life and glory. In the midst stood Man,
Outwardly, inwardly contemplated,
As, of all visible natures, crown, though born
Of dust, and kindred to the worm; a Being,

Both in perception and discernment, first
In every capability of rapture,
Through the divine effect of power and love;
As, more than anything we know, instinct
With godhead, and, by reason and by will,
Acknowledging dependency sublime.

Samuel Taylor Coleridge
1772-1834

The splendors of Coleridge are scarcely to be defined. They brought a
new world of spells and enchantment into English poetry.

In that great poem *Kubla Khan,* part of the verbal magic is due to the
miraculous power, which Coleridge shares with Milton, of lengthening
and shortening lines in such a manner that we are now brought into the
sight of an immensity of forests or of seas, now brought into some secret
sea-cavern where we may hear the enclosed sea-voices, see the glittering
sea-jewelry.

Kubla Khan, after four lines of eights (which, by some secret, have not
the "practical" quality of most eights, but a magical, legendary, far-off
sound), actually shrinks into a six: "Down to a sunless sea."

But, instead of the line seeming shorter (as it is), the alliteration, in
some marvelous manner, seems to extend the line into a long echo, which
lasts long after the word "sea" is silent.

The next two lines, again, are eights; then the following lines extend
themselves, from the sullen mysteriousness of the eights, into a series of
tens (with one eleven adding to the beauty), giving us the wide splendor
of that ancient and lost world of gardens, with its "sunny spots of
greenery."

The next stanza contains a strange variation of female endings and
common endings. The female endings have such a long second syllable
that they have exactly the opposite effect to that obtained by Keats with
his female endings. The dissonance of the endings in these lines:

And 'mid this tumult Kubla heard from far
Ancestral voices prophesying war!

has a mysterious darkening effect.

The next verse has that strange and subtle mixture of lengths to which
I have referred already.

And not one of these lines is stretched or shrunken unduly; each is a
part of;

> . . . the mingled measure
> From the fountain and the caves.

I think that part of the beauty of this miraculous verse is due to the strange narrowing and widening of the *o* and *u* sounds (coming, often, *between* the stresses):

> The shadow of the dome of pleasure
> Floated midway on the waves;
> Where was heard the mingled measure
> From the fountain and the caves.
> It was a miracle of rare device,
> A sunny pleasure-dome with caves of ice!

The alliterative *m* sounds, in this case, give the sound of heavy waters falling in a sullen darkness near to these splendors. The bright *d*'s, in this verse, and the next, give the effect of the bright pleasure-dome with its strange and glittering caves of ice.

But neither the splendors of this wonderful poem (one of the greatest poems in the world) nor the wonders of *The Ancient Mariner* are to be explained. In some parts of *The Ancient Mariner* Coleridge heightens the feeling of impending doom by the contrast between a line of eight syllables, containing a violent caesura, and an irregular-sounding line of seven syllables with practically no caesura, followed by an equally huddled nine-syllable line, which widens again into an eight (widens because of its regularity and its high vowels), then shrinks into a final line of only six syllables:

> Her lips were red, her looks were free,
> Her locks were yellow as gold:
> Her skin was as white as leprosy,
> The Night-mare LIFE-IN-DEATH was she,
> Who thicks man's blood with cold.

In the last line the shrinking from an eight to a six, and the four dull vowels, give us the actual feeling that our blood is shrunken and thick with cold.

Sometimes Coleridge emphasizes the feeling of apprehension, of dread, of fate, by the drumbeat of an internal rhyme. As an example, here is a verse:

> The ice was here, the ice was there,
> The ice was all around:
> It cracked and growled, and roared and howled,
> Like noises in a swound!

The feeling of approaching doom is produced and heightened continually by lengthening the stanza — a device which produces an added quickening. This is a strange freedom in a poem whose ground-stanza is a quatrain. Coleridge, at moments of stress and excitement, alters this to a five-line, to a six-line, to a nine-line verse! And this has the effect of a heart beating, now more and more quickly, now a little slower from dread. It might be said that Coleridge understood, almost better than any other poet, the difference in speed between, say, a quatrain and a sextain. The difference in speed between a couplet (a stage which Coleridge did not use in either of these great poems) and a quatrain is enormous, and this has been but little realized.

But the splendors of Coleridge cannot be defined. They brought a new world into English poetry — a world of magic, not to be explained by rules.

KUBLA KHAN

In Xanadu did Kubla Khan
A stately pleasure-dome decree:
Where Alph, the sacred river, ran
Through caverns measureless to man
    Down to a sunless sea.
So twice five miles of fertile ground
With walls and towers were girdled round:
And there were gardens bright with sinuous rills,
Where blossomed many an incense-bearing tree;
And here were forests ancient as the hills,
Enfolding sunny spots of greenery.

But oh! that deep romantic chasm which slanted
Down the green hill athwart a cedarn cover!
A savage place! as holy and enchanted
As e'er beneath a waning moon was haunted
By woman wailing for her demon-lover!
And from this chasm, with ceaseless turmoil seething,
As if this earth in fast thick pants were breathing,
A mighty fountain momently was forced:
Amid whose swift half-intermitted burst
Huge fragments vaulted like rebounding hail,
Or chaffy grain beneath the thresher's flail:
And 'mid these dancing rocks at once and ever
It flung up momently the sacred river.
Five miles meandering with a mazy motion
Through wood and dale the sacred river ran,

Then reached the caverns measureless to man,
And sank in tumult to a lifeless ocean:
And 'mid this tumult Kubla heard from far
Ancestral voices prophesying war!

    The shadow of the dome of pleasure
        Floated midway on the waves;
    Where was heard the mingled measure
        From the fountain and the caves.
    It was a miracle of rare device,
    A sunny pleasure-dome with caves of ice!

    A damsel with a dulcimer
    In a vision once I saw:
    It was an Abyssinian maid,
    And on her dulcimer she played,
Singing of Mount Abora.
Could I revive within me
Her symphony and song,
To such a deep delight 'twould win me,
    That with music loud and long,
I would build that dome in air,
That sunny dome! those caves of ice!
And all who heard should see them there,
And all should cry, Beware! Beware!
His flashing eyes, his floating hair!
Weave a circle round him thrice,
And close your eyes with holy dread,
For he on honey-dew hath fed,
And drunk the milk of Paradise.

THE RIME OF THE ANCIENT MARINER

PART I

An ancient Mariner meeteth three Gallants bidden to a wedding-feast, and detaineth one.

It is an ancient Mariner,
And he stoppeth one of three.
"By thy long grey beard and glittering eye,
Now wherefore stopp'st thou me?

    The Bridegroom's doors are opened wide,
    And I am next of kin;
    The guests are met, the feast is set:
    May'st hear the merry din."

He holds him with his skinny hand,
"There was a ship," quoth he.
"Hold off! unhand me, grey-beard loon!"
Eftsoons his hand dropt he.

The Wedding-Guest is spell-bound by the eye of the old seafaring man, and constrained to hear his tale.

He holds him with his glittering eye —
The Wedding-Guest stood still,
And listens like a three years' child:
The Mariner hath his will.

The Wedding-Guest sat on a stone:
He cannot choose but hear;
And thus spake on that ancient man,
The bright-eyed Mariner.

"The ship was cheered, the harbour cleared,
Merrily did we drop
Below the kirk, below the hill,
Below the lighthouse top.

The Mariner tells how the ship sailed southward with a good wind and fair weather, till it reached the Line.

The Sun came up upon the left,
Out of the sea came he!
And he shone bright, and on the right
Went down into the sea.

Higher and higher every day,
Till over the mast at noon —"
The Wedding-Guest here beat his breast,
For he heard the loud bassoon.

The Wedding-Guest heareth the bridal music; but the Mariner continueth his tale.

The bride hath paced into the hall,
Red as a rose is she;
Nodding their heads before her goes
The merry minstrelsy.

The Wedding-Guest he beat his breast,
Yet he cannot choose but hear;
And thus spake on that ancient man,
The bright-eyed Mariner.

The ship driven by a storm toward the South Pole.

"And now the STORM-BLAST came, and he
Was tyrannous and strong:
He struck with his o'ertaking wings,
And chased us south along.

With sloping masts and dipping prow,
As who pursued with yell and blow
Still treads the shadow of his foe,
And forward bends his head,
The ship drove fast, loud roared the blast,
And southward aye we fled.

And now there came both mist and snow,
And it grew wondrous cold:
And ice, mast-high, came floating by,
As green as emerald.

The land of ice, and of fearful sounds, where no living thing was to be seen.

And through the drifts the snowy clifts
Did send a dismal sheen:
Nor shapes of men nor beasts we ken —
The ice was all between.

The ice was here, the ice was there,
The ice was all around:
It cracked and growled, and roared and howled.
Like noises in a swound!

Till a great sea-bird, called the Albatross, came through the snow-fog, and was received with great joy and hospitality.

At length did cross an Albatross,
Thorough the fog it came;
As if it had been a Christian soul,
We hailed it in God's name.

It ate the food it ne'er had eat,
And round and round it flew.
The ice did split with a thunder-fit;
The helmsman steered us through!

And lo! the Albatross proveth a bird of good omen, and followeth the ship as it returned northward through fog and floating ice.

And a good south wind sprung up behind;
The Albatross did follow,
And every day, for food or play,
Came to the mariners' hollo!

In mist or cloud, on mast or shroud,
It perched for vespers nine;
Whiles all the night, through fog-smoke white,
Glimmered the white Moon-shine."

The ancient Mariner inhospitably killeth the pious bird of good omen.

"God save thee, ancient Mariner!
From the fiends, that plague thee thus! —
Why look'st thou so?" "With my cross-bow
I shot the ALBATROSS.

PART II

"The Sun now rose upon the right:
Out of the sea came he,
Still hid in mist, and on the left
Went down into the sea.

And the good south wind still blew behind,
But no sweet bird did follow,
Nor any day for food or play
Came to the mariners' hollo!

His shipmates cry out against the ancient Mariner, for killing the bird of good luck.

And I had done a hellish thing,
And it would work 'em woe:
For all averred, I had killed the bird
That made the breeze to blow.
Ah wretch! said they, the bird to slay,
That made the breeze to blow!

But when the fog cleared off, they justify the same, and thus make themselves accomplices in the crime.

Nor dim nor red, like God's own head,
The glorious Sun uprist:
Then all averred, I had killed the bird
That brought the fog and mist.
'Twas right, said they, such birds to slay,
That bring the fog and mist.

The fair breeze continues; the ship enters the Pacific Ocean, and sails northward, even till it reaches the Line.

The fair breeze blew, the white foam flew,
The furrow followed free;
We were the first that ever burst
Into that silent sea.

The ship hath been suddenly becalmed.

Down dropt the breeze, the sails dropt down,
'Twas sad as sad could be;
And we did speak only to break
The silence of the sea!

All in a hot and copper sky,
The bloody Sun, at noon,
Right up above the mast did stand,
No bigger than the Moon.

Day after day, day after day,
We stuck, nor breath nor motion;
As idle as a painted ship
Upon a painted ocean.

*And the Alba-
tross begins to
be avenged.*

Water, water, every where,
And all the boards did shrink;
Water, water, every where,
Nor any drop to drink.

The very deep did rot: O Christ!
That ever this should be!
Yea, slimy things did crawl with legs
Upon the slimy sea.

About, about, in reel and rout
The death-fires danced at night;
The water, like a witch's oils,
Burnt green, and blue and white.

*A Spirit had
followed them;
one of the in-
visible inhabi-
tants of this
planet, neither
departed souls
nor angels;
concerning
whom the
learned Jew,
Josephus, and
the Platonic
Constantino-
politan, Mi-
chael Psellus,
may be con-
sulted. They
are very nu-
merous, and
there is no
climate or ele-
ment without
one or more.*

And some in dreams assured were
Of the Spirit that plagued us so;
Nine fathom deep he had followed us
From the land of mist and snow.

And every tongue, through utter drought,
Was withered at the root:
We could not speak, no more than if
We had been choked with soot.

*The shipmates
in their sore
distress, would
fain throw the
whole guilt on
the ancient
Mariner: in
sign whereof
they hang the
dead sea-bird
round his neck.*

Ah! well a-day! what evil looks
Had I from old and young!
Instead of the cross, the Albatross
About my neck was hung.

PART III

"There passed a weary time. Each throat
Was parched, and glazed each eye.
A weary time! a weary time!
How glazed each weary eye,

*The ancient
Mariner be-
holdeth a sign
in the element
afar off.*

When looking westward, I beheld
A something in the sky.

At first it seemed a little speck,
And then it seemed a mist;
It moved and moved, and took at last
A certain shape, I wist.

A speck, a mist, a shape, I wist!
And still it neared and neared:
As if it dodged a water-sprite,
It plunged and tacked and veered.

At its nearer approach, it seemeth him to be a ship; and at a dear ransom he freeth his speech from the bonds of thirst.

With throats unslaked, with black lips baked,
We could nor laugh nor wail;
Through utter drought all dumb we stood!
I bit my arm, I sucked the blood,
And cried, A sail! a sail!

With throats unslaked, with black lips baked,
Agape they heard me call:

A flash of joy;

Gramercy! they for joy did grin,
And all at once their breath drew in,
As they were drinking all.

And horror follows. For can it be a ship that comes onward without wind or tide?

See! see! (I cried) she tacks no more!
Hither to work us weal;
Without a breeze, without a tide,
She steadies with upright keel!

The western wave was all a-flame.
The day was well nigh done!
Almost upon the western wave
Rested the broad bright Sun;
When that strange shape drove suddenly
Betwixt us and the Sun.

It seemeth him but the skeleton of a ship.

And straight the Sun was flecked with bars,
(Heaven's Mother send us grace!)
As if through a dungeon-grate he peered
With broad and burning face.

Alas! (thought I, and my heart beat loud)
How fast she nears and nears!
Are those *her* sails that glance in the Sun,
Like restless gossameres?

And its ribs are seen as bars on the face of the setting Sun. The Spectre-Woman and her Death-mate, and no other on board the skeleton ship.

Are those *her* ribs through which the Sun
Did peer, as through a grate?
And is that Woman all her crew?
Is that a DEATH? and are there two?
Is DEATH that woman's mate?

Like vessel,
like crew!

Her lips were red, *her* looks were free,
Her locks were yellow as gold:
Her skin was as white as leprosy,

Death and
Life-in-Death
have diced for
the ship's
crew, and she
(the latter)
winneth the
ancient Mari-
ner.

The Night-mare LIFE-IN-DEATH was she,
Who thicks man's blood with cold.

The naked hulk alongside came,
And the twain were casting dice;
'The game is done! I've won! I've won!'
Quoth she, and whistles thrice.

No twilight
within the
courts of the
Sun.

The Sun's rim dips; the stars rush out:
At one stride comes the dark;
With far-heard whisper, o'er the sea,
Off shot the spectre-bark.

At the rising
of the Moon,

We listened and looked sideways up!
Fear at my heart, as at a cup,
My life-blood seemed to sip!
The stars were dim, and thick the night,
The steersman's face by his lamp gleamed white;
From the sails the dew did drip —
Till clomb above the eastern bar
The horned Moon, with one bright star
Within the nether tip.

One after an-
other,

One after one, by the star-dogged Moon,
Too quick for groan or sigh,
Each turned his face with a ghastly pang,
And cursed me with his eye.

His shipmates
drop down
dead.

Four times fifty living men,
(And I heard nor sigh nor groan)
With heavy thump, a lifeless lump,
They fled to bliss or woe!

But Life-in-
Death begins
her work on
the ancient
Mariner.

The souls did from their bodies fly, —
They fled to bliss or woe!
And every soul, it passed me by,
Like the whizz of my cross-bow!"

PART IV

The Wedding-
Guest feareth
that a Spirit is
talking to him;

"I fear thee, ancient Mariner!
I fear thy skinny hand!
And thou art long, and lank, and brown,
As is the ribbed sea-sand.

I fear thee and thy glittering eye,
And thy skinny hand, so brown." —
"Fear not, fear not, thou Wedding-Guest!
This body dropt not down.

But the ancient Mariner assureth him of his bodily life, and proceedeth to relate his horrible penance.

Alone, alone, all, all alone,
Alone on a wide wide sea!
And never a saint took pity on
My soul in agony.

He despiseth the creatures of the calm,

The many men, so beautiful!
And they all dead did lie:
And a thousand thousand slimy things
Lived on; and so did I.

And envieth that they should live, and so many lie dead.

I looked upon the rotting sea,
And drew my eyes away;
I looked upon the rotting deck,
And there the dead men lay.

I looked to heaven, and tried to pray;
But or ever a prayer had gusht,
A wicked whisper came, and made
My heart as dry as dust.

I closed my lids, and kept them close,
And the balls like pulses beat;
For the sky and the sea, and the sea and the sky
Lay like a load on my weary eye,
And the dead were at my feet.

But the curse liveth for him in the eye of the dead men.

The cold sweat melted from their limbs,
Nor rot nor reek did they:
The look with which they looked on me
Had never passed away.

An orphan's curse would drag to hell
A spirit from on high;
But oh! more horrible than that
Is the curse in a dead man's eye!

In his loneliness and fixedness he yearneth towards the journeying Moon, and the stars that still sojourn, yet still move onward; and every where the blue sky

Seven days, seven nights, I saw that curse,
And yet I could not die.

The moving Moon went up the sky,
And no where did abide:
Softly she was going up,
And a star or two beside —

belongs to them, and is their appointed rest, and their native country and their own natural homes, which they enter unannounced, as lords that are certainly expected and yet there is a silent joy at their arrival.

Her beams bemocked the sultry main,
Like April hoar-frost spread;
But where the ship's huge shadow lay,
The charmed water burnt alway
A still and awful red.

By the light of the Moon he beholdeth God's creatures of the great calm.

Beyond the shadow of the ship,
I watched the water-snakes:
They moved in tracks of shining white,
And when they reared, the elfish light
Fell off in hoary flakes.

Within the shadow of the ship
I watched their rich attire:
Blue, glossy green, and velvet black,
They coiled and swam; and every track
Was a flash of golden fire.

Their beauty and their happiness.

O happy living things! no tongue
Their beauty might declare:
A spring of love gushed from my heart,

He blesseth them in his heart.

And I blessed them unaware:
Sure my kind saint took pity on me,
And I blessed them unaware.

The spell begins to break.

The self-same moment I could pray;
And from my neck so free
The Albatross fell off, and sank
Like lead into the sea.

PART V

"Oh sleep! it is a gentle thing,
Beloved from pole to pole!
To Mary Queen the praise be given!
She sent the gentle sleep from Heaven,
That slid into my soul.

By grace of the holy Mother, the ancient Mariner is refreshed with rain.

The silly buckets on the deck,
That had so long remained,
I dreamt that they were filled with dew;
And when I awoke, it rained.

My lips were wet, my throat was cold,
My garments all were dank;
Sure I had drunken in my dreams,
And still my body drank.

I moved, and could not feel my limbs:
I was so light — almost
I thought that I had died in sleep,
And was a blessed ghost.

*He heareth
sounds and
seeth strange
sights and
commotions in
the sky and
the element.*

And soon I heard a roaring wind:
It did not come anear;
But with its sound it shook the sails,
That were so thin and sere.

The upper air burst into life!
And a hundred fire-flags sheen,
To and fro they were hurried about!
And to and fro, and in and out,
The wan stars danced between.

And the coming wind did roar more loud,
And the sails did sigh like sedge;
And the rain poured down from one black cloud;
The Moon was at its edge.

The thick black cloud was cleft, and still
The Moon was at its side:
Like waters shot from some high crag,
The lightning fell with never a jag,
A river steep and wide.

*The bodies of
the ship's crew
are inspired
and the ship
moves on;*

The loud wind never reached the ship,
Yet now the ship moved on!
Beneath the lightning and the Moon
The dead men gave a groan.

They groaned, they stirred, they all uprose,
Nor spake, nor moved their eyes;
It had been strange, even in a dream,
To have seen those dead men rise.

The helmsman steered, the ship moved on;
Yet never a breeze up-blew;
The mariners all 'gan work the ropes,
Where they were wont to do;
They raised their limbs like lifeless tools —
We were a ghastly crew.

The body of my brother's son
Stood by me, knee to knee:
The body and I pulled at one rope,
But he said nought to me."

"I fear thee, ancient Mariner!"
"Be calm, thou Wedding-Guest!

But not by the souls of the men, nor by dæmons of earth or middle air, but by a blessed troop of angelic spirits, sent down by the invocation of the guardian saint.

'Twas not those souls that fled in pain,
Which to their corses came again,
But a troop of spirits blest:

For when it dawned — they dropped their arms,
And clustered round the mast;
Sweet sounds rose slowly through their mouths,
And from their bodies passed.

Around, around, flew each sweet sound,
Then darted to the Sun;
Slowly the sounds came back again,
Now mixed, now one by one.

Sometimes a-dropping from the sky
I heard the sky-lark sing;
Sometimes all little birds that are,
How they seemed to fill the sea and air
With their sweet jargoning!

And now 'twas like all instruments,
Now like a lonely flute;
And now it is an angel's song,
That makes the heavens be mute.

It ceased; yet still the sails made on
A pleasant noise till noon,
A noise like of a hidden brook
In the leafy month of June,
That to the sleeping woods all night
Singeth a quiet tune.

Till noon we quietly sailed on,
Yet never a breeze did breathe:
Slowly and smoothly went the ship,
Moved onward from beneath.

The lonesome Spirit from the South Pole carries on the ship as far as the Line, in obedience to the angelic troop, but still requireth vengeance.

Under the keel nine fathom deep,
From the land of mist and snow,
The spirit slid: and it was he
That made the ship to go.
The sails at noon left off their tune,
And the ship stood still also.

The Sun, right up above the mast,
Had fixed her to the ocean:
But in a minute she 'gan stir,
With a short uneasy motion —
Backwards and forwards half her length
With a short uneasy motion.

Then like a pawing horse let go,
She made a sudden bound:
It flung the blood into my head,
And I fell down in a swound.

The Polar Spirit's fellow-dæmons, the invisible inhabitants of the element, take part in his wrong; and two of them relate, one to the other, that penance long and heavy for the ancient Mariner hath been accorded to the Polar Spirit, who returneth southward.

How long in that same fit I lay,
I have not to declare;
But ere my living life returned,
I heard and in my soul discerned
Two voices in the air.

'Is it he?' quoth one, 'Is this the man?
By him who died on cross,
With his cruel bow he laid full low
The harmless Albatross.

The spirit who bideth by himself
In the land of mist and snow,
He loved the bird that loved the man
Who shot him with his bow.'

The other was a softer voice,
As soft as honey-dew:
Quoth he, 'The man hath penance done,
And penance more will do.'

PART VI

FIRST VOICE

" 'But tell me, tell me! speak again,
Thy soft response renewing —
What makes that ship drive on so fast?
What is the ocean doing?'

SECOND VOICE

'Still as a slave before his lord,
The ocean hath no blast;
His great bright eye most silently
Up to the Moon is cast —

If he may know which way to go;
For she guides him smooth or grim.
See, brother, see! how graciously
She looketh down on him.'

FIRST VOICE

*The Mariner
hath been cast
into a trance;
for the angelic
power causeth
the vessel to
drive north-
ward faster
than human
life could en-
dure.*

'But why drives on that ship so fast,
Without or wave or wind?'

SECOND VOICE

'The air is cut away before,
And closes from behind.

Fly, brother, fly! more high, more high!
Or we shall be belated:
For slow and slow that ship will go,
When the Mariner's trance is abated.'

*The super-
natural motion
is retarded;
the Mariner
awakes, and
his penance be-
gins anew.*

I woke, and we were sailing on
As in a gentle weather:
'Twas night, calm night, the moon was high;
The dead men stood together.

All stood together on the deck,
For a charnel-dungeon fitter:
All fixed on me their stony eyes,
That in the Moon did glitter.

The pang, the curse, with which they died,
Had never passed away:
I could not draw my eyes from theirs,
Nor turn them up to pray.

*The curse is
finally expi-
ated.*

And now this spell was snapt: once more
I viewed the ocean green,
And looked far forth, yet little saw
Of what had else been seen —

Like one, that on a lonesome road
Doth walk in fear and dread,
And having once turned round walks on,
And turns no more his head;
Because he knows, a frightful fiend
Doth close behind him tread.

But soon there breathed a wind on me,
Nor sound nor motion made:
Its path was not upon the sea,
In ripple or in shade.

It raised my hair, it fanned my cheek
Like a meadow-gale of spring —
It mingled strangely with my fears,
Yet it felt like a welcoming.

Swiftly, swiftly flew the ship,
Yet she sailed softly too:
Sweetly, sweetly blew the breeze —
On me alone it blew.

And the an-
cient Mariner
beholdeth his
native country.

Oh! dream of joy! is this indeed
The light-house top I see?
Is this the hill? is this the kirk?
Is this mine own countree?

We drifted o'er the harbour-bar,
And I with sobs did pray —
O let me be awake, my God!
Or let me sleep alway.

The harbour-bay was clear as glass,
So smoothly it was strewn!
And on the bay the moonlight lay,
And the shadow of the Moon.

The rock shone bright, the kirk no less,
That stands above the rock:
The moonlight steeped in silentness
The steady weathercock.

The angelic
spirits leave
the dead
bodies,

And the bay was white with silent light,
Till rising from the same,
Full many shapes, that shadows were,
In crimson colours came.

*And appear in
their own
forms of light.*   A little distance from the prow
Those crimson shadows were:
I turned my eyes upon the deck —
Oh, Christ! what saw I there!

Each corse lay flat, lifeless and flat,
And, by the holy rood!
A man all light, a seraph-man,
On every corse there stood.

This seraph-band, each waved his hand:
It was a heavenly sight!
They stood as signals to the land,
Each one a lovely light;

This seraph-band, each waved his hand,
No voice did they impart —
No voice; but oh! the silence sank
Like music on my heart.

But soon I heard the dash of oars,
I heard the Pilot's cheer;
My head was turned perforce away,
And I saw a boat appear.

The Pilot and the Pilot's boy,
I heard them coming fast:
Dear Lord in Heaven! it was a joy
The dead men could not blast.

I saw a third — I heard his voice:
It is the Hermit good!
He singeth loud his godly hymns
That he makes in the wood.
He'll shrieve my soul, he'll wash away
The Albatross's blood.

PART VII

*The Hermit of
the Wood*   "This Hermit good lives in that wood
Which slopes down to the sea.
How loudly his sweet voice he rears!
He loves to talk with marineres
That come from a far countree.

He kneels at morn, and noon, and eve —
He hath a cushion plump:
It is the moss that wholly hides
The rotted old oak-stump.

The skiff-boat neared: I heard them talk,
'Why, this is strange, I trow!
Where are those lights so many and fair,
That signal made but now?'

Approacheth the ship with wonder.

'Strange, by my faith!' the Hermit said —
'And they answered not our cheer!
The planks look warped! and see those sails,
How thin they are and sere!
I never saw aught like to them,
Unless perchance it were

Brown skeletons of leaves that lag
My forest-brook along;
When the ivy-tod is heavy with snow,
And the owlet whoops to the wolf below,
That eats the she-wolf's young.'

'Dear Lord! it hath a fiendish look —
(The Pilot made reply)
I am a-feared' — 'Push on, push on!'
Said the Hermit cheerily.

The boat came closer to the ship,
But I nor spake nor stirred;
The boat came close beneath the ship,
And straight a sound was heard.

The ship suddenly sinketh.

Under the water it rumbled on,
Still louder and more dread:
It reached the ship, it split the bay;
The ship went down like lead.

The ancient Mariner is saved in the Pilot's boat.

Stunned by that loud and dreadful sound,
Which sky and ocean smote,
Like one that hath been seven days drowned
My body lay afloat;
But swift as dreams, myself I found
Within the Pilot's boat.

Upon the whirl, where sank the ship,
The boat spun round and round;
And all was still, save that the hill
Was telling of the sound.

I moved my lips — the Pilot shrieked
And fell down in a fit;
The holy Hermit raised his eyes,
And prayed where he did sit.

I took the oars: the Pilot's boy,
Who now doth crazy go,
Laughed loud and long, and all the while
His eyes went to and fro.
'Ha! ha!' quoth he, 'full plain I see,
The Devil knows how to row.'

And now, all in my own countree,
I stood on the firm land!
The Hermit stepped forth from the boat,
And scarcely he could stand.

The ancient Mariner earnestly entreateth the Hermit to shrieve him; and the penance of life falls on him.

'O shrieve me, shrieve me, holy man!'
The Hermit crossed his brow.
'Say quick,' quoth he, 'I bid thee say —
What manner of man art thou?'

Forthwith this frame of mine was wrenched
With a woful agony,
Which forced me to begin my tale;
And then it left me free.

And ever and anon throughout his future life an agony constraineth him to travel from land to land;

Since then, at an uncertain hour,
The agony returns:
And till my ghastly tale is told,
This heart within me burns.

I pass, like night, from land to land;
I have strange power of speech;
That moment that his face I see,
I know the man that must hear me:
To him my tale I teach.

What loud uproar bursts from that door!
The wedding-guests are there:
But in the garden-bower the bride

And bride-maids singing are:
And hark the little vesper bell,
Which biddeth me to prayer!

O Wedding-Guest! this soul hath been
Alone on a wide wide sea:
So lonely 'twas, that God himself
Scarce seemed there to be.

O sweeter than the marriage-feast,
'Tis sweeter far to me,
To walk together to the kirk
With a goodly company! —

To walk together to the kirk,
And all together pray,
While each to his great Father bends,
Old men, and babes, and loving friends
And youths and maidens gay!

And to teach,
by his own ex-
ample, love and
reverence to all
things that God
made and
loveth.

Farewell, farewell! but this I tell
To thee, thou Wedding-Guest!
He prayeth well, who loveth well
Both man and bird and beast.

He prayeth best, who loveth best
All things both great and small;
For the dear God who loveth us,
He made and loveth all."

The Mariner, whose eye is bright,
Whose beard with age is hoar,
Is gone: and now the Wedding-Guest
Turned from the bridegroom's door.

He went like one that hath been stunned,
And is of sense forlorn:
A sadder and a wiser man,
He rose the morrow morn.

Percy Bysshe Shelley
1792-1822

It is more difficult to write of the technical beauties of the romantic revival than to explain those of the Augustan age; since with the romantics we are removed from the delights and splendors of architecture, and of the different textures of marble, stone, jewel and silk, to those of the garden and of the forest. It is more difficult to explain the growth of a flower than the growth of the Parthenon, built on a logical plan formed upon the laws of music.

In Shelley's lyrics the actual variations in the texture resemble not so much the differences between silk and marble and stone as the differences between the perfume of lily, dark rose, tuberose, violet and narcissus. These melodic effects are the result, in part, of his vowel schemes, built up, often, on a foundation of two vowels only, or on a foundation of two vowels in which each vowel is used both poignantly and dulled. But the beauty of the poems is often as intangible as the scent of the flowers, and is not to be explained. The great difference between the generation of Shelley and Wordsworth and the generation of Dryden and Pope is the difference between the genius of direction and the genius of construction. With Shelley and Wordsworth, the *direction* was the supreme problem; and the form — which in Shelley at least was usually a marvel of beauty, shaped from within — was often more a matter of genius than the result of a passion for his material. His vowel technique, and his use of assonance and dissonance, the first of which must always come by nature (it cannot be learned), while the second gift, that of assonance and dissonance, is the result of experience — these are among the most skillful and lovely in the language: poignant, variable, subtle, and flawless.

Shelley, unlike most poets, obtains his poignancy almost entirely by the use of sharp vowels — rarely by the use of words beginning with *hard* consonants.

ADONAIS

I weep for Adonais — he is dead!
Oh, weep for Adonais! though our tears
Thaw not the frost which binds so dear a head!
And thou, sad Hour, selected from all years
To mourn our loss, rouse thy obscure compeers,

And teach them thine own sorrow, say: "With me
Died Adonais; till the Future dares
Forget the Past, his fate and fame shall be
An echo and a light unto eternity!"

Where wert thou, mighty Mother, when he lay,
When thy Son lay, pierced by the shaft which flies
In darkness? where was lorn Urania
When Adonais died? With veiled eyes,
'Mid listening Echoes, in her Paradise
She sate, while one, with soft enamoured breath,
Rekindled all the fading melodies,
With which, like flowers that mock the corse beneath,
He had adorned and hid the coming bulk of Death.

Oh, weep for Adonais — he is dead!
Wake, melancholy Mother, wake and weep!
Yet wherefore? Quench within their burning bed
Thy fiery tears, and let thy loud heart keep,
Like his, a mute and uncomplaining sleep;
For he is gone, where all things wise and fair
Descend; — oh, dream not that the amorous Deep
Will yet restore him to the vital air;
Death feeds on his mute voice, and laughs at our despair.

Most musical of mourners, weep again!
Lament anew, Urania! — He died,
Who was the Sire of an immortal strain,
Blind, old, and lonely, when his country's pride
The priest, the slave, and the liberticide,
Trampled and mocked with many a loathed rite
Of lust and blood; he went, unterrified,
Into the gulf of death; but his clear Sprite
Yet reigns o'er earth; the third among the sons of light.

Most musical of mourners, weep anew!
Not all to that bright station dared to climb;
And happier they their happiness who knew,
Whose tapers yet burn through that night of time
In which suns perished; others more sublime,
Struck by the envious wrath of man or god,
Have sunk, extinct in their refulgent prime;
And some yet live, treading the thorny road,
Which leads, through toil and hate, to Fame's serene abode.

But now thy youngest, dearest one has perished —
The nursling of thy widowhood, who grew,
Like a pale flower by some sad maiden cherished,
And fed with true-love tears, instead of dew;
Most musical of mourners, weep anew!
Thy extreme hope, the loveliest and the last,
The bloom whose petals, nipped before they blew,
Died on the promise of the fruit, is waste;
The broken lily lies — the storm is overpast.

To that high Capital, where kingly Death
Keeps his pale court in beauty and decay,
He came; and bought, with price of purest breath,
A grave among the eternal — Come away!
Haste, while the vault of blue Italian day
Is yet his fitting charnel-roof! while still
He lies, as if in dewy sleep he lay;
Awake him not! surely he takes his fill
Of deep and liquid rest, forgetful of all ill.

He will awake no more, oh, never more! —
Within the twilight chamber spreads apace
The shadow of white Death, and at the door
Invisible Corruption waits to trace
His extreme way to her dim dwelling-place;
The eternal Hunger sits, but pity and awe
Soothe her pale rage, nor dares she to deface
So fair a prey, till darkness, and the law
Of change shall o'er his sleep the mortal curtain draw.

Oh, weep for Adonais! — The quick Dreams,
The passion-winged Ministers of thought,
Who were his flocks, whom near the living streams
Of his young spirit he fed, and whom he taught
The love which was its music, wander not, —
Wander no more, from kindling brain to brain,
But droop there, whence they sprung; and mourn their lot
Round the cold heart, where, after their sweet pain,
They ne'er will gather strength, or find a home again.

And one with trembling hands clasps his cold head,
And fans him with her moonlight wings, and cries;
"Our love, our hope, our sorrow, is not dead;
See, on the silken fringe of his faint eyes,
Like dew upon a sleeping flower, there lies
A tear some Dream has loosened from his brain."

Lost Angel of a ruined Paradise!
She knew not 'twas her own; as with no stain
She faded, like a cloud which had outwept its rain.

One from a lucid urn of starry dew
Washed his light limbs as if embalming them;
Another clipped her profuse locks, and threw
The wreath upon him, like an anadem,
Which frozen tears instead of pearls begem;
Another in her wilful grief would break
Her bow and winged reeds, as if to stem
A greater loss with one which was more weak;
And dull the barbed fire against his frozen cheek.

Another Splendour on his mouth alit,
That mouth, whence it was wont to draw the breath
Which gave it strength to pierce the guarded wit,
And pass into the panting heart beneath
With lightning and with music: the lamp death
Quenched its caress upon his icy lips;
And, as a dying meteor stains a wreath
Of moonlight vapour, which the cold night clips,
It flushed through his pale limbs, and passed to its eclipse.

And others came . . . Desires and Adorations,
Winged Persuasions and veiled Destinies,
Splendours, and Glooms, and glimmering Incarnations
Of hopes and fears, and twilight Phantasies;
And Sorrow, with her family of Sighs,
And Pleasure, blind with tears, led by the gleam
Of her own dying smile instead of eyes,
Came in slow pomp; — the moving pomp might seem
Like pageantry of mist on an autumnal stream.

All he had loved, and moulded into thought,
From shape, and hue, and odour, and sweet sound,
Lamented Adonais. Morning sought
Her eastern watch-tower, and her hair unbound,
Wet with the tears which should adorn the ground,
Dimmed the aëreal eyes that kindle day;
Afar the melancholy thunder moaned,
Pale Ocean in unquiet slumber lay,
And the wild Winds flew round, sobbing in their dismay.

Lost Echo sits amid the voiceless mountains,
And feeds her grief with his remembered lay,
And will no more reply to winds or fountains,

Or amorous birds perched on the young green spray;
Or herdsman's horn, or bell at closing day;
Since she can mimic not his lips, more dear
Than those for whose disdain she pined away
Into a shadow of all sounds: — a drear
Murmur, between their songs, is all the woodmen hear.

Grief made the young Spring wild, and she threw down
Her kindling buds, as if she Autumn were,
Or they dead leaves; since her delight is flown,
For whom should she have waked the sullen year?
To Phoebus was not Hyacinth so dear
Nor to himself Narcissus, as to both
Thou, Adonais: wan they stand and sere
Amid the faint companions of their youth,
With dew all turned to tears; odour, to sighing ruth.

Thy spirit's sister, the lorn nightingale
Mourns not her mate with such melodious pain;
Not so the eagle, who like thee could scale
Heaven, and could nourish in the sun's domain
Her mighty youth with morning, doth complain,
Soaring and screaming round her empty nest,
As Albion wails for thee: the curse of Cain
Light on his head who pierced thy innocent breast,
And scared the angel soul that was its earthly guest!

Ah, woe is me! Winter is come and gone,
But grief returns with the revolving year;
The airs and streams renew their joyous tone;
The ants, the bees, the swallows reappear;
Fresh leaves and flowers deck the dead Seasons' bier;
The amorous birds now pair in every brake,
And build their mossy homes in field and brere;
And the green lizard, and the golden snake,
Like unimprisoned flames, out of their trance awake.

Through wood and stream and field and hill and Ocean
A quickening life from the Earth's heart has burst
As it has ever done, with change and motion,
From the great morning of the world when first
God dawned on Chaos; in its stream immersed,
The lamps of Heaven flash with a softer light;
All baser things pant with life's sacred thirst;
Diffuse themselves; and spend in love's delight
The beauty and the joy of their renewed might.

The leprous corpse, touched by this spirit tender,
Exhales itself in flowers of gentle breath;
Like incarnations of the stars, when splendour
Is changed to fragrance, they illumine death
And mock the merry worm that wakes beneath;
Nought we know dies. Shall that alone which knows
Be as a sword consumed before the sheath
By sightless lightning? — the intense atom glows
A moment, then is quenched in a most cold repose.

Alas! that all we loved of him should be,
But for our grief, as if it had not been,
And grief itself be mortal! Woe is me!
Whence are we, and why are we? of what scene
The actors or spectators? Great and mean
Meet massed in death, who lends what life must borrow.
As long as skies are blue, and fields are green,
Evening must usher night, night urge the morrow,
Month follow month with woe, and year wake year to sorrow.

He will awake no more, oh, never more!
"Wake thou," cried Misery, "childless Mother, rise
Out of thy sleep, and slake, in thy heart's core,
A wound more fierce than his, with tears and sighs."
And all the Dreams that watched Urania's eyes,
And all the Echoes whom their sister's song
Had held in holy silence, cried: "Arise!"
Swift as a Thought by the snake Memory stung,
From her ambrosial rest the fading Splendour sprung.

She rose like an autumnal Night, that springs
Out of the East, and follows wild and drear
The golden Day, which, on eternal wings,
Even as a ghost abandoning a bier,
Had left the Earth a corpse. Sorrow and fear
So struck, so roused, so rapt Urania;
So saddened round her like an atmosphere
Of stormy mist; so swept her on her way
Even to the mournful place where Adonais lay.

Out of her secret Paradise she sped,
Through camps and cities rough with stone, and steel,
And human hearts, which to her aery tread
Yielding not, wounded the invisible
Palms of her tender feet where'er they fell:
And barbed tongues, and thoughts more sharp than they,

Rent the soft Form they never could repel,
Whose sacred blood, like the young tears of May,
Paved with eternal flowers that undeserving way.

In the death-chamber for a moment Death,
Shamed by the presence of that living Might,
Blushed to annihilation, and the breath
Revisited those lips, and Life's pale light
Flashed through those limbs, so late her dear delight.
"Leave me not wild and drear and comfortless,
As silent lightning leaves the starless night!
Leave me not!" cried Urania: her distress
Roused Death: Death rose and smiled, and met her vain caress.

"Stay yet awhile! speak to me once again;
Kiss me, so long but as a kiss may live;
And in my heartless breast and burning brain
That word, that kiss, shall all thoughts else survive,
With food of saddest memory kept alive,
Now thou art dead, as if it were a part
Of thee, my Adonais! I would give
All that I am to be as thou now art!
But I am chained to Time, and cannot thence depart!

"O gentle child, beautiful as thou wert,
Why didst thou leave the trodden paths of men
Too soon, and with weak hands though mighty heart
Dare the unpastured dragon in his den?
Defenceless as thou wert, oh, where was then
Wisdom the mirrored shield, or scorn the spear?
Or hadst thou waited the full cycle, when
Thy spirit should have filled its crescent sphere,
The monsters of life's waste had fled from thee like deer.

"The herded wolves, bold only to pursue;
The obscene ravens, clamorous o'er the dead;
The vultures to the conqueror's banner true
Who feed where Desolation first has fed,
And whose wings rain contagion; — how they fled,
When, like Apollo, from his golden bow
The Pythian of the age one arrow sped
And smiled! — The spoilers tempt no second blow,
They fawn on the proud feet that spurn them lying low.

"The sun comes forth, and many reptiles spawn;
He sets, and each ephemeral insect then
Is gathered into death without a dawn,
And the immortal stars awake again;
So is it in the world of living men:
A godlike mind soars forth, in its delight
Making earth bare and veiling heaven, and when
It sinks, the swarms that dimmed or shared its light
Leave to its kindred lamps the spirit's awful night."

Thus ceased she: and the mountain shepherds came,
Their garlands sere, their magic mantles rent;
The Pilgrim of Eternity, whose fame
Over his living head like Heaven is bent,
An early but enduring monument,
Came, veiling all the lightnings of his song
In sorrow; from her wilds Ierne sent
The sweetest lyrist of her saddest wrong,
And Love taught Grief to fall like music from his tongue.

Midst others of less note, came one frail Form,
A phantom among men; companionless
As the last cloud of an expiring storm
Whose thunder is its knell; he, as I guess,
Had gazed on Nature's naked loveliness,
Actaeon-like, and now he fled astray
With feeble steps o'er the world's wilderness,
And his own thoughts, along that rugged way,
Pursued, like raging hounds, their father and their prey.

A pardlike Spirit beautiful and swift —
A Love in desolation masked; — a Power
Girt round with weakness; — it can scarce uplift
The weight of the superincumbent hour;
It is a dying lamp, a falling shower,
A breaking billow; — even whilst we speak
Is it not broken? On the withering flower
The killing sun smiles brightly: on a cheek
The life can burn in blood, even while the heart may break.

His head was bound with pansies overblown,
And faded violets, white, and pied, and blue;
And a light spear topped with a cypress cone,
Round whose rude shaft dark ivy-tresses grew

Yet dripping with the forest's noonday dew,
Vibrated, as the ever-beating heart
Shook the weak hand that grasped it; of that crew
He came the last, neglected and apart;
A herd-abandoned deer struck by the hunter's dart.

All stood aloof, and at his partial moan
Smiled through their tears; well knew that gentle band
Who in another's fate now wept his own,
As in the accents of an unknown land
He sung new sorrow; sad Urania scanned
The Stranger's mien, and murmured: "Who art thou?"
He answered not, but with a sudden hand
Made bare his branded and ensanguined brow,
Which was like Cain's or Christ's — oh! that it should be so!

What softer voice is hushed over the dead?
Athwart what brow is that dark mantle thrown?
What form leans sadly o'er the white death-bed,
In mockery of monumental stone,
The heavy heart heaving without a moan?
If it be He who, gentlest of the wise,
Taught, soothed, loved, honoured the departed one,
Let me not vex, with inharmonious sighs,
The silence of that heart's accepted sacrifice.

Our Adonais has drunk poison — oh!
What deaf and viperous murderer could crown
Life's early cup with such a draught of woe?
The nameless worm would now itself disown:
It felt, yet could escape, the magic tone
Whose prelude held all envy, hate, and wrong,
But what was howling in one breast alone,
Silent with expectation of the song,
Whose master's hand is cold, whose silver lyre unstrung.

Live thou, whose infamy is not thy fame!
Life! fear no heavier chastisement from me,
Thou noteless blot on a remembered name!
But be thyself, and know thyself to be!
And ever at thy season be thou free
To spill the venom when thy fangs o'erflow;
Remorse and Self-contempt shall cling to thee;
Hot Shame shall burn upon thy secret brow,
And like a beaten hound tremble thou shalt — as now.

Nor let us weep that our delight is fled
Far from these carrion kites that scream below;
He wakes or sleeps with the enduring dead;
Thou canst not soar where he is sitting now. —
Dust to the dust! but the pure spirit shall flow
Back to the burning fountain whence it came,
A portion of the Eternal, which must glow
Through time and change, unquenchably the same,
Whilst thy cold embers choke the sordid hearth of shame.

Peace, peace! he is not dead, he doth not sleep —
He hath awakened from the dream of life —
'Tis we, who lost in stormy visions, keep
With phantoms an unprofitable strife,
And in mad trance, strike with our spirit's knife
Invulnerable nothings. — *We* decay
Like corpses in a charnel; fear and grief
Convulse us and consume us day by day,
And cold hopes swarm like worms within our living clay.

He has outsoared the shadow of our night;
Envy and calumny and hate and pain,
And that unrest which men miscall delight,
Can touch him not and torture not again;
From the contagion of the world's slow stain
He is secure, and now can never mourn
A heart grown cold, a head grown gray in vain;
Nor, when the spirit's self has ceased to burn,
With sparkless ashes load an unlamented urn.

He lives, he wakes — 'tis Death is dead, not he;
Mourn not for Adonais. — Thou young Dawn,
Turn all thy dew to splendour, for from thee
The spirit thou lamentest is not gone;
Ye caverns and ye forests, cease to moan!
Cease, ye faint flowers and fountains, and thou Air,
Which like a mourning veil thy scarf hadst thrown
O'er the abandoned Earth, now leave it bare
Even to the joyous stars which smile on its despair!

He is made one with Nature: there is heard
His voice in all her music, from the moan
Of thunder, to the song of night's sweet bird;
He is a presence to be felt and known
In darkness and in light, from herb and stone,
Spreading itself where'er that Power may move

Which has withdrawn his being to its own;
Which wields the world with never-wearied love,
Sustains it from beneath, and kindles it above.

He is a portion of the loveliness
Which once he made more lovely: he doth bear
His part, while the one Spirit's plastic stress
Sweeps through the dull dense world, compelling there
All new successions to the forms they wear;
Torturing th' unwilling dross that checks its flight
To its own likeness, as each mass may bear;
And bursting in its beauty and its might
From trees and beasts and men into the Heaven's light.

The splendours of the firmament of time
May be eclipsed, but are extinguished not;
Like stars to their appointed height they climb,
And death is a low mist which cannot blot
The brightness it may veil. When lofty thought
Lifts a young heart above its mortal lair,
And love and life contend in it, for what
Shall be its earthly doom, the dead live there
And move like winds of light on dark and stormy air.

The inheritors of unfulfilled renown
Rose from their thrones, built beyond mortal thought,
Far in the Unapparent. Chatterton
Rose pale, — his solemn agony had not
Yet faded from him; Sidney, as he fought
And as he fell and as he lived and loved
Sublimely mild, a Spirit without spot,
Arose; and Lucan, by his death approved:
Oblivion as they rose shrank like a thing reproved.

And many more, whose names on Earth are dark,
But whose transmitted effluence cannot die
So long as fire outlives the parent spark,
Rose, robed in dazzling immortality.
"Thou art become as one of us," they cry;
"It was for thee yon kingless sphere has long
Swung blind in unascended majesty,
Silent alone amid an Heaven of Song.
Assume thy winged throne, thou Vesper of our throng!"

Who mourns for Adonais? Oh, come forth,
Fond wretch! and know thyself and him aright.
Clasp with thy panting soul the pendulous Earth;

As from a centre, dart thy spirit's light
Beyond all worlds, until its spacious might
Satiate the void circumference: then shrink
Even to a point within our day and night;
And keep thy heart light lest it make thee sink
When hope has kindled hope, and lured thee to the brink.

Or go to Rome, which is the sepulchre,
Oh, not of him, but of our joy: 'tis nought
That ages, empires, and religions there
Lie buried in the ravage they have wrought;
For such as he can lend, — they borrow not
Glory from those who made the world their prey;
And he is gathered to the kings of thought
Who waged contention with their time's decay,
And of the past are all that cannot pass away.

Go thou to Rome, — at once the Paradise,
The grave, the city, and the wilderness;
And where its wrecks like shattered mountains rise,
And flowering weeds, and fragrant copses dress
The bones of Desolation's nakedness
Pass, till the spirit of the spot shall lead
Thy footsteps to a slope of green access
Where, like an infant's smile, over the dead
A light of laughing flowers along the grass is spread;

And gray walls moulder round, on which dull Time
Feeds, like slow fire upon a hoary brand;
And one keen pyramid with wedge sublime,
Pavilioning the dust of him who planned
This refuge for his memory, doth stand
Like flame transformed to marble; and beneath,
A field is spread, on which a newer band
Have pitched in Heaven's smile their camp of death,
Welcoming him we lose with scarce extinguished breath.

Here pause: these graves are all too young as yet
To have outgrown the sorrow which consigned
Its charge to each; and if the seal is set,
Here, on one fountain of a mourning mind,
Break it not thou! too surely shalt thou find
Thine own well full, if thou returnest home,
Of tears and gall. From the world's bitter wind
Seek shelter in the shadow of the tomb.
What Adonais is, why fear we to become?

The One remains, the many change and pass;
Heaven's light forever shines, Earth's shadows fly;
Life, like a dome of many-coloured glass,
Stains the white radiance of Eternity,
Until Death tramples it to fragments. — Die,
If thou wouldst be with that which thou dost seek!
Follow where all is fled! — Rome's azure sky,
Flowers, ruins, statues, music, words, are weak
The glory they transfuse with fitting truth to speak.

Why linger, why turn back, why shrink, my Heart?
Thy hopes are gone before: from all things here
They have departed; thou shouldst now depart!
A light is passed from the revolving year,
And man, and woman; and what still is dear
Attracts to crush, repels to make thee wither.
The soft sky smiles, — the low wind whispers near:
'Tis Adonais calls! oh, hasten thither,
No more let Life divide what Death can join together.

That Light whose smile kindles the Universe,
That Beauty in which all things work and move,
That Benediction which the eclipsing Curse
Of birth can quench not, that sustaining Love
Which through the web of being blindly wove
By man and beast and earth and air and sea,
Burns bright or dim, as each are mirrors of
The fire for which all thirst; now beams on me,
Consuming the last clouds of cold mortality.

The breath whose might I have invoked in song
Descends on me; my spirit's bark is driven
Far from the shore, far from the trembling throng
Whose sails were never to the tempest given;
The massy earth and sphered skies are riven!
I am borne darkly, fearfully, afar;
Whilst, burning through the inmost veil of Heaven,
The soul of Adonais, like a star,
Beacons from the abode where the Eternal are.

HYMN OF PAN

From the forests and highlands
   We come, we come;
From the river-girt islands,

Where loud waves are dumb
  Listening to my sweet pipings.
The wind in the reeds and the rushes,
  The bees on the bells of thyme,
The birds on the myrtle bushes,
  The cicale above in the lime,
And the lizards below in the grass,
Were as silent as ever old Tmolus was,
  Listening to my sweet pipings.

Liquid Peneus was flowing,
  And all dark Tempe lay
In Pelion's shadow, outgrowing
  The light of the dying day,
  Speeded by my sweet pipings.
The Sileni, and Sylvans, and Fauns,
  And the Nymphs of the woods and the waves,
To the edge of the moist river-lawns,
  And the brink of the dewy caves,
And all that did then attend and follow,
Were silent with love, as you now, Apollo,
  With envy of my sweet pipings.

I sang of the dancing stars,
  I sang of the daedal Earth,
And of Heaven — and the giant wars,
  And Love, and Death, and Birth, —
  And then I changed my pipings, —
Singing how down the vale of Maenalus
  I pursued a maiden and clasped a reed.
Gods and men, we are all deluded thus!
  It breaks in our bosom and then we bleed:
All wept, as I think both ye now would,
If envy or age had not frozen your blood,
  At the sorrow of my sweet pipings.

TO A SKYLARK

Hail to thee, blithe Spirit!
  Bird thou never wert,
That from Heaven, or near it,
  Pourest thy full heart
In profuse strains of unpremeditated art.

Higher still and higher
From the earth thou springest
Like a cloud of fire;
The blue deep thou wingest,
And singing still dost soar, and soaring ever singest.

In the golden lightning
Of the sunken sun,
O'er which clouds are bright'ning,
Thou dost float and run;
Like an unbodied joy whose race is just begun.

The pale purple even
Melts around thy flight;
Like a star of Heaven,
In the broad daylight
Thou art unseen, but yet I hear thy shrill delight,

Keen as are the arrows
Of that silver sphere,
Whose intense lamp narrows
In the white dawn clear
Until we hardly see — we feel that it is there.

All the earth and air
With thy voice is loud,
As, when night is bare,
From one lonely cloud
The moon rains out her beams, and Heaven is overflowed.

What thou art we know not;
What is most like thee?
From rainbow clouds there flow not
Drops so bright to see
As from thy presence showers a rain of melody.

Like a Poet hidden
In the light of thought,
Singing hymns unbidden,
Till the world is wrought
To sympathy with hopes and fears it heeded not:

Like a high-born maiden
In a palace-tower,
Soothing her love-laden
Soul in secret hour
With music sweet as love, which overflows her bower:

Like a glow-worm golden
    In a dell of dew,
Scattering unbeholden
    Its aëreal hue
Among the flowers and grass, which screen it from the view!

Like a rose embowered
    In its own green leaves,
By warm winds deflowered,
    Till the scent it gives
Makes faint with too much sweet those heavy-winged thieves:

Sound of vernal showers
    On the twinkling grass,
Rain-awakened flowers,
    All that ever was
Joyous, and clear, and fresh, thy music doth surpass:

Teach us, Sprite or Bird,
    What sweet thoughts are thine:
I have never heard
    Praise of love or wine
That panted forth a flood of rapture so divine.

Chorus Hymeneal,
    Or triumphal chant,
Matched with thine would be all
    But any empty vaunt,
A thing wherein we feel there is some hidden want.

What objects are the fountains
    Of thy happy strain?
What fields, or waves, or mountains?
    What shapes of sky or plain?
What love of thine own kind? what ignorance of pain?

With thy clear keen joyance
    Languor cannot be:
Shadow of annoyance
    Never came near thee:
Thou lovest — but ne'er knew love's sad satiety.

Waking or asleep,
    Thou of death must deem
Things more true and deep
    Than we mortals dream,
Or how could thy notes flow in such a crystal stream?

We look before and after,
  And pine for what is not:
Our sincerest laughter
  With some pain is fraught;
Our sweetest songs are those that tell of saddest thought.

Yet if we could scorn
  Hate, and pride, and fear;
If we were things born
  Not to shed a tear,
I know not how thy joy we ever should come near.

Better than all measures
  Of delightful sound,
Better than all treasures
  That in books are found,
Thy skill to poet were, thou scorner of the ground!

Teach me half the gladness
  That thy brain must know,
Such harmonious madness
  From my lips would flow
The world should listen then — as I am listening now.

TO NIGHT

Swiftly walk o'er the western wave,
  Spirit of Night!
Out of the misty eastern cave,
Where, all the long and lone daylight,
Thou wovest dreams of joy and fear,
Which make thee terrible and dear, —
  Swift be thy flight!

Wrap thy form in a mantle gray,
  Star-inwrought!
Blind with thine hair the eyes of Day;
Kiss her until she be wearied out,
Then wander o'er city, and sea, and land,
Touching all with thine opiate wand —
  Come, long-sought!

When I arose and saw the dawn,
  I sighed for thee;
When light rode high, and the dew was gone,

And noon lay heavy on flower and tree,
And the weary Day turned to his rest,
Lingering like an unloved guest,
  I sighed for thee.

Thy brother Death came, and cried,
  Wouldst thou me?
Thy sweet child Sleep, the filmy-eyed,
Murmured like a noontide bee,
Shall I nestle near thy side?
Wouldst thou me? — And I replied,
  No, not thee!

Death will come when thou art dead,
  Soon, too soon —
Sleep will come when thou art fled;
Of neither would I ask the boon
I ask of thee, beloved Night —
Swift be thine approaching flight,
  Come soon, soon!

TO ——

Music, when soft voices die,
Vibrates in the memory —
Odours, when sweet violets sicken,
Live within the sense they quicken.

Rose leaves, when the rose is dead,
Are heaped for the beloved's bed;
And so thy thoughts, when thou art gone,
Love itself shall slumber on.

LOVE'S PHILOSOPHY

The fountains mingle with the river
 And the rivers with the Ocean,
The winds of Heaven mix for ever
 With a sweet emotion;
Nothing in the world is single;
 All things by a law divine
In one spirit meet and mingle.
 Why not I with thine? —

See the mountains kiss high Heaven
 And the waves clasp one another;
No sister-flower would be forgiven
 If it disdained its brother;
And the sunlight clasps the earth
 And the moonbeams kiss the sea:
What is all this sweet work worth
 If thou kiss not me?

A LAMENT

O world! O life! O time!
On whose last steps I climb,
   Trembling at that where I had stood before;
When will return the glory of your prime?
    No more — Oh, never more!

Out of the day and night
A joy has taken flight;
   Fresh spring, and summer, and winter hoar,
Move my faint heart with grief, but with delight
    No more — Oh, never more!

From Scene V of CHARLES THE FIRST

A WIDOW BIRD

A widow bird sate mourning for her love
   Upon a wintry bough;
The frozen wind crept on above,
   The freezing stream below.

There was no leaf upon the forest bare,
   No flower upon the ground,
And little motion in the air
   Except the mill-wheel's sound.

From PROMETHEUS UNBOUND

From ACT I

FOURTH SPIRIT. On a poet's lips I slept
   Dreaming like a love-adept
In the sound his breathing kept;
Nor seeks nor finds he mortal blisses,
But feeds on the aëreal kisses
Of shapes that haunt thought's wildernesses.
He will watch from dawn to gloom
The lake-reflected sun illume
The yellow bees in the ivy-bloom,
Nor heed nor see, what things they be;

But from these create he can
Forms more real than living man,
Nurslings of immortality!
One of these awakened me,
And I sped to succour thee.

From *ACT II, SCENE* 2

A Forest, intermingled with Rocks and Caverns. ASIA *and*
PANTHEA *pass into it. Two young Fauns are sitting on
a Rock listening.*

SEMICHORUS I OF SPIRITS

The path through which that lovely twain
    Have passed, by cedar, pine, and yew,
    And each dark tree that ever grew,
    Is curtained out from Heaven's wide blue;
Nor sun, nor moon, nor wind, nor rain,
    Can pierce its interwoven bowers,
    Nor aught, save where some cloud of dew,
Drifted along the earth-creeping breeze,
Between the trunks of the hoar trees,
    Hangs each a pearl in the pale flowers
    Of the green laurel, blown anew;
And bends, and then fades silently,
One frail and fair anemone:
Or when some star of many a one
That climbs and wanders through steep night,
Has found the cleft through which alone
Beams fall from high those depths upon
Ere it is borne away, away,
By the swift Heavens that cannot stay,
It scatters drops of golden light,
Like lines of rain that ne'er unite:
And the gloom divine is all around,
And underneath is the mossy ground.

SEMICHORUS II

There the voluptuous nightingales,
    Are awake through all the broad noonday.
When one with bliss or sadness fails,
    And through the windless ivy-boughs,
    Sick with sweet love, droops dying away
On its mate's music-panting bosom;

Another from the swinging blossom,
    Watching to catch the languid close
    Of the last strain, then lifts on high
    The wings of the weak melody,
'Till some new strain of feeling bear
    The song, and all the woods are mute;
When there is heard through the dim air
The rush of wings, and rising there
    Like many a lake-surrounded flute,
Sounds overflow the listener's brain
So sweet, that joy is almost pain.

                    SEMICHORUS I
There those enchanted eddies play
    Of echoes, music-tongued, which draw,
    By Demogorgon's mighty law,
    With melting rapture, or sweet awe,
All spirits on that secret way;
        As inland boats are driven to Ocean
    Down streams made strong with mountain-thaw:
And first there comes a gentle sound
To those in talk or slumber bound,
    And wakes the destined soft emotion, —
Attracts, impels them; those who saw
    Say from the breathing earth behind
    There steams a plume-uplifting wind
Which drives them on their path, while they
    Believe their own swift wings and feet
The sweet desires within obey:
And so they float upon their way,
Until, still sweet, but loud and strong,
The storm of sound is driven along,
    Sucked up and hurrying: as they fleet
    Behind, its gathering billows meet
And to the fatal mountain bear
Like clouds amid the yielding air.

FIRST FAUN. Canst thou imagine where those spirits live
    Which make such delicate music in the woods?
    We haunt within the least frequented caves
    And closest coverts, and we know these wilds,
    Yet never meet them, though we hear them oft:
    Where may they hide themselves?
SECOND FAUN.   'Tis hard to tell:
    I have heard those more skilled in spirits say,

The bubbles, which the enchantment of the sun
Sucks from the pale faint water-flowers that pave
The oozy bottom of clear lakes and pools,
Are the pavilions where such dwell and float
Under the green and golden atmosphere
Which noontide kindles through the woven leaves;
And when these burst, and the thin fiery air,
The which they breathed within those lucent domes,
Ascends to flow like meteors through the night,
They ride on them, and rein their headlong speed,
And bow their burning crests, and glide in fire
Under the waters of the earth again.

FIRST FAUN. If such live thus, have others other lives,
Under pink blossoms or within the bells
Of meadow flowers, or folded violets deep,
Or on their dying odours, when they die,
Or in the sunlight of the sphered dew?

SECOND FAUN. Ay, many more which we may well divine.
But, should we stay to speak, noontide would come,
And thwart Silenus find his goats undrawn,
And grudge to sing those wise and lovely songs
Of Fate, and Chance, and God, and Chaos old,
And Love, and the chained Titan's woful doom,
And how he shall be loosed, and make the earth
One brotherhood: delightful strains which cheer
Our solitary twilights, and which charm
To silence the unenvying nightingales.

From *ACT II, SCENE 5*

VOICE IN THE AIR, SINGING

Life of Life! thy lips enkindle
  With their love the breath between them;
And thy smiles before they dwindle
  Make the cold air fire; then screen them
In those looks, where whoso gazes
Faints, entangled in their mazes.

Child of Light! thy limbs are burning
  Through the vest which seems to hide them;
As the radiant lines of morning
  Through the clouds ere they divide them;
And this atmosphere divinest
Shrouds thee wheresoe'er thou shinest.

Fair are others; none beholds thee,
　But thy voice sounds low and tender
Like the fairest, for it folds thee
　From the sight, that liquid splendour,
And all feel, yet see thee never,
As I feel now, lost for ever!

Lamp of Earth! where'er thou movest
　Its dim shapes are clad with brightness,
And the souls of whom thou lovest
　Walk upon the winds with lightness,
Till they fail, as I am failing,
Dizzy, lost, yet unbewailing!

ASIA

My soul is an enchanted boat,
　Which, like a sleeping swan, doth float
Upon the silver waves of thy sweet singing;
　And thine doth like an angel sit
　Beside a helm conducting it,
Whilst all the winds with melody are ringing.
　It seems to float ever, for ever,
　Upon that many-winding river,
　Between mountains, woods, abysses,
　A paradise of wildernesses!
Till, like one in slumber bound,
Borne to the ocean, I float down, around,
Into a sea profound, of ever-spreading sound:

　Meanwhile thy spirit lifts its pinions
　In music's most serene dominions;
Catching the winds that fan that happy heaven.
　And we sail on, away, afar,
　Without a course, without a star,
But, by the instinct of sweet music driven;
　Till through Elysian garden islets
　By thee, most beautiful of pilots,
　Where never mortal pinnace glided,
　The boat of my desire is guided:
Realms where the air we breathe is love,
Which in the winds and on the waves doth move,
Harmonizing this earth with what we feel above.

　We have passed Age's icy caves,
　And Manhood's dark and tossing waves,
And Youth's smooth ocean, smiling to betray:

Beyond the glassy gulfs we flee
Of shadow-peopled Infancy,
Through Death and Birth, to a diviner day;
A paradise of vaulted bowers,
Lit by downward-gazing flowers,
And watery paths that wind between
Wildernesses calm and green,
Peopled by shapes too bright to see,
And rest, having beheld; somewhat like thee;
Which walk upon the sea, and chant melodiously!

From *ACT IV*

THE EARTH

The joy, the triumph, the delight, the madness!
The boundless, overflowing, bursting gladness,
The vaporous exultation not to be confined!
Ha! ha! the animation of delight
Which wraps me, like an atmosphere of light,
And bears me as a cloud is borne by its own wind.

THE MOON

The snow upon my lifeless mountains
Is loosened into living fountains,
My solid oceans flow, and sing, and shine:
A spirit from my heart bursts forth,
It clothes with unexpected birth
My cold bare bosom: Oh! it must be thine
On mine, on mine!

Gazing on thee I feel, I know
Green stalks burst forth, and bright flowers grow,
And living shapes upon my bosom move:
Music is in the sea and air,
Winged clouds soar here and there,
Dark with rain new buds are dreaming of:
'Tis love, all love!

From HELLAS

CHORUS: THE WORLD'S GREAT AGE BEGINS ANEW

The world's great age begins anew,
The golden years return,
The earth doth like a snake renew

Her winter weeds outworn:
Heaven smiles, and faiths and empires gleam,
Like wrecks of a dissolving dream.

A brighter Hellas rears its mountains
   From waves serener far;
A new Peneus rolls his fountains
   Against the morning star.
Where fairer Tempes bloom, there sleep
Young Cyclads on a sunnier deep.

A loftier Argo cleaves the main,
   Fraught with a later prize;
Another Orpheus sings again,
   And loves, and weeps, and dies.
A new Ulysses leaves once more
Calypso for his native shore.

Oh, write no more the tale of Troy,
   If earth Death's scroll must be!
Nor mix with Laian rage the joy
   Which dawns upon the free:
Although a subtler Sphinx renew
Riddles of death Thebes never knew.

Another Athens shall arise,
   And to remoter time
Bequeath, like sunset to the skies,
   The splendour of its prime;
And leave, if nought so bright may live,
All earth can take or Heaven can give.

Saturn and Love their long repose
   Shall burst, more bright and good
Than all who fell, than One who rose,
   Than many unsubdued:
Not gold, not blood, their altar dowers,
But votive tears and symbol flowers.

Oh, cease! must hate and death return?
   Cease! must men kill and die?
Cease! drain not to its dregs the urn
   Of bitter prophecy.
The world is weary of the past,
Oh, might it die or rest at last!

John Keats

1795-1821

It may, perhaps, be claimed that some of the moonlit enchanted drowsiness of that miracle of poetry, *The Eve of St. Agnes,* arises from the way in which the lines are blown faintly backward and forward as the result of the difference in *depth,* as well as in *length,* of the pauses occurring in ever-varying places in the lines. And these pauses are largely the result of texture, of the differing lengths of the vowel-sounds which precede them. This, of course, is often the case with poetry (indeed, almost always, excepting when the verse has a herring-backed caesura) — but it is peculiarly so in the case of *The Eve of St. Agnes.* It is a miracle to find the Spenserian meter used so flawlessly, yet without the faintest monotony, in so long a poem. The pattern of the texture varies between magical stretches of calm moonlight (produced by long high vowel-sounds followed by stretching, not sharp, consonants), and menacing shadows (produced by dark vowel sounds) — between delicate arabesques of dim sparkles (produced by the use of faint, yet sharp *t* sounds), and glittering cold airs, dying away again into those shadows. And this pattern is not so regular as to be mechanized: it gives the appearance of being completely natural, the result of instinct alone.

With every poem of Keats the sound and the meter fit the theme in such a manner that they seem inevitable. The goat-footed bucolic rustic sound of the *Hymn to Pan* — goat-footed because of its occasional female endings (not soft, as they are in *Sleep and Poetry,* but hard) — this has the peculiar honeyed sweetness of all Keats' poems. Yet the strange uncouth music of the first verse, so full of the sound of growth, is earthy and forest-rough and harsh as the pipes on which the shepherds play. This harshness is caused by the *a*'s, the rough "ang" of "hang" and "agg" of "jagged," the tuneless *a* of "overshadoweth" placed so close together, though in succeeding lines, and each having its own degree of goatish rankness, of "hairy sound" as Dante would have called it. Much is due, also, to the slowing caused by the *th* and *fe* endings (in the words "the birth, life, death") and, too, by the slowing entanglement of *s*'s (together with the soft *c*) in the line: "Of unseen flowers in heavy peacefulness." In this, and its preceding line — "Eternal whispers, glooms, the birth, life, death" — there is a change from the reverberating circling sound of the first line: "O thou, whose mighty palace roof doth hang," with its deep forest breaths, and the drooping languid sound of the second: "From jagged trunks, and overshadoweth . . ."

If we take the following lines:

The dreary melody of bedded reeds —
In desolate places, where dank moisture breeds
The pipy hemlock to strange overgrowth

we shall see that they are a miraculous fusion of sound and sense, with
the dryness of the external and internal *d* sounds of the first two lines,
the cold variations of the various *e* sounds. "Desolate" is a kind of reversed echo of the sound of "melody," and "bedded" is a sort of dead and
withered, cast-off adjunct of these words. Indeed, in those three lines, the
only living sound seems to lie in the high sound of "places," and in its
darker assonance "strange."

The strange goat-footed female endings, coming from time to time, instead of lengthening the line seem to clip it, to make it harder, quicker,
and more uncouth — so that we are not hearing the peasant's boots falling on a soft soil; we are hearing the hard satyr-hoofs falling on a ground
that is mad and harsh yet honeyed with summer.

LA BELLE DAME SANS MERCI

O, what can ail thee, knight-at-arms,
　　Alone and palely loitering;
The sedge is wither'd from the lake,
　　And no birds sing.

O, what can ail thee, knight-at-arms,
　　So haggard and so woe-begone?
The squirrel's granary is full,
　　And the harvest's done.

I see a lilly on thy brow,
　　With anguish moist and fever dew;
And on thy cheek a fading rose
　　Fast withereth too.

I met a lady in the meads
　　Full beautiful, a faery's child;
Her hair was long, her foot was light,
　　And her eyes were wild.

I set her on my pacing steed,
　　And nothing else saw all day long;
For sideways would she lean, and sing
　　A faery's song.

I made a garland for her head,
　　And bracelets too, and fragrant zone;
She look'd at me as she did love,
　　And made sweet moan.

She found me roots of relish sweet,
　　And honey wild, and manna dew;
And sure in language strange she said,
　　I love thee true.

She took me to her elfin grot,
　　And there she gaz'd and sighed deep,
And there I shut her wild sad eyes —
　　So kiss'd to sleep.

And there we slumber'd on the moss,
　　And there I dream'd, ah woe betide,
The latest dream I ever dream'd
　　On the cold hill side.

I saw pale kings, and princes too,
　　Pale warriors, death-pale were they all;
Who cry'd — "La belle Dame sans merci
　　Hath thee in thrall!"

I saw their starv'd lips in the gloam
　　With horrid warning gaped wide,
And I awoke, and found me here
　　On the cold hill side.

And this is why I sojourn here
　　Alone and palely loitering,
Though the sedge is wither'd from the lake,
　　And no birds sing.

ODE TO A NIGHTINGALE

My heart aches, and a drowsy numbness pains
　　My sense, as though of hemlock I had drunk,
Or emptied some dull opiate to the drains
　　One minute past, and Lethe-wards had sunk:
'Tis not through envy of thy happy lot,
　　But being too happy in thy happiness, —
　　　　That thou, light-winged Dryad of the trees,
　　　　　　In some melodious plot

Of beechen green, and shadows numberless,
    Singest of summer in full-throated ease.

O, for a draught of vintage! that hath been
    Cool'd a long age in the deep-delved earth,
Tasting of Flora and the country green,
    Dance, and Provençal song, and sunburnt mirth!
O for a beaker full of the warm South,
    Full of the true, the blushful Hippocrene,
        With beaded bubbles winking at the brim,
            And purple-stained mouth;
    That I might drink, and leave the world unseen,
        And with thee fade away into the forest dim:

Fade far away, dissolve, and quite forget
    What thou among the leaves hast never known,
The weariness, the fever, and the fret
    Here, where men sit and hear each other groan;
Where palsy shakes a few, sad, last gray hairs,
    Where youth grows pale, and spectre-thin, and dies;
        Where but to think is to be full of sorrow
            And leaden-eyed despairs,
    Where Beauty cannot keep her lustrous eyes,
        Or new Love pine at them beyond to-morrow.

Away! away! for I will fly to thee,
    Not charioted by Bacchus and his pards,
But on the viewless wings of Poesy,
    Though the dull brain perplexes and retards:
Already with thee! tender is the night,
    And haply the Queen-Moon is on her throne,
        Cluster'd around by all her starry Fays;
            But here there is no light,
    Save what from heaven is with the breezes blown
        Through verdurous glooms and winding mossy ways.

I cannot see what flowers are at my feet,
    Nor what soft incense hangs upon the boughs,
But, in embalmed darkness, guess each sweet
    Wherewith the seasonable month endows
The grass, the thicket, and the fruit-tree wild;
    White hawthorn, and the pastoral eglantine;
        Fast fading violets cover'd up in leaves;
            And mid-May's eldest child,
    The coming musk-rose, full of dewy wine,
        The murmurous haunt of flies on summer eves.

Darkling I listen; and, for many a time
  I have been half in love with easeful Death,
Call'd him soft names in many a mused rhyme,
  To take into the air my quiet breath;
Now more than ever seems it rich to die,
  To cease upon the midnight with no pain,
    While thou art pouring forth thy soul abroad
      In such an ecstasy!
Still wouldst thou sing, and I have ears in vain —
  To thy high requiem become a sod.

Thou wast not born for death, immortal Bird!
  No hungry generations tread thee down;
The voice I hear this passing night was heard
  In ancient days by emperor and clown:
Perhaps the self-same song that found a path
  Through the sad heart of Ruth, when, sick for home,
    She stood in tears amid the alien corn;
      The same that oft-times hath
Charm'd magic casements, opening on the foam
  Of perilous seas, in faery lands forlorn.

Forlorn! the very word is like a bell
  To toll me back from thee to my sole self!
Adieu! the fancy cannot cheat so well
  As she is fam'd to do, deceiving elf.
Adieu! adieu! thy plaintive anthem fades
  Past the near meadows, over the still stream,
    Up the hill-side; and now 'tis buried deep
      In the next valley-glades:
Was it a vision, or a waking dream?
    Fled is that music: — Do I wake or sleep?

ODE ON A GRECIAN URN

Thou still unravish'd bride of quietness,
  Thou foster-child of silence and slow time,
Sylvan historian, who canst thus express
  A flowery tale more sweetly than our rhyme:
What leaf-fring'd legend haunts about thy shape
  Of deities or mortals, or of both,
    In Tempe or the dales of Arcady?
  What men or gods are these? What maidens loth?
What mad pursuit? What struggle to escape?
  What pipes and timbrels? What wild ecstasy?

Heard melodies are sweet, but those unheard
  Are sweeter; therefore, ye soft pipes, play on;
Not to the sensual ear, but, more endear'd,
  Pipe to the spirit ditties of no tone:
Fair youth, beneath the trees, thou canst not leave
  Thy song, nor ever can those trees be bare;
    Bold Lover, never, never canst thou kiss,
Though winning near the goal — yet, do not grieve;
    She cannot fade, though thou hast not thy bliss,
For ever wilt thou love, and she be fair!

Ah, happy, happy boughs! that cannot shed
  Your leaves, nor ever bid the Spring adieu;
And, happy melodist, unwearied,
  For ever piping songs for ever new;
More happy love! more happy, happy love!
  For ever warm and still to be enjoy'd,
    For ever panting, and for ever young;
All breathing human passion far above,
  That leaves a heart high-sorrowful and cloy'd,
    A burning forehead, and a parching tongue.

Who are these coming to the sacrifice?
  To what green altar, O mysterious priest,
Lead'st thou that heifer lowing at the skies,
  And all her silken flanks with garlands drest?
What little town by river or sea shore,
  Or mountain-built with peaceful citadel,
    Is emptied of this folk, this pious morn?
And, little town, thy streets for evermore
  Will silent be; and not a soul to tell
    Why thou art desolate, can e'er return.

O Attic shape! Fair attitude! with brede
  Of marble men and maidens overwrought,
With forest branches and the trodden weed;
  Thou, silent form, dost tease us out of thought
As doth eternity: Cold Pastoral!
  When old age shall this generation waste,
    Thou shalt remain, in midst of other woe
Than ours, a friend to man, to whom thou say'st,
"Beauty is truth, truth beauty," — that is all
  Ye know on earth, and all ye need to know.

ODE ON MELANCHOLY

No, no, go not to Lethe, neither twist
  Wolf's bane, tight-rooted, for its poisonous wine;
Nor suffer thy pale forehead to be kiss'd
  By nightshade, ruby grape of Proserpine;
Make not your rosary of yew-berries,
    Nor let the beetle, nor the death-moth be
      Your mournful Psyche, nor the downy owl
A partner in your sorrow's mysteries;
    For shade to shade will come too drowsily,
      And drown the wakeful anguish of the soul.

But when the melancholy fit shall fall
  Sudden from heaven like a weeping cloud,
That fosters the droop-headed flowers all,
  And hides the green hill in an April shroud;
Then glut thy sorrow on a morning rose,
    Or on the rainbow of the salt sand-wave,
      Or on the wealth of globed peonies;
Or if thy mistress some rich anger shows,
    Emprison her soft hand, and let her rave,
      And feed deep, deep upon her peerless eyes.

She dwells with Beauty — Beauty that must die;
  And Joy, whose hand is ever at his lips
Bidding adieu; and aching Pleasure nigh,
  Turning to Poison while the bee-mouth sips:
Ay, in the very temple of Delight
  Veil'd Melancholy has her sovran shrine,
    Though seen of none save him whose strenuous tongue
Can burst Joy's grape against his palate fine;
  His soul shall taste the sadness of her might,
    And be among her cloudy trophies hung.

TO AUTUMN

Season of mists and mellow fruitfulness,
  Close bosom-friend of the maturing sun;
  Conspiring with him how to load and bless
    With fruit the vines that round the thatch-eves run;
To bend with apples the moss'd cottage-trees,
  And fill all fruit with ripeness to the core;
    To swell the gourd, and plump the hazel shells

With a sweet kernel; to set budding more,
And still more, later flowers for the bees,
Until they think warm days will never cease,
    For Summer has o'er-brimm'd their clammy cells.

Who hath not seen thee oft amid thy store?
    Sometimes whoever seeks abroad may find
Thee sitting careless on a granary floor,
    Thy hair soft-lifted by the winnowing wind;
Or on a half-reap'd furrow sound asleep,
    Drows'd with the fume of poppies, while thy hook
    Spares the next swath and all its twined flowers:
And sometimes like a gleaner thou dost keep
    Steady thy laden head across a brook;
    Or by a cyder-press, with patient look,
    Thou watchest the last oozings hours by hours.

Where are the songs of Spring? Ay, where are they?
    Think not of them, thou hast thy music too, —
While barred clouds bloom the soft-dying day,
    And touch the stubble-plains with rosy hue;
Then in a wailful choir the small gnats mourn
    Among the river sallows, borne aloft
    Or sinking as the light wind lives or dies;
And full-grown lambs loud bleat from hilly bourn;
    Hedge-crickets sing: and now with treble soft
    The red-breast whistles from a garden-croft;
    And gathering swallows twitter in the skies.

SONNET: AFTER DARK VAPORS

After dark vapors have oppress'd our plains
    For a long dreary season, comes a day
    Born of the gentle South, and clears away
From the sick heavens all unseemly stains.
The anxious month, relieved of its pains,
    Takes as a long-lost right the feel of May;
    The eyelids with the passing coolness play
Like rose leaves with the drip of Summer rains.
The calmest thoughts come round us; as of leaves
    Budding — fruit ripening in stillness — Autumn suns
Smiling at eve upon the quiet sheaves —
Sweet Sappho's cheek — a smiling infant's breath —
    The gradual sand that through an hour-glass runs —
A woodland rivulet — a Poet's death.

SONNET: TO SLEEP

O soft embalmer of the still midnight,
  Shutting, with careful fingers and benign,
Our gloom-pleas'd eyes, embower'd from the light,
  Enshaded in forgetfulness divine:
O soothest Sleep! if so it please thee, close
  In midst of this thine hymn my willing eyes,
Or wait the "Amen," ere thy poppy throws
  Around my bed its lulling charities.
Then save me, or the passed day will shine
Upon my pillow, breeding many woes, —
Save me from curious Conscience, that still lords
  Its strength for darkness, burrowing like a mole;
Turn the key deftly in the oiled wards,
  And seal the hushed Casket of my Soul.

From ENDYMION

HYMN TO PAN

O thou, whose mighty palace roof doth hang
From jagged trunks, and overshadoweth
Eternal whispers, glooms, the birth, life, death
Of unseen flowers in heavy peacefulness;
Who lov'st to see the hamadryads dress
Their ruffled locks where meeting hazels darken;
And through whole solemn hours dost sit, and hearken
The dreary melody of bedded reeds —
In desolate places, where dank moisture breeds
The pipy hemlock to strange overgrowth;
Bethinking thee, how melancholy loth
Thou wast to lose fair Syrinx — do thou now,
By thy love's milky brow!
By all the trembling mazes that she ran,
      Hear us, great Pan!

O thou, for whose soul-soothing quiet, turtles
Passion their voices cooingly 'mong myrtles,
What time thou wanderest at eventide
Through sunny meadows, that outskirt the side
Of thine enmossed realms: O thou, to whom
Broad leaved fig trees even now foredoom
Their ripen'd fruitage; yellow girted bees
Their golden honeycombs; our village leas

Their fairest blossom'd beans and poppied corn;
The chuckling linnet its five young unborn,
To sing for thee; low creeping strawberries
Their summer coolness; pent up butterflies
Their freckled wings; yea, the fresh budding year
All its completions — be quickly near,
By every wind that nods the mountain pine,
       O forester divine!

   Thou, to whom every faun and satyr flies
For willing service; whether to surprise
The squatted hare while in half sleeping fit;
Or upward ragged precipices flit
To save poor lambkins from the eagle's maw;
Or by mysterious enticement draw
Bewildered shepherds to their path again;
Or to tread breathless round the frothy main,
And gather up all fancifullest shells
For thee to tumble into Naiads' cells,
And, being hidden, laugh at their out-peeping;
Or to delight thee with fantastic leaping,
The while they pelt each other on the crown
With silvery oak apples, and fir cones brown —
By all the echoes that about thee ring,
       Hear us, O satyr King!

   O Hearkener to the loud clapping shears
While ever and anon to his shorn peers
A ram goes bleating: Winder of the horn,
When snouted wild-boars routing tender corn
Anger our huntsmen: Breather round our farms,
To keep off mildews, and all weather harms:
Strange ministrant of undescribed sounds,
That come a swooning over hollow grounds,
And wither drearily on barren moors:
Dread opener of the mysterious doors
Leading to universal knowledge — see,
      Great son of Dryope,
The many that are come to pay their vows
With leaves about their brows!

   Be still the unimaginable lodge
For solitary thinkings; such as dodge
Conception to the very bourne of heaven,
Then leave the naked brain: be still the leaven,

That spreading in this dull and clodded earth
Gives it a touch ethereal — a new birth:
Be still a symbol of immensity;
A firmament reflected in a sea;
An element filling the space between;
An unknown — but no more: we humbly screen
With uplift hands our foreheads, lowly bending,
And giving out a shout most heaven rending,
Conjure thee to receive our humble Pæan,
    Upon thy Mount Lycean!

From SLEEP AND POETRY

As I lay in my bed slepe full unmete
Was unto me, but why that I ne might
Rest I ne wist, for there n'as erthly wight
(As I suppose) had more of hertis ese
Than I, for I n'ad sicknesse nor disese.

            — CHAUCER

What is more gentle than a wind in summer?
What is more soothing than the pretty hummer
That stays one moment in an open flower,
And buzzes cheerily from bower to bower?
What is more tranquil than a musk-rose blowing
In a green island, far from all men's knowing?
More healthful than the leafiness of dales?
More secret than a nest of nightingales?
More serene than Cordelia's countenance?
More full of visions than a high romance?
What but thee, Sleep? Soft closer of our eyes!
Low murmurer of tender lullabies!
Light hoverer around our happy pillows!
Wreather of poppy buds, and weeping willows!
Silent entangler of a beauty's tresses!
Most happy listener! when the morning blesses
Thee for enlivening all the cheerful eyes
That glance so brightly at the new sun-rise.

But what is higher beyond thought than thee?
Fresher than berries of a mountain tree?
More strange, more beautiful, more smooth, more regal,
Than wings of swans, than doves, than dim-seen eagle?
What is it? And to what shall I compare it?
It has a glory, and nought else can share it:

The thought thereof is awful, sweet, and holy,
Chasing away all worldliness and folly;
Coming sometimes like fearful claps of thunder,
Or the low rumblings earth's regions under;
And sometimes like a gentle whispering
Of all the secrets of some wond'rous thing
That breathes about us in the vacant air;
So that we look around with prying stare,
Perhaps to see shapes of light, aerial limning,
And catch soft floatings from a faint-heard hymning;
To see the laurel wreath, on high suspended,
That is to crown our name when life is ended.
Sometimes it gives a glory to the voice,
And from the heart up-springs, rejoice! rejoice!
Sounds which will reach the Framer of all things,
And die away in ardent mutterings.

No one who once the glorious sun has seen,
And all the clouds, and felt his bosom clean
For his great Maker's presence, but must know
What 'tis I mean, and feel his being glow:
Therefore no insult will I give his spirit,
By telling what he sees from native merit.

O Poesy! for thee I hold my pen
That am not yet a glorious denizen
Of thy wide heaven — Should I rather kneel
Upon some mountain-top until I feel
A glowing splendour round about me hung,
And echo back the voice of thine own tongue?
O Poesy! for thee I grasp my pen
That am not yet a glorious denizen
Of thy wide heaven; yet, to my ardent prayer,
Yield from thy sanctuary some clear air,
Smooth'd for intoxication by the breath
Of flowering bays, that I may die a death
Of luxury, and my young spirit follow
The morning sun-beams to the great Apollo
Like a fresh sacrifice.

THE EVE OF ST. AGNES

St. Agnes' Eve — Ah, bitter chill it was!
The owl, for all his feathers, was a-cold;
The hare limp'd trembling through the frozen grass,

And silent was the flock in woolly fold:
Numb were the Beadsman's fingers, while he told
His rosary, and while his frosted breath,
Like pious incense from a censer old,
Seem'd taking flight for heaven, without a death,
Past the sweet Virgin's picture, while his prayer he saith.

His prayer he saith, this patient, holy man;
Then takes his lamp, and riseth from his knees,
And back returneth, meagre, barefoot, wan,
Along the chapel aisle by slow degrees:
The sculptur'd dead, on each side, seem to freeze,
Emprison'd in black, purgatorial rails:
Knights, ladies, praying in dumb orat'ries,
He passeth by; and his weak spirit fails
To think how they may ache in icy hoods and mails.

Northward he turneth through a little door,
And scarce three steps, ere Music's golden tongue
Flatter'd to tears this aged man and poor;
But no — already had his deathbell rung:
The joys of all his life were said and sung:
His was harsh penance on St. Agnes' Eve:
Another way he went, and soon among
Rough ashes sat he for his soul's reprieve,
And all night kept awake, for sinners' sake to grieve.

That ancient Beadsman heard the prelude soft;
And so it chanc'd, for many a door was wide,
From hurry to and fro. Soon, up aloft,
The silver, snarling trumpets 'gan to chide:
The level chambers, ready with their pride,
Were glowing to receive a thousand guests:
The carved angels, ever eager-eyed,
Star'd, where upon their heads the cornice rests,
With hair blown back, and wings put cross-wise on their breasts.

At length burst in the argent revelry,
With plume, tiara, and all rich array,
Numerous as shadows haunting faerily
The brain, new stuff'd, in youth, with triumphs gay
Of old romance. These let us wish away,
And turn, sole-thoughted, to one Lady there,
Whose heart had brooded, all that wintry day,
On love, and wing'd St. Agnes' saintly care,
As she had heard old dames full many times declare.

They told her how, upon St. Agnes' Eve,
Young virgins might have visions of delight,
And soft adorings from their loves receive
Upon the honey'd middle of the night,
If ceremonies due they did aright;
As, supperless to bed they must retire,
And couch supine their beauties, lilly white;
Nor look behind, nor sideways, but require
Of Heaven with upward eyes for all that they desire.

Full of this whim was thoughtful Madeline:
The music, yearning like a God in pain,
She scarcely heard: her maiden eyes divine,
Fix'd on the floor, saw many a sweeping train
Pass by — she heeded not at all: in vain
Came many a tiptoe, amorous cavalier,
And back retir'd; not cool'd by high disdain,
But she saw not: her heart was otherwhere:
She sigh'd for Agnes' dreams, the sweetest of the year.

She danc'd along with vague, regardless eyes,
Anxious her lips, her breathing quick and short:
The hallow'd hour was near at hand: she sighs
Amid the timbrels, and the throng'd resort
Of whisperers in anger, or in sport;
'Mid looks of love, defiance, hate, and scorn,
Hoodwink'd with faery fancy; all amort,
Save to St. Agnes and her lambs unshorn,
And all the bliss to be before to-morrow morn.

So, purposing each moment to retire,
She linger'd still. Meantime, across the moors,
Had come young Porphyro, with heart on fire
For Madeline. Beside the portal doors,
Buttress'd from moonlight, stands he, and implores
All saints to give him sight of Madeline,
But for one moment in the tedious hours,
That he might gaze and worship all unseen;
Perchance speak, kneel, touch, kiss — in sooth such things have been.

He ventures in: let no buzz'd whisper tell:
All eyes be muffled, or a hundred swords
Will storm his heart, Love's fev'rous citadel:
For him, those chambers held barbarian hordes,
Hyena foemen, and hot-blooded lords,

Whose very dogs would execrations howl
Against his lineage: not one breast affords
Him any mercy, in that mansion foul,
Save one old beldame, weak in body and in soul.

Ah, happy chance! the aged creature came,
Shuffling along with ivory-headed wand,
To where he stood, hid from the torch's flame,
Behind a broad hall-pillar, far beyond
The sound of merriment and chorus bland:
He startled her; but soon she knew his face,
And grasp'd his fingers in her palsied hand,
Saying, "Mercy, Porphyro! hie thee from this place:
They are all here to-night, the whole blood-thirsty race!

"Get hence! get hence! there's dwarfish Hildebrand;
He had a fever late, and in the fit
He cursed thee and thine, both house and land:
Then there's that old Lord Maurice, not a whit
More tame for his gray hairs — Alas me! flit!
Flit like a ghost away." — "Ah, Gossip dear,
We're safe enough; here in this arm-chair sit,
And tell me how — " "Good Saints! not here, not here;
Follow me, child, or else these stones will be thy bier."

He follow'd through a lowly arched way,
Brushing the cobwebs with his lofty plume,
And as she mutter'd "Well-a — well-a-day!"
He found him in a little moonlight room,
Pale lattic'd, chill, and silent as a tomb.
"Now tell me where is Madeline," said he,
"O tell me, Angela, by the holy loom
Which none but secret sisterhood may see,
When they St. Agnes' wool are weaving piously."

"St. Agnes! Ah! it is St. Agnes' Eve —
Yet men will murder upon holy days:
Thou must hold water in a witch's sieve,
And be liege-lord of all the Elves and Fays,
To venture so: it fills me with amaze
To see thee, Porphyro! — St. Agnes' Eve!
God's help! my lady fair the conjuror plays
This very night: good angels her deceive!
But let me laugh awhile, I've mickle time to grieve."

Feebly she laugheth in the languid moon,
While Porphyro upon her face doth look,
Like puzzled urchin on an aged crone
Who keepeth clos'd a wond'rous riddle-book,
As spectacled she sits in chimney nook.
But soon his eyes grew brilliant, when she told
His lady's purpose; and he scarce could brook
Tears, at the thought of those enchantments cold,
And Madeline asleep in lap of legends old.

Sudden a thought came like a full-blown rose,
Flushing his brow, and in his pained heart
Made purple riot: then doth he purpose
A stratagem, that makes the beldame start:
"A cruel man and impious thou art:
Sweet lady, let her pray, and sleep, and dream
Alone with her good angels, far apart
From wicked men like thee. Go, go! — I deem
Thou canst not surely be the same that thou didst seem."

"I will not harm her, by all saints I swear,"
Quoth Porphyro: "O may I ne'er find grace
When my weak voice shall whisper its last prayer,
If one of her soft ringlets I displace,
Or look with ruffian passion in her face:
Good Angela, believe me by these tears;
Or I will, even in a moment's space,
Awake, with horrid shout, my foemen's ears,
And beard them, though they be more fang'd than wolves and bears."

"Ah! why wilt thou affright a feeble soul?
A poor, weak, palsy-stricken, churchyard thing,
Whose passing-bell may ere the midnight toll;
Whose prayers for thee, each morn and evening,
Were never miss'd." — Thus plaining, doth she bring
A gentler speech from burning Porphyro;
So woful, and of such deep sorrowing,
That Angela gives promise she will do
Whatever he shall wish, betide her weel or woe.

Which was, to lead him, in close secrecy,
Even to Madeline's chamber, and there hide
Him in a closet, of such privacy
That he might see her beauty unspied,
And win perhaps that night a peerless bride,
While legion'd faeries pac'd the coverlet,

And pale enchantment held her sleepy-eyed.
Never on such a night have lovers met,
Since Merlin paid his Demon all the monstrous debt.

"It shall be as thou wishest," said the Dame:
"All cates and dainties shall be stored there
Quickly on this feast-night: by the tambour frame
Her own lute thou wilt see: no time to spare,
For I am slow and feeble, and scarce dare
On such a catering trust my dizzy head.
Wait here, my child, with patience; kneel in prayer
The while: Ah! thou must needs the lady wed,
Or may I never leave my grave among the dead."

So saying, she hobbled off with busy fear.
The lover's endless minutes slowly pass'd;
The dame return'd, and whisper'd in his ear
To follow her; with aged eyes aghast
From fright of dim espial. Safe at last,
Through many a dusky gallery, they gain
The maiden's chamber, silken, hush'd, and chaste;
Where Porphyro took covert, pleas'd amain.
His poor guide hurried back with agues in her brain.

Her falt'ring hand upon the balustrade,
Old Angela was feeling for the stair,
When Madeline, St. Agnes' charmed maid,
Rose, like a mission'd spirit, unaware:
With silver taper's light, and pious care,
She turn'd, and down the aged gossip led
To a safe level matting. Now prepare,
Young Porphyro, for gazing on that bed;
She comes, she comes again, like ring-dove fray'd and fled.

Out went the taper as she hurried in;
Its little smoke, in pallid moonshine, died:
She clos'd the door, she panted, all akin
To spirits of the air, and visions wide:
No uttered syllable, or, woe betide!
But to her heart, her heart was voluble,
Paining with eloquence her balmy side;
As though a tongueless nightingale should swell
Her throat in vain, and die, heart-stifled, in her dell.

A casement high and triple-arch'd there was,
All garlanded with carven imag'ries
Of fruits, and flowers, and bunches of knot-grass,

And diamonded with panes of quaint device,
Innumerable of stains and splendid dyes,
As are the tiger-moth's deep-damask'd wings;
And in the midst, 'mong thousand heraldries,
And twilight saints, and dim emblazonings,
A shielded scutcheon blush'd with blood of queens and kings.

Full on this casement shone the wintry moon,
And threw warm gules on Madeline's fair breast,
As down she knelt for heaven's grace and boon;
Rose-bloom fell on her hands, together prest,
And on her silver cross soft amethyst,
And on her hair a glory, like a saint:
She seem'd a splendid angel, newly drest,
Save wings, for heaven — Porphyro grew faint:
She knelt, so pure a thing, so free from mortal taint.

Anon his heart revives: her vespers done,
Of all its wreathed pearls her hair she frees;
Unclasps her warmed jewels one by one;
Loosens her fragrant bodice; by degrees
Her rich attire creeps rustling to her knees:
Half-hidden, like a mermaid in sea-weed,
Pensive awhile she dreams awake, and sees,
In fancy, fair St. Agnes in her bed,
But dares not look behind, or all the charm is fled.

Soon, trembling in her soft and chilly nest,
In sort of wakeful swoon, perplex'd she lay,
Until the poppied warmth of sleep oppress'd
Her soothed limbs, and soul fatigued away;
Flown, like a thought, until the morrow-day;
Blissfully haven'd both from joy and pain;
Clasp'd like a missal where swart Paynims pray;
Blinded alike from sunshine and from rain,
As though a rose should shut, and be a bud again.

Stol'n to this paradise, and so entranced,
Porphyro gazed upon her empty dress,
And listen'd to her breathing, if it chanced
To wake into a slumberous tenderness;
Which when he heard, that minute did he bless,
And breath'd himself: then from the closet crept,
Noiseless as fear in a wide wilderness,
And over the hush'd carpet, silent stept,
And 'tween the curtains peep'd, where, lo! — how fast she slept.

Then by the bed-side, where the faded moon
Made a dim, silver twilight, soft he set
A table, and, half anguish'd, threw thereon
A cloth of woven crimson, gold, and jet: —
O for some drowsy Morphean amulet!
The boisterous, midnight, festive clarion,
The kettle-drum, and far-heard clarinet,
Affray his ears, though but in dying tone: —
The hall door shuts again, and all the noise is gone.

And still she slept an azure-lidded sleep,
In blanched linen, smooth, and lavender'd,
While he from forth the closet brought a heap
Of candied apple, quince, and plum, and gourd;
With jellies soother than the creamy curd,
And lucent syrops, tinct with cinnamon;
Manna and dates, in argosy transferr'd
From Fez; and spiced dainties, every one,
From silken Samarcand to cedar'd Lebanon.

These delicates he heap'd with glowing hand
On golden dishes and in baskets bright
Of wreathed silver: sumptuous they stand
In the retired quiet of the night,
Filling the chilly room with perfume light. —
"And now, my love, my seraph fair, awake!
Thou art my heaven, and I thine eremite:
Open thine eyes, for meek St. Agnes' sake,
Or I shall drowse beside thee, so my soul doth ache."

Thus whispering, his warm, unnerved arm
Sank in her pillow. Shaded was her dream
By the dusk curtains: — 'twas a midnight charm
Impossible to melt as iced stream:
The lustrous salvers in the moonlight gleam;
Broad golden fringe upon the carpet lies:
It seem'd he never, never could redeem
From such a steadfast spell his lady's eyes;
So mus'd awhile, entoil'd in woofed phantasies.

Awakening up, he took her hollow lute, —
Tumultuous, — and, in chords that tenderest be,
He play'd an ancient ditty, long since mute,
In Provence call'd, "La belle dame sans mercy":
Close to her ear touching the melody; —
Wherewith disturb'd, she utter'd a soft moan:

He ceased — she panted quick — and suddenly
Her blue affrayed eyes wide open shone:
Upon his knees he sank, pale as smooth-sculptured stone.

Her eyes were open, but she still beheld,
Now wide awake, the vision of her sleep:
There was a painful change, that nigh expell'd
The blisses of her dream so pure and deep,
At which fair Madeline began to weep,
And moan forth witless words with many a sigh;
While still her gaze on Porphyro would keep;
Who knelt, with joined hands and piteous eye,
Fearing to move or speak, she look'd so dreamingly.

"Ah, Porphyro!" said she, "but even now
Thy voice was at sweet tremble in mine ear,
Made tuneable with every sweetest vow;
And those sad eyes were spiritual and clear:
How chang'd thou art! how pallid, chill, and drear!
Give me that voice again, my Porphyro,
Those looks immortal, those complainings dear!
Oh leave me not in this eternal woe,
For if thou diest, my Love, I know not where to go."

Beyond a mortal man impassion'd far
At these voluptuous accents, he arose,
Ethereal, flush'd, and like a throbbing star
Seen mid the sapphire heaven's deep repose;
Into her dream he melted, as the rose
Blendeth its odour with the violet, —
Solution sweet: meantime the frost-wind blows
Like Love's alarum pattering the sharp sleet
Against the window-panes; St. Agnes' moon hath set.

'Tis dark: quick pattereth the flaw-blown sleet:
"This is no dream, my bride, my Madeline!"
'Tis dark: the iced gusts still rave and beat:
"No dream, alas! alas! and woe is mine!
Porphyro will leave me here to fade and pine. —
Cruel! what traitor could thee hither bring?
I curse not, for my heart is lost in thine,
Though thou forsakest a deceived thing; —
A dove forlorn and lost with sick unpruned wing."

"My Madeline! sweet dreamer! lovely bride!
Say, may I be for aye thy vassal blest?
Thy beauty's shield, heart-shap'd and vermeil dyed?

Ah, silver shrine, here will I take my rest
After so many hours of toil and quest,
A famish'd pilgrim, — sav'd by miracle.
Though I have found, I will not rob thy nest
Saving of thy sweet self; if thou think'st well
To trust, fair Madeline, to no rude infidel.

"Hark! 'tis an elfin-storm from faery land,
Of haggard seeming, but a boon indeed:
Arise — arise! the morning is at hand; —
The bloated wassaillers will never heed: —
Let us away, my love, with happy speed;
There are no ears to hear, or eyes to see, —
Drown'd all in Rhenish and the sleepy mead:
Awake! arise! my love, and fearless be,
For o'er the southern moors I have a home for thee."

She hurried at his words, beset with fears,
For there were sleeping dragons all around,
At glaring watch, perhaps, with ready spears —
Down the wide stairs a darkling way they found. —
In all the house was heard no human sound.
A chain-dropp'd lamp was flickering by each door;
The arras, rich with horseman, hawk, and hound,
Flutter'd in the besieging wind's uproar;
And the long carpets rose along the gusty floor.

They glide, like phantoms, into the wide hall;
Like phantoms, to the iron porch, they glide;
Where lay the Porter, in uneasy sprawl,
With a huge empty flaggon by his side:
The wakeful bloodhound rose, and shook his hide,
But his sagacious eye an inmate owns:
By one, and one, the bolts full easy slide: —
The chains lie silent on the footworn stones; —
The key turns, and the door upon its hinges groans.

And they are gone: aye, ages long ago
These lovers fled away into the storm.
That night the Baron dreamt of many a woe,
And all his warrior-guests, with shade and form
Of witch, and demon, and large coffin-worm,
Were long be-nightmar'd. Angela the old
Died palsy-twitch'd, with meagre face deform;
The Beadsman, after thousand aves told,
For aye unsought for slept among his ashes cold.

Sir Walter Scott

1771-1832

PROUD MAISIE

Proud Maisie is in the wood,
  Walking so early;
Sweet Robin sits on the
    bush,
  Singing so rarely.

"Tell me, thou bonny bird,
  When shall I marry me?"
"When six braw gentlemen
  Kirkward shall carry ye."

"Who makes the bridal bed,
  Birdie, say truly?"
"The grey-headed sexton
  That delves the grave duly.

"The glowworm o'er grave and
    stone
  Shall light thee steady;
The owl from the steeple sing
  Welcome, proud lady."

George Gordon, Lord Byron

1788-1824

From ENGLISH BARDS AND SCOTCH REVIEWERS
A Satire

Still must I hear? — shall hoarse Fitzgerald bawl
His creaking couplets in a tavern hall,
And I not sing, lest, haply, Scotch reviews
Should dub me scribbler, and denounce my Muse?
Prepare for rhyme — I'll publish, right or wrong:
Fools are my theme, let satire be my song.

    Oh! nature's noblest gift — my gray goose-quill!
Slave of my thoughts, obedient to my will,
Torn from thy parent bird to form a pen,
That mighty instrument of little men!
The pen! foredoomed to aid the mental throes
Of brains that labor, big with verse or prose,
Though nymphs forsake, and critics may deride
The lover's solace, and the author's pride.
What wits! what poets dost thou daily raise!
How frequent is thy use, how small thy praise!

Condemned at length to be forgotten quite,
With all the pages which 'twas thine to write.
But thou, at least, mine own special pen!
Once laid aside, but now assumed again,
Our task complete, like Hamet's shall be free;
Though spurned by others, yet beloved by me:
Then let us soar to-day: no common theme,
No eastern vision, no distempered dream
Inspires — our path, though full of thorns, is plain;
Smooth be the verse, and easy be the strain.

When Vice triumphant holds her sovereign sway,
Obeyed by all who nought beside obey;
When Folly, frequent harbinger of crime,
Bedecks her cap with bells of every clime;
When knaves and fools combined o'er all prevail,
And weigh their justice in a golden scale;
E'en then the boldest start from public sneers,
Afraid of shame, unknown to other fears,
More darkly sin, by satire kept in awe,
And shrink from ridicule, though not from law.

Such is the force of wit! but not belong
To me the arrows of satiric song;
The royal vices of our age demand
A keener weapon, and a mightier hand.
Still there are follies, e'en for me to chase,
And yield at least amusement in the race:
Laugh when I laugh, I seek no other fame;
The cry is up, and scribblers are my game.
Speed, Pegasus! — ye strains of great and small,
Ode, epic, elegy, have at you all!
I too can scrawl, and once up a time
I poured along the town a flood of rhyme,
A schoolboy freak, unworthy praise or blame;
I printed — older children do the same.
'Tis pleasant, sure, to see one's name in print;
A book's a book, although there's nothing in't.
Not that a title's sounding charm can save
Or scrawl or scribbler from an equal grave:
This Lambe must own, since his patrician name
Failed to preserve the spurious farce from shame.
No matter, George continues still to write
Though now the name is veiled from public sight.

Moved by the great example, I pursue
The self-same road, but make my own review:
Not seek great Jeffrey's, yet like him will be
Self-constituted judge of poesy.

A man must serve his time to every trade
Save censure — critics all are ready made.
Take hackneyed jokes from Miller, got by rote,
With just enough of learning to misquote;
A mind well skilled to find or forge a fault;
A turn for punning, call it Attic salt;
To Jeffrey go, be silent and discreet,
His pay is just ten sterling pounds per sheet:
Fear not to lie, 'twill seem a sharper hit;
Shrink not from blasphemy, 'twill pass for wit;
Care not for feeling — pass your proper jest,
And stand a critic, hated yet caressed.

And shall we own such judgment? no — as soon
Seek roses in December — ice in June;
Hope constancy in wind, or corn in chaff;
Believe a woman or an epitaph,
Or any other thing that's false, before
You trust in critics, who themselves are sore;
Or yield one single thought to be misled
By Jeffrey's heart, or Lambe's Boeotian head.
To these young tyrants, by themselves misplaced,
Combined usurpers on the throne of taste;
To these, when authors bend in humble awe,
And hail their voice as truth, their word as law —
While these are censors, 'twould be sin to spare;
While such are critics, why should I forbear?
But yet, so near all modern worthies run,
'Tis doubtful whom to seek, or whom to shun;
Nor know we when to spare, or where to strike,
Our bards and censors are so much alike.

Then should you ask me, why I venture o'er
The path which Pope and Gifford trod before;
If not yet sickened, you can still proceed:
Go on; my rhyme will tell you as you read.
"But hold!" exclaims a friend, — "here's some neglect:
This — that — and t'other line seem incorrect."
What then? the self-same blunder Pope has got,
And careless Dryden — "Ay, but Pye has not:" —
Indeed! — 'tis granted, faith! — but what care I?
Better to err with Pope, than shine with Pye.

Time was, ere yet in these degenerate days
Ignoble themes obtained mistaken praise,
When sense and wit with poesy allied,
No fabled graces, flourished side by side;
From the same fount their inspiration drew,
And, reared by taste, bloomed fairer as they grew.
Then in this happy isle, a Pope's pure strain
Sought the rapt soul to charm, nor sought in vain;
A polished nation's praise aspired to claim,
And raised the people's, as the poet's fame.
Like him great Dryden poured the tide of song,
In stream less smooth, indeed, yet doubly strong.
Then Congreve's scenes could cheer, or Otway's melt —
For nature then an English audience felt.
But why these names, or greater still, retrace,
When all to feebler bards resign their place?
Yet to such times our lingering looks are cast,
When taste and reason with those times are past.
Now look around, and turn each trifling page,
Survey the precious works that please the age;
This truth at least let satire's self allow,
No dearth of bards can be complained of now.
The loaded press beneath her labor groans,
And printers' devils shake their weary bones;
While Southey's epics cram the creaking shelves,
And Little's lyrics shine in hot-pressed twelves.
Thus saith the preacher: "Nought beneath the sun
Is new;" yet still from change to change we run:
What varied wonders tempt us as they pass.
The cow-pox, tractors, galvanism, and gas,
In turns appear, to make the vulgar stare,
Till the swoln bubble bursts — and all is air!
Nor less new schools of Poetry arise,
Where dull pretenders grapple for the prize:
O'er taste awhile these pseudo-bards prevail;
Each country book-club bows the knee to Baal,
And, hurling lawful genius from the throne,
Erects a shrine and idol of its own;
Some leaden calf — but whom it matters not,
From soaring Southey down to groveling Stott.

Behold! in various throngs the scribbling crew,
For notice eager, pass in long review:
Each spurs his jaded Pegasus apace,
And rhyme and blank maintain an equal race;
Sonnets on sonnets crowd, and ode on ode;
And tales of terror jostle on the road;

Immeasurable measures move along;
For simpering folly loves a varied song,
To strange mysterious dulness still the friend,
Admires the strain she cannot comprehend.
Thus Lays of Minstrels — may they be the last! —
On half-strung harps whine mournful to the blast.
While mountain spirits prate to river sprites,
That dames may listen to the sound at nights;
And goblin brats, of Gilpin Horner's brood,
Decoy young border-nobles through the wood,
And skip at every step, Lord knows how high,
And frighten foolish babes, the Lord knows why;
While high-born ladies in their magic cell,
Forbidding knights to read who cannot spell,
Despatch a courier to a wizard's grave,
And fight with honest men to shield a knave.

Next view in state, proud prancing on his roan.
The golden-crested haughty Marmion,
Now forging scrolls, now foremost in the fight,
Not quite a felon, yet but half a knight,
The gibbet or the field prepared to grace;
A mighty mixture of the great and base.
And thinkest thou, Scott! by vain conceit perchance
On public taste to foist thy stale romance,
Though Murray with his Miller may combine
To yield thy muse just half-a-crown per line?
No! when the sons of song descend to trade,
Their bays are sear, their former laurels fade.
Let such forego the poet's sacred name,
Who rack their brains for lucre, not for fame:
Still for stern Mammon may they toil in vain!
And sadly gaze on gold they cannot gain!
Such be their meed, such still the just reward
Of prostituted muse and hireling bard!
For this we spurn Apollo's venal son,
And bid a long "good night to Marmion."

These are the themes that claim our plaudits now;
These are the bards to whom the muse must bow;
While Milton, Dryden, Pope, alike forgot,
Resign their hallowed bays to Walter Scott.

The time has been, when yet the muse was young,
When Homer swept the lyre, and Maro sung,
An epic scarce ten centuries could claim,
While awe-struck nations hailed the magic name;

The work of each immortal bard appears
The single wonder of a thousand years.
Empires have mouldered from the face of earth,
Tongues have expired with those who gave them birth,
Without the glory such a strain can give,
As even in ruin bids the language live.
Not so with us, though minor bards, content,
On one great work a life of labor spent:
With eagle pinion soaring to the skies,
Behold the ballad-monger Southey rise!
To him let Camoëns, Milton, Tasso yield,
Whose annual strains, like armies, take the field.
First in the ranks see Joan of Arc advance,
The scourge of England and the boast of France!
Though burnt by wicked Bedford for a witch,
Behold her statue placed in glory's niche;
Her fetters burst, and just released from prison,
A virgin phoenix from her ashes risen.
Next see tremendous Thalaba come on,
Arabia's monstrous, wild, and wond'rous son;
Domdaniel's dread destroyer, who o'erthrew
More mad magicians than the world e'er knew.
Immortal hero! all thy foes o'ercome,
For ever reign — the rival of Tom Thumb!
Since startled metre fled before thy face,
Well wert thou doomed the last of all thy race!
Well might triumphant genii bear thee hence,
Illustrious conqueror of common sense!
Now, last and greatest, Madoc spreads his sails,
Cacique in Mexico, and prince in Wales;
Tells us strange tales, as other travellers do,
More old than Mandeville's, and not so true.
Oh, Southey! Southey! cease thy varied song!
A bard may chant too often and too long:
As thou art strong in verse, in mercy, spare!
A fourth, alas! were more than we could bear.
But if, in spite of all the world can say,
Thou still wilt verseward plod thy weary way;
If still in Berkeley ballads most uncivil,
Thou wilt devote old women to the devil,
The babe unborn thy dread intent may rue:
"God help thee," Southey, and thy readers too.

Next comes the dull disciple of thy school,
That mild apostate from poetic rule,
The simple Wordsworth, framer of a lay
As soft as evening in his favorite May,

Who warns his friend "to shake off toil and trouble,
And quit his books, for fear of growing double;"
Who, both by precept and example, shows
That prose is verse, and verse is merely prose;
Convincing all, by demonstration plain,
Poetic souls delight in prose insane;
And Christmas stories tortured into rhyme
Contain the essence of the true sublime.
Thus, when he tells the tale of Betty Foy,
The idiot mother of "an idiot boy;"
A moon-struck, silly lad, who lost his way,
And, like his bard, confounded night with day;
So close on each pathetic part he dwells,
And each adventure so sublimely tells,
That all who view the "idiot in his glory,"
Conceive the bard the hero of the story.

Shall gentle Coleridge pass unnoticed here,
To turgid ode and tumid stanza dear?
Though themes of innocence amuse him best,
Yet still obscurity's a welcome guest.
If Inspiration should her aid refuse
To him who takes a pixy for a muse,
Yet none in lofty numbers can surpass
The bard who soars to elegize an ass.
So well the subject suits his noble mind,
He brays, the laureate of the long-eared kind.

From CHILDE HAROLD'S PILGRIMAGE

ROLL ON, THOU DEEP AND DARK BLUE OCEAN

Roll on, thou deep and dark blue Ocean — roll!
Ten thousand fleets sweep over thee in vain;
Man marks the earth with ruin — his control
Stops with the shore; upon the watery plain
The wrecks are all thy deed, nor doth remain
A shadow of man's ravage, save his own,
When, for a moment, like a drop of rain,
He sinks into thy depths with bubbling groan,
Without a grave, unknell'd, uncoffin'd, and unknown.

His steps are not upon thy paths, — thy fields
Are not a spoil for him, — thou dost arise
And shake him from thee; the vile strength he wields
For earth's destruction thou dost all despise,

Spurning him from thy bosom to the skies,
And send'st him, shivering in thy playful spray
And howling, to his Gods, where haply lies
His petty hope in some near port or bay,
And dashest him again to earth: — there let him lay.

The armaments which thunderstrike the walls
Of rock-built cities, bidding nations quake,
And monarchs tremble in their capitals,
The oak leviathans, whose huge ribs make
Their clay creator the vain title take
Of lord of thee, and arbiter of war —
These are thy toys, and, as the snowy flake,
They melt into thy yeast of waves, which mar
Alike the Armada's pride or spoils of Trafalgar.

Thy shores are empires, changed in all save thee —
Assyria, Greece, Rome, Carthage, what are they?
Thy waters wash'd them power while they were free,
And many a tyrant since; their shores obey
The stranger, slave, or savage; their decay
Has dried up realms to deserts: — not so thou; —
Unchangeable, save to thy wild waves' play,
Time writes no wrinkle on thine azure brow:
Such as creation's dawn beheld, thou rollest now.

Thou glorious mirror, where the Almighty's form
Glasses itself in tempests; in all time, —
Calm or convulsed, in breeze, or gale, or storm,
Icing the pole, or in the torrid clime
Dark-heaving — boundless, endless, and sublime,
The image of eternity, the throne
Of the Invisible; even from out thy slime
The monsters of the deep are made; each zone
Obeys thee; thou goest forth, dread, fathomless, alone.

SHE WALKS IN BEAUTY

She walks in Beauty, like the night
  Of cloudless climes and starry skies;
And all that's best of dark and bright
  Meet in her aspect and her eyes:
Thus mellowed to that tender light
  Which Heaven to gaudy day denies.

One shade the more, one ray the less,
 Had half impaired the nameless grace
Which waves in every raven tress,
 Or softly lightens o'er her face;
Where thoughts serenely sweet express,
 How pure, how dear their dwelling-place.

And on that cheek, and o'er that brow,
 So soft, so calm, yet eloquent,
The smiles that win, the tints that glow,
 But tell of days in goodness spent,
A mind at peace with all below,
 A heart whose love is innocent!

SUN OF THE SLEEPLESS!

Sun of the sleepless! melancholy star!
Whose tearful beam glows tremulously far,
That show'st the darkness thou canst not dispel,
How like art thou to Joy remembered well!
So gleams the past, the light of other days,
Which shines, but warms not with its powerless rays:
A night-beam, Sorrow watcheth to behold,
Distinct, but distant — clear — but, oh how cold!

AND THOU ART DEAD

And thou art dead, as young and fair
 As aught of mortal birth;
And form so soft, and charms so rare,
 Too soon returned to Earth!
Though Earth received them in her bed,
And o'er the spot the crowd may tread
 In carelessness or mirth,
There is an eye which could not brook
A moment on that grave to look.

I will not ask where thou liest low,
 Nor gaze upon the spot;
There flowers or weeds at will may grow,
 So I behold them not:
It is enough for me to prove

That what I loved, and long must love,
   Like common earth can rot;
To me there needs no stone to tell,
'Tis Nothing that I loved so well.

Yet did I love thee to the last
   As fervently as thou,
Who didst not change through all the past,
   And canst not alter now.
The love where Death has set his seal,
Nor age can chill, nor rival steal,
   Nor falsehood disavow:
And, what were worse, thou canst not see
Or wrong, or change, or fault in me.

The better days of life were ours;
   The worst can be but mine:
The sun that cheers, the storm that lowers,
   Shall never more be thine.
The silence of that dreamless sleep
I envy now too much to weep;
   Nor need I to repine,
That all those charms have passed away
I might have watched through long decay.

The flower in ripened bloom unmatched
   Must fall the earliest prey;
Though by no hand untimely snatched,
   The leaves must drop away:
And yet it were a greater grief
To watch it withering, leaf by leaf,
   Than see it plucked to-day;
Since earthly eye but ill can bear
To trace the change to foul from fair.

I know not if I could have borne
   To see thy beauties fade;
The night that followed such a morn
   Had worn a deeper shade:
Thy day without a cloud hath passed,
And thou wert lovely to the last;
   Extinguished, not decayed;
As stars that shoot along the sky
Shine brightest as they fall from high.

As once I wept, if I could weep,
  My tears might well be shed,
To think I was not near to keep
  One vigil o'er thy bed;
To gaze, how fondly! on thy face,
To fold thee in a faint embrace,
  Uphold thy drooping head;
And show that love, however vain,
Nor thou nor I can feel again.

Yet how much less it were to gain,
  Though thou hast left me free,
The loveliest things that still remain,
  Than thus remember thee!
The all of thine that cannot die
Through dark and dread Eternity
  Returns again to me,
And more thy buried love endears
Than aught, except its living years.

SO WE'LL GO NO MORE A–ROVING

So we'll go no more a-roving
  So late into the night,
Though the heart be still as loving,
  And the moon be still as bright.

For the sword outwears its sheath,
  And the soul wears out the breast,
And the heart must pause to breathe,
  And Love itself have rest.

Though the night was made for loving,
  And the day returns too soon,
Yet we'll go no more a-roving
  By the light of the moon.

Robert Burns
1759-1796

BOBBY SHAFTO

Bobby Shafto's gone to sea,
With silver buckles at his knee,
When he'll come home he'll marry
    me,
    Pretty Bobby Shafto.

Bobby Shafto's fat and fair,
Combing down his yellow
    hair;
He's my love for evermair,
    Pretty Bobby Shafto!

YE BANKS AND BRAES O' BONNIE DOON

Ye banks and braes o' bonnie Doon,
    How can ye bloom sae fair?
How can ye chant, ye little birds,
    And I sae fu' o' care?

Thou'lt break my heart, thou
        bonnie bird
    That sings upon the bough;
Thou minds me o' the happy days
    When my fause Luve was true.

Thou'lt break my heart, thou
        bonnie bird

That sings beside thy mate;
For sae I sat, and sae I sang,
    And wist na' o' my fate.

Aft hae I roved by bonnie Doon
    To see the woodbine twine,
And ilka bird sang o' its love;
    And sae did I o' mine.

Wi' lightsome heart I pu'd a rose,
    Frae aff its thorny tree;
And my fause luver staw the rose,
    But left the thorn wi' me.

A RED, RED ROSE

O my luve's like a red, red rose
    That's newly sprung in June;
O my luve's like the melodie
    That's sweetly played in tune.

As fair art thou, my bonnie lass,
    So deep in luve am I;
And I will luve thee still, my dear,
    Till a' the seas gang dry.

Till a' the seas gang dry, my dear,
    And the rocks melt wi' the sun:
O I will luve thee still, my dear,
    While the sands o' life shall run:

And fare thee weel, my only luve!
    And fare thee weel a while!
And I will come again, my luve,
    Though it were ten thousand mile

OPEN THE DOOR TO ME, O
An Irish song altered by Burns

Oh, open the door, some pity to show,
    If love it may na be, O!
Tho' thou hast been false, I'll ever prove true —
    Oh, open the door to me, O!

Cauld is the blast upon my pale cheek,
    But caulder thy love for me, O:
The frost, that freezes the life at my heart,
    Is naught to my pains frae thee, O!

The wan moon sets behind the white wave,
    And time is setting with me, O:
False friends, false love, farewell! for mair
    I'll ne'er trouble them nor thee, O!

She has open'd the door, she has open'd it wide;
    She sees the pale corse on the plain, O,
"My true love!" she cried, and sank down by his side —
    Never to rise again, O!

FOR THE SAKE O' SOMEBODY

My heart is sair — I dare na
    tell,
My heart is sair for Somebody;
I could wake a winter night
    For the sake o' Somebody.
    O-hon! for Somebody!
    O-hey! for Somebody!
I could range the world around
    For the sake o' Somebody!

Ye Powers that smile on virtuous
    love,
    O sweetly smile on Somebody!
Frae ilka danger keep him free
    And send me safe my Somebody!
    O-hon! for Somebody!
    O-hey! for Somebody!
I wad do — what wad I not!
    For the sake o' Somebody!

JOHNNIE, COCK UP YOUR BEAVER

When first my brave Johnnie lad
    Came to this town,
He had a blue bonnet
    That wanted the crown;

But now he has gotten
    A hat and a feather, —
Hey, brave Johnnie lad,
    Cock up your beaver!

BONNIE LESLEY

O saw ye bonnie Lesley
    As she gaed o'er the Border?
She's gane, like Alexander,
    To spread her conquests farther.

To see her is to love her,
    And love but her for ever;
For Nature made her what she is,
    And ne'er made sic anither!

Thou art a queen, fair Lesley,
    Thy subjects we, before thee:
Thou art divine, fair Lesley,
    The hearts o' men adore thee.

The Deil he couldna scaith thee,
    Or aught that wad belang thee;
He'd look into thy bonnie face
    And say, "I canna wrang thee!"

The Powers aboon will tent thee,
    Misfortune sha'na steer thee:
Thou'rt like themsel' sae lovely,
    That ill they'll ne'er let near thee.

Return again, fair Lesley,
    Return to Caledonie!
That we may brag we hae a lass
    There's nane again sae bonnie!

John Clare
1793-1864

HONEY DEW FALLS FROM THE TREE

Honey dew falls from the tree
    Where my Julia walks with me
With her white arm held in mine;
    Luscious smells the eglantine;
In blushes sleeps the rosy briar
    Lit with tiny sparks of fire,
As the red hot sun goes down
    Like a ball to fire the town.

Glow worms fire the dark green grass
    Where my Julia's small feet pass,
And the kingcups rimm'd wi' dew,
    Gold, and white, and pearly blue,
Tap her on her evening track,
    Sandal shoes with ribbons black,

And woodbines with a crimson streak
  Nod against her bonnet peak.

The pearly west glowed golden charms
  While I held Julia in my arms,
Sweet Julia with the eye of dew,
  The heath-bell hasn't one so blue.
Her neck, the lily of the Vale
  Is not so fair and sweetly pale,
Her cheek — the rose cropt in the dew
  Is not so blushing in its hue.

I kissed — yes, I kissed her twice,
  While the little whistling mice
From the hedge ran in and out
  And bounced the silver dews about.
I leaned upon my Julia's cheek
  And could have rested there a week,
But we returned to our repose
  Just as the tall round moon arose.

TO HARRIETT

The tresses of thy glossy hair,
  As dark as is the raven's wing,
When flying in the sunny air
  Beneath the marble clouds of spring,
'Tis dark, nay black as starless night,
Or glossy beauty's softest light.

The thunder tempest near the sun
  Wears awful darkness on its breast;
Thy glossy hair as black, has none
  But softest hues where love could rest.
Thy neck and face were snowy fair,
But beauty was her coal-black hair.

Like darkness in a sunny sky
  It lay upon her neck in light,
As black clouds over sunbeams lie,
  Till her white skin seemed doubly white;
While the rich light in those black eyes
Outshone the sun in summer skies.

THE WINTER'S SPRING

The winter comes; I walk alone,
  I want no birds to sing;
To those who keep their hearts their own,
  The winter is the spring.
No flowers to please — no bees to hum —
The coming spring's already come.

I never want the Christmas rose
  To come before its time;
The seasons, each as God bestows,
  Are simple and sublime.
I love to see the snowstorm hing:
'Tis but the winter garb of spring.

I never want the grass to bloom:
  The snowstorm's best in white.
I love to see the tempest come
  And love its piercing light.
The dazzled eyes that love to cling
O'er snow-white meadows sees the spring.

I love the snow, the crumpling snow
  That hangs on everything,
It covers everything below
  Like white dove's brooding wing,
A landscape to the aching sight,
A vast expanse of dazzling light.

It is the foliage of the woods
  That winters bring — the dress,
White Easter of the year in bud,
  That makes the winter Spring.
The frost and snow his posies bring,
Nature's white spirits of the spring.

THE MAPLE HANGS ITS GREEN BEE FLOWERS

The maple hangs its green bee flowers
All pendant to the summer showers
Above the bluebell's drooping flowers

Where May time tinged the skies —
   My mountain pearl,
   My lovely girl,
   My dearest maid, arise!

The dewy hills, the mossy woods
The cultured fields, the meadow floods,
Green leaves expanding from spring buds
   'Neath skies all crisped and curled —
   My own clear girl,
   And bosom pearl,
   Come forth and charm the world!

Come forth, my own, my charming girl,
With rosy face and teeth of pearl,
Where green grass quakes and rivers swirl
   Through finest scenery —
   My hopes above,
   My fond first love,
   Come out and walk with me!

How purple light delights to dwell
Within the Canterbury Bell
Beside the wood-rail blooming well —
   My mountain maid, arise!
   These flowers we'll view
   In morning dew
   To gladden thy bright eyes.

A dewdrop on the kingcup lies,
While from its root the ground-lark flies,
The sun is mounting up the skies
   And gilds the stretching glade —
   Awake, and come
   Awhile from home,
   And be my own dear maid!

MEET ME IN THE PRIMROSE LANE

Meet me in the primrose lane,
   When moonlight lives above thee:
I'll kiss thy rosy face again
   And everlasting love thee.

Meet me where white clover grows
  In the dewy grass, love.
Meet me where white roses blows,
  And brooks run clear as glass, love.

In the evening I entreat thee
  When the dew is on the brere,
Down the lane of woodbines meet me
  While the brook is running clear,

While the round moon shines so brightly,
  And the diamond star o' even
O'er the lime trees shineth nightly,
  Making earth a lover's heaven.

Among the short white blossom'd clover,
  'Neath the ash tree's shadows there,
While the clouds the moon flies over,
  See me meet my angel fair —

Kiss goodnight — and ease my bosom.
  Rest my hope in slumbers then,
While the dewdrops pearls the blossom,
  And silence sleeps about the glen.

I LOVE THE BLUE VIOLET

I love the blue violet that creeps on the mossy bank,
And wood bell so purple wi' green leaves so glossy rank,
Where wild rabbits caper wi' many a tossy prank
  And show their white tails to the light.
I love the mossy bank of the green hazel bush,
I love the early song o' the brown missel-thrush,
And daisy decked molehills i' beds o' the tassle rush
  I' the middle of summer's delight.

But better than mossy banks twenty time over,
Or wind waving rush beds, the form of my lover,
Sweet Susan, as fair as the clumps o' white clover
  Ever feeding the songs o' the bee,
A' harmless as white legged lambs round the molehills,
Wi' her beauty and truth to o'erflowing the soul fills.
On Susan's white bosom a beauty spot mole kills
  And makes her more dear to me.

Her hair is as dark as the cloud i' the bright morn,
Her bosom's as white as the flower o' the white thorn,
Her lips are as red as the rosebud i' light born,
　And dear is young Susan to me.
I loved her and won her and doatingly love her,
And think her the loveliest all the world over,
And sweeter than rosebuds than red or white clover
　Is bonny young Susan to me.

I HID MY LOVE

I hid my love when young till I
Couldn't hear the buzzing of a fly;
I hid my love to my despite
Till I could not bear to look at light:
I dare not gaze upon her face
But left her memory in each place;
Where'er I saw a wild flower lie
I kissed and bade my love good-bye.

I met her in the greenest dells,
Where dewdrops pearl the wood bluebells;
The lost breeze kissed her bright blue eye,
The bee kissed and went singing by,
A sunbeam found a passage there,
A gold chain round her neck so fair;
As secret as the wild bee's song
She lay there all the summer long.

I hid my love in field and town
Till e'en the breeze would knock me down;
The bees seemed singing ballads o'er,
The fly's bass turned a lion's roar;
And even silence found a tongue,
To haunt me all the summer long;
The riddle nature could not prove
Was nothing else but secret love.

William Barnes

1801-1886

MY LOVE'S GUARDIAN ANGEL

As in the cool-aïr'd road I come by,
 — in the night,
Under the moon-clim'd height o' the sky,
 — in the night,
There by the lime's broad lim's as I did staÿ,
While in the aïr dark sheädes wer' at plaÿ
Up on the windor-glass that did keep
Lew vrom the wind, my true love asleep,
 — in the night.

While in the grey-wall'd height o' the tow'r,
 — in the night,
Sounded the midnight bell wi' the hour,
 — in the night,
There come a bright-heäir'd angel that shed
Light vrom her white robe's zilvery thread,
Wi' her vore-vinger held up to meäke
Silence around lest sleepers mid weäke,
 — in the night.

"Oh! then," I whisper'd, "do I behold
 — in the night,
Linda, my true-love, here in the cwold,
 — in the night?"
"No," she meäde answer, "you do misteäke:
She is asleep, 'tis I be aweäke;
I be her angel brightly a-drest,
Watchèn her slumber while she do rest,
 — in the night.

"Zee how the clear win's, brisk in the bough,
 — in the night,
While they do pass, don't smite on her brow,
 — in the night;
Zee how the cloud-sheädes naïseless do zweep

Over the house-top where she's asleep.
You, too, goo on, though times mid be near,
When you, wi' me, mid speäk to her ear
    — in the night."

THE WIND AT THE DOOR

As day did darken on the dewless grass
  There still wi' nwone a-come by me,
  To stäy a-while at hwome by me;
  Within the house, all dumb by me,
I zot me sad as the eventide did pass.

An' there a win'-blast shook the rattlèn door,
  An' seemed, as win' did mwone without,
  As if my Jeäne, alwone without,
  A-stannèn on the stone without,
Wer there a-come wi' happiness oonce mwore.

I went to door; an' out vrom trees above
  My head, upon the blast by me,
  Sweet blossoms wer a-cast by me,
  As if my love, a-past by me,
Did fling em down — a token ov her love.

"Sweet blossoms o' the tree where I do murn,"
  I thought, "if you did blow vor her,
  Vor apples that should grow vor her,
  A-vallèn down below vor her,
O then how happy I should zee you kern."

But no. Too soon I voun' my charm abroke.
  Noo comely soul in white like her —
  Noo soul a-steppèn light like her —
  An' nwone o' comely height like her —
Went by; but all my grief ageän awoke.

THE RWOSE IN THE DARK

In zummer, leäte at evenèn tide,
  I zot to spend a moonless hour
'Ithin the window, wi' the zide
  A-bound wi' rwoses out in flow'r,
Bezide the bow'r, vorsook o' birds,
An' listen'd to my true-love's words.

A-risèn to her comely height,
　　She push'd the swingèn ceäsement round;
And I could hear, beyond my zight,
　　The win'-blow'd beech-tree softly sound,
On higher ground, a-swayèn slow,
On drough my happy hour below.

An' tho' the darkness then did hide
　　The dewy rwose's blushèn bloom,
He still did cast sweet aïr inside
　　To Jeäne, a-chattèn in the room;
An' though the gloom did hide her feäce,
Her words did bind me to the pleäce.

An' there, while she, wi' runnèn tongue,
　　Did talk unzeen 'ithin the hall,
I thought her like the rwose that flung
　　His sweetness vrom his darken'd ball,
'Ithout the wall, an' sweet's the zight
Ov her bright feäce, by mornèn light.

George Darley
1795-1846

WINDS OF THE WEST, ARISE

Winds of the West, arise!
Hesperian balmiest airs, O waft back those sweet sighs
　　To her that breathes them from her own pure skies,
　　Dew-dropping, mixt with Dawn's engoldened dyes
　　　　O'er my unhappy eyes.
From primrose bed and willow bank where your moss-cradle lies,
O! from your rushy bowers to waft back her sweet sighs —
　　　　Winds of the West, arise.

　　　　Over the ocean blown,
Far-winnowing, let my soul be mingled with her own,
　　By sighs responsive to each other known!
　　Bird unto bird's twin breast has often flown
　　　　From distant zone to zone.
Why must the Darling of the Morn lament him here alone?
Shall not his fleeting spirit be mingled with her own,
　　　　Over the ocean blown!

O BLEST UNFABLED INCENSE TREE

O blest unfabled Incense Tree,
That burns in glorious Araby,
With red scent chalicing the air,
Till earth-life grow Elysian there!

Half buried to her flaming breast
In this bright tree, she makes her nest,
Hundred-sunn'd Phoenix! when she must
Crumble at length to hoary dust!

Her gorgeous death-bed! her rich pyre
Burnt up with aromatic fire!
Her urn, sight high from spoiler men!
Her birthplace when self-born again!

The mountainless green wilds among,
Here ends she her unechoing song!
With amber tears and odorous sighs
Mourn'd by the desert where she dies!

Laid like the young fawn mossily
In sun-green vales of Araby,
I woke hard by the Phoenix tree
That with shadeless boughs flamed over me,
And upward call'd for a dumb cry
With moonbroad orbs of wonder I
Beheld the immortal Bird on high
Glassing the great sun in her eye.
Stedfast she gazed upon his fire,
— Still her destroyer and her sire! —
As if to his her soul of flame
Had flown already whence it came;
Like those that sit and glare so still,
Intense with their death struggle, till
We touch, and curdle at their chill! —
But breathing yet while she doth burn,
The deathless Daughter of the sun!
Slowly to crimson embers turn
The beauties of the brightsome one.
O'er the broad nest her silver wings
Shook down their wasteful glitterings;
Her brinded neck high-arch'd in air
Like a small rainbow faded there;

But brighter glow'd her plumy crown
Mouldering to golden ashes down;
With fume of sweet woods, to the skies,
Pure as a Saint's adoring sighs,
Warm as a prayer in Paradise,
Her life-breath rose in sacrifice!
The while with shrill triumphant tone
Sounding aloud, aloft, alone,
Ceaseless her joyful deathwail she
Sang to departing Araby!

O, fast her amber blood doth flow
   From the heart-wounded Incense Tree,
Fast as earth's deep-embosom'd woe
   In silent rivulets to the sea!

Beauty may weep her fair first-born,
   Perchance in as resplendent tears,
Such golden dewdrops bow the corn
   When the stern sickleman appears:

But O! such perfume to a bower
   Never allured sweet-seeking bee,
As to sip fast that nectarous shower
   A thirstier minstrel drew in me!

Thomas Lovell Beddoes

1803-1849

From DREAM–PEDLARY

If there were dreams to sell,
   What would you buy?
Some cost a passing bell;
   Some a light sigh,
That shakes from Life's fresh crown
Only a roseleaf down.
If there were dreams to sell,
Merry and sad to tell,
And the crier rung the bell,
    What would you buy?

A cottage lone and still,
   With bowers nigh,
Shadowy, my woes to still,
   Until I die.
Such pearl from Life's fresh
    crown
Fain would I shake me down.
Where dreams to have at will,
This would best heal my ill,
    This would I buy.

EARLY FRAGMENTS

I'LL BE AS TRUE

I'll be as true to thee
As odour to the tube-rose, or as honey
Unto its name-sake flower.

HER KISSES

Her kisses are
Soft as a snow-tuft in the dewless cup
Of a redoubled rose, noiselessly falling
When heaven is brimful of starry night.

GRIEF–IN–IDLENESS

Bring me a rose
And I will fill its honey depth with tears
To the blushed brim.

From THE SECOND BROTHER

ACT II, SCENE 1

VALERIA.   I should not say
How thou art like the daisy in Noah's meadow,
On which the foremost drop of rain fell warm
And soft at evening: so the little flower
Wrapped up its leaves, and shut the treacherous water
Close to the golden welcome of its breast,
Delighting in the touch of that which led
The shower of oceans, in whose billowy drops
Tritons and lions of the sea were warring,
And sometimes ships on fire sunk in the blood
Of their own inmates; others were of ice,
And some had islands rooted in their waves,
Beasts on their rocks, and forest-powdering winds,
And showers tumbling on their tumbling self,
And every sea of every ruined star
Was but a drop in the world-melting flood.

Edgar Allan Poe
1809-1849

TO HELEN

Helen, thy beauty is to me
  Like those Nicèan barks of yore,
That gently, o'er a perfumed sea,
  The weary, way-worn wanderer bore
To his own native shore.

On desperate seas long wont to roam,
  Thy hyacinth hair, thy classic face,
Thy Naiad airs have brought me home
  To the glory that was Greece,
And the grandeur that was Rome.

Lo! in yon brilliant window niche,
  How statue-like I see thee stand,
  The agate lamp within thy hand!
Ah, Psyche, from the regions which
  Are Holy Land!

ROMANCE

Romance, who loves to nod and sing,
With drowsy head and folded wing,
Among the green leaves as they shake
Far down within some shadowy lake,
To me a painted paroquet
Hath been — a most familiar bird —
Taught me my alphabet to say —
To lisp my very earliest word
While in the wild wood I did lie,
A child — with a most knowing eye.

Of late, eternal condor years
So shake the very heaven on high
With tumult as they thunder by,
I have no time for idle cares
Through gazing on the unquiet sky;

And when an hour with calmer wings
Its down upon my spirit flings,
That little time with lyre and rhyme
To while away — forbidden things!
My heart would feel to be a crime
Unless it trembled with the strings.

Alfred, Lord Tennyson
1809-1892

The lyrics of this great poet have a singularly pure integrity, impetus (I do not mean speed) and outline.

The age in which he lived was not one which was helpful to his naturally rather conformative character. He was led, by a certain native timidity, into writing verse of a didactic nature which was utterly foreign to his nature.

But how wonderful an artist was he when freed from the heavy, tiresome exigencies of his age. Consider, for a moment, the flawless song *Now sleeps the crimson petal, now the white*. It is a miracle of technique.

Take the first verse. If we examine these wonderful beauties, we shall find that part of the beauty is due to the alliterative *w*'s and *f*'s, placed in such positions in the line as to alter the movement, and that part is due, also, to the dimming from the long *ee*'s of "sleep" to the soft shrinking *e* of "petal," and to the diminishing of the long sound of "winks" to that of the softer, shorter sound of "fin." Nor is this all; much of the perfection is due to the incredible skill with which Tennyson has interspersed one-syllable and two-syllable words, and (but this is hardly necessary to say) to his flawless sense of the varying vowel lengths.

Indeed, the whole poem is one of the miracles of our poetry, as far as texture is concerned.

In the marvelous lyric *Tears, Idle Tears,* part of the unrhymed and deep music of this flawless unrhymed poem, heavy and dark, as if weighted with dew, comes from the fact that in nearly all cases the lines end with a one-syllable word; or, where the line ends with a double-syllable word, the syllables are equal, as in "despair," "regret." In the one case where we find a treble-syllable word ending the line, "underworld," the first and third syllables are equal and balanced, so that the smooth quality of the poem is undisturbed.

Although this poem is unrhymed, the vowels of the end-words of the lines produce a most peculiar effect, with, to take an example, the assonance "fields" coming three lines after the poignant sound of "mean"

("mean" is slightly deeper than "fields," "fields" is a fraction longer than "mean"). There is, too, the lifting sound of "eyes," contrasted with the dark sound of "more" — "no more," the dark drone sound and key-note of the poem, ending each flawless verse. Again, the dark and despairing dissonances ending the second and the last lines of the first stanza, "despair" and "more," with the deeper drop to be found in the third stanza (deeper because the dissonances are placed more closely together) in the words "square" and "more"; these, compared with the assonance in the last stanza, an assonance deeply divided by the varying wavelengths of the words "death" and "regret," all produce an effect nothing short of magical.

THE LOTOS–EATERS

"Courage!" he said, and pointed toward the land,
"This mounting wave will roll us shoreward soon."
In the afternoon they came unto a land
In which it seemed always afternoon.
All round the coast the languid air did swoon,
Breathing like one that hath a weary dream.
Full-faced above the valley stood the moon;
And like a downward smoke, the slender stream
Along the cliff to fall and pause and fall did seem.

A land of streams! some, like a downward smoke,
Slow-dropping veils of thinnest lawn, did go;
And some thro' wavering lights and shadows broke,
Rolling a slumbrous sheet of foam below.
They saw the gleaming river seaward flow
From the inner land: far off, three mountain-tops,
Three silent pinnacles of aged snow,
Stood sunset-flush'd: and, dew'd with showery drops,
Up-clomb the shadowy pine above the woven copse.

The charmed sunset linger'd low adown
In the red West: thro' mountain clefts the dale
Was seen far inland, and the yellow down
Border'd with palm, and many a winding vale
And meadow, set with slender galingale;
A land where all things always seem'd the same!
And round about the keel with faces pale,
Dark faces pale against that rosy flame,
The mild-eyed melancholy Lotos-eaters came.

Branches they bore of that enchanted stem,
Laden with flower and fruit, whereof they gave
To each, but whoso did receive of them
And taste, to him the gushing of the wave
Far far away did seem to mourn and rave
On alien shores; and if his fellow spake,
His voice was thin, as voices from the grave;
And deep-asleep he seem'd, yet all awake,
And music in his ears his beating heart did make.

They sat them down upon the yellow sand,
Between the sun and moon upon the shore;
And sweet it was to dream of Fatherland,
Of child, and wife, and slave; but evermore
Most weary seem'd the sea, weary the oar,
Weary the wandering fields of barren foam.
Then some one said, "We will return no more;"
And all at once they sang, "Our island home
Is far beyond the wave; we will no longer roam."

CHORIC SONG

There is sweet music here that softer falls
Than petals from blown roses on the grass,
Or night-dews on still waters between walls
Of shadowy granite, in a gleaming pass;
Music that gentlier on the spirit lies,
Than tir'd eyelids upon tir'd eyes;
Music that brings sweet sleep down from the blissful skies.
Here are cool mosses deep,
And thro' the moss the ivies creep,
And in the stream the long-leaved flowers weep,
And from the craggy ledge the poppy hangs in sleep.

Why are we weigh'd upon with heaviness,
And utterly consumed with sharp distress,
While all things else have rest from weariness?
All things have rest: why should we toil alone,
We only toil, who are the first of things,
And make perpetual moan,
Still from one sorrow to another thrown:
Nor ever fold our wings,
And cease from wanderings,
Nor steep our brows in slumber's holy balm;
Nor harken what the inner spirit sings,
"There is no joy but calm!"
Why should we only toil, the roof and crown of things?

Lo! in the middle of the wood,
The folded leaf is woo'd from out the bud
With winds upon the branch, and there
Grows green and broad, and takes no care,
Sun-steep'd at noon, and in the moon
Nightly dew-fed; and turning yellow
Falls, and floats adown the air.
Lo! sweetened with the summer light,
The full-juiced apple, waxing over-mellow,
Drops in a silent autumn night.
All its allotted length of days,
The flower ripens in its place,
Ripens and fades, and falls, and hath no toil,
Fast-rooted in the fruitful soil.

Hateful is the dark-blue sky,
Vaulted o'er the dark-blue sea.
Death is the end of life; ah, why
Should life all labour be?
Let us alone. Time driveth onward fast,
And in a little while our lips are dumb.
Let us alone. What is it that will last?
All things are taken from us, and become
Portions and parcels of the dreadful Past.
Let us alone. What pleasure can we have
To war with evil? Is there any peace
In ever climbing up the climbing wave?
All things have rest, and ripen toward the grave
In silence; ripen, fall and cease:
Give us long rest or death, dark death, or dreamful ease.

How sweet it were, hearing the downward stream,
With half-shut eyes ever to seem
Falling asleep in a half-dream!
To dream and dream, like yonder amber light,
Which will not leave the myrrh-bush on the height;
To hear each other's whisper'd speech;
Eating the Lotos day by day,
To watch the crisping ripples on the beach,
And tender curving lines of creamy spray;
To lend our hearts and spirits wholly
To the influence of mild-minded melancholy;
To muse and brood and live again in memory,
With those old faces of our infancy
Heap'd over with a mound of grass,
Two handfuls of white dust, shut in an urn of brass!

Dear is the memory of our wedded lives,
And dear the last embraces of our wives
And their warm tears: but all hath suffer'd change:
For surely now our household hearths are cold:
Our sons inherit us: our looks are strange:
And we should come like ghosts to trouble joy.
Or else the island princes over-bold
Have eat our substance, and the minstrel sings
Before them of the ten years' war in Troy,
And our great deeds, as half-forgotten things.
Is there confusion in the little isle?
Let what is broken so remain.
The Gods are hard to reconcile:
'Tis hard to settle order once again.
There *is* confusion worse than death,
Trouble on trouble, pain on pain,
Long labour unto aged breath,
Sore task to hearts worn out by many wars
And eyes grown dim with gazing on the pilot-stars.

But, propt on beds of amaranth and moly,
How sweet (while warm airs lull us, blowing lowly)
With half-dropt eyelid still,
Beneath a heaven dark and holy,
To watch the long bright river drawing slowly
His waters from the purple hill —
To hear the dewy echoes calling
From cave to cave thro' the thick-twined vine —
To watch the emerald-colour'd water falling
Thro many a wov'n acanthus-wreath divine!
Only to hear and see the far-off sparkling brine,
Only to hear were sweet, stretch'd out beneath the pine.

The Lotos blooms below the barren peak:
The Lotos blows by every winding creek:
All day the wind breathes low with mellower tone:
Thro' every hollow cave and alley lone
Round and round the spicy downs the yellow Lotos-dust is blown.
We have had enough of action, and of motion we,
Roll'd to starboard, roll'd to larboard, when the surge was seething free,
Where the wallowing monster spouted his foam-fountains in the sea.
Let us swear an oath, and keep it with an equal mind,
In the hollow Lotos-land to live and lie reclined
On the hills like Gods together, careless of mankind.
For they lie beside their nectar, and the bolts are hurl'd
Far below them in the valleys, and the clouds are lightly curl'd

Round their golden houses, girdled with the gleaming world:
Where they smile in secret, looking over wasted lands,
Blight and famine, plague and earthquake, roaring deeps and fiery sands,
Clanging fights, and flaming towns, and sinking ships, and praying hands.
But they smile, they find a music centred in a doleful song
Steaming up, a lamentation and an ancient tale of wrong,
Like a tale of little meaning tho' the words are strong;
Chanted from an ill-used race of men that cleave the soil,
Sow the seed, and reap the harvest with enduring toil,
Storing yearly little dues of wheat, and wine and oil;
Till they perish and they suffer — some, 'tis whisper'd — down in hell
Suffer endless anguish, others in Elysian valleys dwell,
Resting weary limbs at last on beds of asphodel.
Surely, surely, slumber is more sweet than toil, the shore
Than labor in the deep mid-ocean, wind and wave and oar;
Oh rest ye, brother mariners, we will not wander more.

From MAUD

A VOICE BY THE CEDAR TREE

A A voice by the cedar tree
B In the meadow under the Hall!
A She is singing an air that is known to me,
C A passionate ballad gallant and gay,
B A martial song like a trumpet's call!
D Singing alone in the morning of life,
C In the happy morning of life and of May,
C Singing of men that in battle array,
E Ready in heart and ready in hand,
D March with banner and bugle and fife
E To the death, for their native land.

Maud with her exquisite face,
And wild voice pealing up to the sunny sky,
And feet like sunny gems on an English green,
Maud in the light of her youth and her grace,
Singing of Death, and of Honour that cannot die,
Till I well could weep for a time so sordid and mean,
And myself so languid and base.

Silence, beautiful voice!
Be still, for you only trouble the mind
With a joy in which I cannot rejoice,
A glory I shall not find.

Still! I will hear you no more,
For your sweetness hardly leaves me a choice
But to move to the meadow and fall before
Her feet on the meadow grass, and adore,
Not her, who is neither courtly nor kind,
Not her, not her, but a voice.

DEAD, LONG DEAD

Dead, long dead,
Long dead!
And my heart is a handful of dust,
And the wheels go over my head,
And my bones are shaken with pain,
For into a shallow grave they are thrust,
Only a yard beneath the street,
And the hoofs of the horses beat, beat,
The hoofs of the horses beat,
Beat into my scalp and my brain,
With never an end to the stream of passing feet,
Driving, hurrying, marrying, burying,
Clamour and rumble, and ringing and clatter,
And here beneath it is all as bad,
For I thought the dead had peace, but it is not so;
To have no peace in the grave, is that not sad?
But up and down and to and fro,
Ever about me the dead men go;
And then to hear a dead man chatter
Is enough to drive one mad.

Wretchedest age, since Time began,
They cannot even bury a man;
And tho' we paid our tithes in the days that are gone,
Not a bell was rung, not a prayer was read;
It is that which makes us loud in the world of the dead;
There is none that does his work, not one;
A touch of their office might have sufficed,
But the churchmen fain would kill their church,
As the churches have kill'd their Christ.

See, there is one of us sobbing,
No limit to his distress;
And another, a lord of all things, praying
To his own great self, as I guess;
And another, a statesman there, betraying
His party-secret, fool, to the press;

And yonder a vile physician, blabbing
The case of his patient — all for what?
To tickle the maggot born in an empty head,
And wheedle a world that loves him not,
For it is but a world of the dead.

Nothing but idiot gabble!
For the prophecy given of old
And then not understood,
Has come to pass as foretold;
Not let any man think for the public good,
But babble, merely for babble.
For I never whisper'd a private affair
Within the hearing of cat or mouse,
No, not to myself in the closet alone,
But I heard it shouted at once from the top of the house;
Everything came to be known.
Who told *him* we were there?

Not that gray old wolf, for he came not back
From the wilderness, full of wolves, where he used to lie;
He has gather'd the bones for his o'ergrown whelp to crack;
Crack them now for yourself, and howl, and die.

Prophet, curse me the blabbing lip,
And curse me the British vermin, the rat;
I know not whether he came in the Hanover ship,
But I know that he lies and listens mute
In an ancient mansion's crannies and holes:
Arsenic, arsenic, sure, would do it,
Except that now we poison our babes, poor souls!
It is all used up for that.

Tell him now: she is standing here at my head;
Not beautiful now, not even kind;
He may take her now; for she never speaks her mind,
But is ever the one thing silent here.
She is not *of* us, as I divine;
She comes from another stiller world of the dead,
Stiller, not fairer than mine.

But I know where a garden grows,
Fairer than aught in the world beside,
All made up of the lily and rose
That blow by night, when the season is good,

To the sound of dancing music and flutes:
It is only flowers, they had no fruits,
And I almost fear they are not roses, but blood;
For the keeper was one, so full of pride,
He linkt a dead man there to a spectral bride;
For he, if he had not been a Sultan of brutes,
Would he have that hole in his side?

But what will the old man say?
He laid a cruel snare in a pit
To catch a friend of mine one stormy day;
Yet now I could even weep to think of it;
For what will the old man say
When he comes to the second corpse in the pit?

Friend, to be struck by the public foe,
Then to strike him and lay him low,
That were a public merit, far,
Whatever the Quaker holds, from sin;
But the red life spilt for a private blow —
I swear to you, lawful and lawless war
Are scarcely even akin.

O me, why have they not buried me deep enough?
Is it kind to have made me a grave so rough?
Me, that was never a quiet sleeper?
Maybe still I am but half-dead;
Then I cannot be wholly dumb;
I will cry to the steps above my head
And somebody, surely, some kind heart will come
To bury me, bury me
Deeper, ever so little deeper.

O THAT 'TWERE POSSIBLE

O that 'twere possible
After long grief and pain
To find the arms of my true love
Round me once again!

When I was wont to meet her
In the silent woody places
By the home that gave me birth,
We stood tranced in long embraces
Mixt with kisses sweeter sweeter
Than anything on earth.

A shadow flits before me,
Not thou, but like to thee:
Ah Christ, that it were possible
For one short hour to see
The souls we loved, that they might tell us
What and where they be.

SONG: A SPIRIT HAUNTS THE YEAR'S LAST HOURS

A spirit haunts the year's last hours
Dwelling amid these yellowing bowers:
    To himself he talks;
For at eventide, listening earnestly,
At his work you may hear him sob and sigh
    In the walks;
    Earthward he boweth the heavy stalks
Of the mouldering flowers:
  Heavily hangs the broad sunflower
    Over its grave i' the earth so chilly;
  Heavily hangs the hollyhock,
    Heavily hangs the tiger-lily.

The air is damp, and hush'd, and close,
As a sick man's room when he taketh repose
    An hour before death;
My very heart faints and my whole soul grieves
At the moist rich smell of the rotting leaves,
    And the breath
    Of the fading edges of box beneath,
And the year's last rose.
  Heavily hangs the broad sunflower
    Over its grave i' the earth so chilly;
  Heavily hangs the hollyhock,
    Heavily hangs the tiger-lily.

CLARIBEL
A Melody

    Where Claribel low-lieth
      The breezes pause and die,
        Letting the rose-leaves fall:
    But the solemn oak-tree sigheth,
      Thick-leaved, ambrosial,
      With an ancient melody
      Of an inward agony,
    Where Claribel low-lieth.

'At eve the beetle boometh
  Athwart the thickest lone:
At noon the wild bee hummeth
  About the moss'd headstone:
At midnight the moon cometh,
  And looketh down alone.
Her song the lintwhite swelleth,
The clear-voiced mavis dwelleth,
  The callow throstle lispeth,
The slumbrous wave outwelleth,
  The babbling runnel crispeth,
The hollow grot replieth
Where Claribel low-lieth.

From THE PRINCESS

TEARS, IDLE TEARS

Tears, idle tears, I know not what they mean,
Tears from the depth of some divine despair
Rise in the heart, and gather to the eyes,
In looking on the happy Autumn-fields,
And thinking of the days that are no more.

Fresh as the first beam glittering on a sail,
That brings our friends up from the underworld,
Sad as the last which reddens over one
That sinks with all we love below the verge;
So sad, so fresh, the days that are no more.

Ah, sad and strange as in dark summer dawns
The earliest pipe of half-awaken'd birds
To dying ears, when unto dying eyes
The casement slowly grows a glimmering square;
So sad, so strange, the days that are no more.

Dear as remembered kisses after death,
And sweet as those by hopeless fancy feign'd
On lips that are for others; deep as love,
Deep as first love, and wild with all regret;
O Death in Life, the days that are no more.

NOW SLEEPS THE CRIMSON PETAL

Now sleeps the crimson petal, now the white;
Nor waves the cypress in the palace walk;
Nor winks the gold fin in the porphyry font:
The fire-fly wakens: waken thou with me.

Now droops the milkwhite peacock like a ghost,
And like a ghost she glimmers on to me.

Now lies the Earth all Danaë to the stars,
And all thy heart lies open unto me.

Now slides the silent meteor on, and leaves
A shining furrow, as thy thoughts in me.

Now folds the lily all her sweetness up,
And slips into the bosom of the lake:
So fold thyself, my dearest, thou, and slip
Into my bosom and be lost in me.

O SWALLOW, SWALLOW, FLYING, FLYING SOUTH

O Swallow, Swallow, flying, flying South,
Fly to her, and fall upon her gilded eaves,
And tell her, tell her, what I tell to thee.

O tell her, Swallow, thou that knowest each,
That bright and fierce and fickle is the South,
And dark and true and tender is the North.

O Swallow, Swallow, if I could follow, and light
Upon her lattice, I would pipe and trill,
And cheep and twitter twenty million loves.

O were I thou that she might take me in,
And lay me on her bosom, and her heart
Would rock the snowy cradle till I died.

Why lingereth she to clothe her heart with love,
Delaying as the tender ash delays
To clothe herself, when all the woods are green?

O tell her, Swallow, that thy brood is flown:
Say to her, I do but wanton in the South,
But in the North long since my nest is made.

O tell her, brief is life but love is long,
And brief the sun of summer in the North,
And brief the moon of beauty in the South.

O Swallow, flying from the golden woods,
Fly to her, and pipe and woo her, and make her mine,
And tell her, tell her, that I follow thee.

COME DOWN, O MAID

Come down, O maid, from yonder mountain height:
What pleasure lives in height (the shepherd sang)
In height and cold, the splendour of the hills?
But cease to move so near the Heavens, and cease
To glide a sunbeam by the blasted Pine,
To sit a star upon the sparkling spire;
And come, for Love is of the valley, come,
For Love is of the valley, come thou down
And find him; by the happy threshold, he,
Or hand in hand with Plenty in the maize,
Or red with spirted purple of the vats,
Or foxlike in the vine; nor cares to walk
With Death and Morning on the silver horns,
Nor wilt thou snare him in the white ravine,
Nor find him dropt upon the firths of ice,
That huddling slant in furrow-cloven falls
To roll the torrent out of dusky doors:
But follow; let the torrent dance thee down
To find him in the valley; let the wild
Lean-headed Eagles yelp alone, and leave
The monstrous ledges there to slope, and spill
Their thousand wreaths of dangling water-smoke,
That like a broken purpose waste in air:
So waste not thou; but come; for all the vales
Await thee; azure pillars of the hearth
Arise to thee; the children call, and I
Thy shepherd pipe, and sweet is every sound,
Sweeter thy voice, but every sound is sweet;
Myriads of rivulets hurrying thro' the lawn,
The moan of doves in immemorial elms,
And murmuring of innumerable bees.

ASK ME NO MORE

Ask me no more: the moon may draw the sea;
   The cloud may stoop from heaven and take the shape
   With fold to fold, of mountain or of cape;
But O too fond, when have I answer'd thee?
     Ask me no more.

Ask me no more: what answer should I give?
   I love not hollow cheek or faded eye:
   Yet, O my friend, I will not have thee die!
Ask me no more, lest I should bid thee live;
     Ask me no more.

Ask me no more: thy fate and mine are seal'd:
  I strove against the stream and all in vain:
  Let the great river take me to the main:
No more, dear love, for at a touch I yield;
      Ask me no more.

THE SPLENDOUR FALLS ON CASTLE WALLS

    The splendour falls on castle walls
      And snowy summits old in story:
    The long light shakes across the lakes,
      And the wild cataract leaps in glory.
Blow, bugle, blow, set the wild echoes flying,
Blow, bugle; answer, echoes, dying, dying, dying.

    O hark, O hear! how thin and clear,
      And thinner, clearer, farther going!
    O sweet and far from cliff and scar
      The horns of Elfland faintly blowing!
Blow, let us hear the purple glens replying:
Blow, bugle; answer, echoes, dying, dying, dying.

    O love, they die in yon rich sky,
      They faint on hill or field or river:
    Our echoes roll from soul to soul,
      And grow for ever and for ever.
Blow, bugle, blow, set the wild echoes flying,
And answer, echoes, answer, dying, dying, dying.

AS THRO' THE LAND AT EVE WE WENT

As thro' the land at eve we went,
  And pluck'd the ripen'd ears,
We fell out, my wife and I,
O we fell out I know not why,
  And kiss'd again with tears.
And blessings on the falling out
  That all the more endears,
When we fall out with those we love
  And kiss again with tears!
For when we came where lies the child
  We lost in other years,
There above the little grave,
O there above the little grave,
  We kiss'd again with tears.

From IN MEMORIAM

L

Be near me when my light is low,
  When the blood creeps, and the nerves prick
  And tingle; and the heart is sick,
And all the wheels of Being slow.

Be near me when the sensuous frame
   Is rack'd with pangs that conquer trust;
   And Time, a maniac scattering dust,
And Life, a Fury slinging flame.

Be near me when my faith is dry,
   And men the flies of latter spring,
   That lay their eggs, and sting and sing
And weave their petty cells and die.

Be near me when I fade away,
   To point the term of human strife,
   And on the low dark verge of life
The twilight of eternal day.

LI

Do we indeed desire the dead
   Should still be near us at our side?
   Is there no baseness we would hide?
No inner vileness that we dread?

Shall he for whose applause I strove,
   I had such reverence for his blame,
   See with clear eye some hidden shame
And I be lessen'd in his love?

I wrong the grave with fears untrue:
   Shall love be blamed for want of faith?
   There must be wisdom with great Death:
The dead shall look me thro' and thro'.

Be near us when we climb or fall:
   Ye watch, like God, the rolling hours
   With larger other eyes than ours,
To make allowance for us all.

LIV

Oh yet we trust that somehow good
   Will be the final goal of ill,
   To pangs of nature, sins of will,
Defects of doubt, and taints of blood;

That nothing walks with aimless feet;
   That not one life shall be destroy'd,
   Or cast as rubbish to the void,
When God hath made the pile complete;

That not a worm is cloven in vain;
  That not a moth with vain desire
  Is shrivell'd in a fruitless fire,
Or but subserves another's gain.

Behold, we know not anything;
  I can but trust that good shall fall
  At last — far off — at last, to all,
And every winter change to spring.

So runs my dream: but what am I?
  An infant crying in the night:
  An infant crying for the light:
And with no language but a cry.

LV

The wish, that of the living whole
  No life may fail beyond the grave,
  Derives it not from what we have
The likest God within the soul?

Are God and Nature then at strife,
  That Nature lends such evil dreams?
  So careful of the type she seems,
So careless of the single life;

That I, considering everywhere
  Her secret meaning in her deeds,
  And finding that of fifty seeds
She often brings but one to bear,

I falter where I firmly trod,
  And falling with my weight of cares
  Upon the great world's altar-stairs
That slope thro' darkness up to God,

I stretch lame hands of faith, and grope,
  And gather dust and chaff, and call
  To what I feel is Lord of all,
And faintly trust the larger hope.

melancholy

Ralph Waldo Emerson
1803-1882

HEROISM

Ruby wine is drunk by knaves,
Sugar spends to fatten slaves,
Rose and vine-leaf deck buffoons;
Thunder-clouds are Jove's festoons,
Drooping oft in wreaths of dread,
Lightning-knotted round his head;
The hero is not fed on sweets,
Daily his own heart he eats;
Chambers of the great are jails,
And head-winds right for royal sails.

BERRYING

"May be true what I had heard, —
Earth's a howling wilderness,
Truculent with fraud and force,"
Said I, strolling through the pastures,
And along the river-side.
Caught among the blackberry vines,
Feeding on the Ethiops sweet,
Pleasant fancies overtook me.
I said, "What influence me preferred,
Elect, to dreams thus beautiful?"
The vines replied, "And didst thou deem
No wisdom from our berries went?"

NEMESIS

Already blushes in thy cheek
The bosom-thought which thou must speak;
The bird, how far it haply roam
By cloud or isle, is flying home;
The maiden fears, and fearing runs
Into the charmed snare she shuns;
And every man, in love or pride,
Of his fate is never wide.

Will a woman's fan the ocean smooth?
Or prayers the stony Parcae soothe,
Or coax the thunder from its mark?
Or tapers light the chaos dark?
In spite of Virtue and the Muse,
Nemesis will have her dues,
And all our struggles and our toils
Tighter wind the giant coils.

Herman Melville

1819-1891

THE WHALE

The ribs and terrors in the whale
  Arched over me a dismal gloom,
While all God's sun-lit waves rolled by,
  And left me deepening down to doom.

I saw the opening maw of hell,
  With endless pains and sorrows there;
Which none but they that feel can tell —
  Oh, I was plunging to despair.

In black distress, I called my God,
  When I could scarce believe Him mine,
He bowed His ear to my complaints —
  No more the whale did me confine.

With speed He flew to my relief
  As on a radiant dolphin borne;
Awful, yet bright, as lightning shone
  The face of my Deliverer God.

My song for ever shall record
  That terrible, that joyful hour;
I give the glory to my God,
  His all the mercy and the power.

THE BERG
A Dream

I saw a ship of martial build
(Her standards set, her brave apparel on)
Directed as by madness mere
Against a solid iceberg steer,
Nor budge it, though the infatuate ship went down.
The impact made huge ice-cubes fall
Sullen, in tons that crashed the deck;
But that one avalanche was all —
No other movement save the foundering wreck.

Along the spurs of ridges pale,
Not any slenderest shaft and frail,
A prism over glass-green gorges lone,
Toppled; nor lace of traceries fine,
Nor pendant drops in grot or mine
Were jarred, when the stunned ship went down,

Nor sole the gulls in cloud that wheeled
Circling one snow-flanked peak afar,
But nearer fowl the floes that skimmed
And crystal beaches, felt no jar.
No thrill transmitted stirred the lock
Of jack-straw needle-ice at base;
Towers undermined by waves — the block
Atilt impending — kept their place.
Seals, dozing sleek on sliddery ledges
Slipt never, when by loftier edges
Through very inertia overthrown,
The impetuous ship in bafflement went down.

Hard Berg (methought), so cold, so vast,
With mortal damps self-overcast;
Exhaling still thy dankish breath —
Adrift dissolving, bound for death;
Though lumpish thou, a lumbering one —
A lumbering lubbard loitering slow,
Impingers rue thee and go down,
Sounding thy precipice below
Nor stir the slimy slug that sprawls
Along thy dead indifference * of walls.

* Dead indifference: Dense stolidity. — AUTHOR'S NOTE

BILLY IN THE DARBIES

Good of the Chaplain to enter Lone Bay
And down on his marrow-bones here and pray
For the likes just o' me, Billy Budd. — But look:
Through the port comes the moon-shine astray!
It tips the guard's cutlass and silvers this nook;
But 'twill die in the dawning of Billy's last day.
A jewel-block they'll make of me to-morrow,
Pendant pearl from the yard-arm-end
Like the ear-drop I gave to Bristol-Molly —
Oh, 'tis me, not the sentence, they'll suspend.
Ay, ay, all is up; and I must up too
Early in the morning, aloft from alow.
On an empty stomach, now, never it would do.
They'll give me a nibble — bit o' biscuit ere I go.
Sure, a mess mate will reach me the last parting cup;
But turning heads away from the hoist and the belay,
Heaven knows who will have the running of me up!
No pipe to those halyards — but aren't it all sham?
A blur's in my eye; it is dreaming that I am.
A hatchet to my panzer? all adrift to go?
The drum roll to grog, and Billy never know?
But Donald he has promised to stand by the plank;
So I'll shake a friendly hand ere I sink.
But — no! It is dead then I'll be, come to think.
I remember Taff the Welshman when he sank.
And his cheek it was like the budding pink.
But me, they'll lash me in hammock, drop me deep
Fathoms down, fathoms down, how I'll dream fast asleep.
I feel it stealing now. Sentry, are you there?
Just ease these darbies at the wrist,
And roll me over fair.
I am sleepy, and the oozy weeds about me twist.

Edward FitzGerald
1809-1883

From RUBÁIYÁT OF OMAR KHAYYÁM OF NAISHÁPÚR

Wake! For the Sun, who scatter'd into flight
The Stars before him from the Field of Night,
   Drives Night along with them from Heav'n, and strikes
The Sultán's Turret with a Shaft of Light.

Before the phantom of False morning died,
Methought a Voice within the Tavern cried,
   "When all the Temple is prepared within,
Why nods the drowsy Worshipper outside?"

And, as the Cock crew, those who stood before
The Tavern shouted — "Open then the Door!
   You know how little while we have to stay,
And, once departed, may return no more."

Now the New Year reviving old Desires,
The thoughtful Soul to Solitude retires,
   Where the WHITE HAND OF MOSES on the Bough
Puts out, and Jesus from the Ground suspires.

Iram indeed is gone with all his Rose,
And Jamshýd's Sev'n-ringed Cup where no one knows;
   But still a Ruby kindles in the Vine,
And many a Garden by the Water blows.

And David's lips are lockt; but in divine
High-piping Péhleví, with "Wine! Wine! Wine!
   Red Wine!"—the Nightingale cries to the Rose
That sallow cheek of hers to incarnadine.

Come, fill the Cup, and in the fire of Spring
Your Winter-garment of Repentance fling:
   The Bird of Time has but a little way
To flutter—and the Bird is on the Wing.

Whether at Naishápúr or Babylon,
Whether the Cup with sweet or bitter run,
   The Wine of Life keeps oozing drop by drop,
The Leaves of Life keep falling one by one.

Each Morn a thousand Roses brings, you say;
Yes, but where leaves the Rose of Yesterday?
   And this first Summer month that brings the Rose
Shall take Jamshýd and Kaikobád away.

Well, let it take them! What have we to do
With Kaikobád the Great, or Kaikhosrú?
   Let Zál and Rustum bluster as they will,
Or Hátim call to Supper — heed not you.

With me along the strip of Herbage strown
That just divides the desert from the sown,
   Where name of Slave and Sultán is forgot —
And Peace to Mahmúd on his golden Throne!

A Book of Verses underneath the Bough,
A Jug of Wine, a Loaf of Bread — and Thou
   Beside me singing in the Wilderness —
Oh, Wilderness were Paradise enow!

Some for the Glories of This World; and some
Sigh for the Prophet's Paradise to come;
   Ah, take the Cash, and let the Credit go,
Nor heed the rumble of a distant Drum!

Look to the blowing Rose about us — "Lo,
Laughing," she says, "into the world I blow,
   At once the silken tassel of my Purse
Tear, and its Treasure on the Garden throw."

And those who husbanded the Golden grain,
And those who flung it to the winds like Rain,
   Alike to no such aureate Earth are turn'd
As, buried once, Men want dug up again.

The Worldly Hope men set their Hearts upon
Turns Ashes — or it prospers; and anon,
   Like Snow upon the Desert's dusty Face,
Lighting a little hour or two — is gone.

Think, in this batter'd Caravanserai
Whose Portals are alternate Night and Day,
   How Sultán after Sultán with his Pomp
Abode his destined Hour, and went his way.

They say the Lion and the Lizard keep
The Courts where Jamshýd gloried and drank deep:
    And Bahrám, that great Hunter — the Wild Ass
Stamps o'er his Head, but cannot break his Sleep.

I sometimes think that never blows so red
The Rose as where some buried Caesar bled;
    That every Hyacinth the Garden wears
Dropt in her lap from some once lovely Head.

And this reviving Herb whose tender Green
Fledges the River-Lip on which we lean —
    Ah, lean upon it lightly! for who knows
From what once lovely Lip it springs unseen!

Ah, my Beloved, fill the Cup that clears
TO-DAY of past Regrets and Future Fears:
    To-morrow! Why, To-morrow I may be
Myself with Yesterday's Sev'n thousand Years.

For some we loved, the loveliest and the best
That from his Vintage rolling Time hath prest,
    Have drunk their Cup a Round or two before,
And one by one crept silently to rest.

And we, that now make merry in the Room
They left, and Summer dresses in new bloom,
    Ourselves must we beneath the Couch of Earth
Descend — ourselves to make a Couch — for whom?

Ah, make the most of what we yet may spend,
Before we too into the Dust descend;
    Dust into Dust, and under Dust to lie
Sans Wine, sans Song, sans Singer, and — sans End!

Alike for those who for TO-DAY prepare,
And those that after some TO-MORROW stare,
    A Muezzín from the Tower of Darkness cries,
"Fools! your Reward is neither Here nor There!"

Why, all the Saints and Sages who discuss'd
Of the Two Worlds so wisely — they are thrust
    Like foolish Prophets forth; their Words to Scorn
Are scatter'd, and their Mouths are stopt with Dust.

Myself when young did eagerly frequent
Doctor and Saint, and heard great argument
   About it and about: but evermore
Came out by the same door where in I went.

With them the seed of Wisdom did I sow,
And with mine own hand wrought to make it grow;
   And this was all the Harvest that I reap'd —
"I came like Water, and like Wind I go."

Into this Universe, and *Why* not knowing,
Nor *Whence,* like Water willy-nilly flowing;
   And out of it, as Wind along the Waste,
I know not *Whither,* willy-nilly blowing.

What, without asking, hither hurried *Whence?*
And, without asking, *Whither* hurried hence!
   Oh, many a Cup of this forbidden Wine
Must drown the memory of that insolence!

Up from Earth's Centre through the Seventh Gate
I rose, and on the Throne of Saturn sate;
   And many a Knot unravel'd by the Road;
But not the Master-knot of Human Fate.

There was the Door to which I found no Key:
There was the Veil through which I might not see:
   Some little talk awhile of ME AND THEE
There was — and then no more of THEE AND ME. . . .

Ah, with the Grape my fading Life provide,
And wash the Body whence the Life has died,
   And lay me, shrouded in the living Leaf,
By some not unfrequented Garden-side.

That ev'n my buried Ashes such a snare
Of Vintage shall fling up into the Air
   As not a True-believer passing by
But shall be overtaken unaware.

Indeed the Idols I have loved so long
Have done my credit in this World much wrong:
   Have drown'd my Glory in a shallow Cup
And sold my Reputation for a Song.

Indeed, indeed, Repentance oft before
I swore — but was I sober when I swore?
    And then and then came Spring, and Rose-in-hand
My thread-bare Penitence apieces tore.

And much as Wine has play'd the Infidel,
And robbed me of my Robe of Honour — Well,
    I wonder often what the Vintners buy
One half so precious as the stuff they sell.

Alas, that Spring should vanish with the Rose!
That Youth's sweet-scented manuscript should close!
    The Nightingale that in the branches sang,
Ah whence, and whither flown again, who knows.

Would but the Desert of the Fountain yield
One glimpse — if dimly, yet indeed, reveal'd,
    To which the fainting Traveller might spring,
As springs the trampled herbage of the field!

Would but some winged Angel ere too late
Arrest the yet unfolded Roll of Fate,
    And make the stern Recorder otherwise
Enregister, or quite obliterate!

Ah Love! could you and I with Him conspire
To grasp this sorry Scheme of Things entire,
    Would not we shatter it to bits — and then
Re-mould it nearer to the Heart's Desire!

.   .   .   .   .   .

Yon rising Moon that looks for us again —
How oft hereafter will she wax and wane;
    How oft hereafter rising look for us
Through this same Garden — and for *one* in vain!

And when like her, oh Sákí, you shall pass
Among the Guests Star-scatter'd on the Grass,
    And in your joyous errand reach the spot
Where I made One — turn down an empty Glass!

TAMÁM

Dante Gabriel Rossetti
1828-1882

LOVE–LILY

Between the hands, between the brows,
  Between the lips of Love-Lily,
A spirit is born whose birth endows
  My blood with fire to burn through me;
Who breathes upon my gazing eyes,
  Who laughs and murmurs in mine ear,
At whose least touch my colour flies,
  And whom my life grows faint to hear.

Within the voice, within the heart,
  Within the mind of Love-Lily,
A spirit is born who lifts apart
  His tremulous wings and looks at me;
Who on my mouth his finger lays,
  And shows, while whispering lutes confer,
That Eden of Love's watered ways
  Whose winds and spirits worship her.

Brows, hands, and lips, heart, mind, and voice,
  Kisses and words of Love-Lily, —
Oh! bid me with your joy rejoice
  Till riotous longing rest in me!
Ah! let not hope be still distraught,
  But find in her its gracious goal,
Whose speech Truth knows not from her thought
  Nor Love her body from her soul.

A NEW YEAR'S BURDEN

Along the grass sweet airs are blown
  Our way this day in Spring.
Of all the songs that we have known
  Now which one shall we sing?
    Not that, my love, ah no! —
    Not this, my love? why, so! —
Yet both were ours, but hours will come and go.

The grove is all a pale frail mist,
   The new year sucks the sun.
Of all the kisses that we kissed
   Now which shall be the one?
     Not that, my love, ah no! —
     Not this, my love? — heigh-ho
For all the sweets that all the winds can blow!

The branches cross above our eyes,
   The skies are in a net:
And what's the thing beneath the skies
   We two would most forget?
     Not birth, my love, no, no, —
     Not death, my love, no, no, —
The love once ours, but ours long hours ago.

THE WOODSPURGE

The wind flapped loose, the wind was still,
Shaken out dead from tree and hill:
I had walked on at the wind's will, —
I sat now, for the wind was still.

Between my knees my forehead was, —
My lips, drawn in, said not Alas!
My hair was over in the grass,
My naked ears heard the day pass.

My eyes, wide open, had the run
Of some ten weeds to fix upon;
Among those few, out of the sun,
The woodspurge flowered, three cups in one.

From perfect grief there need not be
Wisdom or even memory:
One thing then learnt remains to me, —
The woodspurge has a cup of three.

Christina Rossetti
1830-1894

GOBLIN MARKET

Morning and evening
Maids heard the goblins cry:
"Come buy our orchard fruits,
Come buy, come buy:
Apples and quinces,
Lemons and oranges,
Plump unpecked cherries,
Melons and raspberries,
Bloom-down-cheeked peaches,
Swart-headed mulberries,
Wild free-born cranberries,
Crab-apples, dewberries,
Pine-apples, blackberries,
Apricots, strawberries; —
All ripe together
In summer weather, —
Morns that pass by,
Fair eves that fly;
Come buy, come buy:
Our grapes fresh from the vine,
Pomegranates full and fine,
Dates and sharp bullaces,
Rare pears and greengages,
Damsons and bilberries,
Taste them and try:
Currants and gooseberries,
Bright-fire-like barberries,
Figs to fill your mouth,
Citrons from the South,
Sweet to tongue and sound to eye;
Come buy, come buy."

Evening by evening
Among the brookside rushes,
Laura bowed her head to hear,
Lizzie veiled her blushes:

Crouching close together
In the cooling weather.
With clasping arms and cautioning lips,
With tingling cheeks and finger tips.
"Lie close," Laura said,
Pricking up her golden head:
"We must not look at goblin men,
We must not buy their fruits:
Who knows upon what soil they fed
Their hungry thirsty roots?"
"Come buy," call the goblins
Hobbling down the glen.
"Oh," cried Lizzie, "Laura, Laura,
You should not peep at goblin men."
Lizzie covered up her eyes,
Covered close lest they should look;
Laura reared her glossy head,
And whispered like the restless brook:
"Look, Lizzie, look, Lizzie,
Down the glen tramp little men.
One hauls a basket,
One bears a plate,
One lugs a golden dish
Of many pounds weight.
How fair the vine must grow
Whose grapes are so luscious;
How warm the wind must blow
Through those fruit bushes."
"No," said Lizzie: "No, no, no:
Their offers should not charm us,
Their evil gifts would harm us."
She thrust a dimpled finger
In each ear, shut eyes and ran:
Curious Laura chose to linger
Wondering at each merchant man.
One had a cat's face,
One whisked a tail,
One tramped at a rat's pace,
One crawled like a snail,
One like a wombat prowled obtuse and furry,
One like a ratel tumbled hurry skurry.
She heard a voice like voice of doves
Cooing all together:
They sounded kind and full of loves
In the pleasant weather.

Laura stretched her gleaming neck
Like a rush-imbedded swan,
Like a lily from the beck,
Like a moonlit poplar branch,
Like a vessel at the launch
When its last restraint is gone.

Backwards up the mossy glen
Turned and trooped the goblin men,
With their shrill repeated cry,
"Come buy, come buy."
When they reached where Laura was
They stood stock still upon the moss,
Leering at each other,
Brother with queer brother;
Signalling each other,
Brother with sly brother.
One set his basket down,
One reared his plate;
One began to weave a crown
Of tendrils, leaves, and rough nuts brown
(Men sell not such in any town);
One heaved the golden weight
Of dish and fruit to offer her:
"Come buy, come buy," was still their cry.
Laura stared but did not stir,
Longed but had no money:
The whisk-tailed merchant bade her taste
In tones as smooth as honey,
The cat-faced purr'd,
The rat-paced spoke a word
Of welcome, and the snail-paced even was heard;
One parrot-voiced and jolly
Cried "Pretty Goblin" still for "Pretty Polly;" —
One whistled like a bird.

But sweet-toothed Laura spoke in haste:
"Good folk, I have no coin;
To take were to purloin:
I have no copper in my purse,
I have no silver either,
And all my gold is on the furze
That shakes in windy weather
Above the rusty heather."

"You have much gold upon your head,"
They answered all together:
"Buy from us with a golden curl."
She clipped a precious golden lock,
She dropped a tear more rare than pearl,
Then sucked their fruit globes fair or red:
Sweeter than any honey from the rock,
Stronger than man-rejoicing wine,
Clearer than water flowed that juice;
She never tasted such before,
How should it cloy with length of use?
She sucked and sucked and sucked the more
Fruits which that unknown orchard bore;
She sucked until her lips were sore;
Then flung the emptied rinds away
But gathered up one kernel stone,
And knew not was it night or day
As she turned home alone.
   Lizzie met her at the gate
Full of wise upbraidings:
"Dear, you should not stay so late,
Twilight is not good for maidens;
Should not loiter in the glen
In the haunts of goblin men.
Do you not remember Jeanie,
How she met them in the moonlight,
Took their gifts both choice and many,
Ate their fruits and wore their flowers
Plucked from bowers
Where summer ripens at all hours?
But ever in the moonlight
She pined and pined away;
Sought them by night and day,
Found them no more but dwindled and grew grey;
Then fell with the first snow,
While to this day no grass will grow
Where she lies low:
I planted daisies there a year ago
That never blow.
You should not loiter so."
"Nay, hush," said Laura:
"Nay, hush, my sister:
I ate and ate my fill,
Yet my mouth waters still:
To-morrow night I will

Buy more:" and kissed her:
"Have done with sorrow;
I'll bring you plums to-morrow
Fresh on their mother twigs,
Cherries worth getting;
You cannot think what figs
My teeth have met in,
What melons icy-cold
Piled on a dish of gold
Too huge for me to hold,
What peaches with a velvet nap,
Pellucid grapes without one seed:
Odorous indeed must be the mead
Whereon they grow, and pure the wave they drink
With lilies at the brink,
And sugar-sweet their sap."

    Golden head by golden head,
Like two pigeons in one nest
Folded in each other's wings,
They lay down in their curtained bed:
Like two blossoms on one stem,
Like two flakes of new-fall'n snow,
Like two wands of ivory
Tipped with gold for awful kings.
Moon and stars gazed in at them,
Wind sang to them lullaby,
Lumbering owls forbore to fly,
Not a bat flapped to and fro
Round their nest:
Cheek to cheek and breast to breast
Locked together in one nest.

    Early in the morning
When the first cock crowed his warning,
Neat like bees, as sweet and busy,
Laura rose with Lizzie:
Fetched in honey, milked the cows,
Aired and set to rights the house,
Kneaded cakes of whitest wheat,
Cakes for dainty mouths to eat,
Next churned butter, whipped up cream,
Fed their poultry, sat and sewed;
Talked as modest maidens should:

Lizzie with an open heart,
Laura in an absent dream,
One content, one sick in part;
One warbling for the mere bright day's delight,
One longing for the night.

At length slow evening came:
They went with pitchers to the reedy brook;
Lizzie most placid in her look,
Laura most like a leaping flame.
They drew the gurgling water from its deep;
Lizzie plucked purple and rich golden flags,
Then turning homeward said: "The sunset flushes
Those furthest loftiest crags;
Come, Laura, not another maiden lags,
No wilful squirrel wags,
The beasts and birds are fast asleep."
But Laura loitered still among the rushes
And said the bank was steep.

And said the hour was early still,
The dew not fall'n, the wind not chill:
Listening ever, but not catching
The customary cry,
"Come buy, come buy,"
With its iterated jingle
Of sugar-baited words:
Not for all her watching
Once discerning even one goblin
Racing, whisking, tumbling, hobbling;
Let alone the herds
That used to tramp along the glen,
In groups or single,
Of brisk fruit-merchant men.

Till Lizzie urged, "O Laura, come;
I hear the fruit-call but I dare not look:
You should not loiter longer at this brook:
Come with me home.
The stars rise, the moon bends her arc,
Each glowworm winks her spark,
Let us get home before the night grows dark:
For clouds may gather
Though this is summer weather,
Put out the lights and drench us through;
Then if we lost our way what should we do?"

Laura turned cold as stone
To find her sister heard that cry alone,
That goblin cry,
"Come buy our fruits, come buy."
Must she then buy no more such dainty fruit?
Must she no more such succous pasture find,
Gone deaf and blind?
Her tree of life drooped from the root:
She said not one word in her heart's sore ache;
But peering thro' the dimness, nought discerning,
Trudged home, her pitcher dripping all the way;
So crept to bed, and lay
Silent till Lizzie slept;
Then sat up in a passionate yearning,
And gnashed her teeth for baulked desire, and wept
As if her heart would break.

Day after day, night after night,
Laura kept watch in vain
In sullen silence of exceeding pain.
She never caught again the goblin cry:
"Come buy, come buy;" —
She never spied the goblin men
Hawking their fruits along the glen:
But when the moon waxed bright
Her hair grew thin and grey;
She dwindled, as the fair full moon doth turn
To swift decay and burn
Her fire away.

One day remembering her kernel-stone
She set it by a wall that faced the south;
Dewed it with tears, hoped for a root,
Watched for a waxing shoot,
But there came none;
It never saw the sun,
It never felt the trickling moisture run:
While with sunk eyes and faded mouth
She dreamed of melons, as a traveller sees
False waves in desert drouth
With shade of leaf-crowned trees,
And burns the thirstier in the sandful breeze.

She no more swept the house,
Tended the fowls or cows,
Fetched honey, kneaded cakes of wheat,

Brought water from the brook:
But sat down listless in the chimney-nook
And would not eat.

    Tender Lizzie could not bear
To watch her sister's cankerous care
Yet not to share.
She night and morning
Caught the goblins' cry:
"Come buy our orchard fruits,
Come buy, come buy:" —
Beside the brook, along the glen,
She heard the tramp of goblin men,
The voice and stir
Poor Laura could not hear;
Longed to buy fruit to comfort her,
But feared to pay too dear.
She thought of Jeanie in her grave,
Who should have been a bride;
But who for joys brides hope to have
Fell sick and died
In her gay prime,
In earliest Winter time,
With the first glazing rime,
With the first snow-fall of crisp Winter time.

    Till Laura dwindling
Seemed knocking at Death's door:
Then Lizzie weighed no more
Better and worse;
But put a silver penny in her purse,
Kissed Laura, crossed the heath with clumps of furze
At twilight, halted by the brook:
And for the first time in her life
Began to listen and look.

    Laughed every goblin
When they spied her peeping:
Came towards her hobbling,
Flying, running, leaping,
Puffing and blowing,
Chuckling, clapping, crowing,
Clucking and gobbling,
Mopping and mowing,
Full of airs and graces,
Pulling wry faces,

Demure grimaces,
Cat-like and rat-like,
Ratel- and wombat-like,
Snail-paced in a hurry,
Parrot-voiced and whistler,
Helter skelter, hurry skurry,
Chattering like magpies,
Fluttering like pigeons,
Gliding like fishes, —
Hugged her and kissed her:
Squeezed and caressed her:
Stretched up their dishes,
Panniers, and plates:
"Look at our apples
Russet and dun,
Bob at our cherries,
Bite at our peaches,
Citrons and dates,
Grapes for the asking,
Pears red with basking
Out in the sun,
Plums on their twigs;
Pluck them and suck them,
Pomegranates, figs." —

"Good folk," said Lizzie,
Mindful of Jeanie:
"Give me much and many:" —
Held out her apron,
Tossed them her penny.
"Nay, take a seat with us,
Honour and eat with us,"
They answered grinning:
"Our feast is but beginning.
Night yet is early,
Warm and dew-pearly,
Wakeful and starry:
Such fruits as these
No man can carry;
Half their bloom would fly,
Half their dew would dry,
Half their flavour would pass by.
Sit down and feast with us,
Be welcome guest with us,
Cheer you and rest with us." —
"Thank you," said Lizzie: "But one waits

At home alone for me:
So without further parleying,
If you will not sell me any
Of your fruits though much and many,
Give me back my silver penny
I tossed you for a fee." —
They began to scratch their pates,
No longer wagging, purring,
But visibly demurring,
Grunting and snarling.
One called her proud,
Cross-grained, uncivil;
Their tones waxed loud,
Their looks were evil.
Lashing their tails
They trod and hustled her,
Elbowed and jostled her,
Clawed with their nails,
Barking, mewing, hissing, mocking,
Tore her gown and soiled her stocking,
Twitched her hair out by the roots,
Stamped upon her tender feet,
Held her hands and squeezed their fruits
Against her mouth to make her eat.

White and golden Lizzie stood,
Like a lily in a flood, —
Like a rock of blue-veined stone
Lashed by tides obstreperously, —
Like a beacon left alone
In a hoary roaring sea,
Sending up a golden fire, —
Like a fruit-crowned orange-tree
White with blossoms honey-sweet
Sore beset by wasp and bee, —
Like a royal virgin town
Topped with gilded dome and spire
Close beleaguered by a fleet
Mad to tug her standard down.

One may lead a horse to water,
Twenty cannot make him drink.
Though the goblins cuffed and caught her,
Coaxed and fought her,
Bullied and besought her,
Scratched her, pinched her black as ink,

Kicked and knocked her,
Mauled and mocked her,
Lizzie uttered not a word;
Would not open lip from lip
Lest they should cram a mouthful in:
But laughed in heart to feel the drip
Of juice that syrupped all her face,
And lodged in dimples of her chin,
And streaked her neck which quaked like curd.
At last the evil people
Worn out by her resistance
Flung back her penny, kicked their fruit
Along whichever road they took,
Not leaving root or stone or shoot;
Some writhed into the ground,
Some dived into the brook
With ring and ripple,
Some scudded on the gale without a sound,
Some vanished in the distance.

In a smart, ache, tingle,
Lizzie went her way;
Knew not was it night or day;
Sprang up the bank, tore thro' the furze,
Threaded copse and dingle,
And heard her penny jingle
Bouncing in her purse, —
Its bounce was music to her ear.
She ran and ran
As if she feared some goblin man
Dogged her with gibe or curse
Or something worse:
But not one goblin skurried after,
Nor was she pricked by fear;
The kind heart made her windy-paced
That urged her home quite out of breath with haste
And inward laughter.

She cried "Laura," up the garden,
"Did you miss me?
Come and kiss me.
Never mind my bruises,
Hug me, kiss me, suck my juices
Squeezed from goblin fruits for you,
Goblin pulp and goblin dew.
Eat me, drink me, love me;

Laura, make much of me:
For your sake I have braved the glen
And had to do with goblin merchant men."

Laura started from her chair,
Flung her arms up in the air,
Clutched her hair:
"Lizzie, Lizzie, have you tasted
For my sake the fruit forbidden?
Must your light like mine be hidden,
Your young life like mine be wasted,
Undone in mine undoing
And ruined in my ruin,
Thirsty, cankered, goblin-ridden?" —
She clung about her sister,
Kissed and kissed and kissed her:
Tears once again
Refreshed her shrunken eyes,
Dropping like rain
After long sultry drouth;
Shaking with aguish fear, and pain,
She kissed and kissed her with a hungry mouth.

Her lips began to scorch,
That juice was wormwood to her tongue,
She loathed the feast:
Writhing as one possessed she leaped and sung,
Rent all her robe, and wrung
Her hands in lamentable haste,
And beat her breast.
Her locks streamed like the torch
Borne by a racer at full speed,
Or like the mane of horses in their flight,
Or like an eagle when she stems the light
Straight toward the sun,
Or like a caged thing freed,
Or like a flying flag when armies run.

Swift fire spread through her veins, knocked at her heart,
Met the fire smouldering there
And overbore its lesser flame;
She gorged on bitterness without a name:
Ah! fool, to choose such part
Of soul-consuming care!
Sense failed in the mortal strife:

Like the watch-tower of a town
Which an earthquake shatters down,
Like a lightning-stricken mast,
Like a wind-uprooted tree
Spun about,
Like a foam-topped waterspout
Cast down headlong in the sea,
She fell at last;
Pleasure past and anguish past,
Is it death or is it life?

    Life out of death.
That night long Lizzie watched by her,
Counted her pulse's flagging stir,
Felt for her breath,
Held water to her lips, and cooled her face
With tears and fanning leaves:
But when the first birds chirped about their eaves,
And early reapers plodded to the place
Of golden sheaves,
And dew-wet grass
Bowed in the morning winds so brisk to pass,
And new buds with new day
Opened of cup-like lilies on the stream,
Laura awoke as from a dream,
Laughed in the innocent old way.
Hugged Lizzie but not twice or thrice;
Her gleaming locks showed not one thread of grey,
Her breath was sweet as May
And light danced in her eyes.

    Days, weeks, months, years
Afterwards, when both were wives
With children of their own;
Their mother-hearts beset with fears,
Their lives bound up in tender lives;
Laura would call the little ones
And tell them of her early prime,
Those pleasant days long gone
Of not-returning time:
Would talk about the haunted glen,
The wicked, quaint fruit-merchant men,
Their fruits like honey to the throat
But poison in the blood;
(Men sell not such in any town:)

Would tell them how her sister stood
In deadly peril to do her good,
And win the fiery antidote:
Then joining hands to little hands
Would bid them cling together,
"For there is no friend like a sister
In calm or stormy weather;
To cheer one on the tedious way,
To fetch one if one goes astray,
To lift one if one totters down,
To strengthen whilst one stands."

William Morris

1834-1896

THE HOLLOW LAND

Christ keep the Hollow Land
  Through the sweet spring-tide,
When the apple-blossoms bless
  The lowly bent hill side.

Christ keep the Hollow Land
  All the summer-tide;
Still we cannot understand
  Where the waters glide;

  Only dimly seeing them
    Coldly slipping through
Many green-lipp'd cavern mouths,
  Where the hills are blue.

SONG *from* GOLDEN WINGS

GOLD WINGS ACROSS THE SEA

Gold wings across the sea!
Grey light from tree to tree,
Gold hair beside my knee,
I pray thee come to me,
  Gold wings!

Are not my blue eyes sweet?
The west wind from the wheat
Blows cold across my feet;
Is it not time to meet
  Gold wings across the sea?

  The water slips,
The red-bill'd moorhen dips.
Sweet kisses on red lips;
Alas! the red rust grips,
And the blood-red dagger rips,
  Yet, O knight, come to me!

White swans on the green moat,
Small feathers left afloat
By the blue-painted boat;
Swift running of the stoat;
Sweet gurgling note by note
  Of sweet music.

O gold wings,
Listen how gold hair sings,
And the Ladies' Castle rings,
Gold wings across the sea.

I sit on a purple bed,
Outside, the wall is red,
Thereby the apple hangs,
And the wasp, caught by the fangs,

Dies in the autumn night,
And the bat flits till light,
And the love-crazed knight

Kisses the long wet grass:
The weary days pass, —
Gold wings across the sea!

Gold wings across the sea!
Moonlight from tree to tree,
Sweet hair laid on my knee,
O, sweet knight, come to me!

Gold wings, the short night slips,
The white swan's long neck drips,
I pray thee, kiss my lips,
Gold wings across the sea.

IN PRISON

Wearily, drearily,
Half the day long,
Flap the great banners
High over the stone;
Strangely and eerily
Sounds the wind's song,
Bending the banner-poles.

While, all alone,
Watching the loophole's spark,
Lie I, with life all dark,
Feet tether'd, hands fetter'd
Fast to the stone,
The grim walls, square letter'd
With prison'd men's groan.

Still strain the banner-poles
Through the wind's song,
Westward the banner rolls
Over my wrong.

I KNOW A LITTLE GARDEN–CLOSE

I know a little garden-close,
Set thick with lily and red rose,
Where I would wander if I might
From dewy morn to dewy night,
And have one with me wandering.

And though within it no birds sing,
And though no pillar'd house is there,
And though the apple-boughs are bare ·
Of fruit and blossom, would to God
Her feet upon the green grass trod,
And I beheld them as before.

There comes a murmur from the shore,
And in the close two fair streams are,
Drawn from the purple hills afar,
Drawn down into the restless sea:
Dark hills whose heath-bloom feeds no bee,
Dark shore no ship has ever seen,
Tormented by the billows green
Whose murmur comes unceasingly
Upon the place for which I cry.

For which I cry both day and night,
For which I let slip all delight,
Whereby I grow both deaf and blind,
Careless to win, unskilled to find,
And quick to lose what all men seek.

Yet tottering as I am and weak,
Still have I left a little breath
To seek within the jaws of death
An entrance to that happy place,
To seek the unforgotten face,
Once seen, once kissed, once reft from me
Anigh the murmuring of the sea.

SUMMER DAWN

Pray but one prayer for me 'twixt thy closed lips,
   Think but one thought of me up in the stars.
The summer night waneth, the morning light slips,
    Faint and grey 'twixt the leaves of the aspen, betwixt
       the cloud-bars,
That are patiently waiting there for the dawn:
   Patient and colourless, though Heaven's gold
Waits to float through them along with the sun.
Far out in the meadows, above the young corn,
   The heavy elms wait, and restless and cold
The uneasy wind rises; the roses are dun;
Through the long twilight they pray for the dawn,
Round the lone house in the midst of the corn.
   Speak but one word to me over the corn,
   Over the tender, bow'd locks of the corn.

From LOVE IS ENOUGH

Music with singing (from without)

Dawn talks to-day
 Over dew-gleaming flowers,
Night flies away
 Till the resting of hours:
Fresh are thy feet
 And with dreams thine eyes glistening,
Thy still lips are sweet
 Though the world is a-listening.
O Love, set a word in my mouth for our meeting,
Cast thine arms round about me to stay my heart's beating!
 O fresh day, O fair day, O long day made ours!

Morn shall meet noon
 While the flower-stems yet move,
Though the wind dieth soon
 And the clouds fade above.
Loved lips are thine
 As I tremble and hearken;
Bright thine eyes shine,
 Though the leaves thy brow darken.
O Love, kiss me into silence, lest no word avail me,
Stay my head with thy bosom lest breath and life fail me!
 O sweet day, O rich day, made long for our love.

Late day shall greet eve,
 And the full blossoms shake,
For the wind will not leave
 The tall trees while they wake.
Eyes soft with bliss,
 Come nigher and nigher!
Sweet mouth I kiss,
 Tell me all thy desire!
Let us speak, love, together some words of our story
That our lips as they part may remember the glory!
 O soft day, O calm day, made clear for our sake!

Algernon Charles Swinburne
1837-1909

The beauties of Swinburne are so great, and have been so much despised by people who can only understand fashions in poetry, that it is difficult to know where to begin this examination, in order, if possible, to obtain for him a sensible and sensitive hearing, and a true valuation.

Swinburne had one of the most flawless and wonderful vowel techniques in our language.

If the beauties of the poems by Swinburne included in this anthology are denied, it is because the reader has been blinded by a foolish and transitory fashion. At the moment it is fashionable to admire in poetry knuckles, bits of bones and of dead brains, and to detest that genius for the medium which has given mastery, splendor, light and life to the masterpieces of our language. But why should we trouble ourselves about such falsities?

In *August* the feeling of the roundness and the ripeness of the fruit on the lovely apple tree, of the dew, of the green leaves, is conveyed, very largely, by means of the roundness and ripeness of the vowels used. In this poem, as in every work of this great poet, there are the faintest stirrings and blood beats, produced sometimes by the repeated use of the same vowel with different vibration lengths, at other moments by the use of the same consonant ending two consecutive words. Take, for instance, this stanza:

> There were four apples on the tree,
> Red stained through gold, that all might see
> The sun went warm from core to rind;
> The green leaves made the summer blind
> In that soft place they kept for me
> With golden apples shut behind.

Now in this verse, the first line and the last two lines seem to me to be, very faintly, quicker, seem to be, very faintly, shorter (though, in actuality, they are not) than the other lines. This is due to the fact that the use of the *d*'s in "red stained through gold" seems a prolonging or a deepening of the color, whilst there are four consonants together — *d, t, h, r* — none of which can be *lifted;* they are on a level of sound, and this loss of movement makes the sound seem longer. Again, the use of the alliterative *e*'s in "The green leaves" deepens the sound.

But the whole poem is of an incredible subtlety. The wandering from the dark to the dulled *u* sounds, and from these to the warmer, darker depths of the varying *o* sounds, these give a sense of the change to the roundness, warmth and ripeness of the fruit, after the sharpness of the leaves. These effects could only have been produced by one of the greatest of artists in his own medium. Here is another example:

> In the m*u*te Aug*u*st afternoon
> They trembled to some undert*u*ne
> Of m*u*sic in the silver air;
> Great pleas*u*re was it to be there
> Till green t*u*rned d*u*skier and the m*oo*n
> C*o*l*ou*red the c*o*rn sheaves like g*o*ld hair.

Notice, too, the slight slowing produced by the *r*'s in "silver air."

Two stanzas after, the "moon," "noon," "tune" theme is repeated, with fresh subtleties of *o* sounds. Then, in this lovely stanza—

> I lay there till the warm smell grew
> More sharp, when flecks of yellow dew
> Between the round ripe leaves had blurred
> The rind with stain and wet; I heard
> A wind that blew and breathed and blew
> Too weak to alter its one word.

— the slight lengthening caused by the *m*'s in "warm" and "smell," the pause after "sharp," the faint difference, so faint as to be almost imperceptible, between the sounds of "grew" and "dew," of "blurred" and "heard," the movement caused by the different *e*'s in

> A wind that bl*ew* and br*ea*thed and bl*ew*
> Too w*ea*k to alter its one word.

— all these subtleties give a feeling of dew falling on those round ripe leaves, sometimes chilled by a passing air, sometimes not. And this is not *only* a matter of association, though association plays its part in the magic, as well as texture.

And here I leave the great poet of whom Saintsbury has said: "Every weapon and sleight of the English poet — equivalence and substitution, alternation and repetition, rhymes and rhymeless suspension of sound, volley and check of verse, stanza construction, line-and-pause moulding, foot-conjunction and contrast — this poet knows and can use them all. The triple rhyme itself, that springe for the unwary, gives him no difficulty. He seems to revel in variety: the stanzas actually hide, though they never falsify, their heredity of norm."

From ANACTORIA

For who shall change with prayers or thanksgivings
The mystery of the cruelty of things?
Or say what God above all gods and years
With offering and blood-sacrifice of tears,
With lamentation from strange lands, from graves
Where the snake pastures, from scarred mouths of slaves,
From prison, and from plunging prows of ships
Through flamelike foam of the sea's closing lips —
With thwartings of strange signs, and wind-blown hair
Of comets, desolating the dim air,
When darkness is made fast with seals and bars,
And fierce reluctance of disastrous stars,
Eclipse, and sound of shaken hills, and wings
Darkening, and blind inexpiable things —
With sorrow of labouring moons, and altering light
And travail of the planets of the night,
And weeping of the weary Pleiads seven,
Feeds the mute melancholy lust of heaven?
Is not his incense bitterness, his meat
Murder? his hidden face and iron feet
Hath not man known, and felt them on their way
Threaten and trample all things and every day?
Hath he not sent us hunger? who hath cursed
Spirit and flesh with longing? filled with thirst
Their lips who cried unto him? who bade exceed
The fervid will, fall short the feeble deed,
Bade sink the spirit and the flesh aspire,
Pain animate the dust of dead desire,
And life yield up her flower to violent fate?
Him would I reach, him smite, him desecrate,
Pierce the cold lips of God with human breath,
And mix his immortality with death.
Why hath he made us? what had all we done
That we should live and loathe the sterile sun,
And with the moon wax paler as she wanes,
And pulse by pulse feel time grow through our veins?
Thee too the years shall cover; thou shalt be
As the rose born of one same blood with thee,
As a song sung, as a word said, and fall
Flower-wise, and be not any more at all,
Nor any memory of thee anywhere;
For never Muse has bound above thine hair

The high Pierian flower whose graft outgrows
All summer kinship of the mortal rose
And colour of deciduous days, nor shed
Reflex and flush of heaven about thine head,
Nor reddened brows made pale by floral grief
With splendid shadow from that lordlier leaf.
Yea, thou shalt be forgotten like spilt wine,
Except these kisses of my lips on thine
Brand them with immortality; but me —
Men shall not see bright fire nor hear the sea,
Nor mix their hearts with music, nor behold
Cast forth of heaven, with feet of awful gold
And plumeless wings that make the bright air blind,
Lightning, with thunder for a hound behind
Hunting through fields unfurrowed and unsown,
But in the light and laughter, in the moan
And music, and in grasp of lip and hand
And shudder of water that makes felt on land
The immeasurable tremor of all the sea,
Memories shall mix and metaphors of me.
Like me shall be the shuddering calm of night,
When all the winds of the world for pure delight
Close lips that quiver and fold up wings that ache;
When nightingales are louder for love's sake,
And leaves tremble like lute-strings or like fire;
Like me the one star swooning with desire
Even at the cold lips of the sleepless moon,
As I at thine; like me the waste white noon,
Burnt through with barren sunlight; and like me
The land-stream and the tide-stream in the sea.
I am sick with time as these with ebb and flow,
And by the yearning in my veins I know
The yearning sound of waters; and mine eyes
Burn as that beamless fire which fills the skies
With troubled stars and travailing things of flame;
And in my heart the grief consuming them
Labours, and in my veins the thirst of these,
And all the summer travail of the trees
And all the winter sickness; and the earth,
Filled full with deadly works of death and birth,
Sore spent with hungry lusts of birth and death,
Has pain like mine in her divided breath;
Her spring of leaves is barren, and her fruit
Ashes; her boughs are burdened, and her root
Fibrous and gnarled with poison; underneath
Serpents have gnawn it through with tortuous teeth

Made sharp upon the bones of all the dead,
And wild birds rend her branches overhead.
These, woven as raiment for his word and thought,
These hath God made, and me as these, and wrought
Song, and hath lit it at my lips; and me
Earth shall not gather though she feed on thee.
As a shed tear shalt thou be shed; but I —
Lo, earth may labour, men live long and die,
Years change and stars, and the high God devise
New things, and old things wane before his eyes
Who wields and wrecks them, being more strong than they —
But, having made me, me he shall not slay.
Nor slay nor satiate, like those herds of his
Who laugh and live a little, and their kiss
Contents them, and their loves are swift and sweet,
And sure death grasps and gains them with slow feet,
Love they or hate they, strive or bow their knees —
And all these end; he hath his will of these.
Yea, but albeit he slay me, hating me —
Albeit he hide me in the deep dear sea
And cover me with cool wan foam, and ease
This soul of mine as any soul of these,
And give me water and great sweet waves, and make
The very sea's name lordlier for my sake,
The whole sea sweeter — albeit I die indeed
And hide myself and sleep and no man heed,
Of me the high God hath not all his will.
Blossom of branches, and on each high hill
Clear air and wind, and under in clamorous vales
Fierce noises of the fiery nightingales,
Buds burning in the sudden spring like fire,
The wan washed sand and the waves' vain desire,
Sails seen like blown white flowers at sea, and words
That bring tears swiftest, and long notes of birds
Violently singing till the whole world sings —
I Sappho shall be one with all these things,
With all high things for ever; and my face
Seen once, my songs once heard in a strange place,
Cleave to men's lives, and waste the days thereof
With gladness and much sadness and long love.
Yea, they shall say, earth's womb has borne in vain
New things, and never this best thing again;
Borne days and men, borne fruits and wars and wine,
Seasons and songs, but no song more like mine.
And they shall know me as ye who have known me here,
Last year when I loved Atthis, and this year

When I love thee; and they shall praise me, and say
"She hath all time as all we have our day,
Shall she not live and have her will" — even I?
Yea, though thou diest, I say I shall not die.
For these shall give me of their souls, shall give
Life, and the days and loves wherewith I live,
Shall quicken me with loving, fill with breath,
Save me and serve me, strive for me with death.
Alas, that neither moon nor snow nor dew
Nor all cold things can purge me wholly through,
Assuage me nor allay me nor appease,
Till supreme sleep shall bring me bloodless ease;
Till time wax faint in all his periods;
Till fate undo the bondage of the gods,
And lay, to slake and satiate me all through,
Lotus and Lethe on my lips like dew,
And shed around and over and under me
Thick darkness and the insuperable sea.

From THE MASQUE OF QUEEN BERSABE
A Miracle-play

HERODIAS

I am the queen Herodias.
This headband of my temples was
  King Herod's gold band woven me.
This broken dry staff in my hand
Was the queen's staff of a great land
  Betwixen Perse and Samarie.
For that one dancing of my feet,
The fire is come in my green wheat,
  From one sea to the other sea.

AHOLIBAH

I am the queen Aholibah.
My lips kissed dumb the word of *Ah*
  Sighed on strange lips grown sick thereby,
God wrought to me my royal bed;
The inner work thereof was red,
  The outer work was ivory.
My mouth's heat was the heat of flame
From lust towards the kings that came
  With horsemen riding royally.

CLEOPATRA

I am the queen of Ethiope.
Love bade my kissing eyelids ope
 That men beholding might praise love.
My hair was wonderful and curled;
My lips held fast the mouth o' the world
 To spoil the strength and speech thereof.
The latter triumph in my breath
Bowed down the beaten brows of death,
 Ashamed they had not wrath enough.

ABIHAIL

I am the queen of Tyrians.
My hair was glorious for twelve spans,
 That dried to loose dust afterward.
My stature was a strong man's length:
My neck was like a place of strength
 Built with white walls, even and hard.
Like the first noise of rain leaves catch
One from another, snatch by snatch,
 Is my praise, hissed against and marred.

AZUBAH

I am the queen of Amorites.
My face was like a place of lights
 With multitudes at festival.
The glory of my gracious brows
Was like God's house made glorious
 With colours upon either wall.
Between my brows and hair there was
A white space like a space of glass
 With golden candles over all.

AHOLAH

I am the queen of Amalek.
There was no tender touch or fleck
 To spoil my body or bared feet.
My words were soft like dulcimers,
And the first sweet of grape-flowers
 Made each side of my bosom sweet.
My raiment was as tender fruit
Whose rind smells sweet of spice-tree root,
 Bruised balm-blossom and budded wheat.

AHINOAM

I am the queen Ahinoam.
Like the throat of a soft slain lamb
    Was my throat, softer veined than his:
My lips were as two grapes the sun
Lays his whole weight of heat upon
    Like a mouth heavy with a kiss:
My hair's pure purple a wrought fleece,
My temples therein as a piece
    Of a pomegranate's cleaving is.

ATARAH

I am the queen Sidonian.
My face made faint the face of man,
    And strength was bound between my brows.
Spikenard was hidden in my ships,
Honey and wheat and myrrh in strips,
    White wools that shine as colour does,
Soft linen dyed upon the fold,
Split spice and cores of scented gold,
    Cedar and broken calamus.

SEMIRAMIS

I am the queen Semiramis.
The whole world and the sea that is
    In fashion like a chrysopras,
The noise of all men labouring,
The priest's mouth tired through thanksgiving,
    The sound of love in the blood's pause,
The strength of love in the blood's beat,
All these were cast beneath my feet
    And all found lesser than I was.

HESIONE

I am the queen Hesione.
The seasons that increased in me
    Made my face fairer than all men's.
I had the summer in my hair;
And all the pale gold autumn air
    Was as the habit of my sense.
My body was as fire that shone;
God's beauty that makes all things one
    Was one among my handmaidens.

CHRYSOTHEMIS

I am the queen of Samothrace.
God, making roses, made my face
　　As a rose filled up full with red.
My prows made sharp the straitened seas
From Pontus to the Chersonese
　　Whereon the ebbed Asian stream is shed.
My hair was as sweet scent that drips;
Love's breath begun about my lips
　　Kindled the lips of people dead.

THOMYRIS

I am the queen of Scythians.
My strength was like no strength of man's,
　　My face like day, my breast like spring.
My fame was felt in the extreme land
That hath sunshine on the one hand
　　And on the other star-shining.
Yea, and the wind there fails of breath;
Yea, and there life is waste like death;
　　Yea, and there death is a glad thing.

HARHAS

I am the queen of Anakim.
In the spent years whose speech is dim,
　　Whose raiment is the dust and death,
My stately body without stain
Shone as the shining race of rain
　　Whose hair a great wind scattereth.
Now hath God turned my lips to sighs,
Plucked off mine eyelids from mine eyes,
　　And sealed with seals my way of breath.

MYRRHA

I am the queen Arabian.
The tears wherewith mine eyelids ran
　　Smelt like my perfumed eyelids' smell.
A harsh thirst made my soft mouth hard,
That ached with kisses afterward;
　　My brain rang like a beaten bell.
As tears on eyes, as fire on wood,
Sin fed upon my breath and blood,
　　Sin made my breasts subside and swell.

PASIPHAE

I am the queen Pasiphae.
Not all the pure clean-coloured sea
   Could cleanse or cool my yearning veins;
Nor any root nor herb that grew,
Flag-leaves that let green water through,
   Nor washing of the dews and rains.
From shame's pressed core I wrung the sweet
Fruit's savour that was death to eat,
   Whereof no seed but death remains.

SAPPHO

I am the queen of Lesbians.
My love, that had no part in man's,
   Was sweeter than all shape of sweet.
The intolerable infinite desire
Made my face pale like faded fire
   When the ashen pyre falls through with heat.
My blood was hot wan wine of love,
And my song's sound the sound thereof,
   The sound of the delight of it.

MESSALINA

I am the queen of Italy.
These were the signs God set on me;
   A barren beauty subtle and sleek,
Curled carven hair, and cheeks worn wan
With fierce false lips of many a man,
   Large temples where the blood ran weak,
A mouth athirst and amorous
And hungering as the grave's mouth does
   That, being an-hungred, cannot speak.

AMESTRIS

I am the queen of Persians.
My breasts were lordlier than bright swans,
   My body as amber fair and thin.
Strange flesh was given my lips for bread,
With poisonous hours my days were fed,
   And my feet shod with adder-skin.
In Shushan toward Ecbatane
I wrought my joys with tears and pain,
   My loves with blood and bitter sin.

EPHRATH

I am the queen of Rephaim.
God, that some while refraineth him,
  Made in the end a spoil of me.
My rumour was upon the world
As strong sound of swoln water hurled
  Through porches of the straining sea.
My hair was like the flag-flower,
And my breasts carven goodlier
  Than beryl with chalcedony.

PASITHEA

I am the queen of Cypriotes.
Mine oarsmen, labouring with brown throats,
  Sang of me many a tender thing.
My maidens, girdled loose and braced
With gold from bosom to white waist,
  Praised me between their wool-combing.
All that praise Venus all night long
With lips like speech and lids like song
  Praised me till song lost heart to sing.

ALACIEL

I am the queen Alaciel.
My mouth was like that moist gold cell
  Whereout the thickest honey drips.
Mine eyes were as a grey-green sea;
The amorous blood that smote on me
  Smote to my feet and finger-tips.
My throat was whiter than the dove,
Mine eyelids as the seals of love,
  And as the doors of love my lips.

ERIGONE

I am the queen Erigone.
The wild wine shed as blood on me
  Made my face brighter than a bride's.
My large lips had the old thirst of earth,
Mine arms the might of the old sea's girth
  Bound round the whole world's iron sides.
Within mine eyes and in mine ears
Were music and the wine of tears,
  And light, and thunder of the tides.

AUGUST

There were four apples on the bough,
Half gold half red, that one might know
The blood was ripe inside the core;
The colour of the leaves was more
Like stems of yellow corn that grow
Through all the gold June meadow's floor.

The warm smell of the fruit was good
To feed on, and the split green wood,
With all its bearded lips and stains
Of mosses in the cloven veins,
Most pleasant, if one lay or stood
In sunshine or in happy rains.

There were four apples on the tree,
Red stained through gold, that all might see
The sun went warm from core to rind;
The green leaves made the summer blind
In that soft place they kept for me
With golden apples shut behind.

The leaves caught gold across the sun,
And where the bluest air begun
Thirsted for song to help the heat;
As I to feel my lady's feet
Draw close before the day were done;
Both lips grew dry with dreams of it.

In the mute August afternoon
They trembled to some undertune
Of music in the silver air;
Great pleasure was it to be there
Till green turned duskier and the moon
Coloured the corn-sheaves like gold hair.

That August time it was delight
To watch the red moons wane to white
'Twixt gray seamed stems of apple-trees;
A sense of heavy harmonies
Grew on the growth of patient night,
More sweet than shapen music is.

But some three hours before the moon
The air, still eager from the noon,
Flagged after heat, not wholly dead;
Against the stem I leant my head;
The colour soothed me like a tune,
Green leaves all round the gold and red.

I lay there till the warm smell grew
More sharp, when flecks of yellow dew
Between the round ripe leaves had blurred
The rind with stain and wet; I heard
A wind that blew and breathed and blew,
Too weak to alter its one word.

The wet leaves next the gentle fruit
Felt smoother, and the brown tree-root
Felt the mould warmer: I too felt
(As water feels the slow gold melt
Right through it when the day burns mute)
The peace of time wherein love dwelt.

There were four apples on the tree,
Gold stained on red that all might see
The sweet blood filled them to the core:
The colour of her hair is more
Like stems of fair faint gold, that be
Mown from the harvest's middle floor.

John Greenleaf Whittier
1807-1892

From SNOW–BOUND
A Winter Idyl

The sun that brief December day
Rose cheerless over hills of gray,
And, darkly circled, gave at noon
A sadder light than waning moon.
Slow tracing down the thickening sky
Its mute and ominous prophecy,
A portent seeming less than threat,
It sank from sight before it set.

A chill no coat, however stout,
Of homespun stuff could quite shut out,
A hard, dull bitterness of cold,
  That checked, mid-vein, the circling race
  Of life-blood in the sharpened face,
The coming of the snow-storm told.
The wind blew east: we heard the roar
Of Ocean on his wintry shore,
And felt the strong pulse throbbing there
Beat with low rhythm our inland air.

Meanwhile we did our nightly chores, —
Brought in the wood from out of doors,
Littered the stalls, and from the mows
Raked down the herd's-grass for the cows:
Heard the horse whinnying for his corn;
And, sharply clashing horn on horn,
Impatient down the stanchion rows
The cattle shake their walnut bows;
While, peering from his early perch
Upon the scaffold's pole of birch,
The cock his crested helmet bent
And down his querulous challenge sent.

Unwarmed by any sunset light
The gray day darkened into night,
A night made hoary with the swarm
And whirl-dance of the blinding storm,
As zigzag wavering to and fro
Crossed and recrossed the winged snow:
And ere the early bedtime came
The white drift piled the window-frame,
And through the glass the clothes-line posts
Looked in like tall and sheeted ghosts.

So all night long the storm roared on:
The morning broke without a sun;
In tiny spherule traced with lines
Of Nature's geometric signs,
In starry flake, and pellicle,
All day the hoary meteor fell;
And, when the second morning shone,
We looked upon a world unknown,
On nothing we could call our own.
Around the glistening wonder bent
The blue walls of the firmament,

No cloud above, no earth below, —
A universe of sky and snow!
The old familiar sights of ours
Took marvellous shapes; strange domes and towers
Rose up where sty or corn-crib stood,
Or garden wall, or belt of wood;
A smooth white mound the brush-pile showed,
A fenceless drift what once was road;
The bridle-post an old man sat
With loose-flung coat and high cocked hat;
The well-curb had a Chinese roof;
And even the long sweep, high aloof,
In its slant splendor, seemed to tell
Of Pisa's leaning miracle.

A prompt, decisive man, no breath
Our father wasted: "Boys, a path!"
Well pleased, (for when did farmer boy
Count such a summons less than joy?)
Our buskins on our feet we drew;
    With mittened hands, and caps drawn low,
    To guard our necks and ears from snow,
We cut the solid whiteness through.
And, where the drift was deepest, made
A tunnel walled and overlaid
With dazzling crystal: we had read
Of rare Aladdin's wondrous cave,
And to our own, his name we gave,
With many a wish the luck were ours
To test his lamp's supernal powers.
We reached the barn with merry din,
And roused the prisoned brutes within.
The old horse thrust his long head out,
And grave with wonder gazed about;
The cock his lusty greeting said,
And forth his speckled harem led;
The oxen lashed their tails, and hooked,
And mild reproach of hunger looked;
The horned patriarch of the sheep,
Like Egypt's Amun roused from sleep,
Shook his sage head with gesture mute,
And emphasized with stamp of foot.

All day the gusty north-wind bore
The loosening drift its breath before;
Low circling round its southern zone,
The sun through dazzling snow-mist shone.

No church-bell lent its Christian tone
To the savage air, no social smoke
Curled over woods of snow-hung oak.
A solitude made more intense
By dreary-voiced elements,
The shrieking of the mindless wind,
The moaning tree-boughs swaying blind,
And on the glass the unmeaning beat
Of ghostly finger-tips of sleet.
Beyond the circle of our hearth
No welcome sound of toil or mirth
Unbound the spell, and testified
Of human life and thought outside.
We minded that the sharpest ear
The buried brooklet could not hear,
The music of whose liquid lip
Had been to us companionship,
And, in our lonely life, had grown
To have an almost human tone.

As night drew on, and, from the crest
Of wooded knolls that ridged the west,
The sun, a snow-blown traveller, sank
From sight beneath the smothering bank,
We piled, with care, our nightly stack
Of wood against the chimney-back, —
The oaken log, green, huge, and thick,
And on its top the stout back-stick;
The knotty forestick laid apart,
And filled between with curious art
The ragged brush; then, hovering near,
We watched the first red blaze appear,
Heard the sharp crackle, caught the gleam
On whitewashed wall and sagging beam,
Until the old, rude-furnished room
Burst, flower-like, into rosy bloom;
While radiant with a mimic flame
Outside the sparkling drift became,
And through the bare-boughed lilac-tree
Our own warm hearth seemed blazing free.
The crane and pendent trammels showed,
The Turks' heads on the andirons glowed;
While childish fancy, prompt to tell
The meaning of the miracle,
Whispered the old rhyme: "*Under the tree,
When fire outdoors burns merrily,
There the witches are making tea.*"

The moon above the eastern wood
Shone at its full; the hill-range stood
Transfigured in the silver flood,
Its blown snows flashing cold and keen,
Dead white, save where some sharp ravine
Took shadow, or the sombre green
Of hemlocks turned to pitchy black
Against the whiteness of their back.
For such a world and such a night
Most fitting that unwarming light,
Which only seemed where'er it fell
To make the coldness visible.

Shut in from all the world without,
We sat the clean-winged hearth about,
Content to let the north-wind roar
In baffled rage at pane and door,
While the red logs before us beat
The frost-line back with tropic heat;
And ever, when a louder blast
Shook beam and rafter as it passed,
The merrier up its roaring draught
The great throat of the chimney laughed;
The house-dog on his paws outspread
Laid to the fire his drowsy head,
The cat's dark silhouette on the wall
A couchant tiger's seemed to fall;
And, for the winter fireside meet,
Between the andirons' straddling feet,
The mug of cider simmered slow,
The apples sputtered in a row,
And, close at hand, the basket stood
With nuts from brown October's wood.

What matter how the night behaved?
What matter how the north-wind raved?
Blow high, blow low, not all its snow
Could quench our hearth-fire's ruddy glow.
O Time and Change! — with hair as gray
As was my sire's that winter day,
How strange it seems, with so much gone
Of life and love, to still live on!
Ah, brother! only I and thou
Are left of all that circle now, —

The dear home faces whereupon
That fitful firelight paled and shone.
Henceforward, listen as we will,
The voices of that hearth are still;
Look where we may, the wide earth o'er,
Those lighted faces smile no more.
We tread the paths their feet have worn,
    We sit beneath their orchard-trees,
    We hear, like them, the hum of bees
And rustle of the bladed corn;
We turn the pages that they read,
    Their written words we linger o'er,
But in the sun they cast no shade,
No voice is heard, no sign is made,
    No step is on the conscious floor!
Yet Love will dream, and Faith will trust,
(Since He who knows our need is just,)
That somehow, somewhere, meet we must.
Alas for him who never sees
The stars shine through his cypress-trees!
Who, hopeless, lays his dead away,
Nor looks to see the breaking day
Across the mournful marbles play!
Who hath not learned, in hours of faith
    The truth to flesh and sense unknown,
That Life is ever lord of Death
And Love can never lose its own!

Henry Wadsworth Longfellow

1807-1882

THE WITNESSES

In Ocean's wide domains,
    Half buried in the sands,
Lie skeletons in chains,
    With shackled feet and hands.

Beyond the fall of dews,
    Deeper than plummet lies,
Float ships, with all their crews,
    No more to sink nor rise.

There the black Slave-ship swims,
    Freighted with human forms,
Whose fettered, fleshless limbs
    Are not the sport of storms.

These are the bones of Slaves;
    They gleam from the abyss;
They cry, from yawning waves,
    "We are the Witnesses!"

Within Earth's wide domains
  Are markets for men's lives;
Their necks are galled with chains,
  Their wrists are cramped with
    gyves.

Dead bodies, that the kite
  In deserts makes its prey;
Murders, that with affright
  Scare school-boys from their play!

All evil thoughts and deeds;
  Anger, and lust, and pride;
The foulest, rankest weeds,
  That choke Life's groaning tide!

These are the woes of Slaves;
  They glare from the abyss;
They cry, from unknown graves,
  "We are the Witnesses!"

THE DISCOVERER OF THE NORTH CAPE

A Leaf from King Alfred's "Orosius"

Othere, the old sea-captain
  Who dwelt in Helgoland,
To King Alfred, the Lover of Truth,
Brought a snow-white walrus-tooth,
  Which he held in his brown right
    hand.

His figure was tall and stately,
  Like a boy's his eye appeared;
His hair was yellow as hay,
But threads of a silvery gray
  Gleamed in his tawny beard.

Hearty and hale was Othere,
  His cheek had the color of oak;
With a kind of laugh in his speech,
Like the sea-tide on a beach,
  As unto the King he spoke.

And Alfred, King of the Saxons,
  Had a book upon his knees,
And wrote down the wondrous tale
Of him who was first to sail
  Into the Arctic seas.

"So far I live to the northward,
  No man lives north of me;
To the east are wild mountain-
    chains

And beyond them meres and plains;
  To the westward all is sea.

"So far I live to the northward,
  From the harbor of Skeringes-
    hale,
If you only sailed by day,
With a fair wind all the way,
  More than a month would you
    sail.

"I own six hundred reindeer,
  With sheep and swine beside;
I have tribute from the Finns,
Whalebone and reindeer-skins,
  And ropes of walrus-hide.

"I ploughed the land with horses,
  But my heart was ill at ease;
For the old seafaring men
Came to me now and then,
  With their sagas of the seas; —

"Of Iceland and of Greenland,
  And the stormy Hebrides,
And the undiscovered deep; —
Oh I could not eat nor sleep
  For thinking of those seas.

"To the northward stretched the
    desert,
  How far I fain would know;
So at last I sallied forth,
And three days sailed due north,
  As far as the whale-ships go.

"To the west of me was the ocean,
  To the right the desolate shore,
But I did not slacken sail
For the walrus or the whale,
  Till after three days more.

"The days grew longer and longer,
  Till they became as one,
And southward through the haze
I saw the sullen blaze
  Of the red midnight sun.

"And then uprose before me,
  Upon the water's edge,
The huge and haggard shape
Of that unknown North Cape,
  Whose form is like a wedge.

"The sea was rough and stormy,
  The tempest howled and wailed,
And the sea-fog, like a ghost,
Haunted that dreary coast,
  But onward still I sailed.

"Four days I steered to eastward,
  Four days without a night:
Round in a fiery ring
Went the great sun, O King,
  With red and lurid light."

Here Alfred, King of the Saxons,
  Ceased writing for a while;
And raised his eyes from his book,
With a strange and puzzled look,
  And an incredulous smile.

But Othere, the old sea-captain,
  He neither paused nor stirred,
Till the King listened and then
Once more took up his pen,
  And wrote down every word.

"And now the land," said Othere,
  "Bent southward suddenly,
And I followed the curving shore
And ever southward bore
  Into a nameless sea.

"And there we hunted the walrus,
  The narwhale, and the seal;
Ha! 't was a noble game!
And like the lightning's flame
  Flew our harpoons of steel.

"There were six of us all together,
  Norsemen of Helgoland;
In two days and no more
We killed of them threescore,
  And dragged them to the strand!"

Here Alfred the Truth-Teller
  Suddenly closed his book,
And lifted his blue eyes,
With doubt and strange surmise
  Depicted in their look.

And Othere the old sea-captain
  Stared at him wild and weird,
Then smiled, till his shining teeth
Gleamed white from underneath
  His tawny, quivering beard.

And to the King of the Saxons,
  In witness of the truth,
Raising his noble head,
He stretched his brown hand, and
     said
  "Behold this walrus-tooth."

Walt Whitman
1819-1892

STARTING FROM PAUMANOK

I

Starting from fish-shape Paumanok where I was born,
Well-begotten, and rais'd by a perfect mother,
After roaming many lands, lover of populous pavements,
Dweller in Mannahatta my city, or on southern savannas,
Or a soldier camp'd or carrying my knapsack and gun, or a miner in
 California,
Or rude in my home in Dakota's woods, my diet meat, my drink from
 the spring,
Or withdrawn to muse and meditate in some deep recess,
Far from the clank of crowds intervals passing rapt and happy,
Aware of the fresh free giver the flowing Missouri, aware of mighty
 Niagara,
Aware of the buffalo herds grazing the plains, the hirsute and strong-
 breasted bull,
Of earth, rocks, Fifth-month flowers experienced, stars, rain, snow, my
 amaze,
Having studied the mocking-bird's tones and the flight of the mountain-
 hawk,
And heard at dawn the unrivall'd one, the hermit thrush from the
 swamp-cedars,
Solitary, singing in the West, I strike up for a New World.

II

Victory, union, faith, identity, time,
The indissoluble compacts, riches, mystery,
Eternal progress, the kosmos, and the modern reports.

This then is life,
Here is what has come to the surface after so many throes and convulsions.

How curious! how real!
Underfoot the divine soil, overhead the sun.

See revolving the globe,
The ancestor-continents away group'd together,
The present and future continents north and south, with the isthmus be-
    tween.

See, vast trackless spaces,
As in a dream they change, they swiftly fill,
Countless masses debouch upon them,
They are now cover'd with the foremost people, arts, institutions, known.

See, projected through time,
For me an audience interminable.

With firm and regular step they wend, they never stop,
Successions of men, Americanos, a hundred millions,
One generation playing its part and passing on,
Another generation playing its part and passing on in its turn,
With faces turn'd sideways or backwards towards me to listen,
With eyes retrospective towards me.

III

Americanos! conquerors! marches humanitarian!
Foremost, century marches! Libertad! masses!
For you a programme of chants.

Chants of the prairies,
Chants of the long-running Mississippi, and down to the Mexican sea,
Chants of Ohio, Indiana, Illinois, Iowa, Wisconsin and Minnesota,
Chants going forth from the centre from Kansas, and thence equi-distant,
Shooting in pulses of fire ceaseless to vivify all.

IV

Take my leaves America, take them South and take them North.
Make welcome for them everywhere, for they are your own offspring,
Surround them East and West, for they would surround you,
And you precedents, connect lovingly with them, for they connect lov-
    ingly with you.

I conn'd old times,
I sat studying at the feet of the great masters,
Now if eligible O that the great masters might return and study me.

In the name of these States shall I scorn the antique?
Why these are the children of the antique to justify it.

V

Dead poets, philosophs, priests,
Martyrs, artists, inventors, governments long since,
Language-shapers on other shores,
Nations once powerful, now reduced, withdrawn, or desolate,
I dare not proceed till I respectfully credit what you have left wafted
    hither,
I have perused it, own it is admirable, (moving awhile among it,)
Think nothing can ever be greater, nothing can ever deserve more than
    it deserves,
Regarding it all intently a long while, then dismissing it,
I stand in my place with my own day here.

Here lands female and male,
Here the heir-ship and heiress-ship of the world, here the flame of ma-
    terials,
Here spirituality the translatress, the openly-avowed,
The ever-tending, the finalè of visible forms,
The satisfier, after due long-waiting now advancing,
Yes here comes my mistress the soul.

VI

The soul,
Forever and forever — longer than soil is brown and solid — longer than
    water ebbs and flows.

I will make the poems of materials, for I think they are to be the most
    spiritual poems,
And I will make the poems of my body and of mortality,
For I think I shall then supply myself with the poems of my soul and of
    immortality.

I will make a song for these States that no one State may under any cir-
    cumstances be subjected to another State,
And I will make a song that there shall be comity by day and by night
    between all the States, and between any two of them,
And I will make a song for the ears of the President, full of weapons with
    menacing points,
And behind the weapons countless dissatisfied faces;
And a song make I of the One form'd out of all,
The fang'd and glittering One whose head is over all,
Resolute warlike One including and over all,
(However high the head of any else that head is over all.)

I will acknowledge contemporary lands,
I will trail the whole geography of the globe and salute courteously every
    city large and small,
And employments! I will put in my poems that with you is heroism upon
    land and sea,
And I will report all heroism from an American point of view.

I will sing the song of companionship,
I will show what alone must finally compact these,
I believe these are to found their own ideal of manly love, indicating it
    in me,
I will therefore let flame from me the burning fires that were threatening
    to consume me,
I will lift what has too long kept down those smouldering fires,
I will give them complete abandonment,
I will write the evangel-poem of comrades and of love,
For who but I should understand love with all its sorrows and joy?
And who but I should be the poet of comrades?

VII

I am the credulous man of qualities, ages, races,
I advance from the people in their own spirit,
Here is what sings unrestricted faith.

Omnes! omnes! let others ignore what they may,
I make the poem of evil also, I commemorate that part also,
I am myself just as much evil as good, and my nation is — and I say there
    is in fact no evil,
(Or if there is I say it is just as important to you, to the land or to me, as
    any thing else.)

I too, following many and follow'd by many, inaugurate a religion, I de-
    scend into the arena,
(It may be I am destin'd to utter the loudest cries there, the winner's peal-
    ing shouts,
Who knows? they may rise from me yet, and soar above every thing.)

Each is not for its own sake,
I say the whole truth and all the stars in the sky are for religion's sake.

I say no man has ever yet been half devout enough,
None has ever yet adored or worship'd half enough,
None has begun to think how divine he himself is, and how certain the
    future is.

I say that the real and permanent grandeur of these States must be their
    religion,
Otherwise there is no real and permanent grandeur;
(Nor character nor life worthy the name without religion,
Nor land nor man or woman without religion.)

VIII

What are you doing young man?
Are you so earnest, so given up to literature, science, art, amours?
These ostensible realities, politics, points?
Your ambition or business whatever it may be?

It is well — against such I say not a word, I am their poet also,
But behold! such swiftly subside, burnt up for religion's sake,
For not all matter is fuel to heat, impalpable flame, the essential life of
    the earth,
Any more than such are to religion.

IX

What do you seek so pensive and silent?
What do you need camerado?
Dear son do you think it is love?

Listen dear son — listen America, daughter or son,
It is a painful thing to love a man or woman to excess, and yet it satisfies,
    it is great,
But there is something else very great, it makes the whole coincide,
It, magnificent, beyond materials, with continuous hands sweeps and pro-
    vides for all.

X

Know you, solely to drop in the earth the germs of a greater religion,
The following chants each for its kind I sing.

My comrade!
For you to share with me two greatnesses, and a third one rising inclusive
    and more resplendent,
The greatness of Love and Democracy, and the greatness of Religion.

Melange mine own, the unseen and the seen,
Mysterious ocean where the streams empty,
Prophetic spirit of materials shifting and flickering around me,
Living beings, identities now doubtless near us in the air that we know
    not of,

Contact daily and hourly that will not release me,
These selecting, these in hints demanded of me.

Not he with a daily kiss onward from childhood kissing me,
Has winded and twisted around me that which holds me to him,
Any more than I am held to the heavens and all the spiritual world,
After what they have done to me, suggesting themes.

O such themes — equalities! O divine average!
Warblings under the sun, usher'd as now, or at noon, or setting,
Strains musical flowing through ages, now reaching hither,
I take to your reckless and composite chords, add to them, and cheerfully
    pass them forward.

XI

As I have walk'd in Alabama my morning walk,
I have seen where the she-bird the mocking-bird sat on her nest in the
    briers hatching her brood.

I have seen the he-bird also,
I have paus'd to hear him near at hand inflating his throat and joyfully
    singing.

And while I paus'd it came to me that what he really sang for was not
    there only,
Nor for his mate nor himself only, nor all sent back by the echoes,
But subtle, clandestine, away beyond,
A charge transmitted and gift occult for those being born.

XII

Democracy! near at hand to you a throat is now inflating itself and joy-
    fully singing.

Ma femme! for the brood beyond us and of us,
For those who belong here and those to come,
I exultant to be ready for them will now shake out carols stronger and
    haughtier than have ever yet been heard upon earth.

I will make the songs of passion to give them their way,
And your songs outlaw'd offenders, for I scan you with kindred eyes, and
    carry you with me the same as any.

I will make the true poem of riches,
To earn for the body and the mind whatever adheres and goes forward
    and is not dropt by death;

I will effuse egotism and show it underlying all, and I will be the bard of
    personality,
And I will show of male and female that either is but the equal of the
    other,
And sexual organs and acts! do you concentrate in me, for I am deter-
    min'd to tell you with courageous clear voice to prove you illus-
    trious,
And I will show that there is no imperfection in the present, and can be
    none in the future.
And I will show that whatever happens to anybody it may be turn'd to
    beautiful results,
And I will show that nothing can happen more beautiful than death,
And I will thread a thread through my poems that time and events are
    compact,
And that all the things of the universe are perfect miracles, each as pro-
    found as any.

I will not make poems with reference to parts,
But I will make poems, songs, thoughts, with reference to ensemble,
And I will not sing with reference to a day, but with reference to all days,
And I will not make a poem nor the least part of a poem but has refer-
    ence to the soul,
Because having look'd at the objects of the universe, I find there is no
    one nor any particle of one but has reference to the soul.

XIII

Was somebody asking to see the soul?
See, your own shape and countenance, persons, substances, beasts, the
    trees, the running rivers, the rocks and sands.

All hold spiritual joys and afterwards loosen them;
How can the real body ever die and be buried?

Of your real body and any man's or woman's real body,
Item for item it will elude the hands of the corpse-cleaners and pass to
    fitting spheres,
Carrying what has accrued to it from the moment of birth to the moment
    of death.

Not the types set up by the printer return their impression, the meaning,
    the main concern,
Any more than a man's substance and life or a woman's substance and
    life return in the body and the soul,
Indifferently before death and after death.

Behold, the body includes and is the meaning, the main concern, and includes and is the soul;
Whoever you are, how superb and how divine is your body, or any part of it!

XIV

Whoever you are, to you endless announcements!

Daughter of the lands did you wait for your poet?
Did you wait for one with a flowing mouth and indicative hand?
Toward the male of the States, and toward the female of the States,
Exulting words, words to Democracy's lands.

Interlink'd, food-yielding lands!
Land of coal and iron! land of gold! land of cotton, sugar, rice!
Land of wheat, beef, pork! land of wool and hemp! land of the apple and the grape!
Land of the pastoral plains, the grass-fields of the world! land of those sweet-air'd interminable plateaus!
Land of the herd, the garden, the healthy house of adobie!
Lands where the north-west Columbia winds, and where the south-west Colorado winds!
Land of the eastern Chesapeake! land of the Delaware!
Land of Ontario, Erie, Huron, Michigan!
Land of the Old Thirteen! Massachusetts land! land of Vermont and Connecticut!
Land of the ocean shores! land of sierras and peaks!
Land of boatmen and sailors! fishermen's land!
Inextricable lands! the clutch'd together! the passionate ones!
The side by side! the elder and younger brothers! the bony-limb'd!
The great women's land! the feminine! the experienced sisters and the inexperienced sisters!
Far breath'd land! Arctic braced! Mexican breez'd! the diverse! the compact!
The Pennsylvanian! the Virginian! the double Carolinian!
O all and each well-loved by me! my intrepid nations! O I at any rate include you all with perfect love!
I cannot be discharged from you! not from one any sooner than another!
O death! O for all that, I am yet of you unseen this hour with irrepressible love,
Walking New England, a friend, a traveler,
Splashing my bare feet in the edge of the summer ripples on Paumanok's sands,
Crossing the prairies, dwelling again in Chicago, dwelling in every town,

Observing shows, births, improvements, structures, arts,
Listening to orators and oratresses in public halls,
Of and through the States as during life, each man and woman my neighbor,
The Louisianian, the Georgian, as near to me, and I as near to him and her,
The Mississippian and Arkansian yet with me, and I yet with any of them,
Yet upon the plains west of the spinal river, yet in my house of adobie,
Yet returning eastward, yet in the Seaside State or in Maryland,
Yet Kanadian cheerily braving the winter, the snow and ice welcome to me,
Yet a true son either of Maine or of the Granite State, or the Narrangansett Bay State, or the Empire State,
Yet sailing to other shores to annex the same, yet welcoming every new brother,
Hereby applying these leaves to the new ones from the hour they unite with the old ones,
Coming among the new ones myself to be their companion and equal, coming personally to you now.
Enjoining you to acts, characters, spectacles, with me.

XV

With me with firm holding, yet haste, haste on.

For your life adhere to me,
(I may have to be persuaded many times before I consent to give myself really to you, but what of that?
Must not Nature be persuaded many times?)

No dainty dolce affettuoso I,
Bearded, sun-burnt, gray-neck'd, forbidding, I have arrived,
To be wrestled with as I pass for the solid prizes of the universe,
For such I afford whoever can persevere to win them.

XVI

On my way a moment I pause,
Here for you! and here for America!
Still the present I raise aloft, still the future of the States I harbinge glad and sublime,
And for the past I pronounce what the air holds of the red aborigines.

The red aborigines,
Leaving natural breaths, sounds of rain and winds, calls as of birds and animals in the woods, syllabled to us for names,

Okonee, Koosa, Ottawa, Monongahela, Sauk, Natchez, Chattahoochee,
 Kaqueta, Oronoco,
Wabash, Miami, Saginaw, Chippewa, Oshkosh, Walla-Walla,
Leaving such to the States they melt, they depart, charging the water and
 the land with names.

XVII

Expanding and swift, henceforth,
Elements, breeds, adjustments, turbulent, quick and audacious,
A world primal again, vistas of glory incessant and branching,
A new race dominating previous ones and grander far, with new contests,
New politics, new literatures and religions, new inventions and arts.

These, my voice announcing — I will sleep no more but arise,
You oceans that have been calm within me! how I feel you, fathomless,
 stirring, preparing unprecedented waves and storms.

XVIII

See, steamers steaming through my poems,
See, in my poems immigrants continually coming and landing,
See, in arriere, the wigwam, the trail, the hunter's hut, the flat-boat, the
 maize-leaf, the claim, the rude fence, and the backwoods village,
See, on the one side the Western Sea and on the other the Eastern Sea,
 how they advance and retreat upon my poems as upon their own
 shores,
See, pastures and forests in my poems — see, animals wild and tame —
 see, beyond the kaw, countless herds of buffalo feeding on short
 curly grass,
See, in my poems, cities, solid, vast, inland, with paved streets, with iron
 and stone edifices, ceaseless vehicles, and commerce,
See, the many-cylinder'd steam printing-press — see, the electric tele-
 graph stretching across the continent,
See, through Atlantica's depths pulses American Europe reaching, pulses
 of Europe duly return'd,
See, the strong and quick locomotive as it departs, panting, blowing the
 steam-whistle,
See, ploughmen ploughing farms — see, miners digging mines — see, the
 numberless factories,
See, mechanics busy at their benches with tools, see from among them
 superior judges, philosophs, Presidents, emerge, drest in working
 dresses,
See, lounging through the shops and fields of the States, me well-belov'd,
 close-held by day and night,
Hear the loud echoes of my songs there — read the hints come at last.

XIX

O camerado close! O you and me at last, and us two only,
O a word to clear one's path ahead endlessly!
O something ecstatic and undemonstrable! O music wild!
O now I triumph — and you shall also;
O hand in hand — O wholesome pleasure — O one more desirer and
    lover!
O to haste firm holding — to haste, haste on with me.

From SONG OF THE OPEN ROAD

I

Afoot and light-hearted I take to the open road,
Healthy, free, the world before me,
The long brown path before me leading wherever I choose.

Henceforth I ask not good-fortune, I myself am good-fortune,
Henceforth I whimper no more, postpone no more, need nothing,
Done with indoor complaints, libraries, querulous criticisms,
Strong and content I travel the open road.

The earth, that is sufficient,
I do not want the constellations any nearer,
I know they are very well where they are,
I know they suffice for those who belong to them.

(Still here I carry my old delicious burdens,
I carry them, men and women, I carry them with me wherever I go,
I swear it is impossible for me to get rid of them,
I am fill'd with them, and I will fill them in return.)

II

You road I enter upon and look around, I believe you are not all that is
    here,
I believe that much unseen is also here.

Here the profound lesson of reception, nor preference nor denial,
The black with his woolly head, the felon, the diseas'd, the illiterate per-
    son, are not denied;
The birth, the hasting after the physician, the beggar's tramp, the drunk-
    ard's stagger, the laughing party of mechanics,
The escaped youth, the rich person's carriage, the fop, the eloping cou-
    ple,

The early market-man, the hearse, the moving of furniture into the
    town, the return back from town,
They pass, I also pass, any thing passes, none can be interdicted,
None but are accepted, none but shall be dear to me.

III

You air that serves me with breath to speak!
You objects that call from diffusion my meanings and give them shape!
You light that wraps me and all things in delicate equable showers!
You paths worn in the irregular hollows by the roadsides!
I believe you are latent with unseen existences, you are so dear to me.

You flagg'd walks of the cities! you strong curbs at the edges!
You ferries! you planks and posts of wharves! you timber-lined sides! you
    distant ships!
You rows of houses! you window-pierc'd façades! you roofs!
You porches and entrances! you copings and iron guards!
You windows whose transparent shells might expose so much!
You doors and ascending steps! you arches!
You gray stones of interminable pavements! you trodden crossings!
From all that has touch'd you I believe you have imparted to yourselves,
    and now would impart the same secretly to me,
From the living and the dead you have peopled your impassive surfaces,
    and the spirits thereof would be evident and amicable with me.

IV

The earth expanding right hand and left hand,
The picture alive, every part in its best light,
The music falling in where it is wanted, and stopping where it is not
    wanted,
The cheerful voice of the public road, the gay fresh sentiment of the
    road.

O highway I travel, do you say to me *Do not leave me?*
Do you say *Venture not — if you leave me you are lost?*
Do you say *I am already prepared, I am well-beaten and undenied, ad-*
    here to me?

O public road, I say back I am not afraid to leave you, I love you,
You express me better than I can express myself,
You shall be more to me than my poem.

I think heroic deeds were all conceiv'd in the open air, and all free poems
    also,
I think I could stop here myself and do miracles,

I think whatever I shall meet on the road I shall like, and whoever beholds me shall like me,
I think whoever I see must be happy.

V

From this hour I ordain myself loos'd of limits and imaginary lines,
Going where I list, my own master total and absolute,
Listening to others, considering well what they say,
Pausing, searching, receiving, contemplating,
Gently, but with undeniable will, divesting myself of the holds that would hold me.

I inhale great draughts of space,
The east and the west are mine, and the north and the south are mine.

I am larger, better than I thought,
I did not know I held so much goodness.

All seems beautiful to me,
I can repeat over to men and women You have done such good to me I would do the same to you,
I will recruit for myself and you as I go,
I will scatter myself among men and women as I go,
I will toss a new gladness and roughness among them,
Whoever denies me it shall not trouble me,
Whoever accepts me he or she shall be blessed and shall bless me.

From SONG OF MYSELF

A CHILD SAID WHAT IS THE GRASS

A child said *What is the grass?* fetching it to me with full hands;
How could I answer the child? I do not know what it is any more than he.

I guess it must be the flag of my disposition, out of hopeful green stuff woven.

Or I guess it is the handkerchief of the Lord,
A scented gift and remembrancer designedly dropt,
Bearing the owner's name someway in the corners, that we may see and remark, and say *Whose?*

Or I guess the grass is itself a child, the produced babe of the vegetation.

Or I guess it is a uniform hieroglyphic,
And it means, Sprouting alike in broad zones and narrow zones,
Growing among black folks as among white,
Kanuck, Tuckahoe, Congressman, Cuff, I give them the same, I receive
    them the same.

And now it seems to me the beautiful uncut hair of graves.

Tenderly will I use your curling grass,
It may be you transpire from the breasts of young men,
It may be if I had known them I would have loved them,
It may be you are from old people, or from offspring taken soon out of
    their mothers' laps,
And here you are the mothers' laps.

This grass is very dark to be from the white heads of old mothers,
Darker than the colorless beards of old men,
Dark to come from under the faint red roofs of mouths.

O I perceive after all so many uttering tongues,
And I perceive they do not come from the roofs of mouths for nothing.

I wish I could translate the hints about the dead young men and women,
And the hints about old men and mothers, and the offspring taken soon
    out of their laps.

What do you think has become of the young and old men?
And what do you think has become of the women and children?

They are alive and well somewhere,
The smallest sprout shows there is really no death,
And if ever there was it led forward life, and does not wait at the end to
    arrest it,
And ceas'd the moment life appear'd.

All goes onward and outward, nothing collapses,
And to die is different from what any one supposed, and luckier.

WITH MUSIC STRONG I COME

With music strong I come, with my cornets and my drums,
I play not marches for accepted victors only, I play marches for con-
    quer'd and slain persons.

Have you heard that it was good to gain the day?
I also say it is good to fall, battles are lost in the same spirit in which they
    are won.

I beat and pound for the dead,
I blow through my embouchures my loudest and gayest for them.

Vivas to those who have fail'd!
And to those whose war-vessels sank in the sea!
And to those themselves who sank in the sea!
And to all generals that lost engagements, and all overcome heroes!
And the numberless unknown heroes equal to the greatest heroes known!

This is the meal equally set, this the meat for natural hunger,
It is for the wicked just the same as the righteous, I make appointments
     with all,
I will not have a single person slighted or left away,
The kept-woman, sponger, thief, are hereby invited,
The heavy-lipp'd slave is invited, the venerealee is invited;
There shall be no difference between them and the rest. . . .

Do you guess I have some intricate purpose?
Well I have, for the Fourth-month showers have, and the mica on the
     side of a rock has.

Do you take it I would astonish?
Does the daylight astonish? does the early redstart twittering through the
     woods?
Do I astonish more than they?

I AM HE THAT WALKS WITH THE TENDER AND GROWING NIGHT

I am he that walks with the tender and growing night,
I call to the earth and sea half-held by the night.

Press close bare-bosom'd night — press close magnetic nourishing night!
Night of south winds — night of the large few stars!
Still nodding night — mad naked summer night.

Smile O voluptuous cool-breath'd earth!
Earth of the slumbering and liquid trees!
Earth of departed sunset — earth of the mountains misty-topt!
Earth of the vitreous pour of the full moon just tinged with blue!
Earth of shine and dark mottling the tide of the river!
Earth of the limpid gray of clouds brighter and clearer for my sake!
Far-swooping elbow'd earth — rich apple-blossom'd earth!
Smile, for your lover comes.

Prodigal, you have given me love — therefore I to you give love!
O unspeakable passionate love.

DAZZLING AND TREMENDOUS HOW QUICK THE SUN–RISE WOULD KILL ME

Dazzling and tremendous how quick the sun-rise would kill me,
If I could not now and always send sun-rise out of me.

We also ascend dazzling and tremendous as the sun,
We found our own O my soul in the calm and cool of the day-break.

My voice goes after what my eyes cannot reach,
With the twirl of my tongue I encompass worlds and volumes of worlds.

Speech is the twin of my vision, it is unequal to measure itself,
It provokes me forever, it says sarcastically,
Walt you contain enough, why don't you let it out then?

Come now I will not be tantalized, you conceive too much of articulation,
Do you know O speech how the buds beneath you are folded?
Waiting in gloom, protected by frost,
The dirt receding before my prophetical screams,
I underlying causes to balance them at last,
My knowledge my live parts, it keeping tally with the meaning of all things.
Happiness, (which whoever hears me let him or her set out in search of this day.)

From SALUT AU MONDE

My spirit has pass'd in compassion and determination around the whole earth,
I have look'd for equals and lovers and found them ready for me in all lands,
I think some divine rapport has equalized me with them.

You vapors, I think I have risen with you, moved away to distant continents, and fallen down there, for reasons,
I think I have blown with you you winds;
You waters I have finger'd every shore with you,
I have run through what any river or strait of the globe has run through,
I have taken my stand on the bases of peninsulas and on the high embedded rocks, to cry thence:

Salut au monde!
What cities the light or warmth penetrates I penetrate those cities myself,
All islands to which birds wing their way I wing my way myself.

Toward you all, in America's name,
I raise high the perpendicular hand, I make the signal,
To remain after me in sight forever,
For all the haunts and homes of men.

Emily Dickinson
1830-1886

THERE'S A CERTAIN SLANT OF LIGHT

There's a certain slant of
    light,
Winter afternoons —
That oppresses, like the heft
Of cathedral tunes.

Heavenly hurt it gives us —
We can find no scar,
But internal difference,
Where the meanings are.

None may teach it — any —
'Tis the seal despair —
An imperial affliction
Sent us of the air.

When it comes, the landscape
    listens,
Shadows hold their breath —
When it goes, 'tis like the distance
On the look of death.

THERE CAME A WIND LIKE A BUGLE

There came a wind like a bugle —
It quivered through the grass
And a green chill upon the heat
So ominous did pass
We barred the windows and the doors
As from an emerald ghost —
The doom's electric moccasin
That very instant passed
On a strange mob of panting trees,
And fences fled away,
And rivers where the houses ran
Those looked that lived — that day —
The bell within the steeple wild
The flying tidings told —
How much can come
And much can go,
And yet abide the world!

A NARROW FELLOW IN THE GRASS

A narrow fellow in the grass
Occasionally rides;
You may have met him? — did you
    not
His notice sudden is.

The grass divides as with a comb —
A spotted shaft is seen;
And then it closes at your feet
And opens further on.

He likes a boggy acre,
A floor too cool for corn.
Yet when a boy, and barefoot,
I more than once at noon

Have passed, I thought, a whip-
    lash
Unbraiding in the sun —
When, stooping to secure it,
It wrinkled, and was gone.

Several of nature's people
I know, and they know me —
I feel for them a transport
Of cordiality —

But never met this fellow,
Attended or alone,
Without a tighter breathing,
And zero at the bone.

GREAT STREETS OF SILENCE LED AWAY

Great streets of silence led away
To neighbourhoods of pause —
Here was no notice — no
    dissent —
No universe — no laws.

By clocks, 'twas morning, and for
    night
The bells at distance called;
But epoch had no basis here
For period exhaled.

OUR JOURNEY HAD ADVANCED

Our journey had advanced —
Our feet were almost come
To that odd fork in Being's road,
Eternity — by term.

Our pace took sudden awe,
Our feet reluctant led.
Before were cities, but between,
The forest of the dead.

Retreat was out of hope —
Behind, a sealèd route,
Eternity's white flag before,
And God at every gate.

IT WAS NOT DEATH, FOR I STOOD UP

It was not death, for I stood up,
And all the dead lie down —
It was not night, for all the bells
Put out their tongues, for noon.

It was not frost, for on my flesh
I felt siroccos crawl —
Nor fire, for just my marble feet
Could keep a chancel cool.

And yet it tasted like them
    all,
The figures I have seen
Set orderly, for burial,
Reminded me of mine,

As if my life were shaven,
And fitted to a frame,
And could not breathe without a
    key,
And 'twas like midnight, some —

When everything that ticked has
    stopped,
And space stares all around,
Or grisly frosts, first autumn morns,
Repeal the beating ground.

But most like chaos — stopless —
    cool —
Without a chance or spar,
Or even a report of land
To justify despair.

MY LIFE CLOSED TWICE

My life closed twice before its close;
It yet remains to see
If Immortality unveil
A third event to me,

So huge, so hopeless to conceive
As these that twice befell.
Parting is all we know of heaven,
And all we need of hell.

AMPLE MAKE THIS BED

Ample make this bed —
Make this bed with awe —
In it wait till judgment break
Excellent and fair.

Be its mattress straight —
Be its pillow round —
Let no sunrise' yellow noise
Interrupt this ground.

Robert Browning
1812-1889

SONG *from* IN A GONDOLA

THE MOTH'S KISS, FIRST

The Moth's kiss, first!
Kiss me as if you made believe
You were not sure, this eve,
How my face, your flower, had pursed
Its petals up; so, here and there
You brush it, till I grow aware
Who wants me, and wide open burst.

The Bee's kiss, now!
Kiss me as if you entered gay
My heart at some noonday,
A bud that dares not disallow
The claim, so all is rendered up,
And passively its shattered cup
Over your head to sleep I bow.

MISCONCEPTIONS

This is a spray the Bird clung to,
  Making it blossom with pleasure,
Ere the high tree-top she sprung to,
  Fit for her nest and her treasure.
  Oh, what a hope beyond measure
Was the poor spray's, which the flying feet hung to, —
So to be singled out, built in, and sung to!

This is a heart the Queen leant on,
  Thrilled in a minute erratic,
Ere the true bosom she bent on,
  Meet for love's regal dalmatic.
  Oh, what a fancy ecstatic
Was the poor heart's, ere the wanderer went on —
Love to be saved for it, proffered to, spent on!

PORPHYRIA'S LOVER

The rain set early in to-night,
  The sullen wind was soon awake,
It tore the elm-tops down for spite,
  And did its worst to vex the lake,
  I listened with heart fit to break.
When glided in Porphyria; straight
  She shut the cold out and the storm,
And kneeled and made the cheerless grate
  Blaze up, and all the cottage warm;
  Which done, she rose, and from her form
Withdrew the dripping cloak and shawl,
  And laid her soiled gloves by, untied
Her hat and let the damp hair fall,
  And, last, she sat down by my side

And called me. When no voice replied,
She put my arm about her waist,
  And made her smooth white shoulder bare,
And all her yellow hair displaced,
  And, stooping, made my cheek lie there,
  And spread o'er all her yellow hair,
Murmuring how she loved me — she
  Too weak, for all her heart's endeavour,
To set its struggling passion free
  From pride, and vainer ties dissever,
  And give herself to me for ever.
But passion sometimes would prevail,
  Nor could to-night's gay feast restrain
A sudden thought of one so pale
  For love of her, and all in vain;
  So, she was come through wind and rain.
Be sure I looked up at her eyes
  Happy and proud; at last I knew
Porphyria worshipped me; surprise
  Made my heart swell, and still it grew
  While I debated what to do.
That moment she was mine, mine, fair,
  Perfectly pure and good: I found
A thing to do, and all her hair
  In one long yellow string I wound
  Three times her little throat around,
And strangled her. No pain felt she;
  I am quite sure she felt no pain.
As a shut bud that holds the bee,
  I warily oped her lids; again
  Laughed the blue eyes without a stain.
And I untightened next the tress
  About her neck; her cheek once more
Blushed bright beneath my burning kiss:
  I propped her head up as before,
  Only, this time *my* shoulder bore
Her head, which droops upon it still:
  The smiling rosy little head,
So glad it has its utmost will,
  That all it scorned at once is fled,
  And I, its love, am gained instead!
Porphyria's love: she guessed not how
  Her darling one wish would be heard.
And thus we sit together now,
  And all night long we have not stirred,
  And yet God has not said a word!

IN A YEAR

Never any more
  While I live,
Need I hope to see his face
  As before.
Once his love grown chill,
  Mine may strive —
Bitterly we re-embrace,
  Single still.

Was it something said,
  Something done,
Vexed him? was it touch of hand,
  Turn of head?
Strange! that very way
  Love begun.
I as little understand
  Love's decay.

When I sewed or drew,
  I recall
How he looked as if I sang,
  — Sweetly too.
If I spoke a word,
  First of all
Up his cheek the colour sprang,
  Then he heard.

Sitting by my side,
  At my feet,
So he breathed the air I breathed,
  Satisfied!
I, too, at love's brim
  Touched the sweet:
I would die if death bequeathed
  Sweet to him.

"Speak, I love thee best!"
  He exclaimed:
"Let my love thy own foretell, —"
  I confessed:
"Clasp my heart on thine
  Now unblamed,
Since upon thy soul as well
  Hangeth mine!"

Was it wrong to own,
  Being truth?
Why should all the giving prove
  His alone?
I had wealth and ease,
  Beauty, youth —
Since my lover gave me love,
  I gave these.

That was all I meant,
  — To be just,
And the passion I had raised
  To content.
Since he chose to change
  Gold for dust,
If I gave him what he praised
  Was it strange?

Would he loved me yet,
  On and on,
While I found some way undreamed
  — Paid my debt!
Gave more life and more,
  Till, all gone,
He should smile "She never seemed
  Mine before.

"What — she felt the while,
  Must I think?
Love's so different with us men."
  He should smile.
"Dying for my sake —
  White and pink!
Can't we touch these bubbles then
  But they break?"

Dear, the pang is brief.
  Do thy part,
Have thy pleasure. How perplext
  Grows belief!
Well, this cold clay clod
  Was man's heart.
Crumble it, and what comes next?
  Is it God?

Matthew Arnold
1822-1888

PHILOMELA

Hark! ah, the nightingale —
The tawny-throated!
Hark, from that moonlit cedar what a burst!
What triumph! hark! — what pain!

O wanderer from a Grecian shore,
Still, after many years, in distant lands,
Still nourishing in thy bewilder'd brain
That wild, unquench'd, deep-sunken, old-world pain —
Say, will it never heal?
And can this fragrant lawn
With its cool trees, and night,
And the sweet, tranquil Thames,
And moonshine, and the dew,
To thy rack'd heart and brain
Afford no balm?

Dost thou to-night behold,
Here, through the moonlight on this English grass,
The unfriendly palace in the Thracian wild?
Dost thou again peruse
With hot cheeks and sear'd eyes
The too clear web, and thy dumb sister's shame?
Dost thou once more assay
Thy flight, and feel come over thee,
Poor fugitive, the feathery change
Once more, and once more seem to make resound
With love and hate, triumph and agony,
Lone Daulis, and the high Cephissian vale?
Listen, Eugenia —
How thick the bursts come crowding through the leaves!
Again — thou hearest?
Eternal passion!
Eternal pain!

Robert Bridges

1844-1930

NIGHTINGALES

Beautiful must be the mountains whence ye come,
And bright in the fruitful valleys the streams, wherefrom
    Ye learn your song:
Where are those starry woods? O might I wander there,
  Among the flowers, which in that heavenly air
    Bloom the year long!

Nay, barren are those mountains and spent the streams:
Our song is the voice of desire, that haunts our dreams,
    A throe of the heart,
Whose pining visions dim, forbidden hopes profound,
  No dying cadence nor long sigh can sound,
    For all our art.

Alone, aloud in the raptured ear of men
We pour our dark nocturnal secret; and then,
    As night is withdrawn
From those sweet-springing meads and bursting boughs of May,
  Dream, while the innumerable choir of day
    Welcome the dawn.

Gerard Manley Hopkins

1844-1889

In the threadbare minor poetry of the later Victorian and the Edwardian eras, though the technique of the art had recently been enriched by the innovations of Father Gerard Manley Hopkins, these had not yet had time to sink into the consciousness. But now, where these examples have been followed, they have not been understood, and Hopkins has met with the fate of nearly all innovators. Hopkins should never be regarded as a model, since he worked his own discoveries to the uttermost point; there is no room for advancement, or development, along his lines. His imitators have misunderstood his examples, and, ignorant that his rhythmical impetus, his magnificence of texture, are the results, at once natural and cultivated, of the properties of his material acted upon by the impact of his personality, they produce poems with superimposed rhythms, exterior and therefore unliving rhythms, instead of rhythms which live in, under, and over the lines. Unskillful imitations of him have resulted, too, in a complete loss of melody, arising from falsified, clumsy, or too thick vowel-schemes, clumsy and huddled assonance patterns, useless alliterations, and a meaningless accumulation of knotted consonants.

Yet great are the technical wonders from which these imitations have sprung. Not, perhaps, since Dryden and Pope have we had such mountains and gulfs, such raging waves, such deserts of the eternal cold, and these are produced not by a succession of images alone, but by the movement of the lines, the texture, and by Hopkins' supreme gift of rhetoric.

I will not discuss Hopkins' use of sprung rhythm, since, after his own notes on the subject, nothing is left to say. I will dwell, rather, on what at first sight seems the strange imagery (it is of great beauty) of his poems.

Sir Wentworth D'Arcy Thompson, in *Growth and Form,* wrote of a "great Aristotelian theme — the search for relations between things apparently disconnected, and for 'similitude in things to common view unlike.'" Perrin speaks with admiration, in *Les Atomes,* of men like Galileo and Carnot, who "possessed the power of perceiving analogies to an extraordinary degree." Hume declared, and Mill said much the same thing, that all reasoning whatsoever depends on resemblance or analogy, and the power to recognize it.

Hopkins possessed this "power of perceiving analogies" to an extraordinary degree. He had, as Emerson said of Plato, a "genial radiation, skillful to discriminate power from form, essence from accident, and opening by its terminology and definition, high roads into nature."

Hopkins had an acute and strange visual sense, piercing down to the essence of the thing seen, and by endowing it with attributes which at first seem alien, with colors that are sharper, clearer, more piercing than those that are seen by the common eye, he succeeds in producing its inherent spirit.

This acute and piercing visual apprehension, this sharpening and heightening of the thing seen, so as to obtain its essential spirit, produces great beauty in *The May Magnificat.* Here, in the sharply seen image of the "star-eyed strawberry-breasted" thrush — strawberry-breasted because of the freckles on her breast — in the enhanced and deepened color of the "bugle blue eggs" (I presume the image is derived from the deep blue wildflower of that name — bugle, or bugloss), in which the sharp *u* of "bugle" melting to the softer *u* of "blue" gives the reflection and the sisterhood of the deep blue heaven, the flower, and the egg, we have a piercing truth-finding vision.

Both here, in the poems with short lines, and in those long lines that are not "rhythm run to seed: everything is weighed in them" (letter to Robert Bridges, 1882) and in the *Notebooks,* we find this piercing vision. "I see how chestnuts in bloom look like big seeded strawberries" (*Note-*

books). "Antares sparkled like a bright crab-apple tingling in the wind" (*Notebooks*). "As kingfishers catch fire, dragon-flies draw flame" (A Sonnet).

In the first verse of that great poem *The Wreck of the* Deutschland, we have the huge primeval swell of the sea, with its mountain-heights and its hell-depths, and we have the movement before life began, conveyed by technical means.

In the slow and majestic first line, "Thou mastering me," the long and strongly swelling vowels and the alliterative *m*'s produce the sensation of an immense wave getting itself up, rising slowly, ever increasing in its huge power, till we come to the pause that follows the long vowel of "me." Then the wave falls, only to rush forward again.

After this majestic line comes the heaving line "God! giver of breath and bread," ending with the ship poised on the top of the wave. This last effect is caused by the assonances of "breath" and "bread." The sound of "breath" is slightly longer, has slightly more of a swell beneath the surface than "bread," because of the *th*. This pause on the top of the wave is followed by the gigantic straining forward of the waves in the line "World's strand, sway of the sea," an effect that has been produced by the strong alliterative *s*'s, reinforced by the internal *r*'s of "World's strand," followed by the internal *w* of "sway." This line, after the huge tossing up and down from the dulled *a* of "strand" to the higher dissonantal *a* of "sway," ends by sweeping forward still further with the long vowel-sound of "sea," a sound that is more peaceful than that of "strand" and "sway" because of its absence of consonants.

The whole poem is inhabited by a gigantic and overwhelming power, like that of the element that inspired it. The huge force produced by the alliteration in the lines I have analyzed above, and in such a line as "Thou hast bound bones and veins in me, fastened me flesh," has never been exceeded, even by Dryden and by Pope, those masters of the effects that can be produced by alliteration. It is true that the last line I have quoted from Hopkins is necessarily, because of the subject, more static than most of the more magnificent lines of Dryden and Pope, yet Hopkins' line is of an equally giant stature.

At the end of this verse, the huge primeval power, splendor and terror which inhabit it change to the softness and tenderness of "Once again I feel thy finger and find thee" — a line which is equaled in gentleness and sweetness by the lovely line in the ninth verse: "Thou art lightning and love, I found it, a winter and warm." How huge is the contrast between this and the black coldness and opaqueness, like that of savage waters, of the line "And the sea flint-flake, black-backed in the regular blow." The opaqueness of this is caused by the flat assonances, the thick consonants, of "black-backed" and "blow."

In the same verse, we find this line: "Wiry and white-fiery and whirlwind-swivellèd snow." I cannot recall any other English poet who has produced such a feeling of huge and elemental cold as Hopkins.

In the line quoted above, he produces the sensation of watching a wave receding and then plunging forward, by rhyming the first and the fourth word. A higher and more piercing dissonantal *i* precedes the second rhyme, and this feeling of the wave plunging forward is the result, too, of the internal *r*'s which always lengthen a word or else make it flutter. In this case (as in the line "World's strand, sway of the sea") they lengthen it or rather give the feeling of an immeasurable force driving onward.

This relentless and inevitable wave-stretch, this driving onward, contained in the sound of "whirl," is followed immediately by the shrinking sound of "wind," the *i*'s in "wind" and "swivellèd" being dulled with cold.

A lovely movement, a sense that all is well, that all creation is part of a controlled and gigantic design, is given by the internal rhymes and assonances of the twenty-sixth stanza.

The movement of this is like that of a bird flying through the bright air, swooping downward to its nest, then up again through the holy and peaceful light.

We find a lovely floating movement, but this time not like that of a bird flying home through the wide air, but, instead, like that of a bird seeking its nest through the soft dark leaves of a wood, in *Peace*.

It is owing to the reiterations, and to the subtle arrangement of the exquisitely soft and hardly perceptible variations of the *o* and *u* sounds ("wood," "you," "do," "poor," "pure," "good," "plumes," "coo," and "brood") with their higher dissonances "round" and "boughs," that we see the dove circling through the trees, that we hear its soft warm voice. In this poem the form, the texture and the subject form one miraculous whole.

If we compare this with the terror and huge strength of *Carrion Comfort* — perhaps the greatest of Hopkins' sonnets — we shall see the variety of which he is capable.

The great strangeness of this poem is almost entirely a matter of texture. Hopkins recognized this strangeness in nearly all his poems, for he wrote in a letter dated 1879: "No doubt my poems err on the side of oddness. I hope in time to have a more balanced and Miltonic style. But as air, melody, is what strikes me most of all in music, and design in painting, so design, pattern, of that I can inscape is what I, above all, aim at in poetry. Now it is the virtue of design, pattern, or inscape to be distinctive, and it is the vice of distinctiveness to become queer. This vice I cannot have escaped." Later, we find him explaining, ". . . when, on somebody returning me the Euridice, I opened and read some lines, as one commonly reads whether prose or verse, with the eyes, so to say only, it struck me aghast with a kind of raw nakedness and unmitigated violence I was unprepared for: but take breath and read it with the ears, as I always wish to read, and my verse becomes all right."

It is exactly in this raw nakedness and unmitigated violence, in a leonine majesty, that Hopkins' greatness was shown.

THE WRECK OF THE *DEUTSCHLAND*

To the
happy memory of five Franciscan Nuns
exiles by the Falk Laws
drowned between midnight and morning of
Dec. 7th, 1875

PART THE FIRST

    Thou mastering me
   God! giver of breath and bread;
  World's strand, sway of the sea;
   Lord of living and dead;
Thou hast bound bones and veins in me, fastened me flesh,
And after it almost unmade, what with dread,
  Thy doing: and dost thou touch me afresh?
Over again I feel thy finger and find thee.

    I did say yes
   O at lightning and lashed rod;
  Thou heardst me truer than tongue confess
   Thy terror, O Christ, O God;
Thou knowest the walls, altar and hour and night:
The swoon of a heart that the sweep and the hurl of thee trod
  Hard down with a horror of height:
And the midriff astrain with leaning of, laced with fire of stress.

    The frown of his face
   Before me, the hurtle of hell
  Behind, where, where was a, where was a place?
   I whirled out wings that spell
And fled with a fling of the heart to the heart of the Host.
My heart, but you were dovewinged, I can tell,
  Carrier-witted, I am bold to boast,
To flash from the flame to the flame then, tower from the grace to the
    grace.

    I am soft sift
   In an hourglass — at the wall
  Fast, but mined with a motion, a drift,
   And it crowds and it combs to the fall;
I steady as a water in a well, to a poise, to a pane,
But roped with, always, all the way down from the tall
  Fells or flanks of the voel, a vein
Of the gospel proffer, a pressure, a principle, Christ's gift.

I kiss my hand
To the stars, lovely-asunder
Starlight, wafting him out of it; and
Glow, glory in thunder;
Kiss my hand to the dappled-with-damson west:
Since, tho' he is under the world's splendour and wonder,
His mystery must be instressed, stressed;
For I greet him the days I meet him, and bless when I understand.

Not out of his bliss
Springs the stress felt
Nor first from heaven (and few know this)
Swings the stroke dealt —
Stroke and a stress that stars and storms deliver,
That guilt is hushed by, hearts are flushed by and melt —
But it rides time like riding a river
(And here the faithful waver, the faithless fable and miss).

It dates from day
Of his going in Galilee;
Warm-laid grave of a womb-life grey;
Manger, maiden's knee;
The dense and the driven Passion, and frightful sweat;
Thence the discharge of it, there its swelling to be,
Though felt before, though in high flood yet —
What none would have known of it, only the heart, being hard at bay,

Is out with it! Oh,
We lash with the best or worst
Word last! How a lush-kept plush-capped sloe
Will, mouthed to flesh-burst,
Gush! flush the man, the being with it, sour or sweet,
Brim, in a flash, full! — Hither then, last or first,
To hero of Calvary, Christ's feet —
Never ask if meaning it, wanting it, warned of it — men go.

Be adored among men,
God, three-numberèd form;
Wring thy rebel, dogged in den,
Man's malice, with wrecking and storm.
Beyond saying sweet, past telling of tongue,
Thou art lightning and love, I found it, a winter and warm;
Father and fondler of heart thou hast wrung:
Hast thy dark descending and most art merciful then.

With an anvil-ding
And with fire in him forge thy will
Or rather, rather then, stealing as Spring
Through him, melt him but master him still:
Whether at once, as once at a crash Paul,
Or as Austin, a lingering-out swéet skíll,
Make mercy in all of us, out of us all
Mastery, but be adored, but be adored King.

PART THE SECOND

"Some find me a sword; some
The flange and the rail; flame,
Fang, or flood" goes Death on drum,
And storms bugle his fame.
But wé dream we are rooted in earth — Dust!
Flesh falls within sight of us, we, though our flower the same,
Wave with the meadow, forget that there must
The sour scythe cringe, and the blear share come.

On Saturday sailed from Bremen,
American-outward-bound,
Take settler and seaman, tell men with women,
Two hundred souls in the round —
O Father, not under thy feathers nor ever as guessing
The goal was a shoal, of a fourth the doom to be drowned;
Yet did the dark side of the bay of thy blessing
Not vault them, the millions of rounds of thy mercy not reeve even them
        in?

Into the snows she sweeps,
Hurling the haven behind,
The Deutschland, on Sunday; and so the sky keeps,
For the infinite air is unkind,
And the sea flint-flake, black-backed in the regular blow,
Sitting Eastnortheast, in cursed quarter, the wind;
Wiry and white-fiery and whirlwind-swivellèd snow
Spins to the widow-making unchilding unfathering deeps.

She drove in the dark to leeward,
She struck — not a reef or a rock
But the combs of a smother of sand: night drew her
Dead to the Kentish Knock;
And she beat the bank down with her bows and the ride of her keel:
The breakers rolled on her beam with ruinous shock;
And canvas and compass, the whorl and the wheel
Idle for ever to waft her or wind her with, these she endured.

Hope had grown grey hairs,
Hope had mourning on,
Trenched with tears, carved with cares,
Hope was twelve hours gone;
And frightful a nightfall folded rueful a day
Nor rescue, only rocket and lightship, shone,
And lives at last were washing away:
To the shrouds they took — they shook in the hurling and horrible airs.

One stirred from the rigging to save
The wild woman-kind below,
With a rope's end round the man, handy and brave —
He was pitched to his death at a blow,
For all his dreadnought breast and braids of thew:
They could tell him for hours, dandled the to and fro
Through the cobbled foam-fleece, what could he do
With the burl of the fountains of air, buck and the flood of the wave?

They fought with God's cold —
And they could not and fell to the deck
(Crushed them) or water (and drowned them) or rolled
With the sea-romp over the wreck.
Night roared, with the heart-break hearing a heart-broke rabble,
The woman's wailing, the crying of child without check —
Till a lioness arose breasting the babble,
A prophetess towered in the tumult, a virginal tongue told.

Ah, touched in your bower of bone
Are you! turned for an exquisite smart,
Have you! make words break from me here all alone
Do you! — mother of being in me, heart.
O unteachably after evil, but uttering truth,
Why, tears! is it? tears; such a melting, a madrigal start!
Never-eldering revel and river of youth,
What can it be, this glee? the good you have there of your own?

Sister, a sister calling
A master, her master and mine! —
And the inboard seas run swirling and hawling;
The rash smart sloggering brine
Blinds her; but she that weather sees one thing, one;
Has one fetch in her: she rears herself to divine
Ears, and the call of the tall nun
To the men in the tops and the tackle rode over the storm's brawling.

She was the first of a five and came
  Of a coifèd sisterhood.
(O Deutschland, double a desperate name!
  O world wide of its good!
But Gertrude, lily, and Luther, are two of a town,
  Christ's lily and beast of the waste wood:
    From life's dawn it is drawn down,
Abel is Cain's brother and breasts they have sucked the same.)

Loathed for a love men knew in them,
  Banned by the land of their birth,
Rhine refused them. Thames would ruin them;
  Surf, snow, river and earth
Gnashed: but thou art above, thou Orion of light;
  Thy unchancelling poising palms were weighing the worth,
    Thou martyr-master: in thy sight
Storm flakes were scroll-leaved flowers, lily showers — sweet heaven was
    astrew in them.

Five! the finding and sake
  And cipher of suffering Christ.
Mark, the mark is of man's make
  And the word of it Sacrificed.
But he scores it in scarlet himself on his own bespoken,
  Before-time-taken, dearest prizèd and priced —
    Stigma, signal, cinquefoil token
For lettering of the lamb's fleece, ruddying of the rose-flake.

Joy fall to thee, father Francis,
  Drawn to the Life that died;
With the gnarls of the nails in thee, niche of the lance, his
  Lovescape crucified
And seal of his seraph-arrival! and these thy daughters
  And five-livèd and leavèd favour and pride,
    Are sisterly sealed in wild waters,
To bathe in his fall-gold mercies, to breathe in his all-fire glances.

Away in the loveable west,
  On a pastoral forehead of Wales,
I was under a roof here, I was at rest,
  And they the prey of the gales;
She to the black-about air, to the breaker, the thickly
  Falling flakes, to the throng that catches and quails
    Was calling "O Christ, Christ, come quickly":
The cross to her she calls Christ to her, christens her wild-worst Best.

The majesty! what did she mean?
Breathe, arch and original Breath.
Is it love in her of the being as her lover had been?
Breathe, body of lovely Death.
They were else-minded then, altogether, the men
Woke thee with a *we are perishing* in the weather of Gennesareth.
Or is it that she cried for the crown then,
The keener to come at the comfort for feeling the combating keen?

For how to the heart's cheering
The down-dugged ground-hugged grey
Hovers off, the jay-blue heavens appearing
Of pied and peeled May!
Blue-beating and hoary-glow height; or night, still higher,
With belled fire and the moth-soft Milky Way,
What by your measure is the heaven of desire,
The treasure never eyesight got, nor was ever guessed what for the
hearing?

No, but it was not these.
The jading and jar of the cart,
Time's tasking, it is fathers that asking for ease
Of the sodden-with-its-sorrowing heart,
Not danger, electrical horror; then further it finds
The appealing of the Passion is tenderer in prayer apart:
Other, I gather, in measure her mind's
Burden, in wind's burly and beat of endragonèd seas.

But how shall I . . . make me room there:
Reach me a . . . Fancy, come faster —
Strike you the sight of it? look at it loom there,
Thing that she . . . there then! the Master,
Ipse, the only one, Christ, King, Head:
He was to cure the extremity where he had cast her;
Do, deal, lord it with living and dead;
Let him ride, her pride, in his triumph, despatch and have done with his
doom there.

Ah! there was a heart right
There was single eye!
Read the unshapeable shock night
And knew the who and the why;
Wording it how but by him that present and past,
Heaven and earth are word of, worded by? —
The Simon Peter of a soul! to the blast
Tarpeian-fast, but a blown beacon of light.

Jesu, heart's light,
Jesu, maid's son,
What was the feast followed the night
Thou hadst glory of this nun? —
Feast of the one woman without stain.
For so conceivèd, so to conceive thee is done;
But here was heart-throe, birth of a brain,
Word, that heard and kept thee and uttered thee outright.

Well, she has thee for the pain, for the
Patience; but pity of the rest of them!
Heart, go and bleed at a bitterer vein for the
Comfortless unconfessed of them —
No not uncomforted: lovely-felicitous Providence
Finger of a tender of, O of a feathery delicacy, the breast of the
Maiden could obey so, be a bell to, ring of it, and
Startle the poor sheep back! is the shipwreck then a harvest, does tempest
carry the grain for thee?

I admire thee, master of the tides,
Of the Yore-flood, of the year's fall;
The recurb and the recovery of the gulf's sides,
The girth of it and the wharf of it and the wall;
Stanching, quenching ocean of a motionable mind;
Ground of being, and granite of it: past all
Grasp God, throned behind
Death with a sovereignty that heeds but hides, bodes but abides;

With a mercy that outrides
The all of water, an ark
For the listener; for the lingerer with a love glides
Lower than death and the dark;
A vein for the visiting of the past-prayer, pent in prison,
The-last-breath penitent spirits — the uttermost mark
Our passion-plungèd giant risen,
The Christ of the Father compassionate, fetched in the storm of his
strides.

Now burn, new born to the world,
Doubled-naturèd name,
The heaven-flung, heart-fleshed, maiden-furled
Miracle-in-Mary-of-flame,
Mid-numbered He in three of the thunder-throne!
Not a dooms-day dazzle in his coming nor dark as he came;
Kind, but royally reclaiming his own;
A released shower, let flash to the shire, not a lightning of fire hard-
hurled.

Dame, at our door
Drowned, and among our shoals,
Remember us in the roads, the heaven-haven of the Reward:
Our King back, oh, upon English souls!
Let him easter in us, be a dayspring to the dimness of us, be a crimson-
cresseted east,
More brightening her, rare-dear Britain, as his reign rolls,
Pride, rose, prince, hero of us, high-priest,
Our hearts' charity's hearth's fire, our thoughts' chivalry's throng's Lord.

PEACE

When will you ever, Peace, wild wooddove, shy wings shut,
Your round me roaming end, and under be my boughs?
When, when, Peace, will you, Peace? I'll not play hypocrite
To my own heart: I yield you do come sometimes; but
That piecemeal peace is poor peace. What pure peace allows
Alarms of wars, the daunting wars, the death of it?

O surely, reaving Peace, my Lord should leave in lieu
Some good! And so he does leave Patience exquisite,
That plumes to Peace thereafter. And when Peace here does house
He comes with work to do, he does not come to coo,
He comes to brood and sit.

THE MAY MAGNIFICAT

May is Mary's month, and I
Muse at that and wonder why:
Her feasts follow reason,
Dated due to season —

Candlemas, Lady Day;
But the Lady Month, May,
Why fasten that upon her,
With a feasting in her honour?

Is it only its being brighter
Than the most are must delight her?
Is it opportunest
And flowers finds soonest?

Ask of her, the mighty mother:
Her reply puts this other
    Question: What is Spring? —
    Growth in every thing —

Flesh and fleece, fur and feather,
Grass and greenworld all together;
    Star-eyed strawberry-breasted
    Throstle above her nested

Cluster of bugle blue eggs thin
Forms and warms the life within;
    And bird and blossom swell
    In sod or sheath or shell.

All things rising, all things sizing
Mary sees, sympathising
    With that world of good,
    Nature's motherhood.

Their magnifying of each its kind
With delight calls to mind
    How she did in her stored
    Magnify the Lord.

Well but there was more than this:
Spring's universal bliss
    Much, had much to say
    To offering Mary May.

When drop-of-blood-and-foam-dapple
Bloom lights the orchard-apple
    And thicket and thorp are merry
    With silver-surfèd cherry

And azuring-over greybell makes
Wood banks and brakes wash wet like lakes
    And magic cuckoocall
    Caps, clears, and clinches all —

This ecstasy all through mothering earth
Tells Mary her mirth till Christ's birth
    To remember and exultation
    In God who was her salvation,

FRAGMENT: THE FURL OF FRESH–LEAVED
DOG–ROSE DOWN

The furl of fresh-leaved dog-rose down
His cheeks the forth-and-flaunting sun
Had swarthed about with lion-brown
Before the Spring was done.

His locks like all a ravel-rope's-end
With hempen strands in spray —
Fallow, foam-fallow, hanks — fall'n off their ranks
Swung down at a disarray.

Or like a juicy and jostling shock
Of bluebells sheaved in May
Or wind-long fleeces on the flock
A day off shearing-day.

Then over his turnèd temples — here —
Was a rose, or, failing that,
Rough-Robin or five-lipped campion clear
For a beauty-bow to his hat,
And the sunlight sidled, like dewdrops, like dandled diamonds,
Through the sieve of the straw of his hat.

THAT NATURE IS A HERACLITEAN FIRE AND OF
THE COMFORT OF THE RESURRECTION

Cloud-puffball, torn tufts, tossed pillows flaunt forth, then chevy on an air-
built thoroughfare: heaven-roysterers, in gay-gangs they throng; they glit-
ter in marches.
Down roughcast, down dazzling whitewash, wherever an elm arches,
Shivelights and shadowtackle in long lashes lace, lance, and pair.
Delightfully the bright wind boisterous ropes, wrestles, beats earth bare
Of yestertempest's creases; in pool and rut peel parches
Squandering ooze to squeezed dough, crust, dust; stanches, starches
Squadroned masks and manmarks treadmire toil there
Footfretted in it. Million-fuelèd, nature's bonfire burns on.
But quench her bonniest, dearest to her, her clearest-selvèd spark
Man, how fast his firedint, his mark on mind, is gone!
Both are in an unfathomable, all is in an enormous dark
Drowned. O pity and indignation! Manshape, that shone

Sheer off, disseveral, a star, death blots black out; nor mark
           Is any of him at all so stark
But vastness blurs and time beats level. Enough! the Resurrection,
A heart's-clarion! Away grief's gasping, joyless days, dejection.
           Across my foundering deck shone
A beacon, an eternal beam. Flesh fade, and mortal trash
Fall to the residuary worm; world's wildfire, leave but ash:
           In a flash, at a trumpet crash,
I am all at once what Christ is, since he was what I am, and
This Jack, joke, poor potsherd, patch, matchwood, immortal diamond,
           Is immortal diamond.

CARRION COMFORT

Not, I'll not, carrion comfort, Despair, not feast on thee;
Not untwist — slack they may be — these last strands of man
In me ór, most weary, cry *I can no more.* I can;
Can something, hope, wish day come, not choose not to be.
But ah, but O thou terrible, why wouldst thou rude on me
Thy wring-world right foot rock? lay a lionlimb against me? scan
With darksome devouring eyes my bruised bones? and fan,
O in turns of tempest, me heaped there; me frantic to avoid thee and
    flee?

Why? That my chaff might fly; my grain lie, sheer and clear.
Nay in all that toil, that coil, since (seems) I kissed the rod,
Hand rather, my heart lo! lapped strength, stole joy, would laugh, chéer.
Cheer whom though? the hero whose heaven-handling flung me, fóot
    tród
Me? or me that fought him? O which one? is it each one? That night, that
    year
Of now done darkness I wretch lay wrestling with (my God!) my God.

THE WINDHOVER
To Christ our Lord

I caught this morning morning's minion, king-
   dom of daylight's dauphin, dapple-dawn-drawn Falcon, in his riding
  Of the rolling level underneath him steady air, and striding
High there, how he rung upon the rein of a wimpling wing
In his ecstasy! then off, off forth on swing,
  As a skate's heel sweeps smooth on a bow-bend: the hurl and gliding
  Rebuffed the big wind. My heart in hiding
Stirred for a bird — the achieve of, the mastery of the thing!

Brute beauty and valour and act, oh, air, pride, plume, here
Buckle! AND the fire that breaks from thee then, a billion
Times told lovelier, more dangerous, O my chevalier!

No wonder of it: shéer plód makes plough down sillion
Shine, and blue-bleak embers, ah my dear,
    Fall, gall themselves, and gash gold-vermilion.

Thomas Hardy

1840-1928

THE WOMAN I MET

A stranger, I threaded sunken-hearted
        A lamp-lit crowd;
And anon there passed me a soul departed,
        Who mutely bowed.
In my far-off youthful years I had met her,
Full-pulsed; but now, no more life's debtor,
        Onward she slid
    In a shroud that furs half-hid.

"Why do you trouble me, dead woman,
        Trouble me;
You whom I knew when warm and human?
        — How it be
That you quitted earth and are yet upon it
Is, to any who ponder on it,
        Past being read!"
    "Still, it is so," she said.

"These were my haunts in my olden sprightly
        Hours of health;
Here I went tempting frail youth nightly
        To their death;
But you deemed me chaste — me a tinselled sinner!
How thought you one with pureness in her
        Could pace this street
    Eyeing some man to greet?

"Well; your very simplicity made me love you
        Mid such town dross,
Till I set not Heaven itself above you,
        Who grew my Cross;

For you'd only nod, despite how I sighed for you;
So you tortured me, who fain would have died for you!
— What I suffered then
Would have paid for the sins of ten!

"Thus went the days. I feared you despised me
To fling me a nod
Each time, no more: till love chastised me
As with a rod
That a fresh bland boy of no assurance
Should fire me with passion beyond endurance
While others all
I hated, and loathed their call.

"I said: 'It is his mother's spirit
Hovering around,
To shield him, maybe!' I used to fear it,
As still I found
My beauty left no least impression,
And remnants of pride withheld confession
Of my true trade
By speaking; so I delayed.

"I said: 'Perhaps with a costly flower
He'll be beguiled.'
I held it, in passing you one late hour,
To your face: you smiled,
Keeping step with the throng; though you did not see there
A single one that rivalled me there!
Well: it's all past.
I died in the Lock at last."

So walked the dead and I together
The quick among,
Elbowing our kind of every feather
Slowly and long;
Yea, long and slowly, that a phantom should stalk there
With me seemed nothing strange, and talk there
That winter night
By flaming jets of light.

She showed me Juans who feared their call-time,
Guessing their lot;

NOTE. The Lock was a London hospital for syphilis. — E. S.

She showed me her sort that cursed their fall-time,
    And that did not.
Till suddenly murmured she: "Now, tell me,
Why asked you never, ere death befell me,
      To have my love,
      Much as I dreamt thereof?"

I could not answer. And she, well weeting
    All in my heart,
Said "God your guardian kept our fleeting
    Forms apart!"
Sighing and drawing her furs around her
Over the shroud that tightly bound her,
      With wafts as from clay
      She turned and thinned away.

A TRAMPWOMAN'S TRAGEDY

From Wynyard's Gap the livelong day,
    The livelong day,
We beat afoot the northward way
    We had travelled times before.
The sun-blaze burning on our backs,
Our shoulders sticking to our packs,
By fosseway, fields, and turnpike tracks
    We skirted sad Sedge-Moor.

Full twenty miles we jaunted on,
    We jaunted on —
My fancy-man, and jeering John,
    And Mother Lee, and I.
And, as the sun drew down to west,
We climbed the toilsome Poldon crest,
And saw, of landskip sights the best,
    The inn that beamed thereby.

For months we had padded side by side,
    Ay, side by side
Through the Great Forest, Blackmoor wide,
    And where the Parret ran.
We'd faced the gusts on Mendip ridge,
Had crossed the Yeo unhelped by bridge,
Been stung by every Marshwood midge,
    I and my fancy-man.

Lone inns we loved, my man and I,
    My man and I;
"King's Stag," "Windwhistle" high and dry,
    "The Horse" on Hintock Green,
The cosy house at Wynyard's Gap,
"The Hut" renowned on Bredy Knap,
And many another wayside tap
    Where folk might sit unseen.

Now as we trudged — O deadly day
    O deadly day! —
I teased my fancy-man in play
    And wanton idleness.
I walked alongside jeering John,
I laid his hand my waist upon;
I would not bend my glances on
    My lover's dark distress.

Thus Poldon top at last we won,
    At last we won,
And gained the inn at sink of sun
    Far-famed as "Marshal's Elm."
Beneath us figured tor and lea,
From Mendip to the western sea —
I doubt if finer sight there be
    Within this royal realm.

Inside the settle all a-row —
    All four a-row
We sat, I next to John, to show
    That he had wooed and won.
And then he took me on his knee,
And swore it was his turn to be
My favoured mate, and Mother Lee
    Passed to my former one.

Then in a voice I had never heard,
    I had never heard,
My only Love to me: "One word,
    My lady, if you please!
Whose is the child you are like to bear? —
His? After all my months o' care?"
God knows 'twas not! But, O despair!
    I nodded — still to tease.

Then up he sprung, and with his knife —
    And with his knife
He let out jeering Johnny's life,
    Yes; there, at set of sun.
The slant ray through the window nigh
Gilded John's blood and glazing eye,
Ere scarcely Mother Lee and I
    Knew that the deed was done.

The taverns tell the gloomy tale,
    The gloomy tale,
How that at Ivel-chester jail
    My Love, my sweetheart swung;
Though stained till now by no misdeed
Save one horse ta'en in time o' need;
(Blue Jimmy stole right many a steed
    Ere his last fling he flung.)

Thereaft I walked the world alone,
    Alone, alone!
On his death-day I gave my groan
    And dropt his dead-born child,
'Twas nigh the jail, beneath a tree,
None tending me; for Mother Lee
Had died at Glaston, leaving me
    Unfriended on the wild.

And in the night as I lay weak,
    As I lay weak,
The leaves a-falling on my cheek,
    The red moon low declined —
The ghost of him I'd die to kiss
Rose up and said: "Ah, tell me this!
Was the child mine, or was it his?
    Speak, that I rest may find!"

O doubt not but I told him then,
    I told him then,
That I had kept me from all men
    Since we joined lips and swore.
Whereat he smiled, and thinned away
As the wind stirred to call up day . . .
— 'Tis past! And here alone I stray
    Haunting the Western Moor.

AFTER A JOURNEY

Hereto I come to view a voiceless ghost;
  Whither, O whither will its whim now draw me?
Up the cliff, down, till I'm lonely, lost,
  And the unseen waters' ejaculations awe me.
Where you will next be there's no knowing,
  Facing round about me everywhere,
    With your nut-coloured hair,
And gray eyes, and rose-flush coming and going.

Yes: I have entered your olden haunts at last:
  Through the years, through the dead scenes I have tracked you;
What have you now found to say of our past —
  Scanned across the dark space wherein I have lacked you?
Summer gave us sweets, but autumn wrought division?
  Things were not lastly as firstly well
    With us twain, you tell?
But all's closed now, despite Time's derision.

I see what you are doing: you are leading me on
  To the spots we knew when we haunted here together,
The waterfall, above which the mist bow shone
  At the then fair hair in the then fair weather,
And the cave just under, with a voice still so hollow
  That it seems to call out to me from forty years ago,
    When you were all aglow,
And not the thin ghost that I now frailly follow!

Ignorant of what there is flitting here to see,
  The waked birds preen and the seals flop lazily;
Soon you will have, Dear, to vanish from me,
  For the stars close their shutters and the dawn whitens hazily.
Trust me, I mind not, though Life lours,
  The bringing me here; nay, bring me here again!
    I am just the same as when
Our days were a joy, and our paths through flowers.

THE HAUNTER

He does not think that I haunt here nightly;
  How shall I let him know
That whither his fancy sets him wandering
  I, too, alertly go? —

Hover and hover a few feet from him
    Just as I used to do,
But cannot answer the words he lifts me —
    Only listen thereto!

When I could answer he did not say them:
    When I could let him know
How I would like to join in his journeys
    Seldom he wished to go.
Now that he goes and wants me with him
    More than he used to do,
Never he sees my faithful phantom
    Though he speaks thereto.

Yes, I companion him to places
    Only dreamers know,
Where the shy hares print long paces,
    Where the night rooks go;
Into old aisles where the past is all to him,
    Close as his shade can do,
Always lacking the power to call to him,
    Near as I reach thereto!

What a good haunter I am, O tell him!
    Quickly make him know
If he but sigh since my loss befell him
    Straight to his side I go.
Tell him a faithful one is doing
    All that love can do.
Still that his path may be worth pursuing
    And to bring peace thereto.

Rudyard Kipling
1865-1936

THE RUNES ON WELAND'S SWORD

A Smith makes me	The Gold I gather
To betray my Man	Comes into England
In my first fight.	Out of deep Water
To gather Gold	Like a shining Fish
At the world's end	Then it descends
I am sent.	Into deep Water.

It is not given
For goods or gear,
But for The Thing.

The Gold I gather
A king covets
For an ill use.

The Gold I gather
Is drawn up
Out of deep Water.

Like a shining Fish
Then it descends
Into deep Water.

It is not given
For goods or gear,
But for The Thing.

HARP SONG OF THE DANE WOMEN

What is a woman that you forsake her,
And the hearth-fire and the home-acre,
To go with the old grey Widow-maker?

She has no house to lay a guest in —
But one chill bed for all to rest in,
That the pale suns and the stray bergs nest in.

She has no strong white arms to fold you,
But the ten-times-fingering weed to hold you —
Out on the rocks where the tide has rolled you.

Yet, when the signs of summer thicken,
And the ice breaks, and the birch-buds quicken,
Yearly you turn from our side, and sicken —

Sicken again for the shouts and the slaughters.
You steal away to the lapping waters,
And look at your ship in her winter-quarters.

You forget our mirth, and talk at the tables,
The kine in the shed and the horse in the stables —
To pitch her sides and go over her cables.

Then you drive out where the storm-clouds swallow,
And the sound of your oar-blades, falling hollow,
Is all we have left through the months to follow.

Ah, what is Woman that you forsake her,
And the hearth-fire and the home-acre,
To go with the old grey Widow-maker?

THE QUEEN'S MEN

Valour and Innocence
Have latterly gone hence
To certain death by certain shame attended.
Envy — ah! even to tears! —
The fortune of their years
Which, though so few, yet so divinely ended.

Scarce had they lifted up
Life's full and fiery cup,
Than they had set it down untouched before them.
Before their day arose
They beckoned it to close —
Close in confusion and destruction o'er them.

They did not stay to ask
What prize should crown their task —
Well sure that prize was such as no man strives for;
But passed into eclipse,
Her kiss upon their lips —
Even Belphoebe's, whom they gave their lives for!

A ST. HELENA LULLABY

"How far is St. Helena from a little child at play?"
  What makes you want to wander there with all the world between?
Oh, Mother, call your son again or else he'll run away.
  (No one thinks of winter when the grass is green!)

"How far is St. Helena from a fight in Paris Street?"
  I haven't time to answer now — the men are falling fast.
The guns begin to thunder, and the drums begin to beat.
  (If you take the first step, you will take the last!)

"How far is St. Helena from the field of Austerlitz?"
  You couldn't hear me if I told — so loud the cannon roar.
But not so far for people who are living by their wits.
  ("Gay go up" means "Gay go down" the wide world o'er!)

"How far is St. Helena from an Emperor of France?"
  I cannot see — I cannot tell — the Crowns they dazzle so.
The Kings sit down to dinner, and the Queens stand up to dance.
  (After open weather you may look for snow!)

"How far is St. Helena from the Capes of Trafalgar?"
  A longish way — a longish way — with ten year more to run.
It's South across the water underneath a falling star.
  (*What you cannot finish you must leave undone!*)

"How far is St. Helena from the Beresina ice?"
  An ill way — a chill way — the ice begins to crack.
But not so far for gentlemen who never took advice.
  (*When you can't go forward you must e'en come back!*)

"How far is St. Helena from the field of Waterloo?"
  A near way — a clear way — the ship will take you soon.
A pleasant place for gentlemen with little left to do.
  (*Morning never tries you till the afternoon!*)

"How far from St. Helena to the Gate of Heaven's Grace?"
  That no one knows — that no one knows — and no one ever will.
But fold your hands across your heart and cover up your face,
  And after all your trapesings, child, lie still!

John Masefield
b. 1878

SEA–CHANGE

"Goneys an' gullies an' all o' the birds o' the sea
  They ain't no birds, not really," said Billy the Dane.
"Not mollies, nor gullies, nor goneys at all," said he,
  "But simply the sperrits of mariners livin' again.

"Them birds goin' fishin' is nothin' but souls o' the drowned,
  Souls o' the drowned an' the kicked as are never no more;
An' that there haughty old albatross cruisin' around,
  Belike he's Admiral Nelson or Admiral Noah.

"An' merry's the life they are living. They settle and dip,
  They fishes, they never stands watches, they waggle their wings;
When a ship comes by, they fly to look at the ship
  To see how the nowaday mariners manages things.

"When freezing aloft in a snorter, I tell you I wish —
  (Though maybe it ain't like a Christian) — I wish I could be
A haughty old copper-bound albatross dipping for fish
  And coming the proud over all o' the birds o' the sea."

PORT OF HOLY PETER

The blue laguna rocks and quivers,
  Dull gurgling eddies twist and spin,
The climate does for people's livers,
  It's a nasty place to anchor in
      Is Spanish port,
      Fever port,
      Port of Holy Peter.

The town begins on the sea-beaches,
  And the town's mad with the stinging flies,
The drinking water's mostly leeches,
  It's a far remove from Paradise
      Is Spanish port,
      Fever port,
      Port of Holy Peter.

There's sand-bagging and throat-slitting,
  And quiet graves in the sea slime,
Stabbing, of course, and rum-hitting,
  Dirt, and drink, and stink, and crime,
      In Spanish port,
      Fever port,
      Port of Holy Peter.

All the day the wind's blowing
  From the sick swamp below the hills,
All the night the plague's growing,
  And the dawn brings the fever chills,
      In Spanish port,
      Fever port,
      Port of Holy Peter.

You get a thirst there's no slaking,
  You get the chills and fever-shakes,
Tongue yellow and head aching,
  And then the sleep that never wakes.
And all the year the heat's baking,
  The sea rots and the earth quakes,
      In Spanish port,
      Fever port,
      Port of Holy Peter.

From THE EVERLASTING MERCY

THE PLOUGHMAN

O Christ who holds the open gate,
O Christ who drives the furrow straight,
O Christ, the plough, O Christ, the laughter
Of holy white birds flying after,
Lo, all my heart's field red and torn,
And Thou wilt bring the young green corn
The young green corn divinely springing,
The young green corn for ever singing;
And when the field is fresh and fair
Thy blessed feet shall glitter there.
And we will walk the weeded field,
And tell the golden harvest's yield,
The corn that makes the holy bread
By which the soul of man is fed,
The holy bread, the food unpriced,
Thy everlasting mercy, Christ.

The share will jar on many a stone,
Thou wilt not let me stand alone;
And I shall feel (Thou wilt not fail),
Thy hand on mine upon the hale.

William Carlos Williams
b. 1883

ST. FRANCIS EINSTEIN OF THE DAFFODILS
On the first visit of Professor Einstein
to the United States in the spring of 1921

"Sweet land"
at last!
out of the sea —
the Venusremembering wavelets
rippling with laughter —
freedom
for the daffodils!
— in a tearing wind
that shakes
the tufted orchards —

Einstein, tall as a violet
in the lattice-arbor corner
is tall as
a blossomy peartree

O Samos, Samos
dead and buried. Lesbia
a black cat in the freshturned
garden. All dead.
All flesh they sung

is rotten
Sing of it no longer —
Side by side young and old
take the sun together —
maples, green and red
yellowbells
and the vermilion quinceflower
together —

The peartree
with foetid blossoms
sways its high top branches
with contrary motions
and there are both pinkflowered
and coralflowered peachtrees
in the bare chickenyard
of the old Negro
with white hair who hides
poisoned fish-heads

here and there
where stray cats find them —
find them

Spring days
swift and mutable
winds blowing four ways
hot and cold
shaking the flowers —
Now the northeast wind
moving in fogs leaves the grass
cold and dripping. The night
is dark. But in the night
the southeast wind approaches.
The owner of the orchard
lies in bed
with open windows
and throws off his covers
one by one.

From PATERSON, BOOK III

THE LIBRARY

I love the locust tree
the sweet white locust
How much?
How much?
How much does it cost
to love the locust tree
in bloom?

A fortune bigger than
Avery could muster
So much
So much
the shelving green
locust
whose bright small leaves
in June
lean among flowers
sweet and white at
heavy cost.

A cool of books

will sometimes lead the mind to libraries
of a hot afternoon, if books can be found
cool to the sense to lead the mind away.

For there is a wind or ghost of a wind
in all books echoing the life
there, a high wind that fills the tubes
of the ear until we think we hear a wind,
actual
                to lead the mind away.

Drawn from the streets we break off
our mind's seclusion and are taken up by
the books' winds, seeking, seeking
down the wind
until we are unaware which is the wind and
which is the wind's power over us
                to lead the mind away.

and there grows in the mind
a scent, it may be, of locust blossoms
whose perfume is itself a wind moving
                to lead the mind away.

through which, below the cataract
soon to be dry
the river whirls and eddys
                first recollected

Spent from wandering the useless
streets these months, faces folded against
him like clover at nightfall, something
has brought him back to his own
                mind.

        in which a falls unseen
tumbles and rights itself
and refalls — and does not cease, falling
and refalling with a roar, a reverberation
not of the falls but of its rumour
                unabated

      Beautiful thing,
my dove, unable and all who are windblown,
touched by the fire
           and unable,

A roar that (soundless) drowns the sense
with its reiteration
                        unwilling to lie in its bed
and sleep and sleep, sleep
                        in its dark bed.

Summer! it is summer
— and still the roar in his mind is
unabated

A. E. Housman
1859-1936

THE NIGHT IS FREEZING FAST

The night is freezing fast,
    To-morrow comes December,
        And winterfalls of old
Are with me from the past;
    And chiefly I remember
        How Dick would hate the cold.

Fall, winter, fall; for he,
    Prompt hand and headpiece
        clever,
    Has woven a winter robe,
And made of earth and sea
    His overcoat for ever,
        And wears the turning globe.

IS MY TEAM PLOUGHING

"Is my team ploughing
    That I was used to drive
And hear the harness jingle,
    When I was man alive?"

Ay, the horses trample,
    The harness jingles now;
No change though you lie under
    The land you used to plough.

"Is football playing
    Along the river shore,
With lads to chase the leather,
    Now I stand up no more?"

Ay the ball is flying,
    The lads play heart and soul;
The goal stands up, the keeper
    Stands up to keep the goal.

"Is my girl happy
  That I thought hard to leave,
And has she tired of weeping
  As she lies down at eve?"

Ay, she lies down lightly,
  She lies not down to weep:
Your girl is well contented.
  Be still, my lad, and sleep.

"Is my friend hearty,
  Now I am thin and pine,
And has he found to sleep in,
  A better bed than mine?"

Yes, lad, I lie easy,
  I lie as lads would choose;
I cheer a dead man's sweetheart,
  Never ask me whose.

THE CHESTNUT CASTS HIS FLAMBEAUX

The chestnut casts his flambeaux, and the flowers
  Stream from the hawthorn on the wind away,
The doors clap to, the pane is bright with showers.
  Pass me the can, lad; there's an end of May.

There's one spoilt string to scant our mortal lot,
  One season ruined of our little store.
May will be fine next year as like as not:
  Oh ay, but then we shall be twenty-four.

We for a certainty are not the first
  Have sat in taverns while the tempest hurled
Their hopeful plans to emptiness, and cursed
  Whatever brute and blackguard made the world.

It is in truth iniquity on high
  To cheat our sentenced souls of aught they crave
And mar the merriment as you and I
  Fare on our long fool's errand to the grave.

Iniquity it is; but pass the can.
  My lad, no pair of kings our mothers bore;
Our only portion is the estate of man:
  We want the moon, but we shall get no more.

If here to-day the cloud of thunder lours
  To-morrow it will hie on far behests;
The flesh will grieve on other bones but ours
  Soon, and the soul will mourn in other breasts.

The troubles of the proud and angry dust
  Are from eternity, and shall not fail.
Bear them we can, and if we can we must.
  Shoulder the sky, my lad, and drink your ale.

OH WHO IS THAT YOUNG SINNER

Oh who is that young sinner with the handcuffs on his wrists?
And what has he been after that they groan and shake their fists?
And wherefore is he wearing such a conscience-stricken air?
Oh they're taking him to prison for the colour of his hair.

'Tis a shame to human nature, such a head of hair as his;
In the good old time 'twas hanging for the colour that it is;
Though hanging isn't bad enough and flaying would be fair
For the nameless and abominable colour of his hair.

Oh a deal of pains he's taken and a pretty price he's paid
To hide his poll or dye it of a mentionable shade;
But they've pulled the beggar's hat off for the world to see and stare,
And they're taking him to prison for the colour of his hair.

Now 'tis oakum for his fingers and the treadmill for his feet,
And the quarry-gang of Portland in the cold and in the heat,
And between his spells of labour in the time he has to spare
He can curse the God that made him for the colour of his hair.

Francis Thompson
1859-1907

From THE KINGDOM OF GOD

IN NO STRANGE LAND

O World invisible, we view thee,
O world intangible, we touch thee,
O world unknowable, we know thee,
Inapprehensible, we clutch thee!

Does the fish soar to find the ocean,
The eagle plunge to find the air —
That we ask of the stars in motion
If they have rumour of thee there?

Not where the wheeling systems darken,
And our benumbed conceiving soars! —
The drift of pinions, would we hearken,
Beats at our own clay-shuttered doors.

The angels keep their ancient places; —
Turn but a stone, and start a wing!
'Tis ye, 'tis your estrangèd faces,
That miss the many-splendoured thing.

But (when so sad thou canst not sadder)
Cry; — and upon thy so sore loss
Shall shine the traffic of Jacob's ladder
Pitched betwixt Heaven and Charing Cross.

Yea, in the night, my Soul, my daughter,
Cry, — clinging Heaven by the hems;
And lo, Christ walking on the water
Not of Gennesareth, but Thames!

William Butler Yeats
1865-1939

Yeats is one of the world's great tragic poets. His relationships — if he can be said to have any relationships — are with Dante, with Villon, and with Donne, with the poet of *La Vieille Heaulmière,* the poet of such lines as "A bracelet of bright hair about the bone," and the poet of certain passages in *The Inferno.*

Dante, Villon, Donne, and Yeats, each among the greatest in their own way, are not of an equal magnitude (by which I mean size, not grandeur).

With Dante, we saw for the first time, in the passage about Paolo and Francesca, the tragedy of all human love — the tragedy of that for which we had most longed becoming an unescapable part of an eternal hell.

That doom we do not actually find in Yeats. But it is possible to feel, in his poems, that soon another door will open and then shut behind him forever.

In Canto X of *The Inferno,* by means of a few gigantic lines, the whole grave of the world is laid open before us — all human sorrow, all human longing, on fire forever, as Farinata rises from his burning tomb.

To my feeling, nothing in the whole of poetry can compare with the passion, the despair of those lines — not even the passion and despair of

Lear. But it is to such poetry as this that Yeats is most closely related, though his magnitude is of a completely different order.

The passion of Yeats' poems is compressed into verse as strict as mathematics. "Art is a mathematics of the heart," said D. V. Fumet. (This is quoted in Stanislas Fumet's *Le Procès de l'Art*.)

"Poetry inclines above all to the roots of the knowledge of Being," said Charles Maurras, in the preface to *La Musique Intérieure*.

This might have been written of Yeats.

SAILING TO BYZANTIUM

That is no country for old men. The young
In one another's arms, birds in the trees
— Those dying generations — at their song,
The salmon-falls, the mackerel-crowded seas,
Fish, flesh, or fowl, commend all summer long
Whatever is begotten, born, and dies.
Caught in that sensual music all neglect
Monuments of unageing intellect.

An aged man is but a paltry thing,
A tattered coat upon a stick, unless
Soul clap its hands and sing, and louder sing
For every tatter in its mortal dress,
Nor is there singing school but studying
Monuments of its own magnificence;
And therefore I have sailed the seas and come
To the holy city of Byzantium.

O sages standing in God's holy fire
As in the gold mosaic of a wall,
Come from the holy fire, perne in a gyre,
And be the singing-masters of my soul.
Consume my heart away; sick with desire
And fastened to a dying animal
It knows not what it is; and gather me
Into the artifice of eternity.

Once out of nature I shall never take
My bodily form from any natural thing,
But such a form as Grecian goldsmiths make
Of hammered gold and gold enamelling
To keep a drowsy Emperor awake;
Or set upon a golden bough to sing
To lords and ladies of Byzantium
Of what is past, or passing, or to come.

LEDA AND THE SWAN

A sudden blow: the great wings beating still
Above the staggering girl, her thighs caressed
By the dark webs, her nape caught in his bill,
He holds her helpless breast upon his breast.

How can those terrified vague fingers push
The feathered glory from her loosening thighs?
And how can body, laid in that white rush,
But feel the strange heart beating where it lies?

A shudder in the loins engenders there
The broken wall, the burning roof and tower
And Agamemnon dead.
                            Being so caught up,
So mastered by the brute blood of the air,
Did she put on his knowledge with his power
Before the indifferent beak could let her drop?

THE COLLAR–BONE OF A HARE

Would I could cast a sail on the water
Where many a king has gone
And many a king's daughter,
And alight at the comely trees and the lawn,
The playing upon pipes and the dancing,
And learn that the best thing is
To change my loves while dancing
And pay but a kiss for a kiss.

I would find by the edge of that water
The collar-bone of a hare
Worn thin by the lapping of water,
And pierce it through with a gimlet, and stare
At the old bitter world where they marry in churches,
And laugh over the untroubled water
At all who marry in churches,
Through the white thin bone of a hare.

From WORDS FOR MUSIC PERHAPS

CRAZY JANE AND THE BISHOP

Bring me to the blasted oak
That I, midnight upon the stroke,
(All find safety in the tomb.)
May call down curses on his head
Because of my dear Jack that's dead.
Coxcomb was the least he said:
The solid man and the coxcomb.

Nor was he Bishop when his ban
Banished Jack the Journeyman,
(All find safety in the tomb.)
Nor so much as parish priest,
Yet he, an old book in his fist,
Cried that we lived like beast and
　　　beast:
The solid man and the coxcomb.

The Bishop has a skin, God knows,
Wrinkled like the foot of a goose,
(All find safety in the tomb.)
Nor can he hide in holy black
The heron's hunch upon his back,
But a birch-tree stood my Jack:
The solid man and the coxcomb.

Jack had my virginity,
And bids me to the oak, for he
(All find safety in the tomb.)
Wanders out into the night
And there is shelter under it,
But should that other come, I
　　　spit:
The solid man and the coxcomb.

CRAZY JANE REPROVED

I care not what the sailors say:
All those dreadful thunder-stones,
All that storm that blots the day
Can but show that Heaven yawns;
Great Europa played the fool
That changed a lover for a
　　　bull.
Fol de rol, fol de rol.

To round that shell's elaborate
　　　whorl,
Adorning every secret track
With the delicate mother-of-pearl,
Made the joints of Heaven crack:
So never hang your heart upon
A roaring, ranting journeyman.
Fol de rol, fol de rol.

CRAZY JANE ON THE DAY OF JUDGMENT

"Love is all
Unsatisfied
That cannot take the whole
Body and soul";
And that is what Jane said.

"Take the sour
If you take me,
I can scoff and lour
And scold for an hour."
"That's certainly the case," said he.

"Naked I lay,
The grass my bed;
Naked and hidden away,
That black day";
And that is what Jane said.

"What can be shown?
What true love be?
All could be known or shown
If Time were but gone."
"That's certainly the case," said he.

CRAZY JANE AND JACK THE JOURNEYMAN

I know, although when looks meet
I tremble to the bone,
The more I leave the door
    unlatched
The sooner love is gone,
For love is but a skein unwound
Between the dark and dawn.

A lonely ghost the ghost is
That to God shall come;
I — love's skein upon the
    ground,
My body in the tomb —
Shall leap into the light lost
In my mother's womb.

But were I left to lie alone
In an empty bed,
The skein so bound us ghost to
    ghost
When he turned his head
Passing on the road that night,
Mine would walk being dead.

CRAZY JANE ON GOD

That lover of a night
Came when he would,
Went in the dawning light
Whether I would or no;
Men come, men go;
All things remain in God.

Before their eyes a house
That from childhood stood
Uninhabited, ruinous,
Suddenly lit up
From door to top:
All things remain in God.

Banners choke the sky;
Men-at-arms tread;
Armoured horses neigh
Where the great battle was
In the narrow pass:
All things remain in God.

I had wild Jack for a lover;
Though like a road
That men pass over
My body makes no moan
But sings on:
All things remain in God.

CRAZY JANE TALKS WITH THE BISHOP

I met the Bishop on the road
And much said he and I.
"Those breasts are flat and fallen
    now,
Those veins must soon be dry;
Live in a heavenly mansion,
Not in some foul sty."

"Fair and foul are near of kin,
And fair needs foul," I cried.
"My friends are gone, but that's a
    truth
Nor grave nor bed denied,
Learned in bodily lowliness
And in the heart's pride.

"A woman can be proud and stiff
When on love intent;
But Love has pitched his mansion in
The place of excrement;
For nothing can be sole or whole
That has not been rent."

CRAZY JANE GROWN OLD LOOKS AT THE DANCERS

I found that ivory image there
Dancing with her chosen youth,
But when he wound her coal-black
  hair
As though to strangle her, no
  scream
Or bodily movement did I dare,
Eyes under eyelids did so gleam;
Love is like the lion's tooth.

When she, and though some said
  she played
I said that she had danced heart's
  truth,
Drew a knife to strike him dead,
I could but leave him to his fate;
For no matter what is said
They had all that had their hate;
Love is like the lion's tooth.

Did he die or did she die?
Seemed to die or died they both?
God be with the times when I
Cared not a thraneen for what
        chanced
So that I had the limbs to try
Such a dance as there was danced —
Love is like the lion's tooth.

THREE THINGS

"O cruel Death, give three things back,"
Sang a bone upon the shore;
"A child found all a child can lack,
Whether of pleasure or of rest,
Upon the abundance of my breast":
A bone wave-whitened and dried in the wind.

"Three dear things that women know,"
Sang a bone upon the shore;
"A man if I but held him so
When my body was alive
Found all the pleasure that life gave":
A bone wave-whitened and dried in the wind.

"The third thing that I think of yet,"
Sang a bone upon the shore,
"Is that morning when I met
Face to face my rightful man
And did after stretch and yawn":
A bone wave-whitened and dried in the wind.

MAD AS THE MIST AND SNOW

Bolt and bar the shutter,
For the foul winds blow:
Our minds are at their best this
    night,
And I seem to know
That everything outside us is
Mad as the mist and snow.

Horace there by Homer stands,
Plato stands below,
And here is Tully's open page.
How many years ago
Were you and I unlettered
    lads
Mad as the mist and snow?

You ask what makes me sigh, old
    friend,
What makes me shudder so?
I shudder and I sigh to think
That even Cicero
And many-minded Homer were
Mad as the mist and snow.

THOSE DANCING DAYS ARE GONE

Come, let me sing into your ear;
Those dancing days are gone,
All that silk and satin gear;
Crouch upon a stone,
Wrapping that foul body up
In as foul a rag:
I carry the sun in a golden cup,
The moon in a silver bag.

Curse as you may I sing it through;
What matter if the knave
That the most could pleasure you,
The children that he gave,
Are somewhere sleeping like a top
Under a marble flag?
I carry the sun in a golden cup,
The moon in a silver bag.

I thought it out this very day,
Noon upon the clock,
A man may put pretence away
Who leans upon a stick,
May sing, and sing until he drop,
Whether to maid or hag:
I carry the sun in a golden cup,
The moon in a silver bag.

A SONG: I THOUGHT NO MORE WAS NEEDED

I thought no more was needed
Youth to prolong
Than dumb-bell and foil
To keep the body young.
O who could have foretold
That the heart grows old?

Though I have many words,
What woman's satisfied,
I am no longer faint
Because at her side?
O who could have foretold
That the heart grows old?

I have not lost desire
But the heart that I had;
I thought 'twould burn my body
Laid on the death-bed,
For who could have foretold
That the heart grows old?

THE SECOND COMING

Turning and turning in the widening gyre
The falcon cannot hear the falconer;
Things fall apart; the centre cannot hold;
Mere anarchy is loosed upon the world,
The blood-dimmed tide is loosed, and everywhere
The ceremony of innocence is drowned;
The best lack all conviction, while the worst
Are full of passionate intensity.

Surely some revelation is at hand;
Surely the Second Coming is at hand.
The Second Coming! Hardly are those words out
When a vast image out of *Spiritus Mundi*
Troubles my sight: somewhere in sands of the desert
A shape with lion body and the head of a man,
A gaze blank and pitiless as the sun,
Is moving its slow thighs, while all about it
Reel shadows of the indignant desert birds.
The darkness drops again; but now I know
That twenty centuries of stony sleep
Were vexed to nightmare by a rocking cradle,
And what rough beast, its hour come round at last,
Slouches towards Bethlehem to be born?

From A MAN YOUNG AND OLD

THE FRIENDS OF HIS YOUTH

Laughter not time destroyed my voice
And put that crack in it,
And when the moon's pot-bellied
I get a laughing fit,
For that old Madge comes down the lane,
A stone upon her breast,
And a cloak wrapped about the stone,
And she can get no rest
With singing hush and hush-a-bye;
She that has been wild
And barren as a breaking wave
Thinks that the stone's a child.

And Peter that had great affairs
And was a pushing man
Shrieks, "I am King of the Peacocks,"
And perches on a stone;
And then I laugh till tears run down
And the heart thumps at my side,
Remembering that her shriek was love
And that he shrieks from pride.

THE HAWK

"Call down the hawk from the air;
Let him be hooded or caged
Till the yellow eye has grown mild,
For larder and spit are bare,
The old cook enraged,
The scullion gone wild."

"I will not be clapped in a hood,
Nor a cage, nor alight upon wrist,
Now I have learnt to be proud
Hovering over the wood
In the broken mist
Or tumbling cloud."

"What tumbling cloud did you
        cleave,
Yellow-eyed hawk of the mind,
Last evening? that I, who had sat
Dumbfounded before a knave,
Should give to my friend
A pretence of wit."

THE THREE HERMITS

Three old hermits took the air
By a cold and desolate sea,
First was muttering a prayer,
Second rummaged for a flea;
On a windy stone, the third,
Giddy with his hundredth year,
Sang unnoticed like a bird:
"Though the Door of Death is near
And what waits behind the door,
Three times in a single day
I, though upright on the shore,
Fall asleep when I should pray."
So the first, but now the second:
"We're but given what we have earned
When all thoughts and deeds are reckoned,
So it's plain to be discerned
That the shades of holy men
Who have failed, being weak of will,
Pass the Door of Birth again,
And are plagued by crowds, until
They've the passion to escape."
Moaned the other, "They are thrown
Into some most fearful shape."
But the second mocked his moan:
"They are not changed to anything,
Having loved God once, but maybe
To a poet or a king
Or a witty lovely lady."
While he'd rummaged rags and hair,
Caught and cracked his flea, the third,
Giddy with his hundredth year,
Sang unnoticed like a bird.

THE STATESMAN'S HOLIDAY

I lived among great houses,
Riches drove out rank,
Base drove out the better blood,
And mind and body shrank.
No Oscar ruled the table,
But I'd a troop of friends
That knowing better talk had gone
Talked of odds and ends.
Some knew what ailed the world
But never said a thing,
So I have picked a better trade
And night and morning sing:
*Tall dames go walking in grass-
green Avalon.*

Am I a great Lord Chancellor
That slept upon the Sack?
Commanding officer that tore
The khaki from his back?
Or am I de Valéra,
Or the King of Greece,
Or the man that made the motors?
Ach, call me what you please!
Here's a Montenegrin lute,
And its old sole string
Makes me sweet music
And I delight to sing:
*Tall dames go walking in grass-
      green Avalon.*

With boys and girls about him,
With any sort of clothes,
With a hat out of fashion,
With old patched shoes,
With a ragged bandit cloak,
With an eye like a hawk,
With a stiff straight back,
With a strutting turkey walk,
With a bag full of pennies,
With a monkey on a chain,
With a great cock's feather,
With an old foul tune.
*Tall dames go walking in grass-
      green Avalon.*

CRAZY JANE ON THE MOUNTAIN

I am tired of cursing the Bishop,
(Said Crazy Jane)
Nine books or nine hats
Would not make him a man.
I have found something worse
To meditate on.
A King had some beautiful cousins,
But where are they gone?
Battered to death in a cellar,
As he stuck to his throne.
Last night I lay on the mountain,

(Said Crazy Jane)
There in a two-horsed carriage
That on two wheels ran
Great-bladdered Emer sat,
Her violent man
Cuchulain sat at her side;
Thereupon,
Propped upon my two knees,
I kissed a stone;
I lay stretched out in the dirt
And I cried tears down.

JOHN KINSELLA'S LAMENT FOR
MRS. MARY MOORE

A bloody and a sudden end,
    Gunshot or a noose,
For death who takes what man
        would keep,
    Leaves what man would
        lose.
He might have had my sister,
    My cousins by the score,
But nothing satisfied the fool
    But my dear Mary Moore,
None other knows what pleasures
        man

At table or in bed.
*What shall I do for pretty girls
    Now my old bawd is dead?*

Though stiff to strike a bargain,
    Like an old Jew man,
Her bargain struck we laughed and
        talked
    And emptied many a can;
And O! but she had stories,
    Though not for the priest's ear,
To keep the soul of man alive,

Banish age and care,
And being old she put a skin
On everything she said.
What shall I do for pretty girls
Now my old bawd is dead?

The priests have got a book that
   says
But for Adam's sin
Eden's Garden would be there

And I there within.
No expectation fails there,
   No pleasing habit ends,
No man grows old, no girl grows
   cold,
But friends walk by friends.
Who quarrels over halfpennies
   That plucks the trees for bread?
What shall I do for pretty girls
   Now that my old bawd is dead?

THE WILD OLD WICKED MAN

"Because I am mad about women
I am mad about the hills,"
Said that wild old wicked man
Who travels where God wills.
"Not to die on the straw at home,
Those hands to close these eyes,
That is all I ask, my dear,
From the old man in the skies.
          Daybreak and a candle-end.

"Kind are all your words, my dear,
Do not the rest withhold.
Who can know the year, my dear,
When an old man's blood grows cold?
I have what no young man can have
Because he loves too much.
Words I have that can pierce the heart,
But what can he do but touch?"
          Daybreak and a candle-end.

Then said she to that wild old man,
His stout stick under his hand,
"Love to give or to withhold
Is not at my command.
I gave it all to an older man:
That old man in the skies.
Hands that are busy with His beads
Can never close those eyes."
          Daybreak and a candle-end.

"Go your ways, O go your ways,
I choose another mark,
Girls down on the seashore
Who understand the dark;
Bawdy talk for the fishermen;
A dance for the fisher-lads;
When dark hangs upon the water
They turn down their beds.
                    Daybreak and a candle-end.

"A young man in the dark am I,
But a wild old man in the light,
That can make a cat laugh, or
Can touch by mother wit
Things hid in their marrow-bones
From time long passed away,
Hid from all those warty lads
That by their bodies lay.
                    Daybreak and a candle-end.

"All men live in suffering,
I know as few can know,
Whether they take the upper road
Or stay content on the low,
Rower bent in his row-boat
Or weaver bent at his loom,
Horseman erect upon horseback
Or child hid in the womb.
                    Daybreak and a candle-end.

"That some stream of lightning
From the old man in the skies
Can burn out that suffering
No right-taught man denies.
But a coarse old man am I,
I choose the second-best,
I forget it all awhile
Upon a woman's breast."
                    Daybreak and a candle-end.

Walter de la Mare
1873-1956

We move, now, to an exquisite and flawless poet whose honey (sweet as that of Hybla) was gathered from the wildflowers of his native land.

Walter de la Mare is never on a large scale, he is passionless, but he has a peculiar charm which is such a personal quality that it is completely unlike that of any other poet I can think of. His beauty is like that of a friendly fairy, or a child who is only half mortal, and he is utterly original. He seems to have no parentage, although, on the other hand, he is not in the slightest revolutionary. He is at his best in quick, bright rhythms that are not hard, but have a glancing dew-sharp brightness like the glitter of leaves, like the dancing of leaves — in such a poem as *Berries,* for instance, or *Three Jolly Farmers. Old Shellover* is flawless in shape and movement — indeed, the shape and movement are one. In such a poem, again, as *A Widow's Weeds,* we have a half-strange, half-friendly emanation of poetry, a beauty that is concentrated into an image and that then emanates from the image as if it were an air.

It is customary to say of de la Mare that his poems are magical. And, as happens sometimes, this very obvious platitude contains the truth. This poem *is* magic, though the magic can sometimes be traced to the source, to some degree. In this case, it is partly a matter of image, and partly a matter of technique. The movement has within it the echo of that gentle, friendly rain, after which May upshone and leafy June grew green. And to me, part of the beauty lies in the fact that for some reason, not only the fields of May, but also the April rain, seems of gold.

Here again, for some reason, the bees, that are like those in Oberon's meadows, and the poor old widow's bright brown eyes seem, in some strange way, relations.

Then the freshness and the clearness of the texture, the occasional alliterations, the changes from the poignancy of the rhymes and their assonances that end the first three lines — "weeds," "seeds," "deep," to the more secretive, cooler, rounder sound of "drip" (these sounds, and the change between them, are echoed throughout the poem), the change from the sound of "drip" to the warmer vowel sounds of "soon," "June" — all these add to the beauty and magic of this lovely and flawless poem.

THE SCRIBE

What lovely things
  Thy hand hath made:
The smooth-plumed bird
  In its emerald shade,

The seed of the grass,
  The speck of stone
Which the wayfaring ant
  Stirs — and hastes on!

Though I should sit
By some tarn in thy hills,
Using its ink
As the spirit wills
To write of Earth's wonders,
Its live, willed things,
Flit would the ages
On soundless wings
Ere unto Z

My pen drew nigh;
Leviathan told,
And the honey-fly:
And still would remain
My wit to try —
My worn reeds broken,
The dark tarn dry,
All words forgotten —
Thou, Lord, and I.

A QUEEN WASP

Why rouse from thy long winter sleep?
And sound that witchcraft drone in air?
The frost-bound hours of darkness creep,
The night is cold, and bare

Of all that gave thee power to rear
Thy myriad Amazonian host.
All, all are dust. I only, here;
And thou — untimely ghost! —

Prowling, black-orbed, disconsolate,
Questing antennae, quivering wing,
Unwitting of the mortal fate
A human thought might bring

To the mute marvels in thy womb,
Tarrying only summer's heat
To breed a Babylon from the tomb —
As wondrous and exquisite!

Still, now. Thou'rt safe and hidden again;
Thy sombre, astonished piping done . . .
And I, with the hosts that flock the brain,
Back to my self am gone.

THE MARIONETTES

Let the foul Scene proceed:
There's laughter in the wings;
'Tis sawdust that they bleed,
Only a box Death brings.

How rare a skill is theirs —
These extreme pangs to show,
How real a frenzy wears
Each feigner of woe!

Gigantic dins uprise!
  Even the gods must feel
A smarting of the eyes
  As these fumes upsweel.

Strange, such a Piece is free,
  While we Spectators sit,
Aghast at its agony,
  Yet absorbed in it!

Dark is the outer air,
  Coldly the night draughts blow,
Mutely we stare, and stare
  At the frenzied Show.

Yet heaven hath its quiet shroud
  Of deep, immutable blue —
We cry "An end!" We are bowed
  By the dread, "It's true!"

While the Shape who hoofs applause
  Behind our deafened ear,
Hoots — angel-wise — "the Cause!"
  And affrights even fear.

POLONIUS

There haunts in Time's bare house an active ghost,
Enamoured of his name, Polonius.
He moves small fingers much, and all his speech
Is like a sampler of precisest words,
Set in the pattern of a simpleton.
His mirth flows eerily down chill corridors;
His sigh — it is a sound that loves a keyhole;
His tenderness a faint court-tarnished thing;
His wisdom prates as from a wicker cage;
His very belly is a pompous nought;
His eye a page that hath forgot his errand.
Yet in his bran — his spiritual bran —
Lies hid a child's demure, small, silver whistle
Which, to his horror, God blows, unawares,
And sets men staring. It is sad to think,
Might he but don indeed thin flesh and blood,
And pace important to Law's inmost room,
He would see, much marvelling, one immensely wise,
Named Bacon, who, at sound of his youth's step,
Would turn and call him Cousin — for the likeness.

THE KEYS OF MORNING

While at her bedroom window once,
  Learning her task for school,
Little Louisa lonely sat

In the morning clear and cool,
She slanted her small bead-brown
  eyes

Across the empty street,
And saw Death softly watching her
In the sunshine pale and sweet.

His was a long lean sallow face;
He sat with half-shut eyes,
Like an old sailor in a ship
Becalmed 'neath tropic skies.
Beside him in the dust he had set
His staff and a shady hat;
These, peeping small, Louisa saw
Quite clearly where she sat —
The thinness of his coal-black locks,
His hands so long and lean
They scarcely seemed to grasp at all
The keys that hung between:
Both were of gold, but one was small,
And with this last did he
Wag in the air, as if to say,
"Come hither, child, to me!"

Louisa laid her lesson book
On the cold window-sill;
And in the sleepy sunshine house
Went softly down, until
She stood in the half-opened door,
And peeped. But strange to say,
Where Death just now had sun-
ning sat
Only a shadow lay:
Just the tall chimney's round-
topped cowl,
And the small sun behind,
Had with its shadow in the dust
Called sleepy Death to mind.
But most she thought how strange
it was
Two keys that he should bear,
And that, when beckoning, he
should wag
The littlest in the air.

NOD

Softly along the road at evening,
In a twilight dim with rose,
Wrinkled with age, and drenched with dew,
Old Nod, the shepherd, goes.

His drowsy flock streams on before him,
Their fleeces charged with gold,
To where the sun's last beam leans low
On Nod the shepherd's fold.

The hedge is quick and green with brier,
From their sand the conies creep;
And all the birds that fly in heaven
Flock singing home to sleep.

His lambs outnumber a noon's roses,
Yet, when night's shadows fall,
His blind old sheep-dog, Slumber-soon,
Misses not one of all.

His are the quiet steeps of dreamland,
 The waters of no-more-pain,
His ram's bell rings 'neath an arch of stars,
 "Rest, rest, and rest again."

THE HAWTHORN HATH A DEATHLY SMELL

The flowers of the field
 Have a sweet smell;
Meadowsweet, tansy, thyme,
 And faint-heart pimpernel;
But sweeter even than these,
 The silver of the may
Wreathed is with incense for
 The Judgment Day.

An apple, a child, dust,
 When falls the evening rain,
Wild brier's spicèd leaves,
 Breathe memories again;
With further memory fraught,
 The silver of the may
Wreathed is with incense for
 The Judgment Day.

Eyes of all loveliness —
 Shadow of strange delight,
Even as a flower fades
 Must thou from sight;
But oh, o'er thy grave's mound,
 Till come the Judgment Day,
Wreathed shall with incense be
 Thy sharp-thorned may.

OLD SHELLOVER

"Come!" said Old Shellover.
"What?" says Creep.
"The horny old Gardener's fast asleep;
The fat cock Thrush
To his nest has gone;
And the dew shines bright
In the rising Moon;
Old Sallie Worm from her hole doth peep:
Come!" said Old Shellover.
"Ay!" said Creep.

FULL MOON

One night as Dick lay fast asleep,
 Into his drowsy eyes
A great still light began to creep
 From out the silent skies.

It was the lovely moon's, for when
  He raised his dreamy head,
Her surge of silver filled the pane
  And streamed across his bed.
So, for awhile, each gazed at each —
  Dick and the solemn moon —
Till, climbing slowly on her way,
  She vanished, and was gone.

BERRIES

There was an old woman
  Went blackberry picking
Along the hedges
  From Weep to Wicking.
Half a pottle —
  No more she had got,
When out steps a Fairy
  From her green grot;
And says, "Well, Jill,
  Would 'ee pick 'ee mo?"
And Jill, she curtseys,
  And looks just so.
"Be off," says the Fairy,
  "As quick as you can,
Over the meadows
  To the little green lane,
That dips to the hayfields
  Of Farmer Grimes:
I've berried those hedges
  A score of times;
Bushel on bushel
  I'll promise 'ee, Jill,
This side of supper
  If 'ee pick with a will."
She glints very bright,
  And speaks her fair;
Then lo, and behold!
  She had faded in air.

Be sure Old Goodie
  She trots betimes
Over the meadows
  To Farmer Grimes.

And never was queen
  With jewellery rich
As those same hedges
  From twig to ditch;
Like Dutchmen's coffers,
  Fruit, thorn, and flower —
They shone like William
  And Mary's bower.
And be sure Old Goodie
  Went back to Weep
So tired with her basket
  She scarce could creep.

When she comes in the dusk
  To her cottage door,
There's Towser wagging
  As never before,
To see his Missus
  So glad to be
Come from her fruit-picking
  Back to he.
As soon as next morning
  Dawn was grey,
The pot on the hob
  Was simmering away;
And all in a stew
  And a hugger-mugger
Towser and Jill
  A-boiling of sugar,
And the dark clear fruit
  That from Faërie came,
For syrup and jelly
  And blackberry jam.

Twelve jolly gallipots
Jill put by;
And one little teeny one,
One inch high;

And that she's hidden
A good thumb deep,
Half way over
From Wicking to Weep.

A WIDOW'S WEEDS

A poor old Widow in her weeds
Sowed her garden with wild-flower seeds;
Not too shallow, and not too deep,
And down came April — drip — drip — drip.
Up shone May, like gold, and soon
Green as an arbour grew leafy June.
And now all summer she sits and sews
Where willow-herb, comfrey, bugloss blows,
Teasel and tansy, meadowsweet,
Campion, toadflax, and rough hawksbit;
Brown bee orchis, and Peals of Bells;
Clover, burnet, and thyme she smells;
Like Oberon's meadows her garden is
Drowsy from dawn till dusk with bees.
Weeps she never, but sometimes sighs,
And peeps at her garden with bright brown eyes;
And all she has is all she needs —
A poor old Widow in her weeds.

THE SONG OF THE MAD PRINCE

Who said, "Peacock Pie"?
  The old King to the sparrow:
Who said, "Crops are ripe"?
  Rust to the harrow:
Who said, "Where sleeps she now?
  Where rests she now her head,
Bathed in eve's loveliness"? —
  That's what I said.

Who said, "Ay, mum's the word"?
  Sexton to willow:
Who said, "Green dusk for dreams,
  Moss for a pillow"?
Who said, "All Time's delight
  Hath she for narrow bed;
Life's troubled bubble broken"? —
  That's what I said.

Ralph Hodgson
b. 1871

THE BIRD–CATCHER

When flighting-time is on I go
  With clap-net and decoy,
A-fowling after goldfinches
  And other birds of joy.

I lurk among the thickets of
  The Heart where they are bred,
And catch the twittering beauties as
  They fly into my Head.

STUPIDITY STREET

I saw with open eyes
Singing birds sweet
Sold in the shops
For the people to eat,
Sold in the shops of
Stupidity Street.

I saw in a vision
The worm in the wheat,
And in the shops nothing
For people to eat,
Nothing for sale in
Stupidity Street.

THE JOURNEYMAN

Not baser than his own homekeeping kind
  Whose journeyman he is —
Blind sons and breastless daughters of the blind
  Whose darkness pardons his —
About the world, while all the world approves,
  The pimp of Fashion steals,
With all the angels mourning their dead loves
  Behind his bloody heels.

It may be late when Nature cries Enough!
  As one day cry she will,
And man may have the wit to put her off
  With shifts a season still;
But man may find the pinch importunate
  And fall to blaming men —
Blind sires and breastless mothers of his fate,
It may be late and may be very late,
  Too late for blaming then.

THE SONG OF HONOUR

I climbed a hill as light fell short,
And rooks came home in scramble sort,
And filled the trees and flapped and fought
And sang themselves to sleep;
An owl from nowhere with no sound
Swung by and soon was nowhere found,
I heard him calling half-way round,
Holloing loud and deep;
A pair of stars, faint pins of light,
Then many a star, sailed into sight,
And all the stars, the flower of night,
Were round me at a leap;
To tell how still the valleys lay
I heard a watchdog miles away,
And bells of distant sheep.

I heard no more of bird or bell,
The mastiff in a slumber fell,
I stared into the sky,
As wondering men have always done
Since beauty and the stars were one,
Though none so hard as I.

It seemed, so still the valleys were,
As if the whole world knelt at prayer,
Save me and me alone;
So pure and wide that silence was
I feared to bend a blade of grass,
And there I stood like stone.

There, sharp and sudden, there I heard —
    Ah! some wild lovesick singing bird
    Woke singing in the trees?
    The nightingale and babble-wren
    Were in the English greenwood then,
    And you heard one of these?

The babble-wren and nightingale
Sang in the Abyssinian vale
That season of the year!
Yet, true enough, I heard them plain,
I heard them both again, again,

As sharp and sweet and clear
As if the Abyssinian tree
Had thrust a bough across the sea,
Had thrust a bough across to me
With music for my ear!

I heard them both, and oh! I heard
The song of every singing bird
That sings beneath the sky,
And with the song of lark and wren
The song of mountains, moths and men
And seas and rainbows vie!

I heard the universal choir,
The Sons of Light exalt their Sire
With universal song.
Earth's lowliest and loudest notes,
Her million times ten million throats
Exalt Him loud and long,
And lips and lungs and tongues of Grace
From every part and every place
Within the shining of His face,
The universal throng.

I heard the hymn of being sound
From every well of honour found
In human sense and soul:
The song of poets when they write
The testament of Beautysprite
Upon a flying scroll,
The song of painters when they take
A burning brush for Beauty's sake
And limn her features whole —

The song of men divinely wise
Who look and see in starry skies
Not stars so much as robins' eyes,
And when these pale away
Hear flocks of shiny pleiades
Among the plums and apple trees
Sing in the summer day —

The song of all both high and low
To some blest vision true,
The song of beggars when they throw
The crust of pity all men owe

To hungry sparrows in the snow,
Old beggars hungry too —
The song of kings of kingdoms when
They rise above their fortune Men,
And crown themselves anew —

The song of courage, heart and will
And gladness in a fight,
Of men who face a hopeless hill
With sparking and delight,
The bells and bells of song that ring
Round banners of a cause or king
From armies bleeding white —

The song of sailors every one
When monstrous tide and tempest run
At ships like bulls at red,
When stately ships are twirled and spun
Like whipping tops and help there's none
And mighty ships ten thousand ton
Go down like lumps of lead —

And song of fighters stern as they
At odds with fortune night and day,
Crammed up in cities grim and grey
As thick as bees in hives,
Hosannas of a lowly throng
Who sing unconscious of their song,
Whose lips are in their lives —

And song of some at holy war
With spells and ghouls more dread by far
Than deadly seas and cities are
Or hordes of quarrelling kings —
The song of fighters great and small,
The song of pretty fighters all
And high heroic things —

The song of lovers — who knows how
Twitched up from place and time
Upon a sigh, a blush, a vow,
A curve or hue of cheek or brow,
Borne up and off from here and now
Into the void sublime!

And crying loves and passions still
In every key from soft to shrill
And numbers never done,
Dog-loyalties to faith and friend,
And loves like Ruth's of old no end,
And intermission none —

And burst on burst for beauty and
For numbers not behind,
From men whose love of motherland
Is like a dog's for one dear hand,
Sole, selfless, boundless, blind —
And song of some with hearts beside
For men and sorrows far and wide,
Who watch the world with pity and pride
And warm to all mankind —

And endless joyous music rise
From children at their play,
And endless soaring lullabies
From happy, happy mothers' eyes,
And answering crows and baby-cries,
How many who shall say!
And many a song as wondrous well
With pangs and sweets intolerable
From lonely hearths too grey to tell,
God knows how utter grey!
And song from many a house of care
When pain has forced a footing there
And there's a Darkness on the stair
Will not be turned away —

And song — that song whose singers come
With old kind tales of pity from
The Great Compassion's lips,
That make the bells of Heaven to peal
Round pillows frosty with the feel
Of Death's cold fingers tips —

The song of men all sorts and kinds,
As many tempers, moods and minds
As leaves are on a tree,
As many faiths and castes and creeds,
As many human bloods and breeds
As in the world may be;

The song of each and all who gaze
On Beauty in her naked blaze,
Or see her dimly in a haze,
Or get her light in fitful rays
And tiniest needles even,
The song of all not wholly dark,
Not wholly sunk in stupor stark
Too deep for groping Heaven —

And alleluias sweet and clear
And wild with beauty men mishear,
From choirs of song as near and dear
To Paradise as they,
The everlasting pipe and flute
Of wind and sea and bird and brute,
And lips deaf men imagine mute
In wood and stone and clay:

The music of a lion strong
That shakes a hill a whole night long,
A hill as loud as he,
The twitter of a mouse among
Melodious greenery,
The ruby's and the rainbow's song,
The nightingale's — all three,
The song of life that wells and flows
From every leopard, lark and rose
And everything that gleams or goes
Lack-lustre in the sea.

I heard it all, each, every note
Of every lung and tongue and throat,
Ay, every rhythm and rhyme
Of everything that lives and loves
And upward, ever upward moves
From lowly to sublime!
Earth's multitudinous Sons of Light,
I heard them lift their lyric might
With each and every chanting sprite
That lit the sky that wondrous night
As far as eye could climb!

I heard it all, I heard the whole
Harmonious hymn of being roll
Up through the chapel of my soul

And at the altar die,
And in the awful quiet then
Myself I heard, Amen, Amen,
Amen I heard me cry!
I heard it all and then although
I caught my flying senses, Oh,
A dizzy man was I!
I stood and stared; the sky was lit,
The sky was stars all over it,
I stood, I knew not why,
Without a wish, without a will,
I stood upon that silent hill
And stared into the sky until
My eyes were blind with stars and still
I stared into the sky.

Gordon Bottomley
1874-1948

NETTED STRAWBERRIES

I am a willow-wren:
I twitter in the grass on the chimney-top;
The apples far below will never drop
Or turn quite bright, though when

The aimless wind is still
I stand upon the big ones and I peck
And find soft places, leaving spot and speck
When I have munched my fill.

Apples and plums I know
(Plums are dark weights and full of golden rain
That wets neck-feathers when I dip and strain,
And stickies each plumy row),

But past my well-kept trees
The quick small woman in her puffy gown,
That flutters as if its sleeves and skirt had grown
For flying and airy ease,

Has planted little bushes
Of large cool leaves that cover and shade and hide
Things redder than plums and with gold dimples pied,
Dropping on new-cut rushes.

At first I thought with spite
Such heady scent was only a flower's wide cup;
But flower-scents never made my throat close up,
And so I stood in my flight.

Yet over all their sways
A web like those revealed by dawn and dew —
But not like those, that break and let me through
Shivering the drops all ways.

Though I alight and swing
I never reach the things that tumble and crush,
And if I had such long large legs as a thrush
The web would tangle and cling.

William Henry Davies
1871-1940

The beauty of William Davies' poems is due mainly to their fresh
and lovely fancy, and this is enhanced, often, by the shape, which is
clear and rounded as an apple, or has the soft perfection of a bullfinch's
rosy feathers.

The amazing visual beauty and clearness, as of something that has
been washed in dew, is natural to all Davies' poetry. Take, for instance,
these lines in a poem called *Charms:*

> She walks as lightly as the fly
> Skates on the water in July.

The beauty and balance of this is due in part to the assonantal vowels
of "lightly," "fly" and its rhyme "July," in part to the deeper dipping
sound of "water" after the shining sound of "skates," and in part to the
assonance of "water," "walks."

A clear light and color surround all these poems, and often it cannot
be explained, as with these lines:

Ah, little girl with wool,
What are you making now?
Some stockings for a bird
To keep his legs from snow.

The juxtaposition of the idea of the clear feathers of the bird and the white snow gives each a stranger brightness.

How great is the contrast between these brightnesses and happinesses, and the terrible simplicity of such a poem as *Body and Spirit*.

For the most part, Davies looks at Nature with the eyes of the Happy Child in his own poem, which is of a Blake-like innocence and radiance. That poem has the clear colors of the world before sin was known, bathed in the light of a purer heaven than we can know.

FANCY'S HOME

Tell me, Fancy, sweetest child,
 Of thy parents and thy birth;
Had they silk, and had they gold,
 And a park to wander forth,
With a castle green and old?

In a cottage I was born,
 My kind father was Content,
 My dear mother Innocence;
 On wild fruits of wonderment
 I have nourished ever since.

THE HAPPY CHILD

I saw this day sweet flowers grow thick —
But not one like the child did pick.

I heard the pack-hounds in green park —
But no dog like the child heard bark.

I heard this day bird after bird —
But not one like the child has heard.

A hundred butterflies saw I —
But not one like the child saw fly.

I saw the horses roll in grass —
But no horse like the child saw pass.

My world this day has lovely been —
But not like what the child has seen.

SWEET STAY–AT–HOME

Sweet Stay-at-Home, sweet Well-Content,
Thou knowest of no strange continent:
Thou hast not felt thy bosom keep
A gentle motion with the deep;
Thou hast not sailed in Indian seas,
Where scent comes forth in every breeze.
Thou hast not seen the rich grape grow
For miles, as far as eyes can go;
Thou hast not seen a summer's night
When maids could sew by a worm's light;
Nor the North Sea in spring send out
Bright hues that like birds flit about
In solid cages of white ice —
Sweet Stay-at-Home, sweet Love-One-Place.
Thou hast not seen black fingers pick
White cotton when the bloom is thick,
Nor heard black throats in harmony;
Nor hast thou sat on stones that lie
Flat on the earth, that once did rise
To hide proud kings from common eyes;
Thou hast not seen plains full of bloom
Where green things had such little room
They pleased the eye like fairer flowers —
Sweet Stay-at-Home, all these long hours.
Sweet Well-Content, sweet Love-One-Place,
Sweet, simple maid, bless thy dear face;
For thou hast made more homely stuff
Nurture thy gentle self enough;
I love thee for a heart that's kind —
Not for the knowledge in thy mind.

THE BIRD OF PARADISE

Here comes Kate Summers who, for gold,
  Takes any man to bed:
"You knew my friend, Nell Barnes," said she;
  "You knew Nell Barnes — she's dead.

"Nell Barnes was bad on all you men,
  Unclean, a thief as well;
Yet all my life I have not found
  A better friend than Nell.

"So I sat at her side at last,
  For hours, till she was dead;
And yet she had no sense at all
  Of any word I said.

"For all her cry but came to this —
  'Not for the world! Take care:
Don't touch that bird of paradise,
  Perched on the bedpost there!'

"I asked her would she like some grapes,
  Some damsons ripe and sweet;
A custard made with new-laid eggs,
  Or tender fowl to eat.

"I promised I would follow her,
  To see her in her grave;
And buy a wreath with borrowed pence,
  If nothing I could save.

"Yet still her cry but came to this —
  'Not for the world! Take care:
Don't touch that bird of paradise,
  Perched on the bedpost there!' "

BODY AND SPIRIT

Who stands before me on the stairs:
  Ah, is it you, my love?
My candle-light burns through your arm,
  And still thou dost not move;
Thy body's dead, this is not you —
It is thy ghost my light burns through.

Thy spirit this: I leap the stairs,
  To reach thy body's place;
I kiss and kiss, and still there comes
  No colour to thy face;
I hug thee for one little breath —
For this is sleep, it is not death!

. . . . . .

The first night she was in her grave,
  And I looked in the glass,

I saw her sit upright in bed —
　　Without a sound it was;
I saw her hand feel in the cloth,
　　To fetch a box of powder forth.

She sat and watched me all the while,
　　For fear I looked her way;
I saw her powder cheek and chin,
　　Her fast corrupting clay;
Then down my lady lay, and smiled —
She thought her beauty saved, poor child.

Now down the stairs I leap half-mad,
　　And up the street I start;
I still can see her hand at work,
　　And Oh, it breaks my heart:
All night behind my back I see
Her powdering, with her eyes on me.

Gertrude Stein
1874-1946

Gertrude Stein is an illustration of the success, and also of the dangers, of revolution. She is the last writer in the world whom any other writer should take as a model; but her work, for the most part, is very valuable because of its revivifying qualities, and it contains, to my mind, considerable beauty.

"These artists," said Roger Fry in his Catalogue to the second Post-Impressionist Exhibition, "do not seek to imitate life, but to find an equivalent for life. . . . In fact they aim not at illusion but at reality. The logical extreme of such a method would undoubtedly be the attempt to give up all resemblance to natural form, and to create a purely abstract language of form. . . ."

This seems to me applicable to Miss Stein, with her extremely strong visual sense, strengthened, no doubt, by her friendship with the most important painters of her day.

Wordsworth, in the preface to his *Poems* (1815), said of certain processes of creation that these "are carried on either by conferring additional properties upon an object, or abstracting from it some of those which it actually possesses, and thus enabling it to re-act upon the mind which hath performed the process, like a new existence."

Miss Stein does both.

She said to me, in one of our conversations, "The difference between Picasso and inferior painters is that inferior painters put in all the leaves on a tree, with the result that you see neither tree nor leaves. Picasso paints one leaf upon a tree, and you see the life of the tree."

She throws a word into the air, and when it returns to the ground it bears within it the original meaning it bore before custom and misuse had blurred it.

"If we look at an isolated printed word," said William James in *Principles of Psychology*, "and repeat it long enough, it ends by assuming an entirely unnatural aspect . . . its body is indeed there, but its soul is fled. It is reduced, by this new way of attending to it, to its sensational nudity. We never before attended to it in this way, but habitually got it clad with its meaning the moment we caught sight of it, and rapidly passed from it to the other words of the phrase. We apprehended it, in short, with a cloud of associates, and thus perceiving it, we felt it quite otherwise than as we feel it now, divested and alone."

This, I think, is at once the danger and the value of Miss Stein's method. The value is that she does show us the identity of words, deprived of their old smothering associations. Of course every accomplished writer does this to some degree. But Miss Stein goes further than most writers. At the same time, we see objects afresh. Professor James, in another chapter of the book quoted above, says, "The first sensation an infant gets is for him the universe."

The child and the great artist — these alone receive the sensation fresh as it was at the beginning of the world.

From LAND OF NATIONS

Here is a poem.

Amber.
Ambler Curran.
Amber is found on the shores of the Baltic.
Like wild asparagus you must have an eye for it.
    All animals howl.
All animals or a barnyard fowl.
    All animals are stars
    All animals and bars.
    Please pay a monkey a dear or a sweet.
Please pay a lion a pheasant or a street.
    Please recognize a mother a head or an owl.
Please recognize a feather a heather or a soul. Please recognize the
    weather. What do you live for.
    Climate and the affections. Jews quote that.

From SACRED EMILY

Noisy pearls noisy pearl coat.
Arrange.
Arrange wide opposite.
Opposite it.
Lily ice-cream.
Nevertheless.
A hand is Willie.
Henry Henry Henry.
A hand is Henry. . . .

A coral neck and a little song so very extra so very Susie.
Cow come out cow come out and out and smell a little.
Draw prettily.
Next to a bloom.
Neat stretch.
Place plenty.
Cauliflower.
Cauliflower.
Curtain cousin.
Apron.
Neither best set.
Do I make faces like that at you.
Pinkie.

From SCENES

A pale rose is a smell that has no fountain, that has upside down the same distinction, elegance is not coloured, the pain is there.

THE HEAT

I have thought very much about heat. When it is really hot one does not go about in the day time. It is just as well to drink water and even to buy water if it is necessary. So many people diminish. And flowers oh how can flowers be north. They are in the air.

A DAY LOST

In spite of a day a day lost in the heat a day lost in the heat of the hall, in spite of the day lost in the heat of all the heat we know, in spite of words of surprise in spite of mats and strawberries, strawberries in the woods, how prettily I have taught you to say the woods — the poor man's overcoat.

From ACCENTS IN ALSACE

ALSACE OR ALSATIANS

We have been deeply interested in the words of the song.
The Alsatians do not sing as well as their storks.
Their storks are their statuettes.
The rule is that angels and food and eggs are all sold
    by the dozen.
We were astonished. . . .

    All the leaves are green and babyish
    How many children make a family.

THE WATCH ON THE RHINE

Sweeter than water or cream or ice. Sweeter than bells of roses. Sweeter than winter or summer or spring. Sweeter than pretty posies. Sweeter than anything is my queen and loving is her nature.
    Loving and good and delighted and best is her little King and Sire whose devotion is entire who has but one desire to express the love which is hers to inspire.
    In the photograph the Rhine hardly showed
    In what way do chimes remind you of singing. In what way do birds sing. In what way are forests black or white.
    We saw them blue.
    With for get me nots.
    In the midst of our happiness we were very pleased.

D. H. Lawrence
1885-1930

SNAKE

A snake came to my water-trough
On a hot, hot day, and I in pyjamas for the heat,
To drink there.

In the deep, strange-scented shade of the great dark carobtree
I came down the steps with my pitcher
And must wait, must stand and wait, for there he was at the trough be-
    fore me.

He reached down from a fissure in the earth-wall in the gloom
And trailed his yellow-brown slackness soft-bellied down, over the edge
    of the stone trough
And rested his throat upon the stone bottom,
And where the water had dripped from the tap, in a small clearness,
He sipped with his straight mouth,
Softly drank through his straight gums, into his slack long body,
Silently.

Someone was before me at my water-trough,
And I, like a second comer, waiting.

He lifted his head from his drinking, as cattle do,
And looked at me vaguely, as drinking cattle do,
And flickered his two-forked tongue from his lips, and mused a moment,
And stooped and drank a little more,
Being earth-brown, earth-golden from the burning bowels of the earth
On the day of Sicilian July, with Etna smoking.

The voice of my education said to me
He must be killed,
For in Sicily the black, black snakes are innocent, the gold are venomous.

And voices in me said, If you were a man
You would take a stick and break him now, and finish him off.

But must I confess how I liked him,
How glad I was he had come like a guest in quiet, to drink at my water-
    trough

And depart peaceful, pacified, and thankless,
Into the burning bowels of this earth?

Was it cowardice, that I dared not kill him?
Was it perversity, that I longed to talk to him?
Was it humility, to feel so honoured?
I felt so honoured.

And yet those voices:
If you were not afraid, you would kill him!

And truly I was afraid, I was most afraid,
But even so, honoured still more
That he should seek my hospitality
From out the dark door of the secret earth.

He drank enough
And lifted his head, dreamily, as one who has drunken,
And flickered his tongue like a forked night on the air, so black,
Seeming to lick his lips,
And looked around like a god, unseeing, into the air,
And slowly turned his head,
And slowly, very slowly, as if thrice adream,
Proceeded to draw his slow length curving round
And climb again the broken bank of my wall-face.

And as he put his head into that dreadful hole,
And as he slowly drew up, snake-easing his shoulders, and entered
    farther,
A sort of horror, a sort of protest against his withdrawing into that hor-
    rid black hole,
Deliberately going into the blackness, and slowly drawing himself after,
Overcame me now his back was turned.

I looked round, I put down my pitcher,
I picked up a clumsy log
And threw it at the water-trough with a clatter.

I think it did not hit him,
But suddenly that part of him that was left behind convulsed in undigni-
    fied haste,
Writhed like lightning, and was gone
Into the black hole, the earth-lipped fissure in the wall-front,
At which, in the intense still noon, I stared with fascination.

And immediately I regretted it.
I thought how paltry, how vulgar, what a mean act!
I despised myself and the voices of my accursed human education.

And I thought of the albatross,
And I wished he would come back, my snake.

For he seemed to me again like a king,
Like a king in exile, uncrowned in the underworld,
Now due to be crowned again.

And so, I missed my chance with one of the lords
Of life.
And I have something to expiate;
A pettiness.

MOUNTAIN LION

Climbing through the January snow, into the Lobo canyon
Dark grow the spruce-trees, blue is the balsam, water sounds still un-
frozen, and the trail is still evident.

Men!
Two men!
Men! The only animal in the world to fear!

They hesitate.
We hesitate.
They have a gun.
We have no gun.

Then we all advance, to meet.

Two Mexicans, strangers, emerging out of the dark and snow and in-
wardness of the Lobo valley.
What are they doing here on this vanishing trail?

What is he carrying?
Something yellow.
A deer?
Qué tiene, amigo?
León —

He smiles, foolishly, as if he were caught doing wrong.
And we smile, foolishly, as if we didn't know.
He is quite gentle and dark-faced.

It is a mountain lion,
A long, long slim cat, yellow like a lioness.
Dead.
He trapped her this morning, he says, smiling foolishly.

Lift up her face,
Her round, bright face, bright as frost.
Her round, fine-fashioned head, with two dead ears;
And stripes in the brilliant frost of her face, sharp, fine dark rays.
Dark, keen, fine rays in the brilliant frost of her face.
Beautiful dead eyes.

Hermoso es!

They go out towards the open;
We go on into the gloom of Lobo.
And above the trees I found her lair,
A hole in the blood-orange brilliant rocks that stick up, a little cave.
And bones, and twigs, and a perilous ascent.

So, she will never leap up that way again, with the yellow flash of a
  mountain lion's long shoot!
And her bright striped frost-face will never watch any more, out of the
  shadow of the cave in the blood-orange rock,
Above the trees of the Lobo dark valley-mouth!

Instead, I look out.
And out to the dim of the desert, like a dream, never real;
To the snow of the Sangre de Cristo mountains, the ice of the mountains
  of Picoris,
And near across at the opposite steep of snow, green trees motionless
  standing in snow, like a Christmas toy.

And I think in this empty world there was room for me and a mountain
  lion.
And I think in the world beyond, how easily we might spare a million or
  two of humans
And never miss them.
Yet what a gap in the world, the missing white frost-face of that slim
  yellow mountain lion!

BAVARIAN GENTIANS

Not every man has gentians in his house
in Soft September, at slow, Sad Michaelmas.

Bavarian gentians, big and dark, only dark
darkening the day-time torch-like with the smoking blueness of Pluto's
     gloom,
ribbed and torch-like, with their blaze of darkness spread blue
down flattening into points, flattened under the sweep of white day
torch-flower of the blue-smoking darkness, Pluto's dark-blue daze,
black lamps from the halls of Dis, burning dark blue,
giving off darkness, blue darkness, as Demeter's pale lamps give off light,
lead me then, lead me the way.

Reach me a gentian, give me a torch
let me guide myself with the blue, forked torch of this flower
down the darker and darker stairs, where blue is darkened on blueness,
even where Persephone goes, just now, from the frosted September
to the sightless realm where darkness is awake upon the dark
and Persephone herself is but a voice
or a darkness invisible enfolded in the deeper dark
of the arms Plutonic, and pierced with the passion of dense gloom,
among the splendour of torches of darkness, shedding darkness on the
     lost bride and her groom.

Amy Lowell
1874-1925

LILACS

Lilacs,
False blue,
White,
Purple,
Color of lilac,
Your great puffs of flowers
Are everywhere in this my New England.
Among your heart-shaped leaves
Orange orioles hop like music-box birds and sing
Their little weak soft songs;
In the crooks of your branches

The bright eyes of song sparrows sitting on spotted eggs
Peer restlessly through the light and shadow
Of all Springs.
Lilacs in dooryards
Holding quiet conversations with an early moon;
Lilacs watching a deserted house
Settling sideways into the grass of an old road;
Lilacs, wind-beaten, staggering under a lopsided shock of bloom
Above a cellar dug into a hill.
You are everywhere.
You were everywhere.
You tapped the window when the preacher preached his sermon,
And ran along the road beside the boy going to school.
You stood by pasture-bars to give the cows good milking,
You persuaded the housewife that her dish-pan was of silver
And her husband an image of pure gold.
You flaunted the fragrance of your blossoms
Through the wide doors of Custom Houses —
You, and sandalwood, and tea,
Charging the noses of quill-driving clerks
When a ship was in from China.
You called to them: "Goose-quill men, Goose-quill men,
May is a month for flitting,"
Until they writhed on their high stools
And wrote poetry on their letter-sheets behind the propped-up ledgers.
Paradoxical New England clerks,
Writing inventories in ledgers, reading the "Song of Solomon" at night.
So many verses before bedtime,
Because it was the Bible.
The dead fed you
Amid the slant stones of graveyards.
Pale ghosts who planted you
Came in the night time
And let their thin hair blow through your clustered stems.
You are of the green sea,
And of the stone hills which reach a long distance.
You are of elm-shaded streets with little shops where they sell kites and
        marbles,
You are of great parks where everyone walks and nobody is at home.
You cover the blind sides of greenhouses
And lean over the top to say a hurry-word through the glass
To your friends, the grapes, inside.

Lilacs,
False blue,
White,

Purple,
Color of lilac,
You have forgotten your Eastern origin,
The veiled women with eyes like panthers,
The swollen, aggressive turbans of jeweled Pashas.
Now you are a very decent flower,
A reticent flower,
A curiously clear-cut, candid flower,
Standing beside clean doorways,
Friendly to a house-cat and a pair of spectacles,
Making poetry out of a bit of moonlight
And a hundred or two sharp blossoms.

Maine knows you,
Has for years and years;
New Hampshire knows you,
And Massachusetts
And Vermont.
Cape Cod starts you along the beaches to Rhode Island;
Connecticut takes you from a river to the sea.
You are brighter than apples,
Sweeter than tulips,
You are the great flood of our souls
Bursting above the leaf-shapes of our hearts,
You are the smell of all Summers,
The love of wives and children,
The recollection of the gardens of little children,
You are State Houses and Charters
And the familiar treading of the foot to and fro on a road it knows.
May is lilac here in New England,
May is a thrush singing "Sun up!" on a tip-top ash-tree,
May is white clouds behind pine-trees
Puffed out and marching upon a blue sky.
May is a green as no other,
May is much sun through small leaves,
May is soft earth,
And apple-blossoms,
And windows open to a South wind.
May is a full light wind of lilac
From Canada to Narragansett Bay.

Lilacs,
False blue,
White,
Purple,
Color of lilac,

Heart-leaves of lilac all over New England,
Roots of lilac under all the soil of New England,
Lilac in me because I am New England,
Because my roots are in it,
Because my leaves are of it,
Because my flowers are for it,
Because it is my country
And I speak to it of itself
And sing of it with my own voice
Since certainly it is mine.

Robinson Jeffers

b. 1887

HURT HAWKS

The broken pillar of the wing jags from the clotted shoulder,
The wing trails like a banner in defeat,
No more to use the sky forever but live with famine
And pain a few days: cat nor coyote
Will shorten the week of waiting for death, there is game without talons.

He stands under the oak-bush and waits
The lame feet of salvation; at night he remembers freedom
And flies in a dream, the dawns ruin it.
He is strong and pain is worse to the strong, incapacity is worse.
The curs of the day come and torment him
At distance, no one but death the redeemer will humble that head,
The intrepid readiness, the terrible eyes.
The wild God of the world is sometimes merciful to those
That ask mercy, not often to the arrogant.
You do not know him, you communal people, or you have forgotten
   him;
Intemperate and savage, the hawk remembers him;
Beautiful and wild, the hawks, and men that are dying remember him.

I'd sooner, except the penalties, kill a man than a hawk; but the great
   redtail
Had nothing left but unable misery
From the bone too shattered for mending, the wing that trailed under his
   talons when he moved.
We had fed him six weeks, I gave him freedom,

He wandered over the foreland hill and returned in the evening, asking
    for death,
Not like a beggar, still eyed with the old
Implacable arrogance. I gave him the lead gift in the twilight. What fell
    was relaxed,
Owl-downy, soft feminine feathers; but what
Soared: the fierce rush: the night-herons by the flooded river cried fear at
    its rising
Before it was quite unsheathed from reality.

V. Sackville-West

b. 1892

From THE LAND

THE SPRING WAS LATE THAT YEAR

The spring was late that year, I well remember.
The year when first I came on the field of fritillaries;
So late, the cottars meeting in the lanes
Would stop to marvel mildly, with that old
Unplumbed capacity for wonderment
At Nature's whim. The calendar told spring,
But spring was heedless: April into May
Passed, and the trees still wore their livery
Of lean black winter's servants; very strange
Most lovely Easter played three days at summer,
A heavy summer over winter's fields,
Three days, and then was vanished, like a queen
Dropping the lifted flap of her pavilion.

Nightly I leant me at the window-sill,
Telling the chaplet of the slipping days,
But still the lamp streamed wet on polished stones,
And still the nights were empty silences
Robbed of the nightingale; they only held
The slanting strings of rain: Orion marched
Invisible down the hours from dusk to dawn,
Till morning pallor lost him, but the clouds
Hid all his gradual latening; that year
He shot his midnight javelins unseen
And dipped the horizon into other skies,

Lost to the North, till autumn should renew
His captaincy, with Rigel, Betelgeuse,
Aldebaran, and brightest Sirius.

Have we so many springs allotted us,
And who would rob a pauper of his pence?

Then broke the spring. The hedges in a day
Burgeoned to green; the drawing of the trees,
Incomparably pencilled line by line,
Thickened to heaviness, and men forgot
The intellectual austerity
Of winter, in the rich warm-blooded rush
Of growth, and mating beasts, and rising sap.
How swift and sudden strode that tardy spring,
Between a sunrise and a sunset come!
The shadow of a swallow crossed the wall;
Nightingales sang by day. The pushing blade
Parted the soil. The morning roofs and oasts
There, down the lane, beside the brook and willows,
Cast their long shadows. Pasture, ankle-wet,
Streamed to the sun. The tulips dyed their green
To red in cottage gardens. Bees astir,
Fussing from flower to flower, made war on time.
Body and blood were princes; the cold mind
Sank with Orion from the midnight sky;
The stars of spring rose visible: The Virgin;
Al Fard the solitary; Regulus
The kingly star, the handle of the Sickle;
And Venus, lonely splendour in the west,
Roamed over the rapt meadows; shone in gold
Beneath the cottage eaves where nesting birds
Obeyed love's law; shone through the cottage panes
Where youth lay sleeping on the breast of youth,
Where love was life, and not a brief desire;
Shone on the heifer blaring for the bull
Over the hedgerow deep in dewy grass:
And glinted through the dark and open door
Where the proud stallion neighing to his mares
Stamped on the cobbles of the stable floor.
For all were equal in the sight of spring,
Man and his cattle; corn; and greening trees,
Ignorant of the soul's perplexity,
Ignorant of the wherefore and the end,
Bewildered by no transient ecstasy,

But following the old and natural law,
Nor marred nor blazing with a royal excess;
The law of life and life's continuance.

That was a spring of storms. They prowled the night;
Low level lightning flickered in the east
Continuous. The white pear-blossom gleamed
Motionless in the flashes; birds were still;
Darkness and silence knotted to suspense,
Riven by the premonitory glint
Of skulking storm, a giant that whirled a sword
Over the low horizon, and with tread
Earth-shaking ever threatened his approach,
But to delay his terror kept afar,
And held earth stayed in waiting like a beast
Bowed to receive a blow. But when he strode
Down from his throne of hills upon the plain,
And broke his anger to a thousand shards
Over the prostrate fields, then leapt the earth
Proud to accept his challenge; drank his rain;
Under his sudden wind tossed wild her trees;
Opened her secret bosom to his shafts;
The great drops spattered; then above the house
Crashed thunder, and the little wainscot shook
And the green garden in the lightning lay.

Who has not seen the spring, is blind, is dead.
Better for him that he should coffined lie,
And in that coin his toll to Nature pay
Than live a debtor. All things shall pass by
That fret his mind: the shift of policy,
Princes' ambition, wiser governance,
Civilisation's tides. There's dissonance
By our great necessary Babel bred,
Perplexes eager spirits unprepared,
Puts out their seeing eyes, leaves their blind touch
To grope past prejudice and ignorance
Towards solution, as they throw away
Each broken, each successive crutch.
Such truths as we have snared
Into the spread conspiracy of our nets,
Come to us fragmentary from a whole,
As meteorites from space. Now science sets
Two splintered ends together, makes one shred
Corroborate another; now live flesh
Persuades us by its drunken fallacy;

Now the instinctive soul
Takes its short-cut to grace; now blown by gust
Of hazard, truth's entangled in strange mesh,
Else how should poetry,
The runes of divination, superstition
Fastening sharp claw on common circumstance,
Even artifice as neat astrology
Twisting the very stars to fit man's ends,
Mingle some ore with dross of sorcery
Unless the fragment of the whole be part?
There's some relation we may not adjust,
Some concord of creation that the mind
Only in perilous balance apprehends,
Loth, fugitive, obscure.
All else dies in its season; all perplexities,
Even human grief with human body dies,
Such griefs that press so wildly on the heart
As to crush in its shell. But still endure
Nature's renewal and man's fortitude,
A common thing, a permanent common thing,
So coarse, so stated, usual, and so rude,
So quiet in performance, and so slow
That hurrying wit outruns it. Yet with spring
Life leaps; her fountains flow;
And nimble foolish wit must humbled go.

There were so many days that I was given.
But whether of this spring or that? they merge
As travelling clouds across my permanent heaven.

My life was rich; I took a swarm of bees
And found a crumpled snake-skin on the road,
All in one day, and was increased by these.

I have not understood humanity.
But those plain things, that gospel of each year,
Made me the scholar of simplicity.

This once I saw, but not again,
Above the water pocked by rain:
Three mottled eggs in a moorhen's nest,
In a clump of kingcups by the edge
Of the water, in amongst the sedge;
The rain was but an April shower;
The kingcup but a minted flower,
Cup of a king in gold.

Was there not once a king who sought him
The perfect chalice, and bethought him
The breast of Helen for his mould?
A wild bird's nest and Helen's breast,
What lovely things that spring did hold! . . .

Now die the sounds. No whisper stirs the trees
    Her pattern merged into the general web
The shriven day accepts her obsequies
    With humble ebb.

Now are the noiseless stars made visible
    That hidden by the day pursued their track,
And this one planet that we know too well
    Mantles in black.

Then, from the thicket, sang the nightingale,
    So wildly sweet, so sudden, and so true,
It seemed a herald from beyond the veil
    Had broken through.

The common earth's confusion all unseen,
    But worlds revealed in broad magnificence —
That unembodied music thrid between
    Sprang hence, or thence?

Nothing remained of the familiar round,
    Only the soul ecstatic and released
Founted towards the spheres in jets of sound,
    And died, and ceased,

But plangent from the thickets of the thorn
    Broke other voices, taking up the choir,
While Cancer interlaced with Capricorn
    In silent fire,

And all the harmonies were joined and whole,
    Silence was music, music silence made,
Till each was both or either, and the soul
    Was not afraid.

Wilfrid Wilson Gibson
b. 1878

THE GORSE

In dream, again within the clean cold hell
Of glazed and aching silence he was trapped,
And, closing in, the blank walls of his cell
Crushed stifling on him . . . when the bracken snapped,
Caught in his clutching fingers, and he lay
Awake upon his back among the fern
With free eyes travelling the wide blue day
Unhindered, unremembering, while a burn
Tinkled and gurgled somewhere out of sight
Unheard of him till, suddenly aware
Of its cold music, shivering in the light,
He raised himself and with far-ranging stare
Looked all about him; and with dazed eyes wide
Saw, still as in a numb unreal dream,
Black figures scouring a far hillside,
With now and then a sunlit rifle's gleam,
And knew the hunt was hot upon his track —
Yet scarcely seemed to mind somehow just then . . .
But kept on wondering why they looked so black
On the hot hillside, all those little men
Who scurried round like beetles — twelve all told . . .
He counted them twice over and began
A third time reckoning them, but could not hold
His starved wits to the business, while they ran
So brokenly, and always stuck at "five" . . .
And *One, two, three, four, five* a dozen times
He muttered . . . *Can you catch a fish alive?*
Sang mocking echoes of old nursery-rhymes
Through the strained tingling hollow of his head.
And now, almost remembering, he was stirred
To pity them, and wondered if they'd fed
Since he had, or if, ever since they'd heard
Two nights ago the sudden signal-gun
That raised alarm of his escape, they too
Had fasted in the wilderness and run,
With nothing but the thirsty wind to chew,
And nothing in their bellies but a fill
Of cold peat-water, till their heads were light. . . .

The crackling of a rifle on the hill
Rang in his ears and, stung to headlong flight,
He started to his feet and through the brake
He plunged in panic, heedless of the sun
That burned his cropped head to a red-hot ache,
Still racked with crackling echoes of the gun.

Then suddenly the sun-enkindled fire
Of gorse upon the moor-top caught his eye,
And that gold glow held all of his desire
As, like a witless flame-bewildered fly,
He blundered towards the league-wide yellow blaze
And tumbled headlong on the spikes of bloom,
And rising, bruised and bleeding and adaze,
Struggled through clutching spines — the dense sweet fume
Of nutty acrid scent like poison stealing
Through his hot blood: the bristling yellow glare
Spiking his eyes with fire till he went reeling,
Stifling and blinded, on — and did not care
Though he were taken — wandering round and round,
Jerusalem the Golden quavering shrill,
Changing his tune to *Tommy Tiddler's Ground,*
Till, just a lost child on the dazzling hill
Bewildered in a glittering golden maze
Of stinging scented fire, he dropped, quite done,
A shrivelling wisp within a world ablaze
Beneath a blinding sky, one blaze of sun.

Marianne Moore

b. 1887

"Formerly," wrote Sir Arthur Eddington (*The Nature of the Physical World*), "it was freely admitted that the birth of a star was an individual event like the birth of an animal."

I would say that Marianne Moore reverses this way of thinking. To her, the birth of an animal is a cosmic event, like the birth of a star.

She is amongst the most accurate and exquisite observers of our time. "Sir George Beaumont," Coleridge tells us, "learned with advantage to draw from nature through gauze spectacles." For the tender inquirer who is Marianne Moore, these blurring softening encumbrances do not exist. The hummingbird is not better equipped for the piercing down to the deepest essence of the flower than is Miss Moore.

She sees in a flash, reproduces in a flash. And all is delight, containing a kernel of loving wisdom. Nothing is too humble for love, and for the comprehension of its life-source, its delight in living — the joy of the "small desert rat" in its "shining silver house" that to us is only sand.

She examines with an equally loving care how the same creature:

> makes fern-seed
> foot-prints with kangaroo speed.
>
> Its leaps should be set
> to the flageolet . . .

the "fog-colored skin" of the elephant, and, in a later poem, *Melancthon* (which is, to me, her masterpiece), the elephant's trunk:

> that tree-trunk without
> roots, accustomed to shout
> its own thoughts to itself like a shell, maintained intact
> by who knows what strange pressure of the atmosphere; that
>
> spiritual
> brother to the coral-
> plant, absorbed into which, the equable sapphire light
> becomes a nebulous green. The I of each is to
>
> the I of each
> a kind of fretful speech
> which sets a limit on itself; the elephant is
> black earth preceded by a tendril . . .

This, leaving aside its visual beauty and strangeness, is a technical marvel, essence and form being indissoluble. The slow gait of the elephant, its deliberation, these are obtained partly by the short lines which begin each verse, partly by the *t*'s which end each line of the first verse, which seem to bring each line to a full stop, and to produce, between one line and the next, the effect of the space between two gigantic and deliberate footfalls. After these short lines come long lines that seem, by their movement, to carry the lumbering creature into the distance.

This is what Miss Moore's technical genius has produced.

All these poems are infused with a glowing life — not with passion.

"*Quand Pascal place au centre de son système de pensée ce qu'il nomme le coeur,*" wrote Daniel-Rops ("*Mystique et Poésie,*" Fontaine, March–April 1942), "*dans le sens si particulier et si profond qu'il lui donne, ce mot ne veut presque plus rien dire de sentimental. . . . En essence, c'est une faculté de connaissance même, à la fois somme et total de toutes les facultés de connaissance.*"

This is true of Miss Moore.

MELANCTHON

Openly, yes,
with the naturalness
  of the hippopotamus or the alligator
  when it climbs out on the bank to experience the

sun, I do these
things which I do, which please
  no one but myself. Now I breathe and now I am submerged; the blemishes stand up and about when the object

in view was a
renaissance; shall I say
  the contrary? The sediment of the river which
  encrusts my joints, makes me very grey but I am used

to it, it may
remain there; do away
  with it and I am myself done away with, for the
  patina of circumstance can but enrich what was

there to begin
with. This elephant-skin
  which I inhabit, fibred over like the shell of
  the cocoanut, this piece of black glass through which no light

can filter — cut
into checkers by rut
  upon rut of unpreventable experience —
  it is a manual for the peanut-tongued and the

hairy-toed. Black
but beautiful, my back
  is full of the history of power. Of power? What
  is powerful and what is not? My soul shall never

be cut into
by a wooden spear; through-
  out childhood to the present time, the unity of
  life and death has been expressed by the circumference

described by my
trunk; nevertheless I
  perceive feats of strength to be inexplicable after
  all; and I am on my guard; external poise, it

has its centre
well nurtured — we know
      where — in pride; but spiritual poise, it has its centre where?
      My ears are sensitized to more than the sound of

the wind, I see
and I hear, unlike the
      wandlike body of which one hears so much, which was made
      to see and not to see; to hear and not to hear;

that tree-trunk without
roots, accustomed to shout
      its own thoughts to itself like a shell, maintained intact
      by who knows what strange pressure of the atmosphere; that

spiritual
brother to the coral-
      plant, absorbed into which, the equable sapphire light
      becomes a nebulous green. The I of each is to

the I of each
a kind of fretful speech
      which sets a limit on itself; the elephant is
      black earth preceded by a tendril? Compared with those

phenomena
which vacillate like a
      translucence of the atmosphere, the elephant is
      that on which darts cannot strike decisively the first

time, a substance
needful as an instance
      of the indestructibility of matter; it
      has looked at the electricity and at the earth-

quake and is still
here; the name means thick; Will
      depth be depth, thick skin be thick, to one who can see no
      beautiful element of unreason under it?

THE JERBOA

TOO MUCH

A Roman had an
artist, a freedman,
      contrive a cone — pine-cone

or fir-cone — with holes for a fountain. Placed on
the Prison of St. Angelo, this cone
of the Pompeys which is known

now as the Popes', passed
for art. A huge cast
bronze, dwarfing the peacock
statue in the garden of the Vatican,
it looks like a work of art made to give
to a Pompey, or native

of Thebes. Others could
build, and understand
making colossi and
how to use slaves, and kept crocodiles and put
baboons on the necks of giraffes to pick
fruit, and used serpent magic.

They had their men tie
hippopotami
and bring out dapple dog-
cats to course antelopes, dikdik, and ibex;
or used small eagles. They looked on as theirs,
impallas and onigers,

the wild ostrich herd
with hard feet and bird
necks rearing back in the
dust like a serpent preparing to strike, cranes,
mongooses, storks, anoas, Nile geese;
and there were gardens for these —

combining planes, dates,
limes, and pomegranates,
in avenues — with square
pools of pink flowers, tame fish, and small frogs. Besides
yarns dyed with indigo, and red cotton,
they had a flax which they spun

into fine linen
cordage for yachtsmen.
These people liked small things;
they gave to boys little paired playthings such as
nests of eggs, ichneumon and snake, paddle
and raft, badger and camel;

and made toys for them-
selves: the royal totem;
    and toilet-boxes marked
    with the contents. Lords and ladies put goose-grease
        paint in round bone boxes with pivoting
        lid incised with the duck-wing

or reverted duck-
head; kept in a buck
    or rhinoceros horn,
    the ground horn; and locust oil in stone locusts.
        It was a picture with a fine distance;
        of drought, and of assistance

in time, from the Nile
rising slowly, while
    the pig-tailed monkey on
    slab-hands, with arched-up slack-slung gait, and the brown
        dandy, looked at the jasmine two-leafed twig
        and bud, cactus-pads, and fig.

Dwarfs here and there, lent
to an evident
    poetry of frog greys,
    duck-egg greens, and egg-plant blues, a fantasy
        and a verisimilitude that were
        right to those with, everywhere,

power over the poor.
The bees' food is your
    food. Those who tended flower-
    beds and stables were like the king's cane in the
        form of a hand, or the folding bedroom
        made for his mother of whom

he was fond. Princes
clad in queens' dresses,
    calla or petunia
    white, that trembled at the edge, and queens in a
        king's underskirt of fine-twilled thread like silk-
        worm gut, as bee-man and milk-

maid, kept divine cows
and bees; limestone brows,
    and gold-foil wings. They made

basalt serpents and portraits of beetles; the
    king gave his name to them and he was named
    for them. He feared snakes, and tamed

Pharaoh's rat, the rust-
backed mongoose. No bust
    of it was made, but there
    was pleasure for the rat. Its restlessness was
        its excellence; it was praised for its wit;
        and the jerboa, like it,

a small desert rat,
and not famous, that
    lives without water, has
    happiness. Abroad seeking food, or at home
        in its burrow, the Sahara field-mouse
        has a shining silver house

of sand. O rest and
joy, the boundless sand,
    the stupendous sand-spout,
    no water, no palm-trees, no ivory bed,
        tiny cactus; but one would not be he
        who has nothing but plenty.

ABUNDANCE

Africanus meant
the conqueror sent
    from Rome. It should mean the
    untouched: the sand-brown jumping-rat — free-born; and
        the blacks, that choice race with an elegance
        ignored by one's ignorance.

Part terrestrial,
and part celestial,
    Jacob saw, cudgel staff
    in claw-hand — steps of air and air angels; his
        friends were the stones. The translucent mistake
        of the desert, does not make

hardship for one who
can rest and then do
    the opposite — launching
    as if on wings, from its match-thin hind legs, in
        daytime or at night; with the tail as a weight,
        undulated by speed, straight.

Looked at by daylight,
the underside's white,
 though the fur on the back
 is buff-brown like the breast of the fawn-breasted
  bower-bird. It hops like the fawn-breast, but has
  chipmunk contours — perceived as

it turns its bird head —
the nap directed
 neatly back and blending
 with the ear which reiterates the slimness
  of the body. The fine hairs on the tail,
  repeating the other pale

markings, lengthen till
at the tip they fill
 out in a tuft — black and
 white; strange detail of the simplified creature,
  fish-shaped and silvered to steel by the force
  of the large desert moon. Course

the jerboa, or
plunder its food store,
 and you will be cursed. It
 honours the sand by assuming its colour;
  closed upper paws seeming one with the fur
  in its flight from a danger.

By fifths and sevenths,
in leaps of two lengths,
 like the uneven notes
 of the Bedouin flute, it stops its gleaning
  on little wheel castors, and makes fern-seed
  foot-prints with kangaroo speed.

Its leaps should be set
to the flageolet;
 pillar body erect
 on a three-cornered smooth-working Chippendale
  claw — propped on hind legs, and tail as third toe,
  between leaps to its burrow.

David Jones
b. 1895

From THE ANATHEMATA

RITE AND FORE–TIME

We already and first of all discern him making this thing
other. His groping syntax, if we attend, already shapes:
ADSCRIPTAM, RATAM, RATIONABILEM . . . and by pre-application
and for *them*, under modes and patterns altogether theirs,
the holy and venerable hands lift up an efficacious sign.

These, at the sagging end and chapter's close, standing
humbly before the tables spread, in the apsidal houses, who
intend life:
> between the sterile ornaments
> under the pasteboard baldachins
> as, in the young-time, in the sap-years:
> between the living floriations
> under the leaping arches.

(Ossific, trussed with ferric rods, the failing numina
of column and entablature, the genii of spire and triforium,
like great rivals met when all is done, nod recognition across
the cramped repeats of their dead selves.)

These rear-guard details in their quaint attire, heedless of
incongruity, unconscious that the flanks are turned and all
connecting files withdrawn or liquidated — that dead symbols
litter to the base of the cult-stone, that the stem by the
palled stone is thirsty, that the stream is very low.

> The utile infiltration nowhere held
> creeps vestibule
is already at the closed lattices, is coming through each door.

The cult-man stands alone in Pellam's land: more precariously
than he knows he guards the *signa:* the pontifex among his
house-treasures, (the twin-*urbes* his house is) he can fetch
things new and old: the tokens, the matrices, the institutes,

the ancilia, the fertile ashes — the palladic foreshadowings:
the things come down from heaven together with the kept
memorials, the things lifted up and the venerated trinkets.

This man, so late in time, curiously surviving, shows courtesy
to the objects when he moves among, handles or puts aside
the name-bearing instruments, when he shows every day in
his hand the salted cake given for this *gens* to savour all
the *gentes*.

  Within the railed tumulus
     he sings high and he sings low.

    In a low voice
        as one who speaks
where a few are, gathered in high-room
    and one, gone out.

  There's conspiracy here:
     Here is birthday and anniversary, if there's continuity
here, there's a new beginning.
    By intercalation of weeks
        (since the pigeons were unfledged
     and the lambs still young)
     they've adjusted the term
     till this appointed night
        (Sherthursdaye bright)
     the night that falls
     when she's first at the full
     after the vernal turn
     when in the Ram he runs.

  By the two that follow Aquarius
  toiling the dry meander:
      through the byes
    under the low porch
    up the turning stair
    to the high nave

      where the board is
    to spread the board-cloth
    under where the central staple is
    for the ritual light.

  In the high cave they prepare
     for guest to be the *hostia*.

They set the thwart-boards
and along:
        Two for the Gospel-makers
        One for the other Son of Thunder
        One for the swordsman, at the right-board, after;
to make him feel afloat. One for the man from Kerioth,
seven for the rest in order.

They besom here and arrange this handy, tidy here, and
furbish with the green of the year the cross-beams and the
gleaming board.

They make all shipshape
        for she must be trim
                dressed and gaudeous
        all Bristol-fashion here
        for:
                Who d'you think is Master of her?

In the prepared high-room
he implements inside time and late in time under forms
indelibly marked by locale and incidence, deliberations
made out of time, before all oreogenesis

                        on this hill
        at a time's turn
                        not on any hill
        but on this hill.
[On this unabiding rock
                        for one Great Summer
                                lifted up
                        by next Great Winter
                                down
among the altitudes
with all help-heights
                        down
as low as Parnassus
                        (it's Ossa on Pelion now).
Seven templum'd montes
                        under terra-marl.
Senai under.
                        Where's Ark-hill?
Ask both the Idas.
And where:
                        West horse-hills?

Volcae-remnants' crag-*carneddau?*
Moel of the Mothers?
　　the many *colles Arthuri?*

All the efficacious asylums
in Wallia vel in Marchia Walliae,
　　　　ogofau of, that cavern for
　　　　Cronos, Owain, Arthur.
Terra Walliae!
　　　　Buarth Meibion Arthur!
　　　　Enclosure of the Children of Troy!

Nine-strata'd Hissarlik
　　　　a but forty-metre height
yet archetype of sung-heights.

Crux-mound at the node
gammadion'd castle.
Within the laughless Megaron
　　　　the margaron
beyond echelon'd Skaian
　　　　　　the stone
　　　　　　the fonted water
　　　　　　the fronded wood.

Little Hissarlik
　　　　　　least of acclivities
yet
　　　　　　high as Hector the Wall
　　　　　　high as Helen the Moon
who, being lifted up
　　　　　　draw the West to them.

Hissarlik, traversed Hissarlik
　　　　　　mother of forts
　　　　　　hill of cries
small walled-height
　　　　　　that but 750 marching paces would circuit
first revetted of anguish-beights
　　　　　　matrix for West-*oppida*
　　　　　　　　for West-technic
　　　　　　　　for West-saga

down
         under, sheet-darkt Hellespont?
        pack for the Cyclades?
And where, from the potent flotsam, florid she breached,
with spume on her spear-flukes, the great fluked mammals
blow? glaciation cones her own Thebes? loess drifts Leo-
gate?

All *montes*
     with each dear made-height
et omnes colles
      down?
hautes eagle-heights under
low as Lambourn Down?
      As solitary tump, so massif?
Alp, as Bredon
      down?
obedient to the fiery stress
und icy counter-drag
     down, and
there shall be yet *more*
      storm-dark sea?

Lord! what a morning yet may break
on this new-founded Oberland.]

At this unabiding Omphalos
     this other laughless rock
at the stone of division
     above the middle water-deeps
at the turn of time
     not at any time, but
at this acceptable time.
From the year of
     the lord-out-of-Ur
about two millennia.
Two thousand lents again
     since the first barley mow.
Twenty millennia (and what millennia more?)
Since he became
     man master-of-plastic.

Who were his *gens*-men or had he no *Hausname* yet
no *nomen* for his *fecit*-mark
     the Master of the Venus?

whose man-hands god-handled the Willendorf stone
               before they unbound the last glaciation
for the Uhland Father to be-ribbon *die blaue Donau*
               with his Vanabride blue.
O long before they lateen'd her Ister
or Romanitas manned her gender'd stream.

O Europa!
                   how long and long and long and
very long again, before you'll maze the waltz-forms in gay
Vindobona in the ramshackle last phases; or god-shape the
modal rhythms for nocturns in Melk in the young-time; or
plot the Rhaetian limits in the Years of the City.
               But already he's at it
the form-making proto-maker
busy at the fecund image of her.
               Chthonic? why yes
but mother of us.
    Then it is these abundant *ubera*, here, under the species
of worked lime-rock, that gave suck to the lord? She that
they already venerate (what other could they?)
               her we declare?
Who else?
             And see how they run, the juxtaposed forms,
brighting the vaults of Lascaux; how the linear is wedded
to volume, how they do, within, in an unbloody manner,
under the forms of brown haematite and black manganese on
the graved lime-face, what is done, without,
               far on the windy tundra
at the kill
that the kindred may have life.
               O God!
O the Academies!

What ages since
his other marvel-day
               when times turned?
and *how* turned!
When
          (How?
          from early knocking stick or stane?)
the first New Fire wormed
          at the Easter of Technics.
What a holy Saturn's day!
O vere beata nox!

A hundred thousand equinoxes
(less or more)
since they cupped the ritual stones
for the faithful departed.

What, from this one's cranial data, is
like to have been his kindred's psyche; in that they, along
with the journey-food, donated the votive horn? and with
what *pietas* did they donate these among the dead — the life-
givers — and by what rubric?
    Was their oral gloss from a Heidelberg gaffer or did they
emend a Piltdown use, was the girl from Lime Street a butty
of theirs, or were the eight Carmel fathers consanguine or
of any affinity to those that fathered them, that told what
they had heard with their ears of those german to them, before
the palmy arbours began again to pine — and at which of the
boreal oscillations?
                            And before them?
those who put on their coats to oblate the things set apart
in an older Great Cold.
                            And who learned them
if not those whose fathers had received or aped the groping
disciplina of their cognates, or lost or found co-laterals,
on the proto-routes or at the lithic foci?
                            Tundra-wanderers?
or was there no tundra as yet, or not as yet again, to
wander — but grew green the rashes over again? Or was all
once again *informis,* that Cronos for the third time might
see how his lemmings run and hear the cry of his tailless
hare from south of the sixties, from into the forties?
                            For the phases and phase-groups
sway toward and fro within that belt of latitude.
There's where the world's a stage
                            for transformed scenes
with metamorphosed properties
                            for each shifted set.
Now naked as an imagined *belle sauvage,* or as is the actual
Mirriam.
Now shirted, kilted, cloaked, capped and shod, as were the
five men of Jutland, discovered in their peaty cerements, or
as the bear-coped Gilyak is, or was, the other day.
The mimes deploy:
                            anthropoid
                            anthropoi.
Who knows at what precise phase, or from what floriate
green-room, the Master of Harlequinade, himself not made,

maker of sequence and permutation in all things made, called
us from our co-laterals out, to dance the Funeral Games of
the Great Mammalia, as, long, long, long before, these
danced out the Dinosaur?

Now, from the draughty flats
                  the ageless cherubs
pout the Southerlies.
Now, Januarius brings in the millennial snow that makes the
antlered mummers glow for many a hermera.
              The *Vorzeit*-masque is on
that moves to the cosmic introit.
Col canto the piping for this turn.
Unmeasured, irregular in stress and interval, of interior
rhythm, modal.
              If tonic and final are fire
the dominant is ice
              if fifth the fire
the cadence ice.
At these Nocturns the hebdomadary is apt to be vested for
five hundred thousand weeks.
Intunes the Dog:
              Benedicite ignis . . .
Cantor Notus and Favonius with all their south-aisled
numina:
             con flora cálida
             mit warmer Fauna
The Respond is with the Bear:
             Benedicite frigus . . .
Super-pellissed, stalled in crystallos, from the gospel-side,
choir all the boreal schola
            mit kalter Flora
            con fauna fría
Now, sewn fibre is superfluous when Thames falls into
Rhine. Now they would be trappers of every tined creature
and make corners in ulotrichous hide and establish their
wool-cartels as south as Los Millares. Where the stones
shall speak of his cupola-makers: but here we speak of long,
long before their time.
            When is Tellus
to give her dear fosterling
            her adaptable, rational, elect
and plucked-out otherling
           a reasonable chance?
Not yet — but soon, very soon
           as lithic phases go.

So before then?
              Did the fathers of those
who forefathered them
               (if by genital or ideate begetting)
set apart, make other, oblate?

By what rote, if at all
          had they the suffrage:
          Ascribe to, ratify, approve
in the humid paradises
          of the Third Age?
But who or what, before these?
          Had they so far to reach the ground?
and what of the pelvic inclination of their co-laterals,
whose far cognates went — on how many feet? — in the old
time before *them?*
For all WHOSE WORKS FOLLOW THEM
              among any of these or them
dona eis requiem.
          (He would lose, not any one
              from among them.
Of all those given him
          he would lose none.)

          By the uteral marks
that make the covering stone an artefact.
          By the penile ivory
and by the viatic meats.
          Dona ei requiem.
Who was he? Who?
Himself at the cave-mouth
          the last of the father-figures
to take the diriment stroke
          of the last gigantic leader of
thick-felled cave-fauna?
Whoever he was
          Dona ei requiem
sempiternam.
(He would not lose him
          . . . *non perdidi*
ex eis quemquam.)

          Before the melt-waters
had drumlin-dammed a high hill-water for the water-maid
to lave her maiden hair.

Before they morained Tal-y-llyn, cirqued a high hollow for
Idwal, brimmed a deep-dark basin for Peris the Hinge and
for old Paternus.

Long ages since they'd troughed, in solid Ordovician
his Bala bed for Tacitus.
Long, long ago they'd turned the flow about.
But had they as yet morained
      where holy Deva's entry is?
Or pebbled his mere, where
      still the Parthenos
she makes her devious exit?

Before the Irish sea-borne sheet lay tattered on the gestatorial
couch of Camber the eponym
      lifted to every extremity of the sky
by pre-Cambrian oros-heavers
      for him to dream
the Combroges' epode.
In his high *sêt* there.
      Higher than any of 'em
south of the Antonine limits.
Above the sealed hypogéum
      where the contest was
over the great *mundus* of sepulture (there the *ver-tigérnus* was)
here lie dragons and old Pendragons
      very bleached.
His uncomforming bed, as yet
      is by the muses kept.

And shall be, so these Welshmen say, till the thick rotundi-
ties give, and the bent flanks of space itself give way
     and the whitest of the Wanderers
falters in her transit
     at the Sibyl's *in favilla*-day.

Before the drift
     was over the lime-face.
Sometime between the final and the penultimate débâcle.
     (Already Arcturus deploys his reconnoitering
chills in greater strength: soon his last *Putsch* on any scale.)
Before this all but proto-historic transmogrification of the
land-face.
Just before they rigged the half-lit stage for dim-eyed Clio
to step with some small confidence the measures of her
brief and lachrymal pavan.

Before, albescent, out of the day-starred neoarctic night the
Cis-Alclyde pack again came sud of the Mull.
                              Across the watersphere
over the atmosphere, preventing the crystal formations
ambient grew the wondrous New Cold:
                              trauma and thauma, both.
This is how Cronos reads the rubric, *frangit per medium,* when
he breaks his ice like morsels, for the therapy and fertility
of the land-masses.
Or before
              from Eden-dales, or torn from the becked fells
                         transmontane
                         transmarine
the barrier-making flood-gravels
the drumlined clays and the till-drift
                    had bye-wayed and delta'd the mainway
for Tanat and Vyrnwy.
                    Before the heaped detritus
had parted the nymphaean loves
                    of naiad Sabrina and sibylline Dee.
She must marl her clear cascade-locks in dawdling Stour's
English bed
                                                  and she
must glen her parthenogenic waters a shorter cut by Gwen-
frewi's well, before she comes to Wirral.
Before, trans-Solway
              and from over Manannan's *moroedd,* the last debris-
freighted floes echeloned solid from Monapia to Ynys Fôn
                    discharged on Arfon *colles*
what was cargoed-up on Grampius Mons.
                    Off the "strath" into the *ystrad*
out of the "carse" on to the *traeth.*
Heaped amorphous
                    out of Caledonia
into Cambria
                    bound for Snowdonia
transits Cumbria.
                    Long, long, long before
(fifty thousands of winter calends?
fifty thousand calends of Maia before?)
                         the Lord Cunedda
conditor noster
                         filius Æterni, son of Padarn Red
Pexa, son of Tacitus, came south over the same terrain and
by way of the terrain-gaps then modified or determined: for
the *viae* are not independent of geology: that his hobnailed

foederati, his twelve cantred-naming sons and himself, the
loricated leader in his gaffer's purple, might scrape from their
issue *caligae* the mud of Forth into Conwy.

Clyde into Clwyd.
                                        Otadini
over Venedotia
                     and even in Irish Demetia
a Cunedda's Hill.
                    Combroges bore us:
tottering, experienced, crux-signed
                     old Roma
the yet efficient mid-wife of us.

                     Before the slow estuarine alchemies had coal-
blacked the green dryad-ways over the fire-clayed seat-earth
along all the utile seams from Taff to Tâf.

Before the microgranites and the clay-bonded erratics
wrenched from the diorites of Aldasa, or off the Goat Height
in the firth-way, or from the Clota-sides or torn from either
Dalriada, with what was harrowed-out *in via,* up, from the
long drowned out-crops, under, coalesced and southed by
the North Channel.
            As though the sea itself were sea-borne
and under weigh
             as if the whole Ivernian *mare*
directed from hyperboreal control-points by strategi of the
axis were one complex of formations in depth, moving on a
frontage widening with each lesser degree of latitude.

               Heading toward, right astride
to one degree beyond
               Ffraid Sant's fire-track
where Brendan shall cry from his sea-horse
Mirabilis Deus in sanctis suis!

From before all time
              the New Light beams for them
and with eternal clarities
            infulsit and athwart
the fore-times:
             era, period, epoch, hemera.

Through all orogeny:
                      group, system, series, zone.
Brighting at the five-life-layers
                      species, species, genera, families, order.
Piercing the eskered silt, discovering every stria, each score
and macula, lighting all the fragile laminae of the shales.
However Calypso has shuffled the marked pack, veiling with
early the late.
Through all unconformities and the sills without sequence,
glorying all the under-dapple.
Lighting the Cretaceous and the Trias, for Tyrannosaurus
must somehow lie down with herbivores, or, the poet lied,
which is not allowed.
However violent the contortion or whatever the inversion
of the folding.
Oblique through the fire-wrought cold rock dyked from
convulsions under.
Through the slow sedimentations laid by his patient creature
of water.
Which ever the direction of the strike, whether the hade is
to the up-throw or the fault normal.
Through all metamorphs or whatever the pseudomorphoses.

As, down among the palaeo-zoe
                      he brights his ichthyic sign
so brights he the middle-zone
                      where the uterine forms
are some beginnings of his creature.
Brighter yet over the mammal'd Pliocene
                      for these continuings
certainly must praise him:
                      How else, in his good time
should the amorous Silvy
                      to her sweetest dear
her fairest bosom have shown?

                      How else we?
                      or he, himself?
whose name is called He-with-us
because he did not abhor the uterus.
                      Whereby these uberal forms
are to us most dear
                      and of all hills
the most august.

How else her iconography?
How other his liturgy?

            Masters and doctors
of seven-breasted Roma
or of all sites that offer nurture
                of which it is said
Hinc lucem et pocula sacra
               or you of Rhydychen
that have the Lord for your light
answer me.

                            Brighting totally
the post-Pliocene
both Pleistocene and Recent.
                        An aureole here

for Europa's tundra-*beata*
who of duck's bone had made her needle-case.
And where the carboniferous floor
yields from among the elk-bones and the breccia
this separated one
          the data of whose cause is known alone to *him.*

The *egregius*
                     young, toward the prime,
wearing the amulets of ivory and signed with the life-giving
ochre.

             Strayed from among the nine and ninety
Aurignacian *beati*
              that he has numbered
at his secret shearing
             as things made over
             by his Proserpine
                to himself.
When on a leafy morning
             late in June
against the white wattles
             he numbers his own.

As do they
             taught of the herdsman's *Ordinale*
and following the immemorial *numeri*
who say:
          Yan, tyan, tethera, methera, pimp
sethera, lethera, hovera, dovera, dick.

For whom he has notched
his crutched tally-stick
                not at: less one five twenties
                but
at *centum*
                that follow the Lamb
from the Quaternary dawn.
                Numbered among his flock
that no man may number
                but whose works follow them.

Searching where the kitchen midden tells of the decline
which with the receding cold marked the recession of the
Magdalenian splendours.
Yet there he brights fragmented protomorphs
where lies the rudimentary bowl.

                                              How else

multifariam multisque modis
                the splendour of forms yet to come?
How the dish
                that holds no coward's food?
How the *calix*
                without which
                how *the* re-calling?
And there
                where, among the exactly faceted microliths
                lie the bones
of the guardian and friend.
                How else Argos
the friend of Odysseus?
                Or who should tend
the sores of lazars?
(For anthropos is not always kind.)
                How Ranter or True, Ringwood
                or the pseudo-Gelert?
                How Spot, how Cerberus?
(For men can but proceed from what they know, nor is it for
the mind of this flesh to practise poïesis, *ex nihilo*.)
How the hound-bitches
                of the stone kennels of Arthur
that quested the hog and the brood of the hog
                from Pebidiog to Aber Gwy?
How the dog Toby? How the flew'd sweet thunder for
dewy Ida?

And over the submerged dryad-ways
intensively his ray searches
                                    where the alluvium holds
the polished neoliths
and where the long mound inhumes
                        his neolithic loves
or the round-barrow keeps
                        the calcined bones
of these, his still more modern hallows
                        that handled the pitiless bronze.

(Pray for her by whom came war
                        for whose urn-burial
        they made the cist four-square
                        on the bank of the Alaw.)

And over the Cis-padane marls
searching the trapezoidal platforms:
                for but for the Terramare *disciplina*
how should his Mantuan have sung
                the Quadrilateral Plan?

Upon all fore-times
                        From before time
his perpetual light
                        shines upon them.
                        Upon all at once
upon each one
whom he invites, bids, us to recall
when we make the recalling of him
                        daily, at the Stone.
When the offerant
                our *servos,* so theirs whose life is changed
not taken away
                        is directed to say
                        Memento etiam.
After which it is allowed him then to say
                        Nobis quoque.
That we too may be permitted some part with these
like John is!
                        as is Felicity.
                        Through the same Lord
that gave the naiad her habitat
                        which is his proto-sign.

How else from the weathered mantle-rock
and the dark humus spread
(where is exacted the night-labour
　　　　　where the essential and labouring worm
saps micro-workings all the dark day long
　　　　　　　　　　for his creature of air)
should his barlies grow
　　　　　who said
I am your Bread?

John Lehmann
b. 1907

IN A LONDON TERMINUS

Soldier I watch so proudly pass
Beneath the ruined vault of glass,
With eyes the desert wind has blown,
Anonymous, yet always known,
O, in your look and carriage dwell
Mysteries of Heaven and Hell.

There was a time when boyhood saw
The simple truth as living's law,
Even fear could not foretell
The sum that would not come out well,
The paradox no mother planned
Where tank fought tank across the sand;

In those far days, when Egypt's rains
Fell not so red from English veins,
Was innocence so wrong to hold
Concord and joy earth's purest gold,
That now, grown older, must admire
The finer mint from battle's fire?

No, not in vain, for this the prize
The worst that terror could devise;
And yet my heart cannot dispel
Ache for the others — those who fell;
Is the path through gulf and flame
Love's one inexorable claim?

Soldier, the riddles I would read
In the mastery of your head
Do not spell the peace you dreamed
Once, while the scything bullets screamed,
And will but sear the hopes of youth
With their danger-volted truth;

Here, in my trapped perplexity
Turning to Heaven, I only see
The broken girders, empty sky,
Inscrutable to question why
Love's grace must rot by Egypt's sea
That we may grow as we would be.

A DEATH IN HOSPITAL

On the first day, the lifted siege at last
On starving hope: his spirit dropped its load,
And turning once more to the world of friends
    Wept for the love they showed.

Then on the second day, like a black storm
Terror of death burst over him, and pain
Pierced like the jagged lightning, in whose flash
    All he would never gain —

The wine-blue inlets of a home restored,
Peace, and the growth of love in summer's field,
And loaded baskets from a poet's tree —
    Pitiless, stood revealed.

The third night there was battle in the skies:
The tongues of all the guns were hot with steel,
The groaning darkness shuddered, but could add
    No wrench to his ordeal.

The fourth day, when they came with daffodils
And sea-borne fruit, and honey from his home,
They seemed but shadows, where he choked and fought
    There was so little room.

It was the fifth day explanation broke:
There was no fear, nor human longing more,
And all his life in that surprising dawn
    Appeared a dwindling shore

Separate for ever from his tide-kissed boat,
An isle with all its gardens fondly kept
Complete and curious, that belonged to them,
His friends, who stayed and wept.

Elinor Wylie

1885-1928

LAVISH KINDNESS

Indulgent giants burned to crisp
The oak-trees of a dozen shires
Adorning thus a will-o'-the-wisp
With momentary pomp of fires.

The waters of an inland sea
Were magicked to a mountain peak
Enabling dwindled pools to be
Cool to a single swallow's beak.

But whether prodigies of waste,
Or idle, or beneficent,
Such deeds are not performed in haste
And none has fathomed their intent.

Vachel Lindsay

1879-1931

From THE GOLDEN WHALES OF CALIFORNIA
Inscribed to Isadora Bennett Reed

A SHORT WALK ALONG THE COAST
Yes, I have walked in California,
And the rivers there are blue and white.
Thunderclouds of grapes hang on the mountains.
Bears in the meadows pitch and fight.
(*Limber, double-jointed lords of fate,*
Proud native sons of the Golden Gate.)
And flowers burst like bombs in California

Exploding on tomb and tower.
And the panther-cats chase the red rabbits,
Scatter their young blood every hour.
And the cattle on the hills of California
And the very swine in the holes
Have ears of silk and velvet
And tusks like long white poles.
And the very swine, big-hearted,
Walk with pride to their doom
For they feed on the sacred raisins
Where the great black agates loom. . . .

The solid Golden Gate soars up to Heaven.
Perfumed cataracts are hurled
From the zones of silver snow
To the ripening rye below,
To the land of the lemon and the nut
And the biggest ocean in the world.
While the Native Sons, like lords tremendous,
Lift up their heads with chants sublime,
And the band-stands sound the trombone, the saxophone
    and xylophone
And the whales roar in perfect tune and time.
And the chanting of the whales of California
I have set my heart upon.
It is sometimes a play by Belasco,
Sometimes a tale of Prester John.

THE CHANTING OF THE WHALES

North to the Pole, south to the Pole
The whales of California wallow and roll.
They dive and breed and snort and play
And the sun-struck feed them every day
Boatloads of citrons, quinces, cherries,
Of bloody strawberries, plums and beets,
Hogsheads of pomegranates, vats of sweets,
And the he-whales' chant like a cyclone blares,
Proclaiming the California noons
So gloriously hot some days
The snake is fried in the desert
And the flea no longer plays.
There are ten gold suns in California
When all the other lands have one,
For the Golden Gate must have due light
And persimmons be well-done.
And the hot whales slosh and cool in the wash

And the fume of the hollow sea.
Rally and roam in the loblolly foam
And whoop that their souls are free.
(*Limber, double-jointed lords of fate,*
Proud native sons of the Golden Gate.)
And they chant of the forty-niners
Who sailed round the Cape for their loot
With guns and picks and washpans
And a dagger in each boot.
How the richest became the King of England,
The poorest became the King of Spain,
The bravest a colonel in the army,
And a mean one went insane.
The ten gold suns are so blasting
The sunstruck scoot for the sea
And turn to mermen and mermaids
And whoop that their souls are free.
(*Limber, double-jointed lords of fate,*
Proud native sons of the Golden Gate.)
And they take young whales for their bronchos
And old whales for their steeds,
Harnessed with golden sea weeds,
And driven with golden reeds. . . .

And they feed the cuttlefishes, whales and skates
With dates and figs in bales and crates: —
Shiploads of sweet potatoes, peanuts, rutabagas,
Honey in hearts of gourds;
Grapefruits and oranges barrelled with apples
And spices like sharp sweet swords.

ST. FRANCIS OF SAN FRANCISCO

But the surf is white, down the long strange coast
With breasts that shake with sighs,
And the ocean of all oceans
Holds salt from weary eyes.

St. Francis comes to his city at night
And stands in the brilliant electric light
And his swans that prophesy night and day
Would soothe his heart that wastes away:
The giant swans of California
That nest on the Golden Gate
And beat through the clouds serenely
And on St. Francis wait.

THE VOICE OF THE EARTHQUAKE

But what is the earthquake's cry at last
Making St. Francis yet aghast: —

"Oh the flashing cornucopia of haughty California
Is *gold, gold, gold.*
Their brittle speech and their clutching reach
Is *gold, gold, gold.*
What is the fire-engine's ding dong bell?
The burdens of the burble of the bullfrog in the well?
Gold, gold, gold.
What is the color of the cup and plate
And knife and fork of the Chief of State?
Gold, gold, gold.
What is the flavor of the Bartlett pear?
What is the savor of the salt sea air?
Gold, gold, gold.
What is the color of the sea-girl's hair?
Gold, gold, gold.
In the Church of Jesus and the streets of Venus: —
Gold, gold, gold.
What color are the cradle and the bridal bed?
What color are the coffins of the great gray dead?
Gold, gold, gold.
What is the hue of the big whale's hide?
Gold, gold, gold.
What is the color of their guts inside?
Gold, gold, gold.
What is the color of the pumpkins in the moonlight?
Gold, gold, gold.
The color of the moth and the worm in the starlight?
Gold, gold, gold."

Edna St. Vincent Millay

1892-1951

SONNET XIV

Him not the golden fang of furious heaven,
Nor whirling Aeolus on his awful wheel,
Nor foggy specter ramming the swift keel,

Nor flood, nor earthquake, nor the red tongue even
Of fire, disaster's dog — him, him bereaven
Of all save the heart's knocking, and to feel
The air upon his face: not the great keel
Of headless Force into the dust was driven.
These sunken cities, tier on tier, bespeak
How ever from the ashes with proud beak
And shining feathers did the Phoenix rise,
And sail, and send the vulture from the skies . . .
That in the end returned; for Man was weak
Before the unkindness in his brother's eyes.

SONNET XVIII

Here lies, and none to mourn him but the sea,
That falls incessant on the empty shore,
Most various Man, cut down to spring no more;
Before his prime, even in his infancy
Cut down, and all the clamour that was he,
Silenced; and all the rivetted pride he wore,
A rusted iron column whose tall core
The rains have tunnelled like an aspen tree.
Man, doughty Man, what power has brought you low,
That heaven itself in arms could not persuade
To lay aside the lever and the spade
And be as dust among the dusts that blow?
Whence, whence the broadside? whose the heavy blade? . . .
Strive not to speak, poor scattered mouth; I know.

Siegfried Sassoon
b. 1886

THE DUG–OUT

Why do you lie with your legs ungainly huddled,
And one arm bent across your sullen cold
Exhausted face? It hurts my heart to watch you,
Deep-shadowed from the candle's guttering gold;
And you wonder why I shake you by the shoulder;
Drowsy, you mumble and sigh and turn your head . . .
You are too young to fall asleep for ever;
And when you sleep you remind me of the dead.

A LOCAL TRAIN OF THOUGHT

Alone, in silence, at a certain time of night,
Listening, and looking up from what I'm trying to write,
I hear a local train along the Valley. And "There
Goes the one-fifty," think I to myself; aware
That somehow its habitual travelling comforts me,
Making my world seem safer, homelier, sure to be
The same to-morrow; and the same, one hopes, next year.
"There's peacetime in that train." One hears it disappear
With needless warning whistle and rail-resounding wheels.
"That train's quite like an old familiar friend," one feels.

MY PAST HAS GONE TO BED

My past has gone to bed. Upstairs in clockless rooms
My past is fast asleep. But mindsight reillumes
Here in my ruminant head the days where dust lies deep.

Sleep-walkers empty-eyed come strangely down the stairs.
These are my selves — once proud, once passionate with young prayers,
Once vehement with vows. I know not when they died,
Those ignorant selves. . . . Meanwhile my self sits brooding here
In the house where I was born. Dwindling, they disappear.
Me they did not foresee. But in their looks I find
Simplicities unlearned long since and left behind.

Lewis Thompson

1909-1949

BLACK ANGEL

1

One day that black and shining angel who
Haunted my nights in Arles and at Ajmeer,
Monster of beauty loud with cruel gems,
I shall encounter in some lane at noon
Where painted demons have struck dumb the walls.

Perhaps a glance absorbs, unriddles him;
Or he, or I, will follow to such home
As then I seem to have, and (if his height
Of presence do not shatter it roof and floor,
Leaving me dark in a new wilderness
Acrid with blowing smoke, horizonless),
He will have entered in. And though my garland
Shrivel upon his lightning beauty, I have decked him.

Black Peacock harsh with plumes, our sombre legends
Buried you with the Yezidees, or we have mocked you
With the ecstatic irony of red-hot swords.
Now take from me the last shell of my words,
The empty skull, and show me a true body.

2

Mute, inexhaustible music, sweet and mad appalling lyre,
Machine of destiny, enigma, Sphinx!
Hand, lip, life, limb wander your lunar fire
Lost in impenetrable gleaming subtlety.
Your breast — an echoing cithern of black glass;
A holdless precipice, a ladder without rungs
For suffocating rapture — sheer
Vertical cords Apollo's brazen touch
Alone can find: none other wakes
That diamond music. Avid, raving Sun,
Lewd, leonine,
Beat into adamant your meteor dark.
That obstinate anvil, equally, refracts
The cruel, deft and delicate hammer-pulse
To Vulcan clangour — rings
All song to dust. Or else,
Abyss of silence, orchestrates
All bare and bleeding hells.

> The dahlia's crisp and sombre
> Sun and bitter scent,
> Black blood and serpentine
> Of leaf and stem — the
> Dark marriage, Pluto, Proserpina.

O tongueless terror, solitary bell,
Devouring mouth, unborn, undying Youth,
Time you devour — have ever undermined
The last, lean, anguished, agonistic ground

On which Odysseus, Theseus, Herakles,
Faust, Apollonius, every monster or mage,
In desperate, sick and self-exhausting pride
Might stand and still contrive
Against your cheating magic irony —
You the undoing before it can begin,
The never of all their nightmare, all the absurd,
Blind and baroque, laborious suicide
For which, with wonderful tokens, they were born.

> Firm be your sight
> Ever before my eyes:
> You are the Eye that sees
> Yourself by your own light.

The drenching gaze of gold, of marigold eyes,
All calm and all caprice, Edenic wantonness,
Empties to piercing void in whom they light upon
All thought, all faculty. The tawny mane
Of ravelling hair, like gold, like camphor, shakes
A pollen of fresh iridescences
Over the lintel of nervate, warm obsidian,
The shoulders' sweet and solemn, brute and tender span.

Your back is like the secretive lapse and pull
Of wide and sinewy waters. And the firm,
Heavy, elusive loins, mute bell,
Girt with a chain of iron, a shield of polished iron.
The svelte and lusty body subtly bloomed
As if (white-hot) with ash; that silk astringency
Stained at a vine of hair with maddening ichor —
A subtle serpent, tender, gleaming, harsh
With the deep rut of lilt and lightning fire.

A bolt of thunder rises from beneath
The earth, root of the underworld,
Glittering with rigid and relentless bane,
Volcanic, venomous, wielded by Death's
Cold, all-reversing flame —
Satin with freshness like a young and hard blue rose.

Those doors, those vulcan mouths,
Orpheus, dumb horror-stricken harp, affront: Eurydice
(Springtime Proserpina, Ceres) you seek in vain
Beneath the sun or looking back to see
A scatheless image of immortality:

This judgement only if it weigh, bow down the soul
Drenched in the scorching black roke of the bull
Inherits heaven's unfading flowers, the flowering earth.

Terrible luxury, that dour and dark divide:
Black rose, indigo noose, blue satin brazier
Of subterranean fire — the serpent cave
Pulsing and glittering:
Too close and monster-sweet simplicity.

The dizzying maelstrom's void and valsing walls,
Magnetic drag and drive of spinning steel,
Rock, reel, climb, comb, tower and overtower:
Whelming and overwhelming, floorless deeps
Mine, undermine, breath, speech, mind, memory.

What sorrows dumb from the beginning of the world
And dumb for ever, knife always buried first
And hidden in our own heart —
Unfrontiered tenderness and crime
Here, here in the fathomless heart,
Cry (nectar, venom, Angel, Demon), laugh
So terribly out loud!

3

Wordless: skull, rose;
Bull, meteor;
The singing bone.

A thousand lions
Roar like a sun.
The thunderbolt,
His blinding laugh.

A cup of blood
Drinks and drinks up the heart.

ROSE

Iron-red rose-leaf, tinctured with
An acrid blood, a saw-tooth exigence,
Talonned with scorching stripes of wrath:
Tigerish your flower of love and dangerous.

Only the utmost, straitest bound
Of vehemence could have opened the arena where
Your silken, sleepy calm is crowned:
Such massive sweetness fills no smaller air.

H. D.
b. 1886

THE GARDEN

I

You are clear
O rose, cut in rock,
hard as the descent of hail.

I could scrape the colour
from the petals,
like spilt dye from a rock.

If I could break you
I could break a tree.

If I could stir
I could break a tree —
I could break you.

II

O wind, rend open the heat,
cut apart the heat,
slit it to tatters.

Fruit cannot drop
through the thick air;
fruit cannot fall into heat
that presses up, and blunts

the points of pears,
and rounds grapes.

Cut the heat;
plough through it,
turning it on either
        side
of your path.

SEA GODS

I

They say there is no hope —
sand — drift — rocks — rubble of
        the sea —
the broken hulk of a ship,
hung with shreds of rope,
palled under the cracked pitch.

They say there is no hope
to conjure you —
no whip of the tongue to anger
        you —
no hate of words
you must rise to refute.

They say you are twisted by the sea,
you are cut apart
by wave-break upon wave-break,
that you are misshapen by the
    sharp rocks,
broken by the rasp and after-rasp.

That you are cut, torn, mangled,
torn by the stress and beat,
no stronger than the strips of sand
along your rugged beach.

II

But we bring violets,
great masses — single, sweet,
wood-violets, stream-violets,
violets from a wet marsh.

Violets in clumps from hills,
tufts with earth at the roots,
violets tugged from rocks,
blue violets, moss, cliff, river-
    violets.

Yellow violets' gold,
burnt with a rare tint —
violets like red ash
among tufts of grass.
We bring deep-purple
bird-foot violets.

We bring the hyacinth-violet,
sweet, bare, chill to the touch —
and violets whiter than the in-rush
of your own white surf.

III

For you will come,
you will yet haunt men in ships,
you will trail across the fringe of
    strait
and circle jagged rocks.

You will trail across the rocks
and wash them with your salt,
you will curl between sand-hills —
you will thunder along the cliff —
break — retreat — get fresh
    strength —
gather and pour weight upon the
    beach.

You will draw back,
and the ripple on the sand-shelf

will be witness of your track.
O privet-white, you will paint
the lintel of wet sand with froth.

You will bring myrrh bark
and drift laurel-wood from hot
    coasts!
when you hurl high — high —
we will answer with a shout.

For you will come,
you will come,
you will answer our taut hearts,
you will break the lie of men's
    thoughts
and cherish and shelter us.

ORCHARD

I saw the first pear
as it fell —
the honey-seeking, golden-banded,

the yellow swarm
was not more fleet than I,
(spare us from loveliness)

and I fell prostrate,
crying:
you have flayed us with your
    blossoms,
spare us the beauty
of fruit-trees!

The honey-seeking
paused not,
the air thundered their song,
and I alone was prostrate.

O rough-hewn
god of the orchard,

I bring you an offering —
do you, alone unbeautiful,
son of the god,
spare us from loveliness:

these fallen hazel-nuts,
stripped late of their green sheaths,
grapes, red-purple,
their berries
dripping with wine,
pomegranates already broken,
and shrunken figs,
and quinces untouched
I bring you as offering.

O HEART, SMALL URN

O heart, small urn
of porphyry, agate or cornelian,

how imperceptibly the grain fell
between a heart-beat of pleasure

and a heart-beat of pain;
I do not know how it came

nor how long it had lain there,
nor can I say

how it escaped tempest
of passion and malice,

nor why it was not washed away
in flood of sorrow,

    or dried up in the bleak drought
    of bitter thought.

Hugh MacDiarmid
b. 1892

O WHA'S BEEN HERE AFORE ME, LASS

O wha's the bride that cairries the
    bunch
O' thistles blinterin white?
Her cuckold bridegroom little
    dreids
What he sall ken this nicht.

For closer than gudeman can
    come
And closer to'r than hersel,
Wha didna need her maiden-
    heid
Has wrocht his purpose fell.

O wha's been here afore me, lass,
And hoo did he get in?
    A man that deed or I was born
    This evil thing has din.

And left, as it were on a corpse,
Your maidenheid to me?
    Nae lass, gudeman, sin Time
      began
    'S hed ony mair to gie.

But I can gie ye kindness, lad,
And a pair o willin hands,
And ye sall hae my briests like stars,
My limbs like willow wands.

And on my lips ye'll need nae
    mair,
And in my hair forget,
The seed o a' the men that in
My virgin womb hae met . . .

Osbert Sitwell

b. 1892

WINTER THE HUNTSMAN

Through his iron glades
Rides Winter the Huntsman.
All colour fades
As his horn is heard sighing.

Far through the forest
His wild hooves crash and thunder
Till many a mighty branch
Is torn asunder.

And the red reynard creeps
To his hole near the river,
The copper leaves fall
And the bare trees shiver.

As night creeps from the ground,
Hides each tree from its brother,
And each dying sound
Reveals yet another.

    Is it Winter the Huntsman
    Who gallops through his iron glades,
    Cracking his cruel whip
    To the gathering shades?

MRS. SOUTHERN'S ENEMY

    At dusk it is —
        Always at dusk —
           I seem to see again
That grey typhoon we knew as Mrs. Southern,
Spinning along the darkened passages,
Watching things, tugging things,
Seeing to things,
           And putting things to rights.

Oh, would that cruel daylight, too,
Could give us back again
Dear Mrs. Southern,
Dear selfless, blue-lipped Mrs. Southern,
Cross, mumbling and transparent Mrs. Southern,
With her grey hair,
    Grey face,
      And thinly-bitter smile,
In wide blue skirt, white-spotted, and white apron;
On the very top of her head she carried a cap,
An emblem of respect and respectability, while
As though she were a Hindu charmer of snakes,
Her hair lay coiled and tame at the back of her head.
But her actual majesty was really the golden glory,
Through which she moved, a hurrying fly
Enshrined in rolling amber,
As she spun along in a twisting column of golden atoms,
A halo of gold motes above and about her,
A column of visible, virtuous activity.
Her life was a span of hopeless conflict,
For she battled against Time,
That never-vanquished and invisible foe.

She did not recognize her enemy,
She thought him Dust:
But what is Dust,
Save Time's most lethal weapon,
His faithful ally and our sneaking foe,
Through whom Time steals and covers all we know,
The very instrument with which he overcame
Great Nineveh and Rome and Carthage,
Ophir and Trebizond and Ephesus,
Now deep, all deep, so deep in dust?
  Even the lean and arid archæologist,
   Who bends above the stones, and peers and ponders,
    Will, too, be his one day.
Dust loads the dice,
Then challenges to play,
Each layer of dust upon a chair or table
A tablet to his future victory.
And Dust is cruel, no victory despising,
However slight,
And Dust is greedy, eats the very bones;
So that, in the end, still not content
With trophies such as Helen of Troy,
Or with the conquering golden flesh of Cleopatra

(She, perhaps, understood the age-long battle,
For did she not prefer to watch her pearl
Dissolve in amber wine,
Thus herself enjoying
Its ultimate disintegration,
Than let Dust conquer such a thing of beauty?
Was not the asp, fruit-hidden,
The symbol of such understanding?),
He needs must seize on Mrs. Southern,
Poor mumbling, struggling, blue-lipped Mrs. Southern,
For Dust is insatiate and invincible.

OSMUND TOULMIN

The name of Osmund Toulmin, the Gentleman-Jockey,
　Carried a snigger for the respectable:
He had been wrecked on this desolate shore by some deplorable vice:
　What could it have been, yet I wonder?
Red-cheeked was he as an apple, or a muted ventriloquist's dummy,
His eyes were blue and furry as edelweiss, innocent
Enough to separate him from the fault
For which the world shunned him,
Turning aside its glance,
Waiting to laugh till after he passed.
In the plush, lush pleasure world of the 'sixties,
　Under the gaslight flare and flicker,
He had lived like a prince, with Princes,
But his vice had caused him to be thrown into outer darkness,
He was forgotten, had never existed,
But still with polished brown gaiters, in tweeds, exhaling the smell of the
　　　　　stable,
He strutted like a bantam, unashamed, unafraid,
On the blue ledge of the Promenade,
Fixing the deaf man's glare of his eyes on all who approached.

To this day I know not what vice wrecked Osmund Toulmin, the
　　　　　Gentleman-Jockey —
Unless it affords a clue
That he spent long hours on the sands
Watching the flushed schoolgirls playing hockey.

WHAT WAS YOUR DREAM, DOCTOR MURRICOMBE?

What was your dream, Doctor Murricombe,
  As you stumbled through the summer streets, flowering with people,
As you hit at the flies that in their swarms pursued you,
  What was the dream abiding at the back of your eyes,
  As you stared unseeing,
  And swung your stick and mumbled?
I heard your words; what did they mean?
What was your dream that would not let you go,
  Grisly Narcissus, fastened to your fountain,
Drove you continually out into the streets?

The man with his hand at the door was yourself. Never he left you
  As you had left her,
On the bed, dead, with the delicate marking of fingers.
She lay still as you looked over your shoulder,
Waited, as if she were waiting for you to greet her:
  But you were waiting for other meetings.

The Twelve set you free, but never the Three,
They changed to the flies that follow you through summer days,
Buzzing and singing the words that you know so well;
  "What do you want, Frank; Frank, what is it I've done?"
In the quiet voice that was soon to be quiet, you thought, for ever.
  But the Three are the daughters of night, are nourished by darkness,
Blacken all heaven with hell, as you stand again with your hand at the
        door,
Waiting in quiet nevermore to be broken;
  All time stopped flowing in that instant of going.

Now an old man, you stumble and mumble along
Through the streets of the summer, gay with the faces of people,
Unseeing — you see not the blossoming girls
Who, before the figure lay quiet for ever,
Filled your head and your bed.
  You cannot drive off the flies, or the Furies,
Pursuing your carrion,
Tisiphone, the fly,
For one day
  You'll die!

THE BALLAD OF SISTER ANNE

"Sister Anne, Sister Anne,
   You who have always been faithful to me,
Why do you stand there?

"Tell me, run to the window!
   What is it that I hear?
My bed is far from the window and I am restless,
   What is it that I hear?
I do not like to appear too curious
But I *must* know what it is I hear!

"Sister Anne, Sister Anne, I entreat you
   To tell me what it is I hear (I hear).
A new footstep sings to me from the asphalt pavement,
   A new shape patterns old dust.
     You don't hear it, Sister Anne? You must, you must!

"Sister Anne, Sister Anne,
   Run to the window!
     What is it that I hear?
A footstep drawing near and nearer, surely toward
The Grange. Is it the stranger — tall, thin stranger —
   You told me you saw approaching
     Last night in the cards?"

"Miss Wetherby, Miss Wetherby, my love,
   It's only the new butcher's boy at the corner,
     Red as a rose,
Wearing his blue and white striped coat and apron,
Bearing a basket of raw legs and shoulders
To give old people young strength.
   It's only the new butcher's boy at the corner,
     Whistling as he goes."

"Sister Anne, Sister Anne,
   Why do I tremble,
    What is it that I hear?
Perhaps it's Mrs. Shrubfield in her carriage,
Driving down to the Marine Parade and the Pier;
Are her horses sleek still, do the dogs still follow,
   Does she still hold in her eye a tear?"

"Miss Wetherby, my love, you grow uneasy,
  What is there for you to fear
If it were only Mrs. Shrubfield passing near?
    But no,
      It's the grocer's van,
      Varnished, spick and span,
Bringing brown demerara and candy and lump sugar
      And white sifted sugar, sifted fine,
And coffee, roasted and ground daily
      For your convenience and mine."

"Sister Anne, Sister Anne,
  I don't think I'm quite myself today.
Fetch me a thermometer and some sal volatile
      And the medicine-glass with a spout.
      What is it I hear, a sound of singing
— How can it be the alarm-clock ringing
At this hour, on Frances's day out?"

"Miss Wetherby, my love, it is a sound consoling,
      That of a great bell rolling
As it will toll one day for me — and you."

"Sister Anne, Sister Anne!
    Why do I hear the sound of wheels?
      Is it a hearse?
Is it old Miss Vanbrugh at number four
    Who called in Doctor Diggle, the new doctor,
      Did she grow worse?"

"Miss Wetherby, Miss Wetherby, my love,
      Do not yourself distress.
It's only the rumble of Madame Cockburn's van
      Delivering a new dress.
She told me all about it, a dress for Hallows Hall,
A white gown, she said, to be worn at a ball;
      A white cloud —
        Like a shroud."

" 'Like a shroud!' Today you use such odd expressions,
      Sister Anne, Sister Anne,
I think I have a touch of fever, my teeth chatter —
      Is anything the matter,
        Sister Anne?"

"Miss Wetherby, Miss Wetherby,
    I've stretched my neck through the trees from the window
And can tell the truth now."

"Yes, Sister Anne, tell me; tell me
    That it's only once again
The grocer's van,
      The new butcher's boy,
        The dressmaker's man."

"You would like to hear the truth, Madam mine —
    We can do as we like. No one will interrupt us.
There's not a soul in sight, not a sign,
      Not a sign!"

"Sister Anne, Sister Anne!
    What is it gleams in your hand?
Is it the thermometer-case flashing, as you stand
There — but I've never been able to bear people to come near me;
    Don't draw so near!"

"Miss Wetherby, Miss Wetherby, my love,
    It's time to wake you from your dream.
Now I'll tell you what you heard.
    The thin stranger in the cards
Was Death, drawing near and nearer:
    It is Death you feared —
      Try not to scream!"

John Crowe Ransom
b. 1888

CAPTAIN CARPENTER

Captain Carpenter rose up in his prime,
Put on his pistols and went riding out
But had got wellnigh nowhere at that time
Till he fell in with ladies in a rout.

It was a pretty lady and all her train
That played with him so sweetly but before
An hour she'd taken a sword with all her main
And twined him of his nose for evermore.

Captain Carpenter mounted up one day
And rode straightway into a stranger rogue
That looked unchristian but be that as may
The Captain did not wait upon prologue.

But drew upon him out of his great heart
The other swung against him with a club
And cracked his two legs at the shinny part
And let him roll and stick like any tub.

Captain Carpenter rode many a time
From male and female took he sundry harms
He met the wife of Satan crying "I'm
The she-wolf bids you shall bear no more arms."

Their strokes and counters whistled in the wind
I wish he had delivered half his blows
But where she should have made off like a hind
The bitch bit off his arms at the elbows.

And Captain Carpenter parted with his ears
To a black devil that used him in this wise
O Jesus ere his threescore and ten years
Another had plucked out his sweet blue eyes.

Captain Carpenter got up on his roan
And sallied from the gate in hell's despite
I heard him asking in the grimmest tone
If any enemy yet there was to fight?

"To any adversary it is fame
If he risk to be wounded by my tongue
Or burnt in two beneath my red heart's flame
Such are the perils he is cast among.

"But if he can he has a pretty choice
From an anatomy with little to lose
Whether he cut my tongue and take my voice
Or whether it be my round red heart he choose."

It was the neatest knave that ever was seen
Stepping in perfume from his lady's bower
Who at this word put in his merry mien
And fell on Captain Carpenter like a tower.

I would not knock old fellows in the dust
But there lay Captain Carpenter on his back
His weapons were the old heart in his bust
And a blade shook between rotten teeth alack.

The rogue in scarlet and grey soon knew his mind
He wished to get his trophy and depart
With gentle apology and touch refined
He pierced him and produced the Captain's heart.

God's mercy rest on Captain Carpenter now
I thought him Sirs an honest gentleman
Citizen husband soldier and scholar enow
Let jangling kites eat of him if they can.

But God's deep curses follow after those
That shore him of his goodly nose and ears
His legs and strong arms at the two elbows
And eyes that had not watered seventy years.

The curse of hell upon the sleek upstart
That got the Captain finally on his back
And took the red red vitals of his heart
And made the kites to whet their beaks clack clack.

Horace Gregory

b. 1898

From CHORUS FOR SURVIVAL

Waking from sleep we heard the Great Lakes' tide,
clear spray in wind, white blossoming in dark
night bloom, the city's heat behind us, rolling back
miles westward over plains.
　　　　　　　　　　　　Only the sound
of tide, the water leaping these shores,
the lake in wind and in trees over us, the voices
rising in spray, the white tide breaking.

Came Pere Marquette down rivers to the sea,
the inland ocean, bright in wilderness,
sumach and pine.

"Earn heaven for this earth, and iron-blue sky,
the fire-green leaf in the stilled waters —
water, air, fire in my hand, my veins these rivers
flowing to the cross whose flower is man;
the holy tree, blood-red with fruit, the resurrection
waking in this land.

Spring here God's arch, and choir singing praise
through pine and maple crucifix —
                                    the forest
trembling with light: O fiery bough."
                                    The Eucharist in snow,
death's supper underground and the long winter
under foreign stars.

Hart Crane
1899-1932

From THE BRIDGE

AVE MARIA

Venient annis, saecula seris,
Quibus Oceanus vincula rerum
Laxet et ingens pateat tellus
Tiphysque novos detegat orbes
Nec sit terris ultima Thule.
                          — SENECA

Columbus, alone, gazing toward Spain, invokes the pres-
ence of two faithful partisans of his quest. . . .

Be with me, Luis de San Angel, now —
Witness before the tides can wrest away
The word I bring, O you who reined my suit
Into the Queen's great heart that doubtful day;
For I have seen now what no perjured breath
Of clown nor sage can riddle or gainsay; —
To you, too, Juan Perez, whose counsel fear
And greed adjourned — I bring you back Cathay!

Here waves climb into dusk on gleaming mail;
Invisible valves of the sea — locks, tendons
Crested and creeping, troughing corridors

That fall back yawning to another plunge.
Slowly the sun's red caravel drops light
Once more behind us. . . . It is morning there —
O where our Indian emperies lie revealed,
Yet lost, all, let this keel one instant yield!

I thought of Genoa; and this truth, now proved,
That made me exile in her streets, stood me
More absolute than ever — biding the moon
Till dawn should clear that dim frontier, first seen
— The Chan's great continent. . . . Then faith, not fear
Nigh surged me witless. . . . Hearing the surf near —
I, wonder-breathing, kept the watch — saw
The first palm chevron the first lighted hill.

And lowered. And they came out to us crying,
"The Great White Birds!" (O Madre Maria, still
One ship of these thou grantest safe returning;
Assure us through thy mantle's ageless blue!)
And record of more, floating in a casque,
Was tumbled from us under bare poles scudding;
And later hurricanes may claim more pawn . . .
For here between two worlds, another, harsh,

This third, of water, tests the word; lo, here
Bewilderment and mutiny heap whelming
Laughter, and shadow cuts sleep from the heart
Almost as though the Moor's flung scimitar
Found more than flesh to fathom in its fall.
Yet under tempest-lash and surfeitings
Some inmost sob, half-heard, dissuades the abyss,
Merges the wind in measure to the waves,

Series on series, infinite, — till eyes
Starved wide on blackened tides, accrete — enclose
This turning rondure whole, this crescent ring
Sun-cusped and zoned with modulated fire
Like pearls that whisper through the Doge's hands
— Yet no delirium of jewels! O Fernando,
Take of that eastern shore, this western sea,
Yet yield thy God's, thy Virgin's charity!

— Rush down the plenitude, and you shall see
Isaiah counting famine on this lee!

Ah herb, a stray branch among salty teeth,
The jellied weeds that drag the shore — perhaps

To-morrow's moon will grant us Saltes Bar —
Palos again — a land cleared of long war.
Some Angelus environs the cordage tree;
Dark waters onward shake the dark prow free.

O Thou who sleepest on Thyself, apart
Like ocean athwart lanes of death and birth,
And all the eddying breath between dost search
Cruelly with love thy parable of man —
Inquisitor! incognizable Word
Of Eden and the enchained Sepulchre,
Into thy steep savannahs, burning blue,
Utter to loneliness the sail is true.

Who grindest oar, and arguing the mast
Subscribest holocaust of ships, O Thou
Within whose primal scan consummately
The glistening seignories of Ganges swim; —
Who sendest greeting by the corposant,
And Teneriffe's garnet — flamed it in a cloud,
Urging through night our passage to the Chan; —
Te Deum laudamus, for thy teeming span!

Of all that amplitude that time explores,
A needle in the sight, suspended north —
Yielding by inference and discard, faith
And true appointment from the hidden shoal:
This disposition that thy night relates
From Moon to Saturn in one sapphire wheel:
The orbic wake of thy once whirling feet,
Elohim, still I hear thy sounding heel!

White toil of heaven's cordons, mustering
In holy rings all sails charged to the far
Hushed gleaming fields and pendant seething wheat
Of Knowledge — round thy brows unhooded now
— The kindled Crown! acceded of the poles
And biassed by full sails, meridians reel
Thy purpose — still one shore beyond desire!
The sea's green crying towers a-sway, Beyond

And kingdoms
        naked in the
                trembling heart —
Te Deum laudamus
            O Thou Hand of Fire

ATLANTIS

Music is then the knowledge of that which relates to love in harmony and system.

— PLATO

Through the bound cable strands, the arching path
Upward, veering with light, the flight of strings —
Taut miles of shuttling moonlight syncopate
The whispered rush, telepathy of wires.
Up the index of night, granite and steel —
Transparent meshes — fleckless the gleaming staves —
Sybilline voices flicker, waveringly stream
As though a god were issue of the strings. . . .

And through that cordage, threading with its call
One arc synoptic of all tides below —
Their labyrinthine mouths of history
Pouring reply as though all ships at sea
Complighted in one vibrant breath made cry —
"Make thy love sure — to weave whose song we ply!"
— From black embankments, moveless soundings hailed,
So seven oceans answer from their dream.

And on, obliquely up bright carrier bars
New octaves trestle the twin monoliths
Beyond whose frosted capes the moon bequeaths
Two worlds of sleep (O arching strands of song!) —
Onward and up the crystal-flooded aisle
White tempest nets file upward, upward ring
With silver terraces the humming spars,
The loft of vision, palladium helm of stars.

Sheerly the eyes, like seagulls stung with rime —
Slit and propelled by glistening fins of light —
Pick biting way up towering looms that press
Sidelong with flight of blade on tendon blade
— Tomorrows into yesteryear — and link
What cipher-script of time no traveller reads
But who, through smoking pyres of love and death,
Searches the timeless laugh of mythic spears.

Like hails, farewells — up planet-sequined heights
Some trillion whispering hammers glimmer Tyre:
Serenely, sharply up the long anvil cry

Of inchling æons silence rivets Troy.
And you, aloft there — Jason! hesting Shout!
Still wrapping harness to the swarming air!
Silvery the rushing wake, surpassing call,
Beams yelling Æolus! splintered in the straits!

From gulfs unfolding, terrible of drums,
Tall Vision-of-the-Voyage, tensely spare —
Bridge, lifting night to cycloramic crest
Of deepest day — O Choir, translating time
Into what multitudinous Verb the suns
And synergy of waters ever fuse, recast
In myriad syllables — Psalm of Cathay!
O Love, thy white, pervasive Paradigm . . . !

We left the haven hanging in the night —
Sheened harbor lanterns backward fled the keel.
Pacific here at time's end, bearing corn —
Eyes stammer through the pangs of dust and steel.
And still the circular, indubitable frieze
Of heaven's meditation, yoking wave
To kneeling wave, one song devoutly binds —
The vernal strophe chimes from deathless strings!

O Thou steeled Cognizance whose leap commits
The agile precincts of the lark's return;
Within whose lariat sweep encinctured sing
In single chrysalis the many twain —
Of stars Thou are the stitch and stallion glow
And like an organ, Thou, with sound of doom —
Sight, sound and flesh Thou leadest from time's realm
As love strikes clear direction for the helm.

Swift peal of secular light, intrinsic Myth
Whose fell unshadow is death's utter wound —
O River-throated — iridescently upborne
Through the bright drench and fabric of our veins;
With white escarpments swinging into light,
Sustained in tears the cities are endowed
And justified conclamant with ripe fields
Revolving through their harvests in sweet torment.

Forever Deity's glittering Pledge, O Thou
Whose canticle fresh chemistry assigns
To rapt inception and beatitude —
Always through blinding cables, to our joy,

Of thy white seizure springs the prophecy:
Always through spiring cordage, pyramids
Of silver sequel, Deity's young name
Kinetic of white choiring wings . . . ascends.

Migrations that must needs void memory,
Inventions that cobblestone the heart —
Unspeakable Thou Bridge to Thee, O Love.
Thy pardon for this history, whitest Flower,
O Answerer of all — Anemone —
Now while thy petals spend the suns about us, hold —
(O Thou whose radiance doth inherit me)
Atlantis — hold thy floating singer late!

So to thine Everpresence, beyond time,
Like spears ensanguined of one tolling star
That bleeds infinity — the orphic strings,
Sidereal phalanxes, leap and converge:
— One Song, one Bridge of Fire! Is it Cathay,
Now pity steeps the grass and rainbows ring
The serpent with the eagle in the leaves . . . ?
Whispers antiphonal in azure swing.

Wallace Stevens
1879-1955

BANTAMS IN PINE-WOODS

Chieftain Iffucan of Azcan in caftan
Of tan with henna hackles, halt!

Damned universal cock, as if the sun
Was blackamoor to bear your blazing tail.

Fat! Fat! Fat! Fat! I am the personal.
Your world is you. I am my world.

You ten-foot poet among inchlings. Fat!
Begone! An inchling bristles in these pines,

Bristles, and points their Appalachian tangs,
And fears not portly Azcan nor his hoos.

DRY LOAF

It is equal to living in a tragic land
To live in a tragic time.
Regard now the sloping, mountainous rocks
And the river that batters its way over stones,
Regard the hovels of those that live in this land.

That was what I painted behind the loaf,
The rocks not even touched by snow,
The pines along the river and the dry men blown
Brown as the bread, thinking of birds
Flying from burning countries and brown sand shores,

Birds that came like dirty water in waves
Flowing above the rocks, flowing over the sky,
As if the sky was a current that bore them along,
Spreading them as waves spread flat on the shore,
One after another washing the mountains bare.

It was the battering of drums I heard
It was hunger, it was the hungry that cried
And the waves, the waves were soldiers moving,
Marching and marching in a tragic time
Below me, on the asphalt, under the trees.

It was soldiers went marching over the rocks
And still the birds came, came in watery flocks,
Because it was spring and the birds had to come.
No doubt that soldiers had to be marching
And that drums had to be rolling, rolling, rolling.

THE GLASS OF WATER

That the glass would melt in heat,
That the water would freeze in cold,
Shows that this object is merely a state,
One of many, between two poles. So,
In the metaphysical, there are these poles.

Here in the centre stands the glass. Light
Is the lion that comes down to drink. There
And in that state, the glass is a pool.
Ruddy are his eyes and ruddy are his claws
When light comes down to wet his frothy jaws

And in the water winding weeds move round.
And there and in another state — the refractions,
The *metaphysica,* the plastic parts of poems
Crash in the mind — But, fat Jocundus, worrying
About what stands here in the centre, not the glass,

But in the centre of our lives, this time, this day,
It is a state, this spring among the politicians
Playing cards. In a village of the indigenes,
One would have still to discover. Among the dogs and dung,
One would continue to contend with one's ideas.

From NOTES TOWARD A SUPREME FICTION

The President ordains the bee to be
Immortal. The President ordains. But does
The body lift its heavy wing, take up,

Again, an inexhaustible being, rise
Over the loftiest antagonist
To drone the green phrases of its juvenal?

Why should the bee recapture a lost blague,
Find a deep echo in a horn and buzz
The bottomless trophy, new hornsman after old?

The President has apples on the table
And barefoot servants round him who adjust
The curtains to a metaphysical *t*

And the banners of the nation flutter, burst
On the flag-poles in a red-blue dazzle, whack
At the halyards. Why, then, when in golden fury

Spring vanishes the scraps of winter, why
Should there be a question of returning or
Of death in memory's dream? Is spring a sleep?

This warmth is for lovers at last accomplishing
Their love, this beginning, not resuming, this
Booming and booming of the new-come bee.

NOMAD EXQUISITE

As the immense dew of Florida
Brings forth
The big-finned palm
And green vine angering for life,

As the immense dew of Florida
Brings forth hymn and hymn
From the beholder,
Beholding all these green sides
And gold sides of green sides,

And blessed mornings
Meet for the eye of the young alligator,
And lightning colors,
So, in me, come flinging
Forms, flames, and the flakes of flames.

Archibald MacLeish
b. 1892

From CONQUISTADOR

From BERNAL DIAZ' PREFACE

We saw that city on the inland sea:
Towers between: and the green-crowned Montezuma
Walking the gardens of shade: and the staggering bees:

And the girls bearing the woven baskets of bloom on their
Black hair: their breasts alive: and the hunters
Shouldering dangling herons with their ruffled plumes:

We were the first that found that famous country:
We marched by a king's name: we crossed the sierras:
Unknown hardships we suffered: hunger:

Death by the stone knife: thirst: we fared by the
Bitter streams: we came at last to the water:
Towers were steep upon the fluttering air:

We were lords of it all. . . .

THE ARGUMENT

Of that world's conquest and the fortunate wars:
Of the great report and the expectation of honor:
How in their youth they stretched sail: how fared they

Westward under the wind: by wave wandered:
Shoaled ship at the last at the ends of ocean:
How they were marching in the lands beyond:

Of the difficult ways there were and the winter's snow:
Of the city they found in the good lands: how they lay in it:
How there was always the leaves and the days going:

Of the fear they had in their hearts for their lives' sake:
How there was neither the night nor the day sure: and the
Gage they took for their guard: and how evil came of it:

How they were dead and driven and endured:
How they returned with arms in the wet month:
How they destroyed that city: and the gourds were

Bitter with blood: and they made their roofs with gun stocks:

Of that world's conquest and the fortunate wars . . .

From *BOOK 10: AH HOW THE THROAT OF A GIRL*

Ah how the throat of a girl and a girl's arms are
Bright in the riding sun and the young sky
And the green year of our lives where the willows are!

How they were slender with strong breasts and the light of the
Leaves over them! How there were tall men
And the wading lake to their wrists and their wet thighs

Dabbled with sunlight: and they drew the nets
In the green sedge of the shore and they came singing:
The sea-film silvered in the lifting web:

Ah how the land was a good land! and the king of it
Rich and with young wives and with gold and his gardens
Sounding with water: and he went to drink

At noon at the grooved stone by the sheds and the jars were
Choked with the float of the sun: and he ate simnel
And sweet cakes he ate and a kind of partridges:

And none knew his ways or his times with women:
Silent he was and not seen and he came by
Dark: and his desire was in their limbs as an

Odor of plums in the night air and they wakened
Stretching their arms out and between their knees
Delight like the sun's mouth and the water's weight. . . .

From BOOK 13: DAWN ON THE WALL–HEAD THERE

Dawn on the wall-head there: and Montezuma
Clad in the gold cloth: gilded: and he smiled:
He climbed by the stair and smiling and they slew him:

He stood on the stone in the gold in the first light
And the war below: and they fought like dogs in the ditches
Whistling and shrieking: and we heard a sigh as the

Sound in leaves when the storm ends and the pitch of
Rain runs over and far on and the wind is
Gone from the willows and the still leaf drips:

And all at once there were stones and the sky hidden:
And he stood in gold not falling: and he fell:
The lances blurred in the sun as a wheel spinning:

His eyes were lewd with the strange smile: and they yelled as
Fiends in Hell and as beasts: and when we thought it
Least for the bitter fighting he was dead:

All that day and into the dark we fought:
And we lay in the straw in the rank blood and Cortés was
Hoarse with the shouting — "For a man was wronged and a

"Fool to suffer the Sure Aid but to best it and
Fight as he might: and he prayed all of us pardon
And grace if he spoke our hurt: but we were men:

"And we saw well what weapon was our guard:
And now there was none: only the night: and the ways were
Barred before us and the ditches barred

"And the dykes down by the banks and the water breaks
Open and armored and they held the roads:

"And nevertheless we had the choice to take them! . . ."

Robert Frost
b. 1875

OUR SINGING STRENGTH

It snowed in spring on earth so dry and warm
The flakes could find no landing place to form.
Hordes spent themselves to make it wet and cold,
And still they failed of any lasting hold.
They made no white impression on the black.
They disappeared as if earth sent them back.
Not till from separate flakes they changed at night
To almost strips and tapes of ragged white
Did grass and garden ground confess it snowed,
And all go back to winter but the road.
Next day the scene was piled and puffed and dead.
The grass lay flattened under one great tread.
Borne down until the end almost took root,
The rangy bough anticipated fruit
With snowballs cupped in every opening bud.
The road alone maintained itself in mud,
Whatever its secret was of greater heat
From inward fires or brush of passing feet.
In spring more mortal singers than belong
To any one place cover us with song.
Thrush, bluebird, blackbird, sparrow, and robin throng;
Some to go further north to Hudson's Bay,
Some that have come too far north back away,
Really a very few to build and stay.
Now was seen how these liked belated snow.
The fields had nowhere left for them to go;
They'd soon exhausted all there was in flying;
The trees they'd had enough of with once trying
And setting off their heavy powder load.
They could find nothing open but the road.
So there they let their lives be narrowed in
By thousands the bad weather made akin.

The road became a channel running flocks
Of glossy birds like ripples over rocks.
I drove them under foot in bits of flight
That kept the ground, almost disputing right
Of way with me from apathy of wing,
A talking twitter all they had to sing.
A few I must have driven to despair
Made quick asides, but having done in air
A whir among white branches great and small
As in some too much carven marble hall
Where one false wing beat would have brought down all,
Came tamely back in front of me, the Drover,
To suffer the same driven nightmare over.
One such storm in a lifetime couldn't teach them
That back behind pursuit it couldn't reach them;
None flew behind me to be left alone.

Well, something for a snowstorm to have shown
The country's singing strength thus brought together,
That though repressed and moody with the weather
Was none the less there ready to be freed
And sing the wildflowers up from root and seed.

THE TUFT OF FLOWERS

I went to turn the grass once after one
Who mowed it in the dew before the sun.

The dew was gone that made his blade so keen
Before I came to view the levelled scene.

I looked for him behind an isle of trees;
I listened for his whetstone on the breeze.

But he had gone his way, the grass all mown,
And I must be, as he had been — alone,

"As all must be," I said within my heart,
"Whether they work together or apart."

But as I said it, swift there passed me by
On noiseless wing a bewildered butterfly,

Seeking with memories grown dim o'er night
Some resting flower of yesterday's delight.

And once I marked his flight go round and round,
As where some flower lay withering on the ground.

And then he flew as far as eye could see,
And then on tremulous wing came back to me.

I thought of questions that have no reply,
And would have turned to toss the grass to dry;

But he turned first, and led my eye to look
At a tall tuft of flowers beside a brook,

A leaping tongue of bloom the scythe had spared
Beside a reedy brook the scythe had bared,

I left my place to know them by their name,
Finding them butterfly weed when I came.

The mower in the dew had loved them thus,
By leaving them to flourish, not for us,

Nor yet to draw one thought of ours to him,
But from sheer morning gladness at the brim.

The butterfly and I had lit upon,
Nevertheless, a message from the dawn,

That made me hear the wakening birds around,
And hear his long scythe whispering to the ground,

And feel a spirit kindred to my own;
So that henceforth I worked no more alone;

But glad with him, I worked as with his aid,
And weary, sought at noon with him the shade;

And dreaming, as it were, held brotherly speech
With one whose thoughts I had not hoped to reach.

"Men work together," I told him from the heart,
"Whether they work together or apart."

THE SOUND OF THE TREES

I wonder about the trees.
Why do we wish to bear
Forever the noise of these
More than another noise
So close to our dwelling place?
We suffer them by the day
Till we lose all measure of pace,
And fixity in our joys,
And acquire a listening air.
They are that that talks of going
But never gets away;
And that talks no less for
      knowing,

As it grows wiser and older,
That now it means to stay.
My feet tug at the floor
And my head sways to my shoulder
Sometimes when I watch trees sway,
From the window or the door.
I shall set forth for somewhere,
I shall make the reckless choice
Some day when they are in voice
And tossing so as to scare
The white clouds over them on.
I shall have less to say,
But I shall be gone.

DESERT PLACES

Snow falling and night falling, fast, oh, fast
In a field I looked into going past,
And the ground almost covered smooth in snow,
But a few weeds and stubble showing last.

The woods around it have it — it is theirs.
All animals are smothered in their lairs.
I am too absent-spirited to count;
The loneliness includes me unawares.

And lonely as it is that loneliness
Will be more lonely ere it will be less —
A blanker whiteness of benighted snow
With no expression, nothing to express.

They cannot scare me with their empty spaces
Between stars — or stars where no human race is,
I have it in me so much nearer home
To scare myself with my own desert places.

BEREFT

Where had I heard this wind before,
Change like this to a deeper roar?
What would it take my standing there for,

Holding open a restive door,
Looking down hill to a frothy shore?
Summer was past and day was past.
Somber clouds in the west were massed.
Out in the porch's sagging floor,
Leaves got up in a coil and hissed,
Blindly struck at my knee and missed.
Something sinister in the tone
Told me my secret must be known:
Word I was in the house alone
Somehow must have gotten abroad,
Word I was in my life alone,
Word I had no one left but God.

THEY WERE WELCOME TO THEIR BELIEF

Grief may have thought it was grief,
Care may have thought it was care.
They were welcome to their belief,
The overimportant pair.

But whenever the roof came white
The head in the dark below
Was a shade less the color of night
A shade more the color of snow.

No, it took all the snows that clung
To the low roof over his bed,
Beginning when he was young,
To induce the one snow on his head.

Grief may have thought it was grief,
Care may have thought it was care.
But neither one was the thief
Of his raven color of hair.

THE WITCH OF COÖS

I staid the night for shelter at a farm
Behind the mountain, with a mother and son,
Two old-believers. They did all the talking.

MOTHER. Folks think a witch who has familiar spirits
She could call up to pass a winter evening,
But won't, should be burned at the stake or something.
Summoning spirits isn't "Button, button,
Who's got the button," I would have them know.

SON. Mother can make a common table rear
And kick with two legs like an army mule.

MOTHER. And when I've done it, what good have I done?
Rather than tip a table for you, let me
Tell you what Ralle the Sioux Control once told me.

He said the dead had souls, but when I asked him
How could that be — I thought the dead were souls,
He broke my trance. Don't that make you suspicious
That there's something the dead are keeping back?
Yes, there's something the dead are keeping back.

SON. You wouldn't want to tell him what we have
Up attic, mother?

MOTHER.   Bones — a skeleton.

SON. But the headboard of mother's bed is pushed
Against the attic door: the door is nailed.
It's harmless. Mother hears it in the night
Halting perplexed behind the barrier
Of door and headboard. Where it wants to get
Is back into the cellar where it came from.

MOTHER. We'll never let them, will we, son! We'll never!

SON. It left the cellar forty years ago
And carried itself like a pile of dishes
Up one flight from the cellar to the kitchen,
Another from the kitchen to the bedroom,
Another from the bedroom to the attic,
Right past both father and mother, and neither stopped it.
Father had gone upstairs; mother was downstairs.
I was a baby: I don't know where I was.

MOTHER. The only fault my husband found with me —
I went to sleep before I went to bed,
Especially in winter when the bed
Might just as well be ice and the clothes snow.
The night the bones came up the cellar-stairs
Toffile had gone to bed alone and left me,
But left an open door to cool the room off
So as to sort of turn me out of it.
I was just coming to myself enough
To wonder where the cold was coming from,
When I heard Toffile upstairs in the bedroom
And thought I heard him downstairs in the cellar.
The board we had laid down to walk dry-shod on
When there was water in the cellar in spring
Struck the hard cellar bottom. And then someone
Began the stairs, two footsteps for each step,
The way a man with one leg and a crutch,

Or a little child, comes up. It wasn't Toffile:
It wasn't anyone who could be there.
The bulkhead double-doors were double-locked
And swollen tight and buried under snow.
The cellar windows were banked up with sawdust
And swollen tight and buried under snow.
It was the bones. I knew them — and good reason.
My first impulse was to get to the knob
And hold the door. But the bones didn't try
The door; they halted helpless on the landing,
Waiting for things to happen in their favor.
The faintest restless rustling ran all through them.
I never could have done the thing I did
If the wish hadn't been too strong in me
To see how they were mounted for this walk.
I had a vision of them put together
Not like a man, but like a chandelier.
So suddenly I flung the door wide on him.
A moment he stood balancing with emotion,
And all but lost himself. (A tongue of fire
Flashed out and licked along his upper teeth.
Smoke rolled inside the sockets of his eyes.)
Then he came at me with one hand outstretched,
The way he did in life once; but this time
I struck the hand off brittle on the floor,
And fell back from him on the floor myself.
The finger-pieces slid in all directions.
(Where did I see one of those pieces lately?
Hand me my button-box — it must be there.)
I sat up on the floor and shouted, "Toffile,
It's coming up to you." It had its choice
Of the door to the cellar or the hall.
It took the hall door for the novelty,
And set off briskly for so slow a thing,
Still going every which way in the joints, though,
So that it looked like the lightning or a scribble,
From the slap I had just now given its hand.
I listened till it almost climbed the stairs
From the hall to the only finished bedroom,
Before I got up to do anything;
Then ran and shouted, "Shut the bedroom door,
Toffile, for my sake!" "Company?" he said,
"Don't make me get up; I'm too warm in bed."
So lying forward weakly on the handrail
I pushed myself upstairs, and in the light
(The kitchen had been dark) I had to own

I could see nothing. "Toffile, I don't see it.
It's with us in the room though. It's the bones."
"What bones?" "The cellar bones — out of the grave."
That made him throw his bare legs out of bed
And sit up by me and take hold of me.
I wanted to put out the light and see
If I could see it, or else mow the room,
With our arms at the level of our knees,
And bring the chalk-pile down. "I'll tell you what —
It's looking for another door to try.
The uncommonly deep snow has made him think
Of his old song, *The Wild Colonial Boy,*
He always used to sing along the tote-road.
He's after an open door to get out-doors.
Let's trap him with an open door up attic."
Toffile agreed to that, and sure enough,
Almost the moment he was given an opening,
The steps began to climb the attic stairs.
I heard them. Toffile didn't seem to hear them.
"Quick!" I slammed to the door and held the knob.
"Toffile, get nails." I made him nail the door shut,
And push the headboard of the bed against it.
Then we asked was there anything
Up attic that we'd ever want again.
The attic was less to us than the cellar.
If the bones liked the attic, let them have it.
Let them stay in the attic. When they sometimes
Come down the stairs at night and stand perplexed
Behind the door and headboard of the bed,
Brushing their chalky skull with chalky fingers,
With sounds like the dry rattling of a shutter,
That's what I sit up in the dark to say —
To no one any more since Toffile died.
Let them stay in the attic since they went there.
I promised Toffile to be cruel to them
For helping them be cruel once to him.

SON. We think they had a grave down in the cellar.

MOTHER. We know they had a grave down in the cellar.

SON. We never could find out whose bones they were.

MOTHER. Yes, we could too, son. Tell the truth for once,
      They were a man's his father killed for me.
      I mean a man he killed instead of me.

The least I could do was to help dig their grave.
We were about it one night in the cellar.
Son knows the story: but 'twas not for him
To tell the truth, suppose the time had come.
Son looks surprised to see me end a lie
We'd kept all these years between ourselves
So as to have it ready for outsiders.
But to-night I don't care enough to lie —
I don't remember why I ever cared.
Toffile, if he were here, I don't believe
Could tell you why he ever cared himself . . .

She hadn't found the finger-bone she wanted
Among the buttons poured out in her lap.
I verified the name next morning: Toffile.
The rural letter-box said Toffile Lajway.

PROVIDE, PROVIDE

The witch that came (the withered hag)
To wash the steps with pail and rag
Was once the beauty Abishag,

The picture pride of Hollywood.
Too many fall from great and good
For you to doubt the likelihood.

Die early and avoid the fate,
Or if predestined to die late,
Make up your mind to die in state.

Make the whole stock exchange your own!
If need be occupy a throne,
Where nobody can call *you* crone.

Some have relied on what they knew;
Others on being simply true.
What worked for them might work for you.

No memory of having starred
Atones for later disregard
Or keeps the end from being hard.

Better to go down dignified
With boughten friendship at your side
Than none at all. Provide, provide!

Isaac Rosenberg
1890-1918

A WORM FED ON THE HEART OF CORINTH

A worm fed on the heart of Corinth,
Babylon and Rome:
Not Paris raped tall Helen,
But this incestuous worm,
Who lured her vivid beauty
To his amorphous sleep.
England! Famous as Helen
Is thy betrothal sung
To him the shadowless,
More amorous than Solomon.

Wilfred Owen
1893-1918

STRANGE MEETING

It seemed that out of the battle I escaped
Down some profound dull tunnel, long since scooped
Through granites which titanic wars had groined.
Yet also there encumbered sleepers groaned,
Too fast in thought or death to be bestirred.
Then, as I probed them, one sprang up, and stared
With piteous recognition in fixed eyes,
Lifting distressful hands as if to bless.
And by his smile, I knew that sullen hall,
By his dead smile I knew we stood in Hell.
With a thousand fears that vision's face was grained;
Yet no blood reached there from the upper ground,
And no guns thumped, or down the flues made moan.
"Strange, friend," I said, "here is no cause to mourn."
"None," said the other, "save the undone years,
The hopelessness. Whatever hope is yours,
Was my life also; I went hunting wild
After the wildest beauty in the world,
Which lies not calm in eyes, or braided hair,

But mocks the steady running of the hour,
And if it grieves, grieves richlier than here.
For by my glee might many men have laughed,
And of my weeping something has been left,
Which must die now. I mean the truth untold,
The pity of war, the pity war distilled.
Now men will go content with what we spoiled.
Or, discontent, boil bloody, and be spilled.
They will be swift with swiftness of the tigress,
None will break ranks, though nations trek from progress.
Courage was mine, and I had mystery;
Wisdom was mine, and I had mastery;
To miss the march of this retreating world
Into vain citadels that are not walled.
Then, when much blood had clogged their chariot-wheels
I would go up and wash them from sweet wells,
Even with truths that lie too deep for taint.
I would have poured my spirit without stint
But not through wounds; not on the cess of war.
Foreheads of men have bled where no wounds were.
I am the enemy you killed, my friend.
I knew you in this dark; for so you frowned
Yesterday through me as you jabbed and killed.
I parried; but my hands were loath and cold.
Let us sleep now . . ."

FUTILITY

Move him into the sun —
Gently its touch awoke him once,
At home, whispering of fields unsown.
Always it woke him, even in France,
Until this morning and this snow.
If anything might rouse him now
The kind old sun will know.

Think how it wakes the seeds —
Woke, once, the clays of a cold star.
Are limbs so dear-achieved, are sides,
Full-nerved — still warm — too hard to stir?
Was it for this the clay grew tall?
— O what made fatuous sunbeams toil
To break earth's sleep at all?

GREATER LOVE

Red lips are not so red
  As the stained stones kissed by the English dead.
Kindness of wooed and wooer
Seems shame to their love pure.
O Love, your eyes lose lure
  When I behold eyes blinded in my stead!

Your slender attitude
  Trembles not exquisite like limbs knife-skewed,
Rolling and rolling there
Where God seems not to care;
Till the fierce Love they bear
  Cramps them in death's extreme decrepitude.

Your voice sings not so soft, —
  Though even as wind murmuring through raftered loft, —
Your dear voice is not dear,
Gentle, and evening clear,
As theirs whom none now hear,
  Now earth has stopped their piteous mouths that coughed.

Heart, you were never hot,
  Nor large, nor full like hearts made great with shot;
And though your hand be pale,
Paler are all which trail
Your cross through flame and hail:
  Weep, you may weep, for you may touch them not.

Sydney Goodsir Smith

b. 1915

SAAGIN

A demon bydes in the breist in dern,
In the unkent airt
That's neither saul nor mynd nor hert;
And, whiles, like a bairn

Warslan to be born,
Hauds the haill man tense,
His genie struck in the suspense
O' onwyte, dumb at his tide's turn.

Like the globe swings throu equinox
And for a moment spins
Atween twa suns,
Nou in saagin my weird rocks.

THE MANDRAKE HERT

Ye saw 't floueran in my breist
— My mandrake hert —
And, wi a wild wae look,
(O my dear luve!)
Ye reift it scriechan out . . .
And the bluid rins aye frae the torn ruit.

YE SPIER ME

Ye spier me, luve, a question
As we spin throu the abyss
Whar is nae sterne or compass,
Ye spier me what it is
That in the nicht o passion
And the langorie o dawin
Rairs in the tideless ocean
Whar we byde as in a dwaum . . . ?
It is the lava thunderan out
Frae the burst craters o the hert.

DEFEAT O' THE HERT

Borne-heid demoniac
In sleep ye're lain,
At length the raven taks
Her follie's ain.

O black-maned Artemis
The strauchle's dune,
And wi oblivion's kiss
Ye win.

Sidney Keyes

1922-1943

From AGAINST A SECOND COMING

THE WALKING WOMAN

There's a hard wind yet and a sad road
Between the walking woman
And her deadly spouse, the iron lover.
O my hair has fallen and my man
Has fallen and my fruitful time is over:
There is a hard wind and a sad road.

There's a jangled verse, a cry
Beating behind that woman's face.
O my eyes are drowned and my man
Is drowned. Who loves a dead man's grace,
A drowned man's kisses or a blind man's eye?
Cries the unsatisfied, the walking woman.

There's all the angry air, the sea,
Between that woman and her hope:
O once I had a house, a fire
Until my man's proud faring broke
My house and heart. So I'll desire
Lovers of iron or dead men's constancy,
Cries the still passionate, the walking woman.

Carl Sandburg
b. 1878

COOL TOMBS

When Abraham Lincoln was shovelled into the tombs,
    he forgot the copperheads and the assassin . . .
    in the dust, in the cool tombs.

And Ulysses Grant lost all thought of con men and
    Wall Street, cash and collateral turned ashes . . .
    in the dust, in the cool tombs.

Pocahontas' body, lovely as a poplar, sweet as a
    red haw in November or a pawpaw in May, did
    she wonder? does she remember? . . . in the dust,
    in the cool tombs?

Take any streetful of people buying clothes and
    groceries, cheering a hero or throwing confetti and
    blowing tin horns . . . tell me if the lovers are losers . . .
    tell me if any get more than the lovers . . . in
    the dust . . . in the cool tombs.

Allen Tate
b. 1899

LAST DAYS OF ALICE

Alice grown lazy, mammoth but not fat,
Declines upon her lost and twilight age;
Above in the dozing leaves the grinning cat
Quivers forever with his abstract rage:

Whatever light swayed on the perilous gate
Forever sways, nor will the arching grass,
Caught when the world clattered, undulate
In the deep suspension of the looking-glass.

Bright Alice! always pondering to gloze
The spoiled cruelty she had meant to say
Gazes learnedly down her airy nose
At nothing, nothing thinking all the day.

Turned absent-minded by infinity
She cannot move unless her double move,
The All-Alice of the world's entity
Smashed in the anger of her hopeless love,

Love for herself who, as an earthly twain,
Pouted to join her two in a sweet one;
No more the second lips to kiss in vain
The first she broke, plunged through the glass alone —

Alone to the weight of impassivity,
Incest of spirit, theorem of desire,
Without will as chalky cliffs by the sea,
Empty as the bodiless flesh of fire:

All space, that heaven is a dayless night,
A nightless day driven by perfect lust
For vacancy, in which her bored eyesight
Stares at the drowsy cubes of human dust.

— We too back to the world shall never pass
Through the shattered door, a dumb shade-harried crowd
Being all infinite, function depth and mass
Without figure, a mathematical shroud

Hurled at the air — blessèd without sin!
O God of our flesh, return us to Your wrath,
Let us be evil could we enter in
Your grace, and falter on the stony path!

Leonard Clark

b. 1906

THE WALK

for Edmund Blunden

When, head high in corn, I walked with my mother the long, golden
    meadows,
Light on my feet, and sailor-bloused, the whole wide world of summer,
She saw beyond, the dark and looming forest
Deep with its undergrowth waiting to seize all travellers,
But I the easy mouse, happily swaying on ripe wheat-stalks bending
Over the tangled straw-lanes, trodden and wandering among first
    shadows.
My eyes were all shining and open, my ears quick to the nibbling,
But she held my hand tightly, and the touch of her satin
Was lovely and cool to my fingers, her warmth to my wondering
As her watch ticked away and I heard her heart beating,
Till we passed through the stone stile by broken-down barley
And came to the farmhouse where the big, lumbering horses
Were drinking spring water, mouths foam-flecked from harvest.
Secure in the paddock beneath doves round the windows
She suddenly smiled as she looked at my wide eyes
And smoothed down my wild hair in the starred light of evening.

E. E. Cummings

b. 1894

If we take *you are like the snow only* as an example of E. E. Cummings
at his best, we shall see that though we have here no profound meaning,
we have an exquisite poem, with a delicate, hesitating, and fluctuating
rhythm, like the shape and colorlessness of the first flowers, when winter
is about to break into spring. This beauty, this delicate rhythm, this feeling of an early flower scarcely daring to unfold its delicate buds in the
cold wind is obtained not only by the varying length of the lines, but by

the absence of external rhymes, coupled with the use of assonances and an occasional rhyme or dissonance placed with an exquisite subtlety *within* the lines.

To take the first verse:

> you are like the snow only
> purer, fleeter, like the rain
> only sweeter frailer you

the dissonance of "you" taken in conjunction with the assonances "snow" and "only," in the next line with the dissonance of "purer" — these produce a strange, cold, and lovely effect. The sound of "you" is crisp like the petals of the earliest flowers; this sound softens into the deeper sound of "snow" and of "only." "Purer" is less crisp than "you," it is also deeper in sound; but we have the feeling of petals shrinking together in the young cold wind which comes between winter and spring. After the word "rain" comes its assonance "frailer," which has a little trembling movement, half imperceptible.

The internal rhymes placed in exactly the same place in two adjacent lines:

> purer, *fleeter,* like the rain
> only *sweeter* frailer you

— these show us the flower lifting itself up on its delicate stem, after the early spring shower has passed.

Further on in the poem we have the assonances of "resembling" and "trembling" placed in the same line, and giving, to one reader at least, the feeling of the pure narrow outline of the flower-bell; whilst, in the next verse, the far-removed internal rhyme of "little" and, three lines after, "brittle" seems like the faintest green shadow in the delicate bell-shape, as do the assonances of "nothing lingers." Then we have the sharp unripe dissonances, like the unripe cold of early spring, of "marriage" and the deeper, stronger sound of "courage," and the high cold assonances of the *a* sounds in:

> so that against myself
> the sharp days slobber in vain.

After the first verse a kind of faint and almost imperceptible ground-rhythm is formed by the assonance pattern of unsharp *i*'s in "within" and "which," hardly accented at all — a sound which makes us think of a delicate growing thing persisting against the cold, in some half-light, and with that faint green shadow in the heart.

YOU ARE LIKE THE SNOW ONLY

you are like the snow only
purer fleeter, like the rain
only sweeter frailer you

whom certain
flowers resembling but trembling (cowards
which fear
to miss within your least gesture the hurting
skill which lives) and since

nothing lingers
beyond a little instant,
along with rhyme and with laughter
O my lady
(and every brittle marvelous breathing thing)

since i and you are on our ways to dust

of your fragility
(but chiefly of your smile,
most suddenly which is
of love and death a marriage) you give me

courage
so that against myself
the sharp days slobber in vain:

Nor am i afraid that
this, which we call autumn, cleverly
dies and over the ripe world wanders with
a near and careful
smile in his mouth (making

everything suddenly old and with his awkward eyes
pushing
sleep under and thoroughly
into all beautiful things)

winter, whom Spring shall kill

SOMEWHERE I HAVE NEVER TRAVELLED, GLADLY BEYOND

somewhere i have never travelled, gladly beyond
any experience, your eyes have their silence:
in your most frail gesture are things which enclose me,
or which i cannot touch because they are too near

your slightest look easily will unclose me
though i have closed myself as fingers,
you open always petal by petal myself as Spring opens
(touching skilfully, mysteriously) her first rose

or if your wish be to close me, i and
my life will shut very beautifully, suddenly,
as when the heart of this flower imagines
the snow carefully everywhere descending;

nothing which we are to perceive in this world equals
the power of your intense fragility: whose texture
compels me with the colour of its countries,
rendering death and forever with each breathing

(i do not know what it is about you that closes
and opens; only something in me understands
the voice of your eyes is deeper than all roses)
nobody, not even the rain, has such small hands

THE MOON IS HIDING IN

the moon is hiding in
her hair.
The
lily
of heaven
full of all dreams,
draws down.

cover her briefness in singing
close her with intricate faint birds
by daisies and twilights
Deepen her,

> Recite
> upon her
> flesh
> the rain's
>
> pearls singly-whispering.

MY FATHER MOVED THROUGH DOOMS OF LOVE

my father moved through dooms of love
through sames of am through haves of give,
singing each morning out of each night
my father moved through depths of height

this motionless forgetful where
turned at his glance to shining here;
that if (so timid air is firm)
under his eyes would stir and squirm

newly as from unburied which
floats the first who, his april touch
drove sleeping selves to swarm their fates
woke dreamers to their ghostly roots

and should some why completely weep
my father's fingers brought her sleep:
vainly no smallest voice might cry
for he could feel the mountains grow.

Lifting the valleys of the sea
my father moved through griefs of joy;
praising a forehead called the moon
singing desire into begin

joy was his song and joy so pure
a heart of star by him could steer
and pure so now and now so yes
the wrists of twilight would rejoice

keen as midsummer's keen beyond
conceiving mind of sun will stand,
so strictly (over utmost him
so hugely) stood my father's dream

his flesh was flesh his blood was blood:
no hungry man but wished him food;
no cripple wouldn't creep one mile
uphill to only see him smile.

Scorning the pomp of must and shall
my father moved through dooms of feel;
his anger was as right as rain
his pity was as green as grain

septembering arms of year extend
less humbly wealth to foe and friend
than he to foolish and to wise
offered immeasurable is

proudly and (by octobering flame
beckoned) as earth will downward climb,
so naked for immortal work
his shoulders marched against the dark

his sorrow was as true as bread:
no liar looked him in the head;
if every friend became his foe
he'd laugh and build a world with snow.

My father moved through theys of we,
singing each new leaf out of each tree
(and every child was sure that spring
danced when she heard my father sing)

then let men kill which cannot share,
let blood and flesh be mud and mire,
scheming imagine, passion willed,
freedom a drug that's bought and sold

giving to steal and cruel kind,
a heart to fear, to doubt a mind,
to differ a disease of same,
conform the pinnacle of am

though dull were all we taste as bright,
bitter all utterly things sweet,
maggoty minus and dumb death
all we inherit, all bequeath

and nothing quite so least as truth
— i say though hate were why men breathe —
because my father lived his soul
love is the whole and more than all

Sacheverell Sitwell
b. 1897

FISHERMAN

"Do the fish still glitter in the waterpool?"
"No, sir, they are netted and lie ready for your feasting.
They glittered in the water as a star would shine
If it steered into our vision
And through the day, as in the night,
Swam there to follow:
In point of light more brilliant than the race of stars
Shining in one body where it masks the sun,
The fish in this waterpool glitter like that star in air.
They turn like the star would do and lie there to look at you,
High against this glass wall that lies between,
With staring eyes, dreaming,
Then will stretch and spread their fins,
And in a flash be gone,
Where shadow of the trees, or false sun, mars the water,
Safe hidden in this shade or flame.
Here, then, with limp nets we come to look for them,
And the meshes strain and open wide, once in the water,
Till the fish tap at those windows and now float inside."
"Were they lively when you caught them?"
"They leaped and sprang like horses till we held them fast.
We haul at the nets now and pull them out of water
And the fish come out with them like strong springs of silver,
They frisk and leap to get their breath like young horses
Galloping through the fields at early morning,
When the sun is strong already,
And the wind whips, like green rye, the running grassland.
Hold the net tightly as it comes to land,
Sagging, while water lines the strings and drops in runlets,
Safe upon the grass now while the fish still leap!
Close bound within the meshes so they cannot move,
Their lightning fettered, they are lifted shoulder-high
To drown there, stifling in the stiff, cold air."

CHERRY TREE

My salamander in a world of flame,
Safe and breathing,
Come lie beneath this cherry tree,
This green shade heavy hung with coals of fire;
There is only this for coolness while the sun is high —
Zephyr in these branches could never spread his wings,
And rain will never reach us here, so close the boughs,
So dark their shadow that we hide within it —
Grow cool in this shade and then to show your skill
Act the salamander and in the fire lie still,
Let light like honey shine upon your skin:
When you're hot and like a comb of fire
Glide back into this shade,
Bend that heavy branch down with your hand upon its fruit,
Ripe cherries and a honeycomb must make my bread and wine.

From THE RED–GOLD RAIN

ORANGE TREE BY DAY

Sun and rain at work together
Ripened this for summer weather;
Sun gave it colour tawny red
And rain its life as though it bled;
In the long days full of fire
Its fruit will cool us when we tire.
Against the housewall does it grow
With smooth stem like a fountain's flow,
Dark are the leaves, a colder shade
Than ever rock or mountain made;
When the wind plays soft they sing,
For here the birds' songs never ring,
Quite still the fruit that in a golden shower
Will fall one day to flood this tower.

ORANGE TREE BY NIGHT

If you feel for it pressing back the glossy leaves
The fruit looks cold as if its sullen fire is dying,
So red the ember that you scarcely dare to touch it:
And when your fingers close upon its moonlike rind
Chill must be the flavour like a hidden fountain

Whose waters sparkle springing clear from out the rock —
What are its leaves then, but wings, or the wind? —
Wings to hold the fruit high and cool it in the clouds,
Or wind blowing over those hot rocks that hold the water?

"PSITTACUS EOIS IMITATRIX ALES AB INDIS" (*Ovid*)

The parrot's voice snaps out —
No good to contradict —
What he says he'll say again:
Dry facts, dry biscuits.

His voice, and vivid colours
Of his breast and wings,
Are immemoriably old;
Old dowagers dressed in crimpèd satin
Boxed in their rooms
Like specimens beneath a glass,
Inviolate — and never changing,
Their memory of emotions dead;
The ardour of their summers
Sprayed like camphor
On their silken parasols
Intissued in a cupboard.
Reflective, but with never a new thought,
The parrot sways upon his ivory perch —
Then gravely turns a somersault
Through rings nailed in the roof —
Much as the sun performs his antics
As he climbs the aerial bridge
We only see
Through crystal prisms in a falling rain.

From BATTLES OF THE CENTAURS

CENTAURS AND LAPITHÆ

White clouds
(White stallions, white horses tethered),
Make tents and sails and side walls for the banquet:
The trestles are laid: Hippodamia is feasted.

She was born in Argos, where masks of gold
Hide the dead faces in the dead men's tombs:
In beauty as the Argolide, the golden land,
For her skin is saffron, or is smoky amber
Smouldering to the sullen mouth, the red, red lips,
Disdainful, cruel, as a cup of poison
To taint the eyes and kill the souls of men
Caught in the fronds of her, her saffron locks.

She marries Pirithous, King of the Lapithæ:
The gods are invited, all the gods but Mars:
And the Heroes of the days of gold:
And the Centaurs, their neighbours:
The banquet opens.

Round her lie the gods,
And Heroes, Giants and Warriors, who feast their loves,
All happy for an hour, for an immortal breath:
The Centaurs as an army on the grass,
Lie down for the feast, and are men above the trestles
Lifting the wine bowl
To a tune of conches:
Pirithous, beside her, never looks at else
But dwells on her lips, or is lost among her curls.

More wine, more wine, and music while we drink,
Of lute and reed, but not the martial drum;
Let the lute be our hearts on fire that tremble in the heat,
Let the reed be the cooling voice, the agony of the flame;
Music, more music, let us live on fire!

But Mars puts his minions to the kettledrums;
The leaden thunder triumphs;
With his burning blood
Eurythion, a Centaur, leans to Hippodamia,
Pulls her saffron curls to him, with wine stained fingers,
And presses his lips to hers, not unreluctant.
He holds her head above him, as a cup to drink,
And drinks from her lips, and holds her saffron fronds
Looking on her amber skin, her sullen smooth amber,
As parchment with flame behind, as smoke on amber,
And drinks his immortality, his fill of her,
Kissing till the breath goes.

Pirithous sees them, and the Heroes fly to arms,
Hercules, Theseus, the Lapithæ all;

Mars won his stratagem and started war,
Wine stains the trestles, Hippodamia's eyes
Watch her lover go from life to death,
Struck down at her lips;
The breath of her fails in him, he faints and dies
While the dagger shakes,
And Hippodamia, all saffron and all honey,
Smiles for Pirithous with the same red lips.

Eurythion fell, and his body of a Centaur
Sagged, sagged, crumpled,
As though fallen from a cliff;
Other Centaurs dashed their wine bowls down,
The metal battle started, loud the din of armour,
Dented from thrown cups, from emptied bottles hurled
To the breasts of bronze.
The Centaurs held the day until the Heroes found their arms,
And only Eurythion, who drank death from her lips,
Walks in darkness, in the outer world
Waiting for a shadow, another Centaur on the sands,
Or Hippodamia, as he dreamed of her,
Fled from men to meet him,
In her saffron fronds.

The Lapithæ rally, and the Heroes of high names,
In armour of bronze, with horsetail helm
Blown straight with speed, as in the gallop's thunder;
Hercules is with them, in Nemæan coat
Of tawny lion, slain at the Argive wood
And carried to Mycenæ, to the Gate of Lions.

Now they look on dead Eurythion, and form their ranks;
The troop of Centaurs clatter from the tented shade,
From clouds of the hillside to the chestnut land
Of valleys, soft swelling to their smooth, firm breasts,
As ripe a battleground as Hippodamia's hills,
Where died Eurythion, breathing from her lips;
Yellow was the cornland as her waist of amber,
With tassels of the chestnut for her saffron curls.

The true Hippodamia sees the Centaurs die,
One, and then another, and she smiles at this
While proud Pirithous musters the Lapithæ:
They divide, they run with orders: the Hero Theseus,
And Hercules, giant herdsman, are captains of the van
Marching in the summer land, along the corn;

Pirithous, in rear of them, waiting for his time,
Halts with the mainguard: the trumpets sound for battle:
All the Lapithæ, every Hero marches.

A Centaur shows himself, calling with cupped hands,
On a bare hill; higher than the height of man
His voice comes down; and he shouts, but no one answers him,
And calls, calls again, into his conch of fingers,
In deep laid stratagem, lingering to be taken,
For the sides fill with Centaurs. All their troop of horse
Come up to the sky out of the hidden meadow,
Above the panting Lapithæ; they hold huge stones
High in their hands, as high as men on horseback,
And hurl them down the hillside.

But the Heroes close the double horns upon them:
The wings march in: they gather on each flank,
Surround the hills of Centaurs, but the troop has fled,
There is only spring air upon the empty hilltop
And its sight of Arcadia beyond the snows.

While Neptune kisses Ceres, and Hippodamia, missed,
Is called on every wind!
                    O where is Hippodamia?
Is she a prisoner, hidden in the summer?
But wind spells no words, the very groves are mute.

But the Centaurs drew their bows, and many Lapithæ
Felt the feathered arrows and, swan-like, from swan feathers
Sank back on the water, and in ghostly pallor
Floated their souls away upon the stream.
The Heroes march to save them:
                         By laurel and by myrtle,
By leaves of sweet odour, when the fingers press them,
Sent forth, at other times, as sighings on the wind:
Man-high their shade and bruised by the shoulders,
Of bronze to myrtle bough, of aromatic breath
Shed forth as they march, who, coming on the Centaurs,
Turn the whole battle in the river bed,
Hiding in the boulders.
                      Half the race of Centaurs
Perish with arrows: the Lapithæ rally:

And Theseus kills his Centaur: and Pirithous, appeased,
Spares a young Centaur, but has no quarter for the grown,
Remembers Hippodamia, and kills the youth,

Taking that life just given him again,
In no pity for his breathing all the world once more
With its scent in his nostrils, as he sniffed the morning
Standing in the cave mouth, a morning he remembered.
The moon still burned and the Centaur left his love
For a breath of sweet dawn, and watched the waning moon
Go wan and hide. Was it the pallid spectre,
The Centauress, his mother, whom he loved no more,
Deserted for the daylight, for the warmth of life,
His first true love upon the fields and in the cave,
With locks like clover curls, the hue of day
Where noon is brightest, where its wires are gold?
So mother love dies and so the other love comes after,
So day follows night, so at the door of death
Life is on our lips and we walk among our loves,
Living in their glances; but Pirithous gives him peace.
So fell the Centaurs, one and then another
Choked with the sword, while "Hippodamia," hidden,
Echoed in the woods, against the ilex walls.

Mothers of the Centaurs! Look down upon your sons!
They die. They perish. The Centaur blood is finished.
Look down from the clouds for they were born of them.

Heroes and Lapithæ rattle in that wind
In armour of metal, darker than ilex
Beside the lit chestnut with its flaming candles;
They search every glade for Hippodamia, lost,
And hear no sound, but find the print of hooves
Deep on the moss, and deeper from their load
Of Hippodamia, lifted by the stallion;
It is his vengeance and Pirithous, alone,
Goes sword in hand among the lengthening shades.

Dead, dead the darkness, starless, of no moon:
And here lay Hippodamia on the hoof marked moss,
Ringed with that crescent moon a myriad times,
In faunal emblem.
                    Her living pallor
But made more real by her open lips,
Red with blood, as with all her blood,
More lovely, in death, than nectarine alive;
For this was her marriage bed, Pirithous saw her
With amber skin dying, all ripeness still
Of smoky amber, of the nectarine,
As the Centaur killed her, bleeding from his arrow,

With her lovely neck, and all her beauty drawn
To her red, red lips. Her saffron locks
Combed by his fingers, twined for her to die:
Dead before he found her: and her Centaur fled
To safe Arcadia beyond the snows.

Roy Campbell

1901-1957

TO A PET COBRA

With breath indrawn and every nerve alert,
As at the brink of some profound abyss,
I love on my bare arm, capricious flirt,
To feel the chilly and incisive kiss
Of your lithe tongue that forks its swift caress
Between the folded slumber of your fangs,
And half reveals the nacreous recess
Where death upon those dainty hinges hangs.

Our lonely lives in every chance agreeing,
It is no common friendship that you bring,
It was the desert starved us into being,
The hate of men that sharpened us to sting:
Sired by starvation, suckled by neglect,
Hate was the surly tutor of our youth:
I too can hiss the hair of men erect
Because my lips are venomous with truth.

Where the hard rock is barren, scorched the spring,
Shrivelled the grass, and the hot wind of death
Hornets the crag with whirred metallic wing —
We drew the fatal secret of our breath:
By whirlwinds bugled forth, whose funnelled suction
Scrolls the spun sand into a golden spire,
Our spirits leaped, hosannas of destruction,
Like desert lilies forked with tongues of fire.

Dainty one, deadly one, whose folds are panthered
With stars, my slender Kalihari flower,
Whose lips with fangs are delicately anthered,
Whose coils are volted with electric power,

I love to think how men of my dull nation
Might spurn your sleep with inadvertent heel
To kindle up the lithe retaliation
And caper to the slash of sudden steel.

There is no sea so wide, no waste so steril
But holds a rapture for the sons of strife:
There shines upon the topmost peak of peril
A throne for spirits that abound in life:
There is no joy like theirs who fight alone,
Whom lust or gluttony have never tied,
Who in their purity have built a throne,
And in their solitude a tower of pride.

I wish my life, O suave and silent sphinx,
Might flow like yours in some such strenuous line,
My days the scales, my years the bony links,
That chain the length of its resilient spine:
And when at last the moment comes to strike,
Such venom give my hilted fangs the power,
Like drilling roots the dirty soil that spike,
To sting these rotted wastes into a flower.

THE ZULU GIRL
To F. C. Slater

When in the sun the hot red acres smoulder,
Down where the sweating gang its labour plies,
A girl flings down her hoe, and from her shoulder
Unslings her child tormented by the flies.

She takes him to a ring of shadow pooled
By thorn-trees: purpled with the blood of ticks,
While her sharp nails, in slow caresses ruled,
Prowl through his hair with sharp electric clicks,

His sleepy mouth plugged by the heavy nipple,
Tugs like a puppy, grunting as he feeds:
Through his frail nerves her own deep languors ripple
Like a broad river sighing through its reeds.

Yet in that drowsy stream his flesh imbibes
An old unquenched unsmotherable heat —
The curbed ferocity of beaten tribes,
The sullen dignity of their defeat.

Her body looms above him like a hill
Within whose shade a village lies at rest,
Or the first cloud so terrible and still
That bears the coming harvest in its breast.

POMEGRANATES
To Thomas Earp

Sung by the nightingale to birth
Whose ringing pearls were all the dew
With which, the long dry summer through,
The rainless azure fed their dearth —

Pomegranates, colder than the noon,
In whom a maiden breast rebels,
Forcing the smooth gold of their shells
To split with rubies to the noon,

In whose half-opened husks we see,
Where the rich blood of autumn swells,
The membranes and the rosy cells
To which the sunbeam was the bee: —

Like musing brows with patience fraught
Until their secret gems be shown,
And through their inward toil alone
Made royal with a crown of thought: —

As to some poet's labours wed
To dream Golcondas from despair,
Till some pure act of faith or prayer
Shall freeze the crimson tears they shed: —

Like lovers' hearts to ripeness grown
The rapturous red wine they bleed
Is chambered in each lustrous seed
As light within a carven stone.

Warm-flushing through their films of frost
With rosy smiles and crystal teeth
A yielding beauty seems to breathe
Whose language on our lips is lost.

Their speech in coolness dies away,
Thawed by a breath, they change and tremble
As the lips they most resemble
When one red kiss is all they say.

Too fain in fragrance to escape,
Their form eludes the clearest phrase
When Psyche, in a sister's praise,
Would carve her crystals in their shape.

In vain her vision seeks to prove
The secret structure of those grains
Whose dewy membranes and lit veins
Remind her most of those I love.

If new similitudes to try,
Fusing them with her speech, she sips
Those seeds whose death upon the lips
Is half a kiss and half a sigh —

Moulding those phrases with her tongue
That melt as sweetly, by a spell
So transient that she cannot tell
If they be tasted, kissed, or sung —

Their gems so ruddy to the eye
Are snow upon the mouth that sips:
But even when they cheat the lips
And, born of song, in perfume die, —

Are most conspiring with her theme
The true resemblance to disclose,
And tell the secrets of the rose
Whose changing reveries they seem.

THE SNAKE

Damp clods with corn may thank the showers,
But when the desert boulder flowers
No common buds unfold —
A Jove to Danae's bridal showers
Immortal fire and gold,
And high above the wastes will tower
The hydra stem, the deathless flower.

A glory, such as from scant seed
The thirsty rocks suffice to breed
Out of the rainless glare,
Was born in me of such a need
And of a like despair,
But fairer than the aloe sprang
And hilted with a sharper fang.

The heart whom shame or anger sears
Beyond the cheap relief of tears
Its secret never opes,
Save to the loveliest of fears,
The most divine of hopes,
And only when such seeds may find
A tough resistance in the rind —

Hard husks the self-same truth express
As, yielding to the sweet excess
Of hoarded gems within,
They crack to show the rich recess
Our thirsty lips would win,
When ripe grenades that drink the sun
Resolving into rubies run.

So from the old Anchises' tomb
All that the fire could not consume,
The living ichor, flowed,
A serpent from the rocky womb
Where barren death abode,
With lifted crest and radiant gyre
Revolving into wheels of fire.

No rock so pure a crystal rears
But filed with water, thawed with years,
Or by its prophet struck,
Its breast may sparkle into tears
For thirsting hordes to suck.
But it was to a sorer dint
And flashing from a harder flint

That, smitten by its angry god,
My heart recoiling to the rod
Rilled forth its stream of pride,
A serpent from the rifted clod
On rolling wheels to ride,
Who reared, as if their birth were one,
To gaze, an equal, on the Sun.

His eyes like slots of jet inlaid
On their smooth triangle of jade,
Were vigilant with fire,
His armour stripped the sun for braid
And wore the stars for tire
And slid the glory of its greaves
A stream of moonlight through the leaves.

Immortal longings hold his sight
Still sunward to that source of light
Drained from whose crystal spars
His slender current rolls its bright
Alluvium of stars,
And through its winding channel trails
The shingle of his burnished scales.

The news that such a king was crowned
Has made a solitude around
His vigil hushed and calm,
Where, with the fruits of Eden wound,
He girds the stripling Palm
And shares her starry shade with none
Save with the silence and the sun.

His teeth stained crimson with her flowers,
There through the blue enchanted hours
Rocked by the winds to rest,
Her fragrance lulls his folded powers
When slumber sinks his crest
Through his own circles clear and cool
As through the ripples of a pool.

A crystal freshet through whose sluice
The noonday beams their light reduce
To one melodious line,
And flow together like the juice
That circles in the vine,
His frosty ichor drinks the sun
And fuses fire and ice in one.

When by the horror-breathing wraith
The soul is scorched of hope and faith,
This form survives the fire,
The living self no flame can scathe,
The spine, the ringing wire
That silver through its alloy sings
And fresh in each exertion springs.

Blest is the stony ground, where smite
No rains but of the angry light,
And rich beyond all dreams,
Whose stubborn seed will not ignite
Save to such deathless beams
As first through emeralds fire did ray
And into diamonds shot the day:

And blest exchange for vain delight,
For dreams, the tyrants of the night,
And passions — of the day,
Is his whose clear, unchanging sight
Through triumph, change, decay,
In such a serpent's coiled repose
His secret architecture knows.

HORSES ON THE CAMARGUE
To A. F. Tschiffely

In the grey wastes of dread,
The haunt of shattered gulls where nothing moves
But in a shroud of silence like the dead,
I heard a sudden harmony of hooves,
And, turning, saw afar
A hundred snowy horses unconfined,
The silver runaways of Neptune's car
Racing, spray-curled, like waves before the wind.
Sons of the Mistral, fleet
As him with whose strong gusts they love to flee,
Who shod the flying thunders on their feet
And plumed them with the snortings of the sea;
Theirs is no earthly breed
Who only haunt the verges of the earth
And only on the sea's salt herbage feed —
Surely the great white breakers gave them birth.
For when for years a slave,
A horse of the Camargue, in alien lands,
Should catch some far-off fragrance of the wave
Carried far inland from his native sands,
Many have told the tale
Of how in fury, foaming at the rein,
He hurls his rider; and with lifted tail,
With coal-red eyes and cataracting mane,

Heading his course for home,
Though sixty foreign leagues before him sweep,
Will never rest until he breathes the foam
And hears the native thunder of the deep.
But when the great gusts rise
And lash their anger on these arid coasts,
When the scared gulls career with mournful cries
And whirl across the waste like driven ghosts:
When hail and fire converge,
The only souls to which they strike no pain
Are the white-crested fillies of the surge
And the white horses of the windy plain.
Then in their strength and pride
The stallions of the wilderness rejoice;
They feel their Master's trident in their side,
And high and shrill they answer to his voice.
With white tails smoking free,
Long streaming manes, and arching necks, they show
Their kinship to their sisters of the sea —
And forward hurl their thunderbolts of snow.
Still out of hardship bred,
Spirits of power and beauty and delight
Have ever on such frugal pastures fed
And loved to course with tempests through the night.

ON LISA'S GOLDEN HAIR
Translated from Francisco de Quevedo, 1580–1645

When you shake loose your hair from all controlling,
Such thirst of beauty quickens my desire
Over its surge in red tornadoes rolling
My heart goes surfing on the waves of fire.
Leander who for love the tempest dares,
It lets a sea of fire its life consume:
Icarus, from a sun whose rays are hairs,
Ignites its wings and glories in its doom.
Charming its hopes, (whose deaths I mourn) it strives
Out of their ash to form new phoenix-lives
That, dying of delight, new hopes embolden.
Miser, yet poor, the crime and fate it measures
Of Midas, starved and mocked with stacks of treasures,
Or Tantalus, with streams that shone as golden.

UPON A GLOOMY NIGHT
Translated from St. John of the Cross

Upon a gloomy night,
With all my cares to loving ardours flushed,
(O venture of delight!)
With nobody in sight
I went abroad when all my house was hushed.

In safety, in disguise,
In darkness up the secret stair I crept,
(O happy enterprise)
Concealed from other eyes
When all my house at length in silence slept.

Upon that lucky night
In secrecy, inscrutable to sight,
I went without discerning
And with no other light
Except for that which in my heart was burning.

It lit and led me through
More certain than the light of noonday clear
To where One waited near
Whose presence well I knew,
There where no other presence might appear.

Oh night that was my guide!
Oh darkness dearer than the morning's pride,
Oh night that joined the lover
To the beloved bride
Transfiguring them each into the other.

Within my flowering breast
Which only for himself entire I save
He sank into his rest
And all my gifts I gave
Lulled by the airs with which the cedars wave.

Over the ramparts fanned
While the fresh wind was fluttering his tresses,
With his serenest hand
My neck he wounded, and
Suspended every sense with its caresses.

Lost to myself I stayed
My face upon my lover having laid
From all endeavour ceasing:
And all my cares releasing
Threw them amongst the lilies there to fade.

Conrad Aiken
b. 1889

THIS IS THE SHAPE OF THE LEAF

This is the shape of the leaf, and this of the flower,
And this the pale bole of the tree
Which watches its bough in a pool of unwavering water
In a land we shall never see.

The thrush on the bough is silent, the dew falls softly,
In the evening is hardly a sound.
And the three beautiful pilgrims who come here together
Touch lightly the dust of the ground,

Touch it with feet that trouble the dust but as wings do,
Come shyly together, are still,
Like dancers who wait, in a pause of the music, for music
The exquisite silence to fill.

This is the thought of the first, and this of the second,
And this the grave thought of the third:
"Linger we thus for a moment, palely expectant,
And silence will end, and the bird

"Sing the pure phrase, sweet phrase, clear phrase in the twilight
To fill the blue bell of the world;
And we, who on music so leaflike have drifted together,
Leaflike apart shall be whirled

"Into what but the beauty of silence, silence forever?" . . .
. . . This is the shape of the tree,
And the flower, and the leaf, and the three pale beautiful pilgrims;
This is what you are to me.

Robert Lowell
b. 1917

THE GHOST
After Sextus Propertius

A ghost is someone: death has left a hole
For the lead-colored soul to beat the fire:
    Cynthia leaves her dirty pyre
    And seems to coil herself and roll
        Under my canopy,
Love's stale and public playground, where I lie
And fill the run-down empire of my bed.
I see the street, her potter's field, is red
And lively with the ashes of the dead;

But she no longer sparkles off in smoke:
It is the body carted to the gate
    Last Friday, when the sizzling grate
    Left its charred furrows on her smock
        And ate into her hip.
A black nail dangles from a finger-tip
And Lethe oozes from her nether lip.
Her thumb-bones rattle on her brittle hands,
As Cynthia stamps and hisses and demands:

"Sextus, has sleep already washed away
Your manhood? You forget the window-sill
    My sliding wore to slivers? Day
    Would break before the Seven Hills
        Saw Cynthia retreat
And climb your shoulders to the knotted sheet.
You shouldered me and galloped on bare feet
To lay me by the crossroads. Have no fear:
Notus, who snatched your promise, has no ear.

"But why did no one call in my deaf ear?
Your calling would have gained me one more day.
    Sextus, although you ran away
    You might have called and stopped my bier
        A second by your door.

No tears drenched a black toga for your whore
When broken tilestones bruised her face before
The Capitol. Would it have strained your purse
To scatter ten cheap roses on my hearse?

"The State will make Pompilia's Chloris burn:
I knew her secret when I kissed the skull
  Of Pluto in the tainted bowl.
  Let Nomas burn her books and turn
   Her poisons into gold;
The finger-prints upon the potsherd told
Her love. You let a slut, whose body sold
To Thracians, liquefy my golden bust
In the coarse flame that crinkled me to dust.

"If Chloris' bed has left you with your head,
Lover, I think you'll answer my arrears:
  My nurse is getting on in years,
  See that she gets a little bread —
   She never clutched your purse;
See that my little humpback hears no curse
From her close-fisted friend. But burn the verse
You bellowed half a life time in my name:
Why should you feed me to the fires of fame?

"I will not hound you, much as you have earned
It, Sextus: I shall reign in your four books —
  I swear this by the Hag who looks
  Into my heart where it was burned:
   Propertius, I kept faith;
If not, may serpents suck my ghost to death
And spit it with their forked and killing breath
Into the Styx where Agamemnon's wife
Founders in the green circles of her life.

"Beat the sycophant ivy from my urn,
That twists its binding shoots about my bones
  Where apple-sweetened Anio drones
  Through orchards that will never burn
   While honest Herakles,
My patron, watches. Anio, you will please
Me if you whisper upon sliding knees:
'Propertius, Cynthia is here:
She shakes her blossoms when my waters clear.'

"You cannot turn your back upon a dream,
For phantoms have their reasons when they come:
We wander midnights: then the numb
Ghost wades from the Lethean stream:
Even the foolish dog
Stops its hell-raising mouth and casts its clog;
At cock-crow Charon checks us in his log.
Others can have you, Sextus; I alone
Hold: and I grind your manhood bone on bone."

Charles Henri Ford

b. 1913

PLAINT

Before a Mob of 10,000 at Owenboro, Kentucky

I, Rainy Betha, 22
From the top branch of race-hatred look at you.
My limbs are bound, though boundless the bright sun
Like my bright blood which had to run
Into the orchard that excluded me.
Now I climb death's tree.

The pruning-hooks of many mouths
Cut the black-eyed boughs.
The robins of my eyes hover where
Sixteen leaves fall that were a prayer.
Sixteen mouths are open wide,
The minutes, like black cherries,
Drop from my shady side.

Oh, who is the forester must tend such a tree, Lord?
Do angels pick the cherry-blood of folk like me, Lord?

Kenneth Patchen

b. 1911

PASTORAL

The dove walks with sticky feet
Upon the green crowns of the almond tree,
Its feathers smeared over with warmth
Like honey
That drips lazily down into the shadow . . .

Anyone standing in that orchard,
So filled with peace and sleep,
Would hardly have noticed the hill
Nearby
With its three strange wooden arms
Lifted above a throng of motionless people
— Above the helmets of Pilate's soldiers
Flashing like silver teeth in the sun.

W. H. Auden

b. 1907

OUR BIAS

The hour-glass whispers to the lion's paw,
The clock-towers tell the gardens day and night,
How many errors Time has patience for,
How wrong they are in being always right.

Yet Time, however loud its chimes or deep,
However fast its falling torrent flows,
Has never put the lion off his leap
Nor shaken the assurance of the rose.

For they, it seems, care only for success:
While we choose words according to their sound
And judge a problem by its awkwardness;

And Time with us was always popular.
When have we not preferred some going round
To going straight to where we are?

IN MEMORY OF ERNST TOLLER
Died May 1939

The shining neutral summer has no voice
To judge America, or ask how a man dies;
And the friends who are sad and the enemies who rejoice

Are chased by their shadows lightly away from the grave
Of one who was egotistical and brave,
Lest they should learn without suffering how to forgive.

What was it, Ernst, that your shadow unwittingly said?
O did the child see something horrid in the woodshed
Long ago? Or had the Europe which took refuge in your head

Already been too injured to get well?
O for how long, like the swallows in that other cell,
Had the bright little longings been flying in to tell

About the big and friendly death outside,
Where people do not occupy or hide;
No towns like Munich; no need to write?

Dear Ernst, lie shadowless at last among
The other war-horses who existed till they'd done
Something that was an example to the young.

We are lived by powers we pretend to understand:
They arrange our loves; it is they who direct at the end
The enemy bullet, the sickness, or even our hand.

It is their to-morrow hangs over the earth of the living
And all that we wish for our friends: but existence is believing
We know for whom we mourn and who is grieving.

IN MEMORY OF SIGMUND FREUD
Died September 1939

When there are so many we shall have to mourn,
When grief has been made so public, and exposed
To the critique of a whole epoch
The frailty of our conscience and anguish,

Of whom shall we speak? For every day they die
Among us, those who were doing us some good,
      And knew it was never enough but
        Hoped to improve a little by living.

Such was this doctor: still at eighty he wished
To think of our life, from whose unruliness
      So many plausible young futures
        With threats or flattery ask obedience.

But his wish was denied him; he closed his eyes
Upon that last picture common to us all,
      Of problems like relatives standing
        Puzzled and jealous about our dying.

For about him at the very end were still
Those he had studied, the nervous and the nights,
      And shades that still waited to enter
        The bright circle of his recognition

Turned elsewhere with their disappointment as he
Was taken away from his old interest
      To go back to the earth in London
        An important Jew who died in exile.

Only Hate was happy, hoping to augment
His practice now, and his shabby clientèle
      Who think they can be cured by killing
        And covering the gardens with ashes.

They are still alive but in a world he changed
Simply by looking back with no false regrets;
      All that he did was to remember
        Like the old and be honest like children.

He wasn't clever at all: he merely told
The unhappy Present to recite the Past
      Like a poetry lesson till sooner
        Or later it faltered at the line where

Long ago the accusations had begun,
And suddenly knew by whom it had been judged,
      How rich life had been and how silly,
        And was life-forgiven and more humble.

Able to approach the Future as a friend
Without a wardrobe of excuses, without
  A set mask of rectitude or an
  Embarrassing over-familiar gesture.

No wonder the ancient cultures of conceit
In his technique of unsettlement foresaw
  The fall of princes, the collapse of
  Their lucrative patterns of frustration.

If he succeeded, why, the Generalized Life
Would become impossible, the monolith
  Of State be broken and prevented
  The co-operation of avengers.

Of course they called on God: but he went his way,
Down among the Lost People like Dante, down
  To the stinking fosse where the injured
  Lead the ugly life of the rejected.

And showed us what evil is: not as we thought
Deeds that must be punished, but our lack of faith,
  Our dishonest mood of denial,
  The concupiscence of the oppressor.

And if something of the autocratic pose,
The paternal strictness he distrusted, still
  Clung to his utterance and features,
  It was a protective imitation

For one who lived among enemies so long;
If often he was wrong and at times absurd,
  To us he is no more a person
  Now but a whole climate of opinion,

Under whom we conduct our differing lives:
Like weather he can only hinder or help,
  The proud can still be proud but find it
  A little harder, and the tyrant tries

To make him do but doesn't care for him much.
He quietly surrounds all our habits of growth;
  He extends, till the tired in even
  The remotest most miserable duchy

Have felt the change in their bones and are cheered,
And the child unlucky in his little State,
      Some hearth where freedom is excluded,
      A hive whose honey is fear and worry,

Feels calmer now and somehow assured of escape;
While as they lie in the grass of our neglect,
      So many long-forgotten objects
      Revealed by his undiscouraged shining

Are returned to us and made precious again;
Games we had thought we must drop as we grew up,
      Little noises we dared not laugh at,
      Faces we made when no one was looking.

But he wishes us more than this: to be free
Is often to be lonely; he would unite
      The unequal moieties fractured
      By our own well-meaning sense of justice.

Would restore to the larger the wit and will
The smaller possesses but can only use
      For arid disputes, would give back to
      The son the mother's richness of feeling.

But he would have us remember most of all
To be enthusiastic over the night
      Not only for the sense of wonder
      It alone has to offer, but also

Because it needs our love: for with sad eyes
Its delectable creatures look up and beg
      Us dumbly to ask them to follow;
      They are exiles who long for the future

That lies in our power. They too would rejoice
If allowed to serve enlightenment like him,
      Even to bear our cry of "Judas,"
      As he did and all must bear who serve it.

One rational voice is dumb: over a grave
The household of Impulse mourns one dearly loved.
      Sad is Eros, builder of cities,
      And weeping anarchic Aphrodite.

CRISIS

Where do They come from? Those whom we so much dread
As on our dearest location falls the chill
   Of their crooked wing and endangers
   The melting friend, the aqueduct, the flower.

Terrible Presences that the ponds reflect
Back at the famous, and when the blond boy
   Bites eagerly into the shining
   Apple, emerge in their shocking fury.

And we realize the woods are deaf and the sky
Nurses no one, and we are awake and these
   Like farmers have purpose and knowledge,
   And towards us their hate is directed.

We are the barren pastures to which they bring
The resentment of outcasts; on us they work
   Out their despair; they wear our weeping
   As the disgraceful badge of their exile.

O we conjured them here like a lying map;
Desiring the extravagant joy of life
   We lured with a mirage of orchards
   Fat in the lazy climate of refuge.

Our money sang like streams on the aloof peaks
Of our thinking that beckoned them on like girls;
   Our culture like a West of wonder
   Shone a solemn promise in their faces.

We expected the beautiful or the wise
Ready to see a charm in our childish fib,
   Pleased to find nothing but stones and
   Able at once to create a garden.

But those who come are not even children with
The big indiscriminate eyes we had lost,
   Occupying our narrow spaces
   With their anarchist vivid abandon.

They arrive, already adroit, having learned
Restraint at the table of a father's rage;
   In a mother's distorting mirror
   They discovered the Meaning of Knowing.

These pioneers have long adapted themselves
To the night and the nightmare; they come equipped
  To reply to terror with terror,
  With lies to unmask the least deception.

For a future of marriage nevertheless
The bed is prepared, though all our whiteness shrinks
  From the hairy and clumsy bridegroom,
  We conceive in the shuddering instant.

For the barren must wish to bear though the Spring
Punish; and the crooked that dreads to be straight
  Cannot alter its prayer but summons
  Out of the dark a horrible rector.

O the striped and vigorous tiger can move
With style through the borough of murder; the ape
  Is really at home in the parish
  Of grimacing and licking: but we have

Failed as their pupils. Our tears well from a love
We have never outgrown; our cities predict
  More than we hope; even our armies
  Have to express our need of forgiveness.

AS I WALKED OUT ONE EVENING

As I walked out one evening,
  Walking down Bristol Street,
The crowds upon the pavement
  Were fields of harvest wheat.

And down by the brimming river
  I heard a lover sing
Under an arch of the railway:
  "Love has no ending.

"I'll love you, dear, I'll love you
  Till China and Africa meet,
And the river jumps over the
    mountain
  And the salmon sing in the street.

"I'll love you till the ocean
  Is folded and hung up to dry
And the seven stars go squawking
  Like geese about the sky.

"The years shall run like rabbits,
  For in my arms I hold
The Flower of the Ages,
  And the first love of the world."

But all the clocks in the city
  Began to whirr and chime:
"O let not Time deceive you,
  You cannot conquer Time.

"In the burrows of the Nightmare
  Where Justice naked is,
Time watches from the shadow
  And coughs when you would
    kiss.

"In headaches and in worry
  Vaguely life leaks away,
And Time will have his fancy
  To-morrow or to-day.

"Into many a green valley
   Drifts the appalling snow;
Time breaks the threaded dances
   And the diver's brilliant bow.

"O plunge your hands in water,
   Plunge them in up to the wrist;
Stare, stare in the basin
   And wonder what you've missed.

"The glacier knocks in the
     cupboard,
   The desert sighs in the bed,
And the crack in the tea-cup opens
   A lane to the land of the dead.

"Where the beggars raffle the
     banknotes
   And the Giant is enchanting to
     Jack,
And the Lily-white Boy is a Roarer,
   And Jill goes down on her back.

"O look, look in the mirror,
   O look in your distress;
Life remains a blessing
   Although you cannot bless.

"O stand, stand at the window
   As the tears scald and start;
You shall love your crooked
     neighbour
   With your crooked heart."

It was late, late in the evening,
   The lovers they were gone;
The clocks had ceased their chiming,
   And the deep river ran on.

FISH IN THE UNRUFFLED LAKES

Fish in the unruffled lakes
The swarming colours wear,
Swans in the winter air
A white perfection have,
And the great lion walks
Through his innocent grove;
Lion, fish, and swan
Act, and are gone
Upon Time's toppling wave.

We till shadowed days are done,
We must weep and sing
Duty's conscious wrong,
The Devil in the clock,
The Goodness carefully worn
For atonement or for luck;
We must lose our loves,
On each beast and bird that moves
Turn an envious look.

Sighs for folly said and done
Twist our narrow days;
But I must bless, I must praise
That you, my swan, who have
All gifts that to the swan
Impulsive Nature gave,
The majesty and pride,
Last night should add
Your voluntary love.

O FOR DOORS TO BE OPEN

— "O for doors to be open and an invite with gilded edges
To dine with Lord Lobcock and Count Asthma on the platinum benches,
With somersaults and fireworks, the roast and the smacking kisses" —
    Cried the cripples to the silent statue,
    The six beggared cripples.

— "And Garbo's and Cleopatra's wits to go astraying,
In a feather ocean with me to go fishing and playing,
Still jolly when the cock has burst himself with crowing" —
    Cried the cripples to the silent statue,
    The six beggared cripples.

— "And to stand on green turf among the craning yellow faces
Dependent on the chestnut, the sable, and Arabian horses,
And me with a magic crystal to foresee their places" —
    Cried the cripples to the silent statue,
    The six beggared cripples.

— "And this square to be deck and these pigeons sails to rig,
And to follow the delicious breeze like a tantony pig
To the shaded feverless islands where the melons are big" —
    Cried the cripples to the silent statue,
    The six beggared cripples.

— "And these shops to be turned to tulips in a garden bed,
And me with my crutch to thrash each merchant dead
As he pokes from a flower his bald and wicked head" —
    Cried the cripples to the silent statue,
    The six beggared cripples.

— "And a hole in the bottom of heaven, and Peter and Paul
And each smug surprised saint like parachutes to fall,
And every one-legged beggar to have no legs at all" —
    Cried the cripples to the silent statue,
    The six beggared cripples.

Cecil Day Lewis
b. 1904

MY LOVE IS A TOWER

My love is a tower.
Standing up in her
I parley with planets
And the casual wind.
Arcturus may grind
Against our wall: — he whets
A tropic appetite,
And decorates our night.
"What happier place
For Johnny Head-in-Air,
Who never would hear
Time mumbling at the base?"

I will not hear, for she's
My real Antipodes,
And our ingrowing loves
Shall meet below earth's spine
And there shall intertwine,
Though Babel falls above.
Time, we allow, destroys
All aërial toys:
But to assail love's heart
He has no strategy,
Unless he suck up the sea
And pull the earth apart.

IS IT FAR TO GO

Is it far to go?
  A step — no further.
Is it hard to go?
  Ask the melting snow,
  The eddying feather.

What can I take there?
  Not a hank, not a hair.
What shall I leave behind?
  Ask the hastening wind,
  The fainting star.

Shall I be gone long?
  For ever and a day.
To whom there belong?
  Ask the stone to say,
  Ask my song.

Who will say farewell?
  The beating bell.
Will anyone miss me?
  That I dare not tell —
  Quick, Rose, and kiss me.

COME, LIVE WITH ME AND BE MY LOVE

Come, live with me and be my love,
And we will all the pleasures prove
Of peace and plenty, bed and board,
That chance employment may afford.

I'll handle dainties on the docks
And thou shalt read of summer frocks:
At evening by the sour canals
We'll hope to hear some madrigals.

Care on thy maiden brow shall put
A wreath of wrinkles, and thy foot
Be shod with pain: not silken dress
But toil shall tire thy loveliness.

Hunger shall make thy modest zone
And cheat fond death of all but bone —
If these delights thy mind may move,
Then live with me and be my love.

PEGASUS
In memoriam L. B. L.

It was there on the hillside, no tall traveller's story.
A cloud caught on a whin-bush, an airing of bleached
Linen, a swan, the cliff of a marble quarry —
It could have been any of these: but as he approached,
He saw that it was indeed what he had cause
Both to doubt and believe in — a horse, a winged white horse.

It filled the pasture with essence of solitude.
The wind tiptoed away like an interloper,
The sunlight there became a transparent hood
Estranging what it revealed: and the bold horse-coper,
The invincible hero, trudging up Helicon,
Knew he had never before been truly alone.

It stood there, solid as ivory, dreamy as smoke;
Or moved, and its hooves went dewdropping so lightly
That even the wild cyclamen were not broken:
But when those hooves struck rock, such was their might
They tapped a crystal vein which flowed into song
As it ran through thyme and grasses down-along.

"Pegasus," he called, "Pegasus" — with the surprise
Of one for the first time naming his naked lover.
The creature turned its lordly, incurious eyes
Upon the young man; but they seemed to pass him over
As something beneath their pride or beyond their ken.
It returned to cropping the violets and cyclamen.

Such meekness, indifference, frightened him more than any
Rumoured Chimaera. He wavered, remembering how
This milk-white beast was born from the blood of uncanny
Medusa, the nightmare-eyed: and at once, although
Its brief glance had been mild, he felt a cringing
And pinched himself to make sure he was not changing

Into a stone. The animal tossed its head;
The white mane lifted and fell like an arrogant whinny.
"Horses are meant to be ridden," the hero said,
"Wings or no wings, and men to mount them. Athene
Ordered my mission, besides, and certainly you
Must obey that goddess," he cried, and flung the lassoo.

The cyclamen bow their heads, the cicadas pause.
The mountain shivers from flank to snowy top,
Shaking off eagles as a pastured horse
Shakes off a cloud of flies. The faint airs drop.
Pegasus, with a movement of light on water,
Shimmers aside, is elsewhere, mocking the halter.

So there began the contest. A young man
Challenging, coaxing, pursuing, always pursuing
The dream of those dewfall hooves: a horse which ran
Quicksilver from his touch, sliding and slewing
Away, then immobile a moment, derisively tame,
Almost as if it entered into a game.

He summoned up his youth, his conscious art
To tire or trick the beast, criss-crossing the meadow
With a web of patient moves, circling apart,
Nearing, and pouncing, but only upon its shadow.
What skill and passion weave the subtle net!
But Pegasus goes free, unmounted yet.

All day he tried for this radiant creature. The more he
Persevered, the less he thought of the task
For which he required it, and the ultimate glory.
So it let him draw close, closer — nearly to grasp
Its mane; but that instant it broke out wings like a spread
Of canvas, and sailed off easily overhead.

He cursed Pegasus then. Anger arose
With a new desire, as if it were some white girl
To stretch, mount, master, exhaust in shuddering throes.

The animal gave him a different look: it swirled
Towards him, circled him round in a dazzling mist,
And one light hoof just knocked upon his breast.

The pale sky yawns to its uttermost concave,
Flowers open their eyes, rivulets prance
Again, and over the mountainside a wave
Of sparkling air tumbles. Now from its trance
That holy ground is deeply sighing and stirring.
The heights take back their eagles, cicadas are whirring.

The furious art, the pursuer's rhythmic pace
Failed in him now. Another self had awoken,
Which knew — but felt no chagrin, no disgrace —
That he, not the winged horse, was being broken:
It was his lode, his lord, his appointed star,
He but its shadow and familiar.

So he lay down to sleep. Argos, Chimaera,
Athene in one solution were immersed.
Around him, on bush and blade, each dewdrop mirrored
A star, his riding star, his universe,
While on the moonlit flowers at his side
Pegasus grazed, palpable, undenied.

A golden bridle came to him in sleep —
A mesh of immortal fire and sensual earth,
Pliant as love, compulsive as the sweep
Of light-years, brilliant as truth, perfect as death.
He dreamed a magic bridle, and next day
When he awoke, there to his hand it lay.

Wings furled, on printless feet through the dews of morn
Pegasus stepped, in majesty and submission,
Towards him. Mane of tempest, delicate mien,
It was all brides, all thoroughbreds, all pent passion.
Breathing flowers upon him, it arched a superb
Neck to receive the visionary curb.

Pegasus said, "The bridle that you found
In sleep, you yourself made, your hard pursuit,
Your game with me upon this hallowed ground
Forged it, your failures tempered it. I am brute
And Angel. He alone, who taps the source
Of both, can ride me. Bellerophon, I am yours."

THE DOUBLE VISION

The river this November afternoon
Rests in an equipoise of sun and cloud:
A glooming light, a gleaming darkness shroud
Its passage. All seems tranquil, all in tune.

Image and real are joined like Siamese twins:
Their doubles draw the willows, a brown mare
Drinks her reflection. There's no margin where
Substance leaves off, the illusory begins.

You and I by the river contemplate
Our ideal selves, glossed here, crystal-divined:
We yearn to them, knowing one sigh of wind
Will rub these precious figures from the slate.

It is not of their transience I'm afraid,
But thinking how most human loves protract
Themselves to unreality — the fact
Drained of its virtue by the image it made.

O double vision of the autumnal stream,
Teach me to bear love's fusion or diffusion!
O gems of purest water, pure illusion,
Answer my rays and cluster to a theme!

Richard Church
b. 1893

THE MOUNTAIN LAKE

Empty of heart we wait amid the snow,
The feline snow that crouches by the lake,
Empty of heart, except for icy fear
Reflected from unfathomable deeps,
Blue beyond blue, past the inverted pines,
Past mirrored fangs laid bare against the sky,
Past silent air, and silence in the vault,
The iris of the mountain, hiding thought
No human fear might hide, or love reveal
Within the eye, lake of the human soul.

We know this presence. From the valley first
Lifting our eyes toward the mountain wall
We saw the morning tremble in the deep
Where the night's constellations lay dissolved.
We saw the sun, with cautious sword out-thrust,
Creep with that misted blade from height to height,
Testing ravine and bastion and crag
With ringing blows of light. The splintered gold
Broke gaily over forest, lanced the snow
And melted to the valley with delight.

That visible laughter made the earth respond.
An eagle first, immovable above
The highest reach of alp, fluttered its pinions
And then relapsed to stoniness in air.
Larks and cascades competed in their song,
Each conjuring, with throat and rock-foot pool,
A clamour of laughter such as silver makes
Webbed in a girl's gold hair when snaring with it
The first desire of boyhood. From the slopes
Below the alpine panther's drooping pads,
The little cowslips ran like bees disturbed
By a marauding bear. Innumerable flowers
Lifted their heads and flung toward the sun
Their tiny shouts of perfume, breaking together
And deluging the valley with the riot
Of morning-joy indistinguishable from mirth
Of mortal lips and innocence of meadows.

And through this gaiety we took our way
Against the onrush from the slopes above,
Pageant and cavalcade of song and colour,
Dancing and miming of the naked mists
Down through the boulder-rooted woods that stood
Aloof and stubborn, except for the young larches
Who trembled, sighed, and shook their verdant hair.

But all this masquerade from dawn to noon
Borne down against our ascent, could not blind
Our eyes, nor cover the knowledge in our hearts.
We saw, we knew the monster of the ice,
The glacier, the morain of the rocks,
The cleft concealed with a faint feather of snow,
The horror of the silence in the height
Turning to murmur of its own despair.
We knew that as we climbed we should encounter

This powdery spirit like the breath of fear,
Invisible, yet glinting in the air
Above the peak, and shaking through sunshafts
Its venom of resentment on the soul
Of man, of eagle, lark and wild cascade,
The little flowers shouting to the valley,
Frosting them all with leper-touch of terror
Colder than echo, quieter than death.

Louis MacNeice
b. 1907

BROTHER FIRE

When our brother Fire was having his dog's day
Jumping the London streets with millions of tin cans
Clanking at his tail, we heard some shadow say
"Give the dog a bone" — and so we gave him ours;
Night after night we watched him slaver and crunch away
The beams of human life, the tops of topless towers.

Which gluttony of his for us was Lenten fare
Who mother-naked, suckled with sparks, were chill
Though cotted in a grill of sizzling air
Striped like a convict — black, yellow and red;
Thus were we weaned to knowledge of the Will
That wills the natural world but wills us dead.

O delicate walker, babbler, dialectician Fire,
O enemy and image of ourselves,
Did we not on those mornings after the All Clear,
When you were looting shops in elemental joy
And singing as you swarmed up city block and spire,
Echo your thought in ours? "Destroy! Destroy!"

Demetrios Capetanakis

1912-1944

ABEL

My brother Cain, the wounded, liked to sit
Brushing my shoulder, by the staring water
Of life, or death, in cinemas half-lit
By scenes of peace that always turned to slaughter.

He liked to talk to me. His eager voice
Whispered the puzzle of his bleeding thirst,
Or prayed me not to make my final choice,
Unless we had a chat about it first.

And then he chose the final pain for me.
I do not blame his nature: he's my brother;
Nor what you call the times: our love was free,
Would be the same at any time; but rather

The ageless ambiguity of things
Which makes our life mean death, our love be hate.
My blood that streams across the bedroom sings
"I am my brother opening the gate!"

Howard Moss

b. 1922

THE LIE

Some bloodied sea-bird's hovering decay
Assails us where we lie, and lie
To make that symbol go away,
To mock the true north of the eye.
But lie to me, lie next to me;
The world is an infirmity.

Too much of sun's been said, too much
Of sea, and of the lover's touch,
Whole volumes that old men debauch.
But we, at the sea's edge curled,
Hurl back their bloody world.
Lie to me, lie next to me.

For there is nothing here to see
But the mirror of ourselves, the day,
Clear with the odors of the sea.
Lie to me. And lie to me.

Stephen Spender

b. 1909

AFTER THEY HAVE TIRED OF THE BRILLIANCE OF CITIES

After they have tired of the brilliance of cities
And of striving for office where at last they may languish
Hung round with easy chains until
Death and Jerusalem glorify also the crossing sweeper:
Then those streets the rich built and their easy love
Fade like old cloths, and it is death stalks through life
Grinning white through all faces
Clean and equal like the shine from snow.

In this day when grief pours freezing over us,
When the hard light of pain gleams at every street corner,
When those who were pillars of yesterday's roof
Shrink in their clothes: then surely from hunger
We may strike fire, like fire from flint?
And our strength is now the strength of our bones
Clean and equal like the shine from snow
And the strength of famine and our enforced idleness,
And it is the strength of our love for one another.

Readers of this strange language,
We have come at last to a country
Where light equal, like the shine from snow, strikes all faces.
Here you may wonder
How it was that works, money, interest, building, could ever hide
The palpable and obvious love of man for man.

Oh, comrades, let not those who follow after
— The beautiful generation that will spring from our sides —
Let them not wonder how after the failure of banks,
The failure of cathedrals and the declared insanity of our rulers,
We lacked the Spring-like resources of the tiger
Or of plants which strike out new roots to urgent waters.
Through torn-down portions of fabric let their eyes
Witness the admiring dawn explode like a shell
Around us, dazing us with its light like snow.

I THINK CONTINUALLY OF THOSE
WHO WERE TRULY GREAT

I think continually of those who were truly great.
Who, from the womb, remembered the soul's history
Through corridors of light where the hours are suns,
Endless and singing. Whose lovely ambition
Was that their lips, still touched with fire,
Should tell of the Spirit, clothed from head to foot in song.
And who hoarded from the Spring branches
The desires falling across their bodies like blossoms.

What is precious, is never to forget
The essential delight of the blood drawn from ageless springs
Breaking through rocks in worlds before our earth.
Never to deny its pleasure in the morning simple light
Nor its grave evening demand for love.
Never to allow gradually the traffic to smother
With noise and fog, the flowering of the Spirit.

Near the snow, near the sun, in the highest fields,
See how these names are fêted by the waving grass
And by the streamers of white cloud
And whispers of wind in the listening sky.
The names of those who in their lives fought for life,
Who wore at their hearts the fire's centre.
Born of the sun, they travelled a short while toward the sun
And left the vivid air signed with their honour.

SEASCAPE
In memoriam, M. A. S.

There are some days the happy ocean lies
Like an unfingered harp, below the land.
Afternoon gilds all the silent wires
Into a burning music for the eyes.
On mirrors flashing between fine-strung fires
The shore, heaped up with roses, horses, spires,
Wanders on water, walking above ribbed sand.

The motionlessness of the hot sky tires
And a sigh, like a woman's, from inland
Brushes the instrument with shadowing hand
Drawing across its wires some gull's sharp cries
Or bell, or shout, from distant, hedged-in shires;
These, deep as anchors, the hushing wave buries.

Then from the shore, two zig-zag butterflies,
Like errant dog-roses, cross the bright strand
Spiralling over sea in foolish gyres
Until they fall into reflected skies.
They drown. Fishermen understand
Such wings sunk in such ritual sacrifice,

Recalling legends of undersea, drowned cities.
What voyagers, oh what heroes, flamed like pyres
With helmets plumed, have set forth from some island
And them the sea engulfed. Their eyes,
Contorted by the cruel waves' desires
Glitter with coins through the tide scarcely scanned,
While, above them, that harp assumes their sighs.

MEMENTO

Remember the blackness of that flesh
Tarring the bones with a thin varnish
Belsen Theresenstadt Buchenwald where
Faces were a clenched despair
Knocking at the bird-song-fretted air.

Their eyes sunk jellied in their holes
Were held up to the sun like begging bowls
Their hands like rakes with finger-nails of rust
Scratched for a little kindness from the dust.
To many, in its beak, no dove brought answer.

ICE
To M ——

She came in from the snowing air
Where icicle-hung architecture
Strung white fleece round the Baroque square.
I saw her face freeze in her fur,
Then my lips ran to her with fire
From the chimney corner of the room,
Where I had waited in my chair.
I kissed their heat against her skin
And watched the red make the white bloom,
While, at my care, her smiling eyes
Shone with the brilliance of the ice
Outside, whose dazzling they brought in.
    That day, until this, I forgot.
How is it now I so remember
Who, when she came indoors, saw not
The passion of her white December?

MIDSUMMER
To Edith Sitwell

There is midsummer
    Opens all the windows
And drowns the houses
    In fever of dust and rose.

Vibrant transparency above
    The hills, is visible.
All night the stars shake through the silence,
    Tangible, audible.

Clear day, you trail
    Whispers of cherry and rambler.
Sun, you'll gild the leaves to wraiths
    Withered in amber.

Within our distraught gale of time
  My secrecy listens
To a dynamo of summer that revolves
  Generating what glistens —

Noon, the moon, straws of light,
  Ringed pulsations on the lake,
Quietness folded on window sills,
  The loads the reapers make.

Would I might be that bough tonight
  Will dip in dews! And, wrung
From my impregnated phosphorescence,
  Honeyed song of my tongue!

But I am tied on strips of time,
  Caged in minutes, made
By men, exiled from the day's brilliance
  In a deliberate shade.

Only, some moment slips between the bars
  Of the raging machines.
It gleams with eternal rumours
  Of the high, midsummer scenes.

Man is that prison where his will
  Has shut without pity
In a clock eternity,
  In his fist, rose of infinity.

MISSING MY DAUGHTER

This wall-paper has lines that rise
Upright like bars, and overhead,
The ceiling's patterned with red roses.
On the wall opposite the bed
The staring looking-glass encloses
Six roses in its white of eyes.

Here at my desk, with note-book open
Missing my daughter, makes those bars
Draw their lines upward through my mind.
This blank page stares at me like glass
Where stared-at roses wish to pass
Through petalling of my pen.

An hour ago, there came an image
Of a beast that pressed its muzzle
Between bars. Next, through tick and tock
Of the reiterating clock
A second glared with the wide dazzle
Of deserts. The door, in a green mirage,

Opened. In my daughter came.
Her eyes were wide as those she has,
The round gaze of her childhood was
White as the distance in the glass
Or on a white page, a white poem.
The roses raced around her name.

THE VASE OF TEARS

Tears pouring from the face of stone,
Angels from the heart, unhappiness
From some dream to yourself alone —
Let me dry your eyes with these kisses.
I pour what comfort of commonplaces
I can: faint light upon your light alone.
And then we smother with caresses
Both our starved needs to atone.

Cold face creased with human tears. Yet
Something in me tender and delicate
Reads in those eyes an ocean of green water
And one by one these bitter drops collects
Into my heart, a glass vase which reflects
The world's grief weeping in its daughter.

Richard Eberhart
b. 1904

THE HORSE CHESTNUT TREE

Boys in sporadic but tenacious droves
Come with sticks, as certainly as Autumn,
To assault the great horse chestnut tree.

There is a law governs their lawlessness.
Desire is in them for a shining amulet
And the best are those that are highest up.

They will not pick them easily from the ground.
With shrill arms they fling to the higher branches,
To hurry the work of nature for their pleasure.

I have seen them trooping down the street
Their pockets stuffed with chestnuts shucked, unshucked.
It is only evening keeps them from their wish.

Sometimes I run out in a kind of rage
To chase the boys away; I catch an arm,
Maybe, and laugh to think of being the lawgiver.

I was once such a young sprout myself
And fingered in my pocket the prize and trophy.
But still I moralize upon the day

And see that we, outlaws on God's property,
Fling out imagination beyond the skies
Wishing a tangible good from the unknown.

And likewise death will drive us from the scene
With the great flowering world unbroken yet,
Which we held in idea, a little handful.

William Plomer

b. 1903

THE SCORPION

Limpopo and Tugela churned
In flood for brown and angry miles
Melons, maize, domestic thatch,
The trunks of trees and crocodiles;

The swollen estuaries were thick
With flotsam, in the sun one saw
The corpse of a young Negress bruised
By rocks, and rolling on the shore,

Pushed by the waves of morning, rolled
Impersonally among shells,
With lolling breasts and bleeding eyes,
And round her neck were beads and bells.

That was the Africa we knew,
Where, wandering alone,
We saw, heraldic in the heat,
A scorpion on a stone.

John Ciardi
b. 1916

ELEGY JUST IN CASE

Here lie Ciardi's pearly bones
In their ripe organic mess.
Jungle blown, his chromosomes
Breed to a new address.

Was it bullets or a wind
Or a rip-cord fouled on Chance?
Artifacts the natives find
Decorate them when they dance.

Here lies the sgt.'s mortal wreck
Lily spiked and termite kissed,
Spiders pendant from his neck
And a beetle on his wrist.

Bring the tic and southern flies
Where the land crabs run
        unmourning
Through a night of jungle skies
To a climeless mourning.

And bring the chalked eraser here
Fresh from rubbing out his name.
Burn the crew-board for a bier.
(Also Colonel what's-his-name.)

Let no dice be stored and still.
Let no poker deck be torn.
But pour the smuggled rye until
The barracks threshold is outworn.

File the papers, pack the clothes,
Send the coded word through air —
"We regret and no one knows
Where the sgt. goes from here."

"Missing as of inst. Oblige,
Deepest sorrow and remain — "
Shall I grin at persiflage?
Could I have my skin again

Would I choose a business
        form
Stilted mute as a giraffe,
Or a pinstripe unicorn
On a cashier's epitaph?

Darling, darling, just in case
Rivets fail or engines burn,
I forget the time and place
But your flesh was sweet to learn.

In the grammar of not yet
Let me name one verb for chance,
Scholarly to one regret:
That I leave your mood and tense.

Swift and single as a shark
I have seen you churn my sleep;
Now if beetles hunt my dark
What will beetles find to keep?

Fractured meat and open bone —
Nothing single or surprised.
Fragments of a written stone,
Undeciphered but surmised.

THE EVIL EYE

The belief in the Evil Eye is a still-surviving superstition among Italian peasants. One method of detecting its presence is to pour olive oil on a saucer of holy water. The shapes assumed by the oil can then be read by the gifted.

Nona poured oil on the water and saw the eye
   Form on my birth. Zia beat me with bay,
    Fennel, and barley to scourge the devil away.
I doubt I needed so much excuse to cry.

From Sister Maria Immaculata there came
   A crucifix, a vow of nine days' prayer,
   And a scapular stitched with virgin's hair.
The eye glowed on the water all the same.

By Felice, the midwife, I was hung with a tin
   Fish stuffed with garlic and bread crumbs.
   Three holy waters washed the breast for my gums.
Still the eye glared, wide as original sin,

On the deepest pools of women midnight-spoken
   To ward my clamoring soul from the clutch of hell,
   Lest growing I be no comfort and dying swell
More than a grave with horror. Still unbroken

The eye glared through the roosts of all their clucking.
   "Jesu," cried Mother, "why is he deviled so?"
   "Baptism without delay," said Father Cosmo.
"This one is not for sprinkling but for ducking."

So in came meat and wine and the feast was on.
   I wore a palm frond in my lace, and sewn
   To my swaddling band a hoop and three beads of bone
For the Trinity. And they ducked me and called me John.

And ate the meat and drank the wine, and the eye
  Closed on the water. All this fell between
   My first scream and first name in 1916,
The year of the war and the influenza, when I

Was not yet ready for evil or my own name,
Though I had one already and the other came.

Jean Starr Untermeyer
b. 1886

THAW

Abortive tears!
That form but will not flow —
Rising so hard and slow
From that dry well of fears
That was my heart, once warm and sound,
Now the rough cicatrice of the enduring wound.

Oh, break and flood
The hillside of my breast;
Reclaim the unpossesst;
Water and warm the blood;
Release, as this spring rain, the bound
And nigh insentient root, green from the rigid ground!

Peter Quennell
b. 1905

THE SUNFLOWER

See, I have bent thee by thy saffron hair,
  O most strange masker,
Towards my face, thy face so full of eyes,
  O almost legendary monster.
Thee of the saffron, circling hair I bend,

Bend by my fingers knotted in thy hair,
   Hair like broad flames.
So — shall I swear by beech husk, spindle-berry,
To break thee, saffron hair, and peering eye,
   To have the mastery?

Laurie Lee

b. 1914

DAY OF THESE DAYS

Such a morning it is when love
leans through geranium windows
and calls with a cockerell's tongue.

When red-haired girls scamper like roses
over the rain-green grass
and the sun drips honey.

When hedgerows grow venerable
berries dry black as blood
and holes suck in their bees.

Such a morning it is when mice
run whispering from the church
dragging dropped ears of harvest.

When the partridge draws back his spring
and shoots like a buzzing arrow
over grained and mahogany fields.

When no table is bare,
and no breast dry,
and the tramp feeds off ribs of rabbit.

Such a day it is when time
piles up the hills like pumpkins,
and the streams run golden.

When all men smell good,
and the cheeks of girls
are as baked bread to the mouth.

As bread and beanflowers
the touch of their lips,
and their white teeth sweeter than cucumbers.

George Barker

b. 1913

NEWS OF THE WORLD III

Let her lie naked here, my hand resting
Light on her broken breast, the sleeping world
Given into our far from careful keeping,
Terrestrial daughter of a disaster of waters
No master honours. Let her lie to-night
Attended by those visions of bright swords
That never defended but ended life.
My emerald trembler, my sky skipping scullion,
See, now, your sister, dipping into the horizon,
Leaves us in darkness; you, nude, and I
Seeking to loose what the day retrieves,
An immoderation of love. Bend your arm
Under my generation of heads. The seas unfold
My sleepless eye and save it weeping
For the dishonoured star. I hear your grave
Nocturnal lamentation, where, abandoned, far
You, like Arabia in her tent, mourn through an evening
Of wildernesses. O what are you grieving for?
From the tiara'd palaces of the Andes
And the last Asiatic terraces, I see
The wringing of the hands of all the world,
I hear your long lingering of disillusion.
Favour the viper, heaven, with one vision
That it may see what is lost. The crime is blended
With the time and the cause. But at your
Guilty and golden bosom, O daughter of laws,
I happy lie to-night, the fingering zephyr
Light and unlikely as a kiss. The shades creep
Out of their holes and graves for a last
Long look at your bare empire as it rolls
Its derelict glory away into darkness. Turn, tear,
Back. Our fate is in your face. Whom do you love
But those whom you doom to the happy disgrace

Of adoring you with degradations? I garb my wife,
The wide world of a bride, in devastations.
She has curled up in my hand, and, like a moth,
Died a legend of splendour along the line of my life.
But the congregation of clouds paces in dolour
Over my head and her never barren belly
Where we lie, summered, together, a world and I.
Her birdflecked hair, sunsetting the weather,
Feathers my eye, she shakes an ear-ring sky,
And her hand of a country trembles against me.
The glittering nightriders gambol through
A zodiac of symbols above our love
Promising, O my star-crossed, death and disasters.
But I want breath for nothing but your possession
Now, now, this summer midnight, before the dawn
Shakes its bright gun in the sky, before
The serried battalions of lies and organizations of hate
Entirely encompass us, buried; before the wolf and friend
Render us enemies. Before all this,
Lie one night in my arms and give me peace.

TURN ON YOUR SIDE AND
BEAR THE DAY TO ME

Turn on your side and bear the day to me
Beloved, sceptre-struck, immured
In the glass wall of sleep. Slowly
Uncloud the borealis of your eye
And show your iceberg secrets, your midnight prizes
To the green-eyed world and to me. Sin
Coils upward into thin air when you awaken
And again morning announces amnesty over
The serpent-kingdomed bed. Your mother
Watched with as dove an eye the unforgiveable night
Sigh backward into innocence when you
Set a bright monument in her amorous sea.
Look down, Undine, on the trident that struck
Sons from the rock of vanity. Turn in the world
Sceptre-struck, spellbound, beloved,
Turn in the world and bear the day to me.

David Gascoyne
b. 1916

LACHRYMAE

Slow are the years of light:
     And more immense
Than the imagination. And the years return
Until the Unity is filled. And heavy are
The lengths of Time with the slow weight of tears.
Since thou didst weep, on a remote hill-side
Beneath the olive-trees, fires of unnumbered stars
Have burnt the years away, until we see them now:

Since Thou didst weep, as many tears
Have flowed like hourglass sand.
Thy tears were all.
And when our secret face
Is blind because of the mysterious
Surging of tears wrung by our most profound
Presentiment of evil in man's fate, our cruellest wounds
Become Thy stigmata. They are Thy tears which fall.

SEPTEMBER SUN: 1947

Magnificent strong sun! in these last days
So prodigally generous of pristine light
That's wasted only by men's sight who will not see
And by self-darkened spirits from whose night
Can rise no longer orison or praise:

Let us consume in fire unfed like yours
And may the quickened gold within me come
To mintage in true season, and not be
Transmuted to no better end than dumb
And self-sufficient usury. These days and years

May bring the sudden call to harvesting,
When if the fields Man labours only yield
Glitter and husks, then with an angrier sun may He
Who first with His gold seed the sightless field
Of Chaos planted, all our trash to cinders bring.

Stephen Vincent Benét
1898-1943

From JOHN BROWN'S BODY

JOHN BROWN'S PRAYER

Omnipotent and steadfast God,
Who, in Thy mercy, hath
Upheaved in me Jehovah's rod
And his chastising wrath,

For fifty-nine unsparing years
Thy Grace hath worked apart
To mould a man of iron tears
With a bullet for a heart.

Yet, since this body may be weak
With all it has to bear,
Once more, before Thy thunders
    speak,
Almighty, hear my prayer.

I saw Thee when Thou did display
The black man and his lord
To bid me free the one, and slay
The other with the sword.

I heard Thee when Thou bade me
    spurn
Destruction from my hand
And, though all Kansas bleed and
    burn,
It was at Thy command.

I hear the rolling of the wheels,
The chariots of war!
I hear the breaking of the seals
And the opening of the door!

The glorious beasts with many eyes
Exult before the Crowned.
The buried saints arise, arise
Like incense from the ground!

Before them march the martyr-
    kings,
In bloody sunsets drest,
Oh, Kansas, bleeding Kansas,
You will not let me rest!

I hear your sighing corn again,
I smell your prairie-sky,
And I remember five dead men
By Pottawatomie.

Lord God, it was a work of Thine,
And how might I refrain?
But Kansas, bleeding Kansas,
I hear her in her pain.

Her corn is rustling in the ground,
An arrow in my flesh.
And all night long I staunch a
    wound
That ever bleeds afresh.

Get up, get up, my hardy sons,
From this time forth we are
No longer men, but pikes and guns
In God's advancing war.

And if we live, we free the slave,
And if we die, we die.
But God has digged His saints a
    grave
Beyond the western sky.

Oh, fairer than the bugle-call
Its walls of jasper shine!
And Joshua's sword is on the wall
With space beside for mine.

And should the Philistine defend
His strength against our blows,
The God who doth not spare His friend,
Will not forget His foes.

FOR ALL BLASPHEMERS

Adam was my grandfather,
A tall, spoiled child,
A red, clay tower
In Eden, green and mild.
He ripped the Sinful Pippin
From its sanctimonious limb.
Adam was my grandfather —
And I take after him.

Noah was my uncle
And he got dead drunk.
There were planets in his liquor-
     can
And lizards in his bunk.
He fell into the Bottomless
Past Hell's most shrinking star.
Old Aunt Fate has often said
How much alike we are.

Lilith, she's my sweetheart
Till my heartstrings break,
Most of her is honey-pale
And all of her is snake.
Sweet as secret thievery
I kiss her all I can,
While Somebody Above remarks
"That's not a nice young man!"

Bacchus was my brother,
Nimrod is my friend.
All of them have talked to me
On how such courses end.
But when His Worship takes me
     up
How can I fare but well?
For who in gaudy Hell will care?
— And I shall be in Hell.

Karl Shapiro

b. 1913

ELEGY FOR TWO BANJOS

Haul up the flag, you mourners,
   Not half-mast but all the way;
The funeral is done and disbanded;
   The devil's had the final say.

O mistress and wife too pensive,
   Pallbearers and priestly men,
Put your black clothes in the attic,
And get up on your feet again.

Death did his job like a scholar,
   A most unusual case,
Death did his job like a gentleman;
   He barely disturbed the face.

You packed him a handsome carton,
   Set the lid with silver screws;
You dug a dark pit in the graveyard
   To tell the white worms the news.

Now you've nothing left to
  remember,
 Nothing but the words he wrote,
But they'll never let you remember,
 Only stick like a bone in your
  throat.

O if I'd been his wife or mistress,
 His pallbearer or his parish priest,
I'd have kept him at home for-
  ever —
 Or as long as bric-a-brac at least.

I would have burned his body
 And salvaged a sizeable bone
For a paper-weight or a door-stop
 Or a garden flagstone.

I would have heaped the fire
 And boiled his beautiful skull.
It was laden like a ship for travels
 And now is but an empty hull.

I would have dried it off in linens,
 Polished it with a chamois cloth
Till it shone like a brand-new
  quarter
 And felt smooth as the nose of a
  moth.

Or I'd have hung it out in the
  garden
 Where everything else is alive,
Put a queen-bee in the brain case
 So the bees could build a hive.

Maybe I'd have wired the jawbone
 With a silver spring beneath,
Set it in the cradle with baby
 So baby could rattle the teeth.

O you didn't do right by William
 To shove him down that filthy
  hole,
Throw him a lot of tears and Latin
 And a cheap "God bless your
  soul."

You might as well leave off
  mourning,
 His photograph is getting dim,
So you'd better take a long look at
  it
 For it's all you'll ever see of him.

Haul up the flag you mourners,
 Not half-mast but all the way,
The funeral is done and disbanded,
 The devil's had the final say.

Charles Causley

b. 1917

OU PHRONTIS
To E. M. Forster

  The bells assault the maiden air,
  The coachman waits with a carriage and pair,
  But the bridegroom says *I won't be there,*
    I don't care!

Three times three times the banns declare
That the boys may blush and the girls may glare,
But the bridegroom is occupied elsewhere,
I don't care!

Lord, but the neighbours all will stare,
Their temperatures jump as high as a hare,
But the bridegroom says *I've paid my fare,*
I don't care!

The bride she waits by the bed so bare,
Soft as a pillow is her hair,
But the bridegroom jigs with the leg of a chair,
I don't care!

Say, but her father's a millionaire,
A girdle of gold all night will she wear,
You must your foolish ways forswear.
I don't care!

Her mother will offer, if she dare,
A ring that is rich but not so rare
If you'll keep your friendship in repair.
I don't care!

Her sisters will give you a plum and a pear
And a diamond saddle for your mare.
O bridegroom! For the night prepare!
I don't care!

Her seven brothers all debonair
Will do your wishes and some to spare
If from your fancy you'll forbear.
I don't care!

Say, but a maid you wouldn't scare
Now that you've got her in your snare?
And what about your son and heir?
I don't care!

She'll leap she'll leap from the highest stair,
She'll drown herself in the river there,
With a silver knife her flesh she'll tear.
I don't care!

Then another will lie in the silken lair
And cover with kisses her springing hair.
Another the bridal bed will share.
I don't care!

I shall stand on my head on the table bare,
I shall kick my lily-white legs in the air,
I shall wash my hands of the whole affair,
I don't care!

NOTE: The words "Ou Phrontis" were carved by T. E. Lawrence over the door of his cottage at Cloud's Hill, Dorset. They come from the story in Herodotus, on which this poem is based. — C.C.

SAILOR'S CAROL

Lord, the snowful sky
  In this pale December
Fingers my clear eye
  Lest seeing, I remember

Not the naked baby
  Weeping in the stable
Nor the singing boys
  All round my table,

Not the dizzy star
  Bursting on the pane
Nor the leopard sun
  Pawing the rain.

Only the deep garden
  Where green lilies grow,
The sailors rolling
  In the sea's blue snow.

Theodore Roethke

b. 1908

FORCING HOUSE

Vines tougher than wrists
And rubbery shoots,
Scums, mildews, smuts along stems,
Great cannas or delicate cyclamen tips —
All pulse with the knocking pipes
That drip and sweat,
Sweat and drip,
Swelling the roots with steam and stench,
Shooting up lime and dung and ground bones —
Fifty summers in motion at once,
As the live heat billows from pipes and pots.

CHILD ON TOP OF A GREENHOUSE

The wind billowing out the seat of my britches,
My feet crackling splinters of glass and dried putty,
The half-grown chrysanthemums staring up like accusers,
Up through the streaked glass, flashing with sunlight,
A few white clouds all rushing eastward,
A line of elms plunging and tossing like horses,
And everyone, everyone pointing up and shouting!

Robert Graves
b. 1895

THE FLORIST ROSE

This wax-mannequin nude, the florist rose,
She of the long stem and too glossy leaf,
Is dead to honest greenfly and leaf-cutter:
Behind plate-glass watches the yellow fogs.

Claims kin with the robust male aeroplane
Whom eagles hate and phantoms of the air,
Who has no legend, as she breaks from legend —
From fellowship with sword and sail and crown.

Experiment's flower, scentless (he its bird);
Is dewed by the spray-gun; is tender-thorned;
Pouts, false-virginal, between bud and bloom;
Bought as a love-gift, droops within the day.

TIME

The vague sea thuds against the marble cliffs
And from their fragments age-long grinds
Pebbles like flowers.

Or the vague weather wanders in the fields,
And up spring flowers with coloured buds
Like marble pebbles.

The beauty of the flowers is Time, death-grieved?
The pebbles' beauty too is Time,
Life-wearied.

It is easy to admire a blowing flower
Or a smooth pebble flower-like freaked
By Time and vagueness.

Time is Time's lapse, the emulsive element coaxing
All obstinate locks and rusty hinges
To loving-kindness.

And am I proof against that lovesome pair,
Old age and childhood, twins in Time,
In sorrowful vagueness?

And will I not pretend the accustomed thanks:
Humouring age with filial flowers,
Childhood with pebbles?

NEW LEGENDS

Content in you,
Andromeda serene,
Mistress of air and ocean
And every fiery dragon,
Chained to no cliff,
Asking no rescue of me.

Content in you,
Mad Atalanta,
Stooping unpausing,
Ever ahead,
Acquitting me of rivalry.

Content in you,
Invariable she-Proteus,
Sole unrecordable,
Giving my tablets holiday.

Content in you,
Niobe of no children,
Sorrow or calamity.

Content in you,
Helen, foiler of beauty.

LIKE SNOW

She, then, like snow in a dark night,
Fell secretly. And the world waked
With dazzling of the drowsy eye,
So that some muttered "Too much light,"
And drew the curtains close.
Like snow, warmer than fingers feared,
And to soil friendly;
Holding the histories of the night
In yet unmelted tracks.

A LOVE STORY

The full moon easterly rising, furious,
Against a winter sky ragged with red;
The hedges high in snow, and owls raving —
Solemnities not easy to withstand:
A shiver wakes the spine.

In boyhood, having encountered the scene,
I suffered horror: I fetched the moon home,
With owls and snow, to nurse in my head
Throughout the trials of a new spring,
Famine unassuaged.

But fell in love, and made a lodgement
Of love on those chill ramparts.
Her image was my ensign: snows melted,
Hedges sprouted, the moon tenderly shone,
The owls trilled with tongues of nightingale.

These were all lies, though they matched the time,
And brought me less than luck: her image
Warped in the weather, turned beldamish.
Then back came winter on me at a bound,
The pallid sky heaved with a moon-quake.

Dangerous it had been with love-notes
To serenade Queen Famine.
In tears I recomposed the former scene,
Let the snow lie, watched the moon rise, suffered the
        owls,
Paid homage to them of unevent.

THE WINDOW SILL

Presage and caveat not only seem
To come in dream,
But do so come in dream.

When the cock crew and phantoms floated by,
This dreamer I
Out of the house went I,

Down long unsteady streets to a mad square;
And who was there,
Or whom did I know there?

Julia, leaning on her window sill.
"I love you still,"
Said she, "O love me still!"

I answered: "Julia, do you love me best?"
"What of this breast,"
She mourned, "this flowery breast?"

Then a wild sobbing spread from door to door,
And every floor
Cried shame on every floor,

As she unlaced her bosom to disclose
Each breast a rose,
A white and cankered rose.

William Empson
b. 1906

TO AN OLD LADY

Ripeness is all; her in her cooling planet
Revere; do not presume to think her wasted.
Project her no projectile, plan nor man it;
Gods cool in turn, by the sun long outlasted.

Our earth alone given no name of god
Gives, too, no hold for such a leap to aid her;
Landing, you break some palace and seem odd;
Bees sting their need, the keeper's queen invader.

No, to your telescope; spy out the land;
Watch while her ritual is still to see,
Still stand her temples emptying in the sand
Whose waves o'erthrew their crumbled tracery;

Still stand uncalled-on her soul's appanage;
Much social detail whose successor fades,
Wit used to run a house and to play Bridge,
And tragic fervour, to dismiss her maids.

Years her precession do not throw from gear.
She reads a compass certain of her pole;
Confident, finds no confines on her sphere,
Whose failing crops are in her sole control.

Stars how much further from me fill my night,
Strange that she too should be inaccessible,
Who shares my sun. He curtains her from sight,
And but in darkness is she visible.

AUTHOR'S NOTE. First three words from "King Lear." *Our earth* without a god's name such as the other planets have is compared to some body of people (absurd to say "the present generation") without fundamental beliefs as a basis for action. When a hive needs a new queen and the keeper puts one in the bees sometimes kill her. Her *precession* is some customary movement of the planet, meant to suggest the dignity of "procession." The unconfined surface of her sphere is like the universe in being finite but unbounded, but I failed to get that into the line.

INVITATION TO JUNO

Lucretius could not credit centaurs;
Such bicycle he deemed asynchronous.
"Man superannuates the horse;
Horse pulses will not gear with ours."

Johnson could see no bicycle would go;
"You bear yourself, and the machine as well."
Gennets for germans sprung not from Othello,
And Ixion rides upon a single wheel.

Courage. Weren't strips of heart culture seen
Of late mating two periodicities?
Did not at one time even Darwin
Graft annual upon perennial trees?

AUTHOR'S NOTE. Dr. Johnson said it, somewhere in Boswell. Iago threatened Brabantio about gennets. Ixion rides on one wheel because he failed in an attempt at mixed marriage with Juno which would have produced demigods, two-wheeled because inheriting two life-periods.

PART OF MANDEVIL'S TRAVELS

*Chapter 87: "of the faith and beliefe of Prester John,
but he hath not all the full beliefe as we have."*

Done into verse, with comment.

"I feel half an Englishman already."
KING AMANULLAH *after firing off a torpedo.*

Mandevil's river of dry jewels grows
Day-cycled, deathly, and, iron-fruited trees;
From Paradise it runs to Pantarose
And with great waves into the gravely seas.

(Olympe, and Paradise Terrestre the same
Whence, bent to improve, King Alleluiah came.
High (Higher, in fact, as Milton boasted) hurled
Clings to the cold slates of the Roof of the World.)

Spears pierce its desert basin, the long dawn:
Tower, noon, all cliquant, dock-side cranes, sag-fruited:
And, sand-born weight, brief by waste sand upborne,
Leave, gulfed, ere night, the bare plain, deeper rooted.

(Herr Trinckler, there of late, reports of these,
A million acres of dead poplar trees.
Well may new pit-heads to wise A appeal;
Our desolation is of harder steel.)

Antred, of malachite, its boulders thunder:
Involve their cataracts, one known week-end:
Then, deep, a labyrinth of landslides, under
The gravely sea, and seen no more, descend.

(It is cracked mud the motor service dints;
Five clays, diluvian, covered some chipped flints.
Tour well the slag-heaps, royalty, we own
The arid sowing, the tumultuous stone.)

Fish of another fashion the dry sea
Ride: can blast through eddies and sail on:
Can rend the hunters whose nets drag the scree:
Are full good savour: are for Prester John.

(Paradise, like Bohemia, has no coast;
Of bombs and bowlers it has power to boast,
But mail-dark fish, spawned in grit-silted grotto,
Adam comes here for; and recites my motto.)

AUTHOR'S NOTE. *Gravely,* the spelling of the original, means "of gravel" but suggests graves. Milton said

on the snowy top
Of cold Olympus ruled the middle air,
Their highest heaven,

which doesn't fit; the boast was only that the Christian heaven was higher. The Roof of the World is, I believe, the Himalayas; the geography here is as dim as Mandevil's. "Spears (first shoots of the metal trees — of man's use of metal) poke up above ground in the basin of the river during the dawn; the same spears at noon tower like cranes, and before night are engulfed and leave the plain bare; they are upheld only by sand which goes deeper than their roots." I meant the motor service from Baghdad to Haifa, though that is far enough from where Herr Trinckler was. The *week-end* is copied from Mandevil. The *motto* is the King's remark at the beginning (as quoted in the papers).

DOCTRINAL POINT

The god approached dissolves into the air.

Magnolias, for instance, when in bud
Are right in doing anything they can think of;
Free by predestination in the blood,
Saved by their own sap, shed for themselves,
Their texture can impose their architecture;
Their sapient matter is always already informed.

Whether they burgeon, massed wax flames, or flare
Plump spaced-out saints, in their gross prime, at prayer,
Or leave the sooted branches bare
To sag at tip from a sole blossom there
They know no act that will not make them fair.

Professor Eddington with the same insolence
Called all physics one tautology;
If you describe things with the right tensors

All law becomes the fact that they can be described with them;
This is the Assumption of the description.
The duality of choice becomes the singularity of existence;
The effort of virtue the unconsciousness of foreknowledge.

That over-all that Solomon should wear
Gives these no cope who cannot know of care.
They have no gap to spare that they should share
The rare calyx we stare at in despair.
They have no other that they should compare.
Their arch of promise the wide Heaviside layer
They rise above a vault into the air.

NOTE ON LOCAL FLORA

There is a tree native in Turkestan,
Or further east towards the Tree of Heaven,
Whose hard cold cones, not being wards to time,
Will leave their mother only for good cause;
Will ripen only in a forest fire;
Wait, to be fathered as was Bacchus once,
Through men's long lives, that image of time's end.
I knew the Phoenix was a vegetable.
So Semele desired her deity
As this in Kew thirsts for the Red Dawn.

AUTHOR'S NOTE. *That image:* the forest fire is like the final burning of the
world.

HIGH DIVE

A cry, a greenish hollow undulation
Echoes slapping across the enclosed bathing pool.
It is irrotational; one potential function
(Hollow, the cry of hounds) will give the rule.

Holding it then, I Sanctus brood thereover,
Inform *in posse* the tank's triple infinite
(So handy for co-ordinates), chauffeur
The girded sky, and need not dive in it;

Stand, wolf-chased Phoebus, ∅ infinite-reined,
Aton of maggots of reflected girder
(Steeds that on Jonah a grim start have gained)
And need not keep the moment, nor yet murder.

Crashing and gay, musical and shocking,
They (green for hares) however, tear me down,
Rut or retract, by gulfs or rocks. Menacing,
Assuring, their tin reverberant town

"Thicker than water" (cleaned out before solid)
Agglutinate, whose wounds raw air composes,
Shall clot (already has forewarned with olive
These doves undriven that coo, Ark neuroses)

Unless, in act, to turbulence, discerning
His shade, not image, on smashed glass disbanded,
One, curve and pause, conscious of strain of turning
Only (muscle on bone, the rein cone now handed)

Unchart the second, the obstetric, chooses,
Leaves isle equation by not frozen ford,
And, to break scent, under foamed new phusis
Dives to receive in memory reward.

Fall to them, Lucifer, Sun's Son. Splash high
Jezebel. Throw her down. They feast, I flee
Her poised tired head and eye
Whose skull pike-high mirrors and waits for me.

Leave outer concrete for the termite city,
Where scab to bullet and strong brick has grown;
Plunge, and in vortex that destroys it, puppy,
Drink deep the imaged solid of the bone.

AUTHOR'S NOTE. You can give a single mathematical expression for all the movements of the water (so contemplate it all in one act, like God) but this may become impossible either through its getting more movement or less, from its becoming solid or from the splash and eddy made by the diver. These are compared to the two ways down from the diving-board, solid and airy, one of which the man must take; hence to the idea that one must go from the godlike state of contemplation even when attained either into action which cannot wholly foresee its consequences or into a fixed condition, due to fear, which does not give real knowledge and leads to neurosis. A wolf tried to eat the sun in Northern mythology during eclipses. ϕ is a general name for this potential function, Aton the heretical Egyptian sun-god with hands at the ends of its rays; both are connected with the horse-chariot of the classical sun-god. The maggots are the rippling reflections that show the movement of the water and suggest cantering horses. Hare-hunters wore green coats. *Thicker than water* as blood is in the proverb, I am using F. M. Cornford's theory that the order behind the "physical" world was originally thought of as the life-blood of the tribe, so that it changes when that does (there is a fear of society in the feeling that you must take the dive once you have gone up). That is why the water of the tank, taken in contemplation as the universe, is called phusis and agglutinate and liable to clog. A termite city actually uses dung for its concrete, but a scab suggests creatures shapeless if you remove their shells. The puppy was carrying a bone over a bridge, and dived after the reflection and lost the bone.

Dylan Thomas
1914-1953

"Even in religious fervor," said Whitman in his *Notebooks*, "there is always a touch of animal heat." Both religious fervor and animal heat were in the poetry of Dylan Thomas, to a high degree. His poetry was the "pure fire compressed into holy forms" of which one of Porphyry's Oracles spoke.

His was a language "fanned by the breath of Nature, which leaps overhead, cares mostly for impetus and effects, and for what it plants and invigorates to grow." (Whitman, *Notebooks*.) He strips from words their old, used, dulled sleepiness, and gives them a refreshed and awakened meaning, a new percussion.

His voice resembles no other voice; the spirit is that of the beginning of created things: there is here no case of a separate imagination, of invention. From the depths of Being, from the roots of the world, a voice speaks.

Boehme said, "The sap in the tree denoteth pure Deity." So it was with Dylan Thomas. He loved and praised "The force that through the green fuse drives the flower" and the

> animals thick as thieves
> On God's rough tumbling ground.

(He saw the world as God's rough tumbling ground, as a ground for joy and the holy wars of the Spirit.)

With him, all is prayer and praise. Poetry to him is prayer. "When we pray," said the Curé d'Ars, "we should open our heart to God, like a fish when it sees the wave coming." "I am so placed and submerged in his great love, that I seem as though in the sea entirely under water, and can on no side touch, see, or feel anything but water." So said Saint Catherine of Genoa. And so might have said Dylan Thomas.

His earliest poems are of great strangeness. From the obscure beauty of those early poems, he went to the miraculous concentration of such lines as "A grief ago" and to the poignance of "In the white giant's thigh."

In William James' *Principles of Psychology* he quotes Condillac as saying that "the first time we see light, we are it rather than see it." In my *Poet's Notebook* I have a quotation about a painter who paints a tree, becoming a tree. This condensation of essence, this power of "becoming a tree" is one of the powers that make Dylan Thomas a great poet. His poems, at first sight, may appear strange. But if we heard a tree speak to us in its own voice, would not that voice seem strange? His is always the voice of Nature. In the exquisite exactness of the lines —

> my ruffled ring dove . . .
> Coo rooing the woods' praise,
> Who moons her blue notes from her nest
> Down to the curlew herd . . .

— you see the misty softness of the sweet dove's feathers, you hear the misty softness of her cooing.

Though he felt, I think, and perhaps dreaded the conquering hand of Time, and knew that he must die young, he defied, always, death and the world's dust:

> A cock-on-a-dunghill
> Crowing to Lazarus the morning is vanity
> Dust be your saviour under the conjured soil.

His pity for the outcast, his love for those who have received no mercy from life, are great:

> I see the tigron in tears
> In the androgynous dark,
> His striped and noon maned tribe striding to holocaust,
> The she mules bear their minotaurs.

In that great poem *A Refusal to Mourn the Death, by Fire, of a Child in London,* with its dark, magnificent, proud movement, we see Death in its reality — as a return to the beginning of things, as a robing, a sacred investiture in those who have been our friends since the beginning of Time.

Bird, beast, and flower have their part in the making of mankind.
The water drop is holy, the wheat ear a place of prayer. The "fathering
and all-humbling darkness" itself is a begetting force. Even grief, even
tears, are a begetting. "The stations of the breath" are the stations of
the Cross.

WHY EAST WIND CHILLS

Why east wind chills and south wind cools
Shall not be known till windwell dries
And west's no longer drowned
In winds that bring the fruit and rind
Of many a hundred falls;
Why silk is soft and the stone wounds
The child shall question all his days,
Why night-time rain and the breast's blood
Both quench his thirst he'll have a black reply.

When cometh Jack Frost? the children ask.
Shall they clasp a comet in their fists?
Not till, from high and low, their dust
Sprinkles in children's eyes a long-last sleep
And dusk is crowded with the children's ghosts,
Shall a white answer echo from the rooftops.

All things are known: the stars' advice
Calls some content to travel with the winds,
Though what the stars ask as they round
Time upon time the towers of the skies
Is heard but little till the stars go out.
I hear content, and "Be content"
Ring like a handbell through the corridors,
And "Know no answer," and I know
No answer to the children's cry
Of echo's answer and the man of frost
And ghastly comets over the raised fists.

A GRIEF AGO

A grief ago,
She who was who I hold, the fats and flower,
Or, water-lammed, from the scythe-sided thorn,
Hell wind and sea,

A stem cementing, wrestled up the tower,
Rose maid and male,
Or, masted venus, through the paddler's bowl
Sailed up the sun;

Who is my grief,
A chrysalis unwrinkling on the iron,
Wrenched by my fingerman, the leaden bud
Shot through the leaf,
Was who was folded on the rod the aaron
Rose cast to plague,
The horn and ball of water on the frog
Housed in the side.

And she who lies,
Like exodus a chapter from the garden,
Brand of the lily's anger on her ring,
Tugged through the days
Her ropes of heritage, the wars of pardon,
On field and sand
The twelve triangles of the cherub wind
Engraving going.

Who then is she,
She holding me? The people's sea drives on her,
Drives out the father from the caesared camp;
The dens of shape
Shape all her whelps with the long voice of water,
That she I have,
The country-handed grave boxed into love,
Rise before dark.

The night is near,
A nitric shape that leaps her, time and acid;
I tell her this: before the suncock cast
Her bone to fire,
Let her inhale her dead, through seed and solid
Draw in their seas,
So cross her hand with their grave gipsy eyes,
And close her fist.

A REFUSAL TO MOURN THE DEATH, BY FIRE, OF A CHILD IN LONDON

Never until the mankind making
Bird beast and flower
Fathering and all humbling darkness
Tells with silence the last light breaking
And the still hour
Is come of the sea tumbling in harness

And I must enter again the round
Zion of the water bead
And the synagogue of the ear of corn
Shall I let pray the shadow of a sound
Or sow my salt seed
In the least valley of sackcloth to mourn

The majesty and burning of the child's death.
I shall not murder
The mankind of her going with a grave truth
Nor blaspheme down the stations of the breath
With any further
Elegy of innocence and youth.

Deep with the first dead lies London's daughter,
Robed in the long friends,
The grains beyond age, the dark veins of her mother,
Secret by the unmourning water
Of the riding Thames.
After the first death, there is no other.

A WINTER'S TALE

It is a winter's tale
That the snow blind twilight ferries over the lakes
And floating fields from the farm in the cup of the vales,
Gliding windless through the hand folded flakes,
The pale breath of cattle at the stealthy sail,

And the stars falling cold,
And the smell of hay in the snow, and the far owl
Warning among the folds, and the frozen hold
Flocked with the sheep white smoke of the farm house cowl
In the river wended vales where the tale was told.

Once when the world turned old
On a star of faith pure as the drifting bread,
As the food and flames of the snow, a man unrolled
The scrolls of fire that burned in his heart and head,
Torn and alone in a farm house in a fold

Of fields. And burning then
In his firelit island ringed by the winged snow
And the dung hills white as wool and the hen
Roosts sleeping chill till the flame of the cock crow
Combs through the mantled yards and the morning men

Stumble out with their spades,
The cattle stirring, the mousing cat stepping shy,
The puffed birds hopping and hunting, the milkmaids
Gentle in their clogs over the fallen sky,
And all the woken farm at its white trades,

He knelt, he wept, he prayed,
By the spit and the black pot in the log bright light
And the cup and the cut bread in the dancing shade,
In the muffled house, in the quick of night,
At the point of love, forsaken and afraid.

He knelt on the cold stones,
He wept from the crest of grief, he prayed to the veiled sky
May his hunger go howling on bare white bones
Past the statues of the stables and the sky roofed sties
And the duck pond glass and the blinding byres alone

Into the home of prayers
And fires where he should prowl down the cloud
Of his snow blind love and rush in the white lairs.
His naked need struck him howling and bowed
Though no sound flowed down the hand folded air

But only the wind strung
Hunger of birds in the fields of the bread of water, tossed
In high corn and the harvest melting on their tongues.
And his nameless need bound him burning and lost
When cold as snow he should run the wended vales among

The rivers mouthed in night,
And drown in the drifts of his need, and lie curled caught
In the always desiring centre of the white
Inhuman cradle and the bride bed forever sought
By the believer lost and the hurled outcast of light.

Deliver him, he cried,
By losing him all in love, and cast his need
Alone and naked in the engulfing bride,
Never to flourish in the fields of the white seed
Or flower under the time dying flesh astride.

Listen. The minstrels sing
In the departed villages. The nightingale,
Dust in the buried wood, flies on the grains of her wings
And spells on the winds of the dead his winter's tale.
The voice of the dust of water from the withered spring

Is telling. The wizened
Stream with bells and baying water bounds. The dew rings
On the gristed leaves and the long gone glistening
Parish of snow. The carved mouths in the rock are wind swept strings.
Time sings through the intricately dead snow drop. Listen.

It was a hand or sound
In the long ago land that glided the dark door wide
And there outside on the bread of the ground
A she bird rose and rayed like a burning bride.
A she bird dawned, and her breast with snow and scarlet downed.

Look. And the dancers move
On the departed, snow bushed green, wanton in moon light
As a dust of pigeons. Exulting, the grave hooved
Horses, centaur dead, turn and tread the drenched white
Paddocks in the farms of birds. The dead oak walks for love.

The carved limbs in the rock
Leap, as to trumpets. Calligraphy of the old
Leaves is dancing. Lines of age on the stones weave in a flock.
And the harp shaped voice of the water's dust plucks in a fold
Of fields. For love, the long ago she bird rises. Look.

And the wild wings were raised
Above her folded head, and the soft feathered voice
Was flying through the house as though the she bird praised
And all the elements of the slow fall rejoiced
That a man knelt alone in the cup of the vales,

In the mantle and calm,
By the spit and the black pot in the log bright light.
And the sky of birds in the plumed voice charmed
Him up and he ran like a wind after the kindling flight
Past the blind barns and byres of the windless farm.

In the poles of the year
When black birds died like priests in the cloaked hedge row
And over the cloth of counties the far hills rode near,
Under the one leaved trees ran a scarecrow of snow
And fast through the drifts of the thickets antlered like deer,

    Rags and prayers down the knee-
Deep hillocks and loud on the numbed lakes,
All night lost and long wading in the wake of the she-
Bird through the times and lands and tribes of the slow flakes.
Listen and look where she sails the goose plucked sea,

    The sky, the bird, the bride,
The cloud, the need, the planted stars, the joy beyond
The fields of seed and the time dying flesh astride,
The heavens, the heaven, the grave, the burning font.
In the far ago land the door of his death glided wide,

    And the bird descended.
On a bread white hill over the cupped farm
And the lakes and floating fields and the river wended
Vales where he prayed to come to the last harm
And the home of prayers and fires, the tale ended.

    The dancing perishes
On the white, no longer growing green, and, minstrel dead,
The singing breaks in the snow shoed villages of wishes
That once cut the figures of birds on the deep bread
And over the glazed lakes skated the shapes of fishes

    Flying. The rite is shorn
Of nightingale and centaur dead horse. The springs wither
Back. Lines of age sleep on the stones till trumpeting dawn.
Exultation lies down. Time buries the spring weather
That belled and bounded with the fossil and the dew reborn.

    For the bird lay bedded
In a choir of wings, as though she slept or died,
And the wings glided wide and he was hymned and wedded,
And through the thighs of the engulfing bride,
The woman breasted and the heaven headed

    Bird, he was brought low,
Burning in the bride bed of love, in the whirl-
Pool at the wanting centre, in the folds
Of paradise, in the spun bud of the world.
And she rose with him flowering in her melting snow.

FERN HILL

Now as I was young and easy under the apple boughs
About the lilting house and happy as the grass was green,
   The night above the dingle starry,
     Time let me hail and climb
     Golden in the heydays of his eyes,
And honoured among wagons I was prince of the apple towns
And once below a time I lordly had the trees and leaves
     Trail with daisies and barley
   Down the rivers of the windfall light.

And as I was green and carefree, famous among the barns
About the happy yard and singing as the farm was home,
   In the sun that is young once only,
     Time let me play and be
     Golden in the mercy of his means,
And green and golden I was huntsman and herdsman, the calves
Sang to my horn, the foxes on the hills barked clear and cold,
     And the sabbath rang slowly
   In the pebbles of the holy streams.

All the sun long it was running, it was lovely, the hay
Fields high as the house, the tunes from the chimneys, it was air
   And playing, lovely and watery
     And fire green as grass.
   And nightly under the simple stars
As I rode to sleep the owls were bearing the farm away,
All the moon long I heard, blessed among stables, the night-jars
     Flying with the ricks, and the horses
     Flashing into the dark.

And then to awake, and the farm, like a wanderer white
With the dew, come back, the cock on his shoulder: it was all
   Shining, it was Adam and maiden,
     The sky gathered again
     And the sun grew round that very day.
So it must have been after the birth of the simple light
In the first, spinning place, the spellbound horses walking warm
   Out of the whinnying green stable
     On to the fields of praise.

And honoured among foxes and pheasants by the gay house
Under the new made clouds and happy as the heart was long,
   In the sun born over and over,
     I ran my heedless ways,

My wishes raced through the house high hay
And nothing I cared, at my sky blue trades, that time allows
In all his tuneful turning so few and such morning songs
   Before the children green and golden
      Follow him out of grace,

Nothing I cared, in the lamb white days, that time would take me
Up to the swallow thronged loft by the shadow of my hand,
   In the moon that is always rising,
     Nor that riding to sleep
   I should hear him fly with the high fields
And wake to the farm forever fled from the childless land.
Oh as I was young and easy in the mercy of his means,
     Time held me green and dying
    Though I sang in my chains like the sea.

IN THE WHITE GIANT'S THIGH

Through throats where many rivers meet, the curlews cry,
Under the conceiving moon, on the high chalk hill,
And there this night I walk in the white giant's thigh
Where barren as boulders women lie longing still

To labour and love though they lay down long ago.

Through throats where many rivers meet, the women pray,
Pleading in the waded bay for the seed to flow
Though the names on their weed grown stones are rained away,

And alone in the night's eternal, curving act
They yearn with tongues of curlews for the unconceived
And immemorial sons of the cudgelling, hacked

Hill. Who once in gooseskin winter loved all ice leaved
In the courters' lanes, or twined in the ox roasting sun
In the wains tonned so high that the wisps of the hay
Clung to the pitching clouds, or gay with any one
Young as they in the after milking moonlight lay

Under the lighted shapes of faith and their moonshade
Petticoats galed high, or shy with the rough riding boys,
Now clasp me to their grains in the gigantic glade,

Who once, green countries since, were a hedgerow of joys.
Time by, their dust was flesh the swineherd rooted sly,
Flared in the reek of the wiving sty with the rush

Light of his thighs, spreadeagle to the dunghill sky,
Or with their orchard man in the core of the sun's bush
Rough as cows' tongues and thrashed with brambles their buttermilk
Manes, under his quenchless summer barbed gold to the bone,

Or rippling soft in the spinney moon as the silk
And ducked and draked white lake that harps to a hail stone.

Who once were a bloom of wayside brides in the hawed house
And heard the lewd, wooed field flow to the coming frost,
The scurrying, furred small friars squeal, in the dowse
Of day, in the thistle aisles, till the white owl crossed

Their breast, the vaulting does roister, the horned bucks climb
Quick in the wood at love, where a torch of foxes foams,
All birds and beasts of the linked night uproar and chime

And the mole snout blunt under his pilgrimage of domes,
Or, butter fat goosegirls, bounced in a gambo bed,
Their breasts full of honey, under their gander king
Trounced by his wings in the hissing shippen, long dead
And gone that barley dark where the clogs danced in the spring,
And their firefly hairpins flew, and the ricks ran round —

(But nothing bore, no mouthing babe to the veined hives
Hugged, and barren and bare on Mother Goose's ground
They with the simple Jacks were a boulder of wives) —

Now curlew cry me down to kiss the mouths of their dust.

The dust of their kettles and clocks swings to and fro
Where the hay rides now or the bracken kitchens rust
As the arc of the billhooks that flashed the hedges low
And cut the birds' boughs that the minstrel sap ran red.
They from houses where the harvest kneels, hold me hard,
Who heard the tall bell sail down the Sundays of the dead
And the rain wring out its tongues on the faded yard,
Teach me the love that is evergreen after the fall leaved
Grave, after Belovéd on the grass gulfed cross is scrubbed
Off by the sun and Daughters no longer grieved
Save by their long desires in the fox cubbed
Streets or hungering in the crumbled wood: to these
Hale dead and deathless do the women of the hill
Love for ever meridian through the courters' trees

And the daughters of darkness flame like Fawkes fires still.

Ezra Pound

b. 1885

Ezra Pound is one of the greatest living poets.

The *Cantos* included in this book are of the highest interest technically, as well as because of the great beauty of their imagery. Let us take this passage, from *Canto II:*

> And poor old Homer blind, blind, as a bat,
> Ear, ear for the sea-surge, murmur of old men's voices:
> "Let her go back to the ships,
> Back among Grecian faces, lest evil come on our own,
> Evil and further evil, and a curse cursed on our children,
> Moves, yes she moves like a goddess
> And has the face of a god
>   and the voice of Schoeney's daughters,
> And doom goes with her in walking,
> Let her go back to the ships,
>   Back among Grecian voices."

In the sound, in the echo of the second one-syllabled word "sea-surge," of "murmur of old men's voices," we are given an evocation of the fact that the sea-surge is immemorially old, has an immemorable wisdom echoing through time. The "sea-surge" and the "murmur of old men's voices" are then separate entities, but they have come together, and are one, or at least are scarcely separate in the ear of age and wisdom. The whole passage has the movement, the majestic sound of waves breaking in all their different splendor: "And doom goes with her in walking."

In that great line we have the whole sound, gathered throughout the ages, of the sea.

Part of the magic conveying the sound of the sea is obtained by the echoes which come from time to time; the sound of "surge," for instance, is echoed, three lines further on, by the less long sound of "curse," repeated twice, like the sound of a wave gathering itself and spreading outwards: "Evil and further evil, and a curse cursed on our children"; and the sound of "moves" in the line "Moves, yes she moves like a goddess" has, after the interval of two lines, the far deeper echo of "doom," a sound which contains all the hollowness and reverberation of the sea-depths. There is an echo, too, at the end of the lines:

> and the voice of Schoeney's *daughters,*
> And doom goes with her in *walking.*

The whole sound is that of the sea, with all the sea's depth.

The first two *Cantos* are a magnificent achievement. The wide stretch of the sea, the scarcely perceptible movement of the ripples, the clear sea airs, are all conveyed by means of the fluctuating lengths of the opening lines of the first *Canto,* and by the shifting of the first accent from the first syllable to the second syllable of the line; and by the fact also that the second line is only part of a phrase and is therefore part of a terrific sweeping movement, with a pause wherein the wind gathers.

The first *Canto*'s first line finds us sailing over a sea . . . and if there is a more terrific sweeping onward of movement (that is yet perfectly smooth) to be found in all English poetry, I have yet to find it.

A small wave comes in the middle of the sixth line, with the faint stresses, placed in immediate juxtaposition, of "out onward," breaks beneath the ship, and the ship sweeps on again.

Both these opening *Cantos* have the most strangely accurate, sharp, acutely observed visual impressions, like the portrait of the seal in the second *Canto.*

The movement of the ship seems to grow faster, in the second *Canto,* with the shortening of the lines, and with the tight effect of the one-syllabled ending of some of the lines, followed by the strong accent on the first syllable of the next line, alternating with the loosening caused by certain feminine endings:

> Ship stock fast in sea-swirl
> Ivy upon the oars, King Pentheus,
> > grapes with no seed but sea-foam,
> Ivy in scupper-hole.

Indeed, the whole of these two *Cantos* may be said to be a miracle of the transfusion of sense into sound; or rather, of the fusion of the two.

In the first part of the second *Canto,* the first accent of the lines shifts its place perpetually, though the movement is not elaborately contrapuntal.

The reason for the more embodied and hard-outlined movement, for its condensation, may be found in the lines:

> void air taking pelt.
> Lifeless air become sinewed.

In this miraculous poetry Pound, by some enchantment, fuses the sense of the beasts with the sense of the oncoming tempest.

The rhythms have an extraordinary variety, a lovely flexibility and inevitability that is sometimes like the "feline leisure of panthers," or like the fluctuating, flowing, waving sound of the airs coming from some immortal sea. The echoes indeed, and the sounds that originate them, vary, as do the sounds and echoes in certain of Milton's songs, from sea air to sea air, from wave to wave, as the beauty of the line lengthens and then runs back again.

At the end of the second *Canto* we have an example of this consummate power of variation. For after the plunging forward of the ship, after the embodying of the beasts, beasts with fur as thick and dark as clouds, with movements like sinewed lightning, in an air "without tempest," we have this sudden dew-laden peace that is not the result of association alone, but also of the lengthening of the line, the scarcely perceptible beat of the accents, and of what is practically an absence of caesura:

> And we have heard the fauns chiding Proteus
> in the smell of hay under the olive-trees,
> And the frogs singing against the fauns
> in the half-light.
> And . . .

Amid the sad darkness of the mind shown in many of the *Cantos* not included here, the splendor of the passage quoted is amongst the most wonderful poetry that has been written in our time.

CANTO I

> And then went down to the ship,
> Set keel to breakers, forth on the godly sea, and
> We set up mast and sail on that swart ship,
> Bore sheep aboard her, and our bodies also
> Heavy with weeping, and winds from sternward
> Bore us out onward with bellying canvas,
> Circe's this craft, the trim-coifed goddess.
> Then sat we amidships, wind jamming the tiller,
> Thus with stretched sail, we went over sea till day's end.
> Sun to his slumber, shadows o'er all the ocean,
> Came we then to the bounds of deepest water,
> To the Kimmerian lands, and peopled cities
> Covered with close-webbed mist, unpierced ever
> With glitter of sun-rays
> Nor with stars stretched, nor looking back from heaven
> Swartest night stretched over wretched men there.
> The ocean flowing backward, came we then to the place
> Aforesaid by Circe.
> Here did they rites, Perimedes and Eurylochus,
> And drawing sword from my hip
> I dug the ell-square pitkin;
> Poured we libations unto each the dead,
> First mead and then sweet wine, water mixed with white flour.
> Then prayed I many a prayer to the sickly death's-heads;

As set in Ithaca, sterile bulls of the best
For sacrifice, heaping the pyre with goods,
A sheep to Tiresias only, black and a bell-sheep.
Dark blood flowed in the fosse,
Souls out of Erebus, cadaverous dead, of brides,
Of youths and of the old who had borne much;
Souls stained with recent tears, girls tender,
Men many, mauled with bronze lance heads,
Battle spoil, bearing yet dreory arms,
These many crowded about me; with shouting,
Pallor upon me, cried to my men for more beasts;
Slaughtered the herds, sheep slain of bronze;
Poured ointment, cried to the gods,
To Pluto the strong, and praised Proserpine;
Unsheathed the narrow sword,
I sat to keep off the impetuous impotent dead,
Till I should hear Tiresias.
But first Elpenor came, our friend Elpenor,
Unburied, cast on the wide earth,
Limbs that we left in the house of Circe,
Unwept, unwrapped in sepulchre, since toils urged other.
Pitiful spirit. And I cried in hurried speech:
"Elpenor, how art thou come to this dark coast?
Cam'st thou afoot, outstripping seamen?"
　　　　　And he in heavy speech:
"Ill fate and abundant wine. I slept in Circe's ingle.
Going down the long ladder unguarded,
I fell against the buttress,
Shattered the nape-nerve, the soul sought Avernus.
But thou, O King, I bid remember me, unwept, unburied,
Heap up mine arms, be tomb by sea-bord, and inscribed:
A man of no fortune, and with a name to come.
And set my oar up, that I swung mid fellows."

And Anticlea came, whom I beat off, and then Tiresias Theban,
Holding his golden wand, knew me, and spoke first:
"A second time? why? man of ill star,
Facing the sunless dead and this joyless region?
Stand from the fosse, leave me my bloody bever
For soothsay."
　　　　　And I stepped back,
And he strong with the blood, said then: "Odysseus
Shalt return through spiteful Neptune, over dark seas,
Lose all companions." And then Anticlea came.
Lie quiet Divus. I mean, that is Andreas Divus,
In officina Wecheli, 1538, out of Homer.

And he sailed, by Sirens and thence outward and away
And unto Circe.
   Venerandam,
In the Cretan's phrase, with the golden crown, Aphrodite,
Cypri munimenta sortita est, mirthful, oricalchi, with golden
Girdles and breast bands, thou with dark eyelids
Bearing the golden bough of Argicida. So that:

CANTO II

Hang it all, Robert Browning,
   there can but be the one "Sordello."
But Sordello, and my Sordello?
Lo Sordels si fo di Mantovana.
So-shu churned in the sea.
Seal sports in the spray-whited circles of cliff-wash,
Sleek head, daughter of Lir,
   eyes of Picasso
Under black fur-hood, lithe daughter of Ocean;
And the wave runs in the beach-groove:
"Eleanor ἑλέναυς and ἑλέπτολις!"
   And poor old Homer blind, blind, as a bat,
Ear, ear for the sea-surge, murmur of old men's voices:
"Let her go back to the ships,
Back among Grecian faces, lest evil come on our own,
Evil and further evil, and a curse cursed on our children,
Moves, yes she moves like a goddess
And has the face of a god
   and the voice of Schoeney's daughters,
And doom goes with her in walking,
Let her go back to the ships,
   back among Grecian voices."
And by the beach-run, Tyro,
   Twisted arms of the sea-god,
Lithe sinews of water, gripping her, cross-hold,
And the blue-gray glass of the wave tents them,
Glare azure of water, cold-welter, close cover.
Quiet sun-tawny sand-stretch,
The gulls broad out their wings,
   nipping between the splay feathers;
Snipe come for their bath,
   bend out their wing-joints,
Spread wet wings to the sun-film,
And by Scios,
   to left of the Naxos passage,

Naviform rock overgrown,
        algæ cling to its edge,
There is a wine-red glow in the shallows,
        a tin flash in the sun-dazzle.

The ship landed in Scios,
        men wanting spring-water,
And by the rock-pool a young boy loggy with vine-must,
        "To Naxos? Yes, we'll take you to Naxos,
Cum' along lad." "Not that way!"
"Aye, that way is Naxos."
        And I said: "It's a straight ship."
And an ex-convict out of Italy
        Knocked me into the fore-stays,
(He was wanted for manslaughter in Tuscany)
        And the whole twenty against me,
Mad for a little slave money.
        And they took her out of Scios
And off her course . . .
        And the boy came to, again, with the racket,
And looked out over the bows,
        and to eastward, and to the Naxos passage.
God-sleight then, god-sleight:
        Ship stock fast in sea-swirl,
Ivy upon the oars, King Pentheus,
        grapes with no seed but sea-foam,
Ivy in scupper-hole.
Aye, I, Accœtes, stood there,
        and the god stood by me,
Water cutting under the keel,
Sea-break from stern forrards,
        wake running off from the bow,
And where was gunwale, there now was vine-trunk,
And tenthril where cordage had been,
        grape-leaves on the rowlocks,
Heavy vine on the oarshafts,
And, out of nothing, a breathing,
        hot breath on my ankles,
Beasts like shadows in glass,
        a furred tail upon nothingness.
Lynx-purr, and heathery smell of beasts,
        where tar smell had been,
Sniff and pad-foot of beasts,
        eye-glitter out of black air.
The sky overshot, dry, with no tempest,

Sniff and pad-foot of beasts,
        fur brushing my knee-skin,
Rustle of airy sheaths,
        dry forms in the *æther*
And the ship like a keel in ship-yard,
        slung like an ox in smith's sling,
Ribs stuck fast in the ways,
        grape-cluster over pin-rack,
        void air taking pelt.
Lifeless air become sinewed,
        feline leisure of panthers,
Leopards sniffing the grape shoots by scupper-hole,
Crouched panthers by fore-hatch,
And the sea blue-deep about us,
        green-ruddy in shadows,
And Lyæus: "From now, Acœtes, my altars,
Fearing no bondage,
        fearing no cat of the wood,
Safe with my lynxes,
        feeding grapes to my leopards,
Olibanum is my incense,
        the vines grow in my homage."
The back-swell now smooth in the rudder-chains,
Black snout of a porpoise
        where Lycabs had been,
Fish-scales on the oarsmen.
        And I worship.
I have seen what I have seen.
        When they brought the boy I said:
"He has a god in him,
        though I do not know which god."
And they kicked me into the fore-stays.
I have seen what I have seen:
        Medon's face like the face of a dory,
Arms shrunk into fins. And you, Pentheus,
Had as well listen to Tiresias, and to Cadmus,
        or your luck will go out of you.
Fish-scales over groin muscles,
        lynx-purr amid sea . . .
And of a later year,
        pale in the wine-red algæ,
If you will lean over the rock,
        the coral face under wave-tinge,
Rose-paleness under water-shift,
        Ileuthyeria, fair Dafne of sea-bords,

The swimmer's arms turned to branches,
Who will say in what year,
            fleeing what band of tritons,
The smooth brows, seen, and half seen,
            now ivory stillness.
And So-shu churned in the sea, So-shu also,
            using the long moon for a churn-stick . . .
Lithe turning of water,
            sinews of Poseidon,
Black azure and hyaline,
            glass wave over Tyro,
Close cover, unstillness,
            bright welter of wave-cords,
Then quiet water,
            quiet in the buff sands,
Sea-fowl stretching wing-joints,
            splashing in rock-hollows and sand-hollows
In the wave-runs by the half-dune;
Glass-glint of wave in the tide-rips against sunlight,
            pallor of Hesperus,
Grey peak of the wave,
            wave, colour of grape's pulp,

Olive grey in the near,
            far, smoke grey of the rock-slide,
Salmon-pink wings of the fish-hawk,
            cast grey shadows in water,
The tower like a one-eyed great goose
            cranes up out of the olive-grove,

And we have heard the fauns chiding Proteus
            in the smell of hay under the olive-trees,
And the frogs singing against the fauns
            in the half-light.
And . . .

From CANTO LXXIX (THE PISAN CANTOS)

            O Lynx, wake Silenus and Casey
            shake the castagnettes of the bassarids,

the mountain forest is full of light
            the tree-comb red-gilded
Who sleeps in the field of lynxes
            in the orchard of Maelids?

(with great blue marble eyes
        "because he likes to," the cossack)
Salazar, Scott, Dawley on sick call
        Polk, Tyler, half the presidents and Calhoun
"Retaliate on the capitalists" sd/ Calhoun "of the North"
ah yes, when the ideas were clearer
        debts to people in N.Y. city
        and on the hill of the Maelids
in the close garden of Venus
        asleep amid serried lynxes
set wreaths on Priapus Ἴακχος, Io! Κύθηρα, Io!
        having root in the equities
Io!
        and you can make 5000 dollars a year
all you have to do is to make one trip up country
then come back to Shanghai
        and send in an annual report
as to the number of converts
        Sweetland on sick call
        ἐλέησον   Kyrie eleison
    each under his fig tree
        or with the smell of fig leaves burning
so shd/ be fire in winter
with fig wood, with cedar, and pine burrs

        O Lynx keep watch on my fire.

So Astafieva had conserved the tradition
From Byzance and before then
        Manitou remember this fire
O lynx, keep the phylloxera from my grape vines
Ἴακχε, Ἴακχε, Χαῖρε, AOI
        "Eat it not in the under world"
        See that the sun or the moon bless thy eating
κόρη κόρη, for the six seeds of an error
or that the stars bless thy eating

        O Lynx, guard this orchard,
        Keep from Demeter's furrow

This fruit has a fire within it,
        Pomona, Pomona
No glass is clearer than are the globes of this flame
What sea is clearer than the pomegranate body
        holding the flame?
        Pomona, Pomona,

        Lynx keep watch on this orchard
        That is named Melagrana
or the Pomegranate field
        The sea is not clearer in azure
        Nor the Heliads bringing light

        Here are lynxes   Here are lynxes,
        Is there a sound in the forest
                   of pard or of bassarid
        or crotale   or of leaves moving?

           Cythera, here are lynxes
Will the scrub-oak burst into flower?
        There is a rose vine in this underbrush
Red? white? No, but a colour between them
    When the pomegranate is open and the light falls
half through it

        Lynx, beware of these vine-thorns
        O Lynx, γλαυκῶπις coming up from the olive yards,
        Kuthera, here are Lynxes and the clicking of crotales
There is a stir of dust from old leaves
        Will you trade roses for acorns
        Will lynxes eat thorn leaves?
        What have you in that wine jar — ?
        ἰχώρ, for lynxes?

Maelid and bassarid among lynxes;
      how many? There are more under the oak trees,
We are here waiting the sun-rise
    and the next sunrise
for three nights amid lynxes. For three nights
    of the oak-wood
And the vines are thick in their branches
    no vine lacking flower,
No lynx lacking a flower rope
    no Maelid minus a wine jar
this forest is named Melagrana

           O lynx keep the edge on my cider
           Keep it clear without cloud

We have lain here amid kalicanthus and sword-flower
    The heliads are caught in wild rose vine
The smell of pine mingles with rose leaves
        O lynx, be many

of spotted fur and sharp ears.
O lynx, have your eyes gone yellow,
with spotted fur and sharp ears?

Therein is the dance of the bassarids
Therein are centaurs
And now Priapus with Faunus
The Graces have brought Ἀφροδίτην
Her cell is drawn by ten leopards
O lynx, guard my vineyard
As the grape swells under vine leaf
Ἥλιος is come to our mountain
there is a red glow in the carpet of pine spikes

O lynx, guard my vineyard
As the grape swells under vine leaf
This Goddess was born of sea-foam
She is lighter than air under Hesperus
δεινὰ, εἶ Κύθηρα
terrible in resistance
κόρη καὶ Δήλια καὶ Μαῖα
trine as praeludio
Κύπρις Ἀφρόδιτη
A petal lighter than sea-foam
Κύθηρα
aram
nemus
vult
O puma, sacred to Hermes, Cimbica servant of Helios.

T. S. Eliot

b. 1888

The later poems of T. S. Eliot, from *The Waste Land* onwards — at least the longer poems — have been discussed by so many commentators, and at such length, that I prefer, in writing of him, to speak of the technical genius that is evident, also, in the shorter poems (not included in this book, but known to all readers of poetry). His technical genius was not formed gradually, but sprang fully grown, like Minerva from the head of Jove.

We find it in such early poems as *Burbank with a Baedeker, Bleistein with a Cigar:*

A lustreless protrusive eye
Stares from the protozoic slime
At a perspective of Canaletto.
The smoky candle-end of time

Declines . . .

In these lines the impression of slime is given by the many slowing,
dulling *s*'s and the *z* in the first two lines, and by the crawling movement
of these. "At a perspective of Canaletto" has the guttering movement of
a candle that will soon die.

At moments, in the early poems, we find an appalling and terrifying
laughter, apt, at times, to change to that we may know where:

> breastless creatures under ground
> Leaned backwards with a lipless grin.

This laughter is heard in all the poems of this period, excepting in
Gerontion, and sometimes it masquerades as human amusement.

In *Sweeney Erect,* however, we have the "lipless grin" alone, and a
sound as of some laughter heard in Hell. This hellish horror, this echo
of laughter, is heard even in the title *Sweeney Erect,* with its black
shadow:

> Gesture of orang-outang
> Rises from the sheets of steam.

In the companion poem to this, amidst the spiritual and physical horror of the company, where man is part braying beast, part worm, part
ape, or where man is but the worm turned vertebrate —

> Apeneck Sweeney spreads his knees
> Letting his arms hang down to laugh,
> The zebra stripes along his jaw
> Swelling to maculate giraffe —

in the midst of Hell, we find this despairing beauty:

> The host with someone indistinct
> Converses at the door apart,
> The nightingales are singing near
> The Convent of the Sacred Heart,
>
> And sang within the bloody wood
> When Agamemnon cried aloud,
> And let their liquid siftings fall
> To stain the stiff dishonoured shroud.

We may remark on the inspiration of genius that in the lines:

> Apeneck Sweeney spreads his knees
> Letting his arms hang down to laugh . . .

uses, in the first line, minute sharp pin-points of vowels — like the beginning of a pin-point of brain — and, in the next line, produces a gross sagging sensuality by the contrasted dark heavy vowels.

We meet Sweeney again, after a century of material experience, compressed into the mechanism of thirteen years or so, in *Sweeney Agonistes.* But here he and his passive complements have lost the flapping laziness which characterized *Sweeney Erect* and *Sweeney among the Nightingales;* they seethe forward into an unknown future with a boneless movement, interweaving like worms intertwining. This movement continues throughout twenty pages, stopping only once, never hesitating otherwise excepting to change its gear from mood to mood, and even then never raising or lowering itself. The speed, the boneless movement merely seethe sideways or backwards.

The rhythms seem to be ordinary speech rhythms, but the seething intertwining movements give them a world of significance which no ordinary speech rhythms would hold. Eliot has, indeed, done with a terrifying perfection exactly what some of the younger members of the new schools of poetry have tried, and failed, to do. "Doris," whom we have met before, speaks with a gramophone imitation of a human voice, but her "terre-à-terre" friend who bears the significant and horrible name of "Dusty" has a voice which seems actually muffled by the element of which she is a native.

In the second part of this work, we have the attempt of the debased rhythm of modern life to simplify itself into the sound — not arising from, but lowered from the needs of that life — of cannibal drums.

In the second part, we have the concentrated horror of this world reduced to the nakedness of this physical trinity: "Birth, and copulation, and death," whose triumph is reiterated over and over again. In the line "I've been born, and once is enough" we have the attitude of the world towards the spirit.

The rhythm of the earlier *Sweeney Erect* and *Sweeney among the Nightingales* and that of *Whispers of Immortality* is roughly the same, inasmuch as all three poems consist of quatrains on the eight-syllable norm, and only the second and fourth lines of each quatrain rhyme; but there is a significant difference. *Whispers of Immortality* has a certain appalling gallantry, for one thing. Owing to the regular gaps in the rhyme scheme, the movement of each verse in all three of these poems flaps lazily open, then flaps together again, like rags of flesh or of bone, blown away from each other and then blown together again by the empty will of the wind — blown backwards and forwards, yet still adhering to the skeleton.

But in the Sweeney poems the movement seems actually quicker and therefore more living (I have not been able to discover the technical reason for this); that movement comes *only* from outside; the characters, the objects have no volition to reorganize their human shape, whilst in *Whispers of Immortality* there is a hopeless strength, a hopeless persistence.

In *Sweeney among the Nightingales* the whole spiritual state of the characters is conveyed by the actual sound of the first verse:

> Apeneck Sweeney spreads his knees
> Letting his arms hang down to laugh,
> The zebra stripes along his jaw
> Swelling to maculate giraffe.

Here, after the first line, there is only hollowness, blankness, lazy abysses of emptiness, stretches of vacancy, contractions into shrunken nothingness, and, amidst this, the hoarse animal sound of the *a* in "jaw." All this is conveyed by the different wave lengths, the heights and depths of the *a*'s which run through the verse.

In *Whispers of Immortality*, however, we have a despairing attempt on the part of the "breastless creatures under ground" to reorganize their shape, and this is conveyed in the verse by an extremely subtle system of alliteration and of echoes, which, at first, seem accidental.

Here we have agony in eternity, grown out of the pain of mortality; and this is shown, in the last verse, by the gradually rising *a* sounds in the first two lines (the highest *a* echoing that of "penetrate" in the third quatrain): "marrow," "ague":

> He knew the anguish of the marrow
> The ague of the skeleton;
> No contact possible to flesh
> Allayed the fever of the bone.

The high sound sinks again, despairingly, to the echo of "anguish" — the word "contact" then rises again to the high phantom sound of "allayed" — an unreal balance to the word "ague." In this verse, then, as in *Sweeney among the Nightingales,* we have a scheme built up upon *a* sounds; but the balance, and therefore the meaning, is utterly different.

As I have said, *The Waste Land* and the *Quartets* have been analyzed at such length, and by so many, that it is best for any commentator writing now of Eliot to examine other poems.

In *The Hollow Men,* the terrible poem which followed *The Waste Land,* with the epigraph from *The Heart of Darkness* "Mistah Kurtz — he dead," we have another dirge for the world; but this time we have not the voice of the nightingale, nor have we the gigantic reverberations of the thunder echoing over mountains of the last section of *The Waste*

Land. This is not a world in ruins, it is a world dissolving into nothingness. All the rhythms and pulses of life are dead, as we know from the whispering muscleless half-movements of the first section. This is conveyed above all by the use of repetitions instead of rhymes twice in the first verse, and by the use, for a rhyme, of "grass" and "glass" — a rhyme where only one letter is changed. This technical genius conveys the failure of active life. Indeed, in the first two sections, the only trace of movement — and how small it is — lies in the line: "Rat's coat, crowskin, crossed staves," and this is because of the hard *c*'s, the hard *k*, and the dry *t*'s placed near together.

In the fifth section, however, the broken springs make a temporary spurt, only to break at the end of each line, excepting in the hopeless round of "Here we go round the prickly pear," and the three succeeding lines, and in the appalling last verse.

In that great poem *Triumphal March* we have, as I see it, the presentation of the world that is waiting for the coming of Christ — and that is given, in His stead, Caesar, the King of the World — the terrible march onward of "5,800,000 rifles and carbines" and all the other engines of destruction.

Then comes the cry, which we find in all the poems of this great poet — though taking many disguises, sounding through many voices:

> "Please, will you
> Give us a light?
> Light
> Light"

THE WASTE LAND

"Nam Sibyllam quidem Cumis ego ipse oculis meis
vidi in ampulla pendere, et cum illi pueri dicerent:
Σίβυλλα τί Θέλεις; respondebat illa: ἀποθανεῖν Θέλω."

For Ezra Pound
il miglior fabbro.

I. THE BURIAL OF THE DEAD

April is the cruellest month, breeding
Lilacs out of the dead land, mixing
Memory and desire, stirring
Dull roots with spring rain.
Winter kept us warm, covering
Earth in forgetful snow, feeding
A little life with dried tubers.
Summer surprised us, coming over the Starnbergersee

With a shower of rain; we stopped in the colonnade,
And went on in sunlight, into the Hofgarten,   10
And drank coffee, and talked for an hour.
Bin gar keine Russin, stamm' aus Litauen, echt deutsch.
And when we were children, staying at the arch-duke's,
My cousin's, he took me out on a sled,
And I was frightened. He said, Marie,
Marie, hold on tight. And down we went.
In the mountains, there you feel free.
I read, much of the night, and go south in the winter.

What are the roots that clutch, what branches grow
Out of this stony rubbish? Son of man,   20
You cannot say, or guess, for you know only
A heap of broken images, where the sun beats,
And the dead tree gives no shelter, the cricket no relief,
And the dry stone no sound of water. Only
There is shadow under this red rock,
(Come in under the shadow of this red rock),
And I will show you something different from either
Your shadow at morning striding behind you
Or your shadow at evening rising to meet you;
I will show you fear in a handful of dust.   30

> *Frisch weht der Wind*
> *Der Heimat zu*
> *Mein Irisch Kind,*
> *Wo weilest du?*

"You gave me hyacinths first a year ago;
They called me the hyacinth girl."
— Yet when we came back, late, from the Hyacinth garden,
Your arms full, and your hair wet, I could not
Speak, and my eyes failed, I was neither
Living nor dead, and I knew nothing,   40
Looking into the heart of light, the silence.
Oed' und leer das Meer.

Madame Sosostris, famous clairvoyante,
Had a bad cold, nevertheless
Is known to be the wisest woman in Europe,
With a wicked pack of cards. Here, said she,
Is your card, the drowned Phoenician Sailor,
(Those are pearls that were his eyes. Look!)
Here is Belladonna, the Lady of the Rocks,
The lady of situations.   50

Here is the man with three staves, and here the Wheel,
And here is the one-eyed merchant, and this card,
Which is blank, is something he carries on his back,
Which I am forbidden to see. I do not find
The Hanged Man. Fear death by water.
I see crowds of people, walking round in a ring.
Thank you. If you see dear Mrs. Equitone,
Tell her I bring the horoscope myself:
One must be so careful these days.

Unreal City,   60
Under the brown fog of a winter dawn,
A crowd flowed over London Bridge, so many,
I had not thought death had undone so many.
Sighs, short and infrequent, were exhaled,
And each man fixed his eyes before his feet.
Flowed up the hill and down King William Street,
To where Saint Mary Woolnoth kept the hours
With a dead sound on the final stroke of nine.
There I saw one I knew, and stopped him, crying "Stetson!
You who were with me in the ships at Mylae!   70
That corpse you planted last year in your garden,
Has it begun to sprout? Will it bloom this year?
Or has the sudden frost disturbed its bed?
Oh keep the Dog far hence, that's friend to men,
Or with his nails he'll dig it up again!
You! hypocrite lecteur! — mon semblable, — mon frère!"

II. A GAME OF CHESS

The Chair she sat in, like a burnished throne,
Glowed on the marble, where the glass
Held up by standards wrought with fruited vines
From which a golden Cupidon peeped out   80
(Another hid his eyes behind his wing)
Doubled the flames of sevenbranched candelabra
Reflecting light upon the table as
The glitter of her jewels rose to meet it,
From satin cases poured in rich profusion;
In vials of ivory and coloured glass
Unstoppered, lurked her strange synthetic perfumes,
Unguent, powdered, or liquid — troubled, confused
And drowned the sense in odours; stirred by the air
That freshened from the window, these ascended   90
In fattening the prolonged candle-flames,
Flung their smoke into the laquearia,
Stirring the pattern on the coffered ceiling.

Huge sea-wood fed with copper
Burned green and orange, framed by the coloured stone,
In which sad light a carvèd dolphin swam.
Above the antique mantel was displayed
As though a window gave upon the sylvan scene
The change of Philomel, by the barbarous king
So rudely forced; yet there the nightingale   100
Filled all the desert with inviolable voice
And still she cried, and still the world pursues,
"Jug Jug" to dirty ears.
And other withered stumps of time
Were told upon the walls; staring forms
Leaned out, leaning, hushing the room enclosed.
Footsteps shuffled on the stair.
Under the firelight, under the brush, her hair
Spread out in fiery points
Glowed into words, then would be savagely still.   110

"My nerves are bad to-night. Yes, bad. Stay with me.
Speak to me. Why do you never speak. Speak.
            What are you thinking of? What thinking? What?
I never know what you are thinking. Think."

I think we are in rats' alley
Where the dead men lost their bones.

"What is that noise?"
                        The wind under the door.
"What is that noise now? What is the wind doing?"
                        Nothing again nothing.   120
                                        "Do
You know nothing? Do you see nothing? Do you remember
Nothing?"

            I remember
Those are pearls that were his eyes.
"Are you alive, or not? Is there nothing in your head?"
                                        But
O O O O that Shakespeherian Rag —
It's so elegant
So intelligent   130
"What shall I do now? What shall I do?"
"I shall rush out as I am, and walk the street
With my hair down, so. What shall we do tomorrow?
What shall we ever do?"
                    The hot water at ten.

And if it rains, a closed car at four.
And we shall play a game of chess,
Pressing lidless eyes and waiting for a knock upon the door.

When Lil's husband got demobbed, I said —
I didn't mince my words, I said to her myself,   140
HURRY UP PLEASE ITS TIME
Now Albert's coming back, make yourself a bit smart.
He'll want to know what you done with that money he gave you
To get yourself some teeth. He did, I was there.
You have them all out, Lil, and get a nice set,
He said, I swear, I can't bear to look at you.
And no more can't I, I said, and think of poor Albert,
He's been in the army four years, he wants a good time,
And if you don't give it him, there's others will, I said.
Oh is there, she said. Something o' that, I said.   150
Then I'll know who to thank, she said, and give me a straight look.
HURRY UP PLEASE ITS TIME
If you don't like it you can get on with it, I said.
Others can pick and choose if you can't.
But if Albert makes off, it won't be for lack of telling.
You ought to be ashamed, I said, to look so antique.
(And her only thirty-one.)
I can't help it, she said, pulling a long face,
It's them pills I took, to bring it off, she said.
(She's had five already, and nearly died of young George.)   160
The chemist said it would be all right, but I've never been the same.
You *are* a proper fool, I said.
Well, if Albert won't leave you alone, there it is, I said,
What you get married for if you don't want children?
HURRY UP PLEASE ITS TIME
Well, that Sunday Albert was home, they had a hot gammon,
And they asked me in to dinner, to get the beauty of it hot —
HURRY UP PLEASE ITS TIME
HURRY UP PLEASE ITS TIME
Goonight Bill. Goonight Lou. Goonight May. Goonight.   170
Ta ta. Goonight. Goonight.
Good night, ladies, good night, sweet ladies, good night, good night.

III. THE FIRE SERMON

The river's tent is broken: the last fingers of leaf
Clutch and sink into the wet bank. The wind
Crosses the brown land, unheard. The nymphs are departed.
Sweet Thames, run softly, till I end my song.
The river bears no empty bottles, sandwich papers,
Silk handkerchiefs, cardboard boxes, cigarette ends

Or other testimony of summer nights. The nymphs are departed.
And their friends, the loitering heirs of city directors;   180
Departed, have left no addresses.
By the waters of Leman I sat down and wept . . .
Sweet Thames, run softly till I end my song,
Sweet Thames, run softly, for I speak not loud or long.
But at my back in a cold blast I hear
The rattle of the bones, and chuckle spread from ear to ear.
A rat crept softly through the vegetation
Dragging its slimy belly on the bank
While I was fishing in the dull canal
On a winter evening round behind the gashouse   190
Musing upon the king my brother's wreck
And on the king my father's death before him.
White bodies naked on the low damp ground
And bones cast in a little low dry garret,
Rattled by the rat's foot only, year to year.
But at my back from time to time I hear
The sound of horns and motors, which shall bring
Sweeney to Mrs. Porter in the spring.
O the moon shone bright on Mrs. Porter
And on her daughter   200
They wash their feet in soda water
Et O ces voix d'enfants, chantant dans la coupole!

Twit twit twit
Jug jug jug jug jug jug
So rudely forc'd.
Tereu

Unreal City
Under the brown fog of a winter noon
Mr. Eugenides, the Smyrna merchant
Unshaven, with a pocket full of currants   210
C.i.f. London: documents at sight,
Asked me in demotic French
To luncheon at the Cannon Street Hotel
Followed by a weekend at the Metropole.

At the violet hour, when the eyes and back
Turn upward from the desk, when the human engine waits
Like a taxi throbbing waiting,
I Tiresias, though blind, throbbing between two lives,
Old man with wrinkled female breasts, can see
At the violet hour, the evening hour that strives   220
Homeward, and brings the sailor home from sea,

The typist home at teatime, clears her breakfast, lights
Her stove, and lays out food in tins.
Out of the window perilously spread
Her drying combinations touched by the sun's last rays,
On the divan are piled (at night her bed)
Stockings, slippers, camisoles, and stays.
I Tiresias, old man with wrinkled dugs
Perceived the scene, and foretold the rest —
I too awaited the expected guest.   230
He, the young man carbuncular, arrives,
A small house agent's clerk, with one bold stare,
One of the low on whom assurance sits
As a silk hat on a Bradford millionaire.
The time is now propitious, as he guesses,
The meal is ended, she is bored and tired,
Endeavours to engage her in caresses
Which still are unreproved, if undesired.
Flushed and decided, he assaults at once;
Exploring hands encounter no defence;   240
His vanity requires no response,
And makes a welcome of indifference.
(And I Tiresias have foresuffered all
Enacted on this same divan or bed;
I who have sat by Thebes below the wall
And walked among the lowest of the dead.)
Bestows one final patronising kiss,
And gropes his way, finding the stairs unlit . . .

She turns and looks a moment in the glass,
Hardly aware of her departed lover;   250
Her brain allows one half-formed thought to pass:
"Well now that's done: and I'm glad it's over."
When lovely woman stoops to folly and
Paces about her room again, alone,
She smoothes her hair with automatic hand,
And puts a record on the gramophone.

"This music crept by me upon the waters"
And along the Strand, up Queen Victoria Street.
O City city, I can sometimes hear
Beside a public bar in Lower Thames Street,   260
The pleasant whining of a mandoline
And a clatter and a chatter from within
Where fishmen lounge at noon: where the walls
Of Magnus Martyr hold
Inexplicable splendour of Ionian white and gold.

The river sweats
Oil and tar
The barges drift
With the turning tide
Red sails   270
Wide
To leeward, swing on the heavy spar.
The barges wash
Drifting logs
Down Greenwich reach
Past the Isle of Dogs.
        Weialala leia
        Wallala leialala

Elizabeth and Leicester
Beating oars   280
The stern was formed
A gilded shell
Red and gold
The brisk swell
Rippled both shores
Southwest wind
Carried down stream
The peal of bells
White towers
        Weialala leia
        Wallala leialala   290

"Trams and dusty trees.
Highbury bore me. Richmond and Kew
Undid me. By Richmond I raised my knees
Supine on the floor of a narrow canoe."

"My feet are at Moorgate, and my heart
Under my feet. After the event
He wept. He promised 'a new start.'
I made no comment. What should I resent?"

"On Margate Sands.   300
I can connect
Nothing with nothing.
The broken fingernails of dirty hands.
My people humble people who expect
Nothing."
        la la

To Carthage then I came

Burning burning burning burning
O Lord Thou pluckest me out
O Lord Thou pluckest   310

burning

IV. DEATH BY WATER

Phlebas the Phoenician, a fortnight dead,
Forgot the cry of gulls, and the deep sea swell
And the profit and loss.
                          A current under sea
Picked his bones in whispers. As he rose and fell
He passed the stages of his age and youth
Entering the whirlpool.
                          Gentile or Jew
O you who turn the wheel and look to windward,   320
Consider Phlebas, who was once handsome and tall as you.

V. WHAT THE THUNDER SAID

After the torchlight red on sweaty faces
After the frosty silence in the gardens
After the agony in stony places
The shouting and the crying
Prison and palace and reverberation
Of thunder of spring over distant mountains
He who was living is now dead
We who were living are now dying
With a little patience   330

Here is no water but only rock
Rock and no water and the sandy road
The road winding above among the mountains
Which are mountains of rock without water
If there were water we should stop and drink
Amongst the rock one cannot stop or think
Sweat is dry and feet are in the sand
If there were only water amongst the rock
Dead mountain mouth of carious teeth that cannot spit
Here one can neither stand nor lie nor sit   340
There is not even silence in the mountains
But dry sterile thunder without rain
There is not even solitude in the mountains
But red sullen faces sneer and snarl
From doors of mudcracked houses

　　　　　　　　　　　If there were water
　　　And no rock
　　　If there were rock
　　　And also water
　　　And water　　　　　　　　　　　　　　　　350
　　　A spring
　　　A pool among the rock
　　　If there were the sound of water only
　　　Not the cicada
　　　And dry grass singing
　　　But sound of water over a rock
　　　Where the hermit-thrush sings in the pine trees
　　　Drip drop drip drop drop drop drop
　　　But there is no water

Who is the third who walks always beside you?　　　360
When I count, there are only you and I together
But when I look ahead up the white road
There is always another one walking beside you
Gliding wrapt in a brown mantle, hooded
I do not know whether a man or a woman
— But who is that on the other side of you?

What is that sound high in the air
Murmur of maternal lamentation
Who are those hooded hordes swarming
Over endless plains, stumbling in cracked earth　　　370
Ringed by the flat horizon only
What is the city over the mountains
Cracks and reforms and bursts in the violet air
Falling towers
Jerusalem Athens Alexandria
Vienna London
Unreal
A woman drew her long black hair out tight
And fiddled whisper music on those strings
And bats with baby faces in the violet light　　　380
Whistled, and beat their wings
And crawled head downward down a blackened wall
And upside down in air were towers
Tolling reminiscent bells, that kept the hours
And voices singing out of empty cisterns and exhausted wells.

In this decayed hole among the mountains
In the faint moonlight, the grass is singing
Over the tumbled graves, about the chapel
There is the empty chapel, only the wind's home.

It has no windows, and the door swings, 390
Dry bones can harm no one.
Only a cock stood on the rooftree
Co co rico co co rico
In a flash of lightning. Then a damp gust
Bringing rain

Ganga was sunken, and the limp leaves
Waited for rain, while the black clouds
Gathered far distant, over Himavant.
The jungle crouched, humped in silence.
Then spoke the thunder 400
DA
Datta: what have we given?
My friend, blood shaking my heart
The awful daring of a moment's surrender
Which an age of prudence can never retract
By this, and this only, we have existed
Which is not to be found in our obituaries
Or in memories draped by the beneficent spider
Or under seals broken by the lean solicitor
In our empty rooms 410
DA
Dayadhvam: I have heard the key
Turn in the door once and turn once only
We think of the key, each in his prison
Thinking of the key, each confirms a prison
Only at nightfall, aethereal rumours
Revive for a moment a broken Coriolanus
DA
Damyata: The boat responded
Gaily, to the hand expert with sail and oar 420
The sea was calm, your heart would have responded
Gaily, when invited, beating obedient
To controlling hands

I sat upon the shore
Fishing, with the arid plain behind me
Shall I at least set my lands in order?
London Bridge is falling down falling down falling down
Poi s'ascose nel foco che gli affina
Quando fiam uti chelidon — O swallow swallow
Le Prince d'Aquitaine à la tour abolie 430
These fragments I have shored against my ruins
Why then Ile fit you. Hieronymo's mad againe.
Datta. Dayadhvam. Damyata.
      Shantih   shantih   shantih

NOTES for THE WASTE LAND

Not only the title, but the plan and a good deal of the incidental symbolism of the poem were suggested by Miss Jessie L. Weston's book on the Grail legend: *From Ritual to Romance* (Macmillan). Indeed, so deeply am I indebted, Miss Weston's book will elucidate the difficulties of the poem much better than my notes can do; and I recommend it (apart from the great interest of the book itself) to any who think such elucidation of the poem worth the trouble. To another work of anthropology I am indebted in general, one which has influenced our generation profoundly; I mean *The Golden Bough;* I have used especially the two volumes *Atthis Adonis Osiris*. Anyone who is acquainted with these works will immediately recognise in the poem certain references to vegetation ceremonies.

I. THE BURIAL OF THE DEAD

Line 20. Cf. Ezekiel II, i.

23. Cf. Ecclesiastes XII, v.

31. V. *Tristan und Isolde,* I, verses 5–8.

42. Id. III, verse 24.

46. I am not familiar with the exact constitution of the Tarot pack of cards, from which I have obviously departed to suit my own convenience. The Hanged Man, a member of the traditional pack, fits my purpose in two ways: because he is associated in my mind with the Hanged God of Frazer, and because I associate him with the hooded figure in the passage of the disciples to Emmaus in Part V. The Phoenician Sailor and the Merchant appear later; also the "crowds of people," and Death by Water is executed in Part IV. The Man with Three Staves (an authentic member of the Tarot pack) I associate, quite arbitrarily, with the Fisher King himself.

60. Cf. Baudelaire:

> Fourmillante cité, cité pleine de rêves,
> Où le spectre en plein jour raccroche le passant.

63. Cf. *Inferno* III, 55–57:

> si lunga tratta di gente, ch'io
> non avrei mai creduto che morte tanta n'avesse disfatta.

64. Cf. *Inferno* IV, 25–27:

> Quivi, secondo che per ascoltare,
> non avea pianto, ma' che di sospiri,
> che l'aura eterna facevan tremare.

68. A phenomenon which I have often noticed.

74. Cf. the Dirge in Webster's *White Devil.*

76. V. Baudelaire, Preface to *Fleurs du Mal.*

II. A GAME OF CHESS

77. Cf. *Antony and Cleopatra,* II, ii, l. 190.

92. Laquearia. V. *Aeneid,* I, 726:

> dependent lychni laquearibus
> aureis incensi, et noctem flammis funalia vincunt.

98. Sylvan scene. V. Milton, *Paradise Lost,* IV, 140.

99. V. Ovid, *Metamorphoses,* VI, Philomela.

100. Cf. Part III l. 204.

115. Cf. Part III l. 195.

118. Cf. Webster: "Is the wind in that door still?"

126. Cf. Part I l. 37, 48.

138. Cf. the game of chess in Middleton's *Women Beware Women.*

III. THE FIRE SERMON

176. V. Spenser, *Prothalamion.*

192. Cf. *The Tempest,* I, ii.

196. Cf. Day, *Parliament of Bees:*

> When of the sudden, listening, you shall hear,
> A noise of horns and hunting, which shall bring
> Actaeon to Diana in the spring,
> Where all shall see her naked skin . . .

197. Cf. Marvell, *To His Coy Mistress.*

199. I do not know the origin of the ballad from which these lines are taken; it was reported to me from Sydney, Australia.

202. V. Verlaine, *Parsifal.*

210. The currants were quoted at a price "carriage and insurance free to London"; and the Bill of Lading etc. were to be handed to the buyer upon payment of the sight draft.

218. Tiresias, although a mere spectator and not indeed a "character," is yet the most important personage in the poem, uniting all the rest. Just as the one-eyed merchant, seller of currants, melts into the Phoenician Sailor, and the latter is not wholly distinct from Ferdinand Prince of Naples, so all the women are one woman, and the two sexes meet in Tiresias. What Tiresias sees, in fact, is the substance of the poem. The whole passage from Ovid is of great anthropological interest:

. . . Cum Iunone iocos et maior vestra profecto est
Quam, quae contingit maribus', dixisse, 'voluptas.'
Illa negat; placuit quae sit sententia docti
Quaerere Tiresiae: venus huic erat utraque nota.
Nam duo magnorum viridi coeuntia silva
Corpora serpentum baculi violaverat ictu
Deque viro factus, mirabile, femina septem
Egerat autumnos; octavo rursus eosdem
Vidit et 'est vestrae si tanta potentia plagae,'
Dixit 'ut auctoris sortem in contraria mutet,
Nunc quoque vos feriam!' percussis anguibus isdem
Forma prior rediit genetivaque venit imago.
Arbiter hic igitur sumptus de lite iocosa
Dicta Iovis firmat; gravius Saturnia iusto
Nec pro materia fertur doluisse suique
Iudicis aeterna damnavit lumina nocte,
At pater omnipotens (neque enim licet inrita cuiquam
Facta dei fecisse deo) pro lumine adempto
Scire futura dedit poenamque levavit honore.

221. This may not appear as exact as Sappho's lines, but I had in mind the "longshore" or "dory" fisherman, who returns at nightfall.

253. V. Goldsmith, the song in *The Vicar of Wakefield*.

257. V. *The Tempest*, as above.

264. The interior of St. Magnus Martyr is to my mind one of the finest among Wren's interiors. See *The Proposed Demolition of Nineteen City Churches*: P. S. King & Son Ltd.).

266. The Song of the (three) Thames-daughters begins here. From line 292 to 306 inclusive they speak in turn. V. *Götterdämmerung*, III, i: the Rhinedaughters.

279. V. Froude, *Elizabeth*, Vol. I, ch. iv, letter of De Quadra to Philip of Spain:

"In the afternoon we were in a barge, watching the games on the river. (The queen) was alone with Lord Robert and myself on the poop, when they began to talk nonsense, and went so far that Lord Robert at last said, as I was on the spot there was no reason why they should not be married if the queen pleased."

293. Cf. *Purgatorio*, V. 133:

Ricorditi di me, che son la Pia;
Siena mi fe', disfecemi Maremma.

307. V. St. Augustine's *Confessions*: "to Carthage then I came, where a cauldron of unholy loves sang all about mine ears."

308. The complete text of the Buddha's Fire Sermon (which corresponds in importance to the Sermon on the Mount) from which these

words are taken, will be found translated in the late Henry Clarke Warren's *Buddhism in Translation* (Harvard Oriental Series). Mr. Warren
was one of the great pioneers of Buddhist studies in the occident.

312. From St. Augustine's *Confessions* again. The collocation of these
two representatives of eastern and western asceticism, as the culmination
of this part of the poem, is not an accident.

V. WHAT THE THUNDER SAID

In the first part of Part V three themes are employed: the journey to
Emmaus, the approach to the Chapel Perilous (see Miss Weston's book)
and the present decay of eastern Europe.

357. This is *Turdus aonalaschkae pallasii*, the hermit-thrush which I
have heard in Quebec County. Chapman says (*Handbook of Birds of
Eastern North America*) "it is most at home in secluded woodland and
thickety retreats. . . . Its notes are not remarkable for variety or volume,
but in purity and sweetness of tone and exquisite modulation they are
unequaled." Its "water-dripping song" is justly celebrated.

360. The following lines were stimulated by the account of one of the
Antarctic expeditions (I forget which, but I think one of Shackleton's):
it was related that the party of explorers, at the extremity of their
strength, had the constant delusion that there was one more member than
could actually be counted.

367–77. Cf. Hermann Hesse, *Blick ins Chaos:*
"Schon ist halb Europa, schon ist zumindest der halbe Osten Europas
auf dem Wege zum Chaos, fährt betrunken im heiligem Wahn am
Abgrund entlang und singt dazu, singt betrunken und hymnisch wie
Dmitri Karamasoff sang. Ueber diese Lieder lacht der Bürger beleidigt,
der Heilige und Seher hört sie mit Tränen."

402. "Datta dayadhvam, damyata" (Give, sympathise, control). The
fable of the meaning of the Thunder is found in the *Brihadaranyaka—
Upanishad,* 5, I. A translation is found in Deussen's *Sechzig Upanishads
des Veda,* p. 489.

408. Cf. Webster, *The White Devil,* V. vi:

> . . . they'll remarry
> Ere the worm pierce your winding-sheet, ere the spider
> Make a thin curtain for your epitaphs.

412. Cf. *Inferno,* XXXIII, 46:

> ed io sentii chiavar l'uscio
> di sotto all'orribile torre.

Also F. H. Bradley, *Appearance and Reality,* p. 346.
"My external sensations are no less private to myself than are my

thoughts or my feelings. In either case my experience falls within my own circle, a circle closed on the outside; and, with all its elements alike, every sphere is opaque to the others which surround it. . . . In brief, regarded as an existence which appears in a soul, the whole world for each is peculiar and private to that soul."

425. V. Weston: *From Ritual to Romance;* chapter on the Fisher King.

428. V. *Purgatorio,* XXVI, 148.

> "Ara vos prec, per aquella valor
> que vos guida al som de l'escalina,
> sovegna vos a temps de ma dolor."
> Poi s'ascose nel foco che gli affina.

429. V. *Pervigilium Veneris.* Cf. Philomela in Parts II and III.

430. V. Gerard de Nerval, Sonnet *El Desdichado.*

432. V. Kyd's *Spanish Tragedy.*

434. Shantih. Repeated as here, a formal ending to an *Upanishad.* "The Peace which passeth understanding" is a feeble translation of the content of this word.

From FOUR QUARTETS

BURNT NORTON

I

Time present and time past
Are both perhaps present in time future,
And time future contained in time past.
If all time is eternally present
All time is unredeemable.
What might have been is an abstraction
Remaining a perpetual possibility
Only in a world of speculation.
What might have been and what has been
Point to one end, which is always present.
Footfalls echo in the memory
Down the passage which we did not take
Towards the door we never opened
Into the rose-garden. My words echo
Thus, in your mind.
                    But to what purpose
Disturbing the dust on a bowl of rose-leaves
I do not know.
                    Other echoes
Inhabit the garden. Shall we follow?

Quick, said the bird, find them, find them,
Round the corner. Through the first gate,
Into our first world, shall we follow
The deception of the thrush? Into our first world.
There they were, dignified, invisible,
Moving without pressure, over the dead leaves,
In the autumn heat, through the vibrant air,
And the bird called, in response to
The unheard music hidden in the shrubbery,
And the unseen eyebeam crossed, for the roses
Had the look of flowers that are looked at.
There they were as our guests, accepted and accepting.
So we moved, and they, in a formal pattern,
Along the empty alley, into the box circle,
To look down into the drained pool.
Dry the pool, dry concrete, brown edged,
And the pool was filled with water out of sunlight,
And the lotos rose, quietly, quietly,
The surface glittered out of heart of light,
And they were behind us, reflected in the pool.
Then a cloud passed, and the pool was empty.
Go, said the bird, for the leaves were full of children,
Hidden excitedly, containing laughter.
Go, go, go, said the bird: human kind
Cannot bear very much reality.
Time past and time future
What might have been and what has been
Point to one end, which is always present.

II

Garlic and sapphires in the mud
Clot the bedded axle-tree.
The trilling wire in the blood
Sings below inveterate scars
Appeasing long forgotten wars.
The dance along the artery
The circulation of the lymph
Are figured in the drift of stars
Ascend to summer in the tree
We move above the moving tree
In light upon the figured leaf
And hear upon the sodden floor
Below, the boarhound and the boar
Pursue their pattern as before
But reconciled among the stars.

At the still point of the turning world. Neither flesh nor fleshless;
Neither from nor towards; at the still point, there the dance is,
But neither arrest nor movement. And do not call it fixity.
Where past and future are gathered. Neither movement from nor to-
    wards,
Neither ascent nor decline. Except for the point, the still point,
There would be no dance, and there is only the dance.
I can only say, *there* we have been: but I cannot say where.
And I cannot say, how long, for that is to place it in time.
The inner freedom from the practical desire,
The release from action and suffering, release from the inner
And the outer compulsion, yet surrounded
By a grace of sense, a white light still and moving,
Erhebung without motion, concentration
Without elimination, both a new world
And the old made explicit, understood
In the completion of its partial ecstasy,
The resolution of its partial horror.
Yet the enchainment of past and future
Woven in the weakness of the changing body,
Protects mankind from heaven and damnation
Which flesh cannot endure.
                    Time past and time future
Allow but a little consciousness.
To be conscious is not to be in time
But only in time can the moment in the rose-garden,
The moment in the arbour where the rain beat,
The moment in the draughty church at smokefall
Be remembered; involved with past and future.
Only through time time is conquered.

III

Here is a place of disaffection
Time before and time after
In a dim light: neither daylight
Investing form with lucid stillness
Turning shadow into transient beauty
With slow rotation suggesting permanence
Nor darkness to purify the soul
Emptying the sensual with deprivation
Cleansing affection from the temporal.
Neither plenitude nor vacancy. Only a flicker
Over the strained time-ridden faces
Distracted from distraction by distraction
Filled with fancies and empty of meaning

Tumid apathy with no concentration
Men and bits of paper, whirled by the cold wind
That blows before and after time,
Wind in and out of unwholesome lungs
Time before and time after.
Eructation of unhealthy souls
Into the faded air, the torpid
Driven on the wind that sweeps the gloomy hills of London,
Hampstead and Clerkenwell, Campden and Putney,
Highgate, Primrose and Ludgate. Not here
Not here the darkness, in this twittering world.

Descend lower, descend only
Into the world of perpetual solitude,
World not world, but that which is not world,
Internal darkness, deprivation
And destitution of all property,
Desiccation of the world of sense,
Evacuation of the world of fancy,
Inoperancy of the world of spirit;
This is the one way, and the other
Is the same, not in movement
But abstention from movement; while the world moves
In appetency, on its metalled ways
Of time past and time future.

IV

Time and the bell have buried the day,
The black cloud carries the sun away.
Will the sunflower turn to us, will the clematis
Stray down, bend to us; tendril and spray
Clutch and cling?
Chill
Fingers of yew be curled
Down on us? After the kingfisher's wing
Has answered light to light, and is silent, the light is still
At the still point of the turning world.

V

Words move, music moves
Only in time; but that which is only living
Can only die. Words, after speech, reach
Into the silence. Only by the form, the pattern,
Can words or music reach

The stillness, as a Chinese jar still
Moves perpetually in its stillness.
Not the stillness of the violin, while the note lasts,
Not that only, but the co-existence,
Or say that the end precedes the beginning,
And the end and the beginning were always there
Before the beginning and after the end.
And all is always now. Words strain,
Crack and sometimes break, under the burden,
Under the tension, slip, slide, perish,
Decay with imprecision, will not stay in place,
Will not stay still. Shrieking voices
Scolding, mocking, or merely chattering,
Always assail them. The Word in the desert
Is most attacked by voices of temptation,
The crying shadow in the funeral dance,
The loud lament of the disconsolate chimera.

The detail of the pattern is movement,
As in the figure of the ten stairs.
Desire itself is movement
Not in itself desirable;
Love is itself unmoving,
Only the cause and end of movement,
Timeless, and undesiring
Except in the aspect of time
Caught in the form of limitation
Between un-being and being.
Sudden in a shaft of sunlight
Even while the dust moves
There rises the hidden laughter
Of children in the foliage
Quick now, here, now, always —
Ridiculous the waste sad time
Stretching before and after.

Translations from the Chinese by

Arthur Waley

b. 1889

LO-YANG
By the Emperor Chien Wên-ti (A.D. *503–551*)

A beautiful place is the town of Lo-yang;
The big streets are full of spring light.
The lads go driving out with lutes in their hands;
The mulberry girls go out to the fields with their baskets.
Golden saddles glint at the horses' flanks,
Gauze sleeves brush the green boughs.
Racing dawn, the carriages come home —
And the girls with their high baskets full of fruit.

REMEMBERING GOLDEN BELLS
By Po Chü-i (A.D. *772–846*)

Ruined and ill — a man of two score;
Pretty and guileless — a girl of three.
Not a boy — but still better than nothing:
To soothe one's feeling — from time to time a kiss!
There came a day — they suddenly took her from me;
Her soul's shadow wandered I know not where.
And when I remember how just at the time she died
She lisped strange sounds, beginning to learn to talk,
Then I know that the ties of flesh and blood
Only bind us to a load of grief and sorrow.
At last, by thinking of the time before she was born,
By thought and reason I drove the pain away.
Since my heart forgot her, many days have passed
And three times winter has changed to spring.
This morning, for a little, the old grief came back,
Because, in the road, I met her foster-nurse.

THE LADY AND THE MAGPIE
Anonymous. Ninth century A.D. *Written on the back of a Buddhist Scripture.*

"Lucky magpie, holy bird, what hateful lies you tell!
Prove, if you can, that ever once your coming brought good luck.
Once too often you have come, and this time I have caught you
And shut you up in a golden cage, and will not let you talk."

"Lady, I came with kind intent and truly bring you joy;
Little did I think you would hold me fast and lock me in a golden cage.
If you really want that far-off man to come quickly home,
Set me free; I will bear him word, flying through the grey clouds."

HOT CAKE
*Part of a poem by Shu Hsi (c.*A.D. *265–306)*

Winter has come; fierce is the cold;
In the sharp morning air new-risen we meet.
Rheum freezes in the nose;
Frost hangs about the chin.
For hollow bellies, for chattering teeth and shivering knees
What better than hot cake?
Soft as the down of spring,
Whiter than autumn floss!
Dense and swift the steam
Rises, swells and spreads.
Fragrance flies through the air,
Is scattered far and wide,
Steals down along the wind and wets
The covetous mouth of passer-by.
Servants and grooms
Throw sidelong glances, munch the empty air.
They lick their lips who serve;
While lines of envious lackeys by the wall
Stand dryly swallowing.

WINTER NIGHT
By Chien Wên-ti (A.D. *503–551*)

My bed is so empty that I keep on waking up;
As the cold increases, the night-wind begins to blow.
It rustles the curtains, making a noise like the sea.
Oh that those were waves which could carry me back to you!

THE HAT GIVEN TO THE POET BY
LI CHIEN
By Po Chü-i (A.D. 772–846)

Long ago to a white-haired gentleman
You made the present of a black gauze hat.
The gauze hat still sits on my head;
But you already are gone to the Nether Springs.
The thing is old, but still fit to wear;
The man is gone and will never be seen again.
Out on the hill the moon is shining to-night
And the trees on your tomb are swayed by the autumn wind.

THE LITTLE CART
By Ch'ên Tzŭ-lung (A.D. 1608–1647)

The little cart jolting and banging through the yellow haze of dusk;
The man pushing behind, the woman pulling in front.
They have left the city and do not know where to go.
"Green, green, those elm-tree leaves; *they* will cure my hunger,
If only we could find some quiet place and sup on them together."

The wind has flattened the yellow mother-wort;
Above it in the distance they see the walls of a house.
"*There* surely must be people living who'll give you something to eat."
They tap at the door, but no one comes; they look in, but the kitchen is
    empty.
They stand hesitating in the lonely road and their tears fall like rain.

LI FU–JÊN
By Wu-ti (157–87 B.C.)

The sound of her silk skirt has stopped.
On the marble pavement dust grows.
Her empty room is cold and still.
Fallen leaves are piled against the doors.
        Longing for that lovely lady
How can I bring my aching heart to rest?

THE BONES OF CHUANG TZU
By Chang Hêng (A.D. *78–139*)

I, Chang P'ing-Tzu, had traversed the Nine Wilds and seen their won-
    ders,
In the eight continents beheld the ways of Man,
The Sun's procession, the orbit of the Stars,
The surging of the dragon, the soaring of the phoenix in his flight.
In the red desert to the south I sweltered,
And northward waded through the wintry burghs of Yu.
Through the Valley of Darkness to the west I wandered,
And eastward travelled to the Sun's extreme abode,
The stooping Mulberry Tree.

So the seasons sped; weak autumn languished,
A small wind woke the cold.
And now with rearing of rein-horse,
Plunging of the tracer, round I fetched
My high-roofed chariot to westward.
Along the dykes we loitered, past many meadows,
And far away among the dunes and hills.
Suddenly I looked and by the roadside
I saw a man's bones lying in the squelchy earth,
Black rime-frost over him; and I in sorrow spoke
And asked him, saying, "Dead man, how was it?
Fled you with your friend from famine and for the last grains
Gambled and lost? Was this earth your tomb,
Or did floods carry you from afar? Were you mighty, were you wise,
Were you foolish and poor? A warrior, or a girl?"
Then a wonder came; for out of the silence a voice —
Thin echo only, in no substance was the Spirit seen —
Mysteriously answered, saying, "I was a man of Sung,
Of the clan of Chuang; Chou was my name.
Beyond the climes of common thought
My reason soared, yet could I not save myself;
For at the last, when the long charter of my years was told,
I, too, for all my magic, by Age was brought
To the Black Hill of Death.
Wherefore, O Master, do you question me?"
Then I answered:
"Let me plead for you upon the Five Hill-tops,
Let me pray for you to the Gods of Heaven and the Gods of Earth,
That your white bones may arise,
And your limbs be joined anew.
The God of the North shall give me back your ears;

I will scour the Southland for your eyes.
From the sunrise I will wrest your feet;
The West shall yield your heart.
I will set each several organ in its throne;
Each subtle sense will I restore.
Would you not have it so?"
The dead man answered me:
"O Friend, how strange and unacceptable your words!
In death I rest and am at peace; in life, I toiled and strove.
Is the hardness of the winter stream
Better than the melting of spring?
All pride that the body knew
Was it not lighter than dust?
What Ch'ao and Hsü despised,
What Po-ch'êng fled,
Shall I desire, whom death
Already has hidden in the Eternal Way —
Where Li Chu cannot see me,
Nor Tzǔ Yeh hear me,
Where neither Yao nor Shun can reward me,
Nor the tyrants Chieh and Hsin condemn me,
Leopard nor tiger harm me,
Lance prick me nor sword wound me?
Of the Primal Spirit is my substance; I am a wave
In the river of Darkness and Light.
The Maker of All Things is my Father and Mother,
Heaven is my bed and earth my cushion,
The thunder and lightning are my drum and fan,
The sun and moon my candle and my torch,
The Milky Way my moat, the stars my jewels.
With Nature my substance is joined;
I have no passion, no desire.
Wash me and I shall be no whiter,
Foul me and I shall yet be clean.
I come not, yet am here;
Hasten not, yet am swift."
The voice stopped, there was silence.
A ghostly light
Faded and expired.
I gazed upon the dead, stared in sorrow and compassion.
Then I called upon my servant that was with me
To tie his silken scarf about those bones
And wrap them in a cloak of sombre dust;
While I, as offering to the soul of this dead man,
Poured my hot tears upon the margin of the road.

Saint-John Perse
b. 1889
Translated by T. S. Eliot

SONG: UNDER THE BRONZE LEAVES

Under the bronze leaves a colt was foaled. Came such an one who laid bitter bay in our hands. Stranger. Who passed. Here comes news of other provinces to my liking. — "Hail, daughter! under the most considerable of the trees of the year."

For the Sun enters the sign of the Lion and the Stranger has laid his finger on the mouth of the Dead. Stranger. Who laughed. And tells us of an herb. O from the provinces blow many winds. What ease to our ways, and how the trumpet rejoices my heart and the feather adept of the scandal of the wing! "My Soul, great girl, you had your ways which are not ours."

Under the bronze leaves a colt had been foaled. Came such an one who laid this bitter bay in our hands. Stranger. Who passed. Out of the bronze tree comes a great bruit of voices. Roses and bitumen, gift of song, thunder and fluting in the rooms. O what ease in our ways, how many gestes to the year, and by the roads of all the earth the Stranger to his ways. . . . "Hail, daughter! robed in the loveliest robe of the year."

From ANABASIS

I HAVE BUILT MYSELF, WITH HONOUR AND DIGNITY

I have built myself, with honour and dignity have I built myself on three great seasons, and it promises well, the soil whereon I have established my Law.

Beautiful are bright weapons in the morning and behind us the sea is fair. Given over to our horses this seedless earth

delivers to us this incorruptible sky. The Sun is unmentioned but his power is amongst us

and the sea at morning like a presumption of the mind.

Power, you sang as we march in darkness . . . At the pure ides of day what know we of our dream, older than ourselves?

Yet one more year among you! Master of the Grain, Master of the Salt, and the commonwealth on an even beam!

I shall not hail the people of another shore. I shall not trace the great
  boroughs of towns on the slopes with powder of coral. But I have the
idea of living among you.
  Glory at the threshold of the tents, and my strength among you, and
the idea pure as salt holds its assize in the light time.

  . . . So I haunted the City of your dreams, and I established in the
desolate markets the pure commerce of my soul, among you
  invisible and insistent as a fire of thorns in the gale.
  Power, you sang on our roads of splendour. . . . "In the delight of
salt the mind shakes its tumult of spears. . . . With salt shall I revive
the dead mouths of desire!
  Him who has not praised thirst and drunk the water of the sands from
a sallet
  I trust him little in the commerce of the soul. . . ." (And the Sun is
unmentioned but his power is amongst us.)

Men, creatures of dust and folk of divers devices, people of business
and of leisure, men from the marches and those from beyond, O men of
little weight in the memory of these lands; people from the valleys and the
uplands and the highest slopes of this world to the ultimate reach of our
shores; Seers of signs and seeds, and confessors of the western winds, followers of trails and of seasons, breakers of camp in the little dawn wind,
seekers of watercourses over the wrinkled rind of the world, O seekers,
O finders of reasons to be up and be gone,
  you traffic not in a salt more strong than this, when at morning with
omen of kingdoms and omen of dead waters swung high over the smokes
of the world, the drums of exile waken on the marches
  Eternity yawning on the sands.

  . . . In a comely robe among you. For another year among you. "My
glory is upon the seas, my strength is amongst you!
  To our destiny promised this breath of other shores, and there beyond
the seeds of time, the splendour of an age at its height on the beam of
the scales. . . ."
  Calculations hung on the floes of salt! there at the sensitive point
on my brow where the poem is formed, I inscribe this chant of all a
people, the most rapt god-drunken,
  drawing to our dockyards eternal keels!

SUCH IS THE WAY OF THE WORLD

Such is the way of the world and I have nothing but good to say of it.
— Foundation of the City. Stone and bronze. Thorn fires at dawn
  bared these great
  green stones and viscid like the bases of temples, of latrines,

and the mariner at sea whom our smoke reached saw that the earth to the summit had changed its form (great tracts of burnt-over land seen afar and these operations of channelling the living waters on the mountains).

Thus was the City founded and placed in the morning under the labials of a holy name. The encampments are razed from the hills! And we who are there in the wooden galleries,
 head bare and foot bare in the freshness of the world,
 what have we to laugh at, but what have we to laugh at, as we sit, for a disembarkation of girls and mules?
 and what is there to say, since the dawn, of all this people under sail?
— Arrivals of grain! . . . And the ships taller than Ilion under the white peacock of heaven, having crossed the bar, hove to
 in this deadwater where floats a dead ass. (We must ordain the fate of this pale meaningless river, colour of grasshoppers crushed in their sap.)

In the great fresh noise of the yonder bank, the blacksmiths are masters of their fires! The cracking of whips in the new streets unloads whole wainsful of unhatched evils. O mules, our shadows under the copper sword! four restive heads knotted to the fist make a living tuft against the blue. The founders of asylums meet beneath a tree and find their ideas for the choice of situations. They teach me the meaning and the purpose of the buildings: front adorned, back blind; the galleries of laterite, the vestibules of black stone and the pools of clear shadow for libraries; cool places for wares of the druggist. And then come the bankers blowing into their keys. And already in the streets a man sang alone, one of those who paint on their brow the cipher of their god. (Perpetual crackling of insects in this quarter of vacant lots and rubbish). . . . And this is no time to tell you, no time to reckon our alliances with the people of the other shore; water presented in skins, commandeering of cavalry for the dock-works and princes paid in currency of fish. (A child sorrowful as the death of apes — that had an elder sister of great beauty — offered us a quail in a slipper of rose-coloured satin.)

. . . Solitude! the blue egg laid by a great sea-bird, and the bay-leaves at morning all littered with gold lemons! Yesterday it was! The bird made off!
 Tomorrow the festivals and tumults, the avenues planted with podded trees, and the dustmen at dawn bearing away huge pieces of dead palm-trees, fragments of giant wings. . . . Tomorrow the festivals,
 the election of harbour-masters, the voices practising in the suburbs and under the moist incubation of storms,
 the yellow town, casque'd in shade, with the girls' drawers hanging at the windows.

. . . At the third lunation, those who kept watch on the hilltops folded their canvas. The body of a woman was burnt in the sands. And a man strode forth at the threshold of the desert — profession of his father: dealer in scent-bottles.

WE SHALL NOT DWELL FOREVER IN THESE YELLOW LANDS

We shall not dwell forever in these yellow lands, our pleasance. . . .

The Summer vaster than the Empire hangs over the tables of space several terraces of climate. The earth huge on its surface over-flowing its pale embers under the ashes — Sulphur colour, honey colour, colour of immortal things, the whole grassy earth taking light from the straw of last winter — and from the green sponge of a lonely tree the sky draws its violet juices.

A place of stone of quartz! Not a pure grain in the wind's beard. And light like oil. — From the crack of my eye to the level of the hills I join myself, I know the stones gillstained, the swarms of silence in the hives of light; and my heart gives heed to a family of crickets. . . .

Milch-camels, gentle beneath the shears, sewn with mauve scars, let the hills march forth under the facts of the harvest sky — let them march in silence over the pale incandescence of the plain; and kneeling at last, in the fantasy of dreams, there where the peoples annihilate themselves in the dead powder of earth.

These are the great quiet lines that disperse in the fading blue of doubtful vines. The earth here and there ripens the violets of storm; and these sandsmokes that rise over dead river courses, like the skirts of centuries on their route. . . .

Lower voice for the dead, lower voice by day. Such mildness in the heart of man, can it fail to find its measure? . . . "I speak to you, my soul! — my soul darkened by the horse smell!" and several great land birds, voyaging westwards, make good likeness of our sea birds.

In the east of so pale a sky, like a holy place sealed by the blind man's linen, calm clouds arrange themselves, where the cancers of camphor and horn revolve. . . . Smoke which a breath of wind claims from us! the earth poised tense in its insect barbs, the earth is brought to bed of wonders! . . .

And at noon, when the jujuba tree breaks the tombstone, man closes his lids and cools his neck in the ages. . . . Horsetramplings of dreams in the place of dead powders, O vain ways swept away by a breath, to our feet! where find, where find, the warriors who shall watch the streams in their nuptials?

At the sound of great waters on march over the earth, all the salt of the earth shudders in dream. And sudden, ah sudden, what would these voices with us? Levy a wilderness of mirrors on the boneyard of streams, let them appeal in the course of ages! Erect stones to my fame, erect stones to silence; and to guard these places, cavalcades of green bronze on the great causeways! . . .

(The shadow of a great bird falls on my face.)

The publishers have overruled the author's objections in their wish to include these five poems, so representative of Edith Sitwell's work.

Edith Sitwell
b. 1887

INVOCATION
For Alec and Merula Guinness

I who was once a golden woman like those who walk
In the dark heavens — but am now grown old
And sit by the fire, and see the fire grow cold,
Watch the dark fields for a rebirth of faith and of wonder.

The turning of Ixion's wheel the day
Ceased not, yet sounds no more the beat of the heart
But only the sound of ultimate Darkness falling
And of the Blind Samson at the Fair, shaking the pillars
    of the world and emptily calling.

For the gardeners cried for rain, but the high priests
    howled
For a darker rain to cool the delirium of gold
And wash the sore of the world, the heart of Dives,
Raise wheat for the hunger that lies in the soul of the
    poor —
Then came the thunderous darkness

And the fly-like whispering of small hopes, small fears,
The gossips of mean Death — gadflies and gnats, the
    summer world:
The small and gilded scholars of the Fly
That feed upon the crowds and their dead breath
And buzz and stink where the bright heroes die
Of the dust's rumours and the old world's fevers.
Then fell the world in winter.

But I, a golden woman like the corn goddess,
Watch the dark fields, and know when spring begins
To the sound of the heart and the planetary rhythm,
Fires in the heavens and in the hearts of men,
Young people and young flowers come out in the
    darkness.

And where are they going? How should I know? I
    see only
The hierarchies love the young people — the Swan has
    given his snows
And Berenice her wild mane to make their fair hair,
And speaking of love are the voices that come from the
    darkness:

Of the nobler love of Man for his brother Man,
And of how the creeds of the world shall no more divide
    them
But every life be that of a country Fate
Whose wheel had a golden woof and warp, the Day —
Woven of threads of the common task: and light
Tells to that little child, the humble dust,
Tales of the old world's holiness, finds veins of ore
In the unripe wheat-ear: and the common fire
That drops with seed like the Sun's, is fallen from the
    long-leaved planets.

So when the winter of the world and Man's fresh Fall
When democratic Death feared no more the heart's
    coldness
Shall be forgotten,
O Love, return to the dying world, as the light
Of morning, shining in all regions, latitudes
And households of high heaven within the heart.

Be then our visible world, our world invisible!
Throughout our day like the laughing flames of the Sun
Lie on our leaves of life, your heat infusing
Deep in the amber blood of the smooth tree.
The panic splendour of the animal
Is yours — O primal Law
That rules the blood — (the solar ray in the veins,
The fire of the hearth, the household Deity
That shines not, nor does it burn, destroy like fire,
But nourishes with its endless wandering
Like that of the Golden Ones in the high heavens.)

Rule then the spirit working in dark earth
As the Sun and Planets rule the husbandman —
O pride that in each semitone
Of amber blood and bone
Proclaims the splendour that arose from the first Dark!

Be too the ear of wheat to the Lost Men
Who ask the city stones if they are bread
And the stones of the city weep . . .
                              You, the lost days
When all might still be hoped for, and the light
Laid gold in the unhopeful path of the poor —
The shrunken darkness in the miser's heart.

Now falls the night of the world: — O Spirit moving upon
        the waters
Your peace instil
In the animal heat and splendour of the blood —
(The hot gold of the sun that flames in the night
And knows not down-going
But moves with the revolutions in the heavens.)

The thunders and the fires and acclamations
Of the leaves of spring are stilled, but in the night
The Holy Ghost speaks in the whispering leaves.
O wheat-ear shining like a fire and the bright gold,
O water brought from far to the dying gardens!

Bring peace to the famine of the heart and lips,
And to the Last Man's loneliness
Of those who dream they can bring back sight to the blind!
You are the Night
When the long hunt for Nothing is at rest
In the Blind Man's Street, and in the human breast
The hammer of Chaos is stilled.
                              Be then the sleep
When Judas gives again the childish kiss
That once his mother knew — and wash the stain
From the darkened hands of the universal Cain.

HEART AND MIND

Said the Lion to the Lioness — "When you are amber dust —
No more a raging fire like the heat of the Sun
(No liking but all lust) —
Remember still the flowering of the amber blood and bone,
The rippling of bright muscles like a sea,
Remember the rose-prickles of bright paws,
Though we shall mate no more
Till the fire of that sun the heart and the moon-cold bone are one."

Said the Skeleton lying upon the sands of Time —
"The great gold planet that is the mourning heat of the Sun
Is greater than all gold, more powerful
Than the tawny body of a Lion that fire consumes
Like all that grows or leaps . . . so is the heart
More powerful than all dust. Once I was Hercules
Or Samson, strong as the pillars of the seas:
But the flames of the heart consumed me, and the mind
Is but a foolish wind."

Said the Sun to the Moon — "When you are but a lonely white crone,
And I, a dead King in my golden armour somewhere in a dark wood,
Remember only this of our hopeless love:
That never till Time is done
Will the fire of the heart and the fire of the mind be one."

MOST LOVELY SHADE
For Alice Bouverie

Most lovely Dark, my Æthiopia born
Of the shade's richest splendour, leave not me
Where in the pomp and splendour of the shade
The dark air's leafy plumes no more a lulling music made.

Dark is your fleece, and dark the airs that grew
Amid those weeping leaves.
Plantations of the East drop precious dew
That, ripened by the light, rich leaves perspire.
Such are the drops that from the dark airs' feathers flew.

Most lovely Shade . . . Syrinx and Dryope
And that smooth nymph that changed into a tree
Are dead . . . the shade, that Æthiopia, sees

Their beauty make more bright its treasuries —
Their amber blood in porphyry veins still grows
Deep in the dark secret of the rose
And the smooth stem of many a weeping tree,
And in your beauty grows.

Come then, my pomp and splendour of the shade,
Most lovely cloud that the hot sun made black
As dark-leaved airs —
　　　　　　　　Come then, O precious cloud,
Lean to my heart: no shade of a rich tree
Shall pour such splendour as your heart to me.

LULLABY

Though the world has slipped and gone,
Sounds my loud discordant cry
Like the steel birds' song on high:
"Still one thing is left — the Bone!"
Then out danced the Babioun.

She sat in the hollow of the sea —
A socket whence the eye's put out —
She sang to the child a lullaby
(The steel birds' nest was thereabout.)

"Do, do, do, do —
Thy mother's hied to the vaster race:
The Pterodactyl made its nest
And laid a steel egg in her breast —
Under the Judas-coloured sun.
She'll work no more, nor dance, nor moan,
And I am come to take her place.
Do, do.

There's nothing left but earth's low bed —
(The Pterodactyl fouls its nest):
But steel wings fan thee to thy rest,
And wingless truth and larvae lie
And eyeless hope and handless fear —
All these for thee as toys are spread,
Do — do —

Red is the bed of Poland, Spain,
And thy mother's breast, who has grown wise

In that fouled nest. If she could rise,
Give birth again,
In wolfish pelt she'd hide thy bones
To shield thee from the world's long cold,
And down on all fours shouldst thou crawl
For thus from no height canst thou fall —
Do, do.

She'd give no hands: there's naught to hold
And naught to make: there's dust to sift,
But no food for the hands to lift.
Do, do.

Heed my ragged lullaby,
Fear not living, fear not chance;
All is equal — blindness, sight,
There is no depth, there is no height:
Do, do.

The Judas-coloured sun is gone,
And with the Ape thou art alone —
Do,
    Do."

From THREE POEMS OF THE ATOMIC AGE

DIRGE FOR THE NEW SUNRISE

*Fifteen minutes past eight o'clock, on the morning
of Monday the 6th of August 1945*

Bound to my heart as Ixion to the wheel,
Nailed to my heart as the Thief upon the Cross,
I hang between our Christ and the gap where the world
    was lost

And watch the phantom Sun in Famine Street
— The ghost of the heart of Man . . . red Cain
And the more murderous brain
Of Man, still redder Nero that conceived the death
Of his mother Earth, and tore
Her womb, to know the place where he was conceived.

But no eyes grieved —
For none were left for tears:
They were blinded as the years

Since Christ was born. Mother or Murderer, you have
       given or taken life —
Now all is one!

There was a morning when the holy Light
Was young. The beautiful First Creature came
To our water-springs, and thought us without blame.
Our hearts seemed safe in our breasts and sang to the
       Light —
The marrow in the bone
We dreamed was safe . . . the blood in the veins, the sap
       in the tree
Were springs of Deity.

But I saw the little Ant-men as they ran
Carrying the world's weight of the world's filth
And the filth in the heart of Man —
Compressed till those lusts and greeds had a greater heat
       than that of the Sun.

And the ray from that heat came soundless, shook the sky
As if in search of food, and squeezed the stems
Of all that grows on the earth till they were dry
— And drank the marrow of the bone:
The eyes that saw, the lips that kissed, are gone
Or black as thunder lie and grin at the murdered Sun.

The living blind and seeing Dead together lie
As if in love . . . There was no more hating then,
And no more love: Gone is the heart of Man.

Indices

Index of Authors and Titles

Index of First Lines